TOTAL HOTEL MOGEL

ESSAYS ON HOTEL **PROFITABILITY**

Adam Mogelonsky & Larry Mogelonsky

authorHOUSE®

AuthorHouse™
1663 Liberty Drive
Bloomington, IN 47403
www.authorhouse.com
Phone: 833-262-8899

Published by AuthorHouse 09/09/2024

ISBN: 979-8-8230-3178-3 (sc)
ISBN: 979-8-8230-3177-6 (e)

Library of Congress Control Number: 2024916627

Print information available on the last page.

Also by the Authors

Are You an Ostrich or a Llama? (2012)
Llama Rules (2013)
Hotel Llama (2015)
The Llama is Inn (2017)
The Hotel Mogel (2018)
More Hotel Mogel (2020)
In Vino Veritas: A Guide for Hoteliers and Restaurateurs to Sell More Wine (2022)

This book is dedicated to Klaus D. Tenter, my first General Manager and a true hotelier.

(Dedication written by Larry Mogelonsky)

Klaus Tenter passed in May 2024 at the age of 80. As all-encompassing as obituaries are, they often overlook the nuances that make that individual special.

In 1984, I stepped into Toronto's Inn on the Park hotel (a Four Seasons property, demolished several years ago), armed with almost eight years of marketing experience with Procter & Gamble and PepsiCo, plus an MBA in marketing. However, my understanding of the hotel industry was limited to nights spent in various properties and a few conferences that I had planned. Instead of immediately overwhelming me with occupancy or rate data, sales or marketing plans, he proposed a different way of learning the business. He suggested I spend a weekend with my family at the hotel, fully compensated. This guest-oriented initiation was Klaus's way of immersing me in the true essence of hospitality.

The following Monday, he asked me what I had learned, what impressed me the most, and where there were opportunities for improvement. Rather than express this to him as a written document, what I was used to from the corporate world, he dragged me into the morning's executive committee (ECOM) meeting as the first item on the agenda. His point of view was simple: my presentation was as frank as possible and unbiased without knowing any BOH labor challenges, budget issues, or business targets.

For Klaus, the guest was always at the forefront. While our industry is often consumed by acronyms like RevPAR, ADR, TRevPAR, LOS, CRM, CRM and, of course, KPIs, Klaus reminded us of the true essence of our role: hospitality. His unwavering focus on the guest experience was a testament to his passion and dedication to our industry. Whereas hundreds of hoteliers owe a good portion of their industry education to Klaus, don't forget the tens of thousands of guests who owe a good night's sleep to his management.

Klaus' hospitality extended to his home life. At the many dinners we enjoyed at his Toronto home, Klaus was the consummate host, supporting his wife Liz's impressive culinary capabilities with some of the best wines from his extended cellar. You knew that one bottle of first-growth Bordeaux was not a solo venture, and several more would follow. The conversations were numerous, hilarious, and particularly insightful.

As Klaus' health worsened, he maintained his understanding and appreciation of the human condition. We visited him at his winter home in Longboat Key, Florida. We chatted for several hours as he acted as our chauffeur on a guided tour of the surrounding area. He pointed out every restaurant and hotel with a detailed itemization of their successes and improvement opportunities. His knowledge was encyclopedic. Somehow, as we embraced upon departure, I knew it would be our last time together.

CONTENTS

FOREWORD

In the heart of Waikiki and having recently gone through an 18-month renovation, the Halekulani with its 453 rooms and suites represents quintessential Hawaiian luxury.

Hotel Grand Strategy Starts with Your People

A new year means a new mindset. And this will be an interesting period as the entire hospitality sector looks for a fresh start. But where to begin? The obvious answer is that hospitality will always depend on its people, and so you must do your best to inspire your teams to keep learning and keep finding those bold new ideas to advance the organization.

As they say, "People don't leave companies; they leave bad bosses." This is an essential phrase to take to heart now more than ever because modern hotel organizations don't have vast lineups of potential replacements for every rising star or intrepid veteran who departs for one reason or another.

Instead, we portend a rather prickly situation for hotels in the near future whereby our industry has lost its luster amongst youth more inclined to pursue careers in STEM or finance where the prospects of cushy monetary rewards and entrepreneurship are higher. Add to this the stigma that hotels have accrued in the wake of COVID where we are deemed a high-touch workplace and not strictly WFH-enabled (work from home). In this 'brain drain' scenario, traditional property may struggle to find suitable candidates to fill vital operational roles.

We bring forward this hellfire and brimstone outlook because we've seen it too many times throughout the years as asset managers and marketers-for-hire for various hotels. This is not to say that your team of hoteliers is lacking per se, but if profits or revenues aren't following the macro-level recovery trendlines, then it may be a result of a deep, internal rift.

An underlying weakness of the hotel industry itself is that productivity and effective operations hinge upon so many distinct roles acting in harmony where one kink in the chain can reverberate and disrupt throughout. A property runs a lot like an army corps in that regard. This is why when our consultancy (aptly named Hotel Mogel!) undertakes an assignment to help execute the owner or GM's vision, the first thing we look at is the people – the boots on the ground. Without a strong team, any overarching objectives can never be wholly realized.

This brings us to the idea of 'grand strategy' which is a term rooted in the military that can seriously help in the achievement of an owner's targets. It is not the vision itself but a detailed outline of how that vision will be attained across the entire property's operations. An outcome-related metric for a hotel's grand strategy may be TRevPAR (total revenue, including rooms and all other streams).

We all know and use 'strategy' as part of any departmental planning, but the problem therein is that the strategies and goals outlined are too siloed, not properly taking into account the needs of other operations. Instead, grand strategy is how you put the pieces in place to then ensure a seamless execution of all the iterative plans and all enacted in concert with each other.

Working with hotels, when we start having those heady, top-level discussions concerning grand strategy, the 'pieces' are often the hoteliers themselves. While there are always other considerations like renovation projects, new programs to grow RevPAR and the overall sales approach, when it comes to the people we look at the organizational structure and how to maximize performance from each individual. This is accomplished through such things as how best to maximize support for internal directors, how to increase motivation so managers succeed in their roles, succession planning and making sure decision makers aren't stymied by nonstop meetings or emails every day.

These sorts of discussions may seem relatively straightforward, but it's surprising how many senior executives don't sit down for a review on a regular basis. Of course, as a third-party coming in, a consultancy can help to cut through the noise by offering a sounding board and fresh eyes on any number of problems related to organizational structure or other team productivity issues.

Ultimately, though, this grand strategy is something we would encourage all organizations to incorporate into their yearly planning sessions, especially in the face of our current 'great reset' that the hotel industry is facing for the decade ahead.

If Elon Musk Was a Hotelier

What if a person of Elon Musk's character and bravado were to enter the hotel industry? How would they shake things up and presage the next 'gamechangers' to propel hospitality beyond our current challenges?

We are big fans of Elon Musk's business acumen. He is a man of galactic vision and the dogged gumption to make those ideas into reality despite any criticism. Sadly, I did not get in on the Tesla stock boom, but that does not mean I don't ogle every Model S that drives by or enthusiastically read every SpaceX news clipping. But while it's easy to associate such a larger-than-life personality with an intrepid technology company, hotel brands tend to be far more conservative in their approach and evolution.

Maybe it's that as part of hotel management school, we don't really learn about the history of hotels so that we have a reasonable frame of reference. Who was the last true revolutionary actor in our industry?

Looking further back just over a century, it was Ellsworth M. Statler who introduced the original concept of the modern hotel, including individual guestroom baths, lights in closets and daily housekeeping. Fast forward to more contemporary times and could this mantle belong to Ian Schrager with his creation of the boutique luxury hotel some 20 years ago? Perhaps one of our industry's finest minds, Schrager created an entire class of products which have now been imitated in part or in full by all of the top chains. Plagiarism is the best form of flattery, after all. Before him, perhaps the next big industry icon was Isadore Sharp of Four Seasons fame, who redefined the modern luxury property for the modern era.

These individuals deserve all the accolades that they have received, and no doubt there are other examples you can cite of undeniable visionaries who have helped innovate the hotel experience for the benefit of guests as well as owners' wallets. As Canadians always do, we apologize if we've missed anyone who deserves mention.

What a history of hospitality should stress is the need for constant innovation, and indeed no event in the past century may have precipitated that more than the recent pandemic. Now is the time for sweeping changes to how we operate. Now is the time for hospitality's version of Elon Musk to rise to the occasion and show us how to untangle this giant mess.

This starts by shifting how we think. Hoteliers all know that technology is vital, yet we aren't curious enough as to how it can transform rather than simply enhance existing practices. It's thus a matter of asking the right questions.

As a straightforward example, instead of asking your tech vendors how technology can make your front office operations contactless, you might instead ask how software and digital kiosks can wholly replace the front desk. For the rest of the 2020s, all brands must consider whether guests event want the front desk as part of their hotel experience. What would the lobby look like and feel like if the front desk space were reoriented to be something else?

These are the broad matters you should consider, and now is the perfect time to do so. What if the only contact guests want with staff is via their mobile devices or when a specific onsite service is requested? How do you engineer the entire on-property journey to be facilitated from a customer's phone? What cutting-edge programs, like DNA-based medical tourism, can your hotel engage with to generate unique awareness and a whole new set of customers? This requires a profound rethink of housekeeping, front office, F&B, reservations, accounting, and practically every other department where technology may impact SOPs and labor.

Beyond technology-enabled operational mergers, the entire concept of the hotel has to be redefined. Fundamentals of our business model need to be questioned: Why is standard check-out at 11 am and check-in at 4 pm? Yes, this is based on well-established housekeeping shiftwork, but now we have advanced scheduling software to better accommodate guests arriving at all hours of the day and night. This may require you to think about how to turn a room quicker or reconfigure furniture that is difficult to clean or superfluous to the guest journey, like the alarm clock.

Next, consider dynamic pricing models and compression events. We yield room rates, so why not yield F&B, spa, golf, poolside chairs, and fitness times? A dinner reservation at 8 pm is technically more valuable than at 6 pm, so shouldn't customers pay a small surcharge for those timeslots that are in higher demand?

For older properties that are desperately in need of renovation, you might even consider conversions to college dorms, eldercare, rehabilitation facilities or even quarantine centers for those arriving from other countries. This notion reminds me of a property in Western Canada that we worked on several years ago. With see-saw occupancies, depending upon seasonality, a conversion to a long-term care facility delivered superior returns to ownership, with only marginal CAPEX requirements after a proper assessment was completed.

The bottom line is that despite all the recent upgrades we've made in light of the coronavirus and the fear of a deadly new disease in our midst, we are all still reacting to present conditions rather than boldly going in a new direction.

There are still so many systemic challenges ahead for the hotel industry that we cannot simply assume that customers will eventually come back as if it's 2019 again. Maybe the pandemic can still be the wake-up call we need, but who will be our Elon Musk to show us the way?

Dare we say it, but perhaps this mantle now belongs to Brian Chesky, CEO of Airbnb. After capturing the hearts and minds of the whole centennial generation, and with the company already having IPO several years ago, there's no telling what new and innovative products will come about from this extra capital injection. It's definitely worth highlighting that Airbnb's rise to the world leader in accommodations has mostly occurred within the past decade, so with the right idea and the grit to see it through, your brand can realize tremendous success.

General Manager General Marshall

When it comes to lessons in organizational skills, look no further than General George C. Marshall. For reference, he was the Chief of Staff under FDR who coordinated all of the United States' military efforts across both theaters of war during WWII, and then went on to orchestrate what became known as the Marshall Plan to rebuild Europe in the aftermath of that deadly conflict.

His example has important teachings for the hotel industry as travel recovers from COVID. Staffing up and dealing with erratic demand are the top objectives, but there are numerous other initiatives that still need to be pushed forward regardless of how lean a hotel's team must remain during all this.

Much has already been written about General Marshall's inhuman ability to lead and to build command structures that have a healthy 'operational tempo'. As it pertains to hospitality, the pandemic has gutted or jumbled the organizational structure of many hotels, leaving them in limbo when it comes to advancing those projects that will help a property reassert its revenue-generating abilities. But the hierarchal problems were already festering long before a little virus brought us to our knees.

Two Structural Problems

Firstly, hotels have long suffered during the inefficiencies of 'meeting paralysis', where a lack of departmental autonomy or middle manager empowerment has ensured that senior executives are compelled to attend every single conference call or meeting and be carbon-copied on every email thread. Despite your own personal experiences, it has been scientifically proven that humans are horrible multitaskers, so the more people meet, the less real work that actually gets done.

The pandemic has compounded this problem via the proliferation of videoconferences. Making meeting access more convenient has resulted in more meetings and more people attending those meetings who should otherwise be sequestered away revising SOPs or updating rates. Rather than three people directly involved in a problem huddling together in one of the hotel's subbasement breakrooms to hash out a problem, now you have an additional five people on any single email thread to organize a time for a call and those same five people induced to join the videoconference. If that call takes, say, an hour plus an additional ten minutes of administration time, you just lost about six hours in productivity.

Secondly, and related to the first issue of a lack of team empowerment, is a risible misinterpretation of the contemporary push for 'flatter' organizational structures. In other industries, flat has meant more cross-departmental chatter and less siloed projects to serve broader company goals. Many hotels have made their corporate structures flatter by simply cutting out a few middle rungs on the ladder and having everyone report directly to the general manager (or another equivalent position).

This in turn makes the GM the one and only stop-gap for decision making, leading to stalled implementation and, ultimately, stagnating revenues. In such a pseudo-flat structure, operational tempo is compromised because every morsel of approval rests with the GM instead of department directors being empowered to take actions on their own that fit within predefined objectives and KPIs.

Compounding this misconception of 'flat' is often an entanglement of responsibilities at the very top of the ladder – that is, overlapping authority amongst the GM, owner, asset manager and other members of the executive committee. Yes, these stakeholders need to regroup frequently to decide on a strategic vision and long-term asset growth plan but select operations must be defined according to who has the final word. Again and again, we see hotels reach lackluster results in large part because ownership meddles in the day-to-day, reversing or obfuscating briefings given by the GM or another senior team leader. Contrarily, some of the best-run properties are those where the owners are entirely hands-off; they outline RevPAR growth goals, PIP allocations and executive hiring, but the rest is laissez faire.

GM Marshall

While much could be written about Marshall's tenacity and grit, which helped him rise through the army ranks, one of his most admirable qualities was his mandate for simple objectives moving down the chain of command as well as concise reporting going up. There was no point in sending up a detailed recommendation or after-action report longer than about three pages because it would be a waste of time for the superior officer to read it. Ditto for commands; it wasn't the general's job to loiter over one of their colonels but to summarize the directive and let that colonel interpret the optimal actions towards achieving that goal.

How would General Marshall run a hotel if he were a GM? There are a handful of strategic choices he would make to ensure that his team didn't suffer from the two aforementioned structural problems.

These strategic choices might include:

1. *Fewer meetings.* Managers have to be given leeway to not attend or, at the very least, question why their attendance is absolutely necessary. If a concrete answer can't be given, then said manager should maintain the right to say, without judgment, that they 'have real work to do' or that they can't join

'for their own sanity.' This starts by nurturing a culture of honesty as any organization running on fear will prevent these blunt yet legitimate questions from being asked. This also means having the proper methodology in place to share and review concise documents as oftentimes the meeting may not even be necessary in the first place if everyone can elaborate on their thoughts in advance via email or by circulating a concise document.

2. *Shorter meetings.* The only meeting that should come without an agenda is a happy hour roundtable with Scotch in hand, held after the brain juices become too viscous for proper thought around 6pm. Sticking to an agenda by itself can mean fitting an hour-long discussion into half that time, saving everyone to go do some real work. Again, a culture of honesty means that any attendee should be able to politely say, "Can we get back on track here?" Lastly, tardiness should be a criminal offense. If there are four people on a call and one key person is late by five minutes, that's 15 minutes of lost productivity – and minutes add up! Idea: call the meeting a 'standup', limited to half an hour, no more. Regularly scheduled, these short bursts become productive ways of maintaining communications without an HR resource drag.
3. *Know your roles.* If every team member knows exactly what they are responsible for, what projects they must champion and what level of autonomy they have, more gets done and faster. The easiest way to complete this at the managerial level is to write job descriptions and review those lists with the affected team member so that it's clear and so that modifications can be made. At the ECOM level, roles must be clarified so that the meddling problem is negated, while delegation must also be mandated as a core part of a leader's skill set. No topic or scenario within any discussion should ever be adjourned without a key person assigned to resolve any outstanding issues.

If you want to learn more about General Marshall and how his leadership style can help your hotel, you're but one internet search or book purchase away. For now, understand that, for the remainder of the roaring 2020s, the pace of change within the hospitality industry is only going to accelerate; if your organization is too slow to adapt and implement new programs to meet these new trends, then you'll be leaving much-needed revenue on the table. A clear chain of command with departments that are actually empowered to act on their own is the only way forward for the decade ahead.

HOTEL LEADERS

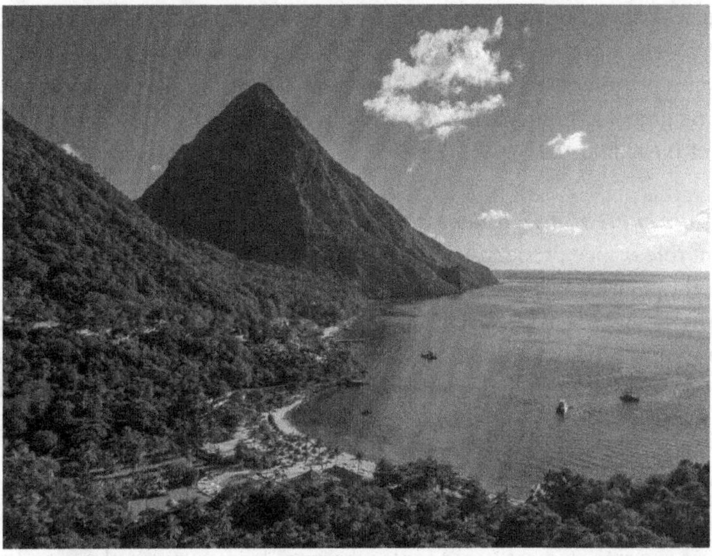

A tropical paradise perfectly situated between the iconic Piton mountains in Saint Lucia, Sugar Beach, a Viceroy Resort nevertheless requires expert technology to uphold its ultraluxury service standards.

View from the Top: An Interview with Shannon McCallum, VP Hotel Operations at Resorts World Las Vegas

Calling Shannon McCallum's career a success is an understatement. As the Vice President of Hotel Operations at Resorts World Las Vegas (RWLV) – which opened in June 2021 as the newest and most technologically advanced casino resort on The Strip – she is responsible for a vast team and even greater number of guests. Yet her career traces back to humble roots in British Columbia, offering an exemplar path that any aspiring hospitality leader can learn from.

Growing up in Kelowna, McCallum fell into hospitality by accident. Living a mile away from a luxury property, she started working there during high school over the weekends and during summertime. Working in hotels not only put her through college, but also inspired her to stay in hospitality as she loved it so much, instead of pursuing law.

Her early experience encompassed 15 years at Canadian Pacific Hotels and Fairmont, including at the Lake Okanagan Resort (managed by Canadian Pacific), opening the Fairmont Vancouver Airport in 1999, and then at the Fairmont Scottsdale Princess. In 2010, she was recruited to join MGM Resorts for the newly opened ARIA Resort & Casino, where all told she has worked at three large luxury Las Vegas Strip hotels over the past 13+ years.

Outside of her duties for RWLV, McCallum is currently a board member for the Nevada Hotel and Lodging Association and past chair of the Nevada Hotel and Lodging Foundation. She is a member of the Hospitality Financial and Technology Professionals Association and was a co-chair of the 2023 HITEC Advisory Council. She is also co-chair of the 2024 Super Bowl Host Committee for Hotels and Housing and she was a prior member of the Forbes Travel Guide Standards Advisory Council representing global gaming properties. She was recognized as Hotelier of the Year for the State of Nevada in 2015.

What is your current assignment at Resorts World?

My current role is Vice President of Hotel Operations at RWLV, overseeing all aspects of the hotel operations with over 1,500 team members. This includes three luxury hotels (Hilton Las Vegas, Conrad Las Vegas and Crockfords Las Vegas), totaling 3,506 rooms and suites combined. RWLV's forecasted hotel revenue alone is north of $300 million for 2023, while the property itself has over 50 restaurants and lounges, a vibrant nightlife as well as a 4,000-seat theatre featuring top A-List entertainment.

Why did you enter hospitality? What factors continue to excite you?

Working in hotels and taking care of people came naturally to me…it never felt like work! It was exciting to meet new people who were from faraway places and to speak about the city or the property. I still get excited walking through our property, hearing our guests having fun, and seeing them enjoying our offerings. As for the present day, hotels are always adapting to changing trends, new menus, updating experiences, and it never gets stale or routine – every day is very different.

Are there any particular individuals or events that spurred your career?
When I was 16, a hotel I worked at hosted a Commonwealth of Nations with a high level of security due to the leaders of the countries in attendance. I clearly remember Margaret Thatcher, the Sultan of Brunei, Rajiv Gandhi and Brian Mulroney who were in attendance, among many other high-level leaders. During the event, I thought to myself, "What a rare opportunity to be involved in such a momentous gathering." It was indeed a very exciting moment for someone my age to be a part of, and there are very few careers that have this ongoing interaction with notable individuals in such an exciting way. I am so fortunate to have taken this path.

Do you believe there is a glass ceiling in our industry?
In the past few decades, there has been an increase of women in executive roles in hospitality. I have never felt a limit to the growth of my career as I have grown my areas of responsibility.

What would you recommend for women currently working in hospitality?
I do feel strongly that building my personal legacy in a positive way, working in a dedicated manner and also treating people well – both internally and externally – played a large part in the opportunities that were open for advancement. I would also emphasize getting involved in the community by joining industry associations and volunteering, as well as building the pipeline of talent for the future of our industry by mentoring up-and-coming individuals. Networking with other hospitality individuals and vendors is always important, while building relationships with my guests over the years and caring about their experiences has also been rewarding.

The SI Swimsuit Edition focused on women's strengths, diversity, and knowledge. You participated and in doing so, becoming the first hotelier in the world to be featured. Tell us about the experience.
When the opportunity to participate in the SI Swimsuit Edition was presented, I was very surprised and happy to see the more diverse conversation and focus of the issue. I was honored to be a part of the conversation that featured women changemakers at Resorts World Las Vegas. Not only was this a great opportunity to show the variety of career paths within hospitality, but also that women are more frequently leading the way than in the past. There is no limit to growth potential and it is exciting to be a role model for young professionals entering into the industry to show them that the opportunities are boundless!

Anything else to add?
The hospitality industry has so much to offer as it can be practiced all over the world and brings new and different experiences every day. There is never a dull moment!

Levering Cinematic Success with Fairmont, The Queen Elizabeth's Barbie® Adventure

The interview was originally published in September 2023, and the indicated status of Fairmont, Queen Elizabeth, in this passage may not reflect current hotel updates.

Fairmont's ambitious *Beyond Limits* campaign embodies the essence of this luxury brand's recognition that accommodations are infinitely more than comfortable beds. The brand-wide campaign epitomizes one of the tenets of the Mille Club, a program we (Hotel Mogel) run designed to inspire any hotelier with lessons from the five-star, thousand-dollar-plus-ADR hotspots around the globe. In short, this timeless tenet is guests want unique experiences.

Right in the heart of Montreal, Canada, Fairmont The Queen Elizabeth is already regarded within the brand and within our home country as among the leading hotels in the 'Augmented Hospitality' movement, having hosted Celeste, a cabaret cirque-in-residence as soon as the pandemic subsided, while everyone in the industry and many others may recall the iconic John and Yoko Bed-In Suite where the song *Give Peace a Chance* was written.

Accordingly, when it came to designing the latest au courant campaign, Fairmont Hotels & Resorts immediately earmarked this property for the creation of the Barbie Dream Suite and accompanying marketing program. To discuss the launch, we asked Philippe Champagne, Fairmont's Regional Director of Sales and Marketing for Eastern Canada to provide us with some further details.

How long did it take from concept through to opening?

The beginning stages of this year-long collaboration between Mattel and Fairmont Hotels and Resorts began several months ago. One of the core values of Barbie is inclusivity, and we needed to make sure to build a complete offer that could be enjoyed across all ages. Team members from several departments were brought together for brainstorming sessions to develop experiences that cater to different audiences – guests from out of town staying at our hotel, local guests, kids, adults, and so on. Our team along with designers who have created all of the different experiences in various areas throughout the hotel – from the Barbie Dream Suite to the Barbie Sweets Shoppe – worked together for about a month to be able to host the first guests staying in the Barbie Dream Suite mid-summer and first Afternoon Tea Experience at Rosélys Restaurant a few days later. We are looking to expand upon the Barbie Dream Experiences at Fairmont The Queen Elizabeth and have more surprises are in store.

The property offers a number of packages. Can you explain the entire program?

Guests can immerse themselves in the pink and playful world of Barbie with a selection of Barbie Dream Experiences to choose from. Stays in the former St-Henri Executive Suite, a two bedroom suite with two full bathrooms, living room, dining area, kitchenette and a powder room starts at $1,499 (price subject to change). Guests can also add to the suite experience a variety of package options including a fabulous tea party, spa day fit for a Barbie girl, birthday celebration or even a slumber party with your best friends.

Alternative Barbie Dream experiences accessible to all are available throughout the hotel. Guests are welcome to raise their PINK-Y during the Barbie Afternoon Tea at Rosélys restaurant every Saturday, sip on Barbie-themed cocktails (or mocktails) at Nacarat Bar and enjoy all the sweet treats from the Barbie Sweets Shoppe at Marché Artisans. A selection of Barbie dolls and accessories with a culinary or travel theme also completes the Barbie offer at Marché Artisans. More surprises in conjunction to the 65th anniversary of Barbie in 2024 will be announced,

What is the guest response? Has demand exceeded the supply?

The response has exceeded our expectations. Because guests need to contact our Barbie Concierge to inquire about availability for the Barbie Dream Suite, we quickly felt the enthusiasm and were able to measure the demand for this new hotel offer. Reservations for the Barbie Afternoon Tea are also very popular, to the point that we needed to increase our order for pink tableware.

What has truly been extra special to experience is seeing the reaction of our guests as soon as they turn the corner and see the Barbie pink door at the end of the corridor on the 17th floor. Guests of all ages are amazed by all the little details that complete the room transformation! Creating unique and memorable experiences for our guests is at the core of Fairmont's *Beyond Limits* campaign and we are so happy to have received such an extraordinary response.

How much extra work does it take housekeeping staff to maintain?

The housekeeping staff is very excited to be part of making this new hotel offer come to life. The cleaning routine is identical to the rest of our 950 hotel rooms; however, we now have to make sure that certain objects are now rose-coloured instead!

With school back in session, do you still have moms and daughters wanting to stay over?

With this year-long partnership, we are offering people of all genders and ages the opportunity to celebrate throughout the year, whether it ties with a special celebration (like a birthday or anniversary) or gives our guests an opportunity to gather and have a fun-filled one-of-a-kind experience.

What lessons did you learn from the process that you could pass on to other hoteliers?

Like always, be bold! I believe that hospitality is much more than just a bed and a shower and that nowadays, hoteliers must integrate unique experiences in both accommodation and F&B. At Fairmont, The Queen Elizabeth, 'Augmented Hospitality' is part of our DNA. It's our vision of creating unforgettable memories for our guests, and we will continue to innovate in this direction because, if you think about it, there really is no limit to what hotels can do as long as there is imagination and audacity.

Senior Team Alignment Critical for Leisure and Group Recovery Success

The article was originally published in May 2021, and the indicated status of Newport Hospitality Group in this passage may not reflect current Company practices.

The recovery in the leisure sector is imminent, and we argue that small groups aren't far behind, given that 'revenge travel' also implies a strong yearning to reconnect and congregate. A return to healthy numbers won't be evenly spread across all hotels, though. It will favor those properties and those organizations that are already prepared for a diverse range of ramp-up scenarios, with others leaving revenue on the table by not having plans in place prior to this next phase.

While hotels could hardly have predicted or prevented the advent of COVID, what we've witnessed in the latter half of 2020 is an industry that's largely reactive to macroeconomic forces. Many operators have hinged their hopes on a near-complete reversal to 2019 demand levels and guest expectations without any earnest consideration for structural innovation and becoming more adaptable to the increased volatility in the market. Luckily, there are a few shining stars that highlight where hospitality needs to be for the decade ahead, and we're excited to present one such case herein.

Newport Hospitality Group (NHG) is a management company that's been operating for 30 years and now has over 50 managed properties in its portfolio spread all along the Eastern Seaboard. Most fascinating for our current conversation is that the organization has some inherent 'antifragility' (to borrow a term from the brilliant statistician and option trader Nassim Taleb) in that it thrives relative to its comp set not only during good times but also during periods of economic turmoil.

Upon reviewing their annual RevPAR growth metrics, they've beaten their respective markets in every year since 2005. Emphasizing this is that during the calendar year of 2020 NHG dropped 7.9% less than the US RevPAR average and the company also added 10 properties to its portfolio. This echoes their relative CAGR for the recession of 2008-09 where they also substantially beat the market.

Success Starts at the Senior Level

In trying to decipher the secret to the longstanding NHG playbook, we had an extensive discussion with Wayne West III, NHG's President. He explained that success during turbulent times hinges upon decisive attention at the senior level combined with a thorough comprehension of the roles and responsibilities for the onsite operator, the corporate office team, and the owner. Finding the best alignment amongst these entities – which may or may not have different goals – is an initial step that is often overlooked.

So much time is spent in planning meetings and getting approval for changes and new initiatives that operations can easily get bogged down through 'decision by committee'. In particular, hospitality is more exposed to this problem than other industries, given our highly vertical organizational structures and lack of monetary empowerment at the property level. These types of inertial situations can easily be exacerbated by conflicting visions and orders stemming from the three-headed,

'Cerberus-like' discord amongst the owners, brand and management company. The key is to find a balance of responsibilities.

"In many ways, the hotel industry's current situation is like a street race," quipped West as he explained how immobility can compromise a hotel's success. "You don't start revving your engine when the light turns green. You rev in neutral so that you can fly out of the gates once the countdown hits zero. This resembles the state of many hotels as we gear up for a roaring Q3 and Q4. At NHG, we established a playbook for swiftly reacting to hard times even before the Great Recession to the point where it's now baked into our culture. All our managed properties have a clear chain of command and are staffed up to handle a surge of both transient guests and group RFPs."

Indeed, one case where having alignment at the senior level is mission critical pertains to the re-emergence of groups, starting with reunions, corporate retreats, and wedding receptions later this fall in advance of larger MICE-type travel sometime in 2022. With those small group gatherings taking place in the autumn or winter, the planning starts in late spring or early summer, and hotels must have a sales team and group rate plan fully set up to win these contracts.

To this end, one reason for NHG's success versus its competitive set in 2020 was because it retained its sales team throughout. This meant that they were fully ready to enter any negotiation with attractive offers and coronavirus-specific programs such as full-floor or section buyouts and operational staff pods to limit cross-exposure.

Emphasizing Succession Planning

To ingrain the first lesson above, far better than a lengthy deliberation over the best possible approach is to implement a reasonably satisfactory course then act quickly to adjust the plan as market conditions evolve. To enable this ability to pivot, onsite leaders must have a certain degree of autonomy and freedom to act within a proscribed framework. But how do you develop a culture of empowerment?

One critical point that West highlighted to that end was succession planning and how many hotels aren't prepared for a return to normalcy because they furloughed too many of their team members. This is especially evident for sales teams, whereby without key managers kept up to speed on a property's event capabilities, each RFP cannot be addressed through a pre-established process. This results in teams constantly playing catch-up and reacting week-over-week to new inquiries rather than looking ahead to new initiatives that will advance the hotel's revenue prospects.

To ensure this type of problem never sets in, NHG prides itself on promoting from within and executive retention, with nearly half of their senior teams staying with the company for over a decade and nearly a quarter staying for over 20 years. A sharp focus on retention like this means that the onsite operators are totally in sync with ownership and the corporate office, intrinsically knowing how to implement the latter's directives and hastily deploy resources to make those changes a reality.

"A property is only as good as its GM," remarked West to close out our talk, succinctly describing how, if the GM gives his or her managers a clear and actionable plan without backtracking or indecisiveness, then success is all but guaranteed. In this sense, nurturing great teams, especially during hard times like the current pandemic, is vital for decreasing conflict and aligning operations prior to periods of increased demand.

Particularly at the senior level, the time to make your organization nimble and imbue a clear command structure for rapid action was yesterday. But, with hindsight being what it is, a close second place would be today. It's never too late to chart a course for a profitable decade ahead, and our hope is that you can learn from this brief examination of NHG to see how you can create a culture of success.

Sense of Community as a Growth Strategy with Andaz Mexico City Condesa

The idea of an urban hotel embedding itself into the surrounding community is nothing new, but for many properties it remains just that: an idea that's talked about in press releases and on the website yet seldom woven into every aspect of the operations and amenities. When a hotel does in fact go through the meticulous process of creating a strong sense of community, the results are nothing short of magical, and this is reflected through a positive impact on guest satisfaction, demand and the ability to grow rate.

Celebrating its one-year anniversary in January 2024, the newly opened Andaz Mexico City Condesa – a Concept by Hyatt serves as the quintessential example of how a hotel can go about fostering this sense of community in order to create spaces that are truly special to both travelers and locals. At 17 stories, this luxury lifestyle hotel consists of 213 residential-style guestrooms, including 20 suites, with a private courtyard, rooftop pool, a 24-hour fitness center, full spa, art throughout the public spaces and five dining options.

In sitting down with General Manager Analía Capurro, we learned that the story of Andaz Mexico City Condesa is as much about what makes this particular property successful as it is a tale about the unique neighborhood that is La Condesa and the current lifestyle hospitality renaissance that's happening throughout Mexico City (CDMX).

A Rapidly Evolving Hotel Landscape

Hailing from Buenos Aires and having been in the Hyatt family for over 20 years, Capurro first moved to CDMX over a decade ago where she almost immediately became enamored by the city while stationed at the Hyatt Regency Mexico City – a landmark property over in the ritzy Polanco neighborhood. During this time and also during the opening of the Andaz Mexico City Condesa, she has witnessed a tremendous shift in the traveler composition to CDMX.

"It used to be that Mexico City was a Monday to Thursday night town, with business travelers coming in for midweek meetings then emptying by the weekend," commented Capurro. "While that segment is still very much alive, Mexico City has come into the global limelight as a leisure destination, cultural center and gastronomic hub, where today weekend occupancies sit above 70% year round. The city is alive!"

Major brands are hardly ignorant of this evolution either, with the luxury and lifestyle segments achieving huge growth in recent years to capitalize on this new demand. Notable recent openings include The Ritz-Carlton, Mexico City in October 2021, Mondrian Mexico City Condesa right across from the Andaz Mexico City Condesa in December 2022, Soho House Mexico City in September 2023, and a handful of boutique homegrown brands like the 49-key Hotel Volga in the nearby neighborhood of Cuauhtémoc that soft-opened in June 2023 followed by the design-centric aparthotel ONTO Tonalá that opened in November 2023. Nor is this trend letting up with a strong development pipeline for CDMX that includes the likes of Park Hyatt and Rosewood over the next few years.

Writing about CDMX as outsiders, it's important to also talk about the international perception of crime in this city – an aspect for which Capurro has observed a steady downswing since she first moved there. Nowadays, all the main tourist areas are safe, while the government has also established special tourism police force with all officers fluent in English and knowledge about insurance claims. Just as the city's commerce, tourism, and development continue to boom, the criminal element will recede even further.

As Goes Condesa-Roma Goes Mexico

With commerce in CDMX centered on the grand avenue of Avenida Paseo de La Reforma, the two neighborhoods immediately south from there, La Condesa and Roma – together as Condesa-Roma – represent the cool capital of Mexico. Gastronomic, fashion, and lifestyle trends start here before spreading nationwide.

As a wellness-oriented example of this, it's in Condesa-Roma where yoga and Pilates first took off in Mexico. To embed itself into this relaxed-yet-avant-garde sensibility, the Andaz Mexico City Condesa paid particular attention to how it designed its services and amenities to attract locals as well as foster a dynamic atmosphere where *capitalinos* and *viajeros* intermingle.

Starting out from the Andaz brand's Wellbeing is Personal mission, the interpretation here was to adapt this motto into monthly programs at its Pasana Spa & Wellness that purposefully introduce locals to the latest wellness and vitality trends while showing the warmth and sense of belonging of Condesa-Roma to travelers. This was achieved by alternating the hotel's regular Saturday classes between contrast therapy – circuits of ice baths, saunas, and breathwork – and barre – a form of dance class that brings in elements of yoga and other low-impact exercises. Capitalizing on an even newer trend, they also now run animal flow classes, which are movement routines focusing on natural transitions for a full-body workout.

To ensure the community stayed engaged, each new offering was first posted on social media for organic awareness. Critically, though, while hotel guests can always learn and then purchase through the app or via on-site QR code, class pricing was not made prohibitive to local attendance, resulting in a 50-50 split for these two segments.

Next, as a fun bit of trivia, Condesa-Roma also has the most dogs (as pets) per capita of any urban area in the world. So, while most properties in CDMX are pet friendly, the Andaz Mexico City Condesa went far beyond mere box-checking in this aspect by developing its outdoor restaurant concept, Wooftop Beer Garden & Canine Club, aimed directly at pet owners coming with their furry companions. Adjacent to this is Bulldog Sports Bar which, per its name, also serves both hominids and canines in an indoor bar and lounge with massive TVs, air hockey and nostalgic arcade games. Whether they're visiting from Los Angeles or New York – two of the property's main feeder cities – or a few blocks away, this differentiated programming is yet one more way that the hotel has built an organic following that compounds to make for healthy year-round revenues.

Being Stewards of the Community

It's often said that the best hotels are not only those that are excellently designed but those that enhance their environs. If there's a single word that encapsulates this, it's stewardship. Condesa-Roma is a neighborhood that tests boundaries and as such the Andaz Mexico City Condesa has strived to be forward-thinking with its wellness and pet friendly amenities.

But this being the culinary capital that CDMX is known for, no discussion of stewardship in this city is complete without a sharp focus on the hotel's core restaurant offerings, especially with every competitor property already at the forefront of gastronomy. Besides an outlet specifically for pet owners, the hotel's signature concept is Cabuya Rooftop, focusing on contemporary seafood and cocktails with panoramas of the downtown skyline and curated music every night. This positioning has earned the terrace restaurant heavy traffic all week with four out of five patrons being local.

Rounding out this keystone offering is the Derba Matcha Café where, per its name, the hotel recruited ostensibly the best pastry chef in CDMX to theme the array of caffeinated beverages and baked goods around this healthy green tea powder. Embracing guest wellness and vitality here, everything is made in-house with no additives from whole foods, and the staff is trained to be able to answer guest inquiries about where the ingredients came from.

Then, as a fifth dining option, the hotel has Pórtico, the newest offering on the first floor, which exclusively focuses on breakfasts during this initial launch period. Finally, spilling out from the lobby are billiards and tables equipped with card games that, alongside the activities within Bulldog Sports Bar, transform the main floor into a hangout for locals every night. What you can observe from all this is that whatever amenity hotel guests opt to use, they become immersed in a lively atmosphere brimming with residents from the area. This serves to amplify their experience in CDMX, which boosts satisfaction and loyalty, while also diversifying revenues away from just ancillary capture by travelers.

Ending with the Guestrooms

Of course, the core revenue generator of a hotel is mostly to be its rooms, so that is where we conclude this overview of how building a product for locals as much as for guests adds to more than the sum of its parts. For the Andaz Mexico City Condesa, wellness yet again is ever-present with the Headspace app available via a brand wide agreement with Hyatt, a custom pillow menu, on-demand exercise equipment, and the minibar outfitted with healthy snacks – for example, avocado chips instead of the expected global brand potato chips – as well as chocolates that are sustainably sourced from within Mexico.

But the property being one block away from the Auditorio Blackberry, a popular live music venue, they added an element of emotional wellness by ensuring all rooms have their own record player with individual records available downstairs. With the Andaz brand's new tagline of 'Indulgence like no one's watching', the Andaz Mexico City Condesa team lensed this as 'Move like no one's watching' by leaning into what their neighborhood has to offer and bundling a DJ experience for hotel guests. In this package, the resident DJ from Cabuya heads down to the guestroom for a personal tutorial on the craft.

Like all the other amenities we've covered, this DJ experience is authentically local, directly aligned with the posh sensibility of the brand and wholly part of a smart strategy that offers either a unique approach to market for travelers or a welcoming hangout for residents of Condesa-Roma. The Andaz Mexico City Condesa has plenty more lessons for the industry as it continues to adapt its programming in lockstep with its rapidly evolving community.

Leading the Culinary Lifestyle Segment with Christopher Hunsberger of Appellation Hotels

Every hotelier knows in their heart of hearts the importance of giving guests a great experience. It's the lifeblood of hospitality. Yet beyond impeccable service and a flawless guestroom, so much of that hotel experience is crafted by what else is happening onsite. This is what we often label as a 'reason-to-visit' which can be a spa, golf, the pool, beach access, proximity to attractions, activities, funky décor or a mix of several of these and more.

In this case, the focus is F&B as that reason to visit, yet normally we would still write about its importance as a part of the overall hotel experience – framed as an ancillary spend, if you will. Appellation changes this dynamic by molding the hotel experience around the culinary, and in doing so is carving out a whole new niche of next-generation approachable luxury.

Beyond just being approachable and upscale, we see Appellation as yet one more intrepid player within the broader, growing movement of lifestyle hotels whereby customers are selecting their accommodations based on those brands that conform with their identities and aspirations. In this case, the subcategory would be 'culinary lifestyle', aiming to create one-of-a-kind, food-centric experiences that guests will not find anywhere else.

To get some insights on what makes this brand tick and how it's filling a previously underserved market, we sat down with Appellation Hotels Co-founder and COO, Chris Hunsberger. Of the two of us, Larry worked with Hunsberger many years ago when he was President of Americas for Four Seasons Hotels and Resorts. Getting caught up, we were eager to learn about his new venture and what lessons apply to every hotelier looking to evolve their brand.

Tell me how you came to be a part of Appellation.

After working together on projects for more than 20 years, my cofounder Chef Charlie Palmer and I wanted to create a true merger of culinary and hospitality – something we have not seen implemented well yet. There are many great hotel restaurants, but nobody has really blended the culinary experience completely into the DNA of a hotel. At the time of our founding, Charlie and I owned and ran a couple of hotels in California that were eventually sold to become the seed capital to start Appellation, turning our vision into a reality by flipping the traditional hotel model and putting culinary at the forefront.

What is your vision for the new brand?

Beyond a culinary-first hotel concept, our hotels honor the brand's namesake, Appellation, which means 'to give a name to a place'. We are setting a new standard for immersion in culinary, culture and community that can only be found here. We have also thoughtfully positioned Appellation's hotels at the 4.5-star service level. We believe luxury hospitality should be world-class while also being approachable and welcoming.

Where are your first properties located and when do you expect to open?

We're focused on only developing hotels in places we love – places with a lot of soul and character. These tend to be high barrier-to-entry markets with an underserved luxury demand. Appellation Healdsburg – right in our hometown in Sonoma County wine country and neighboring our Appellation headquarters – will be our first opening. We are also debuting a hotel and residences in Sun Valley, Idaho for 2025, followed by hotel openings in Petaluma and Pacific Grove, California in 2026.

You mentioned the term approachable luxury. What does this actually mean?

We see approachable luxury as the future of luxury travel. Guests are seeking an impressive but unpretentious setting. Our hotels deliver first-rate services and unique experiences while prioritizing comfort and connection over formality and extravagance. We are creating a welcoming environment with ways for guests to learn new things during their stay, and our staff is genuinely happy to help.

Tell us more about the experiences that you expect to offer.

With a name like 'Appellation' it's imperative that our hotels truly reflect a sense of place. In addition to our own farming operations and working with local purveyors for the best regional ingredients, we also seek out rising culinary talent in the market and bring them onto our team. Similarly, we are building unique Maker Spaces into our lobbies where we invite local makers and artisans to come in and perform their craft as part of our *Crafted at Appellation* immersive learning program. More than anything, we want our guests to feel like they live in the community, even if it's for just a few days. We envision our guests' rubbing shoulders with locals – whether that be at one of our *Crafted at Appellation* classes, over dinner at one of our restaurants or late at night in one of our rooftop lounges.

Who is the primary target audience?
Our audience is curious by nature and looking to discover a destination's deepest roots, while connecting with others – all in a luxury setting. For our guests, food and beverage are not just part of the experience; it is the experience.

Do you have any competitors?
With our 4.5-star positioning and new culinary-first hotel concept, we really see Appellation as carving a new space in the luxury hospitality segment.

Tell us more about your key team.
Appellation is the product of its people. My co-founder and CEO, Chef Charlie Palmer, is a renowned restaurateur with multiple James Beard Awards and 20 Michelin stars to his name. Many of Charlie's protégés and close colleagues have gone on to open some of the best restaurants and most beloved establishments. We've brought in top leaders from all disciplines – guest experience, sales and marketing, finance, human resources, information technology, and development. We've also assembled a team of the best architects, interior designers, procurement specialists and legal experts.

Anything else to finish off?
We are innovating the use of technology in hospitality with our very own technology ecosystem called Appellation Insights. We spent a lot of time and resources to create a truly best-in-class marketing and guest experience platform ensuring a truly frictionless experiential environment for both guests and employees. While comparable hotels typically deploy about a hundred different pieces of tech, Appellation Insights efficiently encompasses one-third of that number. Most importantly, we are using technology to enhance interactions between guests and our staff, and not replace these interactions. Appellation Insights helps free up our team members' time to take on the hospitality-focused services they enjoy most, from guest interactions to surprise and delight experiences.

The Funkiest Southwest Hotel with Lessons for Every Hotelier Worldwide

The concept of a contemporary, boutique motel, either as a new build or retrofit, that commands sizably higher-than-market rates started to become a trend in the 2010s but has grown since the pandemic. Spurred on by a core psychographic of drive-to-vacation culture amongst Gen X and millennials, in the United States we are seeing multi-property brands like Bluebird and Urban Cowboy achieve success by opening exquisitely decorated lodges in sought-after rural areas near major cities. Then there are a host of independents gracing the covers of travel magazines such as The Vagabond Hotel in Miami, The Dive Motel in Nashville, Skyview Los Alamos in California, and Thunderbird in Marfa, Texas.

But perhaps one property stands above the rest by capturing the heart of this trend and then accelerating into a territory unmatched by any other hotel in the world due to its astounding, eccentric, and fun-in-every-way design. This is none other than the Hotel Zazz in Albuquerque, New Mexico which opened in Fall 2022. Right along the famed Route 66, all of the 48 guestrooms are imaginatively decorated with colorful, eclectic finishings, while the public spaces are equally dazzling and funky.

To help give you a better picture about what makes this hotel's soul so unique, they have onsite their own published children's book called "The Zazzy Adventures of Roozy and Raffie" that's a coloring storybook as well as a word search. Visitors who buy the book not only receive a lifetime membership to the 'R&R Club' for 15% off their current and all future stays at Hotel Zazz, but proceeds also support a charity dedicated to educating women and children around the world about the arts, culture and music.

Besides bringing joy to all visitors by literally brightening their day, the combination of a distinctively themed design and genuinely warm service serves as yet one more clear example of how unique hospitality experiences will always triumph no matter the market. And indeed, the market has responded with nonstop acclaim, buzz on social media and high year-round occupancies. In particular, Hotel Zazz is a darling amongst Gen Zers, with their user-generated content organically attracting all the other generations.

Together this represents a fundamental lesson and we were honored to sit down with owner-operator and Chief Experience Officer, Sharmin Dharas, to hear her story about how Hotel Zazz came to be.

Can you start by listing off some of the metrics that highlight just how much guests love Hotel Zazz?

We won eight awards in the first four months of being open! Now that we finished our first year, we have been hitting all the marks when it comes to social media bookings. Yes, SOCIAL MEDIA bookings – ones straight off of Instagram. We have guests slip into our DMs asking us to book their birthday vacation or a staycay. It's been amazing to not only get bookings via a free stream of marketing but to also have that as a direct booking! It's been a win-win. All of our social media is completely purely organic. We do not pay influencers because we feel people should showcase what is the true hotel from their angle. To repeat: not a social influence angle. But I will say it doesn't hurt to have them stay with us and organically give us a shout-out!

When was the moment that you knew you had to go all in on making the zaniest, zazziest hotel?

I love this question. When was the moment you knew you had to go all in on making the zazziest hotel? It was all my life. I grew up on the property. As an only child I wish

I had a park to walk to or neighbors to play with. Instead, I would imagine I had a swing, a playground, a children's dream in the center of the entertainment district. But I really knew it would bring in the ROI when I saw similar properties around the world when I would travel as a student doctor. Back then, boutique hotels weren't a thing; it was renovated hostiles that were. So, I knew we had something when I would see these locations being profitable without any pizzazz.

How did you get funding? How did you get investors to believe in the concept versus more traditional hotel brands?

Funding was a journey. I love sharing this story because it almost didn't happen. We actually put a packet together that showed the old then we added our bold concept. We also showed the market we would target and how much revenue each of the SMERF (social, military, educational, religious, fraternal) would provide within a certain radius. It was hard to get the data because I wasn't part of any of the hospitality associations. It was a lot of research and STR data. At the end of it all, they always care about proforma.

Mind you, I pitched it to them in 2021. This was immediately after we came out of the stay-at-home pandemic. I looked for community banks and pitched it to one who I thought would want to support the project because I had the city councilor call the bank president to get me in. And, well, we did it! We were at the table about to sign the closing documents, then they stopped and pulled the loan from us because, as they said, there were other hotels that were coming into the market. So, here I am in early 2021 with everything lined up to execute, and the local community bank shattered my dreams. But I wanted to be an entrepreneur in boutique hotels, so I found the grit to go find another bank.

Just then, my cousin Rahim told me about another community bank. I asked the VP to meet me for breakfast at a boutique Curio property along with my hotel guru Alan Barmaper. We are all at the table about to order breakfast when I give the VP the prospectus – nicely bound, color print with a cover and back that has all our info – and all he just takes it, sets it aside and looks at the menu to order. After ordering, without looking at the booklet, the VP looks me straight in the eyes and asks me about my vision. This was the first time someone wanted to hear what I had to say versus only the numbers.

When I described how the hotel would be located in the Nob Hill Entertainment District, the VP jumped into a story about how he lived right behind a dumpy old motel there, and about how all his friends in the neighborhood wished there was a boutique hotel in the area for when family would visit – instead of having them shack up in the district's historic, 800-square-feet-tops houses. He knew the site well as it turns out and was sold on the project all before our food arrived. Let me tell you, just like getting pregnant it only takes one!

How did you 'zazzify' the hotel's culture to ensure that every aspect of operations would embody the tone and spirit that you set out to create on a continual basis?

The zazzification of Hotel Zazz happened as the project unfolded. It really started from the discovery of the name. Picture this: it's during the pandemic; I'm on a Zoom call. I had a COVID baby in my arms and I'm telling the branding team that this neighborhood is so eclectic and unique. It's all about local and we just need to add some pizzazz, when my daughter, Shayrooz, attached at my hip looks at me and says "Daazz? Wat's daath?" A lightbulb went on – the baby is right! – it's zazz, the hotel should be called Hotel Zazz.

This girl was genius if she only knew but that was the moment that started the zazzification of everything. We had her tell us what her favorite color was and, like any toddler, it changed daily. So, we went along with it. But the best was when we asked her, "If zazz was an animal, what would it be?" She said Raffie! Naturally, we next asked, "what's Raffie's favorite snack?" She said it was a 'nanana' (baby speak for banana). This was the impetus for the speakeasy golden banana entry!

Without playing favorites, what hotel features or amenities are you fondest about?

The lobby is the first impression, and that's exactly what we did. We made sure that the second you walked in you could use all five senses as well as the sixth sense – that of feelings and introspection. We wanted to make sure you can activate them all. From the second you walk in, you can smell sweet banana slurpee – our signature scent. You hear the tunes that give you the good vibes and you see this tree of life that Shayrooz wanted. Think *Game of Thrones* on steroids with silver. And you tap the golden banana three times to go into the hidden speakeasy that gives you your first taste of whimsical freedom. Let me tell you that the whole thing is an experience. All of our staff love seeing our guests' faces when they tap the golden banana three times and see this wall pop open. It's wild!

You've just opened a spa amenity. What metrics did you use to justify this capex?

I never used capex; I used what would I want to have if I could afford a room at Hotel Zazz. It's so unique to have a full-blown spa on property that you would never expect to see in a motel-style boutique hotel.

Before entering hospitality, you were a licensed medical professional. That's a profound and very uncommon career path. Can you describe what motivated that change?

Yes, I'm a doctor, but I was born into hotel hospitality. I literally watched my parents in the middle of the night get up to check-in a guest. I was trained that sleep doesn't matter; work ethics do. That actually prepared me for medical training (the no sleep aspect), and that medical training got me ready to be a serial entrepreneur who apparently believes in sleep later. Thank god we have massages and spa on property for some R&R!

But the reason why I left medicine was because I was depressed in every way. I was literally dealing with life and death, and I was a people person. I wanted what I saw growing up. Human interaction and storytelling. I knew that this would be the best thing for mental health and happiness. Our number one goal when you get on our property is to have you feel happy. We also took the time to make sure the colors that were selected impacted you in a fun way. Hotel Zazz is a pioneer of chromotherapy; we know colors invoke feelings, so why not make them make you feel fantastic.

What challenges have you had to overcome because of this that others may not have faced?

Being a hotel owner-operator for at least the first two years of a new concept is critical because it allows you the opportunity to make sure the brand is translated and successful. It also allows you to add that extra element of true hospitality that you as an owner can make calls for – for instance, a free bottle of wine or hearing that guests like a certain brand of local chocolates and getting it delivered to them. Also, it's the storytelling component – really tuning in to hear likes and dislikes then amplifying the likes.

The biggest challenge is not having a full grasp on operations like you would from a franchise SOP playbook and just learning as we go. In a way, it's also been a blessing because we are not the standard. Apparently, I am the only solely-woman-owned hotel in New Mexico. That is huge because now I can prove that it can be done. Since hitting the stage at a BITAC event in August 2023, there have been a few women who reached out to me and asked me to help them with their projects. I love that. I love that they have someone that I didn't have. Also, being a minority-owned hotel, most of our staff are from Africa, like me. We hope to eventually grow the Zazz brand and give them some skin in the game so that one day, they can own their own hotel.

What's next for Hotel Zazz? Fingers crossed for a branded hotel in our hometown of Toronto.

Since we opened, we had about five additional requests to open other Zazz properties along with potential owners. It looks like Zanzibar, Dubai, and Arizona will be some of the first, followed by Toronto and Mexico soon after. I am always so god-willing and family-supporting because, without that faith and family, I wouldn't have been able to move through all the hurdles we had to overcome and come out with a zazzy concept!

Checking in at Fairmont Banff Springs and the Luxury Trend for More Intimate Guestrooms

For Canadians, Fairmont is not just a hotel brand but a fixture of our nation's history. In the decades following the country's confederation in 1867, towns that connected the Eastern hubs of Montreal, Toronto, Quebec, and Ottawa with the still-budding Western ports of Vancouver and Victoria were few and far between. It fell up Canadian Pacific – the company that would eventually sell its hotel division to Fairmont Raffles Hotels International, then to Accor in 2016 – to not only build a transcontinental railway, but to erect a series of what we now deem iconic hotels along the route.

The Fairmont Banff Springs, first opened in 1888, is one such gem from this nation-building era. Perhaps a shock to some of you, but the business of hospitality has indeed changed in the past 130 some-odd years, and so too must the 764-key Fairmont Banff Springs reinvent itself from time to time. As such, we were excited to tour the property following its most recent $35 million renovation and then report on what was accomplished and how it fits into a greater industry trend.

This latest refresh was focused on the hotel's luxury guestrooms and suites, including the transformation of Fairmont Gold – an exclusive hotel-within-a-hotel experience. This involved the renovation of the fifth floor, now devoted solely to Fairmont Gold (with some Fairmont Gold rooms on the fourth floor). All Fairmont Gold rooms and suites received upgraded finishes, and a club lounge area with convenient food options and a quiet room was added. A special Fairmont Gold arrival experience was created by restoring the property's original motor court that faces directly onto the mountains and having guests enter through a separate lobby.

Without getting too far into the details just yet, the lesson for readers is how this Fairmont Gold-oriented capital improvement taps into a global trend that's accelerated in the post-pandemic era centered around the 'price inelastic yet experience elastic' hotel consumer.

To fully understand the strategy behind this renovation and how it meets this trend head-on with an elevated guest experience, we sat down with the General Manager at Fairmont Banff Springs, Gregor Resch, in his office on the premises for a casual discussion about the state of the industry and the launching Fairmont Gold at a historic hotel.

Besides his GM duties, Resch is also Regional Vice President, overseeing executive decision-making for all properties in the Canadian Western Mountain Region – including Fairmont Château Lake Louise and Fairmont Jasper Park Lodge in Alberta, and Fairmont Château Whistler in British Columbia – as well as playing a guiding hand in the rebranding and renovation of the Rimrock Resort just up the street from Fairmont Banff Springs, which was only brought under the Accor banner in June 2023.

The Money Value of Time

Turning the financial concept of discounting – for reference, known as the 'time value of money' – on its head, per the sub-heading the big global hospitality trend in the upscale, luxury, and ultraluxury segments is that nightly rates and prices aren't nearly as important as maximizing one's time and experience while visiting a destination. With this in mind, the concept behind Fairmont Gold is to offer luxury guests beautifully appointed rooms with a more intimate club lounge experience.

Touring the results of the renovation and Fairmont Banff Springs executes to the fullest. With a rotunda driveway that jogs around and past the grand frontage of the hotel, every guest's arrival experience is punctuated by a backdrop of the lush forests surrounding the confluence of the Spray and Bow Rivers with the snowcapped Rocky Mountains behind. This is a 'sense of place' in its truest form. Past the new check-in desk and up to the dedicated Fairmont Gold floor area, all guests are treated to the convenience of a 'flexible and delectable' dining space with catered bar service, an adjoining reading room, and windows throughout facing onto Mount Rundle in the distance.

The idea behind a club lounge that Fairmont Gold and other leading brands are investing in is worth exploring some more because it fits into the modern paradigm for exclusivity and the aforementioned flexibility. Really, though, it's peace of mind that consumers are after.

Many guests are willing to pay more for a sense of privacy and having a third space near to their room or suite where they can casually unwind with some light, complimentary refreshments. In this case, those snacks and beverages come along with inspirational mountain views. With the nature of travel and technology nowadays, people's schedules are simultaneously more frenetic and relaxed, so not every meal needs to be an elaborately catered affair. Sometimes it's better for the guest overall enjoyment of a property to facilitate some buffet-style, hands-off foodservice, albeit with an execution that always reflects the culinary team's expertise.

The Economics of Upleveling

It's easy to take a glance at the town of Banff and remark with a 'If you build it, they will come' attitude regarding the establishment of a new hotel product in the luxury category. But as Resch noted, while this latest Fairmont Gold renovation indeed opens up the destination to a new type of traveler, it's never that simple when it comes to getting the project off the ground.

Notably, there was a concern amongst ownership about the reduced gross operating profit (GOP) margins per key for the Fairmont Gold product (roughly 70% GOP) versus the other rooms at Fairmont Banff Springs (roughly 75% GOP). On a per-unit basis, this is true, but the average ADR for Fairmont Gold rooms is north of $450 higher – albeit with a greater suites contribution – meaning that the total volume of revenues is significantly better even with the slight drop of per-key margins.

Not only that but the team has observed that Fairmont Gold guests have a longer length of stay (LOS) and they spend more on ancillaries per guest during their time onsite (TRevPAR). All this is to say that when you look at the metrics holistically, upleveling a section of the hotel makes complete sense.

And while on the topic of ancillaries and TRevPAR, the Fairmont Spa was another spot on our tour. This 48,000-square-foot facility features a gigantic mineral pool treatment rooms and a full exercise area, all with a very Alpine feel and thermal focus. For the summers, they have a sprawling terrace facing the mountains for outdoor yoga. Of note, hotel guests book around a month in advance for any appointments, while the facility also attracts a lot of locals for memberships.

To circle back to the notion of an elevated experience via amenities like an exclusive lounge and access to a world-class spa, what Resch also highlighted as critical for giving Fairmont Gold customers maximum value for their time is the nature by which they book people into these on-prem experiences so that no hotel guest is disappointed. Similar to spa appointments, another unforgettable experience would be to golf on the course that snakes around the river valley, and yet wouldn't it be a shame if a guest were to miss out because the tee time they wanted was no longer available?

To fulfill this need in as frictionless a manner as possible, the team is testing out a property experience management system (PXMS) that can act as a one-stop shop and itinerary planner for guests with connections into Opera, OpenTable (restaurants), Shiji Concept (golf) and Book4Time (spa and activities). This way, the hotel can deliver even more convenience on top of the other amenities catering to this modern shift. Regardless of the technology, it always comes back to the experience, and for this alone the new renovation helps keep this historic property in line with the latest luxury trends and set for many years to come in showing guests the very best of Canada.

Length of Stay Is the Best KPI for Proving the Value of Wellness Investments

The word 'optimization' in today's world implies the use of data and metrics for continuous business improvement, but it also implies making tradeoffs and devoting limited resources to certain goals ahead of others. For today's hospitality world, we are confronted by so many data points, so many partners or siloed interests and so many different activities vying for our attention or capital. To make informed, strategic decisions that will unify various operations towards a common objective, hoteliers and owners must carefully pick the key performance indicators (KPIs) that they will optimize and prioritize.

What KPIs should a hotel focus on improving? This pursuit of optimization only gets more complex with the more operations we add – profit centers such as a wellness center that are very often necessary to drive occupancy as well as diversify away from a purely heads-in-beds model – making business intelligence (BI) and machine learning (ML) instrumental to making sense of it all.

In anticipation of his keynote appearance at Forum Hotel&Spa in Paris, I had the opportunity to sit down with Hans-Peter Veit, Director of Spa & Recreation at Appenzeller Huus Gonten in Switzerland, where we discussed why length of stay (LOS) should be the foremost KPI to optimize for whenever a hotel leader or brand is considering the substantial capex requirements for new wellness assets at their properties.

A Distinguished Spa Career in Focus

To frame the justification for LOS above the numerous other metrics that hotels can track, it's important to first remark on Veit's career in luxury hospitality to see how he arrived at this KPI as the holistic marker of property growth.

Veit started his hotel career as a personal trainer in 1999 at Brenners Park-Hotel & Spa, a historic, five-star wellness-focused property in Baden-Baden dating back to 1834 that's also the first property in the celebrated Oetker Collection. After two years, he moved into spa management, staying at Brenners Park for over 17 years. (As an aside for those unfamiliar with this region, Baden-Baden has been renowned for its healing thermal waters since Roman times, with accounts surviving of Emperor Carcalla visiting the baths in the early third century to cure his arthritis.)

In mid-2009, Veit took on a larger role for the Oetker Collection, acting as the Director of Spa Development for seven years, where he helped manage new resort spa constructions as well as the design of multi-night wellness packages and a variety of onsite programs to meet guest needs. Thereafter, he was the Director of Spa at Victoria-Jungfrau Grand Hotel & Spa in Interlaken for over four years and the Director of Spa & Wellbeing at Grand Resort Bad Ragaz for over three years before joining Appenzeller Huus in Gonten in January 2024.

Observations from Luxury Hotel Management

Taken together, these properties represent the pinnacle of the destination spa world, with time-honored wellness brands that must be upheld through meticulous attention to the available programming and through periodic renovations to ensure lasting quality befitting their prestige. These are hotels that often host the same single occupants, couples, families and groups each year, with guests returning annually because they are treated special and their detailed preferences are remembered.

This level of anticipatory service is only possible when teams remain intact – a clear incentive to prioritize your employees. But the knock-on effect of incredible service is that you have reduced customer acquisition costs because a sizable proportion of your guests are returning and booking direct. Moreover, these returning guests have on average a longer LOS and spend more on ancillaries to increase total revenue per guest (TRevPAR). Given the higher relative costs of operationalizing check-ins and check-outs, increasing LOS in this way is both a reflection of higher topline throughout as well as a cost-cutting measure.

From his tenure at these luxury brands, Veit has many other keen observations on the operational challenges for five-star hotel spas that others may miss, especially those that relate to the human side of wellness service delivery and the personal touch of a caring, devoted and energized spa practitioner.

"When it comes to delivering five-star wellness experiences, everyone at the hotel is as important as the next, from the general manager right down to the receptionist and masseuse," remarked Veit. "All spa team members need time to recharge in order to deliver their best performance and not just average service. For instance, when you allow for too many bookings in the evening, your practitioner may be fatigued by then and won't be able to give a treatment that's reflective of true luxury quality. So, even though the demand may be there for those late-hour appointments, you have to restrict availability in order to preserve both the guest experience and team morale."

This example highlights a tradeoff that only a true wellness veteran would be able to navigate. By optimizing for the highest quality of spa service, the push for maximizing short-term revenues may be sacrificed, but the long-term benefit is that guests remember how the staff treated them, and then become loyal patrons for years to come, serving this LOS-driven objective.

After all, where else but the spa do guests and hotel teams spend so much time interacting? This is a unique quality of a wellness facility versus other onsite touchpoints like the front desk or the restaurant which is often overlooked and difficult to directly quantify. It's this emotional, human connection that results in more return visits, more word of mouth and, ultimately, improvements to all the other metrics that give a full-service property resiliency, with positive changes in ADR, TRevPAR, LOS, direct booking rates, lead times and pace by room type.

Guiding an Enormous Resort Development

While Appenzeller cheese is world-renowned, the canton of Appenzell Innerhoden, much like many other places nestled in vast mountain greenscapes of Switzerland, has quietly gained a devoted following as a wellness destination. The growth of wellness tourism to the country and to this particular district – along with other recent examples of success, such as The Chedi Andermatt, which first opened in December 2013 – became the impetus for Veit's current role helping oversee the Appenzeller Huus Gonten's low nine-figure expansion project, turning the currently 25-room hotel into its own quintessentially Swiss alpine spa village.

The development will include the construction of 80 hotel keys and 42 branded residences spread across a campus of low-rise buildings that each have their own spa amenities and are connected by underground tunnels for access to the primary medi-spa facility. The hotel units will be divided amongst three-star, four-star, and five-star offerings – with certain amenities and facilities exclusive to the luxury customers – while the residences will be operated as serviced apartments with most already presold. Importantly, throughout this entire process, trees will obscure lines of sight with the construction as certain buildings and units are certified as ready for occupancy.

With the spa facilities designed by GOCO Hospitality, the vision was to design a pure Swiss experience, integrating nature wherever possible and even going so far as to use only the original wood from nearby cabins that date back as early as 1602. To build on Veit's understanding of the importance of keeping teams happy in order to generate return visits and increase LOS, budgeted into this construction is *wohngemeinschaft*, from the German for 'shared apartment', although this direct translation doesn't really capture the sense of community inferred by this compound word.

As this outlook relates to Appenzeller Huus Gonten, staffing accommodations are not an afterthought in this development but are central to the planning of attracting top talent to this rural destination. As these employee buildings represent a huge upfront expense in addition to the buildout of a world-class medi-spa, other developers may have opted for minimizing this line item because it doesn't have a direct relationship with returns. And yet, their construction is entirely necessary in order to reflect long-term property health through such metrics as low employee turnover then above-benchmark LOS which as we've shown is the final result of anticipatory service.

What Makes a Medi-Spa

For these shared apartments and with many other intangibles of hospitality capex, Veit and his team have always recognized that the specialized staff required to curate the high-touch and high-tech experiences of a medi-spa all have families and may not be prepared to immediately relocate to Appenzell. Staff buildings with communal kitchens and their own high-end amenities thus become integral to nurturing team bonds and keeping employees for the long-term to enable smooth, efficient operations or so that guests can remain loyal by returning year after year to see the same practitioners.

But what exactly is so specialized about a modern wellness center? In order to drive LOS, of course, guests want great service, but they also need a strong 'reason to visit'.

At Appenzeller Huus Gonten, that reason to visit will be an illustrious, three-story wellness facility with the latest in contrast therapy such as infrared saunas, hyperbaric oxygen tanks and cryochambers, alongside an array of clinicians to administer these treatments as well as physiotherapists and other movement specialists. Part of the design will be to present these experiences in an inviting, non-sterile setting that incorporates natural elements appropriate for the Swiss countryside, and with a bucket list rooftop pool offering awe-inspiring panoramas of the mountains.

Between the clinical staff and state-of-the-art machinery, as well as the lavish fittings, fixings and furnishings, none of this comes cheap. As Veit remarked, he is willing to show a loss on the spa ledger in order to drive room reservations and LOS – the hotel ledger which has the largest margins. After all, it is the wellness facility that will be the main draw for guests to book in the first place, to stay longer and to pay a premium for access to the amenities. In other words, hotel occupancies are being optimized ahead of positive cash flows in the spa, knowing that the latter entity drives business for the former.

"Full service hotels cannot think in terms of silos anymore," added Veit. "Spas should not think only about maximizing profitability within their own operation because this may not best serve the long-term interests of high-paying, loyal hotel guests. Likewise, hotel managers must think about what experiences they are offering in order to build that loyalty and convince guests to stay longer during each visit. This programming and reason to visit comes with a cost, but ensures business longevity, and there's no better way to boost LOS than through wellness."

To conclude our chat, Veit offered one other German word, one that even the famed Swiss hotelier César Ritz used to guide his service approach: *ehrlichkeit* or 'sincerity'. All senior executives and leaders must be honest and upfront with their vision and plans so that they can act in harmony to achieve those lofty goals and build a brand that lasts. Unifying around LOS as a KPI is one foremost way to ensure that everyone from the owner down to the front desk clerk are doing their part to best serve the business.

Creating an Oasis in the City at the Andaz Mexico City Condesa

Come springtime, Mexico City (CDMX) is set ablaze in enchanting swathes of lavender and mauve as the Jacaranda trees enter bloom, littering the parks and grand avenues with flowers and pleasant aromas to contrast the sprawling metropolis all around. Not yet drowning in heat and with cool evenings, April is the perfect time of year to visit the city which itself is entering a hospitality renaissance with tourists discovering this cultural and gastronomic capital while corporate travelers continue to deliver a consistent flow of midweek stays as businesses in CDMX benefits from Mexico's current economic boom.

Against this backdrop, the Andaz Mexico City Condesa is one such newcomer. Tucked just off the main thoroughfare of Avenida de los Insurgentes in the trendy and perfectly safe downtown neighborhood of Condesa-Roma, this hotel of 193 rooms and 20 suites represents a shining example of how dynamic, multi-space programming can drive demand from different segments and boost total revenue by increasing onsite capture per guest (TRevPAR).

Following our first report on this luxury property where we focused on how generating a sense of community can diversify revenues and heighten guest satisfaction, one of this article's coauthored byline (Adam) had the opportunity to revisit the Andaz Mexico City Condesa, both to experience even more of the many gems in CDMX and also to uncover how the management team has created a veritable 'Oasis in the City' with diverse F&B offerings and event spaces.

To fully exploring the Andaz Mexico City Condesa and how it's gone about crafting such a vibrant, TRevPAR-centric hotel, we interviewed both the property's General Manager, Analia Capurro, as well as the Senior Marketing & Communications Manager, Antonio Mejia, discussing how the hotel programs for the leisure, hybrid and group segments across its five signature restaurants and six M&E spaces.

Highlighting the City's Growth

Already getting close to 25 million inhabitants and as a city where north meets south, CDMX is developing and gentrifying at an electric pace due to a variety of converging factors. The nation itself is perhaps the largest beneficiary of the American nearshoring movement while new states and regions continue to open up for tourism and the burgeoning short-term rental market for those who can work remotely. Then, for agriculture, Mexico trumps all but a few – avocados, corn, beans, tomatoes, citrus fruit, chocolate, coffee, and plenty more – while mining is also on the upswing. All this capital inevitably converges on CDMX.

Besides the corporate engine, which has always delivered strong midweek occupancy, Mexico City has arguably the best culinary scene in the Americas, and the word is now out. Much like how the nation's businesses congregate on CDMX, so too does its diverse heritage of regionally specific cuisines. While the city is famous for its al pastor tacos, these are but the tip of the iceberg for what's on hand in any given neighborhood.

Combine this with numerous historical sites and museums, and it's no wonder North Americans are now hopping down in droves for a weekend jaunt or a multi-day stopover before heading out to another lesser-known part of the country that lacks direct flights from the United States or Canada.

Beyond the ever-popular Cancun, Los Cabos and Puerto Vallarta (which all have directs from major cities in the lower 48 and also from other international gateways), think Guadalajara, Mérida, Oaxaca City, Puerto Escondido, San Cristóbal de las Casas in Chiapas, San Miguel de Allende in Guanajuato and Tulum (with its brand new airport that just opened in March), all just a quick flight from the nexus that is CDMX. And to give you a sense of this growth at the luxury end, besides the Andaz Mexico City Condesa, other recent openings included The Ritz-Carlton, Mexico City in October 2021 and Soho House Mexico City in September 2023, with 1 Hotels, Park Hyatt, and Rosewood all having properties in development.

How Different Hotel Spaces Increase Group Spend

The megatrend of megatrends for travel going forward is the prioritization of experiences and the 'monetary value of time' by consumers. While location and price will always be important criteria, hotel guests are increasingly optimizing for experiences over other factors by selecting properties that have outstanding amenities – both in the room and on-premises – so that they have more at their immediate disposal versus having to venture elsewhere.

While there are numerous examples of hotels innovating in this regard, specifically for the Andaz Mexico City Condesa let's focus on how this 'amenitization' affects the group segment. As Capurro pointed out, the property has hosted many multiday events over the past couple of years where the entire itinerary takes place at various venues on the property instead of, for instance, bussing the group to an offsite venue for one or more evening affairs. The hotel's size means it can accommodate large room blocks while facilities like the 24-hour fitness center and the gourmet Derba Matcha Café around the corner from the front desk ensure group guests are well provided for in their spare time.

As one example in particular, Capurro cited a recent 120-someodd-guest wedding where the 17th-floor Cabuya Rooftop – festooned in hanging plants, eclectic furniture and colorful murals – was set up for a daytime ceremony, with the arch and altar positioned next to the pool for a captivating background of CDMX's skyline comprised of the towers along La Reforma and in Polanco further afield. The reception was then held in the main, 6,157-square-foot ballroom capable of handling all banqueting needs, while the full-service Pasana Spa & Wellness on the second floor handled all the bridal party preparations. One breakfast for the group was held at a third space – Pórtico Restaurant, an artsy yet functional space on the first floor that extends into the courtyard – while another utilized a couple breakout rooms.

"From the standpoint of the wedding planner, having everything in one location means peace of mind," commented Capurro. "Shuttling guests to and from offsite venues is often a logistical nightmare, but it's done because planners want to introduce variety to the program in order to make the experience more memorable. Maximizing onsite capture is thus not a matter of building yet another banquet hall. Each space needs its own personality in order to create unique moments in time."

Adding to this, Capurro remarked that, during the sales process, the Andaz

Mexico City Condesa was specifically chosen because its spaces were all unique in both orientation, themed décor, and artwork, thus creating different moods for each individual event on the schedule. Furthermore, because of the property's amenitization, the group block was secured for three nights instead of two, representing a huge bump in the total contract value.

How Different Hotel Spaces Increase Leisure Spend

This prioritization of experiences is equally as strong in the leisure transient and blended travel (bleisure) segments. It all harks back to the desire to have a flexible home base while exploring a destination. For instance, Cabuya Rooftop is a big draw at any hour that it's open (when not booked out for a wedding!), with a sunlit pool, comfy lounge arrangements, a tasty seafood-skewing menu, and a full selection of cocktails and mezcal. It works for families, couples, corporate guests wanting a reprieve, digital nomads who pull out their laptop to fire off some emails, or locals wanting a scenic spot for lunch.

The aforementioned Derba Matcha Café and Pórtico offer yet more varied programming for guests to spread out and change it up without having to leave the premises. Also in the first floor courtyard is La Terrazza, an outdoor extension of Pórtico that's been given a Tulum aesthetic of rustic, natural furnishings centered on two oversized art installations.

And in preparation for a six-week renovation to fully enclose Cabuya Rooftop so that it's rain-resilient, the programming at La Terrazza has been expanded to include a pizza-themed Sunday brunch and extended evening hours. Pasana Spa has likewise introduced a new Indulge in Serenity package, targeting both leisure travelers and local day guests.

It's this sort of dynamic, diverse programming that will convince blended or hybrid travelers to reserve that extra shoulder night around a midweek business trip or persuade their hubby to tag along for 'plus one travel' where one occupant goes off to their meetings for the day while the other uses the onsite amenities. The city is always there for the taking, but when guests are a bit tired, not fully dressed, undercaffeinated, or don't have time to contend with Mexico City's traffic, an oasis is what they want.

When you craft such a place where each space is its own personality, word will inevitably get out and your metrics will improve over time. As a start, you'll notice a gradual increase in length of stay (LOS) and TRevPAR, while the weekday-weekend occupancy ebbs and flows will smooth out, resulting in both a higher average occupancy rate and reduced cost per occupied room (CPOR) as the crunch of having all checkout cleans on a Friday or Sunday will be offset by longer average stays.

In discussing this progression with Mejia, the uptick in ancillary spending also correlates with more return visits and better lead time pacing. As all the onsite activity helps to brand equity, this then translates into a greater volume of direct bookings (RevDirect) versus the OTAs and a reduced need for intensive programmatic ad campaign spending, together boosting net revenues. Taking all these factors into account, the increased demand and heightened perceived value allow a property with a personality like the Andaz Mexico City Condesa to raise rates above benchmarks for even better long-term growth.

In such a place as CDMX, where north meets south and all the timeless history of Mexico comes together, this oasis-in-the-city example is one that everyone should watch as both a perennially healthy business and an experiential trendsetter for hospitality. It all comes back to the programming and the tireless work from team members like Capurro and Mejia to ensure that all the onsite spaces are exceptional in their own way.

The Progressive Luxury Hotel Evolution in Focus with EAST Hotels

The 21st century has already seen immense changes in how people travel and their demands for hotel services and amenities. In focus here is the growth, evolution, and diversification of the luxury segment, wherein we recently sat down with the team behind the rebranding of EAST Hotels, a hotel brand that's emblematic of this modern dynamic and the aspirational nature of travel for the 2020s and beyond. EAST Hotels has launched three hotels in Beijing, Hong Kong and Miami, with several more in the pipeline on multiple continents.

Accelerated by the pandemic, travelers of all demographics and geographics are coming to increasingly prioritize experiences, wellness, eco-conscious hotels, and connecting with like-minded individuals, and they are willing to pay a premium to brands that combine those elements that align with their identities. As discussed with the EAST team, this trend is so mega that the word 'demographic' may soon not really apply as age becomes only one of many contributors towards a consumer's buying decisions, favoring psychographics, interests, and other behavioral qualities to better inform marketing and operations. In a word, brands like EAST are designed for an 'attitude', not a specific age group.

While some luxury brands have veered into the uber-exclusive and stratospherically priced ultraluxury subcategory, other companies are embracing the rise of the knowledge class and HENRYs (high earners, not rich yet) with approachable, wellness-oriented, eco-friendly properties that bring together a global community of alternative thinkers while maintaining the hallmarks of luxury service standards. Most call it 'lifestyle' but we deem this too ambiguous so we've labeled as 'progressive luxury' and it's worth a moment to dwell on its budding nichification away from traditional stalwarts in the luxury category.

Here are the qualities that we associate with lifestyle or progressive luxury:

1. Brands that are, as the word implies, 'making progress' in terms of advancing a better way of living centered around everyday wellness, longevity, and sustainability.
2. Having direct appeal to the knowledge class, denoting people who work in creative, collaborative, largely tech-based, and proliferating industries.

3. Providing amenable spaces that facilitate a sense of community for the now-common lifestyle trend of working from anywhere while also abiding by the tenets of 'quiet luxury' with other spaces for secluded relaxation and privacy.
4. Approachable and flexible interior design that blends the casual and formal with ergonomic furnishings, biophilia, and inspirational artwork or finishes.
5. A strong emphasis on thoughtful, localized, curated and exclusive experiences, understanding that modern consumers often value their time over materialistic gains.
6. Being mission-driven, largely by aligning with wellness practices, healthy living, sustainable practices, locavore, and agrobiodiversity movements, or stewarding traditional cultures.
7. Appealing to other concurrent growth trends in hospitality with appropriate area planning for branded residences and larger guestrooms suitable for multigenerational travel.
8. Ingrained in the brand DNA is the understanding that youth is a mindset and that the attitude of current and near-future luxury guests is one of aligning with purposeful community.

And it's hardly a cookie-cutter approach here. Lifestyle brands like EAST are finding ways to mix these eight tenets to build unique identities that appeal to a cluster of emerging consumer segments.

How EAST Hotels Addresses These Emerging Segments

For reference, the EAST Hotels brand hails from Hong Kong, where its parent company, Swire Hotels, has longstanding experience in luxury hotel development and management via its other established hospitality brand, The House Collective. Embodying the principle that each property is 'Houses Not Hotels', this has been interpreted thus far into three artfully designed, urban luxury gems, including The Upper House in Hong Kong, The Middle House in Shanghai, and The Temple House in Chengdu.

As luck would have it, we were able to find a time that coincided with the availabilities of not one but three members of the dream team behind the rebranding of EAST while they were together in Miami visiting this 40-story, 352-key North American property. All of them hospitality veterans, we met with Dean Winter, Managing Director of Swire Hotels, Teresa Muk, Head of Brand and Strategic Marketing at Swire Hotels, and Toby Smith, Chief Commercial Officer for Swire Hotels.

While The House Collective's brand playbook includes great culinary, the signature Mi Xun Spa, fitness classes with renowned instructors, eco-oriented experiences, fireside talks with tastemakers and a year-round events calendar, EAST takes these all these hallmarks and evolves them for the lifestyle or (our term) progressive luxury niche of alternative thinkers. One prominent way that this is reflected is through the brand's appeal to the wellness-secondary travel segment – guests who are traveling for another purpose but still want to maintain their at-home health regimen while abroad.

Instead of the traditional focus on wellness through spa, EAST's approach is centered more around fitness, nutrition and fostering connections amongst these modern 'glocal' travelers. For instance, the hotel's Run Club brings the community together with regularly scheduled activities like Run and Brunch, and Midnight Runners. As an example from their onsite event series, they've hosted acclaimed speakers focusing on women's health and the new body literacy movement. Especially for corporate guests where the lack of big open time chunks may preclude a visit to the spa, these sorts of 'wellness in between' activities hit a sweet spot.

Here are some other ways that this philosophy is interpreted on premises across EAST properties:

- An architectural and engineering marvel that is the property's Climate Ribbon canopy, creating natural shading to reduce the load on air conditioning units and collecting rainwater for later use
- Filtered water tap in every room, simultaneously reducing single-use plastic (by upwards of 300,000 bottles per year) while also improving guest health by eliminating potentially hazardous pollutants in water as well as exposure to microplastics
- Fulfilling fitness needs with a 24-hour gym, BEAST (Body by EAST), outdoor pool area, EASTudio for multipurpose classes and personal training and complimentary electric bike rentals
- Exceptionally high quality cuisine with locally sourced and organic ingredients wherever possible to enhance flavor and nutrition (and reduce food miles), while minimizing the usage of artificial additives or ultra-processed foods
- Joining the World Wildlife Fund's Sustainable Seafood Business and the WWF's Sustainable Restaurant Association
- Adherence to the company's 2030 Sustainability Goals and Green Kitchen initiative, including onsite food waste treatment via ORCA digesters as well as food waste upcycling procedures such as using unsold bread as malt for craft beer or coffee grounds as onsite vegetable fertilizer
- Biophilic design by incorporating greenscapes throughout and using regenerative materials or those with lower embodied carbon

Environmentalism as a Profit Maker

As can be readily evident from many of these bulleted features, besides wellness-secondary travel, sustainability and eco-consciousness are also in the brand DNA. But rather than treating sustainability as a project where the goal is to meet a minimal threshold, the team at EAST understands that a heartfelt commitment to environmentalism is exactly what the new age cohort of alternative thinkers is looking for in their accommodations. They are willing to pay a premium for supporting aspirational brands.

"It seems like almost every week now, the travel industry is cited as a major contributor to climate change, and as a result, consumers of all demographics and mindsets are highly conscious of the impact they are making," commented Dean Winter. "Still, travel isn't going away; it's too vital for both commerce and individual self-actualization. Instead, smart hotel brands are getting ahead of the curve by becoming true stewards of a greener future. It's a lot more work to approach sustainability from this framework, but it makes dividends when it comes to brand equity, loyalty, and business growth."

Where we distinguish this is in the difference between sustainability and stewardship. The former word denotes a checklist; guests can see that the hotel has attained a passing grade. Think of going paperless, low-flow toilets, or IoT modulation for HVAC units. Don't get us wrong; these are all important, and guests expect them to be handled, but at the same time, no guest is specifically selecting a hotel for those rather invisible features.

Stewardship, on the other hand, is something that guests feel and want to be a part of. It's the makings of bona fide loyalty and the clearest way to show that investments into sustainable design can work out quite lucratively for a brand. EAST demonstrates that through a bolder commitment to these causes, a win for the environment is also a win for all other stakeholders.

The Bright Future for Progressive Luxury

With a pipeline that includes properties in exciting gateway locations around the world, EAST represents the 'next big thing' for hospitality in terms of the lifestyle category and giving guests accommodations that are more than just decent rooms.

For comparison, consider some of the other brands that are actively evolving in this progressive luxury space include: 1 Hotels, Andaz, Appellation, Capella, EDITION, Equinox Hotels, Janu, MGallery, Nobu Hotels, Pendry, SIRO, SLS, Soho House and Viceroy. All of these brands and all of their properties that have a profound 'reason to visit' that brings together service, F&B, wellness, events, activities, art and community in varying combinations that are approachable but still make each stay memorable.

This isn't to say that major chains like Marriott and Hilton aren't keen on this trend. It's an arms race, after all, and luxury hotels have to keep innovating to stay a step ahead. And yet, just as the industry megaliths push into this niche through their soft brands like Autograph and Curio respectively, the growth of relative newcomers like EAST reveals that travelers are nevertheless interested in more than what's being offered by these table names, regardless of both enticing the scale of loyalty programs like Bonvoy or HHonors may be.

Ultimately, this presents a bright future for the entire industry because it shows that there are many different travelers who all want different things – alternatives for alternative thinkers if you will. To conclude our interview with the EAST team, Muk, Smith, and Winter all emphasized that this point of differentiation stems from the passion of the entire team to see it through, and that's what our industry has always been about.

DEVELOPMENT & DESIGN

Launching a new hotel brand that's focusing on immersive, culinary-first experiences, Appellation's first property is aptly located in the heart of California wine country.

Barbell Distribution of Hotel Properties May Be the Future

We're all always asking to some degree where the hotel industry is going. At the ownership level, it's a matter of timing in terms of whether or not to buy, sell, renovate, expand or reflag.

Given the turbulent in market conditions over the past few years, we are all wondering what megatrends will help us guide topline revenue growth so that we have a good flow of topline revenues to then address some of these downstream questions. When is the best time to start a major financial project? How has the pandemic propelled certain trends to guide future investments? Where is there money to be made?

These were just some of the questions that we posed to Michelle Russo, CEO and Founder of HotelAVE, an asset management company that is grappling with the current state of our industry. What we concluded is that hospitality is increasingly moving towards a barbell distribution, with luxury and economy segmentation, and not much in the middle. Below are some of the major talking points from our discussion.

Giving the Hotel Industry a (Financial) Workout

As per the introduction, Ms. Russo immediately drew a parallel between hospitality and a set of barbells by stating, "At one end, you have the luxury resorts and, at the other end, the premium extended stay properties. They are the heavy 'weights' of our industry. The center is thin, a zone of limited investor interest and marginal investment potential. Looking at our post-pandemic business from a strictly financial basis, this middle area is where valuations may not recover to their 2019 peak levels. They will sell at a discount, if at all, and hotels that were challenged pre-COVID perhaps only for land value."

Limited Returns for Property Investments in the Center

Asked about investing in renovations, she replied, "The pandemic just accelerated the pre-existing trends. One must examine the potential for a return on investment. If you own a property with low ceilings, small bathrooms and narrow corridors, you have to start to ask yourself just what sort of rate you can get for this post-renovation. Couple that with HVAC, CAT6 and plumbing infrastructure upgrades, and the analysis may show that there isn't a positive return from any property improvement plan."

A Glimmer of Hope

Ms. Russo continued, "There are a number of relatively new brands that are emerging as successful investment vehicles. Think micro-sized products that can work in the 200 square foot guestroom range or even less, like Yotel, Moxy, and citizenM. They can thrive where there is a need for a lower price point product. Here you can look at more keys in the same floor pad, thereby increasing your yield per square foot. This may be an opportunity for older buildings, again depending upon the infrastructure improvements that are necessary to make the transition into this new product segmentation."

Technology for Improved Guest Service
Asking about the impact of technology on the hotel industry, Ms. Russo remarked, "For transactional functions, technology is actually an improvement over personalized, high-touch guest service. Most guests do not want to wait for check-in or check-out, to make a reservation for dining or room service, or to get on a phone call with someone to have their car brought out of the parking lot. For activities of this nature, technology cannot be beat; guests prefer the speed of automated service. There are many other disciplines where technology can improve the product and also provide cost savings."

Our short conversation concluded with a joint feeling that the transitions in our industry will ultimately strengthen it. Despite recent troubles, the hotel industry is nevertheless ripe for investment if you have done your due diligence to analyze the trends and market demands. Start by thinking in terms of the trend towards this new age barbell-shaped product distribution and where your property or development can fit within those classifications, then allocate capital accordingly.

These Are the Keys to a Healthy Hotel Brand Relationship for the 2020s

The post-pandemic landscape for hotels is one of change, with direct impacts on nearly every department. Given how fast the world is moving nowadays and how quickly guest behavior is evolving, many owners and management companies are rightfully questioning their relationships with their brands. The question of all questions to ask yourself: Is your brand aligned to help your hotel increase revenues, preserve the bottom line and grow asset value during the transitional decade ahead?

While you may feel the big hint within that question as to scrutinizing your franchisee agreement and potentially changing flags, that's not our intent. Rather, it's a matter of getting the most out of your brand, and there are numerous ways to deepen your relationship to maximize success, particularly by focusing on a few key areas.

A Bitter Pandemic Aftertaste
Many franchisees felt pinched by what they perceived as unnecessary and onerous brand mandates related to mitigating COVID, often with increased costs that the properties had to bear. This created some lingering distrust and tension that both sides must first work to repair before going about setting the stage for a prosperous 2020s.

"Both sides need to start by being more upfront, honest and transparent," commented Mark Hope, Vice President of Development and Revenue Strategy at Coast Hotels, when discussing the motivations behind the brand mandates during the pandemic. As further background, Coast Hotels is a boutique, upscale brand with over 40+ flags spread across the West Coast in Canada and the United States, from Hawaii and California through to Alaska and the Yukon.

"Without question, mandates need to be explained as to how, why and when," continued Hope. "Mandates should not be dropped in the laps of franchisee on an overnight basis. They should be done on a realistically planned and timed basis.

Sometimes there needs to be some wiggle room based on the specific franchise. I always look at multiple perspectives – from the guest, from the brand and from the owner's capital spend with an ROI component. And I explain it from that viewpoint."

What should be stressed from the brand side of things is the importance of timing with any mandate. For Coast Hotels, for instance, it may be easier to coordinate a rollout plan for only 40 some-odd hotels where only 30 are franchised – with some having multiple owners – and there's enough bandwidth to talk each through the pending change. However, this gets tougher for bigger franchise companies that have hundreds or thousands of licensees to guide.

While the ball is still in the brand's court to act more transparently coming out of the pandemic as a means of instilling trust, property-level operators would be wise to nevertheless stay attuned with incoming brand directives and be proactive in maintaining a regular rapport.

From our conversation with Hope, he suggested that we treat it like a dance. The tempo goes up; then it goes back down on repeat. With amenity creep and technology creep both bound to accelerate, it's time for the brands to temporarily slow down and listen to the greater franchise communities before righting the ship.

Act as a Customer

Lest you forget that, ultimately, you are the customer and the buck stops with you. Customers have rights, with the brands there to serve your needs. This starts by asking. Prepare a list that brings together needs from every departmental head, then invite your regional brand manager to the property for the executive committee to address each.

For starters, ask your territory rep for similar properties in the region and get introductions so that you can share information and learnings with likeminded colleagues. You can all prosper together, after all. Concurrently, your brands should be able to provide you with market intelligence with particular information pertaining to current issues such as how best to navigate labor shortages.

Then, of course, there are technology considerations for which the entire industry must move at full throttle in order to keep up with evolving demands and automations that can cut costs. Brands are typically the vanguards of new tech, but they should move faster to promote and push these to the franchise level. Ask what new products are brand-approved and how quickly they can move to make introductions or assist with on-prem setup.

Again, it's about asking, then you shall receive. Review how your property is displayed on the brand website, any other vanity URLs beyond your direct purview and on the brand's social media accounts. If there are any issues, make a list and tackle them together with the regional brand manager's team so that your needs are assuaged. Moreover, brands should be supporting your media efforts by lining up press coverage at a regular chip, FAMs if need be or advertiser deals; if they aren't, ask why not.

Act as a Candidate

Let's say you had an upcoming job interview. A good course of action would be to research the prospective company, its competitors and the entire industry so that you are as up to speed as possible with great questions at the ready. This shows preparedness and will make you shine as the best candidate that's wholly worthy of the company's endorsement. The same principle can be applied to your brand relationship.

Due diligence means interviewing operators who are currently part of the brand cohort. Ask how the brand supports their regional efforts, how the brand responds to their needs and the degree to which the brand proactively helps in data mining. While brand cannibalization is always a concern, realistically, there are bigger fish to fry, and it should serve you better to become a consummate student in your brand as well as the specific tactics that have proven fruitful for other local franchisees.

Being proactive also means educating yourself on everything that the brand has to offer, including informational webinars that your team members can attend, online courses that may also offer performance accountability, and regional or national conferences that can also serve as a motivational tool for managers. Do your homework and review your coop plan so that you come back with very thoughtful requests from your regional brand manager. Take advantage of any training programs offered, then participate in brand-related activities, including sales missions.

As previously mentioned, any issues related to new tech solutions that are ready to implement, problems with the website and media relationships will require you to first audit then summarize the situation before addressing it with the brand. Alas, they aren't mind readers, but if you bring forward your concerns in a clearly outlined document then it's hard not to generate a productive discussion with helpful follow-up actions on their part.

Like a Healthy Marriage

From the above, it should be clear that cultivating a better relationship between brand and franchisee will always be a bit of a dance where one partner moves then the other countermoves. But perhaps it should be framed as a healthy marriage, where any dislike is brought forward with compassion and disagreements are tackled constructively.

We touched base with Nicholas Messian, (former) General Manager at the Algonquin Resort, a 233-room property that's a member of Marriott's Autograph Collection located in New Brunswick along the Bay of Fundy close to the border with Maine. "The brand should focus on detailing and explaining why mandates are still relevant for a flagged property. Like being married, it is about managing the evolution of the relationship and therefore finding ways to tweak then enhance the partnership for the benefit of all parties."

To bring this back to the first point about trust, here's a final comment from Anil Taneja, Managing Director of the Palm Holdings Group, a management company with multiple branded and independent properties. "Transparency on why you can or cannot do something to your asset is key, but at the end of the day, this will only buy you time with the brands," added Taneja. "The better the brand, the stronger its ability to dictate without compromise. The more units a brand has, the more infrastructure it has behind it to enforce their mandates; if you want ultimate flexibility within the brand framework, then a soft or newer brand is the way to go."

Do the dance. Be an active customer as well as a worthy job candidate, then together you and your brand will achieve success. It's straightforward but requires a lot of work, nonetheless, so best get started before peak season sidelines any long-term initiatives.

And if the relationship still isn't working after you've put in the necessary work, then and only then is it time to consider going in another direction. This should, of course, be considered a last resort but brands evolve and often there is an emerging sub-brand within your current house of brands that may better fit your target customer, especially in the post-pandemic world where so much about travel has changed within such a short period of time.

How to Elevate the Guest Experience Without Affecting Your Bottom Line

Put yourself in the guest's shoes. Experience your property from hotel research and reservation, through check-in, your actual stay, room cleaning, then check-out, departure and all the post-stay marketing. Now examine every interaction you would have with a member of the hotel team and identify ways in which they can personalize the experience.

What's important in this discussion right now is that, from the customer's perspective, they are primarily concerned with maximizing their own time. Yes, they are cognizant of labor issues and global supply chain hiccups, but that's the property's problem, not theirs. Even with all the post-pandemic bullwhips, they still want service like 2019.

So, how can you personalize the entire guest journey without incurring sizeable labor increases? Examples include a short welcome note delivered in-room upon arrival, a thank you note in the room the night before checking out and a bounce-back coupon attached to the guest's departure folio offering an upgrade or booking discount bonus for the next stay. Three 'old school' ideas, and undoubtedly you can finesse these without a large marginal cost.

Automation to the Rescue

Technology offers tremendous potential for elevating the guest experience without adding to your staffing component. Today's customer is virtually glued to their mobile device. In several properties that we have visited, a welcome note appears on our mobile immediately after check-in both greeting us and asking if there was anything that we needed.

Managed through a trained machine learning platform with support from live agents and escalation protocols, these programs not only improve service levels, but also free up associates to personalize service in other areas.

But technology can do much more than deal with the guest once they arrive on property. In fact, technological advances should be incorporated into every aspect of the guests' journey through your ecosystem, starting with room confirmation.

Your goal is to embrace the guest before they arrive at your front desk. Apart from understanding their time of arrival and mode of transport, you can encourage additional revenue through prepurchase or prearrival reservation of ancillary services such as dining, spa, golf, activities or room amenities. Upselling platforms that can do this are now readily abundant. Rather than looking at this as a merely value-added sales opportunity, most guests will appreciate you identifying both the availability as well as the opportunity to simplify their arrival by making these reservations in advance. Time is more valuable than money, after all.

Thinking Through All Operations

Many properties have a reservations center that operates on a fixed schedule – a common example would be 8am to 8pm in the local time zone. But what happens when a potential guest calls outside of these hours or when the intake team is already tied up serving other customers? Often that call gets diverted to front desk, goes to voicemail or is abandoned.

All three results are unsatisfactory from a guest service standpoint. When the reservations call transfers to a front office associate, that call often leads to unsatisfactory service for onsite guests at the front desk. The cascading effect is that now you have a dissatisfied customer in house, as well as one on the phone who isn't getting your full attention. The cost-effective solution here is artificial intelligence to field basic questions hitting an IVR in combination with an outsourced call center service for overflow. New 'conversational AI' systems are so efficient and personalized that it is hard to differentiate them from a human voice. Often this AI technology will lead to further benefits including streamlined reservations staffing and added sales, not to mention improved customer satisfaction.

Next, have you ever heard of the saying, 'happy wife, happy life'? The same applies to your property! Happy employees lead directly to happy guests. The days of looking at your staff as expendable are over.

Often, it is the little things that count. Yes, every hourly staff member on your team would immediately accept a substantial raise. That is clearly not a financial option. More plausible are several smaller initiatives that can go a long way towards creating an environment that reduces turnover and motivates team support for your guest-enhancing activities. Set a luncheon aside each month for birthdays. Announce the celebrations, provide a cake with small gifts. Significant work anniversaries should be both announced and celebrated with a more formal event where spouses are invited. Here, gifts should reflect the individual's desires, possibly selected from a gift catalog. Support your team as you would your family.

While we're addressing employee satisfaction, your back of house deserves some attention. When was the last time that you entered your property through the service entrance? Does your BOH experience mirror the FOH? What is the level of cleanliness? How cluttered is it? Is there any natural light or revitalizing live plants? When was the last time it was painted? Remember, your team is conditioned through the environment of their workplace. Respect them and the respect will carry forward through their workday.

Still on the topic of BOH, your employee cafeteria needs attention. When was the last time you had a meal there? Better yet, why not hold your next executive committee meeting there? The days of greasy fries and burgers are over. Healthier food options will be appreciated not just for the long-term health of your team, but they will benefit in the short-term by improving moods, nullifying any refined-sugar-induced postprandial slowdown and improving immune systems to reduce sick days.

Satisfaction and Service Standards

Ultimately, what is a satisfied guest? How does this correlate with star rating? Guest satisfaction means at a minimum, performing to the expected standard. You should be looking to do something more.

If you are a select-service property, guest satisfaction might simply imply a quick check-in, a clean guestroom, quiet air conditioning, fast and easy-to-connect internet, a large TV with a good channel selection, ample hot water for the shower, sufficient towels, a comfy bed, morning coffee and express check-out. Meet all these criteria and you've hit the proverbial home run. Remember, though, that this is 'basic' delivery. It does not elevate the guest's appreciation for your product, as it does not differentiate it from your comp set.

So, you must look at little tweaks to see what you can do just a little bit better. Think of ways that technology can, for minimal marginal cost, increase guests' time so they have more of it for other experiences. Think seamless and frictionless, like over-the-top casting for your TVs or mobile keys. Even something like ensuring that your HVAC units have noise levels brought to a minimum can help by giving travelers more peace of mind.

The Key to Great F&B

For properties that go beyond select service, examine all aspects of your operation to see how they can be improved to enhance guest satisfaction. Foodservice deserves your attention as, for most visitors, there is little differentiation between the guestroom and dining room delivery. In the mind of your customer, the restaurant can meaningfully impact the property's overall performance.

Breakfast is the critical component, and we always recommend that a 'Bed and Breakfast' rate be part of your package offering. At a minimum, your restaurant should be able to deliver breakfast promptly with ample quantities. It costs very little extra to make sure that your coffee is hot and contemporary dairy alternatives are available. Now make coffee service memorable by selecting a local supplier who creates an exclusive blend for you – then be sure to let everyone know about it.

Speaking of local suppliers, consider moving select items away from national food suppliers. By creating a local element to your foodservice, you further differentiate your restaurant and enhance guest satisfaction. Start small with local honey, jams and preserves. These can be easily profiled and enhance your breakfast presentation. Re-examine your breadbasket selection to cost-effectively add further points of uniqueness.

Bars are another outlet where local suppliers can create further means to elevate the guest experience. Of course, you have already included several local beers on tap. But why stop there? Explore local distillers for gin, rye, vodka and rum. As a subsequent step, challenge your bar staff to create custom drinks using these ingredients – great for guests and morale.

Authentically Local for All

Local partnerships can go beyond food and beverage suppliers. Dedicate display cases and walls in the lobby or other public corridors to local heritage recognition. Your tourism bureau will be eager to fill the cases with memorabilia.

Guests are always interested in seeing what your area looked like several decades or a century ago. Photos are available, usually free of charge, from your city archives. Print and mount them or load them onto a computer and display them on large monitors. Again, the thought here is that you want the guest to relish their experience with you. Even if they don't have time to peruse it all, they will feel the love.

Memorable impressions are all part of enhancing the guest experience. Once you cover the basics, whatever you can do that is noteworthy and perhaps a little bit eccentric will lead to positive feedback and improved memorability. You have the power to make these modest revisions, so why not consider some of them today?

Long Live the New Business Center

Prior to the pandemic, many had forecasted the business center to be a dead concept for hotels. Relegated to some back corner of the lobby or hidden from the main thoroughfares by a maze of windowless corridors, this amenity has suffered a slow death in the face of laptops, smartphones and all forms of paperless documents. Amongst many other changes, the post-pandemic landscape has evolved corporate and group travel wherein there's a diminished use for a traditional business center.

The business center is experiencing a renewed demand. That is, with so many remote workers, work-from-a-hotel (WFH) incentives and the need for physically distanced office spaces, a retrofit of this amenity may end up being a great long-term project to enhance your value proposition for all travel segments.

Before you start your analysis of how to reinvigorate your business center, you must understand what attracts modern, post-pandemic travelers to these spaces, and this is neatly summarized through the buzzy terminology of one's 'third place' or 'third space'. With the first place being one's home and the second being the office, the next mixes the two.

Prior to COVID, a big part of the USP for Starbucks, aside from great coffee, was offering a cozy respite from the home and the office. Now, you can make a similar argument building upon the success of WFH concepts whereby people will continue to look for hybrid travel options with worktime being easily accessible via dedicated spaces. Another good term to know in this regard is the 'living room' denoting a hotel space that takes on aspects of a members' lounge with comfortable, expansive seating and grab-and-go food options.

Guests will continue to opt for hotels that approach this kind of living room concept where they are comfortable socializing and relaxing in front of a communal television while reading or typing away on their laptops in semi-seclusion. Anything goes, and indeed many of these spaces adjoin some semblance of bar, restaurant or sundry to make dining or imbibing all the more convenient.

Hence, the new business center can work by taking on aspects of both the third place and living room concepts. The foremost problem many hotels face, however, is that the geographic minutia doesn't pan out. That is, many business centers aren't immediately accessible to other areas of interaction like the main entrance, the front desk, the lobby bar, the primary dining outlet, the elevator corridors or any other frequently trafficked footpaths. If this is the case, then the best option may be renovating the spaces closer to check-in to fit into the living room mold – this depends on each property's floorplan.

On the other hand, if the current mothballed business center is reasonably exposed to where your visitors are most likely to walk, then it may be prime for a less expensive makeover that involves an open floor concept and cozy, modular furniture, all with the laptop and mobile device in mind rather than the static desk and printer configuration of old. Importantly here, proximity to a phone charging station is a crucial design factor.

Finally, if the living room concept or office space conversions aren't in the cards for your particular property, then it's time to get creative. Maybe you don't need a business center and this room can be transformed into another dedicated meeting room that can be sold either as part of a group booking or via a third-party site. Maybe you can convert it into additional BOH office space to help keep more of your team working onsite.

Beyond only corporate guests, how might this space be modified to add a new feature for leisure guests? There have been many business centers that have become libraries, games rooms with cards, tables, and a full stack of board games or even arcades with billiards and foosball. Ultimately, there are plenty of options to help leverage this amenity as part of a bigger product refresh. Business center or not, you have the space, so it's just a matter of figuring out how best to use it for the travelers you hope to attract.

The Lobby Bar is Back with a Vengeance

Following a hiatus during the pandemic, we are pleased to see that lobby bars are back in full swing and better than ever, with hoteliers able to use them to differentiate their marketing approach and garner more bookings.

The lobby bar (or rooftop bar) is a point of pride for many properties, and rightfully so as these outlets engender local buzz and amplify the sense of place for incoming travelers. First impressions as they are, it's one thing to approach the front desk to check-in with music billowing the halls from a nearby lounge with most tables occupied by chattering patrons. It's a whole other to be greeted by an empty hall.

Both of us have long been big fans of the multitude of upscale and hobnobbing lounges that hotels have created because of the attention to detail in the décor, F&B, theme and overall vibe at these establishments. They are often attractions in their own right. Importantly, and in contrast to an empty lobby when checking in, this 'scene' acts to boost overall guest satisfaction and word of mouth to draw in more paying guests.

Lobby bars serve an important role as a place for locals and hotel guests to congregate and we can definitively say that such buoyant bar scenes were sadly missed during the pandemic. Without the hubbub, something felt off; it's a void that bleeds into the hotel experience, subtly diminishing one's appreciation for the guestroom product or other amenities.

What we're seeing on the ground right now, though, tells a different story – one of revival. Patrons are increasingly confident about returning to the pre-pandemic lifestyle of gathering at kinetic, close-quarters abodes. Our forecast is that the lobby bar only gets busier and busier as global travel resumes.

How do you take advantage of this emerging renaissance? How do you restart a beverage-driven establishment to be both quantifiably profitable and work intrinsically to boost room reservations? In balancing these two potentially upsides, the latter is one that may not be readily measurable but is perhaps the more critical of the two insofar as driving total revenues for the property and giving your property a zero-base marketing tool.

It's no longer just about thinking of your bar or restaurant as a siloed revenue generator but in its contribution to TRevPAR (total revenue per available room). Does the lobby bar encourage more room reservations? Can the lobby bar positively influence TripAdvisor scores? Are there certain guest profiles that would be more inclined to spend at the lobby bar, thereby giving you a more detailed lookalike audience to hone your marketing efforts? These are a few cross-departments questions to ask.

Design is critical here as your restaurant or bar has to be ready. If you have a renovation planned, the winter is the time to do it before what may be a great summer of travel. Then besides having such an operation already in place, the most crucial thing is having the right staffing. Labor shortages, be as they may, a lack of workers severely limits your topline sales from this outlet, as well as perhaps forcing you to reduce its hours.

To contend, our top recommendation on the labor front is less is more. Food menus should be uncomplicated with only your bestsellers to thus limit requirements in the kitchen and speed up table turns. Likewise, for beverages, it's easier to crack a beer bottle or pour a glass of wine than to prepare an elaborate cocktail, even though the latter may have a price point set at several dollars above such simpler options. While indeed cocktails help to differentiate your product in a unique way, it's a balancing act because of the time drain involved, which may in turn cause patiently waiting patrons not to be so patient anymore and lead them to go elsewhere for the next round.

Next, from a design perspective less is also more as you may be contending with backlogged work orders and supply chain issues that might make complex décor purchases harder to implement. Most guests would simply be happy just to have a home base option at their disposal!

Some hotel brands – many right here in Canada – have great bar components and are poised to make it big as travelers return post-pandemic. In a positive feedback loop sort of way, we stress that it's not just the prospects of some marginal ancillary sales but how a lobby bar can halo back onto the experience for overnight guests to subsequently drive more loyalty and bookings. And that's ultimately what hotels need right now, so consider how your bar, or any restaurant outlet for that matter, can work holistically towards rebuilding your guestroom bookings where most hotels make the majority of their profits.

Lobby Renovations Are an Irrational Expense Yet Essential for the Guest Experience

Summary: As the place where first impressions are codified by guests, the lobby experience must be strong. Thinking broader, a great lobby also contributes to a hotel's overall reason to visit which in turn supports occupancies and higher nightly rates. Moreover, a vibrant lobby is a space where visitors will want to linger, resulting in greater food and beverage sales.

When it comes to any renovation or property improvement plan (PIP), the name of the game in today's ever-uncertain and highly parsimonious hospitality landscape is 'value engineering' in terms of being as cost-effective as possible with any capex. This often means that all expenses have to be justified on a financial statement in terms of their direct and quantifiable attribution to revenue performance, reduction of opex, or increase of net contribution.

And yet, hotels don't quite work that way. Even as data scientists, revenue managers, and the like extol their metrics as the be-all and end-all of operational success, true hospitality nevertheless perseveres as an art form. Our business is one that can never be precisely measured because we deal in human emotions, through what we all refer to as the guest experience.

As a result, there are often expenses that may appear illogical through the scrupulous eyes of the numbers people or a price-sensitive owner, without any immediate or traceable impact on KPIs like TRevPAR or GOPPAR save for how these upgrades will make a guest feel. The lobby is one such area of supposed irrationality, but it deserves a second thought at any property that's starting to allocate funds for a renovation.

Numerous properties that are already in, or aspire to be in, the hospitality hall of fame have this attitude. One program that we have going at our consultancy is called 'The Mille Club' where we apply learning from those hotels around the world that are already charging over a thousand dollars per night ('mille' derived from the Italian for a thousand) to help other brands figure out a strategy for growing their rates to this level and beyond. Without exception, every Mille Club member property has an amazing lobby experience, and putting a plan in motion for creating a similarly elevated ambiance at other hotels is a project that we strongly advise all our clients to undertake.

To convince owners regarding the capex required to make a great lobby, we tell them that sometimes you have to spend a little more in order to make a lot more.

Setting the Tone

Everyone has heard or understands at their core that first impressions are everything. You only get one. In hotel parlance, we call this the 'sense of arrival' to encapsulate the entire onsite arrival from the exterior drive up to the porte-cochere, the uniforms of the valet team, and the manner in which the bellhop assisted with the luggage through to the lobby décor, the artwork, the music billowing out from the adjoining bar and the friendliness of the front desk team during check-in.

Every element here counts, and the best hoteliers sweat over, making each detail perfect and wholly congruent with the hotel's theme in order to elicit a given mood from the visitors, be they travelers with a room upstairs or locals looking to hobnob. The lobby's appearance, layout, flow, lighting, seating, acoustics, and even smell (think fresh flower arrangements or a branded scent) all play a role in setting the tone for a great experience throughout the guest's stay.

Notably, the word 'tone' requires some elaboration in terms of its use borrowed from music. Taken straight from Wikipedia, a musical tone is a steady periodic sound characterized by its duration, pitch, intensity and timbre. What this means for hotels is that the first impression establishes the emotional directionality and elasticity for the remainder of the trip. A great first impression sets the bar high so that the guest is excited and intrigued, while a poor or unremarkable opening encounter puts the guest into an apathetic or defensive mood that is often hard to recover from.

As it relates to the notion of the intangibles within a hotel, a guest who is excited about a vibrant lobby atmosphere is more likely to linger there, more likely to order a cocktail before heading out on the town or more likely to seek out a reservation at the hotel's onsite restaurant instead of going onto Google to search out the nearest hotspot. The opposite is also true; if the lobby doesn't have a vibe or doesn't invite a social scene, then it will be sizably harder to nudge visitors to stick around and spend. We would argue for one scarier step further in that gloomy lobby ultimately discourages guestroom bookings.

A Strong Reason to Visit

What the two of us classify as a hotel's 'reason to visit' goes one step further than the onsite first impression by considering the engagements that a potential customer has before they arrive and what motivates them to book in the first place. Outside of pure price elasticity for pure heads-in-beds operations in the select service and economy segments, what is the core emotional reason for why a guest has selected your property?

While this 'big why' will always have the throughline of 'location, location, location' for any entity in commercial real estate, hotels are a bit of a unique breed. That reason to visit may indeed be a beach or proximity to the convention center, but there's typically something more – the *je ne sais quoi* as the French have so eloquently coined for these seemingly irrational contributors. These intrinsic elements can include but are not limited to a world-class spa, a scenic golf course, a cool pool scene, impeccable guestroom amenities, a Michelin-starred restaurant, curated activities, a fantastical bar, a tony rooftop, a wondrous lobby experience, and yes, old-fashioned guest service.

Within all these components that comprise the overall guest experience, it is difficult to single out the lobby as the key determining factor for why a guest chooses your hotel versus the one across the street or why a guest is willing to pay, for instance, a hundred dollars more per night to have immediate access to your lobby as their temporary home base. Nevertheless, without that gregarious lobby experience, would that reason to visit be quite as strong?

To circle back to the Mille Club, peruse the literature for any hotel with an ADR north of a grand, and you will see that the lobby is typically an architectural marvel in its own right used to market the property. Thematically, some go the more classically lavish route with scintillating chandeliers, ornate marble and gilded balustrades, while others strive more towards nouveau riche with postmodern finishes and artwork that no one really comprehends. Irrespective of the tactics, the emotional gut punch is always the same: this is a 'bucket list' property befitting of a luxury lifestyle and a place that will help you self-actualize on a deeper, limbic plane. In short, the splendor of the lobby gives the onsite experience meaning and that meaning warrants astronomical nightly rates.

If you were to try to quantify this relationship, perhaps the place to start is by reading into magazine editorials, travel writer columns, and guest reviews. Check to see how often the lobby is referenced as worthwhile or a central component that justifies a hotel's nightly rate. While you can evaluate this anecdotally by glancing through some editorials, reading some top-ten lists and scrolling through TripAdvisor, nowadays, one might deploy an AI-driven sentiment analysis tool to interpret the multitude of hotel reviews on the internet to spit out an answer that basically suggests, "Yes, a lobby's design has an impact on occupancy, nightly rates, media impressions and ancillary spend." Prove us wrong.

To Crowd or Not to Crowd

The basis of crowd theory is that people want to go where other people already are. This isn't necessarily because said people are insecure about trying the novel or that they are boringly average. Rather, the presence of a crowd – a scene, if you will – is a mental shortcut that indicates the place is actually good. Hence, creating a scene in your lobby through an orchestra of different tactics and capex serves as a heuristic for visitors to positively evaluate your business, both by locals seeking out their libation as well as by hotel guests looking for reassurance that they are in for a great night's stay.

While this principle is as old as the human race itself, as we progress through the 2020s, there are new evolutions afoot that will influence the future of lobby design. Namely, we must now take into account the digital nomads, the bleisure segment and work-from-anywhere crowd who are knowledge workers enabled by flexible company policy and fast internet connectivity, allowing them to earn their bread while living almost entirely on the road.

That road can be a short-term rental, a cruise ship, or a campsite with a Starlink, and for our purposes, it's our duty as hoteliers to convince these emerging cohorts to select our properties. First and foremost, solid WiFi is obligatory as are accessible power outlets. Next is comfortable seating, as lumbar discomfort is an easy way to dissuade lingering.

But while these design elements also pertain to nonworking visitors in your lobby or at other facilities on premise, maybe it's best to take a step and ask whether or not you want to designate your lobby space as a green zone for remote workers. Might their somewhat antisocial presence detract from others opting to sit down and order a beverage?

This is an important question to answer during the opening stages of a new development or PIP as it will influence the layout and furnishings. While we cannot answer this because the solution is different for every hotel and every brand, we will close with this olive branch: consider carving out a secondary lobby or living room area for these types of guests.

For the former, this might entail a recessed alcove tucked away from the main thoroughfare of the path connecting the entranceway to the front desk. The latter is a bit more upscale and requires some extra operational support. Both of us are big fans of the 'living room' which is a quieter, members-only area wholly separate from the public lobby where snacks and beverages come free of charge. Those members can be any guest with a valid room keycard, only those guests staying in a premium-tier room or as something you sell on a subscription basis. Regardless, a living room should exude privacy and exclusivity, a place where people can concentrate on getting real work done or also engage with like-minded peers should they so desire.

From a pure cost-efficiency perspective, the living room concept, while an opulent lobby, is irrational. Many offer alcoholic refreshments gratis, representing a huge expense, and yet the presence of that living room provides prospective guests with a strong reason to visit that eventually, albeit circuitously, supports healthy occupancies and rate growth. To reiterate, sometimes you have to spend a little more in order to make a lot more, and your lobby is definitely not an area where you should cut corners.

Embracing ADA Compliance as an Underserved Market Gap for Hotel Brands

The hotel industry has exploded with new brands and sub-brands over the past two decades, and this trend isn't going to stop anytime soon. While there are a variety of forces and incentives at play to account for this diversification, one prominent rationale is that emergent brands can better appeal to niche interests, microsegments or customer identities.

We see this with the growth of the extended stay category (such as Home2 Suites by Hilton, Residence Inn by Marriott, Hyatt House) and serviced apartment or aparthotel brands. Others skewing more to the premium and luxury segments have excelled by homing in on a specific value system for communicating their brand equity, be it rigorous sustainability (1 Hotels), extravagant wellness (Aman, Hyatt Andaz, Mandarin Oriental, Six Senses), fitness (Accor's Pullman, IHG's EVEN, Equinox Hotels) or nightlife (Kimpton, Moxy, The W), in addition to the bevy of brands, soft brands and associations tinkering in spaces like lifestyle, design, art and culinary-forward.

While the list of hotel brands across the globe may now require a PhD to effectively memorize and distinguish between each, we posit that there's one major customer cohort that has yet to be properly embraced at the operational and marketing levels – those guests with disabilities. Of course, hotels within the United States must adhere to statutes inscribed by the Americans with Disabilities Act (ADA), but this often comes down to doing the passable minimum insofar as design criteria, training, SOPs or cultural appreciation.

Not to insult any operator, but corporate's efforts in this area often amount to checking a particular box rather than thoughtfully programming with services, amenities, and team training that would make a hotel the brand of choice for disabled or handicapped guests. And yet, the Pew Research Center estimated, based on 2021 census data, that there are over 42 million Americans with disabilities, representing 13% of the civilian, noninstitutionalized population.

This is an untapped market. Not only are the trends indicating that there is a present and growing need for ADA-forward hospitality, but there are also strong opportunities to upsell and cross-sell in order to capture more total revenue from this cohort. And while we started this article by implying change at the brand level, such ADA enhancements need not be corporately governed but can be executed at a specific property to realize many of the same benefits.

The Silver Tsunami

In the introductory section, we were careful to use the word 'cohort' to segment guests with disabilities rather than the more age-specific 'demographic' because such an impairment can strike at any time. Nevertheless, this latter word epitomizes all trends in the 2020s and 2030s, wherein the aging out of the baby boomers indicates a clear need for hotels that can better cater to this market gap.

Namely, the boomer generation is in the process of entering retirement and becoming 'elderly' (we only use this ageist word as a heuristic), with age being the number one risk factor associated with the onset of a minor or severe health condition that may lead to a disability. Yet, unless for past generations, longevity advances over the past few decades have compounded to both extend the lifespans of elderly individuals as well as allow those with disabilities to no longer be housebound by their conditions.

To simplify the past century in reductive terms to get the point across, it used to be that you were healthy and active – that is, you traveled – until you became unhealthy and were immobilized. Life, in this sense, was a dichotomy with a steep and irreversible decline upon illness. While medical insurance for the elderly still acts as an obstacle for many to board a plane or go on a cruise, there are innumerable people who have benefited from modern medicine to live longer and continue exploring the globe well into their sixties, seventies, eighties and beyond. Compounding being the eighth wonder of the world, these longevity advances are only going to get better and better.

This civilization-altering development is best encapsulated by the catchy term 'The Silver Tsunami' denoting the coming wave of gray-haired individuals who will dot every corner of the world, with most of them alive, well and actively traveling. Demographically speaking, the United States isn't quite there yet, but some more advanced countries like Japan, South Korea, and members of the European Union will soon have more than one-third of their populace aged 65 or older. Domestically, the United States Census Bureau estimates that by 2030, approximately 73 million boomers will all be 65 or older.

Stop and think about that for a moment. With age as a leading indicator for practically all chronic diseases or physical impairments, this means that potentially one-third of your future guests will be gracing your halls burdened by a myriad of mobility issues, bad knees, lower back pain, disrupted sleep, heart problems, hearing loss, poor eyesight, compromised immune systems, diabetes or predementia.

Verifying Your Handicapped Services

"Having worked in hospitality for almost 40 years, I thought I understood the requirements for a compliant room until my wife became handicapped, and we grappled firsthand with how inadequate some hotels are," stated Mark Hope, Senior Vice President of Development at Coast Hotels.

During our conversation, Hope detailed many of the design flaws and training errors he's encountered over the years while traveling with his wife. Those are issues that no able-bodied hotelier may really be of the mindset to consider until an actual handicapped guest arrives onsite.

We list these off so that you might learn and adapt accordingly:

- Multiple hotel entrances and exits with only one having a ramp to accommodate a wheelchair, and yet this singular ADA entry isn't clearly communicated on the website or pre-arrival emails
- Particularly for old hotels, the elevators and doors aren't of the recommended width, with ADA stipulates at three inches wider, but these guests need six inches

- Handicapped rooms aren't next to the elevator, and the guest floor corridor has a thick, soft carpet that resists smooth wheelchair motion
- Handicapped rooms aren't equipped with critical features such as a bedrail, toilet grab bar or shower seat, while the floor threshold from bedroom to bathroom is raised or uneven to the point where a wheelchair can't roll into the bathroom (let alone roll under the sink)
- Property management systems not properly demarcating which rooms are for wheelchair-bound guests versus guests with other disabilities, as well as having multiple bed configurations in each
- Certain hotel amenities such as restaurants, spas, meeting spaces, or club lounges aren't easily accessible for handicapped guests, with no communication as such on the website
- Frontline staff aren't trained to deal with disabled guests, often making errors when assigning rooms, giving directions around the hotel, or suggesting local attractions that aren't compliant
- Foodservice areas like a breakfast lounge often don't have a properly accessible table
- Restaurant staff often don't read guest profile information or reservation comments to know that an incoming diner is handicapped so that specific accommodations can be made in advance
- Wanting to do an excursion, few, if any tourism operators offer handicapped transportation
- Hotels not having a compassionate error recovery SOP so that disabled guests can feel valued whenever a problem arises (and they will!)

These points alone could amount to over a year's worth of work to properly address, right down to the cultural adjustments that are necessary to ensure a hotel becomes well-regarded as the destination of choice for disabled travelers. Yet how would a hotel know these particular changes without getting external feedback from an actual handicapped individual? Hence, some form of independent verification or scrupulous self-inspection is needed so that most, if not all, of these issues can be resolved during preconstruction or when planning a PIP, as well as through updated training protocols.

To close our talk, Hope remarked that exceptional service can conquer any fault. He can't expect a property to be perfect, but it's how the onsite teams respond to requests that helps earn his praise and loyalty. For instance, one Boston hotel's handicapped room lacked a bedrail, so rather than shuffle Hope and his wife into another room, a staffer was immediately dispatched to buy then install the device.

Eldercare Services

From the above suggested actions combined with a feasibility study to show the potential opportunity for your own local market, it would be relatively straightforward for an existing brand – especially those within the extended stay or aparthotel categories – to make the case for carving out whole floors or sections devoted to superior ADA compliance. Some destinations may even be able to support hotels with all rooms fully (and verifiably) accessible.

But this only speaks to the marketing prospects of building brand equity amongst disabled travelers; what about upselling additional services? For this, there must be services in place for disabled or dependent guests, blending the divide between short-term hospitality and assisted care facilities or eldercare centers. Finding and maintaining specialized labor will perennially be the biggest challenge, but their services are ones that can be operationalized as an additional charge above the nightly rate.

Here are some ideas for upselling opportunities that are thoughtfully considered for these guests:

- Online packages for adjoining rooms to merchandise family or multigenerational travel where a dependent is assigned the ADA room and the family member is next door
- On-demand access to caregivers with training specific to a particular condition
- Dining and sundry options for specific dietary limitations, such as keto-friendly foods for diabetes
- Offering wheelchair-accessible transportation services
- Sessions with physiotherapists or other rehabilitation practitioners who can guide guests with mobility issues or manage chronic joint pain
- Developing wellness experiences with accessibility in mind regarding time, place and activity

And to close, it should be said that much of this will only be possible with more technology in order to augment the online visibility for a hotel's ADA intentions and to ease the workload on labor. Here are some final thoughts in this aspect:

- Modern booking engines to increase the visibility of ADA rooms and services
- Training a website chatbot to answer questions regarding accessibility
- Stronger data interfaces with a CRM to properly identify guests who may have a disability so that special arrangements can be made in advance
- Connected safety features such as panic buttons to give peace of mind to these guests
- Deploying robot workers to fulfill basic runner functions, reducing wait times for guests and allowing staffers to focus on other tasks

As should be made clear from what's implied by the opening statistic about Americans with disabilities, the Silver Tsunami and some of the relatively cost-effective ways to pivot a property or brand to better accommodate ADA guests, there is an untapped market niche here. If you need one more comparison, just look at the cruise industry and the business they are doing with disabled guests. Above all, being compliant and training your teams to empathize with these guests is simply the right thing to do.

Bibliotherapy and a Possible New Feature for Your Hotel

Who doesn't love a good book? While you have read one of our many other editorials espousing technology, and its myriad benefits for increasing revenues plus ramping up team productivity, sometimes a great hotel differentiator is a bit more 'lo-fi'.

As one can intuit from the word's constituents, bibliotherapy defines the act of finding joy, healing, bliss, or holistic meaning from reading books. Important for the here and now, the pandemic led many to bibliotherapy as a way to cope with the loneliness of isolation and the anxiety induced by a scaremongering media engine. As such, this world event has unquestionably made us more introspective; one that's more willing to open a book and discover its wisdom within.

To swim with the flow of this trending river, a heightened presence of physical books around a hotel may therefore find a receptive audience. Either as a point of differentiation in the guestroom or as part of a dynamic public space like a library living room, the objective here would be to amplify guest satisfaction to drive loyalty as well as give your marketing team one more feature to play with to lure in new customers.

Just as before the pandemic, you need to give people a reason to stay at your property versus your comp set. In that sense, the presence of books isn't in the same pedigree as adding a second golf course or building a new signature restaurant, but they can work more subtly to foster brand endearment.

As an example, we recently stayed at Crockfords at Resorts World Las Vegas. In our room was a strategically placed, coffee table book on oriental carpets. The room was perfect, the TV set huge, the amenities exceptional. The book provided a touchstone and was well-read.

As an in-room amenity, books can help fill an idle hour or two as a guest unwinds in the evening or elects to stay sequestered to avoid the lobby crowds. Or for the abovementioned living room concept, stacks of books foster interactivity with the space where the intent is to have a 'third place' vibe with quieter social dealings mixed with solo business guests.

In deciding between physical books and tablets or e-readers, our vote is decidedly with the former because they add colorful visuals to a space while offering a more tactile, pleasurable reading experience.

On that note, how does one start? For one, the cost of going all new may be prohibitive, so consider used bookstores or other auctions. Then you can go guestroom by guestroom, theming each as the books come in. Alternatively, a public space such as an onsite library requires more advanced planning and critical mass of inventory.

While not an outright revenue builder, appealing to the bibliophile within us may serve more passive ends towards asset growth. As such, bibliotherapy should be one more potential initiative to keep in mind when planning the next physical upgrade to your hotel.

Embracing Hotel 'Lifestyle' by Learning from Retail Brands

Even though retail took a hit during the pandemic, perhaps there's one more drop of tutelage for hotel brands that can be squeezed from this lemon of an industry before every suburban mall is converted into a solar-powered vertical farm. Specifically, we predict that certain 'lifestyle' hotel brands will emerge in the coming decade to dominate the hospitality landscape because of how they mirror an experiential transition by retail brands.

This morsel of instruction comes from how retail shops are adapting to the onslaught of online shopping by making their physical footprint more of a showcase and less of a place for transaction and inventory storage. With everything conveniently available from a customer's home computer, transactional consumerism has found a better home in cyberspace while the on-the-ground storefronts are becoming more 'high touch' – dynamic, more spacious, sensorial, interactive and filled with knowledgeable staff.

As people release all that pent-up energy by venturing out again post-pandemic, hotels should not aim to be more experiential, but also strive to introduce elements of retail into hotels and the ability to 'bring a piece' of that property home in order to continue the relationship. In this sense, making a hotel a retail brand – whether it's clothing, furniture, accessories or any other common form of merchandise – boils down to identity.

The pandemic may have temporarily arrested new hotel development, but in the face of increasing customer hostility towards the staid, cookie-cutter-flagged properties, we predict that the future looks bright for smaller, more meaningful brands to take charge. As companies start to incorporate more service and product differentiation into their overall customer experience framework, your hotel's identity and its value proposition may be imperiled as guests opt for these flashier, niche brands.

As we've explored firsthand on behalf of a select few hotel clients as part of our asset management consulting duties, the paramount objective is still financial survivability. Identity works positively towards this over the long run. You need to imbue a sense of lifestyle – whether through the introduction of elements borrowed from retail or otherwise – to protect your property's reputation and to continually build revenues ahead of market comps. Our hope is that you can be inspired by how a few intrepid retail brands have pivoted in the face of online and on-demand competitors.

Current Retail Crossover Examples

Some laudable examples of this trend include the aforementioned Shinola Hotel in Detroit, which proudly reinforces the company's status as a purveyor of contemporary, American-made sensibility; Atari Hotels with its first prime location in Las Vegas to play upon 1980s nostalgia; the 2015 opening of the Baccarat Hotel & Residences in Midtown Manhattan as a means of generating more North American awareness for the French crystal glassware manufacturer; the 2016 opening of the IKEA Hotel in southern Sweden built next door to the Ikea Museum; and the handful of Equinox Hotels launching to meet the demand for those who want to stay active while traveling.

Then think of the music-driven Hard Rock Hotels as a move to breathe new life into the kitschy restaurants around the world or Bulgari's joint venture with Ritz-Carlton in the early aughts to amplify the prestige of its core jewelry and high-end fashion accessories. On the family front, LEGOLAND Hotels is continuing its rollout in the United States. And so renowned is the Nobu name that the celebrity chef behind these restaurants championing Japanese-Western fusion was able to establish Nobu Hotels in 2009 for which there are already a dozen properties, with Nobu Residences opening in our hometown of Toronto. All this shows that the prestige of a cool hotel can indeed support a retail vertical.

What all these new retail entrants into the industry offer in various forms is the idea of 'aspirational hospitality' where guests can take a piece of their hotel visits home with them to reinforce their identities and lifestyles. Vacation properties can be fun, exciting and memorable while also giving you an idea of what the home life should be.

Trend Just Getting Started

What's the future to bring if this cross-industry symbiosis continues on its current course? Some pie-in-the-sky ideas across a variety of industries include:

- Ferrari® Hotels for car enthusiasts with driving experiences and heaps of onsite memorabilia
- Lindt® Hotels for chocolate lovers offering a full program of pairing and cooking classes
- Apple® unveiling a 'hospitality lab' in Cupertino or downtown San Francisco where guests can stay in rooms with all the latest gadgets as well as test out some that have yet to be released
- E & J Gallo® starting a resort chain to immerse guests in its portfolio of wines through a variety of tastings and educational viniculture-themed activities
- Patagonia® launching its own glamping label where customers select from a global list of curated expeditions with all clothing, equipment, and luxury yurts included
- Lululemon® deepening its sponsoring of yoga retreats by flagging its own wellness resorts
- An international cosmetics company like L'Oréal®, Clinique®, or Estée Lauder® opening a series of chic and boutique properties in alpha-tier cities to cross-promote their full product lines with a plethora of in-room samples readily available

(Note: these are our ideas and do not indicate any accommodation interests of these fine companies.)

For us hoteliers – principally in the independent or boutique luxury segments – what you can learn from this ongoing development is that you must further entrench yourself in the local community, become more experiential and further define your unique identity.

The trend outlined here about corporations from other industries converging on hospitality as a means of brand extension is only just ramping up. To fight this, you must be exceptional in that what you offer is not only different from your competition, but it is congruent with the lifestyle your guests want to live. This is not an easy process at all and one that will take years to properly plan then execute!

Using Green Trends as a Way of Transitioning a Hotel

The green revolution is now firmly upon us. While we are seeing this play out on the global scale with healthy economic incentives for companies directly engaged in renewable energies and shifting away from fossil fuels, ultimately every organization will be compelled to do its part in achieving carbon neutrality, and that includes hotels.

For the decade ahead, therefore, properties that gain a first-mover advantage by embracing climate change initiatives will realize significant cost savings and increased brand recognition. But as this is a huge undertaking, let's look at how green trends can help you dip your toes as the first step towards broader action.

Instead of discussing the reduction of carbon emissions in abstract terms, let's use a recent example to demonstrate how piggybacking off trends can help you shape the future of a property. This past January marked a sizeable year-over-year increase in the awareness for what's known as Veganuary – a portmanteau attempting to heighten the prevalence of a plant-based diet by suggesting people go vegan for a whole month, much like many already do for 'Dry January'.

In this case, hotels could create a menu celebrating Veganuary with two long-term objectives. Firstly, knowing that last January wasn't the greatest for occupancy, any projects undertaken could be tweaked and redeployed for subsequent years, helping make this an 'evergreen' event, especially as the demand for plant-based cuisine becomes more prevalent amongst the general population base. Next, there may come a point in the near future where guests insist on having purely vegan dining options at their hotels, necessitating you to make these menus a permanent fixture of your operations.

For this latter 'sink or swim' scenario, it behooves you to be an early adopter lest you be passed over by the next generation of travelers which is exceedingly sensitive to all matters of ESG (environmental, social and corporate governance). Right now, embracing the green revolution can be interpreted as a largely BOH method of reducing energy combustion through the installation of more efficiency and smart machinery. But as explained through the catchy adage, "Going green to be seen," there's also still a worthwhile marketing angle for any sustainability upgrades you make.

Using the previous example, advertising Veganuary to your target markets and developing a plant-based menu will amount to far less carbon emission reductions when compared to such projects as reconfiguring the guestrooms with smart thermostats or setting up IoT-enabled water recirculation systems. But, unlike the real BOH savers, this trend is guest-facing. It will give your brand cachet amongst a populace that increasingly shuns the copious consumption of the 20th century and wants more environmentally friendly travel accommodations.

What we stress is that now is the time when any green endeavor can be used to generate further appeal for a hotel – before this embrace becomes commonplace and your efforts are no longer buzzworthy. Also, this doesn't have to only be in the restaurant, but maybe you should investigate having all your spa products sourced from local, sustainable suppliers. Or, if you have a golf course, you look to replace your entire fleet of carts with electric vehicles. Even building a few EV recharging stations in your parking lot can give you social marketing credit (but likely not in 2030, even in 2025).

Take heed as this marketing window is rapidly narrowing as green initiatives move in our collective subconscious from value-add to expectation. When it comes to fighting global warming and preventing ecological collapse in the coming decades, this isn't an area where you should wait to be a laggard because it may forever besmirch your brand as one that doesn't care about the environment.

Guests are more forgiving now, but to future proof your organization you must take action in the year ahead and develop a vision for your brand that puts matters of climate change near the top of the list. For this, looking at some of the emerging trends, however fickle, will help you to grow the right culture and reputation among guests so that you are primed for success in the decade ahead.

Hotel Environmental Sustainability Also Means Profit Sustainability

With legislation put forward in Congress aiming to prioritize enforcement and compliance actions that mitigate climate change, it's easy for many of us to get caught out in the sheer divisiveness of the news story and miss the overarching trend. Sustainability and ESG (Environment, Social and Governance) are not only here to stay but, as this national policy demonstrates, leading governments and public authorities around the world are willing to take increasingly bolder actions in the existential fight against climate change.

But political parties being political parties – that is, focused on their own survival above all else – nothing like this comes out of left field. It's preceded by mountains of polling and other population survey data, which, in this case, suggest that global warming is now important enough to enough people to warrant pushing this agenda without the risk of alienating too many voters.

It's a sign of the times and the travel industry is already well in the crosshairs for stricter guidelines regarding emissions and recycling programs. And just as voters are now signaling that they want more environmental action, travelers are likewise becoming highly cognizant of their carbon footprints. As highlighted in the latest report by the World Travel & Tourism Council and Trip.com Group, 69% of travelers surveyed are actively seeking sustainable travel options. Google even now has a dedicated search tool to help users find eco-friendly hotels.

This isn't a novel concept to our industry either; Accor has its Planet 21 program and Marriott has Serve360, while major global inventory buyers are starting to mandate that hotels get in line – for example, Siemens' Green Stay Initiative requiring all corporate stays to be with preferred hotel partners.

All told, this green revolution is no longer something any hotel organization can ignore, but that doesn't mean you can't add some green to your income statements in the process. From our experience working with owners and C-level executives, there are two key territories to help you focus your organization's ESG efforts: those that are guest-facing and those that function behind the scenes.

Real Cost Savings Are Often Invisible to the Guest

Before you can get ahead of the curve, there are some obvious steps that every hotel can take to realize significant cost savings, reduce a property's overall footprint, and develop a roadmap for ongoing improvements. Most of the biggest efficiencies, though, will be realized in the back of house, requiring investments large and small in new capital assets and setting aside budget for future renovations.

Yes, we are talking about the usual suspects of water recycling systems, new energy-efficient laundry machines, low-wattage lighting and IoT thermostats that turn in-room climate controls when the room is unoccupied. While there's an array of projects you can undertake, the first step is to start setting aside a portion of net operating incomes as a reserve fund. The green revolution isn't slowing down and you must be financially nimble.

Concurrently, as strategic advisors, we would next recruit a specialist, screening for someone who understands municipal, regional, and national laws along with any additional credentials, such as being a LEED Green Associate. Not only would this individual help to identify the low-hanging fruit – in this case, the relatively low-cost projects with easy implementation – but they can also conduct a waste audit to assess any property's total greenhouse gas emissions so that there's a firm goalpost in mind for achieving 100% sustainability.

As they say, you can't manage what you don't measure, and this principle applies to any eco-conscious roadmap you develop. A critical part of this management, however, is not just aligning the finances and ordering new capital assets but ensuring that your 'human capital' isn't overloaded. Your engineering team will undoubtedly have a hand in every single sustainability initiative, and unless you are building a new property, you are dealing with a live product, meaning that on any given day there are urgent maintenance tasks and regular system checks that must be performed. Hence, any eco-friendly task scheduling must also be friendly to your engineers' time in order to be realistic and not risk turnover in this department due to workplace stress.

Going Green to be Seen

No guest will ever see the shiny new water-efficient laundry equipment you install that will add thousands of dollars to your bottom line each year, nor will they care to read about these specific upgrades in a press release or in the fine print on your website. What they will see is a stamp of approval from a recognized authority like getting a B Corp Certification or working with an affiliate of the Global Sustainable Tourism Council.

While you may rightfully argue that the primary booking decision for most hotel guests is still one of location, price or brand amenities ahead of sustainability, we argue that any eco-friendly measures you take – as represented by being able to promote said certifications on every consumer channel – will afford your hotel sizeable marketing cachet to both appease this (currently niche) climatarian customer profile and also command higher rates in the process.

Besides the hard work to get some eco-approved logos attached to your brand, there are other ways to use sustainability to drive bookings. Think of climate-conscious restaurant concepts as a 'reason to visit', incorporating biophilic design into the public spaces and guestrooms or going further, like 1 Hotels, where sustainability reverberates through every aspect of the physical structure and operations.

Then, of course, once guests are onsite, you visibility reinforce this belief system by going paperless in favor of apps or in-room tablets, eliminating all single-use plastics (dispensers versus bathroom amenities, for instance), installing more recycling bins to encourage guest waste reduction and looking at ways to reduce food waste by highlighting your food scrap composting or local food bank partnership.

Overall, the customer-facing enhancements you implement should fit a brand narrative that exudes compassion and renewability. For rural properties, for instance, the herb garden that guests walk past may not provide a tenth of the ingredients used in the restaurant, and yet it tells a great story. The same applies for having all meal components locally sourced to drastically curb food miles. The lesson here is that you can and should promote your sustainability efforts.

The Beginning Is the End of the Beginning

To double down on what was stated in the introduction so that its crystal clear, climate change policies are only going to get more and more draconian, thus requiring ongoing vigilance. All it will take is one or two symbolic (like footage of a polar bear wasting away on ever-thinning Arctic ice) or catastrophic events (like the German towns in the Ahr Valley that were literally swept away overnight by flooding in the summer of 2021) to galvanize entire populations into more militant actions.

These proverbial bullets may come in the form of fines, steep carbon taxes for non-net-zero buildings or huge drains on your capex budgets as you are compelled to get caught up, so you must be consummately proactive. Sustainability will be front and center for at least the rest of the decade, but as we've shown, there are ways to make this green revolution work in your favor so that you are driving cost savings while also pivoting to attract this new eco-conscious customer mindset.

Hotel Sustainability Outlook for a New Year Starts with Profitability

Sustainability is the future for hotels, full stop. However profit-conscious or skeptical of international policies you may be, it's becoming exceedingly difficult to fight against the flow of the river, which is an action against human-born climate change. What we argue, though, is that going forward, profitability and sustainability are the same thing.

Every year, the weather gets weirder, and natural disasters become more severe. With hospitality seen as a 'discretionary' industry as compared to, say, agriculture, it will naturally come under increasing scrutiny for its contribution to global carbon emissions. This scrutiny may come from governments through the form of taxation and energy efficiency mandates, or it may come about privately via restricting access to capital for only those properties deemed green or from guests voting with their wallets by only booking those hotels that have passed a third-party sustainability appraisal.

But therein lies a bevy of opportunities for those properties and brands that wholeheartedly embrace this future. On the capital side, for instance, there are now a number of green bond programs and CPACE financing options (this being for the United States, with other countries having similar programs under different names) to help you surmount the upfront capex requirements necessary to bring an existing structure up to date. Then, on the consumer side, room inventory distribution is slowly evolving to offer specific vehicles for letting guests select only those properties that conform to their beliefs in this regard, including even Google, which offers special search highlights to eco-certified properties.

Irrespective of any property improvement plan to better accommodate or anticipate this eco-conscious economy, where do you start? This is a question we often confront when working directly with hotel ownership as asset managers where sustainability is always an objective but it can easily get sidelined by other more pressing matters like erratic occupancies, revenue growth, staffing issues, rolling out new profit centers and upgrading the tech stack. The answer is to start small and start with getting more juice from the squeeze.

What we mean by that analogy is that a lot of properties could become drastically more energy and water-efficient without drastic changes like installing a new heat pump. Instead, there are a series of incremental improvements that hotels can make. In the moment, none may elicit monumental returns, but cumulatively, they are quite powerful and meaningful to the financial bottom line.

Properties can realize big gains through a series of upgrades that include but are not limited to:

1. Setting up a predictive maintenance system to better identify energy-related issues
2. Installing more IoT sensors to more precisely measure then control climate controls and air leaks
3. Low-flow bathroom appliances (toilets, faucets, and showerheads)
4. Upgrading to LED lighting with smarter, motion-activated controls

5. Moving away from all single-use plastics, including surcharged water bottles
6. Using green cleaning products that are often also more universal to reduce cleaning times
7. With 40% of food going to waste, using the whole plant or animal alone can save a ton
8. Smaller plates for buffets that will also reduce your overall food costs
9. In the restaurant, assessing when equipment is actually needed to heighten just-in-time usage
10. Having onsite composting, vermiculture or other types of intelligent food waste recycling
11. Buying renewable energy certificates (RECs) to incentivize more green infrastructure
12. Humidity controls and water submetering with shutoff valves to increase leak prevention
13. Reducing embodied carbon by reupholstering and refinishing furniture versus buying new
14. Stormwater recapture systems to reduce the burden on local drainage infrastructure
15. Developing a standard policy for all contractors regarding sustainability selection criteria
16. If you have onsite laundry, building a plan for heightened water savings
17. If you don't have onsite laundry, discussing with your partner about their sustainability goals
18. Planting native flora species which will naturally reduce irrigation demands
19. If you have a resort, an onsite herb garden or organic farm is always commendable
20. If it allows, solar panels have progressed to now have a reasonable breakeven on cost

That's just 20 without getting into an exhaustive list. But if you did all of them and others incrementally, you would already have a far more profitable physical structure. Moreover, you would be future-proofing your hotel to align with the consumers of tomorrow who are currently willing to pay more each night for the privilege of staying at a sustainable property, rather than being forced into more defensive and reactive steps if you choose to delay the inevitable.

Ultimately, delaying action will put your brand behind those that are pivoting to meet this future outlook on travel, with programs by the major chains, including Accor's Planet 21, IHG's Journey to Tomorrow, Hilton's Travel with Purpose 2030, Hyatt's World of Care and Choice Hotels' Room Be Green. From this last one, a catchy mantra that we've always applied to every hotel's sustainability upgrades is 'going green to be seen'. That is, while most of the actual cost savings will be realized in the back of house, it never hurts to embellish your efforts with clear visual lines to the guest during every part of the customer journey so that your brand cachet becomes synonymous with eco-friendliness.

Listing on the website any big strides you've made or certifications you've accrued, posting to social media with the appropriate hashtags, highlighting your culinary team's food waste reduction efforts, putting information up on the in-room interactive televisions, and displaying usage or waste diversion dashboards so guests can see the property's efforts in real-time. This alone won't happen overnight, but when you think incrementally you can add these touchpoints that will reinforce sustainability as a core facet of your brand. Eventually, with this brand cachet comes the ability to charge more per night as the average consumer comes to recognize and appreciate your brand for its eco-initiatives.

The fact remains that guests are increasingly concerned about their ecological footprints and will come to demand hotels get in line – whether by directly booking eco-friendly hotels, voicing their opinions through the companies they work at or by voting for politicians that favor climate action. This is a gradual change...until it isn't. If recent world events are any indication, guest mindsets can change in an instant with the right motivations.

But rather than view this as a doom and gloom scenario, quite the opposite; all these incremental sustainability changes will set your hotel up for tremendous success and healthier profit margins in the years to come. The key is starting now and getting into a rhythm of making those small, seemingly inconsequential upgrades that will add up to something far greater in the long run.

Embedding Sustainability into a Hotel Starts with Leadership

Organizational structures and job titles grow and evolve the same as every other facet of running a business and adapting to the times. Two decades ago, we may have written about the dawn of online room sales and how hotels would be wise to carve out a 'social media manager' role which was quite novel at the time. Today it's all but anathema to not have a team member solely devoted to this area or specific responsibilities assigned to the marketing director, depending on the size of the company.

With this as context, we argue that the job title of sustainability director is in a similar status within the hospitality industry. Climate change is now at the forefront of people's minds, while travel is continually cited as a major contributor to total carbon emissions. As such, every brand needs a clear plan and must also be increasingly transparent about what's been done to date to win hearts and minds. But every plan relies upon leadership, and with customer sentiment slowly shifting more and more towards ESG values, this presents a clear case for carving out a sustainability role for every hotel.

Of all the places to learn about how to successfully embed sustainability into large-scale hotel operations, few would think to start with Las Vegas. And yet, largely stemming from its desert location, water recycling, and renewable energy programs have been up and running for quite some time at these casino resorts. One property in particular stands out, Resorts World Las Vegas near the north end of the Strip, which as of Fall 2023 is powered by 100% renewable energy.

To learn about how this laudable figure was achieved, we sat down with Brandon Morrison, Director of Sustainability at Resorts World Las Vegas, where he leads the company's commitment to creating positive environmental, economic, and social impact. Reporting to the Vice President of Construction and Facilities, he has direct responsibility for the resort's sustainability strategy and priorities, including the creation of the company's first integrated approach that's designed to deliver market differentiation and strategic business value creation for the resort.

Start by giving us some background on Resorts World Las Vegas's sustainability program.

Our commitment to sustainability has always guided our business operations, with a focus on minimizing environmental impact and promoting efficient practices. Yet defining 'sustainability' is wondrously complicated as it spans a diverse range of topic areas and company objectives. Beyond keeping pace with evolving regulations and consumer preferences, the ability to upset the status quo – and orchestrate purposeful change – is the continual challenge.

The travel and tourism sector – or more colloquially hospitality – is an economic powerhouse, accounting for more than 10% of global GDP. I would argue that no place in the world does hospitality better than Las Vegas, and yet hospitality is a consumption-driven industry. The question becomes, as consumers continue to travel, how do we work to rewrite the narrative of the hospitality industry towards building a better future?

At Resorts World Las Vegas, our sustainability management approach is driven by policies, targets, and performance, all geared towards maximizing the value of our operations. Our environmental management system is ISO 14001 certified, demonstrating a verifiable commitment to innovation and continuous improvement.

How is Resorts World Las Vegas a leader in this area?

Opening the resort while amid a global pandemic, we had a natural and intentional advantage to create the cleanest, safest, and most sustainable integrated resort experience in Las Vegas. All three of the hotel brands within the Resorts World Las Vegas property – Las Vegas Hilton, Conrad Las Vegas, and Crockfords Las Vegas, LXR Hotels & Resorts – have earned Gold Certification under the LEED green building certification program, which is a globally recognized symbol of sustainability achievement and leadership.

Sustainability and green building design were incorporated throughout the entire resort development process. Significant investments – totaling more than one billion dollars – were made towards energy efficiency upgrades. Water-efficient fixtures and technologies were incorporated throughout, both the interior and exterior of the property. Eco-friendly products (such as carpets) and materials (such as paints) were utilized throughout the entire development. To minimize single-use plastics, bulk amenities are utilized in the hotel tower, and water bottle-filling stations are incorporated across the resort.

Since opening the resort in June 2021, this emphasis on sustainability has only increased. We've invested millions in sustainability-related capital projects, with an emphasis on climate action and water efficiency.

Give us some information on electricity and how you manage this utility.

Short of labor, energy spending is typically a hotel's highest operating cost. An average hotel spends nearly $2,200 per available room each year on energy. Resorts World Las Vegas has 3,506 rooms and suites, which would translate to upwards of $8 Million per year in energy costs, given the metric. Aside from the significant financial implications, there is a large environmental impact as well. Globally, hotels account for an estimated 1% of total carbon emissions.

At Resorts World Las Vegas, we take our environmental responsibility seriously. Our commitment to renewable energy – and thus decarbonization – dates to 2019, several years before the resort was set to open. The challenges stemmed, in large part, from construction and supply chain delays. Like many sectors, the solar industry was impacted by the pandemic. Compounding issues – including global supply chain delays and fluctuating raw material costs – placed tremendous pressure on the industry and caused quite a bit of volatility within the solar marketplace. That said, we are proud to announce that we achieved our goal of sourcing 100% renewable power across our entire resort.

Residing in a desert city, how do you conserve water?

Nevada is the driest state in the nation, and Las Vegas is among the fastest-warming cities. Decades of drought coupled with rising atmospheric temperatures have taken their toll on the region's water supply. Yet Southern Nevada leads the nation in water conservation and recycling measures. It is one of the few places on the planet that recycles all indoor water on a community-wide scale. Approximately 99% of indoor water use is recycled, to the tune of nearly 100M gallons of water a day. In contrast to water used indoors, water that is used outdoors cannot be recycled, escaping into the ground or evaporating into the atmosphere.

At Resorts World Las Vegas, we understand the vitality of water stewardship and are committed to using water responsibly and helping the Las Vegas Valley become more resilient to future water resource oscillations through initiatives such as efficient irrigation systems, indigenous landscaping, low flow plumbing fixtures, cooling tower management standards and efficient chemical management. Since opening the resort, sustainability-related capital improvement projects have conserved over 18M gallons of water per year.

What about garbage and recycling?

For an integrated resort of our size, waste management is paramount. Consider this: the average American throws away approximately five pounds of garbage per day. At eight pounds per day, Nevada has the highest national per-person disposal rate. Though waste is easy to produce – and inevitable in modern society – it is not the easiest to manage across 3,506 hotel rooms and suites.

At Resorts World Las Vegas, our efforts start with working to change the definition of waste. Traditionally, waste is anything we throw away. Yet moving forward – towards the notion of a circular economy – waste will become things that have no value. On our docks, waste streams are viewed as a resource, akin to energy or water. We collect more than two dozen different recycling streams. As with many sustainability pursuits, collaboration is key for waste management. We believe that partnerships power progress.

A great example is food waste. Through a partnership with a local livestock farming operation, we can send 100% of our food scraps to the farm, where state-of-the-art systems convert food scraps into livestock feed. This effort is a preferred method of food waste disposal, as endorsed by the (US) Environmental Protection Agency.

How do you weigh the need for sustainability versus the need for profitability?

This is a great question, as many still see an inherent trade-off between choosing a more sustainable future and achieving business growth. Yet today's forward-thinking organizations are seeking to include sustainability in a comprehensive strategy that makes sense for the business. Far from impeding business, sustainability offers considerable benefits. A sustainability-related spend, such as a capital project to reduce energy consumption, is not purely a cost but rather an investment.

As a business, there is an obligation to drive continual value creation. Sustainability is closely linked with efficiency. Embracing sustainability forces companies to look at things differently. System thinking leads to comprehensive analyses of the real situation and thereby opens alternative solutions that can shift a business into greater efficiencies.

Do you have any feedback on the guests' perception insofar as the importance of sustainability?

The world is changing, and with it, our expectations of business. Booking.com publishes an annual 'Sustainable Travel Report' that offers a snapshot of marketplace trends and travelers' mindsets. Per the latest survey, 80% of travelers confirm that traveling more sustainably is important to them. Thus, at a macro level, there is a push towards greater sustainability efforts.

That said, Resorts World Las Vegas provides unprecedented levels of guest comfort and service, with the largest collection of branded Hilton experiences in the world. Underlying these commitments to guest comfort and service is a belief that sustainability can be at the heart of indulgent experiences. Yet we do not sermonize to our guests. While sustainability remains core to our operations, we find everyday opportunities to make a positive impact. In this way, we are choosing on behalf of our guests towards a more sustainable future. Our guests can choose a luxury vacation at Resorts World Las Vegas, knowing that we've made conscious and educated choices on their behalf.

How do you stack up in terms of efficiency when compared to the average home?
Globally, buildings utilize roughly 40% of total energy consumption. An integrated resort the size of Resorts World Las Vegas is no different, in that the facility consumes a lot of resources. Yet as the first new construction integrated resort to open in 10 years, Resorts World Las Vegas had the opportunity to incorporate new technology in ways that have never been attempted on the Strip.

It's easy to become numb to the onslaught of new technologies consistently hitting the market. Consider advancements in smartphones as just one example. In the past decade, advancements in mobile technology and networks have allowed us to do things we never thought possible, including streaming and filmmaking. Now consider this rate of technological change within building technologies and systems. While constructing the property, we were able to incorporate cutting-edge technology and innovation throughout the entire development process.

I'll end with one example: the utilization of building information modelling. Utilizing cutting-edge AI technology, we can create a precise digital twin of our resort. Via this building prototype, we can simulate, predict, and inform facility-related decisions based on real-world conditions and data. Utilizing these technological advancements, we can generate much greater efficiencies, thereby minimizing resource consumption and, thus, our overall environmental footprint.

Spending More to Become the Most Cost-Efficient Hotel Operator

Article originally published in August 2022 and the indicated status of Newport Hospitality Group in this passage may not reflect current company practices.

"You cannot save your way to success. You must invest," is how Andrew Carey, CEO of Newport Hospitality Group (NHG), started our latest interview. As a management company with a portfolio of select and full-service hotels across the Eastern Seaboard, we focused our discussion on what leading management companies such as NHG are doing to continually produce above-benchmark results for their owners during these turbulent past few years.

Entering any market interruption, be it a pandemic or a recession, most hotels, like businesses in practically any other sector, look to tighten the purse strings and cut costs wherever possible. But as Carey demonstrated, pervasive redlining may not achieve the desired result of maximizing returns.

"It's all about knowing where to save and where to staunchly preserve your budgets," continued Carey. "You don't want to dilute services viewed as meaningful to guests or else word of mouth will suffer, nor do you want to accrue a huge maintenance backlog that might result in a bunch of OOS rooms which dampen occupancy maximization once conditions improve. But perhaps the real magic behind our success was keeping our well-oiled sales teams in place so that they were ready to go full bore at working their local markets as restrictions were lifted and traveler confidence returned."

The term that we kept coming back to during our discussion was 'operational maximization', wherein the savviest hotel operators know what combination of costs will deliver the greatest bang for the buck.

The word 'combination' is essential here. For performance optimization, we cannot treat each operation as siloed, mutually exclusive entities. Instead, we must grasp their interdependency and how they all compound in myriad ways to produce the cumulative effect that guests perceive as great service.

That's why aiming to always be cheaper may backfire; cutting ubiquitously can create weak links in the value chain. Regardless of brand or flag, being known for great service pays back manifold through word of mouth, repeat visits, better ability to grow ADR and becoming the top property in a given category for a given territory which then has a positive feedback effect.

Five Elements That Increase Revenues

With the trend towards market consolidation and larger management companies, NHG stands in contrast with 50+ properties under management – almost all of them flagged. The company's size has led to a 'higher touch' approach in terms of:

1. Deployment of bespoke operating strategies
2. Empowerment of local leadership
3. Service-based training attuned to each market
4. Creating a healthy associate-centric culture to mitigate employee turnover
5. Consistent regional sales efforts where local relationships are sustained

Importantly, these five elements do not wholly align with a vision of consummate cost cutting where operators end up shirking in one of these five areas to inevitably compromise RevPAR growth. And speaking of which, from the summer of 2020 onwards – representing the initial reopening from the pandemic – NHG has delivered above-market RevPAR growth, or an index over 100, for 77% of its properties with a companywide compounding annual growth rate of 63% from 2020 to 2021.

This performance figure is what Carey cited as evidence for why not cutting costs and keeping teams intact will result in less revenue lost during tough times and the ability to bounce back faster. In other words, and despite what may be standard practice for other brands or industries, "More often than not, the best hotel operations aren't necessarily the cheapest."

Operational Maximization Reflected Through One Department

To expand further on one other aspect of operating efficiency that Carey mentioned, consider the maintenance backlog leftover from 2020 as many hotels redlined the engineering department to save as much as possible. While some properties closed, others stayed open only to witness a stark change in guest profile whereby guestrooms suffered a lot more abuse resulting in additional maintenance.

Now, to bring a hotel back online in 2022 and deal with any other pandemic-born damages requires a set procedure of systems checks, fire safety, equipment work, parts replacement and so on. Not only does this take time, resulting in a number of OOS rooms that can curtail topline revenues, but it also creates a subsequent bottleneck for getting underway on new projects.

This domino effect may be hard to see when you are caught in the daily clamor of first closing a hotel due to COVID then partially reopening in the wake of the Delta then Omicron variants as well as reskilling associates amidst an agonizing labor shortage. An example of this that we workshopped with Carey was a scenario where a hotel needs to upgrade its hot water system, which can involve the replacement of a dozen or so boilers at a time.

If only it were as simple as evaluating the costs and scheduling the work. First you have to bring your maintenance team back and refamiliarize them with the property, sourcing and training new team members if need be. Then you have to address any higher-priority concerns left over from the pandemic that may affect guest safety or render a room unsellable.

Only now, and if your team has time, can they properly assess the situation, get budgetary approval and put in an order for parts. And even then, due to both global supply chain disruptions and inflation, this order will likely come with greater costs and extra weeks waiting for the new systems to arrive. Altogether, if you wanted the upgraded hot water system online in time for this current summer peak season of 2022, the time to start project execution was in the autumn of 2021.

This same whiplash effect on operational maximization could also be said regarding associate turnover. NHG is an example of a company priding itself on its corporate culture, but this takes decades to build.

During the pandemic, all the furloughs within the hotel industry led many qualified employees and managers to leave in search of better prospects in other areas of the service sector, and they have yet to return. Accelerating its focus on above-market wages, health insurance and benefit packages even in the face of short-term occupancy flatlining, NHG's culture and available pool of skilled associates suffered less, again allowing their properties to build back faster as the pandemic waned.

A Small City Example

In early 2021, NHG bought and ramped up a Home2 Suites by Hilton property in Brunswick, Georgia – a midscale, all-suites brand that specializes in cost-conscious extended stay concepts with flexible guestroom configurations. As you can imagine, Home2 has become a hot commodity in many markets since COVID elevated the need for more total supply in this category.

The numbers from this takeover speak for themselves: even in a turbulent travel year, the Home2 Brunswick still achieved an annual RevPAR in 2021 of almost $83

(18.7% above market based on STAR Report data) with the Q1 2022 numbers already showing even more growth with RevPAR at $105.

Just as Q1 2022's tremendous RevPAR growth represents a managed hotel that is now 'firing on all cylinders', the budgeted 2022 rooms revenue is likewise projected to grow by 40% year over year, with ADR increasing by over 18% year over year. For reference, STAR Report data lists the Home2 Brunswick property at 113.2 on a 100-point index for its 2021 ADR comp set comparison – that is, above market by 13.2% – which is up from the 2020 ADR comp set comparison score of 88.4.

"It's these sorts of growth scenarios that can generate a bit of disbelief, especially when an owner who has thus far self-managed a property reviews our projections," added Carey to conclude our chat. "These results represent the cumulative effect of our hands-on management style where spending more in certain areas disproportionally increases guest scores and revenues, protecting the bottom line. The real secret is knowing where to focus your spend, and despite all the business intelligence software there's still an art to knowing where. Of course, that art comes from experienced leadership at both the local and corporate levels."

So, whatever the macroeconomic situation portends, NHG's case stands as proof that the immediate reaction of cutting costs may not be the optimal move due to the loss of momentum and the cumulative effects on guest service. In other words, preserve your people; they are and will always be the lifeblood of hospitality.

The Next Luxury and Lifestyle Segment Evolutions from NYU IHIIC

Venturing down to the Big Apple for the NYU International Hospitality Industry Investment Conference (IHIIC) is an enlightening must-see event, often a forerunner for many trends that will ripple through every property in every category. The 46th annual, held at the beginning of June 2024 – was no exception. But rather than give a play-by-play on what was said during each panel session, our rationale here is to highlight and expand upon one megatrend that every hotel executive and investor should grasp.

Namely, we are in the midst of a great evolution for what travelers value, what emotionally influences their choice of accommodations, and what else they want to spend their money on. The lifestyle and luxury segments traditionally codify and profit from these tenets. But now, from what we see with the explosion of luxury and lifestyle brands, new properties, and developments within these spaces, even these segments deserve further segmentation.

No two words better encapsulate the sentiment from NYU IHIIC and the general outlook on the hotel industry than 'cautious optimism.' Developers and capital allocators see a bright, long-term future for hospitality. Still, some big, potential bumps along the road are slowing investment in 2024 and leaving a lot of dry powder waiting for a flashing green light, whether that's a clear signal from the Fed of future rate cuts or other positive benchmarks of further economic growth. Still, you can hide a lot in the aggregate, and the continued diversification of lifestyle hotel brands is one such trend.

The Current State of Luxury Categorization

To give you perspective on where we are right now, do you remember when dividing the hotel industry into categories that meant only economy (or budget), midscale, upscale, and luxury? Over the years, as the barbell distribution of hotel categories has fattened both ends of the spectrum, we now have select service, limited service, and (to a lesser extent) extended stay to complement the economy, while on the other end, there's now upper midscale, upscale and upper upscale (this last classification in the chain scale is seeing big year-over-year according to the latest figures by the way).

Through the 'Mille Club', which is Hotel Mogel's internal term to denote our work with and constant research of hotels charging over $1,000 per night, we haven't seen an improved taxonomy within the luxury spectrum. The best we've seen is the partitioning off of the ultraluxury category to denote super-expensive enclaves of the 20-80 key range. Think brands like Aman, Bulgari, Dorchester Collection, Mandarin Oriental, Oetker Collection, One&Only, Raffles, Ritz-Carlton Reserve, Rocco Forte, Rosewood and Six Senses.

Hardly an exhaustive list, each property in these brands, whether urban or resort, reflects flawless service and personalization but also a wholehearted embrace of the in-vogue term 'quiet luxury' where seclusion within a supremely elegant setting is the order of the day. We've seen this category bloom over the past decade, and all indications are that this will continue because it represents the epitome of the 'experience economy' – hyper-personalization, exclusivity, seclusion, immaculate attention to detail, elite access to one-of-a-kind activities.

The word 'lifestyle' has also entered the recent discussion as a pseudo-luxury modifier, but there's no firm delineation of how this reflects rate structure and service offerings. It's used in marketing communications rather liberally by brands that are luxury as well as those that are premium or upscale. Our sense of the word is that it indicates a mindset, not a classification, that is, any hotel in any category that aims to bring together like-minded individuals through a confluence of hotel themes, services, amenities, and curated experiences.

In short, lifestyle primarily focuses on creating a congregation point for a particular psychographic or interest group independent of a hotel classification. Instead, we see growth within the luxury segment within an emerging subcategory that we describe using a novel term that we've borrowed from music—'progressive luxury'.

Defining the Progressive Luxury Category

As its nomenclature implies, progressive is supposed to mean 'making progress'. Hence, progressive luxury represents a new category where the main draw is, like lifestyle, a sense of community for alternative thinkers, wellness-focused travelers, and people who have reoriented their habits around modern high-performance living, all completed with the hallmarks of luxury hotel service. These are properties that are citizens and stewards of their localities.

To give you a baseline for travel demand, here are the secular changes in consumer behavior that progressive luxury is aiming to serve:

- Knowledge workers are supplanting the traditional middle class, where upwardly mobile individuals are rewarded more for creativity, collaboration, tech fluency, and financial acumen.
- Popularity and acceptance of remote work and glocalization whereby people feel a more personal connection to like-minded individuals rather than merely by geographic convenience.
- A longevity focus where 'health is wealth' and people more heavily prioritize work-life balance, quality sleep, food as medicine, stress reduction, and wellness-based discretionary spending.
- On the heels of longevity, society is becoming more ageless with a dissolution of clearcut retirement at 65 and more second careers, emeritus positions, and 'elderpreneurship.'
- Respect and sensitivity for sustainability, eco-consciousness, and living a more 'natural' lifestyle
- Valuing thoughtful experiences, often inwardly focused, over the showier, outward materialistic purchases and conspicuous consumption of past eras, as inscribed by previously mentioned terms such as 'quiet luxury' and 'the experience economy.'
- Branded residences are another vehicle for extended-stay travel. Guests have convenient access to amenities and services, allowing them to maintain their standards of living.
- More multigenerational travel, reorienting area planning around fewer rooms with a higher average square footage.

The prioritization of wellness and well-being is a hallmark of this new categorization and the guests it serves. Whereas wellness in traditional luxury brands may be centered around the spa and gym – think brands like Conrad, Four Seasons, Kempinski, Langham, Montage, Park Hyatt, Ritz-Carlton, Shangri-La, Sofitel, St. Regis, Peninsula and Waldorf Astoria – progressive luxury has placed healthy living, creativity and networking with other HENRYs (high earner not rich yet) in a sophisticated setting at the core of the brand's differentiation.

Of a key range that can be in the 100-250 range, this wellness-oriented lifestyle of a progressive luxury brand transcends the guest suite and pervades every guest-facing operation. To give you a sense of some brands we see evolving in this space, consider ones (however emerging or nascent they may be) like 1 Hotels, Andaz, EAST Hotels, EDITION, Equinox Hotels, Janu, Nobu Hotels, Pendry, SIRO, and Soho House.

Concurrently, to see this evolution in action, you may also look at other niches with a wellness focus like the 'luxury health clinics' of Canyon Ranch or Lanserhof, as well as the 'hip' upper upscale brands such as W Hotels or Virgin Hotels. Yes, we've thrown a lot of names at the wall. Still, the point herein is that there's a new category emerging that's more poignantly targeting health-conscious, eco-conscious, experience-motivated travelers who also happen to be trendy HENRYs or captains of industry. We've labeled this as 'progressive luxury,' but we're open to other nomenclature suggestions!

Lifestyle Total Revenues

What this conference clarified for us was that the luxury segment is more fluid than previously imagined. From all the brand names rifled off above, it should already be evident that there is no longer just one type of luxury customer and that the traditional methodology of segmentation by age and income doesn't work in today's lifestyle-driven economy.

The real secret sauce of progressive luxury and all other luxury subcategories now lies in mixed-use real estate or profit center diversification—what's often termed total revenues on a proforma or the income statement. The principle here is that the hotel room night is often only the first source of revenue from a guest who will ultimately spend 50% to 200% more than their room reservation on ancillaries (dining, spa, activities, excursions, events, gift shop, and so on).

Many of these secondary, non-room revenue sources are harder to forecast accurately during the initial feasibility or development stages. Still, they can be lucrative profit centers and instrumental vehicles for long-term loyalty. This is what we colloquially label as a hotel's 'reason to visit', and it is often pushed through by the passion and sheer will of ownership that sees the intangible benefits beyond the numbers alone may tell.

For instance, can you build a luxury hotel nowadays without a strong wellness program? These spas and guestroom FF&E to realize said programming have a huge capex, and yet they are entirely necessary to attract the type of guests you need to sustain your rates. To give you another sense of the relationship between this diversification of luxury identities and the total revenues from across the entire guest journey, consider the emergence of branded e-commerce like the Mandarin Oriental Shop, Aman Essentials, or, more granularly, Rosewood Asaya's clothing partnership with Sporty & Rich.

It may be a lot to take in all these developments, but what's critical is to consider that mixed-use revenues mean those captured inside the four walls (rooms, dining, spa, parking, etc.) and those beyond (e-commerce, activities, additional services). It's truly a new frontier with luxury representing the hospitality vertical at the forefront of immense change, with hotels developing new products and services to serve this ageless, 21st-century guest mindset. We are eagerly awaiting next year's outing of NYU IHIIC for confirmation on this trend of progressive luxury and to see the latest developments and evolutions that may bring to our incredibly dynamic industry.

Budgeting for Current and Upcoming Hotel Design Trends

This article was originally published in June 2023, and the indicated status of market conditions in this passage may not reflect current events.

Property renovations, improving the physical design of spaces, and upgrading amenities are all inevitable for hotels that want to stay current with guest expectations. The current problem is that brands are simultaneously confronted by market forces that drastically increase the costs of executing any change while navigating some profound, ever-evolving shifts in post-pandemic customer behavior.

Therein, we often have a bit of shopper's paralysis – too much choice that ultimately leads to inaction. And yet, if you don't start making plans for what's coming, you may soon find that it's simply too much and conversion out of the hotel real estate landscape is the only move left. The two of us don't want that to happen, so let's discuss the lay of the land in order for you to better decide what capital investments will maximize your return on investment.

Dealing with the Current Mess

It's 2023, yet we still need to interject the 'C word' into this conversation – COVID. The backlog of maintenance updates, supply chain issues and inflationary cost overruns are all challenges that must be considered with any hotel design update. To give you a better sense of the scenario, Jeremy Buffam, the partner who oversees construction and development at New Castle Hotels & Resorts, an East Coast hotel management company, said it best.

"With FF&E reserves still being replenished, prioritizing capital expenditures is more critical than ever. Many hotels have deferred maintenance that will compete with front-of-house upgrades to improve guest impressions and experiences and, in some instances, meet brand requirements," commented Buffam. "Add the uncertainty that inflation and contractor shortages have added to budgets, and you have a challenging multi-step process to deploy capital dollars effectively. Several brands are looking to push sustainability projects, and the cost of this work and associated ROI will become increasingly important in the years ahead. We expect these initiatives will begin showing up on PIPs soon."

Right now, the choice is clear. There's no point in even thinking about room updates or SOP upgrades if a maintenance issue may impede the sale of a guestroom. But at a certain point in the near future, the pandemic logjam will be fully attenuated while, hopefully, contractor labor shortages and any supply chain headaches will also become non-issues. When that happens, you have to start thinking about the future of hotels and where your brand fits into the new paradigm.

Thinking of the Future

Your first thought about upcoming challenges may lean towards sustainability and updating your hotel to meet the ever-mounting ESG regulations. Indeed, this will be of tremendous importance in the coming years, both for capital assets and construction as well as for financing vehicles, as epitomized by C-PACE financing in the US as well as the EU's green bonds program.

This should definitely be on the list, but there are three other concurrent trends worth your time:

1. *Wellness.* Demand by guests for wellness amenities at hotels is increasing, but how design influences employee wellbeing must also be considered, especially as a means to combat inflationary wages and high turnover rates.
2. *Inflation.* It's all too easy to think of the supply shock that was the pandemic as the only culprit behind the rising prices we've all experienced these past three years, and yet more global forces (like the war in Ukraine, the reshoring of supply chains and shrinking populations in advanced economies) are at play that may make this a perpetual challenge.
3. *Psychographics.* The traditional 'hotels in beds' model was largely based on appealing to certain demographics and levels of wealth. The future portends a shift to people identifying and aligning according to their specific, and often niche, interests.

To help decipher the scope of work involved in navigating this market evolution, we reached out to a longtime colleague and absolutely masterful hotel designer, Alessandro Munge, who is the founder and design director of Studio Munge and has been involved in many new builds and redevelopment projects, specializing in the upscale and luxury end.

"We often think about the luxury sector driving trends and influencing the market," started Munge. "Sure, an element of research and development simmers down from the top-tier projects, but the influence is reciprocal. Activated lobbies and bar lounges with a sense of fun mostly permeated from approachable brands to more established luxury. There's a rising new generation of four and five-star hotels that are much more social and relaxed. Luxury doesn't have to be stiff. Perfectly illustrating that concept is the Pendry brand for which we're designing two properties in Newport Beach and Tampa after successful collaborations in Chicago and San Diego. A great emphasis on social spaces and F&B ultimately creates a multi-layered guest experience that is much more engaging, connective, and profitable for the hotel."

The Hotel Design Gradient

Munge's thoughts support our notion of the 'hotel design gradient' where the in-vogue trends often start at the luxury or boutique categories and then disperse outward into midscale and select service as they gain momentum within the broader consumer landscape. That is, the initial buzz and awareness for something new drives guest demand in a positive feedback loop until the trend shifts from a value-add to a customer expectation.

"For years, we have seen the concept of signature narratives driving the design of more unique boutique properties that evoke a deep sense of place and authenticity, challenging the large conservative brands and hospitality groups to rethink their offering," continued Munge. "The next decade will be about reinvention and helping brands create new standards, redefining the room product and re-exploring what brand fidelity means to the consumer. Because of the economic climate, I foresee many renovation projects soon in the Americas, which aren't always easy to navigate. The guest is more design savvy than ever, so the design community must bridge renovation and innovation smartly."

Indeed, guests are more sensitive to good hotel design than ever before. In an 'experience economy', guests are no longer satisfied by cookie-cutter approaches to interior spaces. And heightened local market competition is also driving this as a bigger factor in the purchasing decision; hotel guests nowadays have so many options and there's so many ways to discover new hotel products that fascinating design can longer be ignored. Hotels need to create both strong digital then onsite impressions in order to respectively drive bookings and guest satisfaction.

"Where we will continue to see new builds is the mix development sector which coincides with evolution within the lifestyle segment," concluded Munge. "It's becoming less and less about the room value as much as it is about the crystallization of a value set. Equinox, 1 Hotel, Proper Hotel, EDITION and Nobu are great examples. And because of the brands' strong appeal, we see an increase in branded residential development. This year, we're completing the first integrated Nobu Hotel, Residences and Restaurant in Toronto. We also just opened the sales office for EDITION Residences Miami Edgewater, the brand's first residence-only property. It shows that brands are still relevant and powerful to lift pricing. However, groups must adapt to the evolving market and demographic. This branded residential concept is proven within the luxury sector. Can it translate to the midscale sector? I believe so, but we need stronger brands with defined statements to carry the torch."

The Bottom Line

To close by circling back to budgeting and incorporating Munge's remarks, the hybrid hotel-residence model should also be on the table. Given the cost of incorporating savvy design principles or building new wellness facilities to meet that growing demand vertical, brands of all categories should consider offsetting those upfront costs with condominium unit sales – a move that can concurrently generate more baseline revenues for your onsite amenities.

While looking at how this hybrid model affects revenue projections is the topic of a whole other conversation, the overall and inescapable fact is that there are profound changes afoot that will impact every hotel segment. These changes are starting slow, until all of a sudden they are an immediate priority. The best bet is to map out your vision for how your property or brand will meet these forthcoming shifts in guest demands and then begin setting aside capex so that you are fully prepared to execute without needing excessive external financing.

Should Hotels Complete a Reserve Fund Study

One of the obligations of moving from a home to a condominium is to take your turn on the board of directors. Don't let anyone fool you into believing that this is a simple,

10-hours-a-month task. The time investment is significantly higher, and even though there is no financial remuneration, your fellow unit owners will treat you as if you're a paid servant. Perhaps this situation strikes closer to home for many of you already.

As we'll examine later on this article, everything is up for grabs as inflation rolls through various sectors of the economy. This is a critical yet still underappreciated variable for today's hotel finances.

Condominium Reserve Fund Studies

Apart from the day-to-day administration, aptly executed by the property manager, the main responsibility of a condominium BOD is to ensure that there are sufficient funds generated through monthly maintenance fees to keep the building operational. The yin and yang of this exercise is balancing the monthly fees versus the quality of service and maintenance expenses. No one wants to see their fees increased, but at the same time, they want to ensure the property is well-maintained. And importantly, no one wants a special, one-time assessment.

While the specific rules vary by state and country, here in our home province of Ontario, Canada legislation mandates that condominium corporations provide adequate funding for long-term repairs and replacement. This is managed through a reserve fund study – an independently developed forecast of expenditures necessary to maintain the building structures. Produced by engineering specialists, this 50-year plan identifies major building systems as well as their forecasted replacement costs and dates. We don't doubt the capabilities of your engineering team, but the emphasis is on 'independent'.

As an example, our building has a roof replacement coming up in just under a decade at a forecasted cost of four million dollars. Rather than have a special assessment when the replacement is due, our owners will pay a much smaller amount each month, setting aside these funds so that when the roof needs a serious overhaul, the funds for this project will be available. As the building is already 20 years old, by the time the roof needs replacement, unit owners will have been paying for some 30 years, which is the expected life of the asset. Our roof is but one of over a hundred items that are identified in the reserve fund study, each with a different dollar value and replacement timeline. Moreover, every few years the replacement study gets updated, reflecting differences between expected and actual life cycles.

Hotel Reserve Studies

Each year, hotel asset managers develop a capital budget outlining what is required for the upcoming year. Capital projects tend to be irregular in nature, resulting in some years being significantly higher in need. Thus, there is a dance of sorts where capital requirements get jockeyed from year to year, often delayed to meet available cash flow from operations or debt service coverage. Most troubling, decisions of this nature are frequently made to fit some hypothetical available capital budget, an extreme need (in other words, it's already broken), or a legal obligation (mostly related to safety). It can all be haphazard and leave hotel owners exposed to uneven annual returns.

A reserve fund study approach would strongly help to eliminate this issue. Instead of asset managers or general managers – who seldom possess an accredited degree in mechanical engineering – making decisions on capital projects, perhaps with the assistance of the maintenance team, a schedule of physical requirements would be available annually with more realistic timelines.

Having a reserve fund study does not force the asset manager to upgrade or replace assets just because they are on the schedule. Rather, it serves as a guideline for budgetary decisions in the present to avoid more drastic measures in the future. In our condominium, we made the decision to move several maintenance items ahead a few years while others have been delayed because their useful life was underestimated.

The Impact of Inflation

Many projected costs of capital asset replacement are still based on the values assessed before average inflation moved from 2% to 5% or even higher. Right now, the narrative around inflation has been centered around commodities and direct-to-consumer goods, and yet it will snowball through nearly every other industry, as we are starting to see in higher costs of new construction.

The impact here is that your long-term capital expenditure budget may be underfunded, failing to anticipate the inflationary pressures on periodic investments like window replacements, new water systems or bathroom renovations. The most dangerous word from the previous paragraph is 'average' because it undermines the erratic variable costs that some materials are encountering as global supply chains ebb and flow. For instance, while the average reported by the news is at around 6-8%, specific goods may be at 25% or more.

This is cause for alarm and yet more one imperative for commissioning a reserve study for your property. For a condo, having the reserve funds allows us to make highly rational decisions without asking our unitholders for additional capital or, more so for commercial real estate, having to plead to a bank for a loan. It's all about preparedness so that any unforeseen, one-time expenses don't stymie your business in a world of hyperinflation.

THE MILLE CLUB

As the premier ultraluxury urban property in Canada, the 77-key Hazelton Hotel in Toronto excels at personalized service with outstanding onsite amenities that include the Valmont Spa and a private film screening room.

With Great Rates Come Great Guest Expectations

Since the pandemic, and for various reasons, hotel rates in many categories have skyrocketed. But does that mean that your current guests – in what can ostensibly still be described as a rebound from the pandemic – are happy guests who are ready to come back within a reasonable timeframe? Would they recommend you to others, either by word of mouth or by word of *mouse*?

While the apt adage for right now is to make hay while the sun shines, it's nevertheless critical to evaluate how guest expectations increase as you yield rates, oftentimes with the two not linearly correlated. From this, we ponder whether there's a long-term risk to your loyalty and, broader, whether we are collectively creating a more mercenary-like disposition amongst travelers when selecting hotel brands.

Price Influences Guest Expectations

Take this basic scenario for instance. A guest checks into a $199 per night room. Their expectations are humble – a quiet night's sleep, controllable air conditioning, a comfortable bed, and a clean bathroom. The price is reasonable based on the rates in the guest's near-past set of hotel experiences. They understand that they have opted for a relatively modest-priced room and have adjusted their standards accordingly. They may even give the room a high rating on TripAdvisor because it offered good perceived value.

Now take this same room and increase the rate to $349 per night, a 75% increase. What are the guest's expectations at this higher rate? Will the same loud-cycling air conditioner, starchy bedsheets, polyester blanket and minimal amenities suffice? Will they be more sensitive to perceived slights by the front-of-house team?

In these cases, the guest's standards may have risen directly to the new price point. That same guest who might have given a five-star review might now rate give two or three stars, wherein it's important to note that guest reviews are emotionally driven and independent of a solid knowledge base of the comp set or brand standards checklist. Nothing has changed insofar as what the operations team delivered. Rather, the guest expects and, really, deserves more at the higher price.

The reality of today's hotel guest is that prices are significantly higher than pre-pandemic rates. Many hotels are enjoying RevPAR levels that were unattainable four years ago. Operators are basking in EBITDA percentages that they have never previously experienced. Ownership is encouraged, eagerly recouping losses incurred during the lockdown era. High fives everywhere! But be wary; guests aren't dumb!

The Never-Content Couple

Consider this anecdotal experience we witnessed firsthand from a recent consulting assignment with an upscale, independent small resort within driving distance from our hometown of Toronto.

In 2019, nightly rates for this property were in the range of $189 to $229 (Canadian) per night. Now, however, we had a couple book with the hotel, and their price for a three-night, double occupancy, standard king room was $389 per night, roughly an 85% increase above where this guestroom would be priced pre-pandemic.

This couple rejected the first three rooms that were offered, as apparently the rooms either smelled of smoke (it was a non-smoking hotel), had mold in the bathrooms, or had views of exhaust stacks from the kitchen. On the fourth try, they were satisfied. Still, the couple noted that the room had a chipped tub and a loose sink. There were also insufficient bathroom amenities requiring a late-evening request to the front desk for additional supplies.

Then came the proverbial straw that broke the housekeeper's back. Coming home in the evening after a day's outing, the couple arrived to find their room just as they left it – uncleaned. When they called the front desk, they were advised (for the first time) that rooms were only cleaned every second day. Demanding a clean room, they were moved again to the 'last clean room available'.

While on paper, the $389 price tag looks good. But are hotels accounting for these hidden costs associated with the burden of moving guests around so haphazardly? Moreover, is there an even-more-hidden effect on the team's morale when such events occur?

Now in your opinion from this story, did the fact that the room was now $389 versus $199 raise the bar? Would these guests have been so nitpicky at the previous, lower rate, or would they be more forgiving? Yes, this is a bit counterfactual, but nonetheless a consideration.

Expectations Versus Chargebacks

Alas, the tale of the never-content couple doesn't end there. Post-stay, their solution was not to write a negative review on TripAdvisor. Rather, they took a more aggressive course of action: they called Mastercard and enacted chargeback protocols.

In chargeback situations, all credit card customers are immediately given priority over merchants – that's how these payment networks first built and continue to build trust, after all. Fighting a chargeback is both time-consuming and with middling success. Moreover, with too many chargebacks, your merchant account is flagged, and higher processing fees may be applied.

While this is arguably a case of friendly fraud, it's still a burden that hotels must devote resources towards. And ultimately, if the chargeback is won by the couple, it may get boiled down and buried within a tabulation on the income statement, often represented by the 'negative review' or 'bad debt' line item and without anyone at corporate having the necessary information to ask what can be done to prevent future incidents.

Chargebacks vary by region and by hotel, but there are lessons to be learned from each one that transpires, both in terms of what types of guests are acting malevolently as well as what the hotel can do to better prevent guests from using the chargeback mechanism as a retaliatory action due to the property not meeting their newly elevated expectations.

These are but a few cautions to consider when raising rates or keeping them at current levels as you start to devise your rate strategy for the future.

The Mille Club: Four-Figure Luxury

In the weird years that immediately followed the pandemic, we were lucky enough to have stayed at properties with daily rates in excess of 1,000 dollars, euros or pounds as part of our consultancy work auditing luxury hotels to improve their topline performance. Any four-figure guest daily hit propels your property into a new snack bracket, and one that plays by a slightly different set of service and amenity requirements. There's prestige, but much, much higher expectations that you must surpass each and every day.

If your property has moved into this Mille Club, it is high time that you recognize this insofar as how you treat your guests. The psychology of hitting four figures in the rate triggers guests to have loftier expectations where a single error can cost you a guest (and likely a high-net-worth guest) for life. (And for reference, we're calling this 'mille' which is Italian for 'thousand' and to distinguish from the 'mile high club' which is a tad different…)

Here is a list for starters that you simply must get right every time if you aspire to grow your rates above $1,000:

1. *Nightly turndown service.* Be prepared to respond to guests who ask your housekeeper to come back at a time that is more convenient to them, even if this means past the normal hours of your team. Don't ask if guests want to eliminate daily housekeeping. If they are concerned about personal interaction, they will certainly let you know. And nowadays you also need good room occupancy tracking to know when rooms are unoccupied so that your team can prepare rooms as invisibly and faster.
2. *Enhanced towels and linens*. Sorry, bedsheets are not to be used as exfoliants! Sheet quality must be up-to-stuff. Familiarize yourself with Frette, Castello or other high-end manufacturers. Linen thread counts are becoming a bit of an arm's race in how they are marketed, too. Towels should be extra thick and never skimp on the quantity. Some guests may wish to reuse towels as an ecofriendly gesture. This is their option and should never be forced unless you are in a drought restriction.
3. *One bottle of each amenity is insufficient.* Two-ounce bottles of shampoo, conditioner and bath gel may not suffice, and you should double the quantity if the service orders on your operations platform are indicating any such evidence of guest requests for additional bathroom amenities. Many hotels are moving towards dispensers for cost as well as ecological reasons. If you are using dispensers (and you certainly should be moving this way), only the finest recognized brands will do in order to make up for their lackluster perception amongst luxury consumers.

4. *Unlimited water.* We visited a hotel where the guest agent leading us to our room was excited to say, "Two bottles of water would be replenished each day free of charge." As the room was 975 euros a night, we naively asked, "And if we need more than two?" The response was that additional bottles of water were available for six euros in our minibar. While the accountants reading this may think this is totally logical, we question the logic at this price point. When you are truly in the Mille Club, you value the customer for a lifetime, not nickel and diming them.
5. *Speaking of minibars, should you really charge for the contents?* We wonder if the days of the grab-it-pay-for-it minibar in the Mille Club are logical. Even if the guest clears it out, which is highly doubtful, the content cost is probably in the 20-buck range. Again, penny-wise actions lead to pound-foolish behavior. Charging seven bucks for a two-ounce bag of potato chips is simply insulting as it assumes the luxury consumer isn't price-conscious. Of course they are! How do you think they became luxury consumers? Your guests will pay the exorbitant price for the chips if they really want it, but it will hit an emotional pain point and be one more factor preventing a return trip.
6. *Streaming services on the TV.* Especially when traveling for an extended period, streaming services such as Netflix, Amazon Prime, or Disney Plus make logical additions. Don't ask me to attempt to synchronize my laptop to the set. I have tried and my success rate is poor. Make it simple; make it easy. The luxury guest values time far more than money, so don't waste their time by making them try to figure out how to log on to your convoluted system or deal with a complex casting solution.
7. *Illuminated makeup mirror.* It's not a 'guy' thing, but women expect them. If you do not have one, commit to the minor capital now. It is a critical differentiator because the lack of a modern vanity mirror setup introduces discomfort in the bathroom experience.
8. *Welcome gift with a handwritten note.* Welcome gifts can be tailored to the guest, the hotel, and thematic events such as the season or a current local festival. They need not be overly expensive, but they need to be there on arrival. No one expects Dom Pérignon, except perhaps at the $5,000 rate level! But a welcome bottle of Prosecco or regional wine makes a difference, accompanied by fruit or baked goods at a minimum.
9. *Better turndown treats.* A two-bit chocolate is just not enough. Something interesting is more appropriate, such as handmade truffles. Packaging and presentation make all the difference; it is the way you deliver it more than its actual value.
10. *Fluffy robes and new slippers.* At turndown, robes should be removed from the closet and placed at the bedside. Slippers can remain in the package as often they are not used, but they should be bedside as well. Your guest should not have to dive into the closet to find these items. It's a small touch, but if

you've made it this far in the article it should be clear that the nuances make all the difference.

11. *Quality, abundant in-room coffee.* Nespresso or Illy machines, of course. But make sure that you have an adequate supply of capsules, both regular or decaffeinated, and never powdered creamer or other overly synthetic additives.
12. *Fresh flowers.* Real, not plastic, please! And these should be supplied both in the room as well as the bathroom. This provides a sense of luxury and brings a natural element into the suite. Remember that smell is an important sense to activate and help shift the mood of your guests.
13. *Personalization starts with a greeting by name.* There is no deeper level to personalization than being addressed by name, as it is the most personal item that any individual holds dear. Your team must learn to recognize your guests and call them by name. It should be easy when they call on the telephone, but often this gets overlooked. Same at the front desk and concierge. Staff training will help, as will technologies that can help you know who is calling, texting, or approaching the front desk.

Above all, be gracious. Remember, guests can stay elsewhere if they choose. They did not select your property because you were a few bucks cheaper than your comp set. Their decision was more complex, reflecting a combination of factors. While many of the items on this list may seem a bit trivial, they are clearly noticeable. Is it enough to limit your repeat business? Perhaps, so why take the risk?

The Mille Club: Across the Entire Guest Journey

We're seeing a trend in post-pandemic luxury – the mantle of attaining then surpassing a thousand dollars per night per room. This is what we have dubbed the 'Mille Club' after the Italian for said four-digit number. If your average daily rate has pushed into the four-figure range or thereabouts, congratulations and welcome. But know that this is something that must be earned because of the psychology that comes with paying above this threshold and because luxury guests have plenty of options nowadays.

As the second entry in this column, the focus is still on what every hotelier can learn from brands that are maintaining $1,000+ ADRs. While such revenues can subsidize elevated staffing and extravagant amenities, we emphasize that a large part of Mille Club membership comes down to the intangibles, the nuances, and scrupulous attention to detail – something that any hotel can set out to achieve no matter the star rating or budget. As per the title of this second outing, we can bring this argument into focus by highlighting examples across each major part of the guest journey.

Start with the Employees

That statement might seem a bit convoluted. So, let's back up a minute. Guest satisfaction is derived from two key elements: product and service. Putting your physical product aside for a moment, guest service is the interaction between your team members and your guests. This means that your employees need to be trained or retrained for their enhanced roles.

Do not expect your team to immediately undertake the changes that may be necessary. Some of them are quite subtle. Encouragingly, most are fully trainable, although the passion for hospitality has to be there. Your role is to facilitate this training program and provide your employees with both the necessary tools and time to accomplish their expanded duties.

Guest Prearrival

It's all about the data. For all guests, both new and repeat, your CRM is invaluable. For new guests, create a storehouse of information. This should include the basics of name, address, reservation source, date, single/double/family occupancy, length of stay, and room type. Should they happen to be a repeat customer, append the latest data to their file, update, and note any commonalities. Note arrival and departure times as well as if transfers were taken. The nuances of the data will inform future service requests as well as what you can do to anticipate needs or create points of personalization; you only need to have the time to look.

Above all, don't wait for the guest to cross your threshold. Communicate your restaurant opening hours and suggest dinner reservations. If a leisure trip or a resort, consider poolside cabanas, spa sessions or golf tee time scheduling to ensure availability and avoid disappointment. Every guest would appreciate a personal assistant of sorts to help set up personalized experiences. Newcomers to your city should be encouraged to rely on you to manage extras such as local or specialized tours. While many of these services provide added revenue opportunities, they also create and establish a relationship while enhancing your property's value.

An often-forgotten part of prearrival is room inspection by a housekeeping supervisor or manager. Simply put, rooms must be perfect. There is no provision for errors. Welcome letters and treats should be planned and in place.

As a supplemental tip, use LinkedIn to learn more about your guest and their interests. Tap your CRM to flag past guest data. Create a welcome gift that shows some unique character with local flavor. Make sure your accompanying handwritten note is genuine. It does not have to be from the GM. At the Boston Harbor Hotel, our welcome gift came from the Executive Chef, knowing that we were a past guest and appreciated his F&B selections.

The Two Parts of Arrival

The welcome experience should be memorable and worthwhile. Armed with a dossier, your reception team can warmly greet the guest personally. The first part takes place in your lobby. Learn to treat every guest as a VIP. Staff needs to warmly greet each guest and step out from behind any barrier such as a front desk. Obtain all necessary credit information. While challenging from a staffing standpoint, each guest in a Mille Club hotel is ushered to their room. And remember, it is all about personalization; know the name of the guest and address them appropriately.

Part two is in the guest's suite. Staff training is important here. Once the room is entered, time should be taken to explain the room's function, in particular any technologies such as WiFi access, television access, casting, IoT room controls and other electronic functions. Breakfast information needs repeating. Minibar function should also be identified, reinforcing those items that are provided to the guest as a convenience at no charge. Remind guests of access to concierge services (both live and on-app). If you do not have an app, at a minimum, give the guest a business card with appropriate contact information. Remind your staff to listen and keep their welcome short as they are on the guest's clock. Once they return to the front desk, they should immediately record any requests or preferences.

For training purposes, we suggest that you roleplay this critical process with every member of your reception staff. After greeting us, the Londra Palace Venezia (Venice) receptionist escorted us to our room, explaining all aspects of the property along the way and as they did not have the electronics in place, gave us a card with a number to text or call 24/7. This was not a substitute for the concierge, but rather a way to reinforce that there was always someone ready to help.

During the Stay

Think extras. How can you make the stay more memorable? Every time the guest uses their in-room telephone, they should be greeted by name. There may not be many, but all requests should be handled expeditiously. For housekeeping, the memorability comes in your turndown service. Your turndown team should be synchronized to complete their tasks while the guest is having dinner and coordinated to avoid any disruption in pre-dinner activities. Apart from housekeeping duties, ensure that they have more than just a traditional chocolate on the pillow. Use your imagination. A personal note (initialed by the housekeeper) is an appropriate touch. Locally made treats trump mass produced items. Stays of more than three nights deserve refreshment of fruit baskets and welcome amenities.

For example, the Halekulani Hotel in Honolulu has a separate turndown amenity for each day of the week, as they recognized that guests would get bored of the same trinket every night during an extended stay. At both The Savoy Hotel (in London) and the Baur au Lac (in Zurich) the minibar was free. Remember, your guests will arrive back at their rooms and may just want a soft drink or a light snack as they get ready for dinner. Charging a few bucks here is an insult.

Then the Departure

If you have planned appropriately, departure is your opportunity to leave a lasting impression. Many guests check out electronically. For those who come to the front desk, remember LIFO (Last In, First Out). We have experienced many poor departures where the team member's focus is solely transactional versus genuine communication with me about my stay and experiences. This critical part of the guest journey is rarely trained and should be a priority as guests will offer profound insights to guide the property and their own return visits.

As a guest departs, think of how you can make lasting memories. Lake Austin Spa Resort provided logoed t-shirts while the Montage Laguna Beach not only provided printout maps of the best route to the airport, but also bottled water, ballcaps, and a brown bag of penny-candy munchies for the drive.

Have you adequately discussed, planned, and budgeted for your guests' departures to leave a lasting impression? You want to establish a warm and continuous relationship with your guests throughout their entire stay. It is labor intensive, but these are the subtleties that you must consider as you aim to grow your ADR in the stratosphere.

The Mille Club: Introducing the Total Revenue Manager

The Mille Club's premise is that guests at this level seek an incredible experience rather than mere accommodations. Instead, hoteliers' offerings compete for guests independent of location, making comp sets typically geographically derived moot. With great rates come great guest expectations.

Current revenue management theory is all about numbers: rate cards, ADR, occupancy, market segments and RevPAR. Its primary focus is maximizing income from rooms' inventory. Typically, it follows a Keynesian (John Maynard Keynes, famed British economist) theory, which inversely correlates price with occupancy. Anticipating future demand, revenue managers work tirelessly to adjust rates to maximize occupancy levels.

Often, this requires strategic input on segment forecasts, competitive analysis, and historical data analysis. In-depth price calibration is critical and appropriate for lower and middle tiers properties. Here, price-sensitive consumers often make buying decisions based on fractions of a dollar. And it makes perfect sense; with fragile inventory such as hotel room nights, an unsold room is a lost product. Moreover, RevPAR, ADR, and GOR are still important benchmarks for the business's real estate and finance sides.

As we have outlined in previous musings, though, revenue management for Mille Club properties is diametrically opposite to that of their lower-priced brethren. Luxury consumers are agnostic to minor price differences, while competitive sets are difficult, if not impossible, to define as they lack close geographic parameters. Then, thanks to the pandemic, historical data provides limited helpful information, especially with all the post-pandemic shifts in the luxury hotel landscape.

What we can say for certain is that luxury guests are price-inelastic but highly experience-elastic. It's the exclusive access, privacy, incredible design, exceptional F&B, activities, and wellness programming that will allow a hotel to ramp up rate by hundreds of dollars above the property down the street.

But whose responsibility is it to coordinate a rate strategy and put some data science behind the numbers that will be presented to the GM? The total revenue manager (TRM for shorthand) is our solution to this quandary for the luxury category.

Classic benchmarks like RevPAR are still important, but rate structures operate more within ranges rather than micromanaged pricing increments. Given the reduced need for minute-over-minute fluctuations by the single dollar. there is less of a need to undertake an in-depth study of the historical RevPAR, rate and OR data that have dominated our industry's analysis for the past few decades.

Accordingly, the TRM examines the rooms division's performance and the total basket of revenue-generating ancillary profit centers. Their efforts are designed to build gross revenue per guestroom. Room rate alone will not determine their success. A collaborative effort is necessary, embracing every guest-facing opportunity.

As a segmentation specialist, the TRM can allow the revenue management system (RMS) to supply accurate insights that will guide the rooms revenue. This frees up time (with the right data connections) to focus on newer stats that take into account the performance of ancillaries and property utilization by each individual room occupant, including:

- *LOS*: length of stay; a metric where increases signal growth in guest satisfaction, loyalty and property utilization as well as reduced costs per room (fewer check-ins and checkout cleans)
- *RevPOR*: revenue per occupied room; giving more information on how overnight guests are spending their money besides only on the room booking
- *RevPAG*: revenue per available guest; teasing out the nuances of how occupants might be spending differently, such as for couples, families or bleisure travelers
- *TRevPAR*: total revenue per available room; very similar to RevPOR but this statistic also incorporates stay-independent income
- *RevPAF/RevPAM*: revenue per available square foot or square meter; getting even more granular in terms of how to optimize all physical spaces

Underpinning all these metrics is the emotional pull a hotel has – the 'reason to visit' for shorthand, if you will. Of primary importance in this regard is F&B. We all know that only a percentage of guests will utilize the spa or golf (if available), but it is guaranteed that guests will eat and drink. However, as hoteliers often joke, "The only reason we're in the restaurant business is because it helps sell rooms."

Nevertheless, the average table cover at many premier restaurants can now represent the equivalent value or a sizable portion of the nightly rate. Therefore, every TRM aims to integrate F&B consumption into every stay by analyzing every stage of the guest journey to see what motivates guests to buy.

This effort begins with examining the promotional offerings, public relations, marketing programs, packages, and direct booking incentives then continues with pre-arrival upselling, check-in sales training, and mid-stay practices. Secondarily, ancillary revenue-generating services, such as the wellness center or golf, are added to the TRM action plan. Gone are departmental silos (or they should be). Finally, through listening to guests' needs, cross-selling related products such as local excursions can now be measured insofar as their tangible effects on sentiment and the ability to drive nightly rate.

While this may sound like an integration of the tasks performed by marketing and the concierge, the goal for all three departments is the same: increasing total guest spending rather than merely focusing on increasing room rates and balancing occupancy levels. And from the guest's perspective, more usage of the property is highly correlated with increased satisfaction, so it truly is a win-win. Whether the RM role evolves into the TRM depends on the skills of the team and redefining roles, but overall it's clear that more attention must be given to ancillaries as a means of driving occupancy and building a healthy profitability mix.

The Mille Club: Potato Chip Pricing Lessons

The Mille Club's premise is that guests at this level are looking for an incredible experience rather than mere accommodations. Instead, hoteliers' offerings compete for guests independent of location, making comp sets typically geographically derived moot. With great rates come great expectations…

But what does this have to do with potato chips? For a moment, let's step away from the hotel environment and visit the grocery store. Shopping here, we are acutely price sensitive. Every item is identified by its price point, with promotional items typically highlighted. Unless you have a few hungry teenagers at home, potato chips are often an indulgence, with many purchases induced through promotional 'end cap' displays. The promotional price may be only a few pennies less than the regular retail. Still, our minds sense a bargain, not to mention the treat factor of hyper-palatable foods reinforcing the favorable buying decision.

Since most of us frequent a grocery store many times a month, we are conditioned to detect minuscule pricing variations. Brand loyalties may result in a purchase at a higher price than a competing product, but we all have a breaking point on price differentials. Thus, our favorite potato chip may be replaced with an alternate when the promotion provides the right level of monetary and emotional inducement.

This trench warfare is a way of life for most grocery goods. Price points are keenly followed, with market share and consumption patterns analyzed to an extent that simplifies our industry's analysis. Packaged goods executives, including those who run potato chip companies, can predict sales differentials based on a ten-cent price spread.

While hotel price points are significantly higher than your one-pound bag of Lay's®, hotel revenue managers working for budget and middle-price properties still fuss over price points – as well they should! We have experienced numerous executive committee meetings where competitive rate analysis is debated to the fraction of a dollar. These discussions are our industry's version of trench warfare.

Consumers have difficulty differentiating brands beyond price point and location for a variety of reasons. The OTAs further encourage price shopping (and loyalty within their own platforms versus direct channels) by reducing every property to a single photo, limited description and price. There's no dynamic website aesthetic or product feel. Even loyalty programs are similarly ubiquitous in aggregating properties, placing economy and luxury hotels within the same query results.

Mille Club Members Are Not Potato Chips

With price points above the thousand-mark, product differentiation is hypercritical, with pricing and location no longer acting as the only top components of the guests' decision making. Unlike potato chips, where $2.99 versus $3.19 per bag (a difference of 20 cents or 6.6%) could lead to a substantial volume shift, pricing for Mille Club properties is much less elastic.

Put another way, luxury hotel guests are *price inelastic but experience elastic.* The only problem is that latter element – the experience – is much harder to directly measure due to all its emotional underwiring. To get a sense of what guests really want and what will compel them to shell out thousands of dollars per stay, we must look to a cluster of factors that include but are not limited to design, staff, privacy, exclusive access, F&B, wellness and activities.

Take this example: Two hotels, one priced at $1,049 per night and the other at $1,119 per night. This is the same 6.6% differential as our potato chip example, yet to the guest, this $70 increment barely registers. Next, consider that the per-night room rate nowadays may only end up being around 50% of the total folio once all ancillaries are tabulated.

Once pricing pushes to four figures, price 'ranges' rather than price 'points' are more relevant. While no public domain research of hotel pricing at this level is available, we hypothesize that a spread of $200, perhaps more, may not trigger cognitive dissonance amongst buyers. If the experience is worth it and one-of-a-kind on this planet, the guests will come.

The implications for the Mille Club property executive are significant. Traditional schools of thought on revenue management and detailed competitive pricing analysis may no longer be relevant. Instead, channel that brain power towards TRevPAR and RevPAG – thinking about ancillary contribution and having great programming 'per available guest' whether that's individuals, couples, families, friends or multigenerational groups.

The focus for onsite management is not simply guest satisfaction but guest enrichment or, more cerebrally, guest 'transformation'. Whether through education, edutainment, wellbeing or wonder, the goal for this echelon of hospitality is to help each traveler improve through lives back at home through self-actualization.

To accomplish this lofty goal, labor allocation switches from BOH-heavy (which can be largely automated) to FOH (guest interface) through having a sizably higher staff-to-guest coverage ratio. Guest personalization is intensified by leveraging in-depth guest profiles and multi-media communication. In all, this is a return to why we started in this business: hospitality. And if you ever find yourself debating the minutia of numbers, take a step back and ask whether you are selling an experience or a bag of potato chips.

The Mille Club: Your Sense of Arrival Is Critical

For those who haven't read the previous Mille Club articles, membership qualification is simple: just offer rates of more than a thousand (hence 'mille') dollars, pounds, Euros or equivalent. Whereas American Express since 1987 espoused the selling line, "Membership has its Privileges™," the opposite applies to your property if it wants to uphold four-figure nightly rates. Aptly expressed, as a member of the Mille Club, *Membership has its Responsibilities.*

If you're hotel is a member and wish to retain this status amongst your guest cohort, you need to understand that luxury guests have options. Yes, there may be a much smaller comp set in your local market for this hotel category, but luxury guests have the capital to go elsewhere, meaning that you aren't competing against only a handful of local outfits, but dare we say the entire world.

This optionality means that the luxury consumer has great expectations, made even more cognizant once they cross the threshold of four digits in the price tag that they see. As such, you need to set aside your knee-jerk-accountant mode of operation and consider the following:

1. Your guests are typically travel-savvy, not geographically confined and cosmopolitan, meaning that they will expect your hotel to deliver the same quality level as the world leader.
2. Your guests have a mindset of high standards set by their own residence(s), meaning that every little detail counts and you must, at the very least, match what they get at their own domicile.

While there is a ton that goes into making all your operations sing in harmony so that you can grow rate to this 'mille' point and then beyond, this entry focuses on only one aspect of the guest experience: the arrival.

Put yourself in your guest's shoes. Think about today's travel experience. Even with business or first-class air, by the time your guests get to your front door, they have experienced crowded airports, ground transfers, and local traffic. With today's typical air traffic delays and security clearances, even the simplest short-haul trip turns into a multi-hour ordeal and perhaps a bit of lower back pain. Your property is not only their destination but a refuge from this travel agony.

Ask yourself when your guests arrive:

- What do they see first?
- What about the other senses (smell, sound, touch, or taste if you offer welcome refreshments)?
- How is the lobby/entry temperature managed: too hot or too cold?
- And importantly, *how* are they greeted by members of your team?

Flowers and Art

For many years, the two of us worked with Four Seasons Hotels & Resorts (mostly Larry). This brand firmly understands the importance of the guest experience. Visiting and working in numerous FSHR properties worldwide, one commonality was the abundance of fresh floral arrangements in the lobby. They are not alone. In Las Vegas, where casinos vie for ultimate wow factors, properties such as Wynn/Encore and ARIA go out of their way to deliver over-the-top floral arrangements that are tourist selfie attractions.

But it is not just flowers that can convey a true and unique sense of arrival. In a property we helped conceive, the William Vale Hotel in Brooklyn, the lobby features an oversized, custom-designed art mural covering more than just one wall. Another property we visited, The Logan in Philadelphia, captures the imagination with art throughout their public areas. The Hazelton Hotel in Toronto, our hometown, has an extensive collection of art, starting with a fascinating sculpture gallery in their lobby and continuing throughout the public areas.

These lobby elements consume ongoing service costs or significant sunk fiscal expenses. An accountant or a naïve hotelier would argue against these expenses as they fail to generate directly measurable revenue. Yet these hoteliers and their owners understand the power of memorable first impressions. These unquantifiable elements make all the difference.

The Ballet of Staff

Apart from the physical space, all arrivals involve greeting your guests. An arrival may include a car valet, doorman, or bellman, as well as a member (or more) of your guest services team. Executing a flawless arrival sequence requires a degree of choreography. If it runs smoothly, the process reassures the guest that their decision is appropriate.

One of the best in our experience is The Savoy in London. The day after we checked in, we watched to see if the treatment we received was flagged as special. It was not, as everyone received the same 'clockwork' greeting, a flawless performance if there ever was one. Another example of perfection was witnessed at the Peninsula Beverly Hills, where the front desk agent, after entering information into the PMS perfunctorily, escorted us personally to our rooms and, in doing so, detailed various aspects of the property. Bravo!

As a member of the Mille Club, take a close look at your lobby from the standpoint of the guest. Understand what they will experience. Use your cellphone, record a video and play it back in your next executive committee. From there, watch how your lobby staff reacts to guests and consider ways to make every guest feel that they have arrived. Now seek suggestions from your entire management team on how you can set a standard that creates immediate, positive memories.

To conclude, first impressions count. Scratch that; they are everything. Mille Club member hotels not only have given them some thought but make them perfect, which requires an ongoing effort.

The Mille Club: The Upside of Crossing Four Digits in Rate

Sometimes, when explaining a concept, it's best to look at the numbers. Before going straight into using hotel rates, we're going to start small with a bottle of run-of-the-mill wine, a product that's also dear to our hearts and many other hoteliers.

While pricing is still a bit of art form, for the sake of round numbers, let's say market research and cost analyses agree that $10.00 is a good direct-to-consumer selling price. But is that what you list it on the shelves for? No, you advertise it as $9.95 per bottle. You take the haircut of five cents, knowing with surety that this minor loss will drive a substantial increase in sales due to the perception of value.

But let's next attribute significant brand leadership to this wine, so much so that they could get away with charging beyond the ten-dollar threshold at a $10.05 price tag without any sacrifice in sales volume, which on paper is just ten cents more than the previous haircut. In this case, though, we mere mortals don't stop to evaluate incrementally with pure-logic thought processing along the lines of, "This brand has marginally better cachet over the ones next to it, so this justifies the ten cents increase." No, we are irrational beings.

For the human brain, the psychological difference between $9.95 and $10.00 is far greater in the consumer's mind than the difference between $10.00 and $10.05. Because the spread for the latter two is perceived as so small, this wine brand may as well start charging $14.95 or $19.95 in order to maximize gross revenues in accordance with where the next psychological threshold might be.

To understand how this applies to hotel pricing, shift the decimal two digits to the right. A lot of work must be done to justify a four-digit nightly rate, but once you do, the sky is the limit.

This doesn't mean you can charge whatever you want without adding more amenities and services to support your ever-loftier Mille Club position. Note: The Mille Club is our name for hotels that levy a nightly rate in excess of a thousand dollars, Euros, pounds, etc. Rather, crossing the $1,000 per night barrier next entails a significant degree of price discovery to establish new rate maximums according to what guests are willing to pay at a given property in a given market. This could be $1,250 per night; it could be $1,495; it could even be $2,195. But, per our wine example, you definitely wouldn't stop at $1,005 per night.

Knowing how far to throttle up rate is still a bit of an art form but there is a plethora of revenue management and business intelligence tools that can help you to accurately forecast where this upper limit will be. This alone should be one more reason to evaluate this aspect of your tech stack.

All this still says nothing about the service expectations of luxury guests, the amenities arms race that exists for five-star properties and how your comp set changes to reflect global competition (instead of only the local market) given that luxury travelers aren't bound by distance or sovereign borders. In other words, it's going to take a lot of hard work to get into the Mille Club, and then even more hard work to flourish and maximize yields once you're a member.

The Mille Club: The Often-Forgotten Sense of Departure

To reprise, the Mille Club: Membership qualification is simple: offer rates of more than a thousand (hence 'mille') dollars, pounds, Euros or equivalent. If you're already there (or very close), or aspire to this lofty room rate level, please read on.

Whereas American Express (since 1987) espoused the selling line, "Membership has its Privileges™," the opposite applies to your property if you want to uphold four-figure-plus nightly rates. Aptly expressed, as a member of the Mille Club, *Membership has its Responsibilities*. The key concept here is that crossing the chasm of four digits in the price tag comes with some serious psychological baggage. In other words, guest expectations jump as well.

Mille Club Comp Sets Lack Geographic Specificity

To start, recognize that once you charge over $1,000 per night your comp set has widened to include not only local competitors but also multiple properties farther afield that the luxury guest has on their radar.

Consider the luxury and HNWI travelers living in Los Angeles looking for a quick getaway. They can travel north to Santa Barbara/Montecito or south to Newport/Laguna Beach. From Beverly Hills or Santa Monica, depending upon traffic, either destination is roughly 90-120 minutes away. So, a Newport-based property should consider properties in Montecito as rightful competitors, even though they are three hours away as the crow flies. Why? Because they are chasing the same target audience.

And that is just the local situation. Luxury guests have the capital and the wherewithal to go anywhere. To build on the previous situation, said traveler may be bored by the drive north to Santa Barbara or south to Laguna Beach, and instead opt for a private charter out of Van Nuys Airport to literally anywhere within flight range – for example, Cabo San Lucas.

The implication is that you aren't just competing against local outfits as most traditional comp sets define them, but pretty much every property worldwide that the luxury guest has previously experienced to establish thereby a baseline expectation for what your experience should be. For all intents and purposes, for the luxury traveler, geography is no longer of primary consideration. Your guests measure you against their standards which are exceptionally high. If you want to play with the 'big boys', you've got to step up to the plate!

Pre-Departure Planning

In a previous article, we discussed the critical sense of arrival and how your guest passes judgment immediately upon entry. By now, we expect that you've already attended to all the important elements of the guest's initial journey into your property. But have you considered and applied the same attention to detail as to their departure?

If you have read or glanced at Nobel laureate behavioral economist Daniel Kahneman's 2011 book, *Thinking, Fast and Slow*, then you may be inclined to believe the endpoint of the guest interaction is even more important than the first impression.

The evidence for this was codified as the 'peak-end rule' wherein people ultimately remember – and are thus emotionally influenced by – primarily the high point and the end point of an experience.

Thus, a property's sense of departure needs some re-examination. For this, Benjamin Franklin said, "By failing to prepare, you are preparing to fail." Guest departure planning starts with gathering data on every check-out planned for that day, learning as much as you can about particular departure needs.

Specific departure communications with the guest should start no later than the afternoon before the end of the stay. Ideally, you will have garnered some information about flights, transportation modes, payment methods, and special needs at check-in. Even if you have this information, a lot can change, so it's always good to reconfirm.

If you are arranging a private car service to the airport, you can develop an appropriate work back schedule to ensure a smooth transition from their guestroom to checkout and then to car service. Here you can manage the process to ensure minimal wait time by having the folio prepared in advance. In most cases, there will be no late items to post, and if there are adjustments can easily be made.

LIFO Front Desk Interaction

Accountants use the inventory term of LIFO, meaning last-in-first-out. Let's apply this terminology to reframe the peak-end rule as it relates to your guest's impressions of your property – that is, their last experience is the first one they will talk about.

Picture this scenario. We're staying at a five-star boutique hotel in London (name redacted) with a rate well above £1,000 per night – a Mille Club member for sure. Here were the exact final words from the front desk agent, "Shall I staple your credit card receipt to the folio?" How does this help us as guests? And does anyone really care about a printed receipt in an era where everything is digitally dispatched? While this lesson applies to all transactional conversations, the bigger goal here is to leave guests on an emotional high.

Now, compare the impression of this to a five-star beachfront resort in Laguna Beach, California, with a comparable rate to the London property. The front desk agent's final words, "I've completed your folio and as well, looked at possible routes for you to take to the airport. Our valet recommends a slightly longer route outlined on this map, which, given the traffic right now, should save 15 to 20 minutes. I've also put two water bottles in your car. Have a safe journey back to Toronto, and we look forward to your return soon." It is immediately obvious that the final impression was enhanced in just a few sentences and extra effort befitting the four-digit nightly rate. And the fact that we remember this conversation some ten years later reinforces the value.

Importantly, our belief is that every luxury guest should be escorted to their transportation, with a simple 'thank you for staying' being sufficient.

Importantly, under no circumstances should a Mille Club guest be asked to recommend or review a property on social media. Their stay with you should be considered confidential. It is strictly their option, not yours to suggest.

Departure Gifts

The goal of your departure program is to enhance the memorability of your property. Emphasizing and teaching about the peak-end rule across all departments will help to instill the overall significance of embellishing your sense of departure.

While every revenue manager would like to have the departing guest book their repeat visit right on the spot, it is probably not the best time to make this request, as it often seems too aggressive. Therefore, what you want to accomplish is to lay the foundation for their next visit. The best way to create a tangible memory of their visit is through a departure gift.

When planning this gift, logistics are important. Understand the guest's departure transportation. For example, if they are traveling by air, a bottle of house wine will probably be given to the taxi or Uber driver, as they will not be able to manage it through carry-on. Funnily enough, we recall a colleague who received a small Swiss-style army knife as a souvenir, only to find it raising red flags at airport security – clearly not the impression that was intended.

Some of the better departure gifts that we received over the years are still on our desks providing continual reminders and 'social proofing' of the properties. With names stated because these properties are all admiral examples to learn from, these departure gifts include:

- A shell coaster from the Halekulani on Waikiki Beach, Honolulu
- An antique key and keychain (which also acted as a door fob) from Crockfords at Resorts World Las Vegas
- A USB memory stick hiding within a real wine bottle cork from the Meritage Resort and Spa in Napa, California

Above all, use your imagination while sticking within the framework of your hotel's theme, and you will find the appropriate approach. It will take time, energy, and some extra costs, but the consequences of not amplifying your sense of departure in this way are far more significant.

The Mille Club: Details, Details, Details

"It's attention to detail that makes the difference between average and stunning." (Francis Attenbury, 1663-1732)

In this installment of the Mille Club column, we are going to address some of the little things that differentiate your property. If your guest can afford to spend a thousand in ADR on your accommodations, their expectations go far beyond a good night's sleep. Their comp set is not just other properties that are in geographic distance, but of equal importance is how you stack up against their own home! To put this another way, luxury hotels should never aim to be 'just like home' but must always strive to be 'better than home', which requires an ever-vigilant eye on the current aspirational trends.

Spend a few minutes browsing any of the recent editions of home and architecture magazines. Guests do not necessarily expect that your property will be featured in *AD (Architectural Digest), Interior Design,* or *Wallpaper.* But pay attention to the clues from these publications. These are the photographs your guests are using to furnish or style their homes. Their expectations for your property are formed accordingly.

As part of our recent oeuvre of strategic consulting assignments, we've had the opportunity to evaluate the FF&E requirements of several new developments. These properties have forecasted rates through a good portion of the year at Mille Club levels. Yet, in the perfunctory budget cutting to meet financial acquisition targets, FF&E design elements were stripped. As the hotel experts on the project, we cannot precisely quantify the impact on daily rates through the elimination of these supposed 'frills'. However, we can say that the delivered end product will not be as we envisioned.

On one consulting assignment, we assumed the role of asset managers for a property on the West Coast. The rooms were large but spartan. As a real estate agent would say, "The property has good bones." But with an empty coffee table in the living room, an empty fridge, a limited amenity package in the bathroom and only a few paintings (and not of any memorable quality or subject matter), the place looked 'desolater and desperate' – that is, to borrow the Latin translation of the word, lacking breath and spirit. The catch was that we could not add to the rooms unless we generated the rates, and yet, without the extras, we could not ask for better rates!

As our opening quotation highlights, it's all in the details. And yet, many of these do not require substantial capex, only a more meticulous attitude that emphasizes the importance of nuance, as well as some SOP rewrites and retraining.

Here is a Mille Club checklist of ten *detailed* items that should be on your radar.

1. *Fresh flowers.* A display in the entry or suite and single flowers in each bathroom. Succulent plants are bathroom alternatives. This is pretty much standard at any Four Seasons property.
2. *Robes and slippers.* As differentiated by season and properly sized for guests, we were first introduced to this at the Lake Austin Spa Resort where, of course, this amenity also included small bedside mats placed at turndown service.
3. *Bathroom amenity kits.* These include makeup remover cloth and pads, shaving cream, disposable razor, toothpaste/toothbrush, comb, nail file and mouthwash, with the Crown Hotel in Melbourne as a great example to emulate in this regard.
4. *Turndown service elements.* Not just chocolate, but something unique; the best we've seen is the Halekulani in Waikiki Beach, which features a different turndown amenity every day of the week, reflecting the average LOS of about seven days.
5. *Taschen books.* On the suite coffee table, with the newly renovated ARIA Sky Suites in Las Vegas having half a dozen to scan through.

6. *Great magazines.* To ponder while enjoying your suite, apart from the design magazines or a local high-end lifestyle magazine, consider others that reflect your property's aesthetic, wherein the Montage brand is highly renowned for this.
7. *The minibar.* Incorporating several interesting treats and non-alcoholic beverages, ideally local and unusual, all of which for Mille Club member hotels should be made available at no charge to the guest, and indeed this is something we instituted at the Villa Eyrie Resort in British Columbia.
8. *A complimentary arrival plate.* If possible, personalized for the individual, wherein we have seen buckets of cold beer and homemade chips, fresh chocolate chip cookies, intricate truffles, fruit plates and combinations thereof – all were appreciated.
9. *Binoculars.* In locations where the sights are spectacular such as the Wickaninnish Inn located in Tofino, British Columbia where they also included heavy-duty rain gear to encourage you to walk the beach regardless of the weather.
10. *A real newspaper in a delivery sleeve.* Digital readers are excellent and no doubt more efficient, but nothing beats the tactile experience of sitting at your dining room table having room service breakfast with a copy of the *Financial Times* or *Wall Street Journal,* as emphasized by a recent stay at The Savoy in London that reinforced the sheer luxury of this minor indulgence. This is Old World for sure, but as long as newspapers are available, this should be a consideration.

The Mille Club: Investing at the Half-Mille Mark

We have written several articles regarding hotels that are part of 'The Mille Club'. But what about those properties that are consistently pushing rates in the $500-999 range, well above the levels that were the norm pre-pandemic: Do the same Mille Club rules apply?

Yes, of course, they do but not at the disproportional levels when you cross the psychological threshold of passing four figures in your sticker price. Many properties have been operating in this 'half-mille' price range for years, with the senior team looking at overarching strategies to support greater and greater rates that will, one day, leap above the $1,000 per night mark. These owners and operators understand that when selling rooms in this half-mille price range, guests are expecting a lot more than the basics.

Getting to a Thousand

Guests are now anticipating a remarkable lobby, a comfortable room with enticing furnishings, a solid service component and upgraded amenities. Further, ancillary activities such as premium dining and spa services play an important part in this half-mille product offering. Above all, it all comes down to service.

But the service standards that are required to edge up towards $995 per night and then sustain rates worthy of five-star, four-figure luxury demand lots of opex and capex retooling of the finances. In short, what are you doing to funnel more of the funds from elevated rates back into the guest experience to reinforce your new rate structure?

And the tricky part about putting money aside for future property improvement plans is that your competitors are likely following the same strategy. If half-mille rates are the new normal for upper upscale properties in your local market and neighboring ones, then you know that guests' expectations have likewise been heightened. Now is not the time to think about any cutback on labor or amenities as so much of getting to $1,000 is momentum based on your good reputation built cumulatively year after year.

A pivot point for example here is that daily housekeeping with turndown service is a must. You need to demonstrate the value within the half-mille range before you can push for a full mille, and this requires getting the operation finely tuned so that it's already in top form by the time you're nearing that four-figure threshold. This is but one instance where you are looking for strong, emotional ways to increase the perceived value of the guest's stay. Often, it's the small touch points like a personalized turndown service that will make the world of difference.

Specific Operations for the Guest Journey

The implementation of turndown service is but one amenity that must be enacted during the half-mille stage in order to achieve proper mille status. As a GM or above-property leader, all your team members must be in sync with your goal of ensuring a memorable, personalized stay with impeccable service. But with so much to do in order to move up the star rating, it's best to break it down into specific departments that are tackled systematically each quarter.

Thinking in terms of the guest journey, here are questions to ask your senior staff:

1. *Pre-arrival.* Have we undertaken effective prearrival programs and system integrations to pinpoint guest arrival time to ensure that their room is ready? Have we detailed guest preferences for prearrival? Have we offered dinner reservations or looked at other guest needs? Will the guest's room be inspected, and will the appropriate unique-to-the-property welcome gift be dispatched? Have you checked your CRM to identify a repeat guest and brief teams on specific personalization attributes?
2. *Arrival.* Is the room ready at the guest's anticipated arrival time? How will you greet the guest upon arrival? What will you do so that the guest will remember you well beyond their stay?
3. *Stay.* Is daily housekeeping in sync with the guest's schedule? Can you work out a way to greet the guest at least once during their stay? How have you made the daily housekeeping turndown service unique to the property?
4. *Departure.* How have you made the departure easy? How have you made it memorable? Have you considered a small token that reprises the property's

key feature, for example, if your property has a strong wine cellar, consider a key chain with an imprinted cork.

5. *Post-Departure.* What can you do to incentivize a return visit? What have you learned about the guest that you can use to encourage this? Are you providing a snack for the road or a departure gift that's emblematic of the hotel?

Beyond hiring outside consultants and interior designers to help devise a full PIP, many of the operational hurdles all come back to using your team's creativity. Some of our most memorable stays were not a function of expensive capex elements, but rather, the attention to detail that we experienced at each of these five milestones of the stay.

Yes, capital expenditures will be critical for getting to $1,000, but it's the opex and the embedded operational wherewithal that will keep you there. As this means hiring, training, writing new SOPs and steering the cultural ship, it's best to proceed diligently and tackle each detail of the guest journey so that you will be ready for full mille membership long before you invest in any sort of renovation.

The Mille Club: Thinking of the Hidden Costs for High Rates

What does it cost? Can you measure its direct effect on net contribution? While the two of us are tremendous fans of helping a hotel evolve into a more data-driven organization, there is nevertheless an art to creating a successful hospitality operation. And nowhere puts this more in focus than the luxury segment where the grandeur, opulence and excess are largely irrational yet wholly necessary to support thousand-dollar rates.

At this point, we could lecture on about Veblen goods, Giffen goods, the rise of the leisure class and other elements of behavioral economics that contribute to a hotel's pricing strategy, perhaps it's better to explain our point via an example. Namely, we are wine nuts, so let's start there. First, let's look at the history of how fine wine has supported fine rates, then circle back to the lesson for every hotelier looking to grow nightly rates, no matter the star rating.

Menu Reminiscing

It's the Winter of 1969. For many north easterners, this meant a trip south, typically by car to Florida. For those of means, Puerto Rico was also a preferred Caribbean destination, being under the American aegis and thus having an air of surety for FITs. With airfares being relatively much more expensive than today, a trip of this nature would not be commonplace, reserved for HNWI travelers.

One such resort catering to Americans, the Dorado Beach Resort (now a Ritz-Carlton Reserve property) offered room rates of over $100 per night, equivalent to roughly $1,000 in today's dollars. Owned (at that time) by the Rockefeller family, it was a hotspot for VIP clients and celebrities. In keeping with their prestigious 'international' status, the resort curated an extensive wine.

As a time-honored Mille Club member, one of the ways the property differentiated itself was with sophistication and a 'European' flair. Back then, for Americans at least, fine wine was still a bit of a mystery. There was a limited appreciation of the nuances of wine-growing regions or grapes, let alone vintages. Recognizing this, the property created a wine list that, at first, educated their customers. To pay off this education, the wine list provided variety insofar as a selection that both demonstrated the restaurant's knowledge while also providing a launch point for intimate guest-sommelier rapport.

As an opening aside to what you can learn from this Mille Club example, examine your wine list. What are you doing to build your guests' basic knowledge and further educate them in an approachable, themed manner? Take a cue from this example and create a reason for your sommelier or wait staff to interact and generate both memorability and profitability.

Then Came Wine Inflation

Examining a page from the 1960s wine list of Red Burgundy, one may be left with a degree of reverse sticker shock, as prices were well below what we are experiencing today, even at your local bottle shop where restaurant markups aren't a thing. When comparing vintages, please keep in mind that this list is 50+ years old, so a 1964 vintage would equate to a 2014-15 today. Nevertheless, we doubt anyone will ever see any vintage of Clos Vougeot under a hundred dollars in any restaurant nationwide.

There are further examples insofar as Bordeaux as well as many other wines. For Mille Club members, the wine list needs vintages that not only reflect your F&B director or sommelier's expertise but also what will match or exceed the guest's expectations. This is, after all, a place where wealthy patrons are anticipating preeminent imports from Europe, so, therefore, they are mandatory towards completing the experience and justifying the nightly rates for the always discerning luxury traveler.

The word we use nowadays to denote this thematic congruence is 'lifestyle'. Thus, the second lesson is that a keen eye for imbuing a sense of lifestyle throughout a hotel can help it escape the challenges of modern-day inflation.

But looking through their Red Great Bordeaux list, it should be noted that these represented some of the rarest wines in the world (their words) and were being offered from the owner's private selection. How about a 1929 Chateau Margaux for $35? An equivalent today would be offering a 1985 Chateau Margaux for $350 instead of its runaway value on the open market.

While it's crazy to look back at how exponential inflation has been for fine wines, the challenge we all face is that keeping up represents a huge carrying cost. And now that senior teams and owners have an ever-scrupulous eye for cost efficiencies, it's becoming harder and harder to rationalize these types of expenses.

How Extravagance Supports High Rates

Mille Club member properties can and should be known for their extravagance, so long as this fits with the brand's core values, theme and desired guest lifestyle. A great cellar is one such element to support that image, provided you flaunt your most exceptional bottles.

This may also be called 'aspirational wines,' where it isn't so much about generating a high volume of sales from listing, say, Chateau Margaux on the list as it is about offering a glimpse into the luxury lifestyle to anchor price everything else.

One bean counter might ask, "This wine is way too expensive to buy and hold, so why not cut it from the menu to boost overall profitability?" But the Mille artist might then counter, "How will we support the image of a luxury hotel and continue to attract our kind of clientele without these kinds of luxury items for guests to behold?" Hence, the third and final lesson is that luxury is irrational, and this requires spending in some areas far above what's necessary to attract the type of guests that you want.

You need fine wines to be called a fine dining establishment and cajole customers to pay elevated prices for that experience. You need to budget for an elaborate lobby PIP to make that space a standout that luxury guests will deem befitting their stature. Even when cheaper ceramic tiles may suffice, you need bathrooms decked out with floor-to-ceiling marble so that luxury guests can see the value for the huge rates. These are but three examples, and yet the takeaway is that to move up in classification you should be prepared to spend, both because your guests will see the difference and because not presenting them with a strong 'reason to visit' will mean they'll go somewhere else.

The Mille Club: Urban Versus Rural Experiences

While there are now numerous hotels around the world that are successfully achieving the one thousand dollars per night level year-round, all Mille members provide incredible lessons for any hotel or brand looking to grow its ADR, whether or not that includes reflagging and a renovation to move up half or a full star rating.

While there is a ton that must happen operationally to justify rates at $1,000+ or even $500+, in this short column we're focusing on the experience, highlighting two examples – one urban and one rural – from North American Four Seasons Hotels and Resorts, a brand that commands four-figure rates at practically every one of its properties. Importantly for you, know that the guests with the monetary flexibility to pay these lofty prices think less in terms of total cost and more in terms of total experience.

Especially for HNW individuals where the price is no object, it's about exclusivity, privacy and self-actualization. What can your hotel offer that is unmatched anywhere else in the world? How are you allowing your guests to rethink a destination they may have been to before? How can you put a unique spin on the physical design, the F&B, the artwork or the activities? How are you making your guests' lives more fulfilling?

Four Seasons understands this, so it behooves all hoteliers to consider actions taken by this brand as examples that they can apply to their business model. Recent media releases from this brand underscore their pursuit of excellence and improving their guest experience. Let's dig in.

Solving the Dilemma of the Minibar

Imagine returning to your hotel room and being charged seven bucks for a can of pop or eight bucks for a small chocolate bar. It's highway robbery. Concurrently, how do you as the hotelier make decisions insofar as the munchies available in the small space afforded to this minifridge and bar top? It is all but impossible to get it correct for every guest. Moreover, the service costs continue to increase.

Enter *The Vaults* at the Four Seasons Boston. There is one located on each of the property's floors. The guest's key opens the door. The Vaults' selection of complimentary snacks and beverages consists of popcorn, chips, movie-sized M&Ms, Swedish Fish, a variety of nuts and dried fruit, flavored sparkling waters, and more.

Here is a guest-oriented solution that provides a strong value-add; the selection is greater without too much sacrifice of convenience (nearby versus in-room). At the same time, this drastically reduces replenishment costs as the servicing cost of an in-room minibar in terms of HPOR often exceeds the purchase price of the snacks dispensed. Moreover, liberating the physical square footage devoted to an in-room minibar means more space for other experience-enhancing guestroom amenities.

Four Seasons Boston's Director of Creative, Jim Peters, remarked, "I was looking for a way to expand the minibar experience for guests, whether on their way out the door to explore the city or snuggling into their Four Seasons bed for the night to watch a movie."

Providing Aspirational Experiences that (Literally) Drive Business

The Four Seasons Resort and Residences Napa Valley positions itself as one of the finest resorts in California, claiming that its onsite Elusa Winery makes it the only resort with a working winery. Fully embracing this with a number of available oenophile-oriented activities and integrations with F&B, not a single guest ever leaves with having a wine-themed experience of a lifetime.

But then Four Seasons outdoes itself as the brand has developed an international program to add new ways for clients to revisit a property and experience it in a new light.

The Four Seasons Driving Experience is the North American adaptation of an event successfully held over in the French Alps – specifically a driving route from the landmark Four Seasons Hotel des Bergues Geneva to the picturesque skiing commune of Megève, France near Chamonix and Mont Blanc. Here, guest can choose their vehicle and follow a multi-day itinerary carefully curated by the Four Seasons team with different experiences and F&B stops along the way provided by local partners.

This addition to the property's list of available experiences at an 'over the top' price point is akin to the presidential suite in a hotel's room repertoire. Marc Speichert, Executive Vice President and Chief Commercial Officer recently noted, "We are bringing the Four Seasons Drive Experience to new, highly sought-after destinations based on a deep understanding of our guests, delivering a luxury experience that reflects the genuine care and empathy that is at the core of Four Seasons."

To close, these are but two examples of how Mille Club members are extending their franchise by enhancing their guest offerings both inside and outside their properties. Each hotel is different; each is a brand. Therefore, what you do to differentiate your onsite experiences is entirely up to you, but what we stress is that the more you differentiate, the more you can ultimately charge.

The Mille Club: Learning from a Luxury Airline

Can hotels learn from an airline? Immediately, we suspect you may have said to yourself: unequivocally, no! And frankly, until a recent trip on Emirates Air, the two of us would have also been in the same camp.

A recent trip changed that. For one of us (Larry), this was a trip to South Africa, Namibi, a and Mozambique over a recent holiday season on Regent Seven Seas Cruises, which included return business class airfare to Cape Town. While many guests elect to select their airline of preference, he (Larry) allowed the cruise line to handle the details. To his pleasant surprise, they selected Emirates via Dubai.

Long admired from afar and now finally having a chance to experience ostensibly the best airline in the world, the first leg of the trip with business class seating was superior to everything we (Larry and his wife) had experienced both domestically and on par with international carrier standards. The second leg on Emirates first class (thanks to an unexpected and complimentary upgrade) was in a league of its own.

Just for perspective, a round trip in Emirates first class from Dubai to Toronto, where we call home, is roughly the price of a new Toyota Corolla. What do you get for this price? And what are the lessons learned for our Mille Club hoteliers?

With Emirates charging what amounts to a Mille Club room night per hour for their first-class experience, undoubtedly with the psyche of luxury travelers there are comparisons taking place between hotels and airlines in terms of what services and amenities are offered. So, what can hotels learn?

1. Service that exceeds your highest expectations.

There are 12 first-class 'cabins', and to call them seats is disrespectful. They are serviced by three or four 'personal assistants'; again, to call them flight attendants would be simply too pedestrian. We were told that they could speak seven languages. Our attendant was able to describe the differences between the Chivas Royal Salute 21-year-old and the Johnny Walker Blue Label offerings, suggesting that the Blue was a better option for the start of the journey due to its hazelnut finish. This level of knowledge is on par with an expert mixologist.

Service is the key to luxury. Too often, we think little of physical enhancements to our room stock or common areas, while coincidentally working to reduce labor costs, often due simply to where it's presented on an income statement or P&L (opex versus capex). Yet, it is that labor pool that differentiates the premium product category. It is your people and the quintessential 'service with a smile' that guests will remember when all is said and done.

2. Consider upgrades to your bathroom amenities.

Emirates supplies their first-class passengers with a substantial amenity kit. We might add that the trip also includes an onboard shower. The products selected are recognized brands, rather than a private label of unknown quality.

As a Mille Club member, consider differentiated bathroom amenities for your premium room categories. As your rates move up, so too should every aspect of your guest journey. These amenities are often inexpensive relative to the proportional increase in room rates that they can reinforce, while also providing an intimate, caring sensibility to this private space by insinuating that you have the guest's hygiene and cosmetic needs covered.

3. Providing gourmet wine options.

The wines on the Emirates flight were mind-blowingly impressive. Suffice it to say that all the wines offered were Grand Cru Burgundies and Second or Third Growth Bordeaux. The port was a 40-year-old tawny. The champagne was 2013 Dom Perignon. Without getting into the details of how altitude and cabin pressure affect the palate, these offers nevertheless add a tasting element to the experience and leave an indelible mark on the memory via sensory activation.

Almost every hotel cannot afford to offer wines of this nature on a complimentary basis. However, Mille Club hotels should consider adding Coravin-dispensed BTG wines to give your dining guests expanded options without having them front the bill for an entire bottle. Not to say they cannot afford the entire bottle, but that drinking less overall is de rigueur (and great for one's health), which makes sampling the way of the future.

4. Are there pajamas in your future?

With a 14-hour flight, Emirates supplied pyjamas. These were distributed once the personal assistant was able to determine an appropriate size. We still have ours and they have now survived a few washings in pretty good condition. Sometimes, as a hotelier, you must add something that differentiates your property, rising above your comp set. This could be that item, both as a souvenir and possibly create that matching pyjama social media moment.

The bottom line is that luxury hoteliers no longer just sell rooms, spa treatments or dining occasions. You sell holistic experiences. As multi-million-mile air travelers, this is the first air experience that was worthy of reporting to our hotelier-focused audience. The challenge we present to our Mille Club readers is: what can you do to make your guests talk about their experience with you? Furthermore, what can you do to enrich your experiences in a meaningful way that allows you to command higher room rates without turning guests off?

The Mille Club: Luxury Demands the Unexpected

A segment that's growing rapidly around the globe is one in which hotels offer accommodations at or above $1,000 per night. With price points in this range and great nominal margins, properties can use their imagination to reinforce their brand equity and enhance the guest's product appreciation. But make no mistake, the competition at the luxury and ultra-luxury levels is just as fierce as ever; it's often not the case of 'can' use so much as 'must' use their imaginations.

In this sense, even if your property is not (yet) at this rate, there is still great learning for you, too. Rates and packages must be competitive, but so must service levels, amenities and onsite programming in order to ensure lasting success.

Obviously, there are numerous ways to go about this, and there's never a silver bullet, panacea or one-size-fits-all solution to all of hospitality. We can, however, deploy the age-old psychology trick of surprising and delighting our guests to endear them to our brands. As we will see in this Mille Club example, embedding these surprises and unexpected services is all but required for modern luxury.

Our recent stay at the Halekulani in Honolulu, Hawaii provides an effective demonstration of this approach. Of the two of us, Larry has visited this property pretty much every year for more than the past decade, except for a COVID-induced break. With 453 rooms, the property is not large in Waikiki Beach terms (the area where the hotel is located), yet at the five-star level this is a fairly significant size. In previous years, we've written about the housekeeping team, which we felt was certainly among the best in the world. On this post-COVID visit, we were wondering if they had maintained this level of excellence.

One week's stay revealed zero housekeeping flaws. Housekeepers at the Halekulani work in pairs, which we suspect is one of the reasons for their exceptional service acumen.

As in the past, each night revealed a different keepsake at turndown, accompanied by a short poetic card. A small tape measure, sand in a bottle, a steel ruler and a book-page clip are examples. All logoed, these small trinkets certainly beat the usual wrapped chocolates or candies. Moreover, they reinforce the brand, something a confection (even a bespoke truffle) can never really hope to accomplish. As we learned from the management team, the Halekulani guest stays an average of 7+ nights. This was the core reason for developing a different turndown trinket for each night of the week.

Yes, the guests delight in receiving something special every evening that differentiates the turndown service and adds that *je ne sais quoi*. But the unexpected part was discovered upon the return from dinner the night before departure. Items carefully arranged on the desk in each of our rooms included a thank-you card from the housekeeping team, eyeglass repair kits, a hardcover book describing the area, and a wall calendar.

While neither of us can comment on whether or not this is solely for repeat guests, to our knowledge, we were not on any VIP list. Asking others at the bar the next day, they confirmed that they too received the same outgoing package of goodies. It's far and above was the luxury guest expects and a wow moment for anyone visiting the hotel.

There are lessons here for your hotel, even if scheduling room attendants in pairs and delivering this upper echelon of SOPs is out of the cards. First, recognize that your housekeepers are a true frontline of your staff. Provide them with the tools to make them part of your loyalty-enhancing team. Encourage them to get involved. Try to find some unique way of creating a lasting impression of your property.

Importantly, lasting impressions harks at the hospitality concept of the 'sense of departure'. We spent so much time crafting great arrival experiences that we may forget that, psychologically speaking, guests may give even more emotional weighting to the moments just before they leave. Hence, turndown chocolate doesn't necessarily work because it's expected and routine. Certainly, with all the bright minds on your team, you can do better!

As a Mille Club member, you've got the financial horsepower – specifically, a greater nominal gross operating profit per available room (GOPPAR) – to make every aspect of your guests' stay memorable from check-in to departure. But for those properties with lower rates that aspire to create similarly delightful moments, there are many other ways to go about this, and oftentimes restraints can be great motivators for coming up with creative solutions.

How Boutique Luxury is Pivoting in the Post-Pandemic

This article was originally published in December 2021, and the status of Rocco Forte Hotels indicated in this passage may not reflect current company practices.

For those with an eye for history, the Forte name reminds one of Baron Forte, the Italian-born, Scottish hotelier that created the Forte brand and the multiple hospitality businesses he helped create. Currently, his son Sir Rocco Forte, together with sister Olga Polizzi, own and operate Rocco Forte Hotels, with 15 properties primarily in Europe (and a few soon to come).

Having stayed in half a dozen Rocco Forte properties over the past few years, it was an honor to have Phillip Haller, then Vice President of Brand Marketing, invite us to lunch in our hometown of Toronto. He assured us that he was not out to scout a North American location for this distinguished brand; rather, he was making the post-coronavirus rounds of key accounts.

Philip is an unabashed admirer of the Rocco Forte brand and he's optimistic for the future of our industry. Thus, our discussions centered on the luxury hotel guest and the changes that COVID has brought about insofar as what the guest is looking for.

Is COVID a game changer for Rocco Forte Hotels?

It is and is not. Business was challenging through the pandemic. Our hope is that the worst is behind us. All our properties are open, and business is coming back strongly. COVID has added an extra level of scrutiny to our housekeeping. It has also brought into closer focus many of the operational aspects of our relationships with our guests. For example, we would normally escort a guest to their guestroom at check-in. Now, we are careful to gauge the guest's need for distancing. But still, we are known for our service. Our guest is coming to our properties, not only for the physical quality of our property but also for the services that they we deliver.

Do you anticipate more technology in the face of a resistance to close personal guest contact?
We are active at implementing technologies that support our luxury mandate. This would include numerous back-of-house programs designed to enhance service implementation and take advantage of economies of scale. And those technologies that guests come to expect, we will implement or already have. What we are adamantly against are those programs that turn our properties into some sort of do it yourself (DIY) venture. If a guest wants to speak to us during their stay we will be there; and if they wish to address their needs through text on their mobile, we will support them in their preferred channels as well. The core concept is to be guest-centric, not cost-cutting.

Is the luxury hotel guest any different now?
There is definitely a sense of pent-up demand. Our more mature guests have missed 12-24 months of activity. Recognizing that they have lost a few seasons, we're determined to make up for lost travel. More youthful guests are eager to explore. Now, they seem to eschew the big brands and instead look for more intimate surroundings with unique experiences. All guests want a hotel experience but also to learn more and be a part of the local environment. Now is not the time to look at economies; now is the time to fulfill and exceed guest expectations.

Looking beyond accommodations, what is a key driver for your properties?
While many of our properties have outstanding spas, incredible relationships with local venues, and some even have golf courses, we think food. Our restaurants are designed to reinforce the perfect hotel experience. They are not cookie-cutter. Each executive chef designs a menu that reflects both the property and the community. Of course, they rely heavily upon local suppliers. We strive to be, as best we can, faithful to the location as well as the needs of our clientele. Our goal is to ensure that everyone who dines with us feels just as special as those who are staying in our accommodations. Think how – in an instant and for a very small sum – you can make an incredible impact on your guest.

How big will Rocco Forte grow?
Years ago, our properties were part of Trusthouse Forte, encompassing many different business entities. We learned our lesson well. Now, it is strictly quality over quantity. We have the Carlton Milan and RF House Milan opening and are always on the lookout for new properties.

The Mille Club: Two Rocco Forte Hotels in One Incredible Trip to Italia

Known to many as the Eternal City, Rome has an uninterrupted history spanning two and a half thousand years. Apart from incredible historical sites, Rome has some of the world's finest luxury hotels, often carved out of grand palazzos that once served members of the royal court of the Papal elite, and all of them adorned with opulent finishings and fine art.

On a typical night in off-peak periods (if Rome even has a low season anymore!), 20 or more properties meet our Mille Club definition, with entry-level rates well over $1,000 (measured in USD, even though these would also be over €1,000), with many double or even triple that amount. And that's often only for the base standard king, with suites and villas running in multiples above that.

We were fortunate to stop in Rome following a business trip and experience the two properties owned by Rocco Forte Hotels, a brand synonymous with Italian elegance. Despite unseasonably cold and rain-soaked spring weather, Hotel de la Ville and Hotel de Russie made us feel beyond welcome with their incredible hospitality.

We asked the Managing Directors of both properties to provide insight into their take on Roman hospitality and the ever-evolving nature of ultraluxury hotels in an alpha-tier city like this one where fierce competition among Mille Club members is fierce.

Part 1: Hotel de la Ville interview with Francesco Roccato, Managing Director for Northern Italy for Rocco Forte Hotels

Why should a discerning guest stay with you?

The Hotel de la Ville boasts an impeccable yet relaxed approach to service. Right from the time our guests make a booking to the time they reach Rome, and even after departure, our guests experience the attentiveness and warmth of the entire team. This is key to attracting new clientele and, at the same time, making them dream to return soon. Moreover, Rocco Forte Hotels enhances the heritage of each destination by choosing unique properties in prime locations, such as the 18th-century palazzo that hosts the Hotel de la Ville.

What are the key differentiators between your property and other luxury properties in the City?

As part of one of the Rocco Forte Hotels pillars, we firmly believe that we make a difference by enhancing the destination with exclusive, authentic, tailormade Roman experiences. This creates a 'fil rouge' or common thread that links the overall experience with the hotel design, the food and beverage offer, and the bespoke suggestions of our local concierge. Another aspect that our guests appreciate about the hotel is the family feeling and the reassuring approach of our dedicated team, which makes them immediately feel welcome and ensures a memorable stay.

How do you ensure that your staff maintains their commitment to excellence that we observed?
I have always strived to establish a good working climate across the entire Hotel de la Ville. I am lucky to have a consolidated team working together since the opening. At Rocco Forte Hotels, we focus on training, cross-training, and career development to have an enthusiastic team. Thus, the team is committed to delivering excellent service and, at the same time, is eager to learn and grow in its career path. We constantly promote a motivated environment aimed at providing excellent service. My motto is, "Treat others how you want to be treated!"

As rates have dramatically increased since the pandemic, how have you ensured the guest receives value?
Since opening in 2019, the Hotel de la Ville has grown its business and consolidated its reputation and awareness. As stated above, we craft customized experiences for our guests that perfectly fit their desires and curiosity and ensure they are looked after throughout their stay. Moreover, we have strong partnerships with local artisans and high-end niche brands strongly linked to the destination. These are part of our appealing gifting program, including a small Roman souvenir for our guests to take home with them.

Can you provide an example of how you and your team anticipate guests' needs during their stay?
Our Concierge and Guest Relations teams contact our guests or their travel agents before arrival to ensure that all their wishes take shape promptly, creating a bespoke itinerary that allows them to discover the destination at its finest. This anticipatory approach makes them feel reassured and more eager to discover the Eternal City's hidden gems!

Part 2: Hotel de Russie interview with Giacomo Battafarano, Managing Director for Southern Italy for Rocco Forte Hotels

Why should a discerning guest stay with you?
Undoubtedly, for our incomparable location! Hotel de Russie is a historical building that houses the monumental gardens designed by Giuseppe Valadier in the 19th century, a green oasis between Piazza del Popolo and Piazza di Spagna in the historic center of the Capital. Fundamental elements are the high level of our professionals which guarantees high standards of services and the strong connection with the destination is a further plus.

What are the key differentiators between your property and other luxury properties in the city?
The brand's philosophy of personalizing the stay and making the experience more exclusive is characterizing. Our guests feel at home away from home.

How do you ensure that your staff maintains their commitment to excellence?
Employee commitment goes beyond mere compliance with job duties. It represents a deep emotional attachment and dedication to the organization. Employees willingly invest their time, effort, and energy to achieve organizational goals when committed.

In Rocco Forte, service excellence is a philosophy. To reach and maintain excellence, we focus on:

1. *Continuous training.*
2. *Creating a positive work environment* is crucial for increasing and sustaining employees' commitment and dedication to a business. It fosters a sense of belonging, motivation, and overall job satisfaction. From the employees' perspective, a positive work environment means feeling valued, respected, and supported by their superiors and colleagues. It involves open communication, trust, and opportunities for growth and development.
3. *Recognizing and rewarding* employee contributions is critical to fostering a positive work environment and enhancing employee commitment.
4. *Lead by example:* Trust begins at the top. Leaders who demonstrate honesty, integrity, and consistency set the tone for the organization. Employees feel secure when leaders keep their promises, admit mistakes, and communicate openly.
5. *Transparent decision-making:* Whenever possible, involve employees in decision-making processes. Explain the rationale behind decisions, even if they are unpopular. Transparency reduces uncertainty and builds trust.
6. *Consistent communication:* Regularly share updates on company performance, strategy, and challenges. Town hall meetings, newsletters, and one-on-one conversations all contribute to transparency.

From employees' perspective, strong leadership is created by communicating the vision, goals, and expectations, giving them trust, transparency, and direction. They understand their role in achieving the objectives and are motivated to contribute. The same can be said from the leaders' point of view: by actively listening to employees' ideas, concerns, and feedback, they can gain valuable insights and make informed decisions.

Finally, yet importantly, promoting work-life balance is critical to fostering a healthy and committed workforce. Striking the right balance between professional and personal commitments can significantly impact an employee's well-being, job satisfaction, and overall productivity.

As rates have dramatically increased post-COVID, how have you ensured the guest receives value?
After the pandemic, the trend of revenge travel spread, and therefore, the unexpressed demand of the period restrictions led to an exponential growth in travel demand.

People have invested more in their well-being and travel. Rome and Italy have always been popular destinations internationally for their historical treasures, quality of life, good food, and art of hospitality. However, due to a very high increase in demand, costs increased.

As a company, we have made many investments, starting with recruiting new staff and continuing with numerous investments, among which the complete refurbishment of the rooms in response to the many requests from our guests staying for longer than just a few nights. The rooms with garden views have been renovated, a unique feature of the Hotel de Russie and the city of Rome.

We have restored the monumental historic garden, the Lobby, and our restaurant, Le Jardin de Russie, internally frescoed by the immersive artist Gio Bressana. The intent is to renovate the entire building by the end of 2025.

Can you provide an example of how you and your team anticipate guests' needs during their stay?

The Hotel de Russie team is involved with its guests from the very beginning, from the booking phase, when we try to understand and find out their expectations and needs to suggest the best accommodation solution for their desired tours and restaurant suggestions.

We have invested in and increased our Guest Relations team, which supports and offers a dedicated, exclusive, and sometimes tailor-made service to all our guests. Furthermore, the Hotel de Russie boasts a very experienced concierge team that is well-connected with the city's historical places, events, tours, and new things to offer.

How Hotels Can Embrace the Technological Age with Sugar Beach IT Director Shearvon Devenish

Every hotelier now knows (or should!) that technology supports all manner of operations. However, outside of the Information Technology (IT) department, it might not be readily understood just how central various systems and hardware have become, in addition to all the complex and meticulous details that must be considered to make it all work.

Coming out of HITEC, a leading hotel trade show, one overarching message was: we are now firmly in a new 'Technological Age' with the likes of ChatGPT and other AI variants only the beginning of what's to come.

Yet, many hotels remain far behind other industries, households and D2C mobile apps when it comes to keeping pace with tech expectations and available services to automate workflows or enhance a brand. The time is ripe for a sea of change to get caught up and realize a healthy return in the process. This, however, may require not only system upgrades but a cultural change where the IT Director and CTO take on a more central role to guide new projects and advise on financial matters.

To offer some incredible words of wisdom for all hoteliers and hopeful vendors to the hospitality industry, at HITEC we met with Shearvon Devenish, Director of Information Technology at Sugar Beach, A Viceroy Property in Saint Lucia, then followed up with him after the tradeshow for this in-depth interview on how this role is shaping the future of hotels.

For background, Sugar Beach is a five-star resort with 130 keys, including villas, beachfront bungalows, and residences. It offers seven restaurants and bars, a full spa and fitness center, and a wide range of both land and water sports, as well as various excursions available. Spread over 100 acres, the grounds stretch from private tropical rainforests to an idyllic white-sand beach with magnificent views of the famous UNESCO World Heritage Pitons. Forbes recently named Sugar Beach as one of the ten best luxury beach resorts in the Caribbean.

Growing up in Saint Lucia, Devenish's career in hospitality as an information systems manager included Hilton properties in Saint Lucia, Barbados, and Venezuela before he joined Sugar Beach, A Viceroy Resort in 2010. This was also while he completed his master's degree in information systems management remotely from the University of Liverpool. It was a delight to hear Devenish speak so eloquently about what the IT role currently includes and where it's headed.

How have you seen the role of IT Director and CTO change over the past decade?

Let's begin with the role of the IT Director. Like the Chief Technology Officer (CTO), their budgets have increased, aiding them to implement new technology to replace services that were previously done manually by staff despite the size of the hotel brand. Technological solutions will eventually become the norm, such as artificial intelligence for booking reservations.

Changes like these assisted brands such as Hilton, Marriott, and Four Seasons to rapidly grow into the chains we know them as today. Boutique hotel companies such as Viceroy have also become quite innovative on the technological front to support their own brand development. Due to how critical technologies have become to maintaining operations and supporting growth, brands have placed a lot of trust in the IT Director to identify these needs, bridge the silo at the local level, implement the new technologies, provide the training, and maintain the relationship with vendors while managing their part of the budget.

The role of the CTO was created to support companies that required a 'captain' to man the ship at the corporate level. In the last decade, CTOs have continued to work with the executive team in planning the IT strategy for expanding the flagship of the company to different states, continents or regions such as the Caribbean, where I live. Their role requires technical engagement with vendors, to understand the business development goals from security compliances introduced by the Payment Card Industry's Data Security Standards (PCI DSS) to the recently passed privacy legislation such as the European Union's General Data Protection Regulation (GDPR) which imposes heavy fines on hoteliers who retain guest's Personal Identifiable Information (PII) without their consent.

The CTOs are firmly at the heart of their respective companies because they support a great percentage of how the vision is communicated in a technological era, be it with the local IT team, vendors, executive branch, asset managers or owners, all to compete within a rapidly changing industry efficiently and securely by obtaining funding and buy-in for the company's growth.

What recent tech projects that you've worked on are you particularly proud of?
Every time my team (Sanique Prospere and Rinaldo Faucher) and I implement a new technology, I'm ecstatic; it's one more outdated, less efficient practice that has been addressed. What I'm most proud of is the expansion of the hotel, and that was done through research, planning, budgeting, procurement, and communication.

I recently designed a wireless network for a nine-bedroom residence at Sugar Beach, which will be called 'Spice of Life'. The residence alone covers 24,000 square feet and will be the largest living accommodation at the resort once the construction is complete. The technology design includes aspects such as cable infrastructure, wireless access points, telephones, security cameras, and network switches, to name a few.

Unlike many of my other projects, network designs for real estate projects are extremely engaging as you near the completion date. It requires IT procurement, continuous meetings with vendors to ensure that the implementation of the technology infrastructure and cabling is completed so you're future-prepared. The build of the data closet, configuration of the network switches with multiple Virtual Local Area Networks (VLANs), all the way to the installation of the various computers, printers, wireless access points and smart technologies for the enjoyment of the end users.

What tech projects are you working on right now? What challenges are you facing with each?
We are currently expanding the outdoor wireless coverage for our 30 residences. The wireless coverage on the inside of the one-to-four-bedroom units is great; however, some of our guests have expressed their desire for an improved coverage when enjoying the outdoor living space, which my team and I will undoubtedly achieve.

Each residence, dependent on the number of rooms, can range from 2,500 to 4,000 square feet. The challenge with this project is the absence of a robust cable infrastructure to the main network switch that is located on the outside of each building. This means that this project requires a WiFi audit to identify the areas with the lowest signal strength, followed by the best physical location to place the wireless units to improve the outdoor coverage in the affected area. All this must be achieved with aesthetics in mind.

Other challenges included the type of wireless access point that would be used; we do have a standard, so there is a vendor that we work with (Cisco Systems). Due to challenges with sourcing the required electronic chips – a key component for building various hardware – we are impacted by the unavailability of certain models, so we do not escape the woes of the global supply chain.

Finally, the budget. The cost of improvements to any residence is incurred by the residence owner, so the design, like anything else, is impacted by the available amount we must spend. I make it my duty to ensure that we perform our due diligence by collating the feedback from our guests, conducting a WiFi audit to validate their claims and tabulating the cost of the recommended hardware or infrastructure (shipping and duties included) in order to address the challenge.

How do you decide what tech projects to prioritize for implementation?

Great question and one that remains at the center of our daily operation because even an ongoing or existing project can be impacted by any challenge that affects the service to our guest or staff. It all depends on where we are with the project and what type of project it is: approved in budget, hardware and/or software, and finally the amount of training required by the end-user.

My projects are usually planned by the end of Q3 and implemented during Q2 and Q3 of the following year. We've found Q1 and Q4 to be extremely hectic with high season and occupancy levels in the Caribbean. As such, we work with department heads during Q3 to share information on solutions that can efficiently improve their operation and then get costing from our vendors. During events such as HITEC, we're able to meet with vendors directly to engage them on what is new, view demos and interact with our local staff to get their feedback – they are the key stakeholders after all.

Once the project's requirements have been met – that is, hardware, software, and funding – we figure out with the key stakeholders a timeframe for implementation. We do not make these decisions without discussing with senior management first.

An example of how another project can be given priority over another would be due to a global change, such as a PCI DSS or GDPR compliance. Projects such as those come with a time frame by which hotels are given stringent deadlines to comply with. Knowing the impact to our business and customers, we pause our existing projects and push these forward to ensure we comply with the global security standard.

How do you interact with other departments so that they're aware of all the tech complexities you face on a regular basis?

I have a beautiful picture in my department that assists with that discussion, and I've coined it the 'big picture'. Every department head has a question – something that they're in dire need of solving. Technology can do a lot and sometimes, technology isn't required because it is an operational challenge, which I'm also happy to assist with. My real concern is being able to actively listen – that skill of being able to hear the question and understand or probe to understand the 'big picture' and then provide the solution immediately or through additional research.

Another key factor is whether the project is a capital expenditure or not. If it isn't part of the budget for the financial year, we need to establish how much of an emergency it is; otherwise, it will be assigned to the department's budget in the next financial year.

How can hotels reorient their processes to more fully embrace technology at their core?

One of the most critical things that I would do would be to restructure their organizational chain. Over the years I've worked across various countries helping hotels achieve this goal.

One of the advantages that I've had was the ability to work with the local executive directly with a dotted line to the corporate office. Today, in many hotels – even during my discussions at HITEC – many hotel managers and hotel financial controllers attended, yet within their companies, IT reports to finance. A simple change of including IT in the main conversation will mean that IT would be furnished with the information required to understand the business's needs and challenges, as well as be able to spend its time efficiently researching solutions and working with vendors to deliver solutions that could positively impact the organization.

Technology isn't slowing down; the most well-known companies are using IT at their core. Two of the world's richest people – Elon Musk and Jeff Bezos – are utilizing technology in every aspect to build on their company's portfolio. It's time to include the IT team in these executive-level conversations.

What hotel technologies are you most excited about right now?

I've been a fan of the use of virtual reality in hospitality for some time now. It answers questions that many travelers have from inception, and unlike the 2D video or image, it takes what Matterport offers on websites and allows travelers to build a better itinerary before arriving at their destination.

I focused on cloud computing when doing my master's degree, and it was because I realized the power the cloud held in making information readily available across the globe. Similarly, for Virtual Reality (VR), it addresses the issue of importing hardware and the cost of hardware for users globally. It makes services like the prearrival check-in and the check-out process more efficient. Because of this, it means staff can focus on other services like improving overall guest satisfaction if executed well.

What other things are you looking forward to?

I'm interested in the introduction of Digital Currencies (DCs). If hoteliers can begin to use DCs at their properties, it would revolutionize the way we do business. And the chatter of Artificial Intelligence (AI) remains; the question is what regulations, like that for a DC, will be placed to ensure it is safe to use. It would help address language barriers between staff and guest, increase hotel occupancy by supporting sales and marketing strategies, and finally, together with DCs, make traveling vastly easier.

Checking the Changes to Hawaiian Luxury with the Halekulani

For those who are unfamiliar, the Halekulani is (pardon the alliteration) a hallmark of Hawaiian hospitality, with the property acting as the keystone for the densely populated beach tourism area of Waikiki in Honolulu. At 453 rooms and suites, the luxury hotel has a time-honored history, first established in 1917 and now comprising five buildings and three signature restaurants, all with an unparalleled onsite experience. Further to this article, the property closed completely for an 18-month renovation at the outset of the pandemic in 2020.

Being regulars at the Halekulani, and true hotel aficionados, we're keenly interested in the impact of senior management changes on a property's operations and performance. Davide Barnes joined the property as Hotel Manager at the beginning of 2023 following an extensive global background in hospitality with senior positions at Benchmark Hospitality, Four Seasons, Hyatt and Shangri-La. Unusual for a hotelier, he also spent five years working as a market leader for Apple at their Cupertino, California headquarters. It was a delight to sit down with Barnes as part of our first return visit to Hawaii following the pandemic to see how the property is fairing and what every hotelier can learn about managing the reopening process after a full-scale PIP.

When you arrived at the Halekulani, what were your top objectives?

Upon arriving at Halekulani, what stood out to me the most was the warmth of the staff and the tranquillity of the property, which I found striking given its location amidst the bustling Waikiki area. The property was closed for some time during the pandemic, and then after reopening business came back much faster than we expected in different ways. My focus has been on operationally making sure that we're able to continue to deliver unrivalled experiences to both our returning hotel guests and our local F&B guests. We've made a lot of progress in reconnecting our guests to everything they've always loved about Halekulani, while also introducing new experiences. At the same time, we're driving consistency and ensuring that the experience guests have now exceeds what they had before.

We (Larry and his wife) have stayed at the Halekulani pretty much once a year. Tell us how you can ensure such a high level of consistently excellent service.

We've made some adjustments on the training front, which have been crucial as we strive to maintain high levels of consistently excellent service. All new employees must go through several days of orientation to learn about the history, hotel culture, and expectations of the hotel before starting their jobs in their departments.

To ensure consistent top-tier service, enhanced communication of details is vital. Each day begins with a morning briefing, attended by a representative from each department. We do a thorough review of our performance from the previous day, as well as a detailed review of all guests arriving the next day. We review everything – from arrival times, past visits, guest preferences – including dietary restrictions, allergies, special celebrations, and even the smallest details like which side of the bed the guest prefers. This detailed and thorough system of communication sets our team for success every day.

Do you have many guests who, like us, make an annual pilgrimage to the Halekulani? Is this loyalty level greater than you have experienced previously in your career?
We have guests who make multiple pilgrimages to Halekulani per year. Every property has some multi-generational guests, but I've never worked at a hotel that has quite so many. I would attribute this high level of loyalty to our team. Most of the team returned after the pandemic and our average employee tenure is 20 to 40 years. One of the benefits to our employees is to see the loyal guests return, and I believe our guests feel the same.

On that note, what advice do you have for other GMs insofar as staff retention, staff training and staff motivation?
The key is to lead from the inside out. If you take great care of your team, this will ensure they take great care of your guests. Everything starts with the team. Something else I find to be positive from a morale standpoint is my view of a flat organization. Everyone works together; there is no bureaucratic structure. Anyone can share an idea; it will be heard and often implemented. For example, a couple of team members approached me a few months ago with an idea for an initiative to support Maui relief. They suggested a market with various arts and crafts created by staff. We moved ahead with the idea and told them we would match all the money that was made from the market. A great success, we raised a substantial donation for the Maui Strong Fund.

How has the West Maui fire disaster affected your operations and bookings?
We have not seen any significant impact on our bookings or operations as it relates to Maui. In terms of staffing, we have hired several people who were displaced and are continuing to find ways to support their community, either financially or with goods and services.

The property was closed for an extensive renovation. Can you discuss some of the rationale for closure versus remaining partially open while work was being undertaken?
When a property is open, there is never a good time to renovate all the guestrooms because you can't deliver the same service experience. Since the experience is so important to us, we saw this as an ideal opportunity to enhance the property without impacting the guests' stay.

How have you embraced technology while at the same time ensuring that you maintain a close personal touch with your guests?
We deploy technology not to replace service but to enhance service and service delivery. Our approach is a high-tech AND high-touch approach. The property has been welcoming guests for over 100 years and technology helps us retain all guest details, expand this data, and help with guest recognition. We realize the importance of guests' technology, so during the renovation, we took the opportunity to increase

the bandwidth to upgrade our WiFi system, added the latest charging stations, and included tablets to all guestrooms allowing easy access to hotel information, the ability to control in-room systems, and initiate service requests such as on-line ordering.

What else should you add?

For all the guests returning, their expectations have changed. The definition of luxury is super subjective now. Luxury to everybody means something completely different. The team's overall emotional intelligence (EQ) is so important, as is their confidence to serve outside of the lines in a way that they're empowered to do the right thing.

Crafting a Luxury Sleep Experience at the Equinox Hotel New York

Does the guarantee of a good night's sleep influence a guest's hotel choice? We say unquestionably yes. With the rise of *sleep tourism* where millions of people are starting to prioritize getting a solid seven hours rest when traveling, hotels all over the world are responding in kind with newfangled or upgraded sleep programs.

However, marketing that a brand cares about a guest's sleep is a world of difference from the program's execution. And as it relates to the execution, there's no better place to look than a luxury hotel that has debuted a sleep program where every single detail has been meticulously completed.

After all, luxury guests may understand the value of being well-rested better than any other guest type. As an example, consider a corporate executive on an important business trip where a great night's sleep ensures a sound mind and good decision-making abilities for the following day's meetings, during which time numerous other people may be directly affected by those meetings' outcomes.

Given how paramount sleep is for guests and how significant a booking driver it can be, it was our pleasure (and duty!) to stay at the Equinox Hotel New York and experience the full depth of the brand's unrivaled sleep program, then report back on what this hotel is doing that's so remarkable. In short, it always comes down to the attention to detail at every level, and it was a delight to speak with Equinox CEO Chris Norton during our time in the Big Apple to help us understand the process behind this property's inception and its focus on sleep.

A Leader in Lifestyle and Luxury

To set the mood, some background on this luxury property is first required. The Equinox Hotel New York opened in July 2019 with 212 rooms and suites as part of the multi-billion-dollar Hudson Yards real estate development. Described as a city within the city, all the gleaming, ultramodern towers have been built on top of the railyards leading into Penn Station, with the Equinox Hotel right across the street from the iconic Vessel art installation, The Shops at Hudson Yards and The Shed, an eight-story art center.

As the first hotel property for Equinox Group, the parent company, the Equinox Hotel New York is the culmination of three decades of growth for the brand which opened its first high-end fitness club in the Upper West Side in 1991 and, amongst others, launched SoulCycle in 2006. Expanding into luxury hospitality was a natural extension, but it nevertheless required an astute vision for how travel behavior is evolving and the emergence of the *lifestyle hotel category*.

Traditional luxury will always have its place, but the lifestyle movement within this segment touches on a profound and wholly 21st-century evolution in that luxury now transcends demographics. Travelers are actively seeking hotel brands whose identities and values are in harmony with their own personal beliefs, with the inception for Equinox Hotels coming about through the recognition that many people of all ages want to maintain their healthy lifestyle while traveling, codified as *high performance living*.

This is reflected by the guestroom amenities such as the Art + Science of Sleep program, by the immediate access to the fitness club, Equinox Hudson Yards; by the bevy of nutritious food options provided by the onsite restaurant, Electric Lemon; and having a world-class onsite wellness center, The Spa by Equinox Hotels.

"Equinox Hotels redefines luxury hospitality for those who embrace high-performance living," commented Norton. "Our concept of luxury transcends the white glove grandeur of the past, focusing on meaningful details and a seamless guest experience. Rooted in the pillars of movement, nutrition, regeneration and community, our modern hospitality offering infuses every stay with purpose. As a luxury hotel, a place intended for rest and rejuvenation, we recognize the profound impact of travel on sleep, a fundamental element of wellbeing. Our guestrooms and sleep program have been developed alongside sleep scientists, offering a science-backed approach that optimizes rest so every guest can get their best night's sleep."

With respect to being a trendsetter in the lifestyle hotel category, an important concept from economics to borrow here is what's called *induced demand*. By raising awareness for what's possible in a luxury, cutting-edge hotel sleep program, Equinox Hotels elevates the entire market for sleep tourism and helps to grow the *total addressable market* (TAM) for the lifestyle category. In other words, this property is definitely not a 'one off'; it's leading the charge on the next big thing in hospitality.

The Art + Science of Sleep in Focus

Until recently, sleep was often treated as auxiliary to good health when compared to diet and exercise. But as more and more research in the past decade in the field of *sleep science* has revealed, it is now widely known that sleep plays an essential role in cognition, mood, bodily fatigue, appetite and immune system functionality. While we all like traveling, the combination of jetlag, grueling hours spent in transit, the unease of being away from home and the ambient noise of a noisy metropolis like New York can all lead to poor sleep quality.

Embracing the design mantra of 'dark, quiet and cool', the finishings and furnishings inscribed by the Art + Science of Sleep program at the Equinox Hotel New York are thoughtfully designed to transform each guestroom into a veritable *sleep chamber* by incorporating all the latest *sleep hygiene* practices so that all guests are guaranteed a fantastic night's rest.

As aforementioned, it's all in the details, and here are some that make this program truly exceptional:

- Light-absorbent and sound-dampening materials such as black marble, dark woods, and stylish insulating wall panels
- Special linens and bedding materials made from toxin-free materials and designed to dissipate bodily heat during sleep and reduce moisture residues
- Best-in-class HVAC and synchronized smart thermostats to accurately modulate ambient temperature without any noise
- Blackout curtains precisely measured to fit each window frame and block out all exterior light
- Circadian-adjusted lighting, such as the stylish amber-hued bedside lamp and ground-level strip lighting built into the bedframe with motion sensor activation
- One-touch dimming and 'lights out' mode buttons adjoining the bed for intuitive room controls
- A smart television with a simplified remote for easy access to the bespoke AM/PM Rituals, constituting time-adjusted, on-demand yoga instructions to reset the body in the morning then calm it back down in the evening
- Custom bathroom amenities by Grown Alchemist, made with natural ingredients to help soothe the skin and relax the body
- A full reimagination to the entire minibar and coffee service amenities dubbed the RoomBar (more on this in a moment)

And as the literal cherry on top, turndown service includes two dark chocolate-covered tart cherries – one of the few foods that's a natural source of exogenous melatonin, the brain's own sleep hormone – delivered under a dapper smoking cloche dome.

An undercurrent to all these room features are some themes that serve as tutelage for any hotel looking to enter the sleep tourism space. Namely, the room is quite high-tech, and yet everything is intuitive and invisible, or, in a word, convenient to the guest. The curtains and lights are seamlessly accessible from the one-touch bedside controls while the in-room tablet acts as a universal access points for all the hotel's services and information on neighborhood attractions.

Together with the essentialist décor and FF&E, the overall impression is a deep-rooted sense of 'peace of mind' – that the hotel has dwelled on every detail to ensure the guest sleeps soundly.

The RoomBar Redefines What the Minibar Can Do

The two of us have long preached the need for a contemporary rethink of the minibar, both as a profit center and as a way to further propel the hotel's branding. Gone are the days where a refrigerator only stocked with mainstays like canned Coca-Cola and one-ounce bottles of Smirnoff will cut it. There's no identity here and nothing that will reinforce the authenticity of the guest experience. Fashioned as the RoomBar, this amenity at the Equinox Hotel New York serves as a quintessential example of how a property can imbue even more lifestyle elements in the room.

Some highlights of the RoomBar that caught our eye include:

- In lieu of basic milk or cream, the Nespresso coffeemaker comes with a collagen powder-infused coconut creamer
- For caffeinated and herbal teas, rather than sort the selection by specific ingredients, these are named according to purpose with Power Up, Recover, Regenerate and Power Down
- Bolstering the high-performance living mantra are exercise accessories like a foam roller, massage ball and small gym bag
- A full array of 80+ health-conscious products for purchase such as functional snacks, niche brand green juices and vitamin packs, all neatly laid out for easy browsing

While the health and exercise focus here likely won't be the best approach for any other brand, the lesson for all hoteliers is that the minibar should be a 'reason to visit' in its own right. Rather than just being a nondescript amenity, the RoomBar is a feature that guests take their time to explore and appreciate, in the process introducing guests to new ways to live healthier back at home.

Looking Ahead to the Future

In speaking with Norton, one challenge that the hotel has overcome is extending its awareness outside of the core fitness-oriented following that stems from the Equinox Group's brand cachet. It's all too easy for a traveler to look at the Equinox Hotel New York and quickly think, "I don't exercise while traveling, so this hotel isn't for me."

True, not everyone has a fitness-primary mindset (right now at least), but everyone sleeps and thus the mission to craft a sleep chamber out of the guestroom is something that resonates with all travelers coming from any origin market. And as previously mentioned, the TAM for sleep tourism is only getting bigger, making the demand for luxury sleep experiences ever greater over time.

Combined with the spa, the restaurant and, yes, the fitness club, the Equinox Hotel New York is a genuine urban wellness hotel and an oasis amongst the hustle and bustle of Manhattan. Outside of this property, Equinox Group has plans to build new hotels in several other alpha-tier cities in the coming years, so be on the lookout for announcements to that effect as you think about how to elevate your own sleep program.

Exploring the Hazelton Hotel Toronto and How In-Room Tablets Are Integral to Modern Luxury

Hotel luxury is a moving target. Of course, the visibility of design trends makes decade-over-decade changes in décor and furnishing relatively easy to call attention to as the engine of this continuous evolution. But let us not forget the underlying 'invisibility' that powerful technologies play in reinforcing the five-star hotel experience.

Frictionless, properly integrated, highly personalized and fully supportive of the well-oiled on-site teams, there's now a complex web of hardware and software that's integral to 21st century luxury, all in order to meet guests' diverse needs via whichever channel or method they prefer. To make the guest-facing side totally uncomplicated and uncluttered, the in-room tablet has assumed an increasingly vital role.

To further unpack this, a fundamental requirement of the guest experience becomes convenience and expediency, together interpreted as 'time saved' and 'no stress whatsoever' or what we hoteliers would classically define as 'great service'. Luxury customers are discerning, after all; they value their time above all else. Moreover, they have options when it comes to their accommodations, not just within localized comp sets but in global destination choice. For this reason, hotels in this category must be exceedingly vigilant with their tech stack innovation in order to facilitate a superior degree of convenience for every point of interaction.

Bringing this principle into focus is the guest room experience. Luxury rooms and suites require a lot of tech, but all of it must now be seamlessly embedded into the environment so that there are only a few universal touchpoints for guests to quickly attain whatever they want in an intuitive and stress-free manner. Hence, it's the guest room tablet that provides immediate access to every on-site service, amenity and room controls.

To demonstrate exactly how the tablet supports the luxury hotel experience, we sat down with Gaurav Dutta, the General Manager for the Hazelton Hotel in Toronto, Canada, to discuss how his hotel stays on the forefront of hospitality, as well as the critical role that INTELITY, the property's tablet platform provider, has played in this development.

About the Hazelton Hotel

The two of us have often mentioned in past articles that we're both from Toronto, so it's with tremendous pride that we get to fawn over an example of the Great White North leading the way in worldwide hospitality. Nestled in the elegant midtown enclave of Yorkville, the Hazelton opened in 2007 with 77 rooms and suites alongside the adjoining signature restaurant, ONE Restaurant. It's also a member of Leading Hotels of the World (for which INTELITY is powering this association's mobile app) and verified by Forbes Travel Guide (who have named INTELITY the organization's official guest engagement and staff management platform).

Other integral hotel amenities include the Spa by Valmont, also housing a heated saltwater pool, and the Norman Jewison Cinema, capable of seating up to 25 guests and famous for its private events during the annual Toronto International Film

Festival. And as a side note on our familiarity with this gem, one of us (Larry) even served as MOD for the property back in the early 2010s.

Bespoke, boutique, and artfully appointed at every turn, this property is quintessential urban ultraluxury. While you are allowed to have your favorites, the Hazelton is quantifiably the best property in the nation, as measured by its top spot on TripAdvisor for the city wherein its reviews are unwaveringly stellar as well as its placement as the #1 hotel in Canada, and #5 in the world for Condé Nast Traveler's Readers' Choice Awards 2023.

"As any veteran hotelier knows, achieving this frequency of positive reviews while ensuring our product and services are at the highest levels requires a mountain of work behind the scenes to make every aspect of the stay absolutely perfect," started Dutta. "It's always in the details and the coordination of those details always comes back to how well the teams work together. Specifically, we've set out to make the Hazelton an oasis in the heart of the city, fulfilling all manner of guest requests flawlessly while also showcasing the best that Toronto has to offer."

Challenges Solved by the Tablet

It's this operating thesis of teams working well together to deliver flawless service that brought INTELITY's solutions into the picture.

Specifically, here are the Hazelton's requirements that had to be met in order for each tablet to effectively convey modern luxury:

1. The platform's guest interface must carry the same *brand standards* and level of sophistication as other digital and physical touchpoints – for instance, by having a direct two-way texting system with one of the property's three Clefs d'Or concierges.
2. Building on the first point, the platform must act as a *one-stop shop*, showcasing every service befitting an ultraluxury hotel, from booking spa treatments, accessing the pillow menu, viewing menus and calling up a bellhop to arranging for event tickets, bringing flowers to the room and scheduling a babysitter.
3. The software must sync with the hotel's *guest experience management system* (GEMS) so that requests can be anticipated and addressed with a hyper-personalized touch.
4. Building on this third point, the software should offer support with *back-of-house operations* to tighten lines of communication and guarantee quality service, either through internal modules that teams can use or through integrations with the PMS (Opera) and the ops platform (HotSOS).
5. A guest's *privacy* must be maintained at all times, both in how the platform uses data and in how service orders are relayed then dispatched.
6. To reach guests at any point in the customer journey, it should connect with the *mobile app*, in this case the one provided by Leading Hotels of the World.

7. It should help the hotel support its core value of *sustainability* by actively working to reduce paper and energy usage (the latter being on the roadmap as more integrations are developed).
8. It must *declutter the guestroom* by connecting various devices and services – for instance, by offering a portal to PressReader so that guests no longer need physical newspapers (which also fits with the hotel's sustainability goals).

With Great Tablet Comes Great Responsibility

As should be clear from these eight points, there's a lot that can be channeled into the tablet to provide the essence of modern luxury, but also a lot that can go wrong by introducing points of guest frustration when something isn't as seamless as it should be. Tablet interfaces are, after all, a reflection of the brand, and a poor experience here can result in a non-returning guest or one who ventures off site instead of spending more onsite — a characteristic that's doubly true for the discerning luxury traveler.

As Dutta cheekily remarked, he and his team are also 'hospitality nerds'. Not only do they marvel at the latest five-star hotel openings around the world, but they also relished the opportunity to source a capable vendor in order to surpass these challenges and ensure that the tablet worked to reinforce the Hazelton's reputation as the best hotel in the city.

Thinking big picture, the case study of the Hazelton's deployment of a strong in-room tablet solution like what INTELITY has offered supports our view that this piece of technology is now indispensable for modern luxury. No matter whether it's Toronto, elsewhere in the Americas, EMEA or APAC, the trends of decluttered, sophisticated and exceedingly convenient hotel experiences are here for good, and that's something every hotel brand should look to pursue.

Voice Channel Resilience and Added Value for Upscale and Luxury Hotels

As consultants, our niche is, per the title, upscale, premium, luxury and ultraluxury hotels and resorts, helping owners solve 'strategic' issues. We put this word in quotations because it means connecting the dots whichever way that is and taking an outsider's perspective on how all operations or distinct data sets integrate for the greater whole, most often anchored around the goal of maximizing profitability.

One counterintuitive observation of recent is that, even in a world of flashy websites and intelligent booking engines, the voice channel is still a very important part of the prebooking and prearrival stages of the journey for luxury guests. While we would never imply that ecommerce isn't critical for hotels or besmirch the scalability that cloud-based tech can provide, preferences change once you start charging a ton of money for a room.

In basic terms, luxury guests want to know what they are getting, and frequently the only way they can gain confidence in the product is through a phone call. For a typical luxury hotel, voice channel revenue can be as much as 20% of total room revenue, and it is the second-most profitable revenue channel, even including the labor costs associated with answering the call.

Joining the Mille Club

For context, one of the biggest trends right now in global hospitality is the proliferation of brands that have no problem sustaining year-round rates above $500, $750, $1,000, $2,000 or even $4,000 per night for a standard king room. Some brands in this category that make hotel nerds like us drool include Aman, Armani, Belmond, Bulgari, Capella, Fairmont, Mandarin Oriental, One&Only, Peninsula, Raffles, Rocco Forte, Rosewood, Six Senses and, perhaps this trend's progenitor, Four Seasons.

Documenting the explosion of hotels appealing to wealthy and high-net-worth individuals (as well as us plebs who opt to splurge on fancy accommodations for a special occasion) is something we do in our regular column called 'The Mille Club' with that middle word denoting the Italian for a thousand. While there are many economic and geopolitical factors contributing to this phenomenon, the focus is on what you can do to become a Mille Club member, wherein sharpening how your voice channel operates is one such task.

What we emphasize throughout this column is that there are certain psychological thresholds, expressed in the form of ever-lofty guest expectations, that exist once your ADR ticks above four digits, although others exist at the half-mille and three-quarters-mille marks. Namely, luxury guests may be price inelastic but they are entirely experience elastic.

These individuals want to maximize their time, no matter the cost, and this means gathering the exact information they need to make a purchasing decision as well as customizing their hotel stays and planning a bespoke itinerary. Despite the recent advances in attribute-based shopping and AI-enhanced tools like chatbots, true customization (for now) can only be achieved by speaking to a live agent. Moreover, there's something irreplaceably wholesome about a human-to-human conversation that's emblematic of real hospitality service.

Rethinking the Call Center

So, you want to increase rates and join the Mille Club? As previously noted, this means building an omnipresent, 24/7 voice channel in order to engage luxury guests during the reservation stage as well as complete customizations and ancillary bookings while on the call. Yes, there's lots of potential here to boost TRevPAR through upselling, but sustaining a well-honed res team still represents a high fixed cost.

And it's not just new bookings that are coming through. Intake teams must also contend with:

- Meal reservations
- Front desk service calls
- Group calls
- OTA confirmation calls (where typically four out of five luxury OTA bookers will call ahead)

To not have these calls roll over to the front desk and potentially compromise onsite service, upscale and luxury hotels need a robust headcount. Yet during the low season, this cost can easily dip from revenue-producing to expense.

We've been brought in by owners and executives in the near past to take a look at how to reduce the payroll, and the best solution involves converting the fixed expense to a variable one. That means recruiting a call center on a per-minute fee – an option that wasn't available many moons ago because these external providers had inferior service and poor conversions relative to the in-house team.

To get some more specificity on this decades-long transition whereby cost-reducing outsourcing partners are now readily available for independents, small groups and other luxury brands that are still scaling up, we engaged John Smallwood, President of Travel Outlook, a call center company whose luxury hotel clients include KSL Resorts and Viceroy Hotel Group.

As education on some of the specific terminology that voice operators use as KPIs, Smallwood added during our discussion about his company, "We average closing more than 65% of the qualified reservations calls we receive, and we also average an 80/30 SLA, meaning that we answer 80% of the calls we receive within 30 seconds. Net abandoned calls are usually less than 5%."

Part of the reason why Mille Club hotel members experience a much higher call volume is due to the convenience of having a human agent complete any manner of customization right on the spot. This has meant that any res team or call center partner has to have custom scripts in order to fulfill specific offerings such as spa rituals, beach rentals, skiing or excursions. Importantly, managers must also establish a seamless process for updating said scripts when there's a special or new feature in order for any reservation agent, internal or external, to effectively sell.

The Future of the Voice Channel

You would think that if convenience is the most important factor then online would rule the day due to the ability for customers to window shop at all hours of the day or night. For most hotels with a limited range of services, this is true.

But when done right, voice will always be more convenient because it allows the customer to get exactly the answers they need to whichever question they have in their mind at that moment rather than scrolling around. Ever on the forefront of how technology can help, Smallwood offered up two advances to consider how to imbue tech into the voice channel for maximal efficiency, ever-better service and further boosts to TRevPAR.

First is the CRM. With easy-to-implement APIs and AI-based connector tools like RPA (robotic processing automation) that solve the problem of double entry, it's no longer the case that the PMS is always the cornerstone of the hotel tech stack. Instead, it's all about knowing who your customer is across the entirety of their spending habits then being able to segment similar guests and find patterns for growing ancillaries, garnering return visits or targeting lookalike audiences.

That's what a well-interfaced CRM can do for you, wherein leading providers like Travel Outlook have their own built-in CRM tools that connect through to hotel marketing databases. To give a sense of what's possible, one protocol that Smallwood has put in place for OTA confirmation calls is to have agents ask all callers for their real email address and phone numbers to see if they want to learn about the best rates and latest information in follow-up communications. From there, the guest profile gets automatically updated in the hotel's CRM, so the property isn't left with a bunch of useless OTA alias emails or duplicate profiles. This technique also works to capture leads for the hotel from callers who don't end up booking at that moment.

The second piece of technology that Smallwood mentioned was conversational AI – a voice bot that recognizes humans and can answer basic questions before passing the call off to a live agent. If a guest just wants to know what time the bar closes, they needn't necessarily wait even 15 seconds in order to get the answer from a human. But if it's a prospective booker with a complex reservation request, the AI can field some initial questions and fill out that information into the corresponding fields to save time for the res agent and for the guest.

For both cases, convenience is enhanced as is total time spent answering the phone. Soon, conversational AI will have the right data integrations to be able to complete basic bookings for the hotel, restaurant, spa or golf independent from any team intervention. Implementing such a tool will be quite the debate for luxury hotels that pride themselves on curating human-to-human interactions as part of their service promise.

To trace back to Travel Outlook's KPIs, if a hotel is able to answer most calls within 30 seconds, then deploying a voice bot might not be necessary. Regardless, to be a Mille Club member the way to add value for luxury guests is to craft an excellent voice channel experience; convenience, responsiveness, customization and knowledge of the product will always be critical. And with every customization request that comes in, there are lessons for how to evolve your ecommerce channels, too.

Forbes Travel Guide Ratings Opinion on the New Relevance of Luxury

Bloomberg Businessweek reported in January 24, 2024 that $1,000 per night was pretty much the de rigueur price point for any hotel room befitting real luxury. Of course, inflation is a contributing factor to this with costs being paid forward to the consumer, but there are many others of significance.

Without going into an entire dissertation on secular trends, there are a plethora of guests from all walks of life and nationalities who are 'price insensitive but highly experience sensitive'. That is, they are willing to pay a premium to get the most out of their time away from home, with a price tag of over $1,000 per night serving a quick litmus test that the services and amenities on hand will match or exceed those expectations.

Another issue related to this litmus test is that the very word 'luxury' has become overused and thus diluted in its connotation. If every brand purports to be luxury, then what's really luxury? That is, how do travelers in this upper-level snack bracket – HNWI (high net worth individuals), business executives or simply those looking for a special occasion – identify which hotel properties consistently deliver value at these elevated price points?

Certainly not from the OTA ratings, where a property can attain a 4.5+ star rating by offering clean sheets, relatively quiet air conditioning, free waffles with artificial maple syrup for breakfast and service with a smile (note: we emphasize that this last one will always be a hallmark of hospitality no matter the brand segmentation). Nor will TripAdvisor provide luxury guests with sufficient data as their ratings are guest-based, and those guests may not necessarily judge a luxury property appropriately on their own experience set.

Enter Forbes Travel Guide, recognized as the world leader in setting the standards that must be achieved for a hotel to be classified as bona fide luxury. Forbes has been in the ratings business since 1958, and with a FTG star rating, there are no half or part levels. A property is ranked as five or four-star, or recommended, with no half measures or leniency mechanisms afforded; you simply are or are not luxury.

To achieve a FTG rating is truly a rarity and an achievement that a property should cherish. Of the roughly 700,000 hotels and resorts in the world, only 0.002% of properties attain this distinction. For the Mille Club traveler who is ever vigilant of the latest luxury hotel openings or renovations in each destination, FTG ratings and magazine coverage articles are essential tools in their product search criteria.

To learn more about this process and how these luxury standards are maintained, we sat down with Amanda Frasier, Forbes Travel Guide's President of Ratings, to discuss how FTG ratings have evolved with the times and continue to recognize the needs of luxury hotel guests.

How exactly has the Forbes Travel Guide rating system changed over time?

Our standards have certainly kept pace with the guests' expectations. The 'bar' for the four- and five-star ratings rises annually. A property that may have achieved a five-star or even a four-star rating half a dozen years ago would probably not maintain this level today without continuous improvements. Of course, physical systems need to work flawlessly and service needs to meet the highest standards. But we go beyond this. Our reviewers are experienced, and in many instances are former luxury hotel GMs. They understand how a hotel works and what defines a luxury property. They are looking for a service that is 'effortless'. In other words, staff is not just going through the motions of service delivery but is performing these tasks in such a way that the guest feels that it is second nature.

Can you explain to our readers what this superior service level is?

There is a certain magical moment that comes when a hotel's staff is so attuned to the guests that they can predict what the guests will need. This effort evolves from experience. It starts with a management team that empowers and encourages staff to anticipate their guest needs and respond accordingly. It can be simple things such as noting their favorite beverage and having it ready to serve, or a turndown service that includes some special elements that reflect the guests' next day. We call this anticipation of needs a true *passion for service.*

How has guest experience entered the Forbes star rating vernacular?
Today, luxury travel is all about experience. The base levels of accommodations are a given. The Forbes five-star guest can be guaranteed a perfectly comfortable room and equivalent service levels. But we're looking for more. We call it, for easy reference, an Instagrammable event or moment. In other words, a stay on your property that is worthy of social media commentary, something that reflects a unique event.

What are the implications for hoteliers hoping to either achieve a five-star rating or maintain their five-star rating?
Never give up. Hire and embrace a team that has a true passion for your guests. Embed the essence of hospitality into every aspect of your business, from housekeeping and valet to concierge and F&B. Decentralize and support decision-making at the guest-contact level. Share your experiences and learn. As a GM or operations manager learn to trust your staff. Be a cheerleader and mentor. You will be amazed at what your team can deliver.

OPERATIONS & LABOR

An iconic Canadian property, The Fairmont Banff Springs epitomizes Rocky Mountain luxury with a world-class golf course, nearby skiing, a thermal spa and onsite programming for a magical experience any time of year.

The Business of 'Busyness' at Hotels

A new phrase that entered the zeitgeist in 2021 was 'Zoom fatigue' for what should be obvious reasons. Besides the strain on your eyes from having to look at the computer screen during yet another conference call, there's far more to unpack here for corporate culture within hospitality.

At the beginning of the pandemic, it was refreshing to see everyone's face as they smiled into their cameras from each respective home office. It alleviated the pandemic panic, the gloom from all the hotel closures and the general loneliness from not being able to gather. Now that this 'COVID moon' phase is long over, we must ask some pragmatic questions about the efficacy of all these video calls. Does everyone really need to attend every meeting? Are daily or weekly standups necessary? Unless someone needs to share their screen, can't we just have a regular phone call and skip the Facetime component?

Addressing the latter question may save your managers from eye burn so that they can devote their precious work hours to looking unimpededly at Excel spreadsheets or one of your various cloud-based operations tools. Answering the former question, though, brings to light some gross inefficiencies that are endemic to many hotel organizations, namely decision by committee occupying too much time and slowing overall progress.

While we would much prefer to quote actual historical figures, there's a line spoken by the late Chadwick Boseman's most famous character, Black Panther or T'Challa of Marvel fame, that demonstrates our argument perfectly. "Two people in a room can get more done than a hundred."

This summarizes much of the profound psychology of group dynamics and groupthink. In many large gatherings, one hierarchically superior voice tends to dominate the conversational flow with numerous others either sycophantically in agreement for whatever reason or hesitant to vocalize their thoughts out of some abstract fear of reprimand. Alternatively, the opposite occurs when an official or unofficial discussion leader seeks out input and consensus from all participants, delaying decision-making and follow-up actions.

These situations are, of course, the extremes but they are nonetheless important to digest because both stymie growth. The answer lies somewhere in the middle and differs for each organization.

Regardless, you start by trimming the fat. Giving the power to your team to make quick decisions and to delegate responsibility greatly expedites the implementation of new plans and new projects; this is immutable although the degree of bestowed power may vary. It can take a lot of time to align multiple executives' schedules. The solution is to let two or three managers hash it out and execute, or at least present a finalized, singular recommendation to those with the right level of authority.

Hotels are notorious for piling on the meetings, starting all the way at the top with the weekly or biweekly executive committee (no offense). Everyone has to attend every meeting when a cursory review of the minutes would suffice – so long as they actually read the minutes.

This is what we classify as busyness in a hospitality sense; team members who justify their roles and salaries within an organization by getting as much facetime, screentime or voice share with colleagues or their superiors. The problem is, of course, that time is scarce. All those minutes spent meeting could well be cycled back into other projects like new initiatives, technology investigations, better guest service and more continued professional development (CPD) to enhance each manager's capabilities while simultaneously reducing their chances of leaving for more fulfilling work.

For many, meeting over-attendance boils down to intrinsic or ingrained insecurity. How will my boss know that I'm working hard if they don't see my face every other day? What will I do with my workdays if I'm not sitting in on these calls and nodding along or voicing my affirmations at the appropriate time? If I'm not on these calls, won't others think I'm slacking off? My boss hasn't given me enough projects to work on, so how will I rationalize my job if I don't make my presence known and constant?

There are some broad ways to address these personal questions, but each requires a fundamental rethink to how your teams are empowered and what their job descriptions really entail.

1. *Fewer meetings and fewer video calls.* This should be readily evident by now. Each attendee should be able to immediately prove why they need to be present. And this applies to general managers or other senior executives whose schedules are consummately overstuffed already. Designate a minute taker so that anyone who can't give a substantive reason can glance over those when they are disseminated. Next, will a mobile call suffice? You can still use Calendly or Google Meets to earmark the time and to serve as a backup for when phone networks are spotty but save your eyes the strain and stick to just voice.
2. *Open-minded work environments.* The boss-employee dynamic is a delicate one, and it's totally natural for subordinates to not want to verbally disagree during a meeting lest they embarrass the boss and suffer the consequences. A good solution is to hold 'office hours' – at the physical office or stated in a memo so that everyone feels as though their superiors are approachable – where anyone can come in to clarify a chosen direction or to voice any trepidations over the current plan. The matter of 'safety' in this instance means that any employee at any level should be able to question or suggest an alternative without reprisal. After all, good ideas can come from anywhere, especially from novices or outsiders who can evaluate scenarios without the bias or blinders of decades working in a single field.
3. *Give your teams more work.* It's often said that if you want something done, give it to the busiest person. After you reduce the total number of meetings and delegate responsibility so that your teams are more empowered to either make fast decisions or coalesce their thought processes into a specific recommendation, you'll soon find that everyone has quite a bit of free time on their hands. Hotels have no shortage of long-term, visionary projects

that are waiting to get greenlit, so to fill this void overload your teams with dense, complex and cranium-straining work, along with review deadlines to keep them all accountable. Another suggestion is to formalize a succession mentorship program as well as internal CPD courses with structured assignments and regular testing. Rewrite each person's job description, then challenge your managers in a sink-or-swim manner and the most likely case is that they will be able to tread water with the best of them.

We cannot wait for a time machine to be invented so that hotels can revert to the way business was in 2019 with its superb guest occupancy numbers covering up much of the past decade's busyness which only served to dampen productivity. Successful hotel organizations going forward will be the ones that save costs by making your teams scrupulously efficient so that you can capably steer the ship while maintaining the leanest possible team.

Adding Some Hospitality to the Next Normal of Videoconferencing

One of the many after effects of the pandemic is the popularity of videoconferencing. Zoom, Google Meets, Skype and Microsoft Teams have made one-on-one meetings easier to attend and more feasible to run.

Given its success and convenience, it's a good bet that videoconferencing will become a permanent aspect of regular business affairs. Now is the time to reflect on how we can improve our communication skills via this medium so that team members are as productive as possible.

As we are in the hotel industry, it's time for us to inject a sense of traditional hospitality into videoconferencing. This will work to boost spirits while also reinforcing a proper sense of attentiveness necessary for when your teams will interact with guests onsite.

As such, here are ten hotel-centric suggestions for getting the most out of videoconferencing.

1. *Review your equipment and location.* Many older laptops lack the RAM to handle or hold video from a camera, while others may have driver conflicts. Those working from their cottages may find that there is insufficient internet bandwidth for videoconferencing. In all cases, audio-only communications may be better as lag or a low framerate can be jarring for recipients.
2. *Know your software.* All videoconferencing programs are slightly different. When dealing with staff, you have likely already subscribed to one application or another. But when it comes to guests, understand that the customer is always king, and you must meet them on their turf. Besides understanding the basic differences between all these programs, one commonality is that it is difficult for multiple people to speak at once, so be especially patient and plan your approach accordingly.

3. *Check your own image.* Lighting and sound are important. Similar to meeting someone in person, what you wear will leave an impression, both for your team and for guests. While it's fun to joke about meeting in your pajamas, the honeymoon phase of videoconferencing is over and perhaps it's time for a dress code to be implemented. Remember, too, you're on camera all the time, so no odd facial expressions, please. I attended a meeting where one of the invitees decided to floss her teeth.
4. *Background check.* If you're working at home, it's often from a desk in a room that might also be a bedroom. But that does not mean we should see an open clothes closet, kids watching TV, or other personal effects. Conversely, the artificial background images available on many applications appear phony and often create odd grayscale bordering effects when you move in your seat. My advice is to treat your background as an extension of your personality, where family portraits and shelves full of books and artwork can also deepen your rapport with other users.
5. *Be punctual.* If you've called a meeting for a specific time, be there a few minutes before to check out your audio, video, and lighting. Don't make attendees wait as this can quickly become a bad habit that others will imitate.
6. *Stick to an agenda.* If you need to, print out the agenda and have it handy for your reference during the meeting. Many people are finding that they have too many video conferencing meetings already, meaning that boredom and frustration abound. Short and sweet ensures that your team's concentration doesn't wander, while perhaps you can also allocate some time at the end of weekly checkups for an open discussion or for others to bring up certain issues you haven't covered.
7. *Avoid wearing headgear.* I know many headsets offer superior sound clarity, but they make you look like a pilot or a taxi dispatcher. This is hospitality, not air travel. You already have the unconscious psychological barrier of video versus in-person to deal with and you don't need another obstacle for effective personal communication.
8. *Consider using the record button.* This may be important if a complex point is being discussed that does not result in a direct and clear next step emerging at the end of the meeting. Proper etiquette also suggests that you take the time to advise participants accordingly so that they don't feel hoodwinked afterward.
9. *Treat the meeting seriously.* Issue a summary or recap of next steps, then send it out within 24 hours of the meeting. With so many younger team members who may not have the necessary self-discipline skills in place, this is critical to keep everyone on track with their objectives and to ensure that all staffers know their specific roles without having to nag.
10. *Get used to it.* While it is hard to imagine a hotel executive committee meeting held regularly this way, it is not out of question. Videoconferencing is here to stay, so you must learn to integrate it as part of the regular workweek.

Two Pizzas for Hotel Manager Meetings

Amidst a labor shortage, hotels worldwide are looking to do more with less, be it digitalizing or automating processes, devising new recruitment strategies, increasing the reward structure to prevent employee churn, or ramping up team productivity by whatever means necessary. All are good ventures, but instead of only focusing on the 'staff' we must also take a sharper look at the 'manager'.

In a lean organizational structure, many managers or supervisors have become, to borrow from baseball, pinch hitters for other departments or all-around utility players able to complete a variety of tasks for a myriad of previously siloed operations. Over the past several years, we've seen revenue managers take on sales roles, ops directors check guests in at the front desk, and GMs change beds. These were short-term measures, of course, but the point is clear: hotelier roles are rapidly evolving, and properties that stalwartly adhere to traditional roles are bound to get left in the dust.

And even as travel numbers tick back up to the pre-COVID golden years, we don't see this 'role amalgamation' reverting. From the owner's ever-pecuniary eye, utility players on the income statement look like more 'utility' – that is productivity – per available player.

But there is one aspect of the average manager's quotidian duties that we've harked on before and deserves repeating. Hotels suffer from too many meetings and too many meeting participants who simply shouldn't be there. The world is moving too fast nowadays, and time is too precious for a decision-by-committee style of administration.

Without writing an entire 300-page dissertation on organizational behavior in the post-COVID era, let's apply a litmus test that we're borrowing from one of the most successful entrepreneurs of the 21st century – Jeff Bezos. Love him or hate him, the man knows how to run a company, and we're sure anyone holding Amazon stock would agree.

This hallowed litmus test that's weaved its way through Silicon Valley is the 'two-pizza rule'. Simply put, any meeting should be attended by no more individuals than can be fed by two whole pizzas.

There's a lot of psychology to unpack here. First, many managers, and even executives, confuse 'busy' or 'work' with realized 'output'. You can table ideas and debate them ad nauseum, but if no decision is made and no subsequent action taken, then it's all for naught. Some managers feel the need to attend every meeting to fill their day and give the appearance of being busy when the whole point of any meeting should be to reach consensus then divide the work up to conquer.

Differentiating between the state of being busy and output should then clue you in to how to reform your company's meetings so that more projects are executed without having to onboard new bodies. Thinking by way of two pizzas, does this person really need to sit in on the meeting? What's their express purpose for attending? Would having them read the meeting minutes suffice? Who is taking these meeting minutes, or at least summarizing the discussion and follow-up steps? Who has seniority to assign or delegate these resultant activities?

This two-pizza rule also applies to video calls. While it may seem polite to include as many managers as possible, let's not forget that humans are naturally horrible multitaskers. So, when you ask someone to attend who doesn't need to be there, they'll end up going on mute and wandering onto unrelated tasks or going into inbox-clearing mode and only performing at mediocre quality levels at best. Again, do these people really need to sit in on the call? Very often, you'll get more done – that is, more output – from two managers hashing it out over the phone than a courteous video call where two managers are compelled to attend and then contribute mere salutations at the beginning and end.

No doubt you may have heard of similar aphorisms that can help make your organization more efficient. We say, "Whatever works."

While the two-pizza rule presents an appetizing visual to make it more memorable, the productivity drives you are currently seeking out in the 'labor' department should be simultaneously conjoined with ways to make your 'manager' time structure more effective – whether they involve food analogies or not. Either way, it's all about attaining a healthier bottom line, for which reducing the number of attendees as well as the frequency of meetings are both great places to start.

An Employee Scorecard to Solve Labor Shortages

A central problem with the hospitality industry's labor crisis is that by framing it as a 'crisis' we are presuming that the shortage will naturally pass by and labor conditions will eventually return to how they were pre-pandemic. Hoteliers have to ride it out and everything will eventually be fine. This is a dangerous mentality; thinking in terms of crises is short-term and the post-pandemic hotel corporate culture requires a long-term solution.

There are several global, decades-long trends at play here, for which COVID was not the cause but an accelerant. For brevity, these can be summarized as:

- Many furloughed hospitality workers reskilled to other parts of the service sector during the pandemic and are reluctant to shift back without sizeable monetary incentives
- Society's acceptance of remote work means that – wages held equal – hotel jobs have to compete against those in many other industries where people have the dual benefits of not having to commute and flexible hours
- Hotel workforces skew old, meaning a higher rate of employees retiring, with many opting to hasten their exit in light of the pandemic
- Natural retirement rates in hospitality are not being adequately offset by youth because the best minds in younger generations are now drawn more toward seemingly higher-paying career prospects in other industries
- As advanced economies continue to gray and lifespans increase, this in turn, expands the demand for high-touch workers at long-term care facilities, with this role a contiguous competitor for hospitality jobs
- Many hotels in advanced economies rely on a labor pool that's largely comprised of immigrants, and while the pandemic temporarily depressed

worker entries, the greater trend is that modern systems favor 'high skill' applicants in STEM or entrepreneurs, both groups being reluctant to work as a 'low skill' front desk clerk, server or room attendant

When you stop and seriously think about these forces, it becomes clear that the real new normal for hotels in the decade ahead is one fraught with ongoing labor headaches. "Where did all the workers go?" we often ask ourselves these days, either in executive committee meetings or to panelists at industry seminars. The answer is 'everywhere' and that's perhaps the most unsettling of all.

A systemic problem requires a systemic solution. Hotels are guest-centric businesses and now we need to become employee-centric to drive team retention by providing a handful of incredible non-wage incentives.

To put another way, treat your employees well and they will in turn pass that goodwill along to your guests. This echoes the golden rule in many ways.

The proof is in how you lead that charge, instilling your managers to act accordingly. A caustic approach from the top will not only be detrimental to the entire organization but also do little to remedy a situation in the long run. There are numerous managerial training programs that can be offered while setting up an internal employee wellness program is also highly beneficial for everyone coming to work at a hotel.

But while training courses and anything wellbeing-oriented takes time to implement and see veritable results, the here and now always starts with the top of the chain of command. What can senior managers, general managers, directors, executives and owners do to instill an employee-centric culture as a means of fighting the labor shortage battle?

Here is a starting checklist to rate yourself on your management approach. Ten items, each scored out of 10, for a final score of 100. Honestly appraise yourself as follows:

1. Are you honest and open to your team? Are you transparent in your approach? Do you work at instilling confidence in your team members? Do they trust you?
2. Are you a walk-around manager? Do you regularly eat in the hotel cafeteria? Have you visited engineering, housekeeping and other BOH functional locations on at least a weekly basis? When was the last time you sat in on a sales or catering presentation?
3. Do you know your employees by name? Do you have regular events where you can meet with them? Can you say that you know them beyond just work? After all, they have families too.
4. Do you consider yourself to be fair and equitable? Do you adequately reward your employees for their efforts?
5. Do you listen to your team members? Do you seek their counsel on issues that relate to their area of expertise and influence? How receptive are you to new ideas?

6. The hotel business is not just ADR, RevPAR and percentage occupancy. Do you understand all aspects of your business? Can you converse with the teams in purchasing, reservations, IT, sales, catering and marketing? Can you use your PMS and complete a check-in? How up to date are you with your own website?
7. Do you motivate your team to better themselves? Do you have to repeatedly ask employees to carry out tasks as instructed? Are your instructions clearly defined both in exact procedure as well as their underlying reason for execution?
8. Do you actively seek to promote from within and encourage this succession planning? Do you have plans that encourage your team members to see their position as part of a career in hospitality rather than just a job? Do you have a program in place to upskill associates into managers?
9. Do you keep abreast of what is happening in your community? Do you encourage your team members to participate through appropriate behaviors such as recognition or compensatory time off?
10. We all know that a bad apple can ruin the basket, as can a bad employee. Are you appropriate, fair and consistent when you deal with these potentially toxic situations? Do your actions set a moral example for the rest of the team?

While many of these are more qualitative than quantitative, the exercise should nevertheless offer some introspection. Let's say an 'A' score is 80 or above, but this is still no excuse for a fixed mindset and not seeking continuous improvement. For everyone else, time to set aside your current approach and re-evaluate. The current labor market demands it!

Reexamining the Communications Hierarchy for Centennial Guests

It seems like just yesterday we were talking about how to adjust your method of communications to better appeal to millennial guests. Now that the first of this cohort is about to turn 40, it's time to turn over a fresh leaf and look at the next rising star in spending power.

When discussing a 'communications hierarchy', what we are first trying to do is rank all forms of communication from most to least influential. It's a matter of guiding potential customers up this ladder, knowing that the more influential the form of communication you are using, the more likely the sale.

Applying for groups as well as transients, this hierarchy is something I've trained hospitality sales associates and managers to use for over two decades now. It dictates that when you want to create a sense of trust, devotion or urgency, you elevate the communication medium to one that's more intimate. If only it were that simple which this latest grouping of travelers!

Traditionally, the communication hierarchy would comprise, in descending order:

1. In-person meetings
2. Videoconferencing
3. Handwritten notes
4. Phone calls with quiet backgrounds
5. Phone calls with noisy backgrounds
6. Personalized emails
7. Personalized text messages
8. Social media direct messages
9. One-to-many digital or print messages

Love them or hate them, the youngest demographic will soon have the spending power to make or break your hotel's revenues, so it's important your team is communicating with them the right way to maximize the L2B ratio as well as guest satisfaction.

Centennial Characteristics

While much as already been said about the millennials and their 'unique' problems, know that the centennials (otherwise known as Gen Z or the iGeneration) can be even more confounding for us boomers and Gen Xers (and even older millennials) in terms of their thought processes and methods of communication. This will require an astute understanding of their preferred mediums, particularly favoring channels for rapid mobile communications – essentially messaging platforms – over phone calls, voicemails or emails.

Not holding back any punches, millennials are often labeled as entitled, nonconfrontational, overly sensitive and a bit flaky but also whip smart and ingeniously intuitive. The same can also be said for their successors. The centennials represent the most intelligent generation yet; the problem is they know it and it's already gotten to their heads!

Growing up without ever knowing a time before cell phones and social media has made them think differently than us old farts. The broadest inference from this is that they are all inherently tech-fluent and have therefore come to expect everything to be accessible through their phones. For your customers, digital payments, mobile service requests and all necessary information must be available to appeal to this demographic. Also beware if your app or website doesn't have a seamless interface as this creates brand distrust.

Critically, as is being increasingly researched and documented, social media is not a replacement for face-to-face communication and the relationship skills developed therein. Ergo, one big problem amongst centennials is that they've grown up in an environment that espouses the former as a direct substitute for the latter, often leading to poor social skills such as bad eye contact during meetings, being afraid to pick up the phone for a sales call or hiding behind their voicemails.

Centennial Communications Hierarchy

Despite these annoyances, for your centennial workforce I'm optimistic; with the right explanation and a touch of empathy these skills can be trained. For your guests, the customer isn't always right but they're still in charge.

In other words, you can't compel them to conform to your desired communication medium but instead must meet them where they're most comfortable. This often results in young guests avoiding phone calls with your reservationists or not responding to emails while simultaneously replying without hesitation to messages received via WhatsApp or FB Messenger. While in times past, I would coach sales managers to always opt for a phone call and, if that didn't work, push for a meeting (or at the very least a Skype chat).

Due to the contributing factors for this profound generational shift, the communication hierarchy needs to be amended as follows:

1. In-person meetings
2. Personalized text messages
3. Social media direct messages
4. Videoconferencing
5. Personalized emails
6. Phone calls with quiet backgrounds
7. Phone calls with noisy backgrounds
8. Handwritten notes
9. One-to-many digital or print messages

Meeting face-to-face will always be the most powerful way to develop rapport, but alas time is fleeting. As such, SMS comes second as it's a direct way to reach your sales target, but you aren't triggering them by demanding an on-the-spot answer like you would unconsciously communicate with a phone call. Also of note here is that handwritten notes, while previously valuable due to their oldfangled connotations, have shown to have little effect on centennials, primarily because they don't open their mail!

There are many implications for your operations here and making the transition in your sales or reservations protocols is a major task our consultancy helps hotels undertake. Critically, you need a strong guest messaging platform that can filter all incoming inquiries onto one system so that your team can then seamlessly coordinate the requests across multiple shifts and different personnel. Such platforms must, of course, be able to send outbound replies back on the guest's preferred channel.

Beyond this, it is a balancing act of understanding who each guest is so that you can best cater to their specific needs in a manner by which they want to communicate. Just as digital mediums are still evolving, so too must you be observant to how centennials adjust their behaviors and on a regional basis. No doubt we will soon be updating this communications hierarchy yet again!

The Real Cost of Housekeeping Is the Replacement

The biggest line item for nearly every hotel's operating costs is the housekeeping department. That isn't going to change any time soon as rooms need to be cleaned in order for them to be resold. Yet, we strive to continuously optimize this expenditure, be it through overtime reduction, inflationary wage controls, automation, or other smart labor management tools.

The two of us caution, though, that there is a hidden cost here that hoteliers aren't properly weighing within their analyses – the resources spent in finding replacement workers. There's a lot of talk about the increasing costs of running a property and how hourly wages need to be kept in check, but perhaps this is the lesser of two evils.

Just think about what happens when a housekeeper leaves in terms of total replacement costs:

- Your property may not be able to clean all rooms and make them available for resale, limiting occupancy and gross revenues
- There may be interruptions or full cessations of specific services impacting guest satisfaction
- There may be interruptions or full cessations of amenities impacting ancillary revenues
- Human resources must spend more time on recruitment and screening of new hires
- Paid overtime increases while these overworked room attendants are more likely to burn out or accrue an illness that leads to short-term disability leave
- You may have to use sign-on incentives for new hires
- Veteran team members must devote time to onboard the new hires
- And when veteran team members depart, you incur a loss of leadership, which can stymy training, team morale, accounts payable (impacting supplier relationships) or brand innovation

All told the cost of letting a good team member quit is greater, in all but a few cases, than the cost of keeping pace with local market wage benchmarks (or national benchmarks in the case of the more mobile managerial roles).

Turnover is thus the critical challenge for hotel labor across all positions within the organizational structure. Before the pandemic, housekeepers were in short supply. Now, they are still sparse, while executives must also contend with supply shortages and churn in other departments as well as amongst the managerial ranks. To resolve this scourge, we need to fundamentally rethink our approach to employee incentivization.

This rethink starts by more scrupulously examining the turn cost of turnover in relation to what it takes monetarily to keep apace with market wages or comparatively fair compensation. Beyond this, hotels must look to non-wage incentives and technology to help right the ship.

To close with some tips and tricks, hoteliers should consider the following:

1. Use big data labor reports first to understand how their wages and salaries for key roles compare to market benchmarks, and then actually use this information to stay ahead of competitors
2. Deploy smart labor management tools to incentivize housekeepers through such features as seniority-based room cleaning orders, flexible shiftwork scheduling and 'cloning' alerts
3. Cash tips for room attendants dropped precipitously during the pandemic, yet now there are a few QR-based digital tipping platforms that can help hotels reactivate this financial incentive
4. Take employee wellness seriously by making it a process of continuous reevaluation, focusing on nutritious staff meals, mental health programming, group exercise classes, teambuilding offsites and redesigning back-of-house spaces to incorporate more uplifting, 'green atmospheric' design

The End of Daily Housekeeping Marks the End of Traditional Hospitality

Let's dig up the now classic hotel ops debate: To clean or not to clean. By the title, it should be clear where we stand (especially for upscale or luxury hotels). Nevertheless, with labor issues omnipresent for hospitality – both supply and cost – this will always be an issue to decide.

Are you considering changing your brand standards to only offer daily housekeeping on demand or for an extra fee? It's a big question with lots of contributing variables. This article is not meant to be a polemic against the global industry shift away from offering daily housekeeping, but more of a 'buyer beware' in that there is a profound loss to the overall hotel experience that will result, regardless of any post-pandemic or generational changes in customer expectations.

In today's climate of spasmodic and market-specific labor shortages, we have heard many arguments that go against daily housekeeping as well as meaningful discussions in favor of cleaning only on a check-out basis.

The three strongest ones are:

1. Eliminating stayover cleans or offering them only by request is the only way to contend with current labor conditions, both insofar as staffing challenges and inflationary costs.
2. Whether it's due to the rising number of Gen Y+Z customers, business travelers who barely use the room or hotel guests on average just don't value daily cleaning, or even turndown service, with certain categories like luxury and resort properties as exceptions.
3. To a lesser extent, technology has now caught up whereby opting in for daily cleaning can be both automated on the individual room cleaning assignment level and, potentially, upsold with frictionless updates to the guest folio.

Penny Wise Pound Foolish?

This discourse is largely happening as a by-product of the COVID era, as many of guests still fear that having a housekeeper in their suite who may leave behind some sort of viral residue, despite all the work that cleaning product suppliers have done to upgrade their sanitization solutions and to ramp up general awareness. Our opinion is that, while there are still some guests who will be forever triggered by the mere thought of COVID, the concern is gone. The world wants to travel as unencountered as is physically possible.

As for trying to mitigate the rising costs of doing business, this is where we see problems in a 'penny wise, pound foolish' sort of way. Despite the work that alternative accommodation providers like Airbnb have done to change the general perception about this service, we firmly believe that daily housekeeping is a core differentiator for traditional hotel products.

Hotels are in the hospitality business, and yet increasingly it's the accountants who are running the show, using metrics that may not wholly account for the gamut of emotions of each guest as they traverse the grounds from check-in to check-out. While we respect the enticement of reduced costs through cutting the most expensive and labor-intensive department, this is the very foundation of our business that is being questioned.

Think deeply about this question: what separates a room for rent from a hotel guestroom? While the answer may differ for brands at the select service and economy spectrum, our belief is that, once we give up housekeeping, we've thrown in the proverbial towel (pun intended).

Over the long run, if you remove housekeeping then what is your brand promise? For example, if a mid-tier brand no longer offers daily housekeeping, then what other core services will they have to keep guests loyal besides points?

The Eyes and Ears of the Hotel

Mark our words: housekeeping is vital to our industry. Firstly, room attendants are a key touchpoint with the guest. They are our eyes and ears on the guestroom floors. By getting into every room every day, they protect our asset and also help us to protect the guest. Good housekeepers identify maintenance issues when they are minor – say, a leaky faucet – and summon an engineer before the issue becomes more serious (possibly to the point where the room needs to be taken out of service, thereby impacting revenues).

By their visibility alone, it is near impossible for a guest to create an act of malfeasance that would harm the property, themselves or other guests. And indeed, there are a few very significant and unspeakable examples of this. On this note, we also wonder if there is a fiduciary responsibility by the innkeeper to protect their guests' welfare through regular inspection. Not being legal experts, we'll set this one aside.

Secondly, there are now several brands that entice guests to forgo housekeeping in return for increased loyalty point accumulation. On an apples-to-apples comparison, this looks good; it promotes more onsite amenity utilization in the way that the guest wants. But we ask: who ultimately pays for these points? When you factor in all the knock-on effects and hidden costs, the burden falls on the individual property.

The Hidden Costs of Forgoing Daily Cleans

Sometimes costs are counterintuitive. You would think that sunsetting stayover cleans would be a great and universal cost saver for hotels in the midscale and premium categories. But oftentimes (and as we have verified firsthand with ops teams when conducting a property evaluation for a client), the lack of daily touch-ups to the room results in sizeable cost overruns and time pressure for check-out cleans.

These overruns, as measured by extra minutes per room, can lead to an inability to turn all the rooms around in time for resale that same day. The end result is you can't max out occupancy on certain days of the week.

This change of events harks at the core of the cost-efficiency problem. Big brands may be shooting themselves in the foot with their scrupulous cost-cutting ventures. On paper, they are saving on wages, but a deeper analysis may reveal that the benefit to gross revenue optimization outweighs increased costs of wages as well as reducing housekeeper turnover by providing better job security through more hours each week.

Ultimately, and this is still our opinion, the death of daily housekeeping will spell the death of brand differentiation. When this happens, you may as well convert every mid-tier property into select service then just have an AI engine choose the nightly rates according to demand indicators, with only a skeleton crew onsite and regional management to optimize GOPPAR.

A hotel world without housekeeping is not the industry that hoteliers have entered, at least not in a traditional sense. Even though times are changing, we must nevertheless decide what are the immutable parts of the hotel experience. Review our arguments and prove us wrong about daily housekeeping being one of those parts.

How Will Tipping Work in a Cashless Hotel

The deployment of cashless payment solutions, a necessary commercial change, spurred by the pandemic is now continuing post-pandemic. Indeed, many businesses have taken the additional step of banning the use of cash altogether. But there's a problem here as this approach disrupts our service tipping mode. This may result in demoralized staff or lead to costly wage increases.

Hotels are only as good as their service delivery which ultimately depends on our frontline teams to execute. But for many who depends on tips for their livelihoods (at least here in a North American capacity), how will they be motivated to give some genuine 'service with a smile' if their critical tip component of their wage package is eliminated?

This is obviously a concern for the restaurant, but it still affects room attendants, bellhops or many other guest-facing roles. Without the ability for said workers to collect gratuities, they may be less motivated to perform above expectation while on the clock or, worse; they may decide to seek another employer who can provide this largely cash-based perk.

Thinking quite broadly and over the very long-term, as we slowly transition to a cashless society, tipping may become less common to the point where it deters people from entering the industry, thereby restricting the overall labor pool. While punching in a tip percentage into a credit card PED is just as easy as leaving a few extra bills on the table; the issue is that the electronic records make it far easier for the tax department to verify a server's real earnings – that is, less disposable income resulting in one less reason to start at the bottom of the hospitality rung.

Here are some other thoughts to consider if your hotel decides to go permanently cashless:

- Eliminating cash has the strong benefit of helping reduce fraud because every transaction will require some form of personal verification
- A fully cashless hotel opens you up to a myriad of cybersecurity threats, so it behooves you to audit your systems to identify any gaps where data breaches may occur
- A fully cashless hotel also opens you to more card-not-present transactions where chargebacks can become a huge nuisance, meaning that you should only PCI-compliant payment methods
- Without having the ability to accept cash, you can get rid of that gaudy ATM in the lobby, and come to think of it you can also get rid of the front desk as these first emerged as glorified cash registers, instead opting for a tablet-based, PMS-synced app with roving front desk agents
- Customers arriving at your restaurant must be well-informed that no cash payments are allowed so that you don't run into any problems when the bill comes, and of course you should set up solutions that allow hotel guests to easily add F&B charges to their folios
- To compensate for the cash gratuity dilemma in the restaurant, add other non-monetary perks to the job to keep your teams motivated
- While disseminating tips via EFT is more time-consuming for your accounting department than just handling out an envelope full of cash at the end of each week, there are quite a few automation platforms that can now be deployed

What the Data Reveals About Key Pre-Stay Questions You Can Automate

There's no panacea to the labor crisis hotels currently face. Instead, the best solutions are often the ones that help you to continuously improve the productivity of your existing team. This is why the two of us persistently extol automation, especially those solutions that are easy to onboard and offer a series of nifty applications well beyond their original aim.

Many of us may try to shrug off staffing woes as a transitionary consequence from all that pent-up travel demand post-pandemic. Economic trends suggest the exact opposite. Our present labor challenges are not temporary; they will be a topic of discussion for the rest of the decade!

This puts automation and great tech platforms front and center, where, per the title, we see great strides being made in pre-stay guest communications. In looking for those nifty applications, it's important to consider how a hotel's pre-stay comms fit into the greater tech ecosystem, where you should always look to deploy those platforms that are not one-off solutions but have a robust feature your organization can grow into over several quarters or longer.

When it comes to pre-stay guest communications, hoteliers should be able to digitize what customers are asking about and then analyze this data to determine how to improve operations or anticipate service needs. To help shed some light on what guests are talking about in advance of their stays, we worked with Bruno Saragat, a product specialist at ReviewPro, a Shiji Group brand, to get aggregated data so that you can make rational inferences to drive product enhancements.

The Need for Automating Pre-Stay

To start, let's breakdown this part of the customer journey, which covers both before guests book (for clarity, what we will heretofore refer to as the 'prebooking' phase) and before guests arrive (the 'prearrival' phase).

Guest behavior differs slightly for these two stages of the journey but the needs for both stakeholders (hotels and customers) should be obvious.

1. *Prebooking.* Immediate answers to questions prevent 'reservation abandonment' by keeping customers engaged in order to secure more room revenues
2. *Prebooking.* Automating responses about your facilities and amenities to deliver this information immediately will increase guest confidence to drive package bookings and ancillary spend
3. *Prearrival.* Quick answers to questions demonstrate high quality guest service to set the pace for a great stay and, ultimately, better post-departure satisfaction scores
4. *Prearrival.* Automating repetitive questions saves your front desk time from having to verbally answer these through live chat, over the phone or once the guest is onsite

With these broad benefits covered, what specific questions are most commonly asked by guests? How can knowing these top guest inquiries be used to improve the hotel product?

While automating responses via a chatbot is indeed highly advantage, where ReviewPro also shines is in the next step – performing semantic analysis to inform what hotel teams should focus on and where to allocate budget. So, let's dive into the data that Saragat provided, which was tabulated using a sample of anonymized aggregate data from over 650 properties using ReviewPro's AI-driven Hotel Chatbot system.

Key Inferences from the Data

What we looked at was the 'volume of conversation' numbers concerning specific topics brought up by guests during prebooking and prearrival then tagged by the system to categorize them.

Reservation doubts.

- By far the biggest category of questions posed by customers pertained to online booking issues, prepayment or problems with the reservation process in general.
- Hotel brands should thus pay extra attention to making their messaging crystal clear on every prebooking channel, be it the website, an OTA or within a standardized response within a live chat.
- As well, if a particular error is found to be commonly cited by guests, this can indicate an immediate upgrade to the booking engine or website to make the reservation process more frictionless in order to avoid abandonment.

Property and guestroom facilities.

- Questions about what was available onsite and in the room represented the penultimate inquiry for the prebooking stage and the third-most for the prearrival stage.
- In both cases, quick answers can be make or break for securing the booking or incremental pre-stay revenues from guests.
- Much like reservation doubts, if your own data indicates specific amenities or facilities as frequently asked about, this may also mean they aren't visible enough on the front-end website or another marketing channel.

Parking and transportation services.

- Interestingly, this came in third at the prebooking stage but not in the top ten for prearrival, encompassing airport pickups or drop-offs, directions, car rentals, taxi services, parking location and valet services.
- What we gather from this is that many guests prioritize the logistics of getting to a property into their booking decision.
- Moreover, this finding may also suggest the setup of various transportation services as a paid add-on (run internally or through a partner) as well as the perceived value of bundling parking in packages or blasting the word 'free' if you offer any services complimentary to visitors.

Pet policy, check-in and check-out.

- Coming in as the fourth, fifth and sixth most frequent for the prearrival stage, it's clear from this that seemingly basic questions like, "When's check-in?" are still very much top of mind.
- But there's also an opportunity here where you can use the semantic data to help sell add-ons. For example, if a high number of guests are indicating a preference for a late check-out, then maybe it's time to package this service or offer it as an automated upsell prompt whenever a guest requests it or even asks what the standard check-out time is.
- As for pets, if you're getting lots of inquiries related to bringing dogs into the rooms, this data can support the move to carve a section of the hotel as a pet-friendly room category (and charging an additional cleaning fee).

Nearby places.

- As another intriguing inference, questions about area attractions and what's in the immediate vicinity came in second for the pre-arrival stage, only slightly behind guests asking about the cancellation policy.
- Similar to our suggestion about all things transportation, popular inquiries here can indicate modifications to your front-end website and onsite (be it an in-room tablet or other display screen) messaging about what to do nearby as well as the setup of experiential packages or new partnerships with neighborhood vendors.
- Knowing that this is a popular question for prearrival but not necessarily for pre-booking can also indicate that most guests aren't mentally ready to consider filling out their day plans right at the time of booking, and too much information at this pre-booking stage may lead to reservation abandonment.

From Questions to Revenues

Guests ask questions because they care about getting an answer. And behind most questions is a 'silent majority' of other guests who had the same thought on their mind but didn't bother to reach out. By itself, this principle suggests that all questions posed throughout the entire customer journey should be encouraged, commended, aggregated and analyzed to inform future product developments.

As you can see from some of the inferences derived from the data supplied by ReviewPro, it should be clear that pre-stay guest inquiries offer an end-to-end opportunity for improvement. If lots of customers are asking about valet, perhaps it's time to set this up and charge for it (as an add-on or bundled). If the data shows that incoming travelers are keenly focused on visiting one particular nearby site, building a value-added package around this attraction will surely be well-received.

If there's a mantra to remember from all this, it's that revenues are built one question at a time. Beyond the prospects of using automated tools like a chatbot to prevent booking abandonment and save your team time, getting more data on what guests are asking helps to focus your resources and more effectively answer, "What do we do next to grow the brand?"

The Post-Pandemic Hotel Experience from the Experience Expert

This article was originally published in December 2020, and Joe Pine's indicated opinions at the time of this writing may not reflect current positions or trends.

As COVID continues to upend travel and rewrite daily habits, hotels must nevertheless continue to differentiate their products to better appeal to guests in the next normal and build revenues. While much needs to be done insofar as safety upgrades and facilitating a contactless customer journey through tech enhancements, it all inevitably comes down to the guest experience.

And so, I turn to the man himself who coined the phrase 'The Experience Economy,' Joe Pine. A thoroughly affable man based out of Minneapolis, his ongoing writing, speaking engagements and work with businesses from all sectors reveal that we mere mortals are in the amidst of a great transformation from the 20th century, service-centric approach to how we treat customers, and into one where time is the key value-add.

As organizations come to familiarize themselves with the psychological principles underpinning the experience economy, it becomes increasingly clear that the future of any company depends on how well they treat their stakeholders and how they can enrich the livelihoods of consumers. While most hoteliers are already well-versed in the need for a memorable guest journey to drive satisfaction, rate, loyalty and return visits, it's nonetheless refreshing to hear it from the commander-in-chief of experiences to see what else brands can do in the face of so much pandemic-generated uncertainty.

Is the experience economy still relevant in today's current environment?

Absolutely! The experience economy isn't going away; if anything, the coronavirus has accelerated the shift from goods and services to experiences as the predominant economic offering. For the pandemic makes us realize that, at least in the first world, we don't need more stuff. We have enough stuff! What we really value are the experiences that give life meaning and experiences with our loved ones, our friends or even our colleagues.

Of course, so very many of those experiences are not possible right now, as anywhere people gather is a place most people don't want to be. But people are social beings and crave experiences. So right now, we are shifting those experiences from 'out there' to 'in here', from the physical to the digital, from the public to the communal. When the pandemic winds down through herd immunity via one or more vaccines, then physical experiences will come roaring back (as they already have to the limited capacity governments allow).

Service culture has been the mainstay of hotels, particularly at the luxury end. How does that work in a world of contactless accommodations?

Oh, the *service* can work perfectly well in a contactless environment! Many hotel services were already contactless, such as cleaning rooms, setting out amenities, preparing breakfast and so on. Now it will accelerate the trend of checking in and opening guestrooms via an app and other ways of contactless service.

So much of the hotel experience, though, happens in the encounter between guests and staff, and the latter will have to work even harder to make personal connections and create meaningful encounters in a time when people don't want to touch others. They will need to fully understand that their work *is* theatre and act in a way that engages guests no matter what distance exists between them. Services are about the 'what' – the functional activities workers perform – while experiences are about 'how' those activities are done. Workers can turn any mundane interaction into an engaging encounter by focusing on how they do what they do.

More of the experience will be delivered digitally, accelerating the trend that started with premium channels on the TV, videos on demand, Alexa voice units in the room, robot delivery and so on. And that will make every personal encounter even more important to the overarching experience.

Post-COVID, what changes do you anticipate the consumer will expect insofar as experiences?

There will be lingering effects for many people, perhaps most, regarding all the hygiene aspects that hotels embraced so quickly – particularly when people realize that they are so much less likely to catch the flu as well. So, they will want to be safe from any sort of virus or 'catchable' disease, which means that part of the experience hotels offer will need to be 'safety theatre'. That is, not just ensuring that the hotel is safe (first for employees, then for guests), but assuring guests by *showing* that the place is safe.

The other thing I think will become more important as personal encounters are lessened is for the hotel experience overall to be more personal – that is, customized to each individual guest. The guiding light here, I think, is Carnival Cruise's Ocean Medallion program, which enables a personal itinerary for each guest (or family) on a cruise. For example, micro-geographically pinged order history data can tell the operator that when you are on the pool deck with your kids that your favorite drink is an iced tea with no lemon, then when you are at the bar with your buddies, it's a mojito, and in the restaurant with your spouse it's a glass of Shiraz.

What can hoteliers do to recapture the magic of experiences?

Hoteliers should be preparing now for a post-COVID world. First, they should (already!) be refreshing their places to make a great first impression, including the safety theatre I mentioned earlier. Second, they must redesign their offerings, in particular working hard to provide more engaging, memorable and remarkable experiences by making them robust, cohesive, personal, dramatic, and even transformative (as we put it in our 2020 re-release, "The Experience Economy: Competing for Customer Time, Attention, and Money"). Finally, hoteliers should be looking to renew their capabilities to provide new possibilities for the guest experience, in particular, digital capabilities.

Anything else that you want to add?
Well, one major trend in tourism right now fits well with the last two imperatives I just mentioned – transformational travel. People are most open to change when they get out of their daily routines, so seeking self-change while traveling is proving to be a big opportunity to which hotels can cater.

A Decade Ahead for Post-Pandemic Hotel Experiences

Guest expectations and desires have changed coming out of the pandemic – that's a no-brainer. But thinking beyond the pent-up demand that's being released during this present travel recovery period, how do you evolve your brand for the near future? Your managers and frontline staff are all likely overworked (and that won't change any time soon!), so you need a clear vision about the long-term before devoting any capex or implementing any changes that will distract your team from other crucial tasks.

This brings us to the concept of the Experience Economy, which was forged in the ante-COVIDian times by Jim Gilmore and our current interviewee, Joe Pine. What this concept proscribes for hotels is to not only think about 'heads in beds' but how to imbue more positive emotionality into the experience, from pre-arrival and onsite through to post-stay and continuing the relationship. You aren't selling guestrooms so much as you're selling the pleasure of having a great place to stay. For this, there are innumerous ways to 'experiencize' your property or your brand, so many in fact that there's likely a book or two written on the matter!

More recently, Joe Pine has taken the idea of the Experience Economy one step further through what's called the Transformation Economy. As aided by modern technology, this concept describes how it's no longer just about how businesses can deliver great experiences but how these brands can improve the livelihoods of their customers. To offer an abstract hospitality example, a day at the spa represents a great 'wellness' experience, but if it's accompanied by some take-home lessons for the guest then this one touchpoint may work to enhance this guest's 'wellbeing' for the long run. With this in mind, let's learn from the experience master.

Based on what you've seen, what brands in the hotel or restaurant space are at present properly capitalizing on the Experience Economy?
High-end hotels are the ones that tend to get it and have the money to do much of it well. I'm thinking of the Ritz-Carlton, Fairmont, Four Seasons, Oriental Mandarin and, of course, The Peninsula. L'Ermitage Beverly Hills is a boutique hotel that uses technology well, including never having cleaning staff knock on the door when you're in the room.

In restaurants, there are a number that follow my long-held prescription to charge admission for the experience, including Next in Chicago, Trois Mec in Los Angeles, Open Concept in St. Louis and Noma in Copenhagen. In fact, Nick Kokonas, the co-founder of Next, created the software platform Tock, a booking platform that lets other restaurants charge admission. And I'll mention SevenRooms, a great platform for knowing restaurant guests and their preferences.

Can you cite any examples of brands using technology to enhance an onsite experience?

Number one in the world at this is Carnival Corporation with its Ocean Medallion system on Princess Cruises. This experience platform elevates the guest experience for everyone on board by knowing everyone, their desires and preferences, and what they like to experience. I'd also point to the theme park industry for how to bring technology into experiences of all stripes, including 3D virtuality, augmented reality, projection mapping, IoT devices, and on and on the list goes.

Picture yourself in a hotel in five years. What technologies are in place to enhance the experience beyond what's currently deployed?

I expect the room itself to be a platform for a customized guest experience. Everything will adapt and morph to my needs, wants and desires, which the experience platform will have learned from past visits and carefully pay attention to this current stay. For example, no more going through the guide of channels on the TV; it will present the channels I tend to watch most, which would never take up more than one screen's worth of space. Today, I'd be happy when there's enough light somewhere in the room to read, and the lighting of the future will match the intensity, the color, ideally, the locality to what I prefer most. And the customizable bed will be preset to how I like to sleep.

Switching to this idea of the transformation economy, how will this change the hospitality industry?

I think going beyond staging experiences to guiding transformations has great promise for the hospitality industry. In fact, transformational travel is already one of the fastest-growing sectors! There are primarily three facets to it. First is personal transformation, where people may be seeking mindfulness, digital detoxing, skills enhancement, or mental, physical, emotional, and spiritual growth. Second is family transformations, heading outside of the home environment to enhance the relationships with their spouses, children and loved ones. And finally, societal transformations, where people desire to be a force for change in the world. Even when the primary purpose of travel is not for transformations, hospitality companies of all stripes should search for the aspirational jobs that guests have to do.

What are some initial steps that hotels and restaurants can take to get involved?
The first thing I always say is that companies need to understand what business they are in. If hotels and restaurants think of themselves as in the service business, providing only 'time well saved', then they will, over the long term, become commoditized. But ascend to the proposition that you are in the experience business, offering 'time well spent', and that will jumpstart your ability to thrive in today's Experience Economy.

It probably doesn't make sense to think of yourselves as in the transformation business directly – that right now is for fitness centers, medical clinics, life coaches and so forth – but do recognize the transformation potential of your experience offerings. As we wrote in "The 'New You' Business" in a recent issue of the *Harvard Business Review*, you can become one part of a total solution that people use to achieve their aspirations. And if you work hard to employ an experience platform that learns about each individual guest, you will be able to uncover not only the functional, emotional and social jobs they want done in hospitality, but the aspirational jobs as well. Then, you can find your role in fulfilling those jobs for your individual guests.

Addressing the Slow Burn Challenge of Hotel Operations Succession Planning

For the decade ahead, hotel companies face a generational challenge – namely, a lack of strong succession planning to protect a property or brand's legacy. Yet because this problem isn't as clearly defined as the before and after of 'The Great Resignation', senior teams may not prioritize a slow burn issue like the gradual depletion of bright young minds from our industry as these candidates opt for other career paths due to a variety of intermingled factors.

This is precisely why succession planning should be addressed now, whereupon cultural and operational changes will then have a progressively positive effect on a hotel's ability to retain talent even as the industry confronts a series of abrupt demographic changes.

"One thing we all know well is that the industry must be agile and able to pivot quickly at all times," commented Janis Clapoff, the managing director of El Encanto, a Belmond Hotel in Santa Barbara, California. "Succession planning prepares us for a quick response and gives us that resilience during challenging times. At Belmond, we have identified the importance of mentoring in our organization to preserve brand integrity and reputation. Mentoring also shows high-performing employees that the company is interested in their growth and development."

Successional Causes

For context, it's important to first understand why large swaths of the hospitality industry may continue to suffer from ongoing labor shortages, both for frontline staffers as well as for managers possessing strong enough skills and tenacity to one day become executive leaders. Knowing the causes helps define the framework for effective actions.

As an opening caveat, though, we say 'may' because this is a complex situation that varies by location and (gasp!) we may be wrong about the durability of these factors. Actually, the two of us hope we are wrong because if all these causes compound, the result will be a dire brain drain over the long run.

Starting back from the opening paragraph, while the media alerted the world during the latter half of the pandemic about this Great Resignation, for hotels in many markets, a better label would have been 'The Great Reskilling' as the furloughs combined with lingering fears over COVID spread and the haphazard stop-start nature of the reopening efforts compelled many to pivot and retrain for other jobs within the broader service sector.

Concurrently and more systemically to hospitality, our salaries just can't compare to other industries like finance, technology, or real estate. Now well into the post-pandemic era, every company must also contend with the dreaded 'H' word – hybrid. While other industries by their very nature can better facilitate remote work and flexible hours, so much of hotel operations is hands-on and in-person that this is impossible for us to do on a consistent basis.

Next, when you consider the mindsets of Gen Y and Gen Z, surveys reveal that, on average these younger cohorts feel strongly about corporate values related to ESG (environmental, social and governance) and DEI (diversity, equity, and inclusion), and are willing to sacrifice higher compensation to work for a company that aligns with their beliefs. Particularly as the climate crisis deepens and travel is singled out as a primary contributor of carbon emissions, hotels that aren't sustainable may soon be deemed as undesirable places to apply for a job, with any robust monetary incentive met only with apathy.

Generational Solutions

Whichever way you feel on these issues, it's much tougher to fight the river than to flow with it. That is, for every one of the causes there is a feasible solution, albeit one that's never a quick fix but part of an ongoing virtuous circle of change management. Getting back to basics means getting down to core values and firmly embedded processes.

"Initially, we consider the business needs. We identify that handful of key positions that need a robust plan in place where an absence would present significant operational issues if the position became vacant," stated Stephen Johnston, the managing director for The Boston Harbor Hotel. "After the business needs have been addressed, we consider the needs of the individuals. It is never a precise science. Some managers are happy with where they are; not everyone aspires to be a general manager. Others are highly ambitious and feel the need for continuous upward movement. If these signs, a willingness to take on more responsibility, are ignored and individuals don't receive opportunities to grow, they will lose faith in the business and seek opportunity elsewhere."

To contrast Johnston's systematized approach, the two of us often hear complaints about the perceived entitlement of younger hires who often deem themselves worthy of being a GM within six months of onboarding. While this may be a result of growing up in an era of pervasive social media and instant gratification, what's critical is to lay out the lines of personal progress and expectations more transparently for performance. From there, continuing professional development (CPD) with gamified elements combined with the personal touch of direct mentorship will more than offset any communication or work style differences between novice and veteran.

"Succession planning starts with knowing your team and their aspirations," added Vikram Sood, the managing director of The Inn at Rancho Santa Fe north of San Diego, California. "Some activities to encourage this effort include a formal mentor-mentee program with monthly check-ins to allow leaders to really understand their team members that have an aspiration to grow, the use of a bench strength worksheet that tracks all the information surrounding a team member's growth aspirations and providing honest feedback throughout the year. Never just use the formal review system."

Technological Succession

The cultural side is a process, but so much of hospitality nowadays involves an interconnected web of management systems that we would be remiss to exclude a minor note on technology's role in succession planning. Namely, there are two critical progressions at play that will help hotels improve their talent retention efforts.

First, the migration to the cloud means that this is less loss of records whenever a manager leaves or during a turnaround situation because the information is restored remotely instead of offline within hard drives and Excel files. This means that new personnel or recruited teams can have immediate access to accurate metrics or forecasts and are never demoralized by having to sort through inconsistencies or devote significant time to data re-entry.

Second and simultaneous to the implementation of cloud-based platforms, various disparate vendors are amalgamating their graphical user interfaces or developing strong data feeds into other systems. The result is that younger hires who are accustomed to sleek, intuitive systems such the apps that they're already familiar on their phones don't feel bogged down by having to cross-check a dozen screens every workday – an effect now described as 'dashboard fatigue' – and can have all the insights they need to plan their next move all in one place.

Ultimately, the slow-burn challenge of planning for the next generation of hoteliers may be rooted in organizational culture, but investments in technology cannot be ignored as a contributing factor either. Every hotel is different, so the exact needs are also different. Nevertheless, having an outlook of constantly supporting young hires and actively listening to their needs is what ensures that your property or brand's legacy is protected for years to come.

Framing Hotel Operations with the Peak-End Rule

If you haven't read Nobel laureate Daniel Kahnemn's 'Thinking, Fast and Slow' (2011), don't worry; its applications for hotels, while manifold, can be neatly summarized. Notably, this book goes at length to explain the 'peak-end rule' based on psychology experiments conducted in the decades prior by Kahneman and his collaborator, Barbara Fredrickson. With travelers rediscovering the world of hotels in the post-pandemic era, you should learn this principle and think about how it may apply to your brand.

The peak-end rule describes a shortcut that the human brain uses to condense information about past experiences in order to save space for other functions and present experiences. Unlike how a computer compresses code by (more or less) evenly omitting repeating or algorithmically decipherable data to reduce the number of megabytes taken up, the brain focuses on preserving two key moments within a broader memory or experience – the peak and the end.

We all live and breathe the 'guest experience,' but really this term is a bit of a simplification. What we actually mean is the sequence of mini-experiences the guest encounters from pre-stay to post-departure that are evaluated in one's mind to determine an overall appreciation for the brand.

Focus on the Departure Experience

The 'peak' in this rule may be more complex to define and to create, but the 'end' is clear as day – the check-out and departure. So much emphasis is put on the check-in experience that we may be neglecting other aspects of operations that may, psychologically speaking, have a substantial influence on how your brand is remembered, reviewed and recommended.

That's not to say that checking in isn't critical; great first impressions set the pace for a great stay and will buffer the peak by allowing for a higher high (a good check-in) or suppressing what maximal can ever be attained (a mediocre or bad check-in). In this sense, it works a lot like compound interest. But the human brain isn't so simple, with the peak-end rule revealing why you must also improve the departure experience to optimize satisfaction.

Here are some thoughts:

- A proud and sincere 'thank you' always goes a long way
- Introduce a bit of theater into your gratitude by making it a grand team gesture
- Personal farewells from a senior manager or a team member who had extensive contact with the guest
- Departure gifts in the form of unique mementos related to the property, the brand or a specifi experience that the guest partook in
- Departure gifts in the form of snacks and drinks for the road
- Refreshment beverages available during the check-out process
- Any kind of surprise and delight

- So often, check-out is depressed by the transactional part of it, implying that you should aim to use technology to shift the guest folio settlement away from the physical check-out
- If the last thing you are giving a guest on check-out is their invoice, then you are leaving them on a sour note that should be avoided or masked by something else

To reiterate from the opening paragraph, a brand's ability to curate an exceptional departure experience is further complicated by guests who want a contactless check-out, settling their folios via their phones and eschewing direct contact with the front desk. If you don't know when guests are leaving, how do you tailor a great departure so that they leave on a positive note?

Tech to the Rescue

Integrations are allowing you to home in on the mini-experiences that are bringing down the average in the guest's mind. Sitting with the aforementioned contactless check-out, perhaps the same technologies that facilitate the online folio settlement and check-out can also send a ping to the front office team so that they are aware of an imminent departure.

Maybe that online check-out can be equipped with a message prompting the departing guest to head somewhere to receive their gift or snacks. Or maybe the solution lies in how brands manage the post-departure aspect of the customer journey. There are lots of options to get creative.

Next, think of the departure as the end of the end, with the overall stay as the aggregate of a bunch of different experiences, each having its own peak and end. How can you map this using internal systems or hotel review platforms? This will help you look beyond the departure to build higher peaks and thus create a more positively remembered onsite experience.

In the Restaurant

On our ledgers, onsite F&B is kept separate from the rooms, but they are jumbled together in the guest's mind. Hence, a great dining experience halos positively back onto the perception of the rooms.

Taking the peak-end rule into account, while an amuse bouche or complimentary breadbasket may come standard at your signature dining outlet, these both start off the experience rather than end it. Yes, a great start allows for a loftier zenith, but to create a lasting upbeat sentiment amongst patrons, consider, for example, a few free house-made truffles presented after the bill.

Such a small gift helps to shift the end from the check (transactional) to a sweet, thoughtful dessert (memorable). This would go over even better if you can identify beforehand whether it's the guest's final night at the hotel – yet another reason for better PMS-POS integrations.

Traditionally this post-meal gift is the mint's role, but there are a few key differences between these two presentations. Truffles are far more elaborate than mints and, when combined with the made-in-house aspect, they really drive home the implication that you truly care. Next, present them after instead of alongside the bill so that the truffles are the final thought and not the dent in the guest's wallet. It doesn't have to be truffles per se; Greek hotels excel at crafting a strong finish with restaurants often leaving a complimentary small bottle of raki (a digestif) on the table for you to enjoy after settling up.

A whole book could be written on how hotels have gone to great lengths to create memorable peaks and pleasant endings, often without ever having heard of the peak-end rule. Beyond the restaurant, how can you apply this psychological lesson to other services? What tech can you deploy to get granular on all these mini-experiences? The point throughout is to focus on these two aspects of the hotel journey and seek out ways to elevate just one element for lasting results.

SALES & MARKETING

With over 3,500 rooms across three different hotels, Resorts World Las Vegas offers an incredible selection of dining, gaming, retail and entertainment options, requiring a literal army to run and astute marketing leadership.

Hotels Need to Measure More Than Just Revenue

Hoteliers live and breathe guest experience. That's what we're classically trained in, but most of that is absorbed as a soft skill or codified in an SOP paper manual. For the past couple years since the pandemic compelled our industry to automate processes, though, data science has now converged to offer us strong business intelligence tools to digitalize all these moments to propel profits and brand advocacy forward. But in order to build the dream, we have to stop thinking only in terms of topline revenues.

We've all attended the weekly pickup meetings where we scrutinize the key stats of occupancy, RevPAR, and ADR benchmarked against a predefined competitive set in tandem with production from discounts, incentives, and active promotions. We're not advocating that this practice be abandoned; rather, it should be upgraded, with major market forces and demand curves factored into these standups in a streamlined, digestible manner.

In essence, you want to imbue enough digitized and quantifiable measurements into your operations so that your hotel becomes a data company. From there, you can test hunches or use a machine learning algorithm on your data set to find the interstitial relationships between all the real goals like revenues, reviews, and return visits so that you can discern whether you are actually improving. These are tasks we are excited to tackle on behalf of hotel clients because there's so much that can be recorded nowadays to help drive operational success, however, that is defined.

Restaurant Soft Metrics

A hypothetical restaurant offers a simplified example of this before we circle back to the multifaceted operations at a given hotel. For a dining outlet, easy metrics may include gross revenue per day broken down by food and alcohol, average revenue by timeslot or average revenue per cover. You may even want to get more granular and go dish by dish or drink by drink, as well as total covers by time by day, average turn time, percent of covers that ordered dessert, and so on. All these can be observed if you have good management software

But what would softer observations tell you about meal satisfaction like the average tip amount left or how many dishes went unfinished? You likely already know that someone who didn't tip and didn't clean their plate was likely dissatisfied and won't be coming back willingly any time soon. It's not a certainty, of course, but smoothed out over hundreds or thousands of similar covers will give you a more accurate picture of what's impeding loyalty and all the benefits that come along with having a strong customer base. These might be hard to record, though, and you may only get qualitative answers from your supervisors.

Other questions may require a big data set to infer more complex answers like if there's a relationship between certain food orders and alcohol spend. For instance, if you find that two or three dishes consistently result in minimal beverage spend then what's your case for keeping them on the menu? Do tables of four spend more per person than tables of two? This can suggest configuration changes.

The question is why. What indicators from these soft metrics can you use to incrementally improve guest satisfaction and revenues?

Hotel Reviews as a Soft Metric

In a search to measure what really matters and what can influence hotel revenues, sentiment analysis tools become instrumental because with a lean team you don't have the time to ask about then accurately act upon anecdotal inferences like the lack of tips or unfinished meals as indicators for dining satisfaction. While integrations take time to complete, there are nevertheless lots of preexisting 'soft data' points for you to scrutinize, which we define as any recordable events that may influence bookings and overall satisfaction but aren't necessarily direct inputs to either.

The clearest of these data sets are your online reviews. Besides addressing those one-star TripAdvisor reviews, are there any popular keywords that can be used to augment your marketing materials. Aggregated mentions may even inform what will increase look-to-book ratios, how to build meaningful packages or promotions and where to earmark future capex to drive long-term asset value.

Are you using in-stay surveys for error recovery? What measurements will signal to you that you have indeed recovered, besides not seeing a negative online review pop up? As an idea, you could test a loyalty subscription prompt after a negative in-stay survey then measure the relationship between who signed up and additional onsite revenue capture. This would require some more integrations into your PMS or whichever system is housing your guest profile data, but luckily the technology exists to do this.

Becoming a Data Company

Going a step further requires you to think of your business not as a hotel brand but as a data company first. How are you using your paid search, website analytics, and booking engine analytics to get a better sense of the customer purchase pathway in terms of any points of friction or where people are looking for peak versus off-peak? Are you able to set up either the front-end website or the booking engine with A/B testing to more precisely determine what works best for driving on-the-spot conversions? Can you deploy an AI to perform up-to-the-minute yield management so that you can improve your abilities to maximize rates relative to market?

By thinking in terms of getting data on everything, you can then see why technology advancements like attribute-based selling (ABS), guest messaging chatbots, AI-driven phone IVRs and in-room voice controls are important.

For ABS, if you were to reconfigure each room category's text-based features into a database, then you could see which of these amenities are motivating sales. This can lead to a reordering of those features or new room classifications.

Likewise, with chatbots or anything voice-related, you are in essentially digitizing guest requests that would typically be handled by a live agent, via direct message on social media or within an email exchange. Getting more data on what people are asking and when will help to reduce inquiry abandonment and drive conversions.

There's a ton that can be done, so for now just think about what data you are recording as well as where that data is being stored. Beyond augmenting the service that current guests receive and derive more revenues from customers who find you, big data will ultimately help with forward-looking travel intent and efficiently discerning lookalike audiences to optimize tight marketing budgets.

Per the title and as you can hopefully see, there's a lot more than just measuring revenue that can contribute to a better bottom line. It's an exciting time for hotel technology, and we're looking forward to helping properties realize tremendous success with it all!

Tech-Driven Segmentation for Bleisure and Beyond

A hotel's future can no longer be sufficiently bucketed into only leisure, corporate, and groups. Hoteliers know this, but the obstacle nowadays is too much information. There are legacy systems that are difficult (and expensive) to integrate and lots of disjointed guest profiles – also known as data silos. Nevertheless, the need for system consolidation and unified guest profiles, particularly at the enterprise level, becomes all the more critical with the renewed drive for customer segmentation.

Emerging segments abound. Bleisure is classically inscribed for business-primary guests who then extend their stay to see the area or experience a property's amenities. Similar but different, workcations came to the limelight during the pandemic to describe those knowledge workers who can get their projects done remotely, oftentimes eschewing the home desk for a change of scenery at a nearby hotel. Then there are the straight-up digital nomads who have no office shackles and, as the name implies, prefer a more itinerant lifestyle.

These trends are reaching the mainstay at the exact moment that hotels need more guests. While there are lots of stats showing that travel numbers will defy the economic gravity of a recession, the reactionary throttling of household discretionary spending – namely vacations – tends to only reveal itself as a lagging indicator. Meanwhile, midweek occupancies aren't looking so hot as companies are loathe to give up the huge cost savings from the videoconferencing boom by returning to the days of overly generous corporate travel budgets.

Regardless, the overarching trend for the rest of the decade is that travel experiences are more widely valued across all demographics, but guest behaviors and guest demands have both undergone radical shifts. Brand loyalty is eroding and top-of-funnel marketing is more expensive, meaning more attention must be given to specific psychographic targeting in order to tap into market niches. Further, with operational costs going up, hotels must drive more revenue per guest (TRevPAR) through packaging, upselling and cross-selling of amenities.

Put another way, segmentation in this manner is to know your customer (KYC) more deeply in aggregate so that any hotel can optimize performance without cost overruns. Segmentation lets a brand identify the most fruitful sales channels, the highest TRevPAR guest types, opportunities to anticipate service requests, and agile, cost-effective marketing tactics.

Here are some examples of how tech-driven segmentation can you optimize revenues:

- If you use the OTAs, do you devote the advertising budget to Expedia or Booking when the former produces more bookings but, in analyzing your internal systems, the latter has a longer LOS and more significant F&B spend at the restaurant?
- How about a peak summer weekend at a seasonal property that has sold out in the past with high-TRevPAR leisure couples, and this year, the sales manager has brought forward a wedding RFP where the group occupancy is guaranteed, but the actual per-guest spend may be lower.
- Suppose you want to develop a wine lover package that's exclusive to past guests who have been identified as such via past package purchases, welcome amenity purchases or restaurant spend history, yet how would you do this nimbly if your POS data isn't currently cleaned and merged with guest profile data from the PMS, CRS, or GEMS?

To get accurate predictions for these sorts of differential segment-versus-segment situations, data integration into one central storehouse becomes an ever-critical and ongoing task to complete these calculations in a timely and labour-light manner.

Bleisure is an even tougher nut to crack because you are trying to change the standard business traveler behavior of arriving, focusing on the work then departing as quickly as possible. Conquering this obstacle requires contextual data – that is, the how and when behind your conversion funnel.

For instance, a business guest makes a reservation two months prior to the date of arrival but only opens your room upgrade offer message that's sent seven days out. Or maybe your automated prearrival email-based upselling isn't working, but SMS offers sent out three days prior are converting.

Testing for then getting differential context like this requires a lot of well-oiled techs to do without overloading your reservations or revenue teams. But the benefits are long-lasting. If you can start by figuring out the bleisure segment and what compels these guests to buy, then you can apply the same methods and systems to solving any other segment.

Above all, we stress that the future of hotel operations will progressively be influenced by the hunt for greater and greater TRevPAR and more granular KYC in order to micro-target specific audiences. Bleisure is a great place to start for this grand goal because it will help drive midweek and off-peak revenues, both places where most hotels could use a little boost.

Ending Seasonality One Week at a Time

The seasonal ebbs and flows of occupancy are real. Rural resorts endure this challenge and must make grand adjustments in staffing to accommodate budgetary fluctuations.

But while necessary measures must be enacted, wouldn't it be great to instill within your hotel a bit of marketplace immunity? That is, give your guests a reason to stay with you during any sort of off-season, irrespective of price incentives.

What you need are one-of-a-kind programs, and this is a key objective in our consulting practice, where we look at how to make a hotel such a unique experience that guests will want to stay there despite it not being the 'ideal' time of year for that locale. In the North American and Western European setting, this means building programs outside of the traditional summer and early shoulder peak travel seasons.

For this, you must appeal to customers' demands for something exceptional beyond what they already get when the kids are off school during summer and the weather typically cooperates. Travelers are using the OTAs to research new drive-to destinations and you cannot depend on return visits for the sake of returning; if you don't have a unique experience, guests will look elsewhere.

The beauty herein is that it is a very creative exercise in figuring out what makes each hotel unique to thereby discern what this typically one-off event will be to draw guests in. All of this planning is conducted well before any marketing efforts and ideated in concert with the promotions team, so that you have an early litmus test for what will actually work.

What we caution here is that slow and steady wins the revenue race. Even though you likely have many periods throughout the calendar year where occupancy isn't ideal, you have to pick your targets at the outset and not overextend yourself. Less is definitely more and as such, you should only target a week per quarter in any given year because customer mindsets are very hard to reverse all at once.

Based upon my work in setting up these events to help grow occupancy during the off-season and end any drastic seasonal downturns, below are a handful of key considerations, for which we are open to discussing these in more depth on a property-by-property basis.

1. *Plan far ahead.* For any new program, you should aim to have the bones of that event in place at least six months ahead of the actual date or dates when it runs. This is critical so that the marketing team has time to devise an appropriate plan, get approval for the budget and hone the messaging while you iron out the operational details.
2. *Theme is crucial.* Any event or weekly course of events you plan must seem like a natural fit for your hotel and your territory. This 'theming' makes the sales and marketing process along with any secondhand word-of-mouth drastically easier.
3. *Exclusivity matters.* Whether you decide to go with a tasting dinners' program, a wellness seminar, or form a limited partnership with a local provider, you need a good selling hook to wrap around your pricing and packaging. Strive

for an experience guests cannot easily attain anywhere else and you'll be off to a good start.

4. *Target past guests.* It's an age-old mantra that getting existing customers to act on your promotions is far easier than new ones, and this applies here, too. Email lists, CRMs, sales records and newsletters are your best friend in making the necessary announcements, but only if people are given sufficient notice to plan their travel ahead of time. That said, with people being digitally marketed to death, you have to engage them electronically on a one-to-one level with unique offers that demonstrate you know who they are.
5. *Shoulder season creep.* Rather than start a program in the middle of your off-peak season, consider experimenting first in a week that adjoins your current shoulder season. Focus on a week that traditionally paces below average but is a logical extension to your current high demand periods. This will also make it easier from a staffing perspective.
6. *Live and learn.* While there are numerous tales of unbridled success for these events in their first year of operation, the majority take several to ramp up. Plan for a small-to-medium sized event in your first outing so that you never sacrifice on service delivery. From there, you can improve each subsequent program with a grander scale and heavier promotional efforts to fill your loftier expectations. Finally, once the event has developed some cachet, only then can you move it to a weaker time slot that's deeper into the slow season.

Blended Travel as a Huge Growth Opportunity with Words of Wisdom from Marriott

Call it bleisure or hybrid travel; then look at emerging segments like the work-from-anywhere digital nomads or workcations. Overall, the hotel industry for the rest of the 2020s will see a demise of the days of wholly separated meeting and events (M&E) and leisure travel segments, giving away to a mixture of the two as travel becomes more experiential and purposeful. It behooves hotels to adjust their commercial strategy and property improvement plan (PIP) to meet this trend, with some guidance from what the Marriott team has observed to help you navigate this great shift.

Suppose a business professional visits another city for a convention then sticks around for the weekend to catch up with friends. Or a nomad executive opts to have an extended stay in a certain market for lifestyle reasons then fits in some meetings with clients who happen to be in the area. Or maybe a conference attendee's spouse decides to travel with them, with one working while the other enjoys the hotel's amenities and works remotely. All are possible nowadays as are plenty others.

Whatever the intent, travel going forward will increasingly blend the two primary purposes of business and vacation. And that will mean new ways for hotels to incentive emerging customer segments, drive longer length of stay (LOS), upsell add-ons, encourage direct bookings through bespoke offers and grow ancillary spend per guest (TRevPAR or RevPAG). This, of course, has profound implications on services, amenities, operations, spatial design and renovations.

To get a sense of just how big this opportunity is for hotel brands and certain properties as well as highlight some examples of success, we sat down with Julius Robinson, Marriott International's Chief Sales & Marketing Officer for the United States and Canada. The key takeaway is that based on what Marriott is forecasting, both on a per-property level and across entire markets, blended travel has only just started to ramp up its impact on the hotel industry.

The Current Boom of Blended Travel

First off, why is the best term to describe this progression 'blended travel'? This was the opening point of distinction that Robinson highlighted during our time together and it's important for readers to note. For one, 'bleisure' is a bit too much of an industry insider's term, but more importantly, it doesn't fully encapsulate all the various primary and secondary travel purposes that people are mixing and matching as they design their personal itineraries. That's where 'blended' comes in; it's simple and universal.

Edge cases aside, one of the clearest primary travel purposes for the 2020s is business travel – this being one of the market segments that continue to proliferate in the post-pandemic era even as others have normalized. According to 2023 report by the Global Business Travel Association (GBTA), this segment is expected to recover to its pre-pandemic total of $1.4 trillion this year then continue to grow to nearly $1.8 trillion by 2027. Moreover, from the surveyed business traveler respondents, 62% say they are more frequently blending business and personal travel than they did in 2019, with 42% adding additional leisure days to their business trips, and 79% of these travelers staying at the same accommodations for the business and vacation portions of their trips.

However promising these metrics sound, they can brush over so many emotional aspects of travel that really come into focus in light of the pandemic's lockdown policies and the concurrent growth of remote or flexible work arrangements. Namely, humans strive for social, in-person bonds; that's baked into our DNA. As recent events have shown, our well-being suffers when we are isolated, and company executives are now fully aware of the detrimental effects of poor mental health on productivity and team retention.

So, because remote work is also a trend that's here to stay due to its personal incentives center around better work-life balance, hotels will therefore play a profound role going forward in facilitating those personal connections when most employees working out of their home offices and don't regularly see each other face-to-face.

"What we've seen is that the role of MICE hotels has changed substantially in the face of remote work," commented Robinson. "Whereas before, events were mostly designed around a single-purpose conference or event venue, now the demand and planning is for more dynamic, experiential spaces that can help facilitate teambuilding, group activities, breakout sessions, and collaboration. In more ways than one, hotels are becoming a company's best friend to foster team bonds when every employee is remote or hybrid."

Blended Travel Across Generations

The growth of flexible or fully remote work arrangements is but one trend that's feeding the resurgent demand for corporate and MICE travel. As Robinson revealed, this is only the beginning as numerous markets all over the continent are seeking consistent growth in M&E of all sizes. During the initial stages of recovery, most group demand was for SMEs, but this year large meetings are back, with a strong pace of bookings for the next few years.

The nature of M&E has changed, though. Planners are requesting nontraditional venues, such as outdoor setups, complex audiovisual, elaborate F&B stations to demonstrate local culinary excellence and reimagined creative spaces. As an example (to boast our own national pride for Canadian ingenuity!), at the Muir, Autograph Collection in Halifax, groups can combine a meeting space with a rental of the hotel's 36-foot private yacht. For another example, Gaylord National Resort & Convention Center recently unveiled Harbor Social as a purpose-built networking space with shuffleboard, air hockey tables, duckpin bowling and a sports bar. It's open to the public, but can also be sold as a breakout space.

In a word, Robinson said that travelers are looking for 'moments' – those micro-meetings and novel experiences that only hotels with a wide range of amenities can provide. As psychology has shown, when you change the setting, you change the energy by creating space for new moments to form. This is why traditional dinner party etiquette dictates that a good host should never serve dessert in the same room as the main course. That's also why events that utilize multiple venues on a property tend to be much more satisfying for individual attendees and, ultimately, more beneficial for the host company.

Supporting this trend for more experiential, moment-driven venues, we also find ourselves living in a very interesting time in history where we have four different generations in the workplace: baby boomers, Gen X, millennials, and Gen Z. All have different values and travel motivations, and yet it is the younger generations that are driving much of this present evolution as hotels look to engage Gen Z with shorter sessions and gamified, interactive activities.

"Millennials and Gen Z really want to know a destination," noted Robinson. "They want localized events from their host hotels. But when it comes to incentivizing longer LOS, hotels need to keep them informed on local happenings during the prearrival phase to help them build out their itineraries."

Marriott's Guidance to Grow Blended Travel Revenues

With access to aggregate demand data and intimate knowledge of what's working at various properties across the United States and Canada, Robinson offered some great advice for hotels looking to boost their blended travel revenues, Whether that's incentivizing the shoulder nights of before or after a conference, or better accommodating the 'plus one travel' persona with more onsite ancillaries to fill out one's day while the spouse is in session, this approach typically comes down to a combination of sharpened use of technology and a PIP.

The Marriott team's local reps will offer bespoke advice and best practices to sales personnel, looking at market trends or popular types of F&B programs, but it's deeper than that. As an example of where automation enters the picture, the Sheraton Orlando Lake Buena Vista has become a popular destination for meetings because corporate travelers can bring their families who can hang out by the pool or go to the kids camp during the day, but also because as a perk planner can opt for complimentary, electronic tickets to Walt Disney World Resort for the entire group block.

Deeper than this and what integrated business intelligence (BI) can tell operators about ancillary utilization, the Marriott team also conducts site inspections and an in-depth consultation before any FF&E upgrades to help refresh a property to meet blended travel demands while also being reflective of the brand and locality. For another Florida example, the recent renovation at the JW Marriott Marco Island Beach Resort included a new restaurant concept, 10K Alley, as a pseudo-Dave & Buster's with arcades, bowling and mini-golf. It fulfills the need for dynamic breakout spaces, but significantly because it's all indoors it also helps the resort for M&E during the sweltering, off-peak summer weeks.

As a final case study of where a PIP can intentionally drive blended travel revenues, Robinson discussed The Westin Washington, DC Downtown where a newly transformed, wellness-oriented space on the lower level with no windows was fitted with an elaborate lighting system so that these meeting spaces would resemble natural sunlight to refresh the mood of all conference attendees. But as these spaces are designated as wellness, they also have flexibility functionality for when events aren't in session.

Ultimately, as you can see from these examples, blended travel presents a lot of opportunities for those hotels that embrace its experiential, flexible, energetic qualities on the strategic level. This may require some capex to bring your spaces up to date, but the rewards will be there insofar as revitalizing underperforming or non-revenue-generating parts of the hotel.

And as this trend progresses and as Robinson emphasized, guests will continue to crave dynamic events and want to design itineraries that combine business purposes with personal extensions or other ancillary add-ons. But hotels have to meet travelers with great amenities and spaces, as well as with seamless technology to integrate all these experiences, in order to realize big gains from blended travel.

Forecasting Fundamental Made Flexible by Great Technology

In hotel revenue conference sessions, they're now calling it 'The Taylor Swift Effect'. Within moments of announcing the next locations for her Eras Tour, hotel rates in the chosen cities spiked, often three or four times higher than normal for the given dates, as fans rushed to secure accommodations. Behind the scenes, it was the adept combination of forward-demand-driven revenue management systems (RMSs) and their revenue director masters that let some properties swiftly (pun intended) seize the moment to ensure no income was left on the table.

While this effect, if you can even call it that, is an outlier, it speaks to the broader trend of just how unpredictable forecasting for hospitality can be in today's era of rapidly evolving guest segments and sweeping changes to customer behavior.

For instance, at the beginning of 2023, many portended a recession on the horizon, with both FITs and business travel plateauing after the post-pandemic revenge travel was satiated during the previous year while companies were bound to tighten their wallets as they opted for videoconferencing over in-person meetings. Both of us were somewhat in this camp and, oh, how we were wrong. Leisure? Fully back to 2019 levels. Corporate? Crushing it. Groups? It might as well be the 'Year of the Conference'.

Still, despite our own humility in not being totally in the money with our predictions, what we can offer is guidance on how the macro-trends will likely influence travel for the year ahead. Primarily, we emphasize that the classical approach to forecasting both the demand side (bookings) and the supply side (necessary opex) still very much applies, but that hoteliers need an added layer of flexibility that can only really be facilitated by the deployment of sophisticated, interconnected technologies.

Forecasting Fundamentals

Before proffering any thoughts on the future, it's critical to note that the overall process to planning for next year is still very much intact, with human oversight being the visionary judicator for how to execute any strategies that will drive reservations as yielded as possible and ancillary spend, no matter how erratic the forecast-to-actual ratio becomes.

Typically, the forecast is generated internally by the sales team that develops a group budget based on known business projected on a (hopefully) weekly timeline along with some estimates from citywide events. Tour operators and corporate sales are also included based upon month-over-month quotas from each key account along with other promotional activities that modeling suggests will be productive.

It's a lot of work but a relatively straightforward process. While the goal from ownership or the executive level is always to be bullish on rate, revenue on the books is still revenue, and it's often better to lock in a slightly discounted income source than to risk empty rooms that could've been sold.

Segmented Customer Trends for Next Year

Now the fun part of suggesting how travel will progress through the course of next year, and then scrubbing the entire internet when we are proven wrong. Jokes aside, our goal is to give a wide berth for each of the following so that you can plug and play how they apply to your own business model.

1. *Hybrid travel.* Call it bleisure or remote work, or workcations, or digital nomadism. Whatever the specifics, the bigger trend is that there are now more tech-enabled knowledge workers than ever before, with pandemic-born policies enabling this cross-generational cohort to be more flexible with the where and when behind their given jobs. It behooves every hotel brand to look at strategically promoting leisure as an add-on to any business or group trip, using a combination of price incentives and frictionless merchandising technologies to accomplish this. While uptake may be relatively minor, a win is a win; finding ways to activate your bleisure travel using the latest business intelligence (BI) and RMS tools, and then incorporating this into your forecasts will give you resilience during any purported downturn.
2. *Meaningful meetings.* Everyone thought groups were dead with the rise of Zoom and Teams. But as we soon learned, nothing replaces a great handshake. Instead, the purpose behind M&E has shifted. Gone are the road warrior, one-night-only affairs, replaced by more dynamic and experiential gatherings with a longer LOS on average. We attribute the adjective 'meaningful' to describe this transition, wherein winning that next contract may require a justification from your sales team for how your hotel will enhance the event's purpose. Especially given the rapid turnaround time on RFPs that many group travel planners are expecting nowadays, this may seem like a burden, and yet that 'how' often inscribes enhanced BEOs, more space rentals and larger room blocks. Nowadays, you can in fact use best-in-breed sales and catering platforms in combination with robotic processing automation (RPA) to automate many of the rote tasks necessary to get a proposal together then itemize tasks once the deal is done.
3. *Channel transparency.* With the sheer onslaught of online travel resources that both leisure and corporate shoppers must compare rates and brands, guests as a whole are more agnostic than they were before the pandemic and, in many cases, the look-to-book ratio remains agonizingly short. This is where flexibility comes in as hotels must have both a tech ecosystem and a cultural disposition that favor being nimble in responding to abrupt market changes. This is also where segmentation comes into effect, as comp sets are no longer static and can vary by guest type. For example, when it comes to groups, a downtown hotel with a conference center may be competing against other centrally located properties with spacious meeting facilities in other cities, while at the same time, the leisure segment's comp set is entirely hyperlocal. Many of the latest BI or RMS vendors can offer support in this segmented benchmarking, while there's also an entirely new subcategory of event intelligence platforms that are purpose-built for this task.

The Supply Side of Forecasting

While the three trends speak to traveler evolutions, in hospitality it's always a bit of a dance between demand forecasts and keeping your supplies as efficiently allocated as possible so that you simultaneously never have cost overruns due to lower-than-expected property utilization or aren't optimizing revenue because you didn't anticipate occupancies at that level.

On the one hand, having intelligent and automated inventory management and procurement systems will help to smooth out the supply chains so that you are always in the Goldilocks zone – not too low where services may be compromised and not overstocked where you have an onerous carrying cost.

But with the biggest line item being labor, that's where your attention should fall. An example where you can go wrong here would be an attempt to curtail housekeeping wages that results in an inability to turn rooms around during a high-demand weekend and the hotel can't maximize occupancy. Tighter labor costs can be achieved using the latest systems that can review past inputs from a variety of on-premises and comp set data sources to equate forecasts more precisely with actuals.

"Smaller hotels, especially owner-operated businesses, may ask "Why do I need labor management software?" Labor management tools like Hotel Effectiveness are essential because these properties have fewer team members in total, which means each labor error or missed optimization opportunity has a substantial negative impact on a P&L," added Adam Glickman, (former) VP of Brand Strategy at Actabl, the parent company of Hotel Effectiveness.

"For properties around or under 150 rooms, using labor forecasting tools to derive reductions in turnover rates, fewer no-show shifts and savings from unqualified overtime can easily produce big, incremental gains in total profitability. For less than the cost of a shift per week, owners can see direct productivity and overtime benefits, as well as have additional peace of mind, especially in markets with more junior and inexperienced managers working day-to-day in the business."

Ultimately, whether there's a slowdown or if we keep on motoring, the macro forces are beyond your control. What is, though, should be incorporated into your plans. Know the fundamentals of how forecasting works, rethink how some of the changes in consumer behavior may continue to evolve travel, and then use the latest and greatest tech to stay as flexible as possible.

Creating the Entertainment Capital within the Entertainment Capital of the World

Las Vegas is a city that lives on reinvention to keep drawing ever-larger crowds to this oasis in the desert that, for full transparency, wouldn't even exist if it weren't for the entertainment industry. While the world's entertainment capital started out with gaming, shows, and conventions, in recent decades, it has also become a culinary mecca and now a world-class sports destination.

In the post-pandemic era, more hotels across the globe are looking to expand upon their core rooms ledgers with leisure and entertainment (L&E) components. This is a natural progression of the push for more F&B, wellness, and other ancillaries to help drive revenue per guest (TRevPAR) during a time when global occupancies are forecasted to be normalizing. So, with more competition in the hospitality L&E from around the world, Vegas must reinvent itself yet again.

Perhaps no other resort on The Strip epitomizes the need for strong L&E programming than Resorts World Las Vegas (RWLV). Launched during the pandemic, this 3,506-key property has had the uphill battle of competing against established players as well as cultivating the best possible lineup of talent, nightlife, and F&B outlets to provide consumers with a veritable 'reason to visit'. Adding to these challenges, RWLV has partnered with Hilton Hotels and has to position its three different room products in ascending order: Hilton, Conrad and Crockfords (also marketed as part of Hilton's LXR Hotels & Resorts brand).

All this hinges on raising awareness and marketing to feed the sales funnel across all segments. And with a property this large and this multifaceted, it requires a clear vision and strategic approach to handle marketing successfully.

For this, we interviewed Ronn Nicolli, Chief Marketing Officer for RWLV, to learn about his approach to managing an operation of this magnitude, how L&E has become an integral part of the revenue mix and what he's done to craft a new casino resort brand in a crowded market. In a few short years, the RWLV marketing team has turned the resort's brand into ostensibly the entertainment capital of The Strip for it to stand apart from the pack. Let's see how Mr. Nicolli has done just that.

To start, can you give us some background on your career and your role at RWLV?
I moved to Las Vegas from Youngstown, Ohio, and found myself getting a job as a street team promoter for Wynn Nightlife. I had previously earned a degree in marketing and approached nightlife with a serious business mindset from the start. I then made a seamless transition from a nightlife focus to a property focus as I transitioned from Vice President of Lifestyle Marketing and Vice President of Zouk Las Vegas to the Chief Marketing Officer of Resorts World Las Vegas (RWLV).

My involvement in the building and opening of RWLV was key to getting the new property (66 floors) off the ground. Opening a new resort in Vegas is never easy, especially opening the first ground-up casino in over a decade and within a newer world of marketing and consumer behavior. Since RWLV opened in June 2021, we launched a refreshed brand campaign, 'Rule the World,' which has had a massive impact on branding and marketing the property. RWLV has become a known name to Vegas enthusiasts everywhere and a frequented destination for many influential hospitality and thought leaders.

Building on this, how has the revenue mix for Las Vegas casino resorts changed over the past two decades? What are some of the forces that are making both L&E, F&B and spa critical nowadays versus only gaming?
Vegas continues to evolve as it always has. In 2002, gaming revenue on the strip was just 42% of revenue versus 2012. That number went down to 36%, and in 2022, it was at 29%. The new Vegas consumer is looking for an array of experiences that include more than gaming. Elements of entertainment, culinary arts and lifestyle amenities like the spa have become more prevalent in spending. The development of the Strip has also contributed to that as newer builds have transitioned from casino properties to casino hotels with other offerings on the property.

The gaming element is always part of the allure of coming to Vegas, but as other domestic cities have started opening up casinos Vegas must continue to innovate and elevate its level of hospitality to evolve with our consumers and to surpass the competition.

In your own words, what makes RWLV such a unique place for guests to stay?
RWLV embodies the definition of modern luxury. It's approachable, and not intimidating; it has life and energy, along with a high level of hospitality and service. Underlying all that is a palpable feeling of human inclusion. It's the type of place to celebrate an occasion, a weekend away or to come out to The Strip for a locals-only experience – something that is often lost amidst the pursuit for tourists.

With so many different operations and target customer segments, guiding the marketing for a property like RWLV is like steering an aircraft carrier. What's your approach when deciding where to focus your attention and that of your team's resources?
This is very tough because we all run into the challenges of budget, resources and audience segmentation. For the first true year of operation, our goal was purely domestic. We then wanted to expand further into Canada and Mexico, so North America became the next big push for year two. As we continue to raise our brand awareness, South America, Europe, and the Middle East will be next on the radar. The true goal is to be in a position at year five or six of operation where we have an efficient, effective, and truly global awareness of RWLV's brand identity. We want to grow into the position where a consumer can understand with simple messaging that we are a modern luxury and are the entertainment capital of The Strip.

RWLV has three different hotel brands: Hilton, Conrad and Crockfords. How do you differentiate each of these three hotel products in terms of branding, positioning and awareness?
Technically we're still in our infancy as our domestic brand for RWLV. Having the three other brands creates consumer confusion regarding different options and price points. With Hilton as a 4-star, Conrad as a 4.5-star and Crockfords as a 5-star, tiering

up requires a concerted effort to distinguish the experiential elements to support the price points at each.

RWLV has become renowned as the best resort on The Strip for entertainment, which has required extensive marketing campaigns to reinforce this branding. What was the strategy behind this direction and what were the key steps in bringing this recognition to life?
The first kind of messaging that we went out to consumers was based on entertainment, which has become a perennial focus and pillar for RWLV. It was easy to communicate at a time when we didn't have a live and active resort because we were marketing during preopening. It then evolved into a partnership where the artists became ambassadors of the brand, which has helped us through the opening and to become who we are today. Strategically, from the outset this direction has cemented us with the consumer as being one of the best entertainment properties in the world. Entertainment is continually changing, especially with artists from touring, releasing music and in general, so we're actively talking with our ambassadors to support their artistry as well as evolve our marketing strategy.

What's in the near future for Las Vegas in terms of a further evolution of the revenue mix, marketing channel mix and demographic shifts?
Events like F1 are reshaping the global perception of Las Vegas to maintain its appeal amongst consumers worldwide. The Super Bowl in February 2024 was perhaps the final step in cementing Vegas as a sports entertainment city. This is something that no one could've predicted two decades ago, least of all when I was just getting started. Some of the core conventions that are looking to grow in size and popularity continue to attract the business consumer. With the Sphere opening and other festivals finding their home in Las Vegas, we've maintained the city as an entertainment capital of the world, and there will be a lot of work for RWLV to make sure we keep pace with this rapidly growing market.

Ambassadorship is the Tech-Driven Authentically Local

In the post-pandemic era, it's important that hotels align their brand visions for the decade before we're all too deep in the weeds of servicing onsite guests. One trend throughout the 2010s was the drive for delivering a 'locally authentic' experience and this will definitely reemerge for the 2020s, but successful properties will be those that take it a full step further.

In the previous decade, being authentic meant, in broad terms, welcoming guests and enriching their journeys by offering their new perspectives of the local culture, cuisine and heritage. Through the use of the time-honored term of 'ambassadorship', hotels must now explore how they can become true hosts to a city or area for incoming travelers – those people who may be venturing off their home bases for the first time in years.

Whereas authentically local would inscribe the choices of what to put on the restaurant menu, what products to source at the spa and how to theme the lobby furnishings, becoming an ambassador also pertains to service in terms of knowing how adventurous each guest's taste buds are or what spa treatment to recommend based on their other travel activities and when to offer said treatments. Rather than passively offering guests a glimpse into what makes the area special, ambassadorship requires more an active role in personalizing the experience.

Ambassadorship also equals peace of mind because guests will feel reassured that their specific requests are being handled. As a simple leisure scenario, picture yourself going on an international vacation with your loved one. You're in a foreign city and country and don't know what attractions to visit and which stores are recommended, on top of a myriad of other questions that would require some digging online. Instead, wouldn't it be great to know that your host hotel has your back the whole way?

In the past, luxury brands have provided this kind of omniscience by deploying an army of staffers, but this model won't jive in the post-pandemic, hyper-labor-efficient market conditions. Still, many would decry that their properties are already excelling at this through high-touch personalization with a backbone of disparate SaaS applications supporting a largely 20th-century method of servicing guests.

Ambassadorship must be natively tech-driven and funneled through a skeleton crew of adept, thoroughly knowledgeable personnel. Moreover, hotels must be proactive in the prearrival stage to ensure incoming guests have everything that they need and to make arrangements on their behalf. This sets the pace for a great onsite experience in lieu of the outdated 'reactive' process of waiting for guests to reach out to you with their inquiries.

Done right, hotels can utilize integrated platforms and build a versatile CRM to connect the entire guest journey that also offers a clear counterargument to the largely self-serve nature of home sharing accommodation providers such as Airbnb. In this sense, we can use the success of home sharing as both an example of what to emulate and where hotels need to be in order to survive well in the future.

Let's break this down to see how ambassadorship represents the new full-service model:

1. Home sharing platforms offer a direct, two-way ***messaging service*** with the accommodation host, and hotels must do the same. Brands should be using a chatbot to immediately respond to the simpler questions –which represent the majority of inquiries – then bouncing the more complex ones onto your front desk or concierge. Ditto for the voice channel where booking engines are available 24/7 and so too must your intake team be ready at all hours in order to win the business.
2. Speaking of booking engines, these should no longer be only for rooms, particularly if we want to continue to push guests towards our websites from the OTAs. Customers should be able to plan their ***entire trip itinerary*** from these portals, starting with dining reservations and spa appointments

through to arrival amenities and perhaps a few 'surprise and delight' freebies such as their preferred complimentary welcome refreshment or departure gift.

3. Physically getting to an accommodation booked through a home-sharing platform is mostly a laissez-faire ordeal. So, why can't hotels offer bespoke, point-to-point guidance on ***transportation*** to and from the rail station or airport, as well as recommendations on how to get to the city or region? As a guest's perception of your arrival experience can depend on the agony of how one arrives at the hotel, why leave this to chance? Besides better integrations to flight trackers so that you know exactly when your guests are expected to arrive, such innovations as autonomous vehicles are just around the corner, which could drastically bring down the costs of shuttle services. Grandiose, for now, perhaps a present-day possibility would be a flight tracker integration so that you know when guests are expected to arrive and can be ready with a warm welcome.
4. The future of travel will be more purpose-driven. Planning a guest's itinerary or making ***local recommendations*** has traditionally fallen under the purview of the concierge, but the time is right for building a 'pick your own adventure' program of bundled, turnkey half-day and full-day activities. This will require deeper integrations with third-party operators as well as a rethink of what onsite or offsite services are most meaningful for guests based upon their given travel purpose. For instance, a late-afternoon, post-meeting relaxation package with a whiskey tasting, revitalizing nosh and back massage will have vastly different appeal from a daylong sightseeing tour that includes timed entrances to exclusive local events.
5. The ***post-stay relationship*** is where home sharing hosts are weakest. The platform does the brunt of this, focusing more on exploring new destinations rather than return visits. For hotels, traditionally the last interaction between guest and staff was often a checkout at the front desk where the final bill was confirmed, representing an emotionless, transactional touchpoint. Now with contactless checkout, hotels can transform this into a meaningful 'thank you' gesture followed by a series of one-to-one messages based upon what a guest utilized while onsite. With a fully integrated CRM, this messaging can be sentient insofar as knowing when to push for additional sales and when to simply keep past guests up to date on the latest happenings.

There are many other ways you can build upon this concept of being an ambassador to your guests in order to drive brand reputation, awareness and, ultimately, revenues. The key is to think about not just what amenities you offer to augment the onsite experience (as supported by your tech stack), but also how you can help guests throughout the entire purchasing pathway. Be proactive instead of reactive. Do that and you may find yourself rapidly becoming the brand of choice for the next cohort of travelers.

Competing with Short-Term Rentals for Leisure and Small Groups

With travel back on track post-pandemic, hoteliers would be wise to closely follow the performance of home sharing platform bookings relative to traditional hotels and the total accommodations market. It's undeniable that short-term rentals are becoming highly influential, both in terms of being the brands of choice for many travelers as well as trendsetters that hotels will inevitably have to emulate. On that note, what can hotels do to take back market share from this rapidly growing sector?

With leisure transients first out of the gate to feed the recovery revenue pipeline, the next related segment to consider small, primarily leisure groups. One area where short-term rentals have already influenced travel behavior is in how leisure customers think about their occupancy demands.

Before, if you were traveling, say, as two couples, you would simply ask for two rooms in a hotel, with or without a special request to have them collocated. The question was only 'what' hotel to select. Now, such travelers are likely to first consider the option of getting a shared space with two bedrooms through an alternate lodging provider. The question has become a 'why' select a hotel at all.

In this initial bout of what's being dubbed Revenge Travel 2.0, we will see many different rationales for small groups of leisure travelers, from couples getaways to multigenerational family reunions. For all cases going forward, hotels now need a compelling reason for answer the why before even getting to the what. The goal here is revenue by adapting to these new demands and the steps you can take to quickly pivot as well as set up your hotel for long-term success.

The Customer's Perspective

To start, reframe the question in the first paragraph from the perspective of a brand-agnostic customer. Not loyal to one hotel brand or another, what accommodation will offer me the most 'value' in terms of rates, spaces, convenience, and location? As an exercise, this can help you to think more objectively about the inherent advantages of your short-term rental competitors and what operational changes or promotions would be meaningful to these guests.

Here are some notes on these alternate lodging providers and what you can do with these elements:

1. *Rates.* Home-sharing units have gained the reputation of offering more square footage per dollar over hotels. While we're all advertising the best-rate guarantee to incentivize customers to book direct, it's now time to conduct an analysis of how your rates stack up with these other accommodations. You may find that an adjustment to your rate strategy is in order.
2. *Spaces.* Home sharing units offer a diverse range of accommodations in terms of configurations, amenities, and décor. Hotels can thus work to create unique touchpoints in each room or even subcategories that have different FF&E configurations. One note is that part of the appeal of a traditional hotel is the guarantee of certain features no matter the exact room; this

brand standard 'peace of mind' should be adhered to and reinforced through marketing.

3. *Convenience.* Even post-pandemic, guests are increasingly favoring more contactless exchanges built into their hotel stays – mobile check-in, mobile room keys, guest comm apps with digital concierge, in-room voice bots versus calling downstairs, mobile check-out and so on. Yet some guests and managers still prefer not to bypass the front desk as a core aspect of the onsite experience. The key is to offer the flexibility for guests to choose.
4. *Location.* While your hotel is situated where it is, consider how home-sharing platforms have long touted their inventory as being 'embedded in the community'. Can't you do the same? Hotels often have some of the best locations in town with immediate access to main sights and transportation options. Start by really embellishing these two, then wax in-depth about all the other hyperlocal (roughly within three blocks) businesses that guests should note, both for convenience (groceries and pharmacies) and experiences (restaurants and shopping).

Those four points are brushing over a literal ton of work to properly pivot a brand, but they are critical right now as hotels look to maintain pricing power by not diluting rates as travel options explode. From our experience overseeing hotel sales and marketing, we can offer a few more general tips to help you maximize bookings for the year ahead.

- *Bundle wherever you can.* Besides learning from home-sharing providers, another big goal this year should be to focus on increasing total spending per guest and not just RevPAR. Corroborating that, our past work from numerous asset management assignments has shown a direct relationship between property utilization and satisfaction – the more you motivate guests to use your amenities, the more revenue you earn and the more likely they are to revisit or recommend. Bundling and packaging creates added value to optimize that total spend.
- *Frame it as free.* There is something very powerful in the word 'free' in terms of drawing eyeballs. Before throwing freebies into your packages or extra nights, consider that many of the services you already offer as brand standards can be reframed as complementary perks, including flexible cancellations and refunds as well as perhaps such features as parking, valet, concierge, business center workspaces, pool access or beach access.
- *Make the numbers simple.* What's easier for your brain to understand: 67% of the time or every two out of three times? Most of us prefer the latter because it's simpler to visualize, and this same principle applies to your discounts and promotions. If you are trying to build midweek occupancy while the corporate segment is still nascent, consider the reframing of a '25% off for four nights or more' into a 'stay three nights and get a fourth-night free' type of ad so that the mental math isn't a barrier.

Obviously, this is still barely cracking the surface. Nevertheless, if you apply these principles to both single-room leisure transients and multi-room leisure groups, you will undoubtedly win over more guests who otherwise would go elsewhere.

Buy Now Pay Later Yet One More Convenience Evolution

From gold, cash and certified checks through to credit cards, digital wallets and cryptocurrencies, the world of payments now contains a litany of terminology, acronyms, governing bodies, networks and technologies. As obvious as it may be, what you should remember is that the one factor all these entities have in common is humans trying to find an ever-quicker and trusted way of exchanging resources.

With hotels as no exception, payments will always evolve in the direction of fast, fair, and frictionless – the three Fs. Digital wallets like Apple Pay and Google Pay fit the bill (pun intended) because they allow consumers to forego carrying around a physical wallet while preserving simplicity and safety. Likewise, the current shift to QR-code portals powered by single sign-on (SSO) functionality and (soon) biometric payment portals will come to be preferred by hotel guests because they are even more of the three Fs, albeit not without their kinks that still need to be ironed out.

This brings us to the burgeoning array of Buy Now, Pay Later (BNPL) platforms and how they can help hotels increase revenues by enhancing the overall convenience to the guests. As an evolution from more classical methods of payment finance, these tailored pay-over-time platforms have been shown to increase conversion and total spending (in retail, often called 'cart size'), and there's no reason why they can't do the same for hotels if you stay cognizant of their drawbacks. Without namedropping any specific vendors and getting into apples-to-apples feature comparisons, what matters most are the psychological principles underpinning BNLP and why these systems are important right now.

The Macroeconomics of Why Now

Despite any recent reworkings of the exact definition of a recession by various institutional authorities, depending on who you ask we are either on the precipice or already deep into one. This current state of the economy is significant for any fintech discussions because an increasing number of hotel customers will be struggling with personal finances and thus more strongly influenced by adaptive, pay-as-you-go schemes that hotels, or any merchant for that matter, can extend.

Don't get us wrong; we are not harbingers of doom with this recession talk. In fact, we're futuristic optimists, especially for hospitality. Despite this suggested decline in disposable income for the near term, travel will increasingly become a defining aspect of people's lives over the next decade. Call it 'purposeful travel' or 'the intrinsic need for memorable experiences', but with the ability to move freely about the world taken away from all of us due to the COVID lockdown, everyone now wants to get out there and self-actualize through travel.

Young, old, leisure, corporate, luxury or regular schmo, we all want to travel.

And travelers will opt for any means necessary to make this dream a reality, including opting for those hospitality brands that offer interest-free BNPL options – brands that give them even more of an 'urge to splurge' if you will. And note here that while luxury consumers may be more apathetic to this pay-over-time evolution, this does not preclude them from rate comparisons or being attracted to value-added packaging.

BNPL as a Part of a Brand Vision

From a psychological standpoint, this flexibility reduces the immediate stress for the payee. For people who want to travel but are struggling to pay the bills, ponying up for a weeklong hotel vacation or any other form of reservation can be a deeply traumatic event, so much so that it may delay or deter a booking altogether. With the advent of zero-interest payment financing, these BNPL platforms may be preferred over the higher credit card interest. In this sense, offering pay-over-time checkout options acts as a way to garner more trust and convert more reservations on the spot. It can also drive more direct bookings versus the OTAs that may not be willing to offer these forms of installment transactions.

Still, there's a crucial, cold and wholly pragmatic business question that you have to ask yourself at this juncture. Given the socioeconomic framework that governs the type of hotel guests more likely to be incentivized by BNPL availability, does this psychographic conform with your brand vision? This is a polite way of inquiring if, by enabling people who stand a greater chance of delinquency, are you also inviting a less-than-savory lot that may cause more problems than they are worth?

Many BNPL providers have been criticized for performing softer credit checks than credit card operators, with words like 'predatory' often thrown around by their detractors who foresee consumers surpassing an untenable threshold of debt through the accrual of regular credit card, household and now BNPL bills. From our experience as asset managers and owners' representatives, there is a nonnegligible correlation, albeit loose, between the guests who haggle over payment terms or nightly rates and those who end up initiating chargeback disputes, complaining on online review websites, leaving the room in a disorderly state to bog down a housekeeper's cleaning schedule or worse. Review your own guest data, but this is our experience thus far.

You have to decide what brand you want to be, what types of guests you hope to attract and whether or not BNPL will complement that direction. For any brand that is economy, select service, limited service, midscale or drives much of its current revenues from the OTAs, our recommendation is to investigate platforms that do indeed offer BNPL functionality.

Guest profiling issues notwithstanding, merchants need not worry about delinquencies per se, but the trade-off is that BNPL platforms charge hotels a significantly higher merchant discount rate (MDR) over traditional credit card interchange fees – often more than 1% extra – which will ultimately cut into your margins. And that MDR only increases with the degree of risk assumed by the BNPL provider.

If It Ain't Broke...

When undertaking any consulting assignment in the realm of hotel technology, one of the core mantras we apply is, 'If it ain't broke, don't fix it'. That is, for tech hotel stacks, while it is entirely possible to rebuild your systems and interfaces from the ground up, it's most likely not feasible. You have a live and highly fragile product – guestrooms that need to be sold, serviced and cleaned every day of the yearly calendar – but, significantly, you have the 'human stack' to consider.

While the current labor crisis is generally lensed around the dearth of available associates, it is also affecting the IT department. These professionals are a rare find and an increasingly expensive one to keep from jumping ship to another property, brand or industry where the salary and upward career prospects may be more lucrative. So, while it's all swell to talk about then plan to bolt-on a new layer of payment financing, does your IT team have the bandwidth to properly vet, install, build the required interfaces, develop SOPs and maintain this new technology product?

However mature the APIs are or how straightforward an SDK is, all this still needs to be configured on the merchant, or hotel, side. Even after accounting for factors like the larger MDR along with the potential for a boost to funnel conversions and cart size, there are hidden labor costs that may be too much at this juncture, especially for smaller brands with only a fire team of technologists to call upon.

Deepen Your Existing Partnerships

With these human factors in mind, the BNPL pivot for the immediate term – for at least until this travel recovery period is ongoing and labor persists in its logjam – is to first ask what your existing vendors can do in this regard. It's not just about what platforms are the most compelling for your guests, but also what ones are the easiest for your teams to set up then regularly operate.

In this regard, one niche technology where we foresee BNPL reaching rapid scale in hospitality is via card-not-present (CNP) payment platforms. While it would be great to see the myriad of website booking engines (WBEs) offer user-friendly interfaces for selecting BNPL versus payment in full via a convenient dropdown-style widget, these may not be ready for a few business cycles given the obstacles of requiring real-time connections with the PMS, CRS, POS or payment gateway.

Instead, most CNP platforms already offer hotel teams an intuitive and secure portal through which to manually prepare installments with manager notifications of both successful and missed payments, albeit most of these features were intended for parsing out large group masters or event folios. It's a classic case of a 'workaround' where CTA messaging can be prominently placed on the WBE telling guests to use the voice channel to inquire about BNPL options. As well, a key word to remember here is 'secure', whereby these CNP platforms, if they meet PCI DSS standards, can also offer protection from chargeback losses.

Still, the point remains. With time as the limiting resource for most hotels, deepening your relationships with your existing vendors is the best path forward. Reach out to them; attend their user conferences; educate yourself on their new features and their near-term roadmaps. If or when you decide that Buy Now, Pay Later is in the cards for your brand, you will have to move quickly to adopt new practices in order to gain awareness amongst travelers as the brand of choice for tailored payment financing.

Attribute-Based Selling is Now Urgently Needed for Hotels to Survive

As per the title, the point here is to explain why attribute-based selling (ABS) is mission-critical for the decade ahead. To properly understand this, though, we must first look at a landmark event in hospitality that occurred in early December 2020.

We all watched the Airbnb IPO as the home-sharing platform debuted to a \$100+ billion market capitalization on its opening day. For reference, that's more than its closest compartment of Booking Holdings at roughly \$85 billion or the likes of Marriott, Hilton, IHG, and Wyndham combined. Understanding what led to Airbnb's gargantuan valuation will help tell you the direction of traveler behavior and what you need to do in the coming years to stand a chance against this industry titan.

Some might be quick to shrug off Airbnb's stock price as mere post-pandemic tech company hype. After all, the company doesn't own (yet!) any of the inventory listed on its platform, so in that regard, it's no different from an OTA or a major brand that only takes a paltry ownership stake in any of its flagged properties. But unlike other recent IPOs in that sector, Airbnb has an easily digestible USP for consumers that's evident by analyzing its loyalty metrics versus competition.

Without getting into the numbers – which you can verify yourself through a number of third-party resources like Transparent – Airbnb users spend more time on its website than users on an OTA or a brand.com and they are much more likely to arrive directly onto the website instead of coming via a Google search, referral or paid ad. So, why are Airbnb users more loyal? Why has it quickly become the platform of choice for accommodation searches?

Perhaps you answer these questions by saying that Airbnb has a better user interface than others, both for desktop and mobile. Or maybe it's the two-way rating system that engenders a profound sense of trust between host and guest. A third explanation might be that Airbnb isn't the actual operator, thereby enabling it to keep costs down, even while scaling, because it doesn't have to allocate cash towards operations like a front desk or concierge. Drill deeper, though.

Listings on Airbnb are perceived as more unique and more exceptional than what one will find through an OTA or by booking directly. This makes searching for the right room, apartment, or house a fun activity in its own right – what I call a 'sense of discovery' – while at the same time giving a diverse range of users a higher degree of confidence that the platform will have an accommodation that suits their specific needs or travel behaviors.

Airbnb may list a few standard double-bed hotel rooms or king-bed private rooms to appease the midweek corporate traveler who fits the typical 'heads in beds' mold. But the platform also has a vast assortment of villas to host mid-sized groups with their own common spaces and 'ghost hotels' which are mostly just Ikea-furnished condominium units with a full kitchen and onsite laundry.

In other words, what makes Airbnb so powerful is its flexibility in accommodating a worldwide emergence of travelers who are fed up with the cookie-cutter big box hotels and how each of its listings comes with its own set of features or attributes.

This becomes a positive feedback loop. As more consumers opt to use Airbnb, they come to expect more unique accommodations across the board and have the ability to query based upon specific attributes, rather than still viewing this as a value-add.

Thus, if hotels and resorts want to survive in the coming decade, they have to adopt an ABS model, where it's no longer just about the bed size but also any number of other in-room features. Some of these to consider are:

- Adjoining rooms or configurable spaces for cribs or remote work
- Technological enhancements and IoT integrations
- Connected rooms with shared common areas
- Key amenities like a jacuzzi, terrace or private pools
- Unique furnishings or artwork
- Proximity to the elevator
- Proximity to amenities
- View orientation or high floor versus low floor
- Club or loyalty floor access
- Kitchenettes or in-room laundry
- Enlarged work desks or workstations
- Fireplaces

This is just a broad and brief start of the attributes that hotels should start to consider for promoting and upselling their products. Important to understand is that many properties already have many exceptional room types; it's now a matter of coding them as such in the PMS or CRS and giving customers the ability to search in an ABS fashion (and not just the traditional rooms-first manner).

Thinking in terms of an ABS model, Airbnb's market cap is less a signal of its strength as a pure *accommodations* company and more as a *data* company. This is because with each new search and reservation made through its ABS-oriented inventory database, Airbnb is better than its competitors at learning about each traveler's accommodation preferences. It can then leverage that data to develop more accurate travel recommendations and predictions about what other travel-adjacent or non-travel products its users will want in the future. Ultimately, it is the value of this data that will lever further partnerships and greater use of their platform.

Gone are the days where your guests are content with merely a standard, cookie-cutter hotel room. They want variety; they want their accommodations to feel different from one territory to the next, perhaps even from one floor to the next! And therein lies the opportunity for hotels to not only appease this popular trend but also boost ancillary revenues, position rooms for better ADR growth and increase the overall segment diversification for long-term asset stability. It's a necessary evolution of our industry, so best look to the world leader in accommodations to see what else you can learn.

Streaming Service Teachings for Building Direct Channel Revenues

With hundreds of millions of global subscribers to the likes of Netflix, Amazon Prime, Apple TV, Disney+, Paramount, Hulu or any other, the common features of the user interfaces for these streaming services are subtly influencing what the average customer expects when browsing through other digital platforms. As such, implementing design changes to your brand.com can not only provide a better path to booking directly but also increase total revenue (GOR).

We only use the first three of those mentioned above, but some of the shared elements they have include:

- Fast load times
- Image-first browsing
- Near endless content
- Short text snippets and descriptions
- Video previews or trailers
- Categories and subcategories
- Suggested films or shows
- Search functions that also contain AI-driven suggestions

While obviously a hotel's website won't approximate anywhere near the volume of content as a streaming service – nor should it – what's remarkable about these platforms is how easy it is for the user to both quickly find what they want to watch, or take pleasure from simply flipping through the plethora of options. As we know, time on site is a powerful metric that increases the likelihood of booking and overall brand loyalty; now should be the time to bolster your hotel's digital presence.

You need to present something different to stand out. Curating great packages, F&B, onsite amenities, activities, nearby attractions, and all other manner of experiences in a fun and digestible format on your website will give your marketing team more toys to play with and ultimately help seal the deal.

Then, there's the ability to optimize GOR. As a customer moves through the booking engine, if the teachings from streaming services are followed, then any ancillary revenue streams could be presented in a manner that encourages more spending per guest at the prearrival stage. As an example, you should be able to prompt guests about dining reservations immediately after they've confirmed their dates and desired room. For the time being, you may also want to emphasize that spots are limited due to social distancing constraints, so booking now is important to guarantee a preferred time.

Likewise, displaying your room products on your brand.com in an appropriately tiered manner to guide viewers through broad then more narrowly defined category features will help to reduce decision fatigue so that customers can better see the value of your suites or top-level rooms. Finally, simply updating your website frequently with news, local events and activities, service offerings, blog posts, and more information on area attractions will help turn your site into a hub for guests to reference later.

Recognizing that some design features may be out of your control if you are part of a chain or group with corporate control, the bottom line is that websites are living, breathing entities that need constant updating. Thinking in terms of a streaming service will, therefore, help guide your approach to the next phase of upgrades that you make.

To help give you some direction, here are a few words of wisdom for getting started:

1. *Content is king.* Just as your owners have a property improvement plan (PIP), you must also have a process in place for allocating regular blocks of time to update your website for the course of a given year. This means that resources are set aside not only for loading new rates and packages but also for nice-to-have projects like the aforementioned nearby activities.
2. *You need a content curator.* Managing a website is a full-time job, and you really need a jack of all trades who can do a bit of copywriting, front-end design, website development, photography, SEO and social media to ensure your site has the best possible content. The larger the hotel, the more budget there is for task specialization.
3. *Create a frictionless experience.* Netflix is able to load a high-resolution movie within seconds, so why is your website struggling with a series of thumbnail images? Obviously, there are numerous reasons for slow page loads but, as noted in the intro, the expectation increasingly favors speed. Moreover, frictionless in this sense can also mean more intuitive ways to access content or complete transactions.
4. *Recommendations.* Where I see the gold standard of hotel websites evolving over the next couple years is in catering bespoke content and upsell opportunities to customers based on their search and purchase history. This need not be some fancy AI-driven software either, but it is certainly data-driven. For example, why offer a discount on a spa treatment to a customer who is in the process of buying a golf package? Instead, serve up some F&B options at the clubhouse for after their round or reframe the spa offer in terms of a post-game massage.

Super-commuters as a Revenue Source for Urban Properties

It's becoming increasingly clear that remote work will become a permanent fixture for many people's work lives. Much has already been discussed about how this trend will affect hotels going forward, but there's one other implication here that can help salespersons set up lucrative programs for business travelers – that is, corporate contracts geared for the 'super-commuter'.

We've all witnessed the real estate market undergo a profound shift away from urban centers to the booming, and often cheaper, suburban and exurban abodes where the prospects of more space per square foot abound. Since the beginning of the pandemic, professionals from numerous sectors have been enabled to upgrade to a larger footpad far away or simply hunker down at the cottage due to changes in a company's work-from-home policies and deeper rural penetration of speedier internet services.

For some time now, many company policies have reverted back to pre-pandemic conditions, compelling people to return to the nine-to-five grind at a central locale. After all, most of us are suffering from videoconferencing fatigue while larger corporations are recognizing some of productivity losses associated with a remote workforce – namely, a lack of effective collaboration.

Enter the super-commuter, a term denoting a professional who journeys well over an hour (possibly over two hours) to reach a given destination, often in an urban center, for work, but only at an infrequent rate of once per week or twice a month. With such a long drive or train ride, the return trip may be too much to undertake following a long, grueling day at a physical office location. Instead, wouldn't it be better if the parent company hoisted said employee up at a nearby hotel for the night, thus allowing the fatigued worker to hit the road with fresh eyes the following morning?

While this may seem to be just another use case within the purview of a general corporate rate agreement, it's important to highlight what differentiates the super-commuter from other guests within the business segment. As a start, many of these long-haul travelers will be arriving at their respective offices via their own personal vehicles in lieu of a car service to and from airports or train stations. Hence, such amenities as free parking (or vouchers), valet and snacks for the road should be packaged into a rate to make it more attractive.

Secondly, in all but a few cases super-commuters will be visiting their own places of business for collaborative sessions rather than dropping in on clients' offices for training seminars or prospective clients to give a sales pitch. This slight change in modality may necessitate higher demand for office spaces within hotels that can facilitate small group projects.

As an example, a late afternoon brainstorm in a downsized company headquarters may spill over into the evening hours. For a change of scenery, several members then decide to regroup back at the super-commuter's hotel suite, assembling for a roundtable discussion in a connected room or a meeting venue downstairs that can be conveniently booked by the hour via an app.

As hotels search for ways to reinvigorate this stagnant segment, appealing to the needs of the super-commuter may be one possibility that works in tandem with or mutually exclusive to the currently in vogue programs focusing on working from a hotel (WFH). From that previous scenario, you can thus see how a WFH rethink of your suites or connected rooms can have legs beyond the immediate behaviors associated with our current pandemic state of mind.

While this niche traveler disposition is obviously not a game-changer by any means, the near future of successful hotels will be marked by finding those pockets of revenue during the industry's gradual return to healthy occupancy numbers. A small win is still a win. If you happen to own or operate an urban hotel looking to negotiate some new corporate contracts, then factoring in the specific desires of the super-commuter may help you get the business.

From Gift Shop to the Post-Pandemic Gift Experience

While perhaps we can see COVID simply as a disruptive anomaly, a more interesting perspective would be to view it as a supercharged catalyst for changes that would have taken place regardless. Nowhere is this more apparent than the damage it's done to the travel and retail sectors.

For the latter, we've long been inundated with forecasts about the coming retail apocalypse, and only now when that decades-long evolution has been compressed into a matter of months do we consider adaptive measures. Given this rapid transition, what are you going to do with your hotel's gift shop?

For many of the properties we helped asset manage, our top-level analyses showed that the gift shop wasn't worth the cost of maintaining it. While sales volumes were often above variable costs (barely), the hoteliers we worked with never fully integrated the opportunity costs involved with what else that space could be used for and how the gift shop amplified the guest experience.

Imagine converting a gift shop near the lobby entrance into a small café or a grab-and-go sundry. Which would generate more sales volume? And more importantly, which would be of more everyday utility to your visitors, be they overnight guests, event attendees or locals?

Alternatively, many have tried to make something special out of their gift shops by stocking products from regional producers that can't be found elsewhere. The goal here is a noble one – to service the demand for 'authentically local' experiences. Yet, few consider the amount of time needed to set up these partnerships and maintain inventory levels relative to the number of customers who pass by.

We are in no way condemning the promotion of local goods, we ask you to think broader. In order to get greater customer volume, you need something special to draw them in.

But do you notice the pattern here? It's all about the holistic experience you provide. The modern gift shop is not an independent sales vertical for tchotchkes and touristy trinkets; it exists as part of an ecosystem of revenue generators, all of them working in harmony to amplify the onsite journey.

If there's another consequence of COVID and the retail apocalypse, it's that it has catalyzed our entrance into the experiential age. Storefronts are no longer places mainly for transactions – all that can occur online via Amazon, eBay or Shopify. And indeed, many would now prefer online purchases because it's far more convenient. Rather, physical shops are places where customers can discover new merchandise, interact with brands and educate themselves about how certain products will benefit their well-beings.

With this in mind, what if the future of your gift shop was not a 'shop' but instead an 'experience'? In this new model, no inventory is kept within sight nor can visitors even walk out with an item. Think of it like an Ikea showroom where you provide a guided journey from kiosk to kiosk to show the best of what a specific product can do (with one-way markers on the floor to promote physical distancing). There's no cash register, only a single, knowledgeable clerk with an iPad to facilitate touchless payments. If a guest purchases an item, it can delivered to their room within 24 hours or shipped worldwide for an extra fee.

Next, consider the 'gift' aspect. A store designed for immediate transactions is more or less one set up for people to treat themselves in that moment. Suppose you have a couple staying at your hotel, and the husband sneaks off during his wife's spa appointment to peruse your wares. On top of having an item sent to the room, you could coordinate gift wrapping and a specific time of delivery better to fulfill the 'surprise and delight' factor. And if you are able to gift wrap an onsite souvenir, there's definitely a way to do it for those back home.

Above all, when you think about transforming this space into a showroom, if nothing else, you are adding another point of entertainment so there's more to differentiate your onsite experience from other properties and to make the guest's journey more memorable to thereby cajole return visits and positive word of mouth. This is a base level of the 'halo effect' or synergy that can be manifest if done right.

The gift shop is but one more operation that you need to rethink from the ground up. Ruminate about what a 'gift experience' can be that's true to your brand and your locality, and you may just find a viable profit-maker in the next normal.

Haunted Hotels as an Important Marketing Lesson

Not exactly a new trend per se, but recently, haunted hotels – under the broader banner of ghost tourism – have gained a niche following, with many promoting stories of their spooky pasts as a means of drumming up free eyeballs and, hopefully, bookings. The underlying marketing lesson is that you have to have a shtick, and this goes far beyond just haunted hotels.

Do a quick Google search, and you'll realize that there are numerous lists for such abodes or ghost tours, and it is indeed becoming a cottage industry of hospitality. As a caveat here, some properties are on the losing end of this trend because their grounds acted as a scene of a truly gruesome event – likely combined with a total lack of renovations and FF&E replacements over the decades – instead of a more fictionalized recount.

As it relates to the shtick of the matter, the impresarios behind each haunted hotel have essentially found a way to cut through the noise of marketing a hotel in a world of limited operating budgets and accommodation commoditization.

Compounding this is the whole commodification dilemma where hotels are slowly being reduced to base products without meaningful differentiation amongst disparate brands. With so many aggregated and now wholly dominant travel search websites – OTAs, tour operators, metasearch and alternate lodging platforms as four big ones – the value of any specific brand is being diluted, often to the point of total interchangeability in the guest's eyes. When that happens, it becomes a race to the bottom with customers only looking for ever-cheaper beds.

Hence, a potential solution to both of these problems is in finding said shtick – something poignant, terse and viscerally stirring that can be used for grassroots, zero-base promotional efforts. If you can find that one unique thing that differentiates your properties from the comp set – or, better, one that can motivate customers to consider routing their entire trip itinerary around a stay at your hotel – then this can serve as a powerful brand story that carries memorability and hinders apples-to-apples commodity comparisons.

While it would be difficult (to say the least) to engineer a hotel to be deemed haunted, there are innumerous other ways to stand apart from the crowd. Some properties need only promote their location, be it proximity to key attractions or centers of commerce, or picturesque views that are wholly embellished in every piece of sales collateral. Other brands aim to find uniqueness through exceptional F&B, wellness or activities (onsite such as an adjacent golf course or through local partners).

You need something to cut through the noise, but then once you have identified it you have to wholly embrace it through simplified messaging. True, a hotel can be many things to many people. However, to get people to show an initial interest so that they choose to devote more attention to your full slate of offerings, you need that one thing.

Luxury's Next Competitor Is Not a Hotel

This article was originally published in February 2021, and Regent Seven Seas Cruises's indicated positioning at the time of this writing may not reflect current company practices.

Every hotel property aspires to be luxury in one way or another, even as the word 'luxury' has become a bit overused in the past decade. As such, there are always new entrants testing out concepts and evolving various features, amenities or service offerings, all in an attempt to get one step ahead of the curve. The pandemic has, of course, shifted priorities but the pursuit of luxury still remains as a means of capturing guests' hearts.

Concurrent to this arms race amongst traditional hotels – and now also alternative accommodations – it is important that hospitality brands consider those accommodations not bound by land. Cruise lines are also evolving and diversifying in the wake of COVID, particularly as they try to cover as many traveler niches as possible, including several different types of luxury such as what's addressed herein. As we all look to recover from this world-shaping crisis, hotels must take a more holistic approach to evaluating market forces and their competition.

Launching the Seven Seas Splendor

This is one event from the anteCOVIDian times that still has significance for hoteliers. Aggressively promoted through social media channels, the christening of the Regent Seven Seas Splendor was an hour-plus YouTube segment dedicated to the company, its staff and the ship. Watching this unfold, we could not help wondering at the tremendous organization that unfolded to not only construct this vessel, but importantly the efforts required to bring this product into the marketplace.

While the coronavirus has cast a big question mark over its long-term success, what's important to remember here is the larger trend – the expansion of the luxury cruise segment.

This being a hotel publication, you may wonder why we are lavishing so much attention on a product launch that is not a hotel property. Fact is, that as hoteliers, there is a great deal of learning that we can glean from this singular event, as well as from the cruise industry's overall response to the pandemic. If you are managing or owning a luxury hotel or resort, this new ship and others like it will soon become a significant competitor; just think of it as 375 rooms added into your comp set.

The Seven Seas Splendor once again raises the bar on 'accessible luxury'. By accessible, we mean prices that run at roughly $2,000+ per night (meals, alcohol, and excursions included), which is a sweet spot for the luxury accommodation market segment. Of note, there is an even higher category of accommodations that we cheekily call 'no-holds-barred-luxury', such as a $5,000+ per night, multiple-bedroom villa-for-rent somewhere along the Mediterranean.

Consider for a moment, a comparison between an eight-day cruise and the same length of stay on a leisure holiday hypothetically in one, two, or three different luxury properties. Let's say your budget is $2,000 per day for a hotel, including three meals, alcoholic beverages, gratuities, and taxes.

These days that is not really all that extravagant and probably not enough for five-star, land-based accommodations in Europe on an all-inclusive financial cost basis. Yet, that's roughly the price range for a luxury, small boat tour (1,000 passengers or less). And remember, the cruise makes it significantly easier on the traveler – unpacking only once and coordinating your needs with exemplary service, not to mention that this all-inclusive price may also comprise day excursions, entertainment, airfare and transfers.

Three Key Lessons

Rest assured that, for the decade ahead, this form of luxury is indeed a competitor to any traditional hotel that you must take into consideration when planning ahead.

Here are three quick takeaways you can learn from this particular ship and other newer, luxury cruise liners of its ilk.

1. *Don't reinvent the wheel.* The new Seven Seas Splendor is virtually identical in design to its sister ship, the Seven Seas Explorer, which launched some five years earlier (and a ship that Larry has journeyed upon). This made the new

ship much more cost-effective to design and faster to build. It also means that the staff familiar with one ship are almost effortlessly interchangeable, thereby reducing onboarding costs. From a marketing standpoint, it also means that guests of one ship will be eager to experiment with the new one as well.

2. *Remember your target audience.* Study trends in design but steer away from the cutting edge. Unlike many new hotel designs, this ship's design elements are tasteful yet far from revolutionary. Often, hoteliers seek to try 'something completely new' in design, perhaps to be provocative from a public relations standpoint. Yet in doing so, they forget that it is the guest that is the ultimate judge and jury. While now taking into account physical distancing measures, you should design appropriately if your core guest demographic is conservative and likely in the age range of 60 to 80 with a high net worth.
3. *Lever your past guests from the entire chain to the new destination.* You're only new once, so make a big deal of it. As a past guest of a sister ship, not a week went by without an email bulletin on the progress and routing. Such new property or program announcements are low-hanging fruit for loyalty patronage. Wouldn't a regular guest in one city opt for staying at the same hotel brand in another? Wouldn't a loyal guest be keen for a return visit if you offer them exclusive or advanced access to a new onsite amenity? As a classic marketing tactic, look to drum up your base before attempting to reach wholly new audiences.

Many people are eagerly awaiting the day when they can get their vaccines then start cruising again, and therein lies tremendous learning opportunities for hotels on what products and services travelers really want. To the captain and crew of this new ship – and to the members of your hotel team – we wish you smooth sailing and hopefully no rogue waves like what we endured last year.

Cruise Lines as the Other Elephant in the Room for Hotels

As the hotel industry gradually morphs into the more-encompassing 'accommodations industry', we hoteliers still can't shake how much home sharing has changed our game. But these alternate accommodations aren't the only elephant that traditional hotel brands should fear.

While a plethora of evidence has now shown how sharing economy platforms like Airbnb, Vrbo, Homestay, and a host of others are eating away at the leisure customer base for traditional hotels – especially amongst the younger demographics – cruise lines represent another primary threat, this time at the older end of the spectrum.

Let's start from a personal angle. As one half of our consulting team, Larry here is easing into his soon-to-retire-maybe-years. Even prior to the pandemic, he felt it was about time he started seriously considering a cruise or two for his vacation in lieu of staying at a series of hotels. The rationale was both for the convenience factor as well as for the hotel consultancy insofar as understanding where properties can emulate cruise lines to improve performance. Thus, his first voyage was a jaunt through the Baltics followed by a two-week trek the following winter through Central America and another half-dozen trips since then.

Now, to grasp why cruise lines are a danger for traditional hotels shortly, you must also look at their inherent value proposition, for which many factors are near-impossible for hotels to replicate:

- *Convenience.* Cruise lines let you visit numerous places without the hassle of planning the itinerary yourself or bouncing from guestroom to guestroom and securing all the additional forms of transportation. Many travelers have a strong distaste for living out of a suitcase. A cruise means unpacking just once.
- *Entertainment.* The variety of onboard dining outlets, shops, shows, facilities and other interactive experiences is insurmountably greater than almost any individual, land-based property save for only the largest of casinos.
- *Cost.* Even though I was doing luxury cruises, a quick apples-to-apples comparison for doing similar trips with only hotels at a comparable pricing tier resulted in significantly more spent for the latter when everything was added up.
- *Service.* Within the scale of these ships as well as several other market forces, cruise lines can afford to have more personalization technology deployment and a much higher staff-to-guest ratio, both of which inevitably lead to better service delivery.

And the reason why cruise lines matter more so now than ever before for hotels can be summed up in three words – aging baby boomers. We're at a tipping point where most boomers are empty nesters who are easing into retirement. This means they have more time on their hands as well as more disposable savings built up from decades of hard work in their careers.

Moreover, there's a bit of boomer #FOMO (fear of missing out) at play here whereby, as they retire, members of this age group have quickly realized their own mortality and now want to experience the innumerous beauties of the world as soon as possible. Lastly, and building upon the fading vitality component, there is a threshold age for which personal travel insurance becomes disdainfully high, with the chaperoned nature of cruises offering a means by which to extend one's sightseeing lifespan.

All these factors combined can spell doom for any hotel that relies solely on the continued patronage of a primarily boomer clientele.

While developing strategies to shift your hospitality brand's appeal to a younger audience is the subject of another article and something we work strategically with our consulting practice's hotel clients to solve, there are still a few big takeaways from the success of cruise lines that you can apply to your property.

To sum them up, here are five trends for you to consider:

1. *Fully planned and exclusive daytime excursions.* Remove the pain of guests having to map out their daily itineraries by setting up programs that do this for them in as safe a manner as possible. This can be done on a one-on-one basis, or you can partner with a local operator. Key here is to ensure that your guests actually know that these services are available!
2. *Living like a local.* This is one of the main value propositions for home-sharing accommodations, but it applies to cruises as well. When passengers disembark, they are likely given a few hours or, at most, one full day to explore a city or area – hardly enough to get a true sense of what makes the region special. In the new decade, authenticity is the new luxury. This is an irreplaceable advantage for hotels in that you can build neighborhood partners and experiences, so guests get a true flavor of how locals live.
3. *Travel coordination assistance.* The biggest gripes of moving from hotel to hotel are schlepping your own bags, arranging your transportation, unpacking then repacking and having to check-in at each individual property. It's exhausting. Hotels that develop contactless travel assistance programs to thereby imbue more of that convenience factor will see huge gains in overall satisfaction, loyalty and word of mouth.
4. *Tour group contracts.* Building upon the idea of heightened convenience, you might want to look into some options regarding partnerships with tour operators or nearby hotels, so you are more inclusive for those guests who are booking through third-party guided travel companies.
5. *Medical tourism.* As the population ages, so too does its demand for wellness resorts and all other health-minded value-adds. There's something to be said about planting yourself in a far-off, singular destination and committing yourself to a specific regimen designed to boost one's physical fitness and mental acuity. There's no reason why your property can't start building programs related to this, even at the urban or select service levels.

While these ideas are the 1% inspiration, you still need the 99% perspiration to get them fully operational for your hotel. This will undoubtedly require a lot of work, particularly in the front office, and we would advise that you investigate your options sooner rather than later because the lucrative baby boomers aren't getting any younger!

FOOD & BEVERAGE

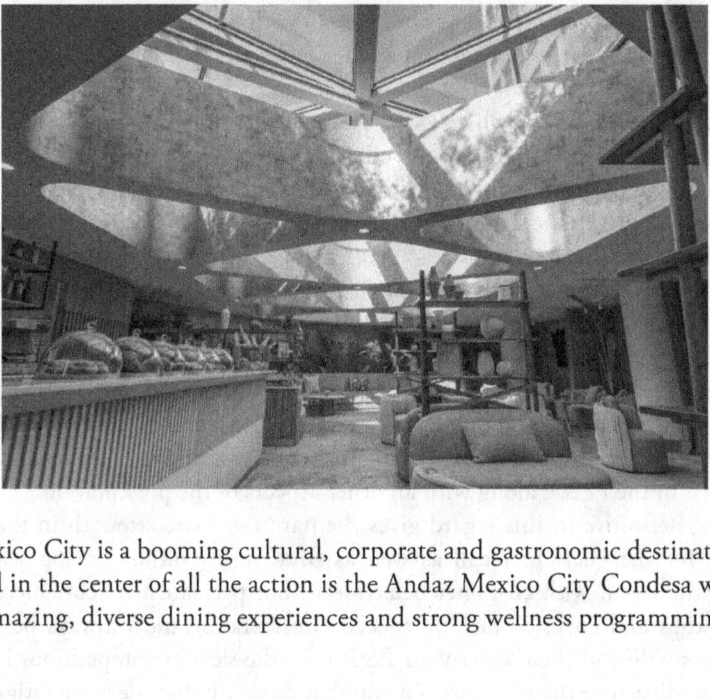

Mexico City is a booming cultural, corporate and gastronomic destination, and in the center of all the action is the Andaz Mexico City Condesa with amazing, diverse dining experiences and strong wellness programming.

Less is More for the New F&B Strategy

With the pandemic behind us, hotels have, in many ways, been given carte blanche to relaunch their rooms product, their restaurants, their spas, and any of their revenue-e generating services. To focus solely on F&B, a minimalist approach will ultimately be profitable as guests continue to realign their shopping habits.

One of our key mantras our consulting firm has always been, "It's better to do one thing great than a bunch only good." The bottom line is you want to be memorable and this can only happen if you stand out. While it's the safe bet to aim to appease everyone without disparaging any particular demographic or psychographic, for your foodservice this can often result in many dishes that are of reasonable quality but not of the 'you have to dine here' caliber.

Why the Need to Stand Apart

It's that latter camp that's critical. Customers are saturated with digital advertisements, so you have to derive unique ways to stand apart from the comp set. From a marketing perspective, having an incredible in-house restaurant cuts through the noise and helps to produce a 'halo' back onto your room reservations. The best way to boost the prestige of your restaurant is not by throwing everything on the menu and seeing what sticks, but in offering a highly selective shortlist that focuses the guest's attention on only the best representations of your culinary team.

This may require some reining in of your executive chef. As extremely creative individuals, your senior F&B team may have the natural inclination to experiment, often resulting in a hemorrhaging of the menu with an increasingly eclectic variety. Aside from mounting ingredient and storage costs, a key problem we've dealt with during past asset management engagements is that such a boundless approach dilutes the theme of the restaurant, which then decreasing memorability and word of mouth.

Instead, suppose you challenged your chefs to limit the full menu – appetizers, mains and desserts – to a total of a dozen items. This would force the team to choose only their finest creations, perhaps merging in elements from other runners up. Furthermore, this resolves the issue of 'shopper's paralysis' where, in the case of food outlets, patrons become psychologically overwhelmed by the multiplicity of options, leading to increased average time per cover and decreased meal satisfaction (optionality often equates to added stress and lingering doubts about choosing the best entry).

Having fewer items on the menu thus means you have to concurrently think hard about what your restaurant wants to be – its theme or genre of cuisine and how this is reflected in the FF&E along with all other aspects of the presentation.

Being definitive in this regard gives the narrative extra strength in that it will be easier for the guest to recall as well as find in any online or app search. To speak to the latter, with customer behavior all but permanently reoriented around delivery apps and curbside pickup, special consideration must always be given to how diners will find then select your F&B over the slew of competition. Having a simple and digestible theme – with a menu that doesn't induce decision fatigue – will greatly enhance sales via these blooming channels. In other words, you have to hone your restaurant's elevator pitch so that its messaging is easily transferrable across all mediums – apps, third-party websites and word of mouth.

The Bottom Line

While it is impossible to draft an entire F&B strategy in a single editorial, especially without factoring in specific geographic concerns, what we stress is that, with so much rapid redirection of customer habits, you have to cut through the noise. Once you have adopted a pseudo-minimalist approach for your signature restaurant, you can then look at how this model can be applied to your catering, room service, sundry and other foodservice amenities.

You must be fully prepared to welcome guests with something that's truly worth leaving the house for. In this sense, less is more can also be adapted for other operations as a means to achieving a profitable hotel by end of year.

This Is Why You Keep Your Restaurant's Signature Dish

Chefs are creative individuals and we're continually blown away by what these professionals can do when challenged to explore their passion. But a restaurant needs some marketing sensibility if it going to thrive, especially in a hotel or urban capacity where there are numerous other independent and more agile operations to compete with.

While some executive chefs are themselves tremendous impresarios or, dare we say, celebrity chefs, many others need to be reined in so that the menus are in stride with what the market wants and so that they fit with the dining outlet's theme for an easily digestible brand narrative. One aspect of this is whether or not to replace the most popular dish, something we recently encountered at a property for which we were asset managers.

The argument in favor of this substitution was that a new season called for a whole new menu in order to truthfully advertise it as such. And as political as any other organization, most of the senior team at the resort did not want to besmirch their camaraderie with the executive chef by testing his ego. But even though it may not be the chef's favorite, if it's the guests' favorite then isn't that what counts?

This is where we had to step in and apply some marketing wisdom as well as some statistics. The item deemed most popular was corroborated against POS sales data, and a myriad of anecdotal evidence scraped from online reviews to verify it as a bona fide 'signature dish' (although if we had a social media aggregating platform, this could likely have been used as well).

From there, it was a matter of explaining that many people don't just choose or suggest a restaurant solely by its ambiance or culinary style. Friends will say to one another, "Go [here] and make sure to try [this dish]." The two thoughts are intrinsically linked. Or, a follow-up question to an inquiry about where to eat may be, "What should I order when I get there?" Such dialogue helps to paint a more vivid picture of the experience diners will have when they ultimately arrive, thereby helping to convince them to go there in the first place.

Hence, when an executive chef presents a new menu to me, we are very hesitant to replace a top-earning item, even if that chef insists that 'people are bored with that one' or 'it's out of season'. Quite the contrary, the reason why it's bringing in the revenues is because it's perennially popular or an olive branch of consistency to the unadventurous. In removing that item, you may in fact be turning off customers who are coming specifically for it.

Just imagine the feeling of abject dissatisfaction when a first-time guest is enticed to visit one of your dining outlets because of a singular, must-try dish, only to arrive and not see it on the latest menu. However much a server attempts to assuage said patron with a, "Don't worry as this new one is similar," or "It will be back in season very soon," that customer isn't coming back ever again. It thus becomes a matter of expectation management, particularly as a restaurant's reputation may be bolstered by that signature dish.

Finally, there's the halo effect to consider. Namely, in a group scenario, one person may be gung-ho about trying your infamous signature dish, so much so that they convince the rest of the more easygoing party to eat there. In this case, if you lose the dish then the whole party may end up elsewhere.

Just as we are skeptical about removing top performers from the menu, so too must you be. However, this does not preclude a totally rigid outlook on seasonal changes, and we would advise starting with the 80/20 rule whereby the bottom 20% of your dishes should almost definitely be on the chopping block. Beyond that, there are many other ways to balance a restaurant's approach between unbridled creativity and marketing wherewithal, but please consider the ramifications of replacing any such cash cow.

Soft-Tech for F&B to Meet Lasting Remote Worker Demand

Post-pandemic travelers are booking hotel stays and swarming back to restaurants with a vengeance! If the current trends hold true, it's a great time to be a hotelier or restaurateur. So, let's drill into a subset within this 'Revenge Travel 2.0' to see where you can optimize revenues at your dining outlets.

Lots of trends born during the pandemic will eventually fall by the wayside, but many are here with us permanently. Specific to this conversation, the benefits to the individual of remote work will ensure that it becomes a lasting fixture of our society. Enabled by the ubiquity of video calls, a digital nomad's hours are flexible, allowing for such conveniences as being able to look after the kids or dog, and you no longer have the burden of the daily commute or unproductive watercooler talk in the office. Provided their output doesn't suffer, they can fit in a leisurely, morning yoga class or spend an hour's break reading outside in the sun – most of said interruptions already proving to be strong wellness positives.

Above all for you, remote workers can clock in from anywhere, so they may as well clock in while eating and drinking at your restaurant. That said, this burgeoning cohort has some specific behaviors that will require you to adjust your operations, of which a lot falls under the domain of 'soft tech' or minor upgrades and adjustments to existing systems in order to better appease this group.

The key in writing this is speed and cost – fast and cheap modifications that you can make in anticipation of the impending surge. Below are some considerations, keeping in mind that these will also halo onto other diner mindsets in terms of helping drum up more sales amongst those looking for midrange meals, small group gatherings and high-end experiences.

1. *Unthrottled WiFi.* This one is a no brainer but many outlets don't advertise it, leaving potential customers questioning whether that's the case. Don't leave any doubts in their minds. If you have a spotty connection, then get it fixed or watch as remote workers come once and never return. Related to this is ease of access to WiFi, where having to ask the server can subtly hinder said team member's time. Have cards or other signage at the ready.
2. *It's an SEO game.* There are quite a few keywords that are specific to the digital nomad based on their exceptional demands. They're looking for cafés with suitable work setups, or they're searching for places open now with takeout available. You'd be surprised how often the hours of operation on 'Google My Business' are out of date. Revising the words that you use to get better search prominence should be a recurrent task, and it's not just for paid search but also your website, social media, reservation platforms, and food delivery apps.
3. *Flexible hours of operation.* Building on the last point, with lockdowns and hospitality labor shortages causing so many disruptions, people will be checking to make sure you're open at the time they want to eat. Remote workers like off-peak hours like brunch, mid-afternoon or late night when it isn't so busy and they can spread out. Although this is more operations than tech, you can use data to determine which off-peak periods will be more likely to be profitable based on the added labor costs and scheduling challenges.
4. *Deeper analytics.* Again, to segue from the last point, remote workers differ in the times of day they prefer as well as what they want to order. With richer analytical platforms and more data feeding into them, you can get a better sense at what the top sellers are at any given moment. These inferences can then be used to better inform labor requirements and to further refine SEO as well as to develop promotions and upsell tactics.
5. *Faster customer communications.* Like numerous other customer service-related businesses, hotel and restaurant guests now want immediate answers, often without ever talking to a team member prior to arrival – and this is doubly true for digital nomads. Critical here is to prevent 'inquiry abandonment' where a customer moves on because you didn't respond fast enough. For this, wholly

integrated guest comms apps are essential so that you can efficiently chat with any patron on any platform. Chatbots are also incredible to instantaneously handle all the basic questions that would otherwise bog down a team member. And also consider outsourcing your reservation line so that customers aren't left waiting for a hurried server to pick up the phone or – gasp! – forced to leave a voicemail.

6. *Summer means outdoor dining and pet friendly.* Less so tech than what your physical space will allow, if you got it then you better flaunt it. This means more attention to SEO, homing in on terms like patios, rooftop terraces, poolside lounges, beach access and sidewalk seating. Remote workers are always keen on inspirational spaces to spend several hours so be sure to highlight any rental fees, day passes and F&B packages as well as great photography to tell the story. On a related note, the amount of dog owners bloomed during the pandemic and they're often looking for pet friendly restaurants to park themselves with their furry friend. This depends on what's allowed in your municipality and your business's specific policy, but if you have the greenlight then be sure you're promoting it.
7. *Platform and app promotions.* Limited marketing budgets mean your reach is only ever so big. Plus, tech savvy patrons will be browsing through these offers, so check to see what's available to breach new audiences. Such promotional vehicles are also great testbeds for whatever inferences your analytics can dig up as well as those generated through the best source available: directly asking your customers.

Breakfast in the Age of Intermittent Fasting

Let's all just take a break from the constant negative news cycle and the rest of worldly distresses. While we're at it, let's take a break from eating, too.

After all, the 'new normal' that is so lauded must also encompass 'new' ways of thinking. Today's tidbit focuses on the ways in which food habits are changing, specifically for the traditional first meal of any given day.

While your F&B team has already gone through a tremendous amount of work to set itself up for all manner of other changes to adapt to the times, we're sorry to say but more will likely be needed to meet the demands of ever-persnickety eaters.

No doubt your culinary artists have already worked hard at adjusting your hotel restaurant's breakfast menu to meet the demands of vegan and keto eaters with more plant-based and no-carb options, respectively. But one dietary trend that always seems to elicit a shoulder shrug is intermittent fasting. That is, how do you adapt the profit-making vehicle that is breakfast service for those customers who no longer eat breakfast?

While this may seem like an esoteric topic, the bevy of medical claims supporting this regimen as a healthy form of weight loss, boosting the immune system and organ repair (read: autophagy) is rapidly convincing many to become ardent followers. The theory goes that by giving your GI tract a break from digestion – the most common form being the 8-16 or an eight-hour window of eating followed by 16 hours of fasting – it then allows your body more time to focus on repair and fat breakdown. "You can't fix a car with the engine on," as they say.

The most common meal that then gets excluded from this diet is the first one of the day. And the problem therein for we hoteliers is that breakfast is a cornerstone of the packages we sell and our rate programs. While it may not be a big concern right now, this is one of many future-proofing scenarios we pose to other executives when helping consult on the strategic direction for a property.

What happens when this meal is no longer an incentive to augment the guest experience but an unwanted product that fails to drive satisfaction and, worse, becomes unprofitable? What do you do when your B&B package or breakfast meal voucher doesn't work? Aside from shifting to a 'bed and lunch' offer, the quick answer is to both enhance your morning beverage offerings, and then to look at the atmosphere you have created in the restaurant during these hours.

For the former, even though intermittent fasters likely won't eat breakfast, they're still going to want coffee, tea, water or some form of juice to tide them over until their 8-16 regimen gives them the green light for solid food consumption. To this end, you must look to be exceptional in one or more of the liquid categories.

Perhaps you partner with a single-origin coffee supplier or local roaster so that you can produce some truly flavorful drip without any added sugar or cream necessary to blunt the harshness of most other percolated (that is, burnt) coffees. Or maybe it's a niche tea provider. Then look to specialty waters or other zero-calorie sodas. Lastly, on the juice front, this can be far more than simply orange, apple, grapefruit and a few of the standard smoothie blends. Add some unique ingredients, powdered boosters or look into green juicing.

As to creating a more inviting environment – one that people would want to start their mornings in regardless of whether or not they are eating – this requires a deft hand and likely some capital expense. To give you some ideas here, think about what people do and want besides food at these hours.

In a modern sense, this definitely means fast and free WiFi so that they can read the news or perform any number of their other phone-based morning rituals. Along these lines, make sure to factor in the business traveler who may be bringing their laptop to the table, in which case power outlets shouldn't be kept out of sight. Interior design also plays a part here as the right mix of soothing and intriguing colors, furnishings, and lighting can go a long way to making guests want to linger.

All told, while this particular dietary trend may still be niche, the reason we bring it to your attention is that the solutions you implement for it will ultimately benefit all other diners, so it's a worthy exercise whether you eat breakfast or not.

From B&B to B&L for a Hotel Package

The bed and breakfast (B&B) bundle is the classic of classic packages that nearly any hotel can use to help build revenues. But there are cultural forces at work that may soon compel you to offer more flexibility in how you motivate room reservations with food.

This relates to the growing popularity of 'intermittent fasting'. In the past decade, a mountain of evidence has shown that giving your body time off from eating has dramatic health benefits. This may come as anathema for many of you, especially after so many decades of snack industry-subsidized studies proclaiming how constant foraging 'boosts the metabolism'. In lieu of a full glossary of biochemistry to explain how intermittent fasting helps your health, let's just say that you can't fix a car with the engine on.

Some intrepid members of the budding biohacking community achieve a desired state of intermittent fasting by foregoing meals for 24-72 hours once a month or so, but the most common form is the 8:16 where you eat all your daily calories in an eight-hour stretch then leave 16 hours off to rest the digestive organs. And in an 8:16, the most frequently omitted mealtime is breakfast.

So, how do you sell a B&B package to an intermittent faster who doesn't care two shakes of a jam jar about your breakfast service? Luckily, this movement is still growing and doesn't seem to have much stickiness amongst boomers who were all raised in a culture of three square meals per day. Still, the younger generations among us are exceedingly health-conscious, and it's not like all your boomer guests are going to pick up the slack by purchasing extra breakfasts. You have to start thinking about these generational and cultural shifts, particularly as they take on an exponential, snowballing growth curve.

To open the brainstorm, let's revert back to the fantastic word 'flexibility.' If you know your costs around lunch service, then you can easily create a B&L package as an option for those abstaining from the first meal of the day. It will likely be more than your B&B, but with a sound rate strategy that takes into account the psychological principle of anchor pricing, you can succeed on both fronts.

A huge concern, though, stems from the standard get-up-and-go behavior. You have breakfast, get ready for the day and head out, whether it's for business meetings or touring about town. Sticking around for lunch thus wouldn't be a much-vaunted perk. Instead of lunch, how about an F&B voucher that's applicable to any meal? This could be offered as part of its own package or available upon request within a B&B reservation.

Next, consider modifications or substitutions to your breakfast service offerings that will indeed appeal to the peculiarities of the intermittent fasting cohort. A carby, fatty breakfast is off the table, but what about a healthy 'smoothie' augmented by a few choice naturopathic supplements? The abbreviation of B&S doesn't quite have the allure of B&B, and let's not even consider what using the acronym for a 'breakfast and juice' package. All staffing shortages aside, an 8:16 can often start at 10:30am or 11am, so extending the hours of operation may work as a viable option – call it 'breakfast and brunch'.

Drilling deeper, if people are skipping a solid breakfast and only having a coffee, then what can you do to augment your coffee service? Single-origin coffee is in vogue, so perhaps you can be bold (pun intended) and put a tasting of three shots of percolated goodness on the menu instead of only offering your drip one full cup at a time. Dairy milk is also now considered unhealthy, creating a demand all types of plant-based alternatives from soy and almond to oat and whatever other head-turner you can source. Then there are all the recently commercialized coffee health additives like MCT oil and chaga mushroom powder that you can start selling as add-on boosters.

The point is to find creative ways to shift your F&B program to meet the market where it currently is as well as where it is headed so that your brand is adaptable to any trend or tipping point.

To close, our first suggestion is to stay on top of the news and look for what cultural shifts you think will influence travelers from beyond the hotel industry. Intermittent fasting is just one, as is the future customer's increasing demand for environmental sustainability or (from within our industry) expediting the check-in process with mobile keys. From there, it's a matter of flexibility; not forcing a new practice onto all guests but giving them the option to stick with what has worked or by trying something fresh.

This is, of course, all dependent on your specific brand's needs and market positioning. For now, just consider what you can do to set up a B&L in parallel with your B&B and see what happens.

Don't Buck the Plant-Based Trend

It's a slow, relentless march towards zero-carbon emissions for all businesses in all industries. While the goal of 'net zero' has been given a far-off deadline like 2035 or 2050, many corporations are already pivoting so that they can improve operational efficiencies – minimizing the 'green premium' as it is known in economics – as well as capitalize upon any trendsetter cachet. The beginning of October saw two major announcements in the F&B space that hoteliers should be conscious of.

Cadbury® is debuting a 'plant milk' line of chocolate bars, priced above their regular dairy-based products with the broader idea being that steady growth will fuel process efficiencies over time to bring the green premium down to zero or even below the cost of dairy. On the same footing, even McDonalds® has experimented with its at-the-time buzzworthy McPlant® Burger, in addition to the launch of a new franchise location in the UK that promises to be net zero in its emissions.

Long ago – in the anteCOVIDian times – we wrote about how 'fast food was where food trends go to die'. What this really means is that by the time major restaurant chains have embraced a trend, that trend has already reached the mainstream with enough justifiable support to warrant a large-scale rollout. National or multinational chains can't afford to take the same risks that, say, a food truck can because a failure would be felt by numerous stakeholders, affecting the share price and costing jobs.

Hence, every new product launch must first be market-tested, which is where independent restaurants – whether housed in a hotel or otherwise – should exist. We must constantly stay one step ahead of the chains, through innovative recipes, higher quality ingredients and superior presentation (both on the plate and overall ambiance). If we don't, then what reason do guests have for choosing our eateries and paying an elevated price plus tip instead of going to the nearest fast food location?

For these two current pieces of news, it is yet more evidence that the plant-based food trend is not one any hotel can ignore. If big brands are pivoting to this space, then it's a sign that you must as well. Particularly amongst the more sensitive younger consumers (who will ultimately inherit the warmer planet that's left for them), plant-based options should be readily apparent on the menu but also have a tasty, innovative twist that a cut above what would be found elsewhere.

And this is more than just presenting the optionality of vegan dishes. Everything now matters when it comes to achieving net zero, from how ingredients are sourced to offsetting energy costs. This starts with an assessment of what can be done as well as a plan for how to execute these changes gradually over the next decade.

There are many ways to go about this transition and we've helped hotel clients navigate these waters successfully as part of our consulting practice. For now, what we stress is, first, to understand that this trend is here to stay and, second, adopt an attitude of innovation.

Plant-Based is Just an Extension of Data-Based

Vegan, vegetarian, flexitarian, dairy-free, gluten-free, ovo-pescatarian, fruitarian – there are lots of diets out there and, significantly, more and more people are adjusting their habits away from the starchy, fried and meat-focused Standard American Diet (SAD). The data underpins any operational changes made to accommodate this societal shift.

Yes, the rise of all these new diets is not just about the food but how you use your guests' eating preferences to build richer profiles and analytics. Hence, there's a big lesson within this trend for how hotels can enhance personalization or marketing for future success.

Regardless of where you stand, the numbers don't lie. Whether it's for personal health, for ethical reasons or to help in the fight against climate change, people are opting for more plant-based eating at an accelerating rate. Travelers vote 'with their wallets' as they say, and hotels that are perceived as offering better plant-based dining options will be more likely to grow brand equity and revenues from this burgeoning group of eaters.

But while this trend may be taking place on a national or global level, how do you know if it applies to your specific property or brand? Does it apply to only the leisure segment or will it influence the hotel selection for groups and corporate travel?

That is, what data points can you measure to indicate whether or not a wholehearted investment into this space will be meaningful to future guests?

Small Example for Big Data

A seemingly trivial scenario here can help to illustrate the broader issue. Suppose your hotel plans to host an outdoor summer barbecue event (with a hefty entrance fee and accompanying room package) for one of Father's Day, Independence Day, Labor Day or any other gloriously humid weekend. Think beer, burgers, smoked brisket, sticky chicken drumsticks, potato salad, mac'n'cheese and any other cholesterol-laden comfort food your culinary team wants to whip up.

For this event, your marketing team plans to keep promotions at near-zero costs. The first rollout is for the hotel's opt-in email pool of past guests followed by other newsletter subscribers then onto social media, using a feature image of a giant blackened piece of beef on the hot grills to tantalize the eyeballs.

Next, suppose that, prior to launching this campaign, you performed some guest profile analytics that also incorporated POS data from all onsite restaurants and found that (hypothetically) 10% of customers in the opt-in email pool (after filtering for repeat patrons to give it some behavioral credence) have only ever ordered vegetarian dishes while staying at your property, or have specified plant-based substitutions or other comparable adjustments for their meals.

While this does not guarantee that said guests are strictly vegan, it is still a non-negligible correlation worth further investigation and testing. From this, we can therefore ask whether this 10% will be positively influenced by your visual meat-based messaging or turned off from said attending said event. While 10% is hardly a majority, the war for revenues is won a single skirmish at a time, so you should not ignore this psychographic shift.

Maybe it's time to lead with a more 'dietary agnostic' image and highlight your vegan menu options in the messaging. Other options would be to A/B test the hypothesis if software allows or segment the 10% off and use a more personalized, plant-forward advertisement design to drive conversions.

Data-Driven Capex Decisions

Getting POS data merged directly into the correct guest profile in such a way as to generate the reports that can answer the vegetarian question from the scenario above is a tall order. But it's coming, or at least it's possible if you have the right technology in place and your IT team has time to build the appropriate interfaces. And this is only the start of the inferences we can make once a hotel has unified guest profiles set up.

Rather than commanding by diktat that the executive chef put more plant-based options on the menu for this summer event, you can arrive at the conversation armed with the necessary data to support this direction and avoid any clash of egos. No more hunches and conjecture; again, the numbers don't lie.

Beyond a one-off or annual event are capex decisions for the long-term. Suppose your property is overdue for a new restaurant concept. If this 10% of assumed vegetarians is modeled to be growing year over year, how might this inform hotel package design, restaurant remodeling, catering menus, sundry inventory sourcing, minibar stocking and room service? Perhaps now is the time to start thinking about a purely plant-based dining outlet, knowing with some semblance of certainty that your customers are also moving in this direction and will be receptive to your product evolution.

Thinking Beyond Food Trends

Consider these advanced analytical intersections and how they might apply to other emerging trends like the drive for sustainability, experiences and the growth of wellness travel. We know that these are all macro-trends, but how can get more granular data on each trend to properly inform and adjust your operations or brand messaging?

Sustainability holds the promise of tremendous savings in energy costs but, for instance, do your customers want to hear about it in your outbound communications? Is sustainability verifiably meaningful to your current customers as a value-add or do they simply expect you to meet governmental guidelines without being 'in your face' about it? Similarly, in the post-pandemic era, travel has become more 'purposeful' but which specific activities or amenities are driving the majority of cross-selling activations to then inform future service developments? Again, what experiences are meaningful in terms of driving new bookings?

It all goes back to the data and getting it all amalgamated so that you can start posing complex questions and build personalized offers or advise on big, new initiatives that require serious capex.

If you aren't keen on considering a flexitarian diet for the health benefits or for the climate, just remember that such a move cuts far deeper than your own beliefs. It's about your guests and driving the topline. For the decade ahead, the growth of plant-based eating is but one more rationale for hotels to start connecting disparate databases for increased revenue opportunities and guest retention.

A Hotel Restaurant Framework for Low-Sugar Healthy Indulgences

Whereas fat was the scourge of dieting in decades past, today's nutritional plans and trends like keto or paleo espouse low carb and low sugar regimens as the foremost method for weight loss and maintaining insulin sensitivity. In particular, refined or added sugar has been singled out as the one food to cut out to achieve a wide array of health benefits including, as is being researched, staving off dementia-related, end-stage diseases like Alzheimer's which is now colloquially called 'Type-3 Diabetes'.

Adding to this is the science around circadian-based eating, wherein consuming sugar at night compounds the ill effects of a sugar rush on the body by potentially disrupting sleep. Fashionable dietary systems like intermittent fasting or mantras like 'don't eat within three hours of going to sleep' reinforce the awareness for the health benefits of not consuming dessert or curbing evening sugar intake.

All this leaves restaurants and hotels in a predicament. If these trends continue, the entire dessert course may be on the chopping block and along with it a good portion of the digestif or post-meal alcohol sales. Psychologically speaking, meal satisfaction is largely a product of the time spent at a table; any reduction here due to the modern customer's distaste for dessert may thus have knock-on effects for a hotel's word of mouth and how an overnight guest eating in-house perceives their overall hotel stay.

Ultimately, this is a challenge to be treated like any other, and hotels will persevere by adapting just as they've done countless times before. Undoubtedly the low-sugar trend is already on the minds of every pastry chef. What we can offer is a simple framework or operating territory for healthier indulgences that are lower in sugar through which to focus the team's attention. Just as artists of previous eras often produced their most seminal work when commissioned by a patron with a very specific agenda, by limiting your chefs' field of view onto just a handful of ingredients, they will deliver masterful results.

The five dessert components that we've singled out based on our own nutritional and wellness research are fruit, nuts, honey, dark chocolate and cheese. The first and third may at first glance contradict our low-sugar creative brief, so best read on.

In describing what you can do with each of these, one other characteristic of note with the low-sugar craze is that it overlaps with a steady increase of customer knowledge and curiosity around specific compounds within certain foods. As an example of this progression, recall the word 'anthocyanin' which is now commonly known to denote a prominent class of antioxidants found primarily in dark berries (and promoted as such), yet this level of awareness was hardly the case a mere five years ago.

Therefore, it's our belief that alongside your restaurant's adaptation to healthier times comes an opportunity for enhancing the meal experience through customer education about why you selected a given ingredient. On this front, we will throw in a few pointers to show you just how far down the wellness rabbit hole you can go.

Fruit

Otherwise known as nature's candy, numerous restaurants already do brisk business off of simple sliced varieties artfully arranged for a dessert platter. Importantly for intact fruit, their insulin-spiking effects are buffered by the presence of fiber, water, polyphenols and flavonoids.

One way to get creative here is to opt for sourcing more exotic, regional or seasonal species – ones that guests may see in the grocery store but are too intimidated to sample or learn how to prepare. This hints at culinary classes, giving guests expertise that they can bring home with them. Another way to proceed is by focusing on those fruits lowest on the glycemic index, advertising it as a slow carb alternative.

Finally, one matter to note is that any form of mechanical processing, such as blending into a smoothie or purée, dislodges the fruit's sugars from its fibers and antioxidants, spiking blood sugar levels faster as a result. As a sciency aside, this processing can also increase food waste by releasing the fruit's own polyphenol oxidase, the enzyme in bananas, apples, avocados and others that causes quick browning and spoilage upon contact with air.

Nuts

As the natural yang to fruit's yin, this sweet and savory combination stands the test of time, albeit nowadays with far more substitutions for those with allergies. Besides scavenging for rare breeds from across the globe or making your own house-made nut butter blends, the one term we will add to this conversation is sprouting.

That is, nuts being the seeds of a tree often contain mildly toxic molecules on their coatings like phytic acid and tannins in order to ward away would-be predators. Soaking nuts for a full day then dehydrating them helps to remove most of these. And while this extra step is laborious, adding the term 'sprouted' on the menu will command guest's attention and justify the surcharge.

Honey

The fruit of the bees comes in near-endless varieties based upon whatever flowers the insects happen to be pollinating. Tastings are thus the name of the game, where the emphasis is not on delivering a large serving of each type but on the more experiential aspects – pairings, presentation, and some sage tableside guidance from the server.

While honey may appear to violate the low-sugar rule, in its raw, unadulterated (and non-counterfeit) form it is the exception due to its high minerality, antimicrobial contents, and diverse array of modulating types of sugar like trehalose. If there's one type of honey worth calling it, manuka is prized for containing strongly antibacterial molecules where concentrations are marketed by a UMF (unique manuka factor) rating scale.

Chocolate

To curb insulin spikes, dietitians might recommend sticking with 85% cacao or above, but this is perhaps a bit too prescriptive; lowering the cutoff to 70% dark chocolate will allow your team to introduce more flavors, especially from the aforementioned fruits and nuts. This also hints as chocolate tastings, while much more can be said about dark chocolate and wine pairings. And lest we forget that chocolate fondue is always incredible.

To further limit refined sugar, sugar alcohol should be considered as an artificial sweetener like erythritol, maltitol, or xylitol that stimulates the palate without affecting the body in the same way as sucrose. As another science aside, cacao has more recently come under fire for its heavy metal content, but this too can be solved by adding a pinch of a chelating agent like activated charcoal or food ash (which can be made from parts of plant ingredients that would normally go to waste) to bind up those harmful atoms and prevent their absorption into the bloodstream.

Cheese

Now onward to the full savory side of things, many of us forget that dessert need not be sweet. Anyone who has experienced real French cuisine knows the unbridled bliss of the after-entrée cheese course where a full board of camembert, brie, blues, aged goat, mimolette, comté, tomme and a host of other regional delicacies are laid out for nibbling – always accompanied by exquisite wine, of course.

Bringing it all together, a cheeseboard with fruits, nuts or honey as accoutrements may typically appear on the appetizer end of the menu, but a curated selection of cheeses for desserts can be a great upsell when given the right marketing panache. As our final sciency aside, while blue cheeses are often detested for their stinky qualities, certain compounds made by the mold used to turn the dairy that color are now being studied for eliciting more vivid dreams when consumed closer to bedtime. Bon appetit et fais de beaux rêves!

Bringing in Blue Zone Foods

We all make New Year's resolutions and succumb to the perfunctory promises of self-improvement for the following 12 months. We bet that staying in shape or incorporating some form of healthier eating habits tops the list.

Importantly, if you have dietary resolutions, no doubt your guests do, too. And they'll be looking for hotels to accommodate their needs accordingly. With most diets continually trending in the direction of healthier, cleaner, organic, local, more plant-based and many other modern criteria, it's important that hotel restaurants periodically renew their menu to keep apace of this demand.

On a fundamental level, this should be done to ensure that hotel restaurants are adequately providing for their guests by offering acceptable foods to meet their various dietary restrictions. But it can also mean increased revenues.

Innovations insofar as creative new dishes that are vegan or using only organic and locally sourced ingredients can command greater price points as well as help to attract high-end clientele. This can have a 'halo' on rooms revenue as product differentiation in the F&B space can give guests a heightened reason to stay with you over the competition. Any resultant prestige can thus be factored into potential RevPAR growth and also garner more local awareness.

All told, with dietary habits changing so quickly nowadays, this is not something you can ignore. But there's one other emerging trend that may perhaps be more to your liking than, say, expensively converting a kitchen to be entirely plant-based.

As per the title, we are referring to foods from our planet's renowned Blue Zones, those semi-isolated and largely agrarian regions peppered across multiple continents where the inhabitants quite often reach triple digits of lifespan. Based on a lot of research from various agencies as well as an eponymous book on the subject, the five key zones identified are:

- The islands of Okinawa, Japan

- The island of Sardinia, Italy
- The island of Ikaria, Greece
- The Nicoya Peninsula in Costa Rica
- The town of Loma Linda in California, particularly its Seventh Day Adventist population

The idea of blue zone foods came about during a late 2019 strategic planning session for a resort where my consultancy was recruited to help relaunch the signature dining outlet. During this meeting, it was deemed that going wholly vegan didn't fit with the overall brand nor target demographic, but that some measures towards healthier, plant-based food options needed to be incorporated in order to fit with the long-term vision of moving into the wellness space.

By adding a single dish on the menu, it helped us address this demand without any additional strain on the kitchen team or increasing ingredient costs. In this instance, the item we added was a 'Blue Zone Minestrone' that echoed the traditional hearty Sardinian soup with a variety of vegetables, beans, whole grain pasta and fresh herbs simmering away for hours on end and perfect for a filling winter lunch. Moreover, inserting the actual words 'blue zone' into the title garnered a lot of attention from patrons who then inquired about what it meant, and subsequently praised our efforts upon learning about the longevity-inducing abilities of said foods.

Although blue zone foods are indeed mostly plant-based, my hope in bringing this to your attention is so that you know there are other variations upon the broad progression towards vegetarian, flexitarian and vegan lifestyles that you can deploy to gain a marketing edge over your competitors. And if you have any blue zone recipes at the ready, we'd love to give them a try!

Leveraging the Ancestral Diet Trend to Upgrade Your Hotel Breakfast

Like fashion, dieting has its trends that come and go. It used to be low-fat everything, while now many of us are all about low carb to blunt those insulin spikes. Full continental breakfasts are still a mainstay; just now their presence is padded by the likes of avocado toast, overnight oats or superfood smoothies. To those without a firm understanding of nutrition, it may seem a bit haphazard, but underneath every new menu unveiling is a hidden trail of scientific research suggesting a healthier path forward.

One of the latest dietary trends that have emerged attempts to answer the question, "Before the agricultural revolution, what would our ancestors have eaten to keep themselves healthy through all four seasons?" Slightly controversial because of how it repudiates veganism and the larger push for plant-based eating, ancestral eating is grounded by the anthropological evidence that the human species has always been an 'opportunistic omnivore' – that we are flexible scavengers as well as crafty fishers and tenacious hunters.

Without getting too far into the weeds of what our paleolithic cousins ate (although weeds like purslane were on the menu for our ancestors), this meant that in summer and early autumn, we laid traps and gorged on wild fruit, while in winter, we tracked down great beasts then found a way to fire roast every last morsel of flesh. Nothing went to waste. With animal husbandry in its infancy, any dairy that was eaten was either as raw milk or as a microbially diverse, fermented product like kefir. Similarly, grains and pseudocereals were at the 'hobbyist farmer' stage at this point and only ever consumed in a slow, yeast-worked form.

Besides the overarching lesson in eschewing ultra-processed foods and opting for more organic ingredients, the tenets of ancestral dieting can be applied to any F&B outlet to differentiate the operation from competitors, offer menu items that are science-backed to support better health and appeal to the growing subculture that's willing to pay a bit more for paleo-approved options.

Here are several to consider that will put you on the right track.

1. *Wild berry cultivars.* What's happened over the past few centuries is that we've started breeding fruits for bigger yields and heightened sweetness to boost profits and palatability. The consequence is that our fruits now have an unnaturally high amount of sugar and reduced antioxidant levels; they aren't as 'nutrient dense' as their wild progenitors. Make no mistake: consuming any fruit is a step in the right direction (except for diabetics). But if you are to opt for 'nature's candy', why not consume the best possible version of it? With berries highlighted for their low fructose content (that's the type of sugar that can overload the liver) and high amounts of polyphenols, let's consider blueberries – irrefutably one of the healthiest foods on the planet. Whether organic or not, most blueberries that reach the market are of the highbush cultivar which has been engineered for its large size and high sugar content. Restaurants can thus wow their patrons by sourcing the antioxidant-laden lowbush varietal (often sold as frozen from Nova Scotia), which is a fraction of the size but has a mystifyingly deep indigo color.
2. *Sourdough bread.* With F&B outlets now having to label items as gluten-free as well as come up with alternatives for celiacs such as chickpea-based pastas, researchers have simultaneously started investigating why people in Southern Europe and the Levant can regularly indulge in grains well into their nonagenarian years without any chronic issues while we North Americans will feel bloated and lethargic after one or two portions of bread. While there are numerous other contributing factors from the revered Mediterranean diet, one culprit on this side of the pond is that we don't let yeast do its thing. Bread that is mechanically processed over a few hours doesn't give the microbes enough time to chew away at the gluten. This process takes days, with the yeast breaking down those gut-irritating proteins with the fermented byproduct of acid for that unmistakable sour taste. While working with sourdough requires patience and, therefore, is an added cost for a commercial kitchen, the word itself is highly

marketable, and you needn't limit yourself to only bread, with sourdough pizza and pasta both in vogue.

3. *Soaked or sprouted nuts.* One important aspect of evolution to understand is that while animals avoid getting eaten by running away, plants fight back through chemical warfare. Flora don't want you to eat their young, and they coat their seeds with compounds that can be highly toxic (or indigestible) to a would-be scavenger to allow the next generation to flourish. With this in mind, we often forget that nuts are the seeds of trees and that the outer layer is laced with antinutrients that can present problems when consumed in large quantities. The solution that our ancestors came up with was to simply soak nuts in water for half a day or a full 24 hours so that the tannins and phytic acid would dissolve away from the shell. A step further was to cycle the nuts through several periods of wet and then dry conditions so that the seeds would sprout (this works for beans, too). From there, you simply dehydrate the nuts back to their dry form. Again, this is a slow and costlier process, but adjectives like 'soaked' or 'sprouted' come with a justifiable surcharge.
4. *Goat or sheep dairy.* Shifting into the animal kingdom, we have already mentioned kefir which does wonders for restoring the gut microbiome. What nutritionists have found, though, is that the milk of goats and sheep is significantly healthier for us than that from cows, with further anthropological evidence pointing to an earlier domestication point for these two species over the larger livestock. Goat and sheep dairy products naturally contain more medium-chain triglycerides (MCTs) which are keto-friendly and help to promote metabolic flexibility for a healthier liver. Moreover, unlike cows of Northern European pedigree that contain the potentially harmful A1-casein protein, goat and sheep milk or cheese won't have this, making both safer for those who feel bad after drinking regular cow's milk.
5. *Nose-to-tail burgers or sausages.* One core mantra espoused by ancestral dieters is that our ancestors ate every part of an animal; the nose, the offal, the oxtail and every other bit of sinew was often boiled down into a collagenous stew. It follows that we should all be eating more organ meats because gram-for-gram these are technically the most nutrient-dense foods on the planet. North America is a bit of an oddity in this regard because we are one of the only places on the planet where you can't regularly find these cuts on the menu. Italians have trippa alla parmigiana (tripe); a common street food in Turkey is kokoretsi (spit-roasted offal); and you can easily find barbecued chicken hearts at any Thai night market. We aren't asking you to go full Liver King with your menu, but luckily meat producers are starting to incorporate the healthier organs into a form that's palatable for Canadians and Americans by grinding offal products into burgers and sausages. It's but one way to ease your guests into these foods.
6. *Intermittent fasting.* We close not on a particular ingredient but on a way of eating that's gaining popularity. On a traditional hunt, our ancestors

likely went long periods without any food, with study after study showing the huge health benefits of giving your digestive tract regular breaks from meals. Thinking existentially about your F&B revenues and how they fit into the greater profitability mix at a hotel, as this trend gains ground what happens when a large number of your guests no longer eat breakfast and thus aren't motivated by your B&B offers? The obvious answer is to have incredible coffee service, but alas the idea around fasting is something every hotelier will have to confront insofar as how it affects foodservice revenues and hotel packaging.

Invasivorism as the Next Food Trend for Hotels

The English language sure loves its neologisms. (Don't look this one up in your dictionary. It's not there…yet.) The one in the title adds an 'ism' onto 'invasivore' where this latter word is ascribed to species that have been accidentally or purposefully introduced into a foreign environment where there are no natural predators to keep their numbers in check, thus diminishing biodiversity. Foremost examples are the African cane toads that have ravaged the Australian continent and the zebra mussels that have similarly become endemic to the Great Lakes.

Specific to you, it's important for hoteliers keep tabs on these sorts of trends because, in the relentless progression of global climate change, customers will continue to demand more from their travel brands to help foster a culture of sustainability. Right now, environmentalism is largely a value-add to make guests feel good about their hotel selections (with the ability to command a few extra dollars in rate for the privilege). There may come a time soon, though, when sustainability is scored, and businesses failing to get a good grade are shunned by prospective bookers.

Invasivorism for hotel restaurants amounts to putting these foods on the menu as a means to:

1. Help build an economic system around the farming and the consumption of invasivores
2. Reduce the stigma of eating these species by transforming them into palatable dishes
3. Raise awareness for the need to cull invasivores to bring indigenous species back into balance
4. Offer a point of differentiation to help with the marketing and PR of your F&B program
5. Round out a brand-wide sustainability initiative that incorporates numerous departments

As you can already tell, the first of these five is hardly easy at present because the supply chains just aren't there. This will change. Think back around two decades when the phrase 'authentically local' was first gaining steam. Stocking inventory from local providers back then required lots of effort because each relationship had to be set up one-to-one and we just didn't yet have the critical mass of adjustable manufacturers to cost-effectively engage in small batch productions.

Now, living local, buying local and eating local are all but the expectation from hotels, albeit they still require a hefty load of setup and care. We foresee invasivorism taking a similar trajectory with hotels benefited from their larger procurement networks to take advantage of this trend.

Personal demand for climate action often begins with an awareness campaign for the 'charismatic megafauna' like a reminder about how few panda there are left, a news story about the recent extinction of the northern white rhino or a video of an emaciated polar bear struggling to find solid footing on a patchwork of half-melted ice blocks. Likewise, invasivorism will start with a ramp up in access to and the edible acceptance of one of the largest provocateurs. Our bet is on the four types of Asian carp invasive to the Mississippi River system – slimy and a pain to debone, but still a suitable substitute for salmon or tuna when minced and sauced.

Not merely a soylent green alternative, invasivorism has applicability for haute cuisine, too. People opt for sophisticated fine dining experiences not only to attain satiety but also to be inspired by the chef's wild, esoteric ingredient combinations as well as having something to talk about with friends at the next dinner party. This last reason may as well be called bragging rights, so give your restaurants something to brag out.

To close, to merge together the haute cuisine element with the awareness and education ones, you are approaching an experience that can be classified as 'transformative' – leaving the guest better off than when they arrived at your hotel. By promoting the ingestion of foods that are not native to a land – in sharp contrast to local eating and the direct opposite of indigenous eating – you are inspiring your customers to reframe the environmental conversation and making them feel good in the process for their active contribution.

If you build enough of these sustainability-related experiences into your brand – of which invasivorism is one possible inclusion – your guests will adore you for it and be willing to pay above market for the opportunity to stay with you.

The One Profit Center Your Hotel Is Missing Is Water

"Will that be still or sparkling?" as a question asked by servers is about to get far more complicated, and it has profound implications for not just onsite restaurants but for all instances in your rooms where guests directly interact with water – namely, bottles, sink and shower.

For those who just want the TLDR, here's our thesis:

1. As wellness becomes a central facet of society, there's growing awareness for the hidden dangers lurking within our water supplies and their long-term health effects.

2. This concern can justify additional onsite filtration capex or upscale bottling as branded features to drive nightly rates or supplemental revenues in the room and at the restaurant.
3. Concurrently, as ESG takes hold, hotels will have to upgrade their water management systems and eliminate single-use plastics, presenting yet two more marketable brand features.
4. The bottom line is that water is no longer just water but is rife with innovation, trends and technologies to aid in ramping up both sustainability practices as well as human longevity.

The Problem

The rationale for wanting ever-cleaner water comes down to what biologists and physicians call hormone or endocrine disruptors. We have completed enough longitudinal population studies to draw statistical causality between the long-term exposure from such substances like heavy metals, pesticides, herbicides, bisphenols in canned goods, phthalates in cosmetics, solvents in sunscreens and even prescribed medications leftover in our water supplies that all have detrimental health effects like mood disorders, chronic inflammation, obesity and low testosterone levels.

This is what human longevity pundits would codify as a 'death by a thousand cuts' problem. The acute exposure to something hazardous like glyphosate or atrazine (both are herbicides sprayed on non-organic crops that leech into our foods and animal feed) won't register a noticeable effect, any yet chronic, decades-long ingestion will accelerate other negative health conditions by jumbling the proper ratio of our bodily chemicals and preoccupying the immune system.

Excising these chemicals from our lives is a huge, existential challenge made even worse by the fact that the unnatural stuff we humans produce also affects other species, potentially leading to bioaccumulation up the food chain, mutations, or environmental degradation. For instance, some compounds in non-mineral sunscreens (often in addition to being hormone disruptors) have been shown to bleach coral reefs, helping propel the movement for 'reef safe' products.

As governments and corporations become more draconian with their environmental policies, cleaning up the water will undoubtedly gain more attention, necessitating upgrades at municipal facilities, at individual buildings and for commercially sold products. For the everyday consumer, the combination of this ever-growing focus on ESG with each new scientific analysis that reaches the airwaves on a particular health hazard will drive more and more people to reconsider drinking regular tap water.

This will be reflected at home with the purchasing of advanced filtration units like a kitchen reverse osmosis system, a hard water filter for the showerhead or something more mobile like a filtered water pitcher. And as one does in private, one will expect the same (or better) for public spaces, meaning that there may soon be a time when your guests will grimace at the server's mere mention of unfiltered tap water, the presence of only soft, single-use plastic bottled water in the room (which often contain leeched phthalates) or the lack of any additional shower water filtration.

The Opportunity

Hardly a glass-half-empty situation where your hotel will inevitably have to absorb the mandated capex, this is the perfect application of the blue ocean strategic thinking (both puns intended).

That is, deploying advanced water filtration systems within the guestrooms can become a visible and marketable room feature so that you can lure in the growing wellness-minded crowd or possibly command a higher nightly rate. Then in the restaurant, with the right explanation guests will be more than willing to pay a reasonable fee for having bottles of filtered still or sparkling, or by procured a trusted supplier in this space. At the very least, it will enhance the meal experience.

For in-room upgrades, the two of us have long ragged on hotels that overcharge for bottled water. One thing we are entirely sure of: single-use plastic bottles are a dinosaur and they simply must go, both for the hormone disruption reason as well as to appease climatarians.

Now let's say you instead source a high-end bottled water supplier that uses either hard plastic or aluminum in a graphically pleasing manner; this can help to justify the price tag of what we would consider overcharging the guest. Moreover, a mineral water selection could be part of the new minibar stock as you rethink this oft-staid amenity.

While thinking about water bottles, you can also consider these as branded souvenirs – a nice gesture for guest satisfaction but also one that will help with 'social proofing' due to their utility outside of the household. Common on cruise ships nowadays is to provide each cabin with a metal refillable water bottle and then have pure water pump stations all over the boat (caveat: this may not be as practical for hotels that deal with a much more transient guest).

Such initiatives are obviously not for every hotel organization, but we are witnessing a continual climb in wellness-driven guests for which these sorts of health-boosting amenities are meaningful, both in their brand selection and for generating ancillary spend.

So, perhaps you test the waters (apologies, these water puns just flow) by carving out a new 'wellness room' category after renovating a single floor, installing vitamin C shower filters and a reverse osmosis tap with an aluminum bottle next to it for refilling, alongside other upgrades like smart lighting, HEPA air filters and exercise equipment.

Then taking the long view on ESG, we know that environmentalism will become both increasingly important for guests (especially from the younger generations) while governments will simultaneously be ramping up bylaws. Together, this means there is a clear and present case for conducting a study on the cost and breakeven point of installing new water saving or water recycling systems. Much like how you can market purified water to guests, we would argue that right now sustainability can also be leveraged as a marketing tool to garner the advocacy of these customer mindsets and to drive rate.

The Future

To end, let's give you one totally-out-there possibility to show where the market for high-end water may be headed. Bear with us while we riff through some chemistry, while the overall point is that this omnipresent fluid offers many layers of technologies that you can capitalize upon.

Hardly mainstream science just yet, but there is emerging evidence that 'deuterium-depleted water' (DDW) can help to improve the piezoelectric structuring of gel-state water within our cells and mitochondria to optimize protein folding and boost energy levels. For reference, deuterium is an isotope of hydrogen that combines with oxygen to form 'heavy water' denoted as D20 versus regular water which is H20, where these atomic-level disturbances to the fluid's structure are caused by heavy water's sharper bond angle over light water (120 degrees for the D-O bond versus 135 degrees for H-O bonds).

In most water supplies – save for glacial runoff and fresh mountain spring water – heavy water naturally exists only around 150 parts per million. Still, this is another death-by-a-thousand-cuts issue.

Thus, using special machinery (which are on the market today) to remove D2O and create purified DDW or 'light water' can theoretically work over a long period of time it may improve health. Fascinatingly, the impetus for investigating DDW as a salve came from the bathing waters beneath the Sanctuary of Our Lady of Lourdes in France, which have long been sought out for their 'miraculous' healing abilities.

All this is to say that *water is not just water anymore*. There are innovations happening and new ways to use the latest water trends to build revenues for your hotel. Maybe in a decade a server at a fine dining establishment can get away with asking the table, "With that be still, sparkling or deuterium-depleted water?" Mind you, the latter entry in this sci-fi case would be priced far higher than the former two.

For now, though, know that there are steps you can take to use something so commonplace and vital to our lives as water to augment the guest experience. Wellness-minded customers want it and the ESG mandates are soon to follow, so get started today.

Where Have All the Breadbaskets Gone?

Before the pandemic, it was quite customary in restaurants to whet the appetite with the tableside delivery of a breadbasket or some variation of a small loaf of bread as a welcome to the establishment. There has always been a positive symbolism with this act, as breaking bread not only increases meal satisfaction by alleviating any hunger pangs but also implies a deeper sense of trust and camaraderie.

There's more here on the psychological and monetary front. The bread serves as a timing delay tactic, giving the kitchen more time to prepare the selected appetizers and mains while simultaneously easing the diners into the setting and prompting them to linger with an opening cocktail or wine order. In this manner, the breadbasket may slow the table turn but ultimately improve the revenue per cover.

Now, in the post-pandemic world, we can't help but notice that bread service at our favorite restaurants is no longer free, with prices ranging from $4 to $12 per order. Obviously, this has been commonplace throughout Europe for quite some time; it nevertheless requires an adjustment for those who aren't used to the surcharge. We understand the need to hold the line on costs; after all, the bread course is not free as it has to be either baked in-house or bought from a local supplier.

In our opinion, though, there is still something magical about sitting down at the restaurant dining table and having the wait staff deliver fresh bread. It cements the welcoming atmosphere and creates a sense of arrival. For those who have an in-house bakery, it demonstrates the creativity of your staff.

To now discover bread on the menu, gawk at the price, think about all the health reasons why we should not consume bread, and then opt to reject or accept it seems like setting the meal off to a very unsatisfactory start. True, it's a minor grievance as people are likely to weigh their mains, drinks and company over mere bread, but first impressions are powerful, nonetheless.

Further, we also wonder if anyone has done an analysis of TripAdvisor scores between those restaurants with complimentary bread service versus those with bread as a paid menu item. It would be difficult to quantity but perhaps there's a way to get some anecdotal feedback from servers in terms of how many times on the average night they are asked about the bread service or what's entailed in its menu price.

So, is this penny wise, pound foolish? Or is it a sign of the times (at least here in North America where it used to be mostly gratis), reflecting the need to recoup past losses or a throughput from all the current staff shortages? What position does your restaurant take on this dough-y matter?

Your Bartender Is Your Real Hotel Concierge

How do guests learn about what's happening on the property once they arrive? You already know where we are going with this one.

One clear victor in the post-pandemic era has been the hotel bar, whether off the lobby, tucked away from non-guests or up on the roof. People love the ability to reconnect and socialize with some unique and colorful cocktails thrown into the mix. The infamy of a good hotel bar makes it the natural converging point for out-of-towners looking for the latest and greatest, both about the incumbent hotel and the destination at large.

But wait. Isn't telling your incoming guests about the amenities onsite the job of all that great technology you're using? Yes, but sometimes guests don't read the confirmation email, are ignoring your prearrival communications and are too 'apped-out' to want to download your hotel app. You must always stay cognizant of the 'context' of a particular guest.

Both of us are planners of the militant variety, mapping our hotel itineraries months in advance. Both of us work frenetically to achieve the hallowed ground of inbox zero every Friday. Others like to play it by ear and have 25,000 unread emails just sitting there. For people of this latter disposition, all your tech may be for naught because you misread their 'context' of wanting to be sold once onsite or after arrival and likely by a real person where the chat about the amenity or the experience is part of the fun of it all.

Newer tech pieces like contextual digital signage are helping address this challenge in a labor-light answer, but you still need every at-bat to get those hits in – that is, to maximize revenue per guest – with the cross-training of your server team a great way to build that ancillary spend. Now we get to the next problem: how do you motivate your bartenders, mixologists, and servers to care about anything other than the cuisine and beverages that will directly pad their own pockets via higher average guest covers and better tips?

The first answer has everything to do with culture and company policy. Have you built an organization where servers are part of the restaurant or the hotel? Are you taking the time to explain to them the 'halo effect'? That is, from the guest's point of view, experiences at the restaurant spill over onto the perception of the entire hotel. Are you incorporating hotel happenings into stand-up meetings for the server team or as part of team tasting and training sessions? You can also incentivize them by rewarding good team members with comped room nights, free spa treatments or gift shop vouchers so that they can speak from the heart about these amenities. Just a few ideas…

An important caveat here is for those properties that have third party-managed restaurants, likely in place to maintain a lower-cost operating model. In these cases, there is little you can do besides bringing this issue up with your management partner. And as strategic advisors, one of the big questions we have helped owners to answer on past consulting assignments is whether these third-party F&B outlets are serving the greater whole or not. That is, are owner profits ultimately suffering because the outsourced restaurant isn't adequately representing the hotel or feeding business back to the rooms?

Next, there's the power of technology, in this case, the bulletins, app-based checklists and blackboard training tools you have likely mandated as an adaptation to pandemic operations. All these tools can be used for 'bite-sized learning' or the insertion of tiny bits of information to remind your teams about your amenities and subtly nudge them to mention them in conversations with guests. The key here is to keep it simple and as brief as possible with your messaging.

The third key area pertains to all the tactics you can deploy to drive guests to the restaurant, knowing that the customer-staff interactions in that outlet will inevitably lead to more guest utilization of other amenities. Likely, you are already giving this your full attention, but it nevertheless deserves yet more of your time regarding such labor-light activations like app-based drinks or appetizers, F&B packaging that specifically highlights off-peak traffic to the restaurant and in-room personalized digital promotions.

In sum, it's all about knowing what the trend is, then looking at how your various piece of tech can help you capitalize upon it without requiring more labor.

Right now, the hotel bar is experiencing a revival while guests who are over-satiated by screens are reverting to the 'old school' method of asking a real person what they should do or where they should go. There are plenty of ways to make this work for your topline growth.

Innovation Inspiration Happening at the Hotel Lugano Dante's Bar

Implementing operational change is always difficult, and yet from the guest's perspective it's often the little touches that make the experience exceptional. In this case, why care about something as small as a new beverage offering? We point to the 'halo effect' where, in the guest's mind, non-room amenities echo back onto overall property satisfaction.

This brings us to our friend, Carlo Fontana, owner and operator of the Hotel Lugano Dante in Lugano, Switzerland and its onsite Flamel Restaurant and Bar which prides itself on being at the cutting edge of bar technology. The mission at Flamel is to highlight the local Swiss tastes while elevating the concept of mixology by having every single drink component produced entirely in-house.

The Equipment

At the center of Flamel's mixology tech is a BuchiRotavapor® R-300 rotary evaporator, a pharmaceutical-grade alcohol distiller, costing approximately $16,000 plus accessories. The rotary evaporator allows the restaurant to bring new flavors into its drinks by extracting the 'soul' of each ingredient.

Picture the Rotavapor as a modern still; it works under vacuum so that the evaporation point of each liquid occurs around room temperature. The result is that fragrances are kept intact.

While this price tag may induce sticker shock, it's an example of pain now, profit later. The equipment costs and training were all amortized, but after that only small quantities of externally purchased bottles were required, resulting in an average internal bottle production cost of 50% versus wholesale purchases.

The Training

Following standard recipes with some experimentation, Flamel uses this equipment to make its own gins, absinths, malts and liquors. Not only is the bar team allowed to become mixologists by crafting wild new cocktails, but they are also immersed in the classical teachings of how vacuum distillation works.

Given the complexity of making literally everything from scratch, training of the five-person team is continuous and was fraught with mistakes at the program's outset. Fontana notes, though, that this training encourages an ongoing dialogue amongst the team, distillers and other craftsmen, offering a profound bonding experience that severely curtails turnover. The process acts as a deeper form of continuing professional development by incentivizing the team to learn the technical skills of processing the raw materials into beverage ingredients.

The Ingredients

With everything produced onsite, the only inputs are pure Swiss grain alcohol, with 98% of other ingredients also from Switzerland and the remaining 2% of raw spices sourced from around the world. Besides distilling different types of citrus fruit, many of the herbs used come from the hotel's nearby urban garden, while the team is constantly challenged to infuse unusual ingredients like jalapeño, black garlic and horseradish.

Even with this laboratory mindset, management nevertheless keeps the menu approachable with twists on classic cocktails – a negroni made from self-produced liqueurs or an old fashioned with Swiss rye whiskey and diluted with birch water. Bonus points here on the sustainability front as this push for everything local has sharply minimized food miles insofar as the procurement of exotic raw materials.

For its bar ice, Flamel uses a technique called 'directional freezing' where microfiltered water is put in large insulating containers, and after about 48 hours blocks of crystalline ice are formed with impurity residues at the bottom that can be separated out. Such blocks melt much more slowly and can be stored in the freezer instead of having to be thrown away every night as is the case in most cocktail bars.

The Results

Being avant-garde to the nth degree certainly generates that wow factor, but Fontana isn't afraid to admit that it can alienate the less adventurous visitors. The key to overcoming this challenge has been to wholly embrace the concept at every touchpoint of the hotel's messaging so that guests are aware of how different Flamel is well before they arrive. Setting this expectation ensures that the surprise always skews positive when the finished blend is served at the table.

The core philosophy here reinforces a mantra that the two of us deploy: try to appeal to everything and resonate with no one. Flamel isn't for everyone and that's entirely why it works.

Epicurean Ventures for the Travel Recovery

Interview originally published in December 2020 and the indicated opinions by Marc Bauer, formerly of Epicurean Atlanta at the time of this writing may not reflect current company practices.

We've always espoused the mantra that the core of any property's success is their F&B. Some golf, some are into wellness, but everyone eats. As demonstrated by a property we acted on as asset manager a few years ago, a property can even overcome deficiencies in their rooms' product through a focus on exceptional dining.

Now imagine a clean slate; an opportunity to build a hotel from scratch with a focus on food. This is the basis for the Epicurean Hotel opening this summer in Atlanta, Georgia. The Atlanta property follows the 2014 launch of the Epicurean in Tampa, Florida. Built by Mainsail Lodging & Development, both properties are operated within Marriott's Autograph Collection.

A Zoom call with Marc Bauer, the Epicurean Atlanta's General Manager, gave us some insight into the new property. We met Marc several years ago when he was the GM at the Hotel Duval in Tallahassee. His enthusiasm was both contagious and encouraging.

In brief, the property occupies one of three towers that comprise a full city block (3.5 acres) just south of the city's Marriott Suites and Four Seasons properties. The other towers – one being offices, the other a condominium – all surround a public plaza. Consistent with the trend towards development of the downtown core, these structures replace a dubious collection of parking lots and light commercial ventures.

The 16-story Epicurean Atlanta features 178 rooms including 22 suites. At the core of the property is a culinary demonstration kitchen capable of 'enter-learning' – a clever portmanteau of entertainment plus learning. With its classroom-style configuration, the room can host 100 attendees. Reverence, the signature restaurant, seats 127, and is ably curated by Executive Chef Ewart Wardhaugh, who brings an international hand to the kitchen.

In the following interview, we look at how to create a food-centric hotel through the lens of the expected travel recovery as guests re-emerge from the pandemic restrictions.

Is this a culinary adventure wrapped in a hotel or a hotel that features great F&B?

If we've learned one thing from the past year, it's that a hotel has to be more than a place to grab a few hours of rest. We like to think of our property as culinary-centric. Hotels must create experiences and generate revenue beyond the guestroom, and the best way to do this is through food and beverage. Another great advantage of being a food destination is community presence in that we want the property to be a destination for locals.

So, does the restaurant pay homage to food?

Yes, absolutely, but more importantly the origins of the food and beverage. The growers, makers and fishers. At Reverence, diners will experience regional cuisine with a locavore focus. Being blessed by our location in the heart of Georgia, we can furnish just about everything that is consumed within an easy driving distance. Our menus will reflect this with seasonal revisions as well as specials based upon immediate availability.

Tell us about your demonstration kitchen.

We call it a culinary theatre. To be successful, you have to deliver an experience to your guests. Picture a typical group event. Delegates meet for the business part of their get-together, usually followed by a social function such as a dinner. Now imagine the effect when the social function is replaced by mixology or cooking demonstration where everyone is participating. There are demonstration kitchens in the area, but we believe we will be the largest and certainly the most modern from a technological standpoint.

How are you welcoming guests?
First, we reimagined the arrival experience. The Epicurean journey begins with a complimentary glass of wine or craft beer, check-in is completed on a tablet in the guestroom. The kitchen is not hidden but behind a glass partition wall, so diners can gain a better understanding of preparation techniques.

What new technologies are you incorporating?
We want to be contactless, but at the same time, retain a personalized touch. As mentioned, arriving guests will be checked in on tablets. We will also adapt many guest-centric technologies such as in-room Google Nest and Volara voice-based activation allowing for customizable experiences.

What about your guestrooms?
Modern and comfortable, of course, but we also wanted to extend the foodie experience here as well. Instead of the usual minibar with outrageous pricing, we are offering an artisan pantry which will feature local producers' products – soft drinks, craft beer, snacks and so on – at prices that are more reasonable.

Any last words?
The pandemic has afforded us the opportunity to capitalize upon a wealth of great talent in the city. As we are building our team from scratch, we will search out individuals committed to exceptional service and who identify as food centric. We're excited about the opportunity.

Future Foods for Hotels

Food and beverage for hotels is at a bit of an inflection point. On the one hand, we are still contending with all the inflationary wages, short staffing and supply chain headaches left over the pandemic. On the other, we have a recession year ahead of us where we still need to derive profits from the onsite eatery (or at least use the chef-driven restaurant concept to support hotel bookings).

Innovation is the only way forward, and hopefully there's a trend here that inspires you. Therein, the two of us trust that you are already investigating some of in vogue fusion cuisine trends, more vegetable-centric meal options, the umami punch of incorporating mushrooms or, for larger hotels, how to revitalize a public area with a food hall concept.

Thinking beyond cyclicals, one other existential and secular issue that many hotels we've worked with are facing is the schism between healthy and more 'traditional' eaters. There are those longstanding guests that want a burger and fries, and will complain whenever the price goes up or if you change a single dish on the menu. At the same point, kowtowing to only this old guard will alienate the growing number of people who want their on-premises dining option to be organic, vegan, vegetarian, gluten-free, dairy-free, raw, locally sourced, or any other form of wellness-branded.

You can venture into this wellness F&B space, but after the new ingredient costs are considered who knows if it's actually profitable! (Measuring whether or not is subject to a whole other article on POS data usage where, for the time being we recommend you focus on deeper integrations.)

With all this in mind, here are some buzz terms to get you thinking:

1. *Tea:* Who would've thought, right? Most F&B outlets pride themselves on their coffee service, but tea offers a tremendously diverse selection by which to enhance the meal experience. There are the caffeinated blends, or single origin versions, of green, white, black, oolong and orange, but when designing a modern tea program there is now much more appreciation for high-end herbal and functional blends.
2. *Generation Zilch:* This is a new nickname for the late-millennial and centennial cohorts that is gaining steam as a way of describing their comparatively clean forms of vice. Whether driven by the economics of the times or awareness of the detrimental health effects, young people today are minimizing or abstaining from drinking regularly and smoking (even vaping). As alcohol is where the margins are, you need to start thinking of pivoting to other beverage enhancements like tea, mocktails, smoothies or restorative tonics. And while mentioning these often-unctuous tonics, the palates of younger generations have a significantly appreciation for spicy foods, as led by the sriracha craze, in addition to aromatic and highly marketable spice blends like five spice (China), shichimi (Japan), za'atar (Levant), baharat (Middle East) or garam masala (India).
3. *Zero Artificial Additives:* A sub-movement within the healthy eating trend is a greater awareness for the slow-acting, harmful effects of unnatural food processing, coloring agents, emulsifiers and preservatives. Next time you're at the grocery store, look on the back for things like potassium sorbate, carrageenan, polysorbate 80, autolyzed yeast extract, or maltodextrin. Perhaps the biggest push right now is around removing industrialized seed oils like grapeseed, sunflower, soybean, corn, canola or, worst of all, hydrogenated vegetable oil (the science here is beyond scope, but they have been shown to be dangerous, especially when put under high heat). All told, there may soon come a day when your server puts a bottle of olive oil down on the table, only for the guest to ask if it's been cut with a seed oil where any uncertainty in the response will yield scoffs of disgust.
4. *Cleaner Meats:* Yes, people are edging more towards plant-based, flexitarian or plant-forward, but concurrently they are also asking restaurants for more literature about where they are sourcing their meats. Are your eggs free run, free range or pasture-raised? Is your fish certified as sustainably sourced? Is your butter grass-fed? Is your red meat grass-fed...and grass-finished? Do you list the exact farm where your animal products are from? Obviously, this level of detail will differ by restaurant and target audience, but these

modifiers are still important for some customers. Importantly, they very often let you charge more.

5. *Lab-Cultured Meats:* While plant-based meats are still gaining traction, there is another emerging alternative to factory-farmed animals where the science is paving the way. Currently, only Singapore legally allows for lab-made animal imitations to be sold direct to consumer, but it's only a matter of time before this trend snowballs. Given the increasing costs of animal husbandry and the mounting awareness of the inhumane conditions for livestock on big factory farm, it's only a matter of time before the FDA or other regulatory bodies start to seriously consider legalization.
6. *Invasivorism:* An 'invasivore' is someone who seeks to eat animals or plants that are not indigenous to a given area (as opposed to a 'locavore'). This is a form of climate activism whereby customers are helping support the reorientation of supply chains around the consumption of species that are harmful to the environment. In the United States, for instance, there's a movement to try and get people to eat Asian carp which has had a destructive impact on the Mississippi river system.
7. *Regenivorism:* Slightly newer than an invasivore, a regenivore denotes a person who selects foods specifically for their ability to help regenerate the local ecosystem. As a step beyond sustainable sourcing, regenivorism may involve eating a product made from upcycled waste – for example, specialty mushrooms grown in compost. Herein you may be noticing the larger trend which is that climatarians are gaining ground as a more vocal minority of the population and environmentalism is only bound to grow in the coming years. Right now, it's more about marketing cachet, but times may soon change as weird weather events become more frequent.
8. *Automation Always:* To contend with ever-changing costs, digital menus are a boon as you can update pricing instantaneously and without the cost of reprinting menus. Moreover, restaurants need tech to contend with the temporal shifts to eating patterns resulting from remote work. These sorts of customer-facing and largely web-based improvements already abound to help speed up the ordering process and encourage more total spend per table. Hence, it's important to always consider what else you can use your software for to ensure that your servers' time is spent more productively by better servicing in-house guests. Then for the more futuristic-minded, we are seeing companies deploy ceiling-mounted robotic arms for food assembly. Call us crazy, but just recently McDonald's debuted its first 'mostly automated' location in Fort Worth, Texas. Robots working in the kitchen will happen sooner than you think!

TECHNOLOGY

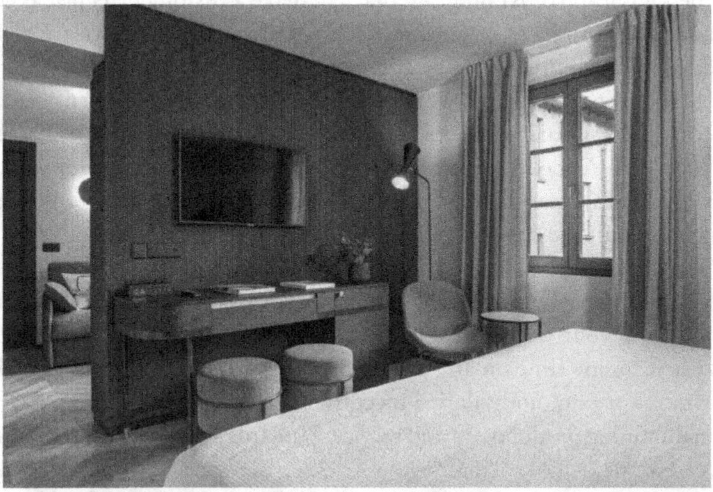

A short funicular ride down from lakeside Lugano's main train station, the 91-room Luganodante is as creative as they come, going so far as to distill its own liquors in-house for cocktails at its signature restaurant, Flamel, using herbs grown on the rooftop.

Tech Doesn't Replace But Supports Guest Communications

Hotels are back to pre-pandemic times before contactless communication was a necessity. But the future will see a balance of teams and tech from here out.

First off, nothing replaces the human touch, and we've yet to see a machine learning messaging app or AI program that can make a customer feel just as confident in a product as a direct interaction with a live representative. This we are saying even in the face of so much innovation post the pandemic.

But this being a tech-centric world and one where guests expect customer service to be exceedingly fast, various pieces of software can make your team insurmountably better at their jobs. A cool term to remember here is a 'centaur' mode of work, where, like the mythological creature, the horse (AI) does all the grunt work while the human body atop it does all the creative thought. That's where we are inevitably heading.

There are so many angles to approach the subject of how technology enhances guest communications, but the foundational objective – if you haven't already initiated this – is enabling your front office team to be able to respond to any guest request from anywhere at any time on any platform. This becomes critical in a world where remote work is a strong, non-salaried incentive to keep employees as well as a crucial need for maintaining productivity and service standards amidst the forthcoming travel recovery.

The pandemic was a time of lean teams – that is, fewer people able to handle guest communications – and the enabling of remote work. These are here to stay. Together, the result is the need for an unbreakable backbone of technology to run a hotel while still keeping net operating income above water. In the case of internal and external communications, you need automation to keep labor costs down and to stop miscommunication from resulting in service errors that can lead to refund losses or bad online reviews. The only way to achieve this harmony in the new normal is to constantly investigate what you can do to improve it and reinvent it.

Consider the work-from-home model for a moment, which may still be necessary for the aforementioned reason of heightened manager flexibility. To operate in this way and never sacrifice good communications, there are already several mature vendors that can route all incoming messages to one dashboard so your team can answer from the office or from home, at night or on weekends, and all with tracking features for managers. Guests expect immediate responses, and you better give them what you want, or they're gone.

The next and equally critical aspect you simply must have is integration. A customer service rep talking with a guest – whether by phone, text or email – must be able to put requests directly through to the department affected as well as be able to update the guest's profile within the PMS or CRM so that the personalization data is captured and remembered. Without this seamless transfer, you are creating bottlenecks that will inevitably overload the skeleton crews that have to process all these work orders. And the department that renders the service should also have accountability tracking with escalation parameters in order to prevent recovery situations from occurring.

In tandem to these essential aspects of tech integration are fancier, yet still incredibly powerful, tools like a chatbot. Crucial here is to look for a system that can ping and shift to a live agent when any request becomes complex. Thinking in terms of the 80/20 rule, AI is fantastic for handling the basics like answering where you are located, what your hours of operations are, what onsite amenities you have and other top-twenty questions, as well as reservations if you link the booking engine. Nowadays these are all simply distractions for your team who should instead be focusing on solving intricate requests or focusing on the guests who are physically on property at that very moment.

The fourth broad item where tech can make an impact relates to your concierge services. The foremost question to keep on the back of your mind for this is: how is your team better than a Google search? Because that's who you are competing against! You want your concierge to be able to provide exclusive recommendations and deals with local business, while several active software providers can also help to keep your team and your guests up to date with all the best events happenings in your area.

Fifth and finally, consider your satisfaction scores which we previously hinted at with a mention of 'bad online reviews'. Everyone knew before the pandemic that a few one-star critiques at the top of the pile on TripAdvisor could spell doom for future bookings. This is still true, if not even more so given how sensitive some guests are. Rather than delivered post-departure, if you have quick, automated surveys built in the prearrival or post-check-in parts of the guest journey, you can better identify then correct negative experiences before they become irremediable.

All told, there's a lot here to consider adding to your tech stack. Of course, specific needs vary on a property-by-property basis. This will indubitably require a thorough assessment with the overarching goal of having the technology do wonders in the background so that your team isn't bogged down by the minutia and can focus on the flawless service delivery for those visitors already onsite.

Prioritizing the Human Stack to Enable Tech Growth

Hotel executives are well aware of the challenges that cumbersome tech stacks and siloed data have created. And yet the overall direction of the industry will continue to demand more and more technology adoption – both for labor efficiencies and revenue growth – further complicating all the platforms in use and necessary interfaces.

The core problem may not be with the software ecosystems we've built up over the decades, however, but with the business practices that have crept into our companies and are now out of alignment with the rapid pace of innovation that the post-COVID, hyper-capitalist world requires. Hence, even before any new vendor evaluations or tech stack redevelopment, hotels should first look at their 'human stack' to find all the team inefficiencies that are stifling expedient change.

Learning from Big Tech

Evaluating the human stack is something that the two of us have leaned into as part of any consulting assignment we undertake under the banner of our 'Teams N Tech' (TNT) auditing program. When an owner or C-level executive first comes to us with a technology problem or growth-oriented directive, we often find that the hindrance is deeper – that the real problem lies in how the various teams make decisions, how workflows (or working blocks of time) are managed and interdepartmental politics.

One of most salient problems is overcrowded meetings where the efficiencies of the medium are lost due to too many participants. The more attendees you add, the longer it takes to align on a time then get underway while everyone waits for the tardy joiner. Then the more people you have, the longer it takes to require consensus and the more hesitant some participants will be with their thoughts.

Fans of symbology and shorthand principles to help with memorability, the two of us have frequently deployed the 'two pizza rule' as famously named and used by Amazon. No meeting should have more participants than can be adequately fed by two whole pizzas. Abiding by this rule thus requires more purpose to meetings – clear agendas and justifiable roles for each attendee.

Closely related to this, another huge time suck is simply having too many meetings when an email or management-by-exception style of empowerment will suffice. For this, we can learn from Shopify's recent 'calendar purge' mandate. The company removed all recurring meetings with more than two employees. Then Wednesdays were declared meeting-free while all big team meetings were confined to Thursdays.

Propelling this was the inference that many meetings in larger organizations – as well as the busywork arranging for these meetings – tend to become vehicles for maintaining the status quo rather than assemblies where decisions are made promptly. Any hotel can also succumb to this 'statis creep'.

Rethinking Meeting Design

The overall lesson we can learn from Amazon and Shopify is that meeting design needs a rethink in order to maximize each team member's productivity. The need for this organizational revamp has become all the more critical with a remote, hybrid or flexible working arrangement – something that many hotel companies have considered or implemented in order to incentivize employees to stay.

In fact, it goes deeper than that. People have largely entered our industry to be guest-facing and to do the meaningful work of directly helping guests. Poorly managed meetings can detract from this goal, which then negatively impacts motivation, raises job-related stress, and can be a factor in turnover.

You also need to consider where those meetings are taking place. Oftentimes the fluorescent-lit, drab back-of-house offices where hoteliers meet seldom elevate moods like those front-of-house public spaces imbued with natural light and more pleasant furnishings.

Various technologies – albeit combined with policy shifts – can help to shift the

Five Ws of meetings so that your human stack then has the bandwidth to keep pace with the tech that society now demands.

1. *Why.* Meetings should either be all hands in which case they are announced via a company bulletin far ahead of the chosen date or they abide by the two pizza rule. For stand-up meetings that involve associates, mobile operations platforms are quite adept nowadays at disseminating all the nuts and bolts so that the physical, in-person time can be best spent on the proactive, teambuilding activities that will boost motivation and performance.
2. *What.* No meeting should occur without an agenda. Bulleted topics can be proposed and edited within any calendar setting tool so that every attendee is aligned prior to the chosen time. And contextual naming matters: if it's a managers' happy hour without an express purpose, then it's not a meeting and should not be labeled as such so that attendees enter with the right mindset.
3. *When.* Part of the inefficiency with meetings is the minutia of back-and-forth email threads as everyone announces when they are free. Calendly has become an invaluable tool for two parties to quickly find the optimal time by simply sending a link or embedding it within an email signature. For multi-party scheduling, consider something like Doodle that can let everyone vote on availabilities so that the meeting leader can then declare the final time.
4. *Who.* Deciding on meeting attendees should be very easy as you can now use Asana, Slack, Wrike or another project management platform to only involve direct assignees for a given task. Such software can concurrently reduce email inbox bloat, confining the chatter to individual project threads. Then for executive committee meetings, much of the reporting can be easily generated then disseminated from within the PMS, POS, RMS or other system so that the senior team can review on its own time and not see it all for the first time during the actual meeting.
5. *Where.* Hinted at above when comparing BOH to FOH, the setting can help to raise energy levels and maximize in-person productivity. This may necessitate a larger renovation down the road so that teams have an inspirational space all to themselves, but in the meantime, you should aim to place meetings away from the office desk so that there's a change of scenery and to involve a bit of a walk to get the heart going. Teams should be empowered to use guest meeting rooms by first checking the appropriate management software to see if they are free.

After Meetings Then What

Using all the time management software and workplace policy adjustments that you can muster, your human stack should be singing your praises and ready to roll out new services, amenities, or tech adoptions that will advance the company's goal. People will be more energized and have more time for 'flow' – the state of focused concentration that results in higher intrinsic motivation, fulfillment, and skill development, as elucidated by Mihaly Csikszentmihalyi's seminal 2014 book of the same name.

With much of the email fatigue and interruptive busywork now gone, what can you then look at doing? To circle back to the introduction, more tech will be needed; only now will your team have time to evaluate, implement, and learn it all in a relatively brisk, stress-free fashion, with an eye towards even more automation in order to make your team's ever-more guest-facing.

Considering automation as a consummate process, we close with some areas to consider:

- End-to-end PMS and POS integrations, allowing for rich, centralized guest profiles for better analytics, personalized service and real-time connections with ancillary profit centers like restaurants, spa, golf, events, and activities so that there's less offline paper pushing by managers to reconcile all this previously disparate information
- Advanced business intelligence platforms that can incorporate operational data points to give you accurate predictive recommendations of what tasks are eating away at your teams' time, where the labor savings are and which are likely to be the morale-eroding culprits
- Omnichannel outbound messaging platforms that you can cascade through a series of channels to reach guests on their preferred communication medium, all with the end goal of reducing the need for front desk agents to restate these nuts and bolts
- Machine learning chatbots to handle repetitive questions posed on your website live chat, via text and on social media, with some systems even capable of handling reservations
- Conversational AI that's intelligent enough to accurately replicate a human voice for incoming calls to replace the IVR and, like chatbots, handle basic inquiries before passing the customer off to a live agent
- Call centers to outsource your reservation and service calls as well as offering quality reporting to keep track of conversions and call abandonment, freeing up managers' time in trying to source and supervise your own agents while also redirecting calls away from the front desk so that those associates can focus on in-house guests
- In-room tablets and mobile apps that act as a single point of control for service requests, hotel information, virtual concierge and additional purchases
- Payroll and accounts payable automation so that an executive isn't needed to authorize every minor payment, thereby freeing up time and also helping with supply chain management

Process Innovation as the Core Engine for Hotel Technology Implementation

Reflecting on the few years, have you noticed that the pace of the world has seemed to become relentlessly fast? At first, it was easy to chalk this up to playing catch-up from the temporary slowdown of daily life that was the pandemic. But this current tempo is the real new normal, especially with the dawn of publicly available generative artificial bits of intelligence like ChatGPT that are implied to be the provocateurs for widespread creative destruction in both travel and hospitality.

The feats already accomplished by these pseudo-strong AIs can bestow a deep sense of powerlessness, not because of any near-future doomsday scenario but because they are indicative of a far larger trend for the hotel industry. To give you a sense of this rapidity, check out Korea-based MyRealTrip's AI Trip Planner, an itinerary platform built in just two days using ChatGPT.

And with this technological renaissance, travelers' expectations are likewise evolving at an accelerating pace, so much so that a wide swath of businesses are soon to be left behind by the invisible hand, whether that's reflected through financial stagnation, rate commoditization, an inability to keep talent or insufficient CAPEX to revitalize the physical assets.

Maybe the two of us are getting a bit hokey by opening with a feeling, an abstraction, and a prophecy rather than cold, hard statistics, many of which have been carved up to show that all is quiet on the hotel front. But we foresee a series of converging existential problems – recessionary impacts, perpetual staffing shortages, a downsized corporate segment, leisure segment brand apathy, a generational brain drain into other sectors, the aging out of the baby boomers and unwieldy legacy tech stacks, to name a few.

Righting the ship to meet all these challenges will take years, shrewd planning, vision, and gumption. Yet none of that will happen if a hotel's underlying engine – that is, how its people get work done – hasn't had its oil checked since the 1990s. This is where 'process innovation' becomes instrumental to success.

Teams and Tech

From our past and present assignments where we work with independent upscale and luxury hotel owners to chart a course and avoid this existential torpor, what we found is that, while upgrading a brand's technology is instrumental to modern hospitality, the way teams work is equally if not even more important to success. To this end, we productized this observation as the Teams N Tech (TNT) Audit that looks specifically at the top issues clogging up the organizational engine in both arenas with process innovation recommendations so that the whole team can pick up the pace.

Here's what happens in many cases. A property has gone through the iterative, oft painstaking and consummative process of upgrading its tech stacks, yet its human stacks remain firmly stuck in the 20th century. Departmental silos are common, leading to goal misalignment, office politics that waste resources, lowered morale and reduced overall productivity. Meanwhile, team empowerment and agile decision-making exist in name only, without the proper policy framework to prevent homogenized groupthink outcomes.

Too much time is wasted on meetings, emails, and reports that no one reads, and that's before any tech stack automation that we may suggest. The result is that the deployment of new technology is stifled by all these process logjams. Thus, fix the process and you fix the tech implementation.

Though we would always advocate the prudence in 'measuring twice and drilling once', there is a cutoff point where inaction in the face of rapidly evolving market conditions leads to both significant opportunity costs – notably, lost revenue from not maximizing per-guest spend or from guests going elsewhere – and an inability to get caught as those market changes start to accelerate in pace.

This is to say, what's the point of rolling out the perfect technology solution two years from now if, in the interim, you've lost guests to your competitors, failed to generate healthy ancillary spend from those customers that remain and are turning over good team members every year due to their frustrations with how the business operates?

Automating Meetings

By now, you may think this article is a bait and switch in that you were expecting to read about technology only to discover a passage about culture. In the 2020s, these are one and the same. Hence, an improvement to how your teamwork will enable them to reach decisions faster as to budgets for tech exploration, which vendors to select and the workflow necessary to get systems implemented.

One huge wrench in nearly every hotel's engine is that the average manager is drowning in meetings, sucking up their available time and energy for self-directed 'real work'. And this insight is hardly revelatory, with the likes of Shopify's calendar purge enacted in early January or (one of our favorites) Amazon's two-pizza rule which states that if the attendees of a meeting cannot be adequately fed by two decent size pies, then there are too many attendees.

Finding the best fit differs by organization, but here are some policy guidelines we've deployed:

Shorter Meetings. Asking first if an hour timeslot can be compressed into half an hour, then look at early adjournments (50 minutes versus an hour; 25 minutes versus half an hour) so attendees have time to reflect

Structured Meetings. Every gathering should have a detailed agenda that is followed sequentially, while every attendee should have a specific purpose for being present with specific tasks assigned to those attendees at the meeting's conclusion (if not, then they shouldn't be there) as well as a designated minute-take for others who couldn't attend to read in

Clustered Meetings. An open calendar where meetings can be slotted in whenever isn't how you maximize individual productivity because people need dedicated blocks of time to attain a 'flow state', so instead bunch meetings on specific days of the week, don't schedule recurrent meetings unless they are absolutely critical and empower teams to send only one representative

Normalized Solo Time. Aside from letting teams divide and conquer, hotel cultures must work to change the act of declining invitations to something that's accepted to protect each manager's time, especially if these meetings interfere with this team member's 'flow blocks' or dedicated periods of deep, concentrated, creative work that should also be visible on a shared calendar

Email Process Innovation

The majority of hotel tech is sharply focused on building consolidated or integrated systems that merge data sets from multiple departments. Then to fill in the gaps you have middleware, customer data platforms (CDP) and now robotic process automation (RPA). When we are referring to process innovation, however, we aren't homing in specifically on the digital transformation tools that are enabling hoteliers to become software-first operators, but rather more broadly and crudely to anything that will increase the rate at which business is conducted.

Yet this speed improvement very often involves technology, even so far as using certain platforms to reduce the sheer volume of electronic information we face daily and streamline our attention. One of the culprits is the time suck of too many meetings, for which the solution is a combination of a shared, cloud-based calendar, an online calendar booking platform and a cultural shift away from 'meeting for any reason possible, even when a well-written memo will suffice'.

Then, naturally, you must consider how that well-written memo will be disseminated. Email perhaps? Most managers are receiving hundreds of fresh ones in their inboxes every day and an attached PDF is likely to get lost in the shuffle. Besides all the marketing communications from third parties diverting the team's attention, also compounding this second-time suck of too many emails are the ongoing back-and-forth message threads between two people that also have a handful of other managers copied.

The underlying problem here is psychological; continuous email threads are interruptive to the real work that advances business goals, both for the two or three active correspondents as well as for all other silent witnesses. Individual job satisfaction is largely derived from helping create achievable measurable results, and the two of us highly doubt that anyone would be fulfilled if all they ever did in life was attain the illusory 'inbox zero'.

Hence, part of team empowerment means trusting that associates and managers will dutifully respond to emails addressed only to them so that colleagues or superiors don't need to be copied to keep everyone accountable. Aside from unsubscribing from everything, this policy shift may be the second biggest action to reducing email volume and thereafter everyone's stress levels.

Next, part of normalizing solo time means that managers should have the freedom to ignore their inboxes for several hours at a time to concentrate on specific assignments, like crafting a memo that articulates a topic eloquently and succinctly with clearly identifiable next steps. Of course, there are a handful of apps you can encourage your teams to use that help train one's focus.

This is also where project management software comes in, giving any company the ability to compartmentalize any project by tasks and subtasks so that this well-written memo needn't even generate a single email but merely uploaded it to the right thread. Such process management software is also great for tracking meeting agendas and meeting follow-up activities.

Conclusion

While it would be great to prognosticate about, for instance, how future-forward technologies like BingAI or the metaverse will impact travel search and guest booking behavior, what's far more important at this time is to take stock of the fundamental workflows that will liberate your teams' time so that they can take advantage of the latest and greatest.

The world isn't slowing down, and the only way for any hotel to keep pace is to start moving faster. From our consultancy's TNT Audits, we know that means more efficient meetings, more efficient communications, and more efficient decision-making. While achieving this often involves tech, like nearly every other aspect of hospitality, it's the people that ultimately matter the most.

Hotel Operations Platforms Now Enable 'Utility Players'

Venturing down to the HITEC tradeshow was fraught with obstacles that hindered it from achieving the highs of its anteCOVIDian outings. It competed for attendees with another concurrent conference, and perhaps the greatest concern is that many technology vendors, much like the hotels they are serve, are operating on lean budgets with just-in-time delivery of new features and sales through one-off video calls that defeat the purpose of a maintaining an expensive booth presence.

Still, the hotel industry marches on and tech suppliers are here to help, especially when it comes to economically mitigating the ongoing labor shortages that are palpable in just about every travel market across the globe.

The first layer of the tech stack is, of course, the PMS, for which vendors have already rolled out features to assist with mobile bookings (for guests) and mobile management (for team members on the go). The best PMS suppliers are aiding on the staffing front by enhancing the prearrival experience – either natively or through better integrations to bolt-on platforms – to both present customers with better upsell opportunities (room upgrades or attribute-based sales) and to secure as much ancillary revenue on the books as possible (dining reservations, spa appointments, golf rounds and so on).

Besides revenue optimization, what's critical in a labor-deprived world is to have a crystal-clear picture of what service your guests will want to utilize prior to their arrival. That way, you can plan accordingly and don't end up in a situation where you can't provide, with money is inevitably left on the table.

One recent firsthand experience illustrating this was while traveling to a Californian resort where, due to staffing shortages, the signature restaurant had to close at 10 pm even though there was a rush of late dinner walk-ins from in-house guests who were more than keen on drinking well past the midnight hour. The eatery was kept lightly staffed due to various forces, and the manager, in the hours or days prior, had to make a judgment call on overtime allotment based upon the information they had at the time – that this particular evening would likely peter out by 10 pm as it had in the near past when reviewing historical data.

However, over two hours of bar tabs were lost in this instance due to a probabilistic shift scheduling snafu. Whether it was actually the property's 'fault' or simply a fallout from macroeconomic forces is beyond any single manager's control.

But had the hotel worked to secure those seating times in the weeks before the evening in question – via strong booking engine software, prearrival emails or proper voice channel follow-up – then the restaurant director would've anticipated this late-hour need and likely reacted by finding the necessary staff to keep the drinks (and revenues) flowing.

This example brings us forward to the second layer of the tech stack, which is the hotel operations platform, giving managers an intuitive and tabulated interface through which to oversee key tasks like housekeeping, maintenance work orders and guest requests. Crucially here is how these systems have now evolved to facilitate what the two of us dub as 'utility players' or those frontline staffers who can complete jobs across multiple departments.

Unionized hotels aside, we first borrowed this baseball terminology to describe how hotels were keeping the lights on during the worst days of the pandemic with each remaining member of the skeleton crew performing a variety of previously siloed duties. With the pandemic waning and demand returning, the need for labor is back but the silos should decidedly not return.

The hotels poised for success over the coming decades are those that start to blend departments (and their supportive technologies), both to save costs on labor inefficiencies and to heighten service through better, more integrated communications channels. The hotel operations platform is the enabler for this evolution because most are equipped with specific features to shuffle tasks around amongst employees as well as establish escalation criteria, tracking metrics and gamification.

There's a lot of overlap in functionality for these systems, so we stress that you consider what the executive team wants as well as what the managers using these platforms can handle. For them, learning how to work within two interfaces (the PMS and the ops platform) is easier than having five or more partly connected applications open. Consolidation is key to maintain daily active usage.

Then from the employee's perspective, having a system that can enable utility work will help to reduce on-the-job confusion as well as boredom, in turn assisting with talent retention and stymie the labor churn that plagued our industry since mid- 2020. Such ops platforms let a hotel rebuild their teams and simultaneously motivate them through exposure to numerous and varied tasks, making the employee experience more dynamic as well as revealing where said staffer would be best suited for career advancement.

Without getting too far into the weeds of examining select features that may be offered by one vendor or another, what's important for now is to understand this broad trend and how hotel tech is progressing in sync with what properties need to navigate the untested waters ahead. If you weren't able to make it to a HITEC, we encourage you to reach out to vendors working within this hotel operations management space to see how they can help maximize team productivity so that you can realize all of the abovementioned benefits.

Automation Is Key for Attention, Team Retention and Data Comprehension

If there was a single overarching theme to this past summer's HITEC, it was that every tech vendor is working on clever and cost-conscious ways to help hotels solve the ongoing labor shortage. Our suspicion, though, is that this current crisis will take at least several years to abate due to all the workers who have permanently reskilled into other service sector jobs combined with our on-average lower pay-scale incentivizing younger candidates towards other industries.

Deepening a hotel's automation is the only path forward, with numerous benefits that we will explore in this article.

Much focus has already been given of late to various technologies that are helping hospitality organizations ramp up associate and manager productivity, but often this isn't lensed correctly nor is the calculation taking all factors into account. We all know that automation 'saves time'. From there it's a matter of computing the time per task multiplied by the wage of the staffer executing said task. That's the obvious part of justifying a new hardware or software deployment.

However, what's perhaps even more important than the time saved through automation is the mental energy saved. And this is where the real win-win comes in; your team gains time to offer more quality, 'high touch' service for guests and their morale improves synchronously. Critically for managers, this energy can be redirected towards those projects that require more thoughtful deliberation, such as forecasting and comprehending the loads of data generated in any given period.

Interruptive Workflows

If you've read our past work or heard either of us speak, then you know that we've spoken ad nauseum about the problem of too many meetings in hotel organizational culture. If everyone is meeting all the time to groupthink problems or give status reports, there aren't enough solid, uninterrupted chunks in a given day to focus on the real work – the 'knowledge work' as it is often described – that will actually advance business goals.

Hungarian-American psychologist Mihaly Csikszentmihalyi articulated this perfectly in "Flow" (2014) whereby a state of focused concentration on only one project results in higher intrinsic motivation, job fulfillment and skill development. Despite what you may believe, humans are horrible multitaskers; we merely pretend to do this but are in fact single-tasking between our email inboxes, our text messages, social media, news websites and that SOP guideline you've been trying to polish for the past two hours. All that constant bouncing from task to task inevitably leaves us drained and disengaged, making for a silent factor in lowered team retention.

More recently, bestselling author Cal Newport's "A World Without Email" (2021) builds on the concept of task immersion for optimized performance by exploring some of the detrimental effects of modern email communication through what he has coined as 'attention capital'. Namely, in a world where there's an overwhelming abundance of communication, attention to any one thing is what drives production and value. More specific to hotels, when team members are expected to always be 'on' as measured by email response times, we are inducing a chronic level of background stress into our line of work as well as preventing our managers from entering a state of flow for big projects and delivering more accurate forecasting.

It's no wonder that European countries are starting to penalize texting and other forms of communication to employees after work hours. The emotional reprieve each evening is much needed to preserve one's mental health.

But this benefit is also reciprocal for the hotel. With more focused work via a reduction of email notifications or other tasks that can be migrated to an automation platform, hotels can increase morale, positively affecting both associate and manager retention. In the era of the Great Resignation, the interruptive nature of email systems is but one more contributor to hospitality's labor woes and should thus be a serious topic to address entering the next business cycle.

Automation as a Process

Whatever your cost-benefit analysis reveals for the earnout point for new SaaS platform, it's much harder to calculate the mental energy saved by automating various interruptive workflows. Once you understand just how important these technologies are for emotional well-being, then forget the analysis and implement it literally yesterday!

Attaining a heightened level of automation so that your teams gain time and aren't bogged down by multitasking will not happen overnight or is there a universal panacea for all your woes. It requires a staggered approach, with a process of constant reevaluation and a timeline for implementation.

Speaking of staggered, here are some cool automation that we saw for you to consider:

- End-to-end PMS and POS integrations, allowing for rich, centralized guest profiles for better analytics, personalized service and real-time connections with ancillary profit centers like restaurant, spa, golf, events and activities

so that there's less paper pushing by managers to reconcile all this previously disparate information
- Advanced business intelligence platforms that can incorporate operational data points to give you highly precise forecasting models and prescriptive recommendations of what tasks are eating away at your teams' time as well as which are likely to be the morale-eroding culprits
- Labor efficiency tools that can deploy artificial intelligence to help you develop more accurate budgets as well as take much of the data comprehension onto the cloud when it was previously offline (that is, within an Excel spreadsheet on a manager's desktop)
- Omnichannel outbound messaging platforms that you can cascade through a series of channels to reach guests on their preferred communication medium
- Machine learning chatbots to handle repetitive questions posed on your website live chat, via text and on social media, with some systems even able of handling reservations
- Conversational AI that's intelligent enough to accurately replicate a human voice for incoming calls to replace the IVR and, like chatbots, handle basic inquiries before passing the customer off to a live agent
- Call centers to outsource your reservation and service calls as well as offering quality reporting to keep track of conversions and call abandonment, freeing up managers' time in trying to source and supervise your own agents while also redirecting calls away from the front desk so that those associates can focus on in-house guests
- In-room tablets and mobile apps that act as a single point of control for service requests, hotel information, virtual concierge and additional purchases

You can't implement all of these at the same time. And yet you really need them all in order to have breathing room to look ahead to what new trends will emerge in the next five years or so. Hence, it's a matter of evaluating what you can do now, what you can do in a month's time, and what you will (reluctantly) have to wait for in the future.

Automation and Forecasting

Circling back to the problem of emails, there are many other lo-fi tactics that can help. To chip away at the mountain of emails, reduce CCs and unnecessary notifications where you are not a direct report. Next, make stand-up meetings routine, agenda-driven and as short as possible so that you minimize the back and forth over one-off meeting setup (using scheduling or time management software for all else). Then to truly enable knowledge work, allow for half-day and full-day chunks where managers are not expected to be checking their inboxes, devoting this time for projects that require flow.

The inescapable truth is that hotel operations going forward need to be lean in order to maintain margins and not run into labor issues. This new reality demands automation tools to reduce the interruptive workflows that are tearing apart your managers' days and preventing any semblance of flow from being attaining.

Without those dedicated two-hour blocks, there's no time to properly peruse the multitude of data to deduce actionable inferences for further cost efficiencies or revenue opportunities. Moreover, if your IT team must contend with the daily inbox-clearing grind, they, too, won't have time to tackle the setup of new software interfaces so that data can seamlessly flow into your enterprise business intelligence platform for further data comprehension.

When's the Time to Fire a Guest

To close out on a more jocular, albeit controversial note, suppose you have solved many of the challenges introduced by the convergence of our current labor crisis and interruptive workflows. Next comes evaluating which guests are causing the majority of the problems and, when the emotional strain on your team is properly considered, actually have a negative ROI. That is, with the right data connections, can you forecast when a guest isn't worth the trouble?

In an 80/20 kind of way, there are likely only a handful of past and present guests who fit this bill – the ones who make repeated, small requests and still leave a tepid TripAdvisor review. But you won't know how to tackle this problem without a solid business intelligence platform that can compute revenues versus total labor per guest.

Until that time, workflow automation is the goal for the near future in order to ramp up your team's attention capital. Especially with the inestimable benefit of reducing stress to increase team retention, it's not just about doing a direct cost analysis for what you will save on paper by deploying a new piece of technology; it's about the mental energy saved that can be redirected towards more complex and compelling projects – such as forecasting – that have long-term, positive outcomes.

The Three Domains of Protecting Hotel Payments and Revenues

With so many difficulties from the pandemic still playing out, the upcoming years for hospitality will mark a dedicated stretch of time for continuing to streamline processes and staying lean on the labor front while increasing productivity. This means automating wherever possible, simplifying the daisy chain of enterprise software, deploying better tech to help augment the guest service and finding creative ways to keep costs down amidst still-ambiguous demand forecasts.

There's a lot that can be done to fit these lofty goals, but where to start? New advances within the payment industry touch on all of these aspects with immediate applicability, so it's worthwhile to see how the latest and greatest can help a hotel property. In particular, we emphasize that many of these developments represent 'low hanging fruit' – relatively frictionless business upgrades that will elicit incremental cost savings and productivity gains, representing a quick win to give your organization some buffer to then tackle large-scale projects.

At the forefront of the payment world is a concerted effort to rein in fraud – which hurts both the merchant and the processor – by rolling out additive layers of credit card verification and transaction flexibility. When you tally all the expenses associated with a fraudulent reservation – room opportunity cost, cleaning costs, representment costs, processor penalties and so on – a single case can amount to roughly 250% of the total booking value. To help fight this, a key practice that requires a full explanation and a discussion on the bigger picture of payment evolution is Three Domain Secure or 3-D Secure (3DS).

How 3DS Works

This isn't anything revolutionary as this protocol is already in use and standardized for Europe, Africa, Australia and Russia – going on for almost two decades in some territories. But it's soon set to take hold of the North American market, which will breathe new life into the prospect of 3DS as a global standard as well as what's deemed a passing grade by payment card industry data security standards (PCI DSS) to in turn prevent interchange rate hikes.

Without getting into all the different acronyms and definitions for the payment industry (for which they are legion), what the three domains refer to are the broad-level delineations of parties involved in authorizing payments and move funds over:

1. Merchant (in this case, a hotel), acquiring (merchant's) bank and payment gateway
2. Cardholder and issuing (cardholder's) bank
3. Interoperability networks such as credit card processor

The current system has payments verified within the first and second domains via the payment gateway interacting with an internet-based access control server that then separately parlays with the third domain to authorize the release of the funds from the cardholder's account. Now with 3DS, customers at a merchant's payment terminal are automatically brought to an issuer's internal verification portal where a distinct user authorization key or text-delivered, one-time password must be inserted to complete the transaction.

This extra step helps to shift the burden of liability for fraudulent payments from the merchant to the issuing bank. Genuine fraud, or the unauthorized use of a card, is inordinately minimized while friendly fraud, or claiming a chargeback after services were adequately rendered, is also somewhat thwarted. Significantly for our industry, where many hotels have of recent become prime targets for fraud, this means a lot of relief not immediately palpable from comparing annual income statements because that aforementioned 250% of total booking value is often buried under several disparate line items.

In cases of genuine fraud at hotels, while nowadays a fraudster may gain access to a guest's 16-digit card number, expiry date, and security code on the back, it's extraordinarily rare that they will also know the secondary passcode required for the issuer's 3DS verification portal. And for friendly fraud chargebacks, the input of this

3DS user authorization key subsequently raises the evidential threshold necessary to prove that the merchant acted in bad faith, increasing the likelihood for the acquiring party (that's you) to win a dispute.

The Bigger Picture

Why are we homing in on 3DS of all things affecting the hotel industry? As hinted at in the intro, compared to all the other challenges that hotels will have to confront in the coming years – guest expectations coming out of the pandemic, new service demands requiring hefty capex and tackling climate change through sustainability upgrades, to name three – getting your payment systems in order is a fairly simple task that's a steppingstone towards successfully operating in the new normal.

To drive profitability for the rest of the 2020s, you can no longer rely on a huge topline revenue figure to pad your gross profit and net operating income (NOI). The decade ahead will be defined by leaner, turnkey operations – fewer team members on hand to complete repetitive tasks and mandating more productivity from those that remain.

The only way forward is through automation in order to maintain a healthy NOI while occupancy forecasts in key segments remain in their respective nadirs or, worse, are one big question mark. Some hotels have already discerned ways to buoy profits and service debt with peak-period occupancies in the 25% to 40% range so that they are also somewhat immune to the stubborn labor shortage challenges that will continue to plague us for at least the next few business cycles.

Your front office team no longer has the time to manually transfer payment cards from a gateway into the property management system (PMS); this action also being in breach of PCI compliance standards. Your accountants likewise don't have time to prepare documentation in order to properly dispute upwards of 5% of all room reservation. Thirdly, with erratic revenue projections and opaque forward-looking travel demand data, you can no longer afford to incur fraudulent charges (sometimes docked as negative revenues) or have your processing fees go up, even by a few basis points, because you, the merchant, have been deemed high risk according to the latest PCI DSS covenants.

The Future of Payments

The broader theme behind our push for 3DS adoption is that its implementation will ultimately help reduce direct costs, administrative time and negative revenues. With this heightened level of transactional security also comes the flexibility to enact further upgrades to your payment ecosystem.

First off is 3DS2 which attempts to solve the friction induced by requiring a second password inserted into a separate frame prompted from the issuer by only requiring one when a challenge algorithm deems a transaction of high risk after reviewing a guest's payment history and other contextual data. As well, this contemporary version allows developers to keep the auxiliary passcode wholly with a hotel's branded app so that the (mostly mobile) guest experience isn't perturbed.

After this, the big phase will be doing all this while eliminating the physical payment card itself. Many payment platforms capable of handling 3DS2 customer pass-throughs are similarly adept at facilitating transactions straight from a digital wallet that verifies transactions based on what a customer has (phone) and is (face scan or thumbprint) and not necessarily what the customer knows (password). Think Apple Pay, Google Pay, WeChat Pay and a host of other mobile payment services.

And let's not even get into where cryptocurrencies fit into all this! The bottom line is that the sooner you upgrade your hotel's payment apparatus, the sooner you can start cushioning your NOI then move on to solving far tougher challenges. In this sense, 3DS or 3DS2 is a fantastic first step.

Mobile Check-In Technology Enhancements Beyond Just Checking In

The check-in experience is perennially under the microscope because first impressions are everything. When you consider the context of the guest that's arriving – jetlagged, lower back pain from being crammed like sardines into an airplane, stressed from being in a foreign city – it makes sense to prioritize upgrading this aspect of the hotel stay, particularly when there are so many tech vendors who can help you solve the challenges of long lineups and disgruntled travelers who may not want to deal with a front desk agent.

First and foremost, we must mention the non-mobile upgrades because they are important, too. Yes, certain guest segments would likely prefer to check-in and out directly from their phones and remain largely invisible to the front office team. Consider the solo corporate traveler who wants to be as efficient as possible with their time or members of the younger generations who are, to hyperbolize just a bit, addicted to their phones and may even get minor anxiety from having to contend with the front desk. Then there are luxury hotels or resorts where meeting the guests at check-in is a set way to set the tone for an enjoyable stay.

For all these instances where mobile check-in is out of the running, a good first step is developing strong data connections to a business intelligence or a dedicated labor management platform. Such systems would be able to give you actionable insights on the exact times when front desk agents are most needed so that you can staff efficiently while also preventing those dreaded lineups. Moreover, bringing in the data from the mobile app will give you better intelligence on the average check-in time, letting you attenuate housekeeping schedules. As this is but one function that these platforms perform to help finesse operating costs, they are worth investigating regardless of whether you're going mobile or not.

Next, for economy, select service and midscale properties, the advent of check-in kiosks offers a healthy middle ground between front desk clerk and fully mobile. While a number of vendors now incorporate proper biometric verification so that falsified identities are not a concern and so that guests can more frictionlessly get their keycards, what we stress again is guest context. Many travelers will be fully zoned out by the time they arrive in the lobby – not exactly a mood conducive to upselling. But kiosks are just a screen where there's no pressure that you're keeping someone waiting.

In other words, like the website, the newsletters, the social media posts and the dedicated prearrival upselling platform, kiosks facilitate 'window shopping'. Some customers want to evaluate their potential purchases from afar, without the perceived discomfort of monopolizing the staffer's time or any semblance of 'decision fatigue' from having to choose on the spot likely at a moment of weariness. The same guest who says, "I'll think about it," then never does after being prompted by a front desk clerk about add-ons may instead spend a few extra seconds evaluating some promotional offers at a kiosk.

With all this background, we can circle back to what the latest is with mobile check-in where the concepts of intelligent labor management, biometric identification and window shopping all apply.

Like kiosks, mobile apps have progressed to the point where remote identification can be completed in a secured manner. This is an important step to look at integrating as, again, consider the context of a tired traveler who just wants to check-in from their phones but then gets frustrated because they still have to visit someone in the lobby to verify their passport. Call it the mission to be 'incrementally frictionless'.

And with that as the goal, another captivating feature for mobile check-in is the ability to geofence so that the software can interpret estimated time of arrival to then coordinate onsite activities. As a simplified example, suppose that a guest who purchased a chilled bottle of champagne as a welcome amenity is discovered to be checking in from the airport and you know that on average it takes half an hour to get to your hotel. This alone would help to guide smoother timing of the required service order to the room through the ops platform.

Key here is 'smoother' wherein tight labor controls are a consummate goal for hotel management. Once you understand how geofenced check-ins can help to more accurately time service delivery, it lets you get more creative with what welcome amenities you can possibly offer as well as what the arrive experience looks like.

Then just like the kiosks, the app interface is yet another way to upsell and cross-sell without the subconscious pressure of keeping real people waiting. Therein you can test different offers or the specific ordering of offers to see what resonates the most. To be clear, we aren't talking about night-and-day revenue growth, but a win is a win, and if you can incrementally drive a few percentage points each quarter for suite upsells or additional F&B orders, then that's still worth celebrating.

To close, it's important to mention the actual hardware that facilitates the mobile check-in process. Your door locks may need some upgrading, which is a potential scheduling roadblock for the low season. Therein you have to decide about whether to allow for silent near-field communications so that guests can enter the guestroom simply by approaching the door or if you require an extra point of security – and friction – by making them open the hotel app before the door can be unlocked. Moreover, you will also need backup procedures in place for when a guest's phone dies. Like anything in this regard, permitting mobile check-ins has its uses and its tradeoffs, but we hope this clears up a few points.

Introducing Integrated Business Intelligence and Its Game-Changing Potential for Hotels

As they say, there are the problems you see and the ones you don't. Many hotels may be operating under certain assumptions carried over from decades of routine and tradition that integrated data analysis can now reveal to be flawed or wholly false, all of it silently sapping the bottom line.

This is where Business Intelligence (BI) comes in. These platforms blossomed from a need to gain more visibility on these unknown challenges by feeding loads of data into one system then generating comprehensive reports for executives to make better decisions. More recently, machine learning has been introduced to further augment the cost-saving and revenue-generating power of these systems.

Coming out of HITEC, the world's foremost hotel technology trade show, we can report that hotel-focused BI is about to experience a seismic shift in its decision-making sophistication. New integrations are enabling numerous other data points to be computed to help hospitality organizations realize stable growth in the years ahead.

Leading the way is the new company Actabl which brings together software solutions ProfitSword (enterprise-level business intelligence), Hotel Effectiveness (labor management), ALICE (operations) and Transcendent (asset management and capex). We sat down with Steven Moore, Actabl CEO, to discuss the specifics of how building this integrated platform will enhance business practices from property-level and group finances all the way down to team dynamics and individual SOPs.

"Imagine a platform that brings together financial data, accounting, procurement, labor, guest profiles, guest satisfaction, information from daily operations and specifics from every profit center with external factors like competitive set benchmarks and industry trends," stated Moore. "That's what we're building at Actabl. We're combining these under one roof – four solutions with over 250 integrations – and serving them up in a digestible format, allowing hoteliers to challenge their current approach with precise data to see what's working and what isn't."

The Current State of BI

We often talk about each department in a hotel as a 'silo'. In its present state, BI helps to eliminate those silos by merging data from different inputs that not one single department or manager can observe on their own.

These platforms take in metrics like ADR, RevPAR, occupancy, GSS, guest segmentation, dining spend and amenity utilization to produce inclusive health scores and inferences to help managers improve sales efforts, staffing, marketing campaigns and capex decisions, amongst others. For executives, BI has and continues to create a strong sense of trust – giving leaders the right data to make faster and more specific decisions while knowing throughout that the data supports these choices.

Many properties simply cannot thrive without this top-level analysis to finesse operations and budgets. By removing these silos, BI lets hotels see how all profit centers – like rooms, dining, parking, spa or golf – interconnect to help optimize labor needs and reveal other areas for cost savings as well as discern what motivates more total guest spend for an increased topline.

Underspend Versus Overspend

"How do you know if your property is doing well?" posed Moore during our interview. "For the past two decades, answering this has meant reviewing such key metrics as internal and external benchmarks for the nightly rate, RevPAR, escalation events, TripAdvisor scores and so on. But these are often the symptoms without necessarily revealing the root cause of any pain. With enough data, though, hotels can identify and treat the source, so that they know exactly where they are underspending or overspending and apply just the right allotment of resources to move the needle."

What Moore discussed with us was what we came to describe as a 'Goldilocks zone of hotel management'. Each hotel has different goals – and those goals are constantly changing! – meaning that there's no one-size-fits-all playbook for hospitality. Modern BI lets hotels find the underspend or overspend to then know where that middle zone of bliss truly is.

This Goldilocks concept harks back all the way to the classical economic theory of 'marginal utility'. To illustrate this concept in a simple form, think about eating several donuts. The first is a symphony of sweetness on your tongue; the second is a muted delight; by the third, you're sick of eating said doughy treat altogether (well, most of us are). With all donuts created equal, once our base hunger needs are satisfied our taste centers derive diminishing returns from each subsequent bite, and the same psychology can be applied to hospitality experiences.

As a hotel example, slightly exceeding your brand standards in room cleaning may elicit cheers from your guests but going completely over the top with your housekeeping SOPs may not garner proportionally better praise. In such cases, you would be wise to only slightly exceed your brand standards then divert the extra energy to another project. Sure, you could keep spending in this one area; beyond a certain point, however, the average guest won't notice or care.

The problem with these Goldilocks situations has always been that there was no way to accurately measure when enough was enough so as to optimize for the challenge of marginal utility and diminishing returns. As such, hotels get bogged down with cost overruns or other inefficiencies that can impede brand momentum and new program that would be rolled out had there been a more effective allocation of capital.

That's about to change. With the integrated BI powered by Actabl, hotels can use their resources as efficiently as possible to improve their bottom lines, setting the stage for dramatic outperformance of the competition.

How to Win with BI

One of the main ways that a hotel can win with integrated BI is through forecasting precision. Armed with the actual operational data delivered through the ALICE front office and housekeeping modules, Actabl offers hoteliers proscriptive metrics so that they know exactly what next month's budget should be and do not incur costs where they shouldn't. Then via the capital asset management tracking functionalities within the Transcendent product, capex planning can now be directly compared with opex, making preventative maintenance even more preventative.

Returning to the previous example, executive housekeepers and GMs might ask whether they are overspending or underspending in this department. Until now, this has commonly been a defensive play, where the minimum threshold is broadly established by ensuring that all dirty rooms are cleaned according to brand standards and ready for sale to meet occupancy demands. The only real way to know if more spending was needed was when rooms were still dirty by check-in time, guests complained or overtime pay exceeded projections.

With integrated BI, you can test granular ideas for iterative improvements, such as how the insertion of new SOPs into a cleaning checklist that's pushed to the ALICE app on a room attendant's mobile phone might impact both labor per room (costs) and TripAdvisor scores (satisfaction) within ProfitSword, where the AI can then calculate the best balance between additional effort and real results.

Going a step further, said AI can be trained with specific housekeeping rules engines so that you can, for instance, model how effective individual room attendants are at cleaning on specific floors. With Actabl's latest addition, Hotel Effectiveness, hoteliers can go a step further by optimizing their labor allocation and spend across their portfolios, An end-to-end solution measuring the true value of changes to operational SOPs then allows for adjustments to labor in order to optimize for efficiency and the bottom line.

Playing Offense

They say that the best defense is a good offense; the feedback loops offered by integrated BI represent how this can become a reality for hotel operations. We bring up housekeeping because labor is perhaps the most salient issue of the day. Optimizing within this department is just the tip of the iceberg based on what we learned from Moore about the vision for Actabl and its ability to let hotels go on the offense in the form of sampling improvements.

To start, incorporating operational data gives a more accurate property health score then, as described above, lets you test variables to help solve the attribution problem and develop a feedback loop for increasing stakeholder value. This is a huge topic and one that we will explore in further depth to fully flesh out all the possibilities for this development.

To close, think about TRevPAR – that is, knowing which guest profiles are the most lucrative to your organization. Over the past few years, we've been big proponents of this under the generic maxim that more onsite spending equates to more guest satisfaction and more overall profits.

Not only do BI platforms let you put some math behind this principle but they can also tell you which specific parts of each operation are underperforming and give you the tools to improve. With technology this powerful, the only limit then becomes your own ideas and what questions you pose.

Hotels Now Have a Critical Need for One-Stop Shop Platforms

Often the personal can speak to the universal, so let's start with a personal story of a 120-room, independent hotel that we were recently helping to resolve some tech issues. The key goal put forth by the managing director was to merge all guest data into a unified guest experience management system so that the property could ramp up packaging and upselling (pre-arrival and onsite) in order to drive total revenue per guest (TRevPAR).

The problem was that the tech stack had become needlessly complex as single-use pieces were added iteratively over the years. This siloed approach not only led to increased total ongoing software fees, but the IT team had to spend more time maintaining integrations while the options for new pieces were constrained by the established interfaces of the current systems. Moreover, too many different systems had created data bottlenecks and the end users — onsite teams mostly comprising twenty-something guest service agents and managers — were stressed out by having to cross-reference so many databases.

Sound familiar? It's a situation all of us are confronting in some way as the industry's need for automation has bloomed over the past few years. In this case, the managing director was looking for us to evaluate then help implement yet one more platform to act as this ***single source of truth*** for guest profile data, but our solution was to first take a step back and look for a vendor that could solve the present-day challenge then also offer room to grow as systems were consolidated quarter over quarter.

The hotel tech stack is one seeking minimalism, not further expansion, especially given the risk of creating ***zombie platforms*** that your teams are too busy to learn or use on a regular basis. The years ahead are thus about finding a ***one-stop shop*** that offers a versatile range of tools to make things simple for both sales and marketing, as well as operations.

On this note, we were impressed by the latest platform offered by INTELITY because its GEMS (Guest Experience Management System), in addition to its core ticketing functions, had the ability to quickly take on this single-source-of-truth role, as well as help fill some gaps that would have otherwise required the extra cost of single-use system deployments.

For you as the reader, what's critical to understand is some top-level criteria for evaluating tech going forward — specifically what to look for in a one-stop shop so that you can build a roadmap for consolidation around a handful of platforms to serve all your current needs and help you grow TRevPAR.

What Can You Do with a Single Source of Truth

What impressed us most about the platform — and what you should always evaluate any provider on — was the richness of GEMS in its ability to copy, clean and merge guest data from the PMS, POS, any other F&B systems, spa booking software, operations platform, and the hotel guest app. Once you have that, the possibilities are only as good as the ideas, questions, and inferences your managers have.

For this property case study, we were also working with the F&B director to cultivate an exquisite wine program. Oenophiles as the two of us are, we saw an opportunity to build TRevPAR by identifying then targeting past guests whose data revealed them as probably being fellow wine enthusiasts. This alone required some analytics around past package purchases, onsite restaurant purchases (total wine spend, specific bottles bought, and so on) and any wine-related arrival amenities that were successfully upsold.

The strategy from there was to refine a list of customers, then target them with an exclusive and high value-add, wine-focused package that brought together past F&B purchases, in-room services and a bespoke experience. Moreover, we also applied this data query to our automated upselling, knowing that sometimes guests simply weren't ready to consider additional purchases at the time of reserving a room. It seems simple, but before this transition, the creation and targeting for something like this would all have to be done using offline exported sheets in Excel.

How Unified Platforms Help Save Labor

Thinking about how a one-stop shop can help build topline revenues is still less than half the battle in a labor-tight market, especially when you're having problems fulfilling service orders. Here's what we found in INTELITY — both from its back-of-house platform and from its guest-facing app — so that you can use this as a guide for your own endeavors:

1. *The hotel app that teams like to use.* From the point of view of the onsite content managers, it's all about having the ability to automate service requests as well as execute no-code updates on the fly within the CMS. Further, having the app directly connected into the GEMS with data ported from the operations platform allowed both the front office manager and executive housekeeper to anticipate high-volume periods for less overtime and faster service overall.
2. *The hotel app that guests prefer to use.* By far the most popular use for the app was for F&B, and yet much of this was a straight displacement of orders previously put through the phone system. While on paper it could be seen as a net-zero, this pass-through nevertheless meant that the front desk team wasn't constantly interrupted by all these in-house guest calls, whether it was for F&B or other complimentary services. Secondly, we found that cart size was larger for app orders than for phone orders, suggesting that guests will

spend more with a hotel when they can browse online without feeling rushed by having a live person on the other end.

3. *Reframing the mobile check-in experience.* If you look at many of the current online registration and mobile check-in procedures, it can be quite a cumbersome flow from the guest's perspective. Instead, identification verification can now be completed within the app well in advance of a guest's stay, then geolocation proximity algorithms can detect on the day of arrival that the guest is now onsite (or is approaching the hotel) and automatically drop the mobile key into the hotel app, as well as ping the appropriate teams for any welcome amenity requirements. This requires a complex series of connections between the app, security platform, operations platform, door locks and the PMS, but it can now be done, all to improve the guest check-in experience and boost labor efficiencies.
4. *Pitching in for tech stack gaps.* Opting for a handful of robust platforms oftentimes means that certain departments doggedly request standalone solutions to meet all of their specific needs. Part of our job was thus to deftly handle the change management insofar as convincing siloed teams of the merits of system consolidation with all the productivity gains that would be achieved — for instance, by temporarily filling the role of a service and work order system. What we've often found on tech consultations is that the search for a single-use system that can meet the department's every single requirement can take upwards of a full year, all the while the team suffers in lost productivity. The cost of capital is now too great for this type of waiting game, and it's better to have a versatile, centralized platform that pitches in wherever needed.

To close, and add to that fourth point, these one-stop shop platforms give hotels the ability to reduce subscription fees by not needing a bunch of standalone solutions, but, perhaps more significantly, they allow for *utility players* where labor and managers can be flexibly distributed across multiple operations at any given time, both to meet the needs of any given day in a labor-tight world and also as motivation to deter employee turnover.

That's where the future of hotel labor is headed. Wages are only going to keep rising and the need to intelligently drive revenue per guest is also becoming all the more crucial, so you need to start thinking holistically about how your entire tech stack can grow in this direction.

This Is Why You Need Great Tech-Enabled Hotel Employee Experiences

Since well before the pandemic, hotels have been in the midst of an 'operations revolution', largely by deploying better and better technology to automate mundane tasks so that teams can be more guest-facing and deliver more personalized experiences.

Along the way, though, we have created a bit of a monster that has only now reared its head as labor supply issues have been priority number one.

The statistic that best encapsulates this issue comes from a study published in 2019 by the University of California, Irvine, which found that the average office worker switches between different screens or tasks *566 times per day*. Not only does all this multitasking prevent 'flow' – that is, the time-efficient generation of high-quality output per employee – but each little screen or task switch also induces a morsel of stress, all of which accumulate throughout the workday like a death by a thousand cuts.

We get it. Hotel operations are complex, necessitating lots of systems to render services complete. At the same time, however, your employees are overwhelmed by dashboards, apps, reports, data, and all sorts of screens they must check daily. This is undeniably a cause for the high rates of turnover we see in hospitality and perhaps also a supplemental reason for why we cannot even attract good Gen Y+Z (millennials and centennials) talent to the industry in the first place.

Something has to give. Luckily, the most salient answer to the problem of too much tech is yet more tech, or rather smarter tech, that consolidates information and actions under one intuitive screen so that teams can get back to *monotasking*. For this, we have Robert Stevenson, CEO of INTELITY, a next-gen provider of operations and guest-facing technologies, to thank for demoing the company's brand-new INTELITY R5 platform and all the neat tools it has to help your hotel get its teams motivated.

Prioritizing the Employee Experience for Next-Gen Hoteliers

The two of us are keen evangelists of all the latest strides to make wellness a cornerstone of hospitality, both for FOH as a tool to generate more revenues from guests and for BOH as a means of combating the post-pandemic mental health crisis by improving employee wellbeing. It's this latter point where exceptionally designed operations platforms enter the picture because good tech works to boost the holistic *employee experience* (EX).

Significantly, younger generations are more attracted to inclusive work environments with robust wellbeing programs in place. So, to attract the next generation of hoteliers, organizations must examine every way possible to make the job more suitable for Gen Y+Z, for which adopting smarter tech is one of the low-hanging fruit.

But why should EX be a top priority right now? It's a tough sell in an economic landscape where surpassing a given profitability benchmark is still uncertain, and the push for greater efficiency is the foremost goal of C-level executives. We argue that efficiency and profitability are wholly dependent on EX, especially in a workplace culture that increasingly values wellness.

Here are three big-picture challenges that we discussed with Stevenson as they relate to technology:

- Per the aforementioned mental health crisis, lowered employee morale due to tech frustrations translates into more presenteeism (lost productivity, suboptimal onsite performance and more errors made), absenteeism (impacting other costs like overtime payout) and, of course, turnover.

- The ongoing hotel labor shortage is leading to inflationary wages and salaries, meaning that you need every nonwage incentive at your disposal to buttress this cost, including a consolidated tech stack that reduces the mental workload required to wield it.
- As the two digitally fluent generations raised on seamless graphical user interfaces (GUIs), Gen Y+Z employees don't like going back to outdated GUIs at all, further demotivating them and cajoling them to quit.

As we see it, the inability to retain talent is the core issue holding a hotel back from continuous success, precisely because it creates discontinuity. Without a solid team in place – especially one that fosters the next generation of hoteliers – you end up with service gaps and also leadership gaps as managers leave for competitors offering a better EX, all of which erode profitability and operational efficiency.

Turnover also comes with a sizeable, albeit hidden, *replacement cost, which includes recruitment costs, more time spent screening candidates, onboarding new hires, sign-on bonuses, offering above-market wage incentives to stay competitive,* and project stalls due to loss of leadership.

Attention Management Through Good Tech

Especially for the Gen Y+Z that are already eternally distracted by the likes of Instagram, TikTok and WhatsApp, the constant shifting of their cognitive resources amongst the various hotel systems can be a major performance drain and jobsite stressor. Hence, if efficiency boils down to better time management, then integrated tech – like what we saw with INTELITY's R5 platform – provides better attention management, as encapsulated by three broad utilities.

1. *Working spheres.* This is the term that Stevenson offhandedly used to denote software design consolidation where similar tasks are clustered onto a single viewing screen with all nonessential information omitted to focus the mind on what's important in that very instant. This heightened focus, as enabled by all-in-one platforms, is what will free up your associates' time to be great hosts for guests or allow managers to make headway on those revenue-generating projects.
2. *Reducing busywork and invisible work.* Bringing all the various operations under one roof by integrating, cleaning and structuring the data from departments ranging from front office, housekeeping and maintenance to F&B, spa, retail, golf, valet, concierge, events and meetings will help to diminish the busywork of cross-referencing multiple systems and the invisible work of having to spend extra time behind the scenes getting caught up because there are so many workflow interruptions. Again, this liberates time for more service personalization or working on projects that will add long-term value.

3. *Utility players and flexible hours.* In a world of ever-decreasing labor supply, hotels are starting to rotate workers through different roles and across variable shifts depending on where demand is strongest, while also using the prospects of a more dynamic, cross-departmental workplace as a tool to retain talent. All this hinges, though, on the ability to streamline underlying processes so that team members can be 'plug and play' wherever they are needed with direct supervision.

The key throughout is that as technology becomes the foundation of smooth service delivery, all the older, siloed tech platforms no longer work because you need your supervisors' and managers' attention devoted to other matters impacting the guest experience. In this sense, it's the strong 'no touch' backbone of technology that will enable the next phase of 'high touch' hospitality.

The Future of the Front Desk

We close by focusing on one example of how tech will evolve the hotel experience – the front desk – that the two of us discussed with Stevenson in terms of how INTELITY's customizable hotel app shifts certain tasks away from hotel teams so that there's more time available for revenue-generating ones.

Currently, the front desk functions primarily to execute *transactional conversations* including perfunctory actions like authorizing credit cards, verifying passwords, handing out keys, directing guests to facilities and settling folios at check-out. These types of interactions don't build rapport nor do they endear guests to the brand.

Instead, we can now largely transfer these transactional conversations onto the guest-facing hotel app by allowing the app to do the following:

- Enable mobile check-in with passport verification
- Secure the NFC or BLE mobile keys
- Act as a repository for all property information and available amenities
- Provide instant access for on-demand services
- Cross-sell onsite experiences to amplify a guest's stay
- Enable mobile checkout with folio settlement

By offloading all this from the day-to-day of the front desk team, said frontline employees can then move – both figuratively and literally – to the front of the desk, assuming the role of a 'welcome team' and 'hosts' who now have an unrushed, casual chat with guests.

These genuine conversations are the lifeblood of true hospitality because they actually augment the guests' experiences as well as give the staff a chance to ask about how to further personalize the stay or present additional services the guests may want to purchase. And all the while, the physical front desk might be converted into a complimentary refreshment station, further enhancing the sense of arrival.

Ultimately, hospitality is and will always be about people. But if hotels continue to struggle in attracting and retaining great young hires by not heeding the call for EX innovation, guest service will be what suffers, greatly impacting the bottom line. And because next-gen hoteliers are digitally fluent, so too must your tech stack also keep pace with what these stakeholders demand.

Driving Direct Bookings in the Era of Integrated Systems

In an ideal world, your hotel would turn off distribution to online travel agencies, sourcing all guests from direct channels and maximizing net revenues. But in reality, OTAs today are likened to a necessary evil to both raise awareness with new customers and generate bookings from guests who have no previous experience with your brand.

Now, however, new advances in property-level systems are enabling hotels to rethink how they incentivize direct bookings, learn more about guests from owned channels and, ultimately, drive traffic away from the commission-heavy OTAs. Importantly, any resultant increase in net revenues from this concerted effort will be needed as financial wiggle room for future capital expenditures in the face of a rapidly changing hospitality landscape.

We say 'concerted' because this is more than just technology; it also involves marketing strategy, onsite team training and other operations. While there's lots you can do – and indeed, guest intelligence and agile hotel marketing are subjects for an entire masterclass – here are three main 'rules' centered around data integrations for you to consider prioritizing to realize significant gains in direct bookings.

Why Right Now

It's a given that your hotel is making far less off of an OTA booking than from a reservation made through an owned channel, with commissions varying depending on what you negotiated. What you have to remember is that an OTA customer is not your customer...yet!

When an OTA guest checks in, their email is opaque – aliased – which makes it difficult to enroll them into your loyalty program or communicate with them for upselling additional services like room upgrade or F&B. While undoubtedly you have workshopped several different 'mousetraps' to get these guests to hand over some more personal information, the risk right now is that the OTAs are doing a really good job that keeping their customers loyal to them. Once habits are instilled, they're very difficult to change.

Namely, Booking and Expedia both have their own rewards programs that prioritize destination over any property or brand in particular, meaning that even a specific hotel search may yield competitive offers that behaviorally deter even the thought of hotel brand loyalty. More recently, the OTAs have become trendsetters with deploying new technologies like GPT-based travel planning plugins to imbue additional layers of convenience into their platforms.

In other words, it's almost getting to be too late; the user interface on the OTAs is too robust, too flexible and too valuable for guests to bother looking elsewhere but perhaps Airbnb. Some hotels may end up doomed to rely on hefty commissions eroding gross margins, a disloyal customer base that they know little about and constant problems with cancellations, no shows, chargebacks and reconciliation issues.

Rule #1: Never Give Guests an Excuse to Book Anywhere Else

Rate parity means you can't undercut the OTAs on price, but there are ways to get creative and still abide by the terms of these agreements. It's never a one-size-fits-all approach, so here are some ideas to ensure your hotel can compete on price with the OTAs while still adding value to the direct booking as well as the direct booking experience.

- Promoting your *best rate guarantee* is a half measure because it requires an extra morsel of time on the part of the guest to bring to your attention. You need a clear and real-time picture of when the OTAs are running promotions – both those that your revenue director controls and those that the OTA runs themselves – so that you direct channel lists the same price as what's on an OTA and nothing higher. This will require good intelligence from your revenue management system (RMS) and perhaps some AI-based automatic rate adjustments to make happen.
- Another important aspect that the leading RMS vendors can now offer is the interpretation of vast sums of *forward-looking demand data* so that your rates can remain nimble with respect to the comp set or any compression events. You have to be able to react in an instant in order to optimize revenues and not drive traffic to the OTAs because they're displaying a slightly lower price by being just a touch faster.
- Next, consider your *channel manager* and which room types and room packages you send to the OTAs. Yes, your contract says you must give them the same rates as what you list on direct channels, but there may be some room to breathe (pun intended) around which specific room categories you push out. Notably, you may decide to keep all the premium rooms and suites for direct guests, then combine this with an extra, non-price incentive like offering a 'same day complimentary upgrade upon availability.' Other areas where value can be added, depending on the terms in your OTA contract, include prepaid noncancellable rates, free breakfasts, all-inclusive rates or packaged specials that bundle local attractions.

Rule #2: Know Your Guests and Their Lookalikes

It's not like the problem of opaque information from OTA guests is new, and tech vendors have made incredible strides over the past few years to let you hone the leisure transient funnel and enhance each phase of the customer journey so that you can still get a good picture of what motivates your guests. Furthermore, what we learn about our guests is invaluable in developing lookalike personas and microsegments to guide marketing efforts and future promotions.

- Outside any discussions of programmatic advertising or other top-of-funnel awareness campaigns, the first real touchpoint with your guests is the website. Whether or not you have control over any modifications to the front-end design, it's nevertheless important to know about the latest enhancements to the *website booking engine* (WBE). Not only are the user interfaces becoming more adaptable, but you have more user behavior data to tell you where customers are dropping off as well as what additional incentives are working to lock in the bookings when those shoppers return.
- If you have control over your front-end website and can add a prominent 'Book Now' button, then great, do that. But as a bolt-on to the site, adding *live chat functionality* may be more likely as an approvable project. Guests will have questions and the more you can answer them and engage them, the more likely they are to prefer the direct channel. And for efficiency's sake, nowadays you can deploy a chatbot that can be trained to answer most of the repetitive questions before handing over the reins to a live agent to complete the booking or handle complex requests.
- While we, as people in the industry, know quite well the benefits of our loyalty programs, numerous other 'average consumers' have no clue nor do they see a long-term future with your brand. They're mercenaries who want immediate gratification. Luckily, there are a handful of *rewards platforms* that can help entice direct reservations in the moment while remaining compatible with your loyalty program.
- And to circle back to the title of the article, *integrating systems* is a must. This can improve the performance of the rewards you present, the intelligent guidance your RMS gives you and the packaging flexibility you are able to present within the WBE. The more you clean and combine the data, the more actionable insights you will have to see what's working. Even broader, think in terms of revenue per guest, wherein additional integrations from the point of sale (POS) can tell you what's driving ancillary spend to further refine those guest inferences that will guide the messaging to lookalike audiences.

Rule #3: Information Capture for the Onsite Experience

This is likely to be your best chance to get the guest's real email, phone number or social media account for future marketing efforts. It goes without saying that this largely depends on how good the onsite experience is, but a great stay is no guarantee that the OTA guest converts into one of yours.

- Outside of all things tech, *online staff training* is your ace in the hole, both by delivering exceptional guest service to build positive rapport as well as treating every customer interaction as a way to remind them to book directly. Are they prompting guests about your loyalty program? Do they know the specific advantages so that they can speak about them passionately? Are you incentivizing your front desk agents to obtain the real email address from

OTA guests by offering them, for example, 10% off their next stay? While a lot of this can be done in person, facilitating this education through an online portal is more efficient and scalable.

- Another great point to discuss the loyalty program is through *digital signage*, be it in the display, a public area display or a check-in kiosk. All can be configured to raise awareness or even include a specific mousetrap like a QR-code-based promotion for a free drink at the bar that requires a real email address to be activated.
- A third area that may need some retooling is the *Wi-Fi login portal*. Most are already set up to show a host of available add-ons, but there are now a few upselling platforms that can be bolted on to A/B test different offers and incentives to see what's working to drive ancillary spend.

It Takes a Village

As trite as it may be to say, we (hotels) are all in this fight together. It's often far too easy to fall into a prisoner's dilemma type of attitude whereby, in anticipation of your competitors undercutting your rates, you preemptively lower your rates, then your competitors do the same and the entire market spirals down into commoditization.

Instead, understand that there are passive, cooperative benefits to enhancing your efforts to drive direct bookings. These efforts will undoubtedly help other hotels – in your comp set and in other markets – but their efforts will also boost your own direct reservations ratio over the long run as the average consumer slowly but surely becomes more aware of why booking direct is always the best way to go. It's a bit like karma, and you have to trust that if we all work together on this problem, then together it will course correct and every hotel will realize healthier net revenues.

How Great Survey Design Impacts Hotel Operations and Long-Term Hotel Value

As consultants who are often brought on by hotel owners to represent their interests as asset managers, one of the first tasks we undertake to familiarize ourselves with the brand or property is to peruse the reviews and other feedback data. We mean 'peruse' in its literal definition; we read through the entirety of TripAdvisor, OTA reviews, and other survey channels, never settling for the aggregate metrics as presented. What we're looking for in all this is, in a word, 'significance' or what's truly meaningful for the guest.

Working as asset managers, our primary goal isn't simply to move the online rating from, for instance, a 4.5 out of 5 to a 4.6 or a 4.7, but to figure out what guests like the most about a hotel and what factors are its weakest links. We want to embellish the good and eliminate the bad in order to maximize occupancy, loyalty, return visits and the ability to grow rate. As every hotelier knows, however, guests perceive hotels in a highly emotional way, which means that what may negatively affect satisfaction doesn't necessarily correlate one-to-one with cost.

Perusing reviews and surveys gives you a far deeper sense of a hotel's 'value-engineered ROI' – that is, the fixes, be they capex or opex, that will give you the most bang for your buck. For example, from a former assignment several years back for a West Coast resort, we discerned from reviews that the walls between guestrooms were rather thin, which hindered return visits for some guests due to it being 'noisy' at certain times during the night. Without tearing the place down to cram in more insulation, the most cost-effective solution was to festoon the rooms with heavy drapes, carpets, door sweeps, and other soundproofing materials and then monitor comments to see if the problem went away (it did).

From these types of value-engineered solutions, it follows that the more feedback a hotel gets, the more of this 'significance' a management team can leverage as insights to decide best what capital or operational improvements will deliver the most positive impact from the perception of the guest.

With this in mind, it was a delight to sit down with Jeff Robbins, founder of GuestInsight, to learn about what hotels can do to rapidly scale their total guest engagement so that management can make more informed decisions as to which projects will have the most ROI.

Yes, GuestInsight offers a great platform to help hoteliers collect, analyze and automate their guest feedback. But what really excited us about talking with Robbins was learning about the people behind the product. They bring with them over two decades of deep experience in survey design – something that's seldom taught in hospitality school – and apply this expertise daily via ongoing customer support so that hotels can realize the benefit of asking the right questions that engage guests in the right way.

The Great Review Reset

Like any conversation we have with hoteliers and others active in hospitality technology, it starts and ends with a state of the industry. Where we began with Robbins is something we all experienced; the big 'P' word causing a before-after schism in how reviews are perceived. Notably, in our post-pandemic world, guests are much more sensitive to craving good reviews within the near past.

First, this was out of fear of COVID and wanting to know about how hotels were keeping guests safe. Next, this morphed into using reviews as a litmus test for how service levels were changing during the recovery period. Now, it is guests wanting to know if the onsite experience is keeping pace with the inflation of nightly rates. The pattern throughout is that the hospitality world is moving a mile a minute, and with this 'Great Review Rest,' hotels need a persistent stream of fresh reviews in order to raise customer confidence and spur new bookings.

The problem here is and has always been engagement rates. How do hotels keep pace with the speed of society where the desire for fresh reviews remains at an all-time high? Besides the post-departure guest-facing side of all this – namely, engaging guests who've had a positive experience to elicit more positive reviews online with TripAdvisor or one of the OTAs – the flip side of the coin for engagement is completed surveys directly to the hotel, which will ultimately influence capex and opex decisions. Either way, hotels need a 'quantity of quality' in engagement in order to attain a better 'decision efficiency'.

Great Survey Design to Fight Feedback Abandonment

As mentioned in the nighttime noise example, oftentimes the best solution from an ROI perspective doesn't involve a full-scale renovation or adding elaborate new amenities. It's about addressing those issues that guests perceive to be particularly irksome. But you can only prioritize these with a large enough sample size of feedback and by asking the types of questions that will generate relevant responses or data.

Without formal training in feedback design, survey psychology and statistical analysis, most hotel brands (and both authors included!) have largely treated feedback abandonment rates as something that cannot be sizably improved – a kind of 'it is what it is' challenge. Moreover, for most hotels, once the actual survey content is set, updates to said content are infrequent or there isn't much thought about A/B testing questions or prompts to optimize for engagement and abandonment reduction.

Some survey design tips that Robbins suggests based on current work with GuestInsight clients include:

- Messaging that demonstrates respect for the guest's time and inbox
- Messaging that clearly defines the ask in terms of reason and time expectations
- Stating outright how important the effort of collecting feedback is for the hotel
- Being transparent about recruiting an experienced outside agency to manage the process
- Mentioning how the guest's anonymity and privacy will be protected
- Having a responsive survey interface with reliably quick load times
- Not bundling the feedback request with a sales effort
- Having an alert mechanism in place so that teams can immediately tackle an error recovery situation or when the surveys are used for post-departure requests like making another booking
- Being cognizant of a team's overall 'alert fatigue' when setting up said alert mechanisms

Above all, Robbins emphasized that surveys must be structured in a way that accomplishes the research goals with the least amount of effort required by the guest according to these three principles:

1. *Question sequencing* that prioritizes specified feedback goals:
2. Question wording or *question format selection* with precise and concise language to elicit results
3. Flexibility in adapting the survey with *seasonal or monthly updates* to the questions in order to test new ideas as well as stress certain facilities or services

Any Tool Still Needs Human Judgment

With any discussion of feedback, it's inevitable for AI to enter the picture, either as natural language processing (NLP) to help scale sentiment analysis or another form of machine learning (ML) that finds patterns in the multitude. And as any IT professional knows, the amount of data hotels currently have is becoming overwhelming; AI will be pivotal to help guide the judgment of managers. From the above tips, though, what's apparent is that these technologies are just tools; they believe the need for veteran oversight to help hotels maximize the usage of the totality of data for any algorithm to chew on.

Hence, the act of setting up then updating questionnaires shouldn't be the sole responsibility of the hotelier who isn't formally trained in survey design and cannot provide this oversight or human judgment. While one option can be continuing professional development to provide this internal education, oftentimes the more accessible route is to get external help in guiding, shaping and continually adapting a brand's surveys.

The risk nowadays is that if feedback response rates remain low, then the data won't be big enough for an AI to accurately interpret. Simultaneously, of course, some of that 'significance' also won't rise to the top to present those value-engineered solutions that will inform operational planning and future investments in a meaningful way that will increase long-term asset value.

Californian Case Study

To close, Robbins offered one generalized case study worth going through. Working with a 120-room independent property in Silicon Valley, the GuestInsight platform was able to drastically ramp up the number of completed surveys, with a year-to-date total of 819 internal completed surveys compared to 12 reviews on TripAdvisor, 67 on Google and 193 on Booking.

With over 20 times the number of surveys versus TripAdvisor reviews, this uptick in both the quantity and pace at which data was accumulating meant that the hotel was able to rapidly spot a significant trend from its declining scores and guest comments. Specifically, the breakfast offering was changed during the pandemic and was initially positively received, so the hotel kept it in place. But during the late spring months, this perception shifted and was quickly spotted by the metrics which started to trail off at the same time.

From this observation, amidst the hectic summer period, the team was able to upgrade its breakfast service back to and beyond its pre-pandemic levels, and this positive, cost-effective change was reflected in the post hoc responses. Overall, these sorts of minute-by-minute inferences are only possible when there's proper survey design in place to maximize response rates and the amount of data received. And when you spot enough of these trends, you ensure that no issue goes unnoticed and that the hotel is maximizing satisfaction to thereafter influence brand advocacy, the ability to grow ADR and, specifically for owners, long-term asset value.

All Hail Hotel QR Codes

After a frenetic week at HITEC, it's clear that one trend firmly embedded in the hospitality landscape for the next few years is the QR (quick response) code. Riding on the back of guests demanding everything contactless from the pandemic, software developers have now come back with quite a few functional and lucrative applications for this trendy tech.

Before expanding on some use cases, it's important to reflect on both the pre-COVID applications of QR codes and, critically, their overall perception. In the anteCOVIDian times, like the two of us, you may have thought of these matrix barcodes as nothing more than a fad or even an obstruction from otherwise accepted and routine mediums of commerce. Think of paper menus as a quick and convenient way of conveying what's on offer at a restaurant (if it ain't broke, right?).

Just as few accurately predicted the pandemic, few could have foreseen just how central this technology would become. The overarching lesson here is that while you are allowed (dare we say, encouraged) to have strong opinions on a subject, you must be open to change in the face of new information – 'strong opinions, loosely held' as they say in the investing world. The virus represented that new information that pushed QR codes into the limelight, so much so that now they are a de facto part of our phone-centric society.

Ruminating on this shift, ask yourself what other trends you are reluctant to embrace even as the social fabric evolves around you. For the more cerebral hotelier to consider, there may also be a morsel of 'technological determinism' at play here, with the new functionality, feature, platform or device influencing the grand direction of civilization and relegating the non-adapters to the scrapheap of history. It's worth an evening Scotch to ponder how this may play out over the decade ahead.

Basic QR Advantages

While QR codes are already ubiquitous, it's important to run through the fundamentals for why they have persisted even as the pandemic has ended. These matrix barcodes are:

- *Socially accepted,* which encourages further usage of the technology
- *Convenient* and frictionless after all the improvements made over the past few years
- *Contactless* and therefore safe for those still worried about physical distancing
- *Relatively cheap* where, once the setup is complete, print costs are minimized

Given these four advantages, QR codes will continue to find new uses for hotels. With any new feature or proposed application for this tech, you should always evaluate it from the guest's perspective according to these fundamentals to better predict if it will work as intended.

Taking QR to the Next Level

These use cases require a bit more explanation for how these work, but the end goal throughout is always one of heightened convenience, personalization or optimizing revenue per guest. (The following three use cases are ones that are currently deployed and we'll be happy to point you in the right direction of some prospective vendors who can help you out.)

1. *Incentivizing app downloads.* Hotels want guests to use their apps because these apps tend to be great tools for increasing spend, expediting service requests and augmenting engagement for better GSS. But here in the 2020s, we're all 'apped out' and thus resistant to yet one more company trying to cajole us into downloading yet one more mobile app. We need a spark, which QR codes can provide in the form of bespoke onsite offers – think happy hour drink promos advertised at the front desk – that automatically take customers to the app download page.
2. *Upselling and cross-selling.* Building on the first point, several vendors now allow hotels to use QR codes to not only offer bespoke promotions that boost impulse buying, but the matrix barcode redirects can also be set up with a single sign on (SSO) so that customer authentication doesn't act as a point of friction in the sales process. As an example, consider a QR code set up on the 15th or 16th hole at a golf resort with a message that encourages players to order ahead of time so that the total order is fully ready by the time they get to the clubhouse. Upon activation, the QR code takes users directly to the appropriate restaurant ordering page where, due to SSO mechanics from a previous interaction with the app, those users are already known, thereby enhancing data collection and personalization. The result is smoother service, faster food delivery and greater spend; everybody wins.
3. *Getting around OTA email aliases.* Despite what hoteliers may say out in public, in private we all hate the OTAs. They're stealing our business in more ways than one, foremost of which is the email aliases they use that stymie loyalty incentivization, remarketing campaigns and lookalike audience analytics. This is where QR codes present a nifty trick. Any app download or sign-on incentive can be programmed to require a real email (not an OTA alias) as well as the guest's phone number for verification. Then, behind the scenes the phone number will be used to cross-reference and update a guest profile with their correct email.

While we are always game for a fireside chat about the applications of NFTs or another futurist technology for hotels, from the above three use cases it should be apparent that QR codes are far more fitting for the harried hotelier amidst this current travel recovery phase. This technology can speed up service, help reduce a lot of the busywork and grow guest revenues across a variety of profit centers. This isn't necessarily anything new; when you make something more convenient – like the shift from cash to credit cards – people are bound to spend more liberally.

To end with a caveat emptor, always evaluate your deployment of this technology from the four core abovementioned utilities because there are some instances where old school remains in vogue. For instance, while the two of us have embraced what QR codes can do, one area where we're still holding out is the physical food and drink menus at high-end dining establishments. There's something about caressing a heavy cardstock and glancing over the grooves of embossed, expertly typeset branded text that delights the senses and adds to the overall meal experience. Prove us wrong!

QR Codes Have So Much More Potential for Hotels

The quick ready or matrix barcode has proven itself resilient beyond a mere pandemic fad. First they were a novelty, or often a joke, in the anteCOVIDian times before gaining widespread adoption due to their contactless utility. Then as we shifted out of the pandemic, their benefits for saving on printing costs and labor efficiency were also too good to ignore. Together, this technology determinism has solidified the QR code's place in hotels for the next half a decade at least, and yet their full potential hasn't been unlocked.

With the travel recovery craziness sunsetting back into relative normalcy for demand and labor forecasting (that is to say, we now know that labor will be constantly in short supply), it's time to look ahead to the future and how we can better use this technology that's been embraced, albeit often reluctantly, by both hospitality brands and our customers.

While the two of us both relish a good fireside chat about all things web3, crypto, longevity tech and super-sustainability projects, these are rather far-off aspirations – and thus unobtainable in the near-term – for most properties largely because of labor shortages in the IT department. When considering both your tech stack and your 'human stack', available resources for the calendar year dictate that it's better to augment what you already have, which in this case is the QR code and the bevy of vendors doing incredible things to help you use it to optimize service and conversions.

The Digital Restaurant Menu Experience

To gain adoption, a QR experience must be more convenient or contextual than current customer habits, or it must dangle a carrot that's too good for the guest to refuse – for example, offering a promotion to offset a high-friction app download that also captures first-party data. This grand idea of the guest experience is often too ambiguous, so it's better to drill down to specific operations to derive quantifiable improvements.

We thus start in the restaurant where QR-accessible menus have shown tremendous value for:

1. Saving on printing costs

2. Dealing with erratic supply chains that require sudden menu omissions or pricing increases
3. Reducing labor involved with handing out physical menus
4. Lowering average table turn time
5. Offering guests a frictionless BYOD ordering experience
6. Expediting the payment process
7. Increasing tipping in a now-cashless society
8. Getting more data on specific orders and special requests
9. More precise geolocation of food order delivery
10. Analytics of order fulfillment to improve service and guide staffing decisions

This all said, there are objections. Here, you encounter the growing lamentations over on-prem QR overload, particularly if these are plastered as signage everywhere, as well as the concern of the loss of genuine interactions between customers and brand representatives (be that a server or associate).

But perhaps one of the most often customer-side complaints against QR menus is that patrons can't see the full menu in one snapshot. This can hurt the branding for high-end restaurants where a thick cardstock or leatherbound menu backing adds to the experience, but more significantly the nuisance of pinching in or scrolling through the menu off a phone can result in items getting missed, amounting to lost revenues and more time spent by servers compensating for this issue.

The solution here is to work towards a better mobile menu experience, with the following as possibilities for you to figure out what can work with your team's current bandwidth:

- Knowing that linking to a static PDF is no longer acceptable customer service, the next option is to connect a QR to an HTML-based menu, nullifying the pinching issue (and at a low cost as most websites are already mobile-responsive) but not quite for the scrolling drop-off
- To prevent said scrolling drop-off from negatively affecting beverage revenues, you need to prioritize your alcohol offerings by putting them at the top or first connecting to a landing page that broadly delineates for food and beverage options
- Now think in terms of tabulated menus similar to online ordering apps where this sectioning facilitates less scrolling and more visibility on desired food or beverage categories, although this refinement often can't be done without bugs for the browser version
- To drive app downloads and thus provide a better digital menu experience, you need nudges like putting the WiFi password right need to the matrix barcode which redirects to the app download page (although this likely won't be enough of an incentive versus going straight into the browser version)
- As abovementioned, app downloads can be required to access certain promotions or freebies, which can be further rationalized for multi-operation

hotels where the app provides a convenient path to purchase for not only the restaurant but also room service, spa, gift shop, golf tee times, virtual concierge, housekeeping, activities or maintenance orders
- App or HTML, the wider trend is that menus are becoming more interactive, so expect to see such additions like on-click images, cinemagraphs or GIFs of dishes, curated UGC and promotional or announcement pop-up banners (possibly with an 'order now' functionality that puts an order directly through to the kitchen instead of waiting on the server)

Connecting the Guestroom and Onsite Amenities

As we transition to the QR experience version 2.0, it's only natural that this coincides with the deployment of more IoT devices and the evolution towards a bona fide connected room.

This tech can indeed offer a series of contextual and filtered actions to enhance the in-room experience, including but not limited to:
- Placing a matrix barcode by the door to facilitate express check-out by already knowing the room number
- This same QR placed by the door could also be used for guests to signal when they are departing for the day to schedule a stayover clean and to notify the smart thermostat for energy savings
- In a now-cashless society, branded QRs can increase total tips (and provide tracking on those tips) to offer a non-wage incentive for keeping room attendants versus competitors who don't have an easy pathway for guests to leave a tip
- Speaking of housekeeping, if your brand is going the opt-in route, QRs can act as a fluid portal for on-demand cleaning services (perhaps even prompting an app download in the process)
- To help mollify the QR overload and physical signage objections, QRs can be inserted on digital displays like TVs – an action which also helps address several of the security concerns whereby hackers can use false QR codes to install malware on unsuspecting phone
- As a future use case, QRs on interactive TVs can be used for content-as-a-service (CaaS) advertising where hotels get a slice of the clickthrough bids and conversion value

Next, for on-demand amenities, the versatility of QRs allow hotels to maintain service in a labor-light operative model by letting guests order whenever and from wherever they want. Especially for full-service properties, some possibilities include:
- Because resort staff is reduced and often can't spend time patrolling a beach for orders, location-specific QRs can be used to call food or drinks to a chaise or cabana without the guest needing to walk up to the bar

- QRs can be used alongside image-driven advertisements for onsite experiences where access then links directly back to the right webpage of curated activities (or, even better, to prompt an app download)
- Finally, to readdress the concern that frictionless ordering via QR codes will render hotel associates into mere fulfillment agents, it's important to consider how you can channel the time savings from this tech into service improvements, either through actual product enhancements that may not have been possible given previous labor limitations or retraining so that staff can engage guests on a non-transactional level

Having made it this far, you can tell that some use cases may apply to your organization and some do not. It really comes down to the last bullet point in that hotels can never lose sight of the human element in service-oriented business. Any QR functionality you set up must ultimately never take away from the guest experience, but add convenience and increase amenity awareness so that your teams can focus their limited time on other product evolutions.

Attribute-Based Shopping for Hotels in the Wake of the AI Craze

Artificial intelligence (AI) is at the forefront of hospitality technology. In looking at specific tasks where it can be deployed, a very lucrative application is attribute-based shopping (ABS). Alongside other pursuits like dynamic pricing and adept channel management, the ability for hotel guests to select individual rooms, configurations, services, add-ons, and ancillaries in an a la carte manner has long been sought after as a way to bolster net revenues (some postulate by as much as 10% for the average property) without any significant upleveling of the physical product, and now with some AI bolted on this newly unlocked value may finally be achieved.

Before diving into why AI works for ABS and why your brand may need it, two prominent obstacles need to be addressed, both from the transient guest's perspective as well as from the hotel manager's side of things. While many have thus far blamed legacy systems as the hindrance, this is hardly the case as leading industry vendors have all deeply considered ABS modules as a way to provide more value for their clients. Instead, the challenges are mainly psychological.

Stating the Objections

From the guest's point of view, it's a matter of 'shopper's paralysis.' You give a guest four room types and they have no problem selecting which one fits their needs and budget. You give a guest those same four room types along with varied check-in times, F&B packages, high floor or low floor, close or far from the elevator, ocean view or no ocean view and others like these, and it becomes too much. Instead of making a choice, the user abandons the cart and goes elsewhere for their accommodation needs.

How about solving this with a purchasing sequence within the internet booking engine (IBE) so that these variables act akin to a prix fixe menu? This can work, but then you must also consider the stepchild of shopper's paralysis – decision fatigue. Especially when it comes to the psychological pain of putting money on the line, making a decision is the most energetically taxing function that our brain performs. Ergo, the more monetary decisions you laden a guest with, the more displeasing the booking process becomes and, again, the more likely they are to abandon the cart. In this case, the customer may already be exhausted having compared upwards of 20 to 30 different lodging options, and throwing ABS on top of that would be overkill.

Onto the back office and the situation is one that every hotelier around the world can relate to – room blocks and VIPs. Hoteliers need to maintain control over where they place guests right up to the last few weeks before arrival so that they can maintain flexibility for accommodating a big group contract that came in or someone that deserves a higher-tier room based on their loyalty status. For these cases, ABS would 'lock' specific rooms and possibly create more work for managers who then have to untangle groups or VIP requests around these upsold ABS room assignments.

How AI Helps ABS

The mechanics of A/B testing different options and offers as they relate to machine learning (ML) presents a profitable avenue for both incremental revenues and insights to guide future capital improvements or a full-property renovation.

At its core, ML is just pattern recognition based off of a multitude of data – namely, thousands upon thousands of guest interactions with a specific brand as well as those derived systemwide from all hotels using a vendor's platform – then optimizing to better fit that pattern towards a given outcome. In a general sense, the more data a machine has, the more patterns it can decipher and the better it can fit its behavior towards that stated goal.

So, if the objective is to maximize the number of bookings, the AI may determine that the best route is to not deploy ABS within the IBE. Why exactly? Answering that isn't within the machine's purview, but the human overseer may judge from the insights found by A/B testing different purchasing sequences that it's because of shopper's paralysis interfering with conversion maximization. Contrarily, if the objective is to optimize for revenue per room reservation, then the AI may find that compromising slightly on occupancy with well-sequenced ABS of the rooms inventory alongside other saleable products delivers a better overall topline.

There are indeed some prominent vendors who have built incredible online shopping experiences that incorporate elements of ABS and ML directly into the IBE. Getting into specifics for all the possibilities and advantages for specific hotels would take pages, but rest assured, they've found a way to thread the needle between customer decision fatigue and net revenue maximization. When considering how a prix fixe menu relates to the entirety of the guest journey, the two other areas where A/B testing can occur are within a prearrival upselling platform as well as within the hotel app for when the guest is onsite. Again, vendors are on the case, especially for the former of the two, where ML can also observe the optimal day out from arrival for when guests are most likely to spend time on ancillaries or individual rooms.

Separate from all the transient merchandising considerations, another prominent area where AI is reaching the forefront is in robotic processing automation (RPA), wherein a machine can be trained to connect disparate systems together when a strong interface doesn't exist or there are problems structuring the data. While not expressly a function that current vendors can solve for right now, with ML's core purpose being pattern recognition, RPA should be considered as a means of observing the behavior behind all group bookings so that a hotel has a better sense of what that segment's volume will be according to pace reports and when the best time is to serve up ABS offers.

Why ABS Needs to Start Now

We've talked a bit in abstract about what the machine can do with the user interaction data it is provided, but we haven't yet emphasized how the machine learns. It's relatively easy to understand what A/B testing is or even how a Monte Carlo experiment can work to deliver a range of possible revenue outcomes with a high confidence interval. What's more difficult is, like the obstacles, the human factor of being patient with the learning process.

That is, it takes time for the machine to test within a given range of variables in order to decipher what actually works to get guests to purchase more at any given moment as well as deliver actionable insights that can be used by hotel teams to improve product messaging, contextual delivery, sequencing, packaging, new types of onsite programming or capital expenses that maximize returns.

Because all this hinges on big data sets, every digital interaction that your guests currently have with your hotel where all the booking variables aren't being recorded then tested is an opportunity that's lost. This will likely require a lot of deliberate thought about what IBE, CRS and upselling platform you are using to start putting ML behind your online shopping experience, but it's a task that should be undertaken quickly because otherwise lots of money is being left on the table.

Data Maturation Represents the Essential Reason for Deploying Machine Learning Today

From the recent articles that Oracle Hospitality has published on both how machine learning (ML) works as well as some of its key applications, there is a single term that all hoteliers should remember when deciding how to commercialize this type of artificial intelligence (AI). This term is 'data maturation' and, as the name suggests, you need time to let the ML occur. You need to give the computers time to sift through the reams of training data to test variables and find the patterns that will then lead to the algorithms and models to advance business goals.

As with so many other aspects of hotel operations (and life for that matter!), time is the limiting resource. Significantly, we must remain cognizant of the large gap in learning between machines and humans because this difference can often twist our judgment about how quickly AI applications can be brought to fruition for a property or companywide.

From what we understand about consciousness, the knowing ape that is *homo sapiens* learns largely by causal inference. As a crude example of this contrast, let's say you encounter an ash-ridden husk of a burnt-down house. You will very likely know intuitively that a fire was the culprit after only one occasion of this and without directly witnessing the fire itself.

Computers learn about correlation not causation. Without enough datapoints on this current ash-ridden house and other similar instances from the past, the machine cannot say with a high degree of confidence if it was an unseen fire that burned the house down or if the house first collapsed via another mechanism and the ash formed thereafter.

What computers need to get from the 0% to 85%, then to 95% and 99.999% (the 'five nines' as they call it) confidence intervals are observations. It needs to analyze different variables across as many instances as possible in order to develop a probabilistic model of how the world works, and then it needs to test and retest that model in order to refine how well it fits with real world outcomes.

Just as a child doesn't become a mature adult overnight, from this previous sentence two important actions are implied:

1. *Deeper data connections.* The more fields of data points, the AI has that are associated with a given observation, the better it can evaluate hidden patterns amongst the vastness of numbers in order to build more accurate algorithms and models. Besides other key benefits of integrating various systems, the use cases for ML mean that APIs, CDPs and other unified platforms should remain a top priority for a hotel's commercial strategy.
2. *Multivariate testing.* Better data interfaces will yield more characteristics around a given observation, but the machine also needs more observations overall. Apart from the size of the initial training data, to learn and become increasingly accurate, the machine needs to A/B test and examine how people respond to its current modeling. Because this requires guests or customers to interact with measurable aspects of a hotel such as the website or mobile app, the more time that passes, the more physical interactions the machine can use to hone the model.

This last part drives home the point that you need to develop a plan for deploying ML now and thinking in terms of data maturation over the long run.

To close with an example from Norl and how data maturation affects prearrival upselling revenues, let's say your hotel has designed its pre-stay funnel to include an 'upgrade your stay' confirmation email that's sent out upon reservation and also seven days out from arrival. While the days out part is something upon itself that can be tested by the computer in order to optimize open rate and conversions, for simplicity we're going to start from upon landing within the upselling platform.

Let's say you present the user with three basic offers: add breakfast (F&B), upgrade to a suite (rooms), or purchase a spa voucher (wellness). At the start of ML deployment, all three offers are presented equally in the first, second and third positions, with customer #1 seeing F&B in the top left, rooms in the middle, and wellness in the top right, while customer #2 might see rooms in the top left, wellness in the middle and F&B in the top right.

If customer #1 chooses to add breakfast, is this because they wanted breakfast or because the F&B offer was in the first position? If customer #2 also chooses to add breakfast when it appears in the third position, is this enough evidence to determine that the F&B offer is what guests want or is the sample size too small?

At this point, there are so many variables, obvious or otherwise, to make a causal determination. What if both guests just want some form of food offer while onsite and don't care if it's breakfast, lunch, dinner or a ubiquitous food voucher, but they chose breakfast because it was the only F&B option? What if the photography for the breakfast offer was palpably more colorful and drew the eyes toward it better than the other two? What if the breakfast offer was significantly cheaper than the other two and it was chosen because of its inexpensiveness? What if both customers entered the upselling platform right before dinnertime around 5pm and it was their hunger that was driving their decision?

Even with only three offers, there are too many variables to tease out any correlation, let alone causation, at this point. The only way to make any sense around these questions is to test, test and retest. And because all your potential guests aren't going to visit your website or open a prearrival email all of sudden once you have your ML tool in place, it will take time for the observations to accumulate and for the model to mature, so best start accumulating now!

How Generative AI Maximizes the Direct Channel with Tata Crocombe

Article originally published in October 2023 and the indicated activities or results for Tata Crocombe's hotel properties at the time of this writing may not reflect current company practices.

The public debut of ChatGPT in late 2022 and the subsequent hype cycle afterwards certainly spurred a lot of thought from hoteliers about to use these large language models (LLMs) to improve the hotel business on multiple fronts – the onsite experience, BOH efficiencies, recruitment and, for today's case, getting guests to book direct in lieu of third-party channels.

Perhaps no hotel owner understands just how revolutionary generative artificial intelligence (GenAI) will be more than Tata Crocombe. Rather than just a vendor promoting its products into the vast expanse that is the hospitality technology marketplace, Crocombe offers hotelier experience stemming from the firsthand results of experimenting and deploying GenAI at his private island resort and two beach resorts in the Cook Islands in the South Pacific, respectively the Aitutaki

Lagoon Private Island Resort, The Rarotongan Beach Resort & Lagoonarium, and Sanctuary Rarotonga.

We first sat down with Crocombe at HITEC after he delivered a presentation on the seemingly innumerous ways that GenAI can be iteratively embedded into various operations and technologies. Crucial here is the word 'iterative' as contemplating the sheer power of ChatGPT and its ilk can be overwhelming insofar as rethinking every entrenched process at a hotel in one fell swoop.

Rather, Crocombe's presentation demonstrated the various ways that he has currently implemented GenAI as well as the other areas where he's charted a course for successive rollouts over the coming quarters and years once the initial use cases have been ironed out. As he emphasized, however, probably the most profound way that a hotel can deploy GenAI right now is by using a machine learning (ML) chatbot or conversational AI (for the voice channel) to enhance the website booking experience as a means of driving direct bookings.

All other variables held constant, quickly scaling your technologies to support the biggest possible channel shift is the best value to drive profitability in the next few business cycles because of the resultant bump in net revenues with marginal opex increases.

The Generative Game Is Afoot

In the pursuit of greater and greater GOPPAR and, ultimately, net operating incomes (NOI), there is no clearer place to look for a quick win than in growing net revenues by reducing customer acquisition costs (CAC). This objective is achieved by increasing the percentage of direct business significantly by winning guests to book online directly with the hotel rather than a third-party distribution partner, and in the process reducing commissions to the OTAs that can be as high as 28% down (comprised of a 15% standard commission, a 3% preferred commission and a 10% members commission) to the direct CAC which can come in as low as 2%.

Every prudent executive committee, marketing director or revenue manager has likely already given some thought to their channel conversion strategy and how chatbots figure into this mix of tactics. But with Booking Holdings and Expedia both rapidly incorporating ChatGPT into their travel planner toolkits to help keep more customers loyal to their platforms, it's now or never for many hotel brands.

This is an arms race that hotels cannot lose ground in because, when combined with their own loyalty programs, the OTAs are building defensive moats. Once their GenAI tools are ironed out, it will be hard to reverse the value they are extracting from the global hotel industry.

Booking Holdings and Expedia have set the current standard for online bookings, though. If hotels want to increase their direct booking percentage, they have to out-service these competitors by making the reservation experience more efficient and pleasurable than that on an OTA. This requires hoteliers to never accept the status quo for how their website or booking engine works, as guests may want in their hearts to book direct but end up going back to an OTA because the hotel's brand.com was poorly built or more expensive than the third party.

This last aspect related to channel management touches on an important point before getting into the specifics of chatbots – concerted efforts. An AI agent is not a panacea; it must be deployed in tandem with an array of other tactics, some online and others not, that will together make for a better reservation experience.

To give you a specific example here, Crocombe developed for his properties a landing page called What Room is Best for Me that has helped guests work out for themselves where they want to stay, adding an element of gamification and 'sense of discovery' to the customer journey. This was combined with a thorough upgrade to the website with lots of new information, imagery, and virtual room tours, as well as direct booking promotions, including 15% off on accommodations and then 10% off on restaurant, bar, spa, and gift shop purchases.

Next, even before testing and launching the chatbot, Crocombe observed that there are guests that want to deal with a human and those that are happy to parlay with a bot. So, his team connected a 24/7 live chat and recruited a reservations center in the Philippines so that going forward this blended model would facilitate flexibility for any guest's preferences.

How Direct Chatbots Help You Win

Crocombe offers a shimmering ray of hope, though, in that a well-trained LLM-based AI will always be superior to whatever offering the OTAs present because no third party will ever be able to give the same level of detail, the focused passion, calibration of responses and connectivity into all hotel operations as a first-party system can.

Significantly, this new generation of AI tools is 'democratized' in that they are available to any property for sometimes as low as $20 per month, thereby leveling the playing field and allowing any independent hotel or vacation rental a better-than-fighting chance against the multinational brands or, our industry's common enemy, the OTAs.

That said, the training and interfacing for any chatbot for conversational AI falls squarely on the hotel's marketing and IT teams to elevate it through testing and retesting to that 95% confidence interval wherein guests are always satisfied with the GenAI's answers and come to trust the hotel's machine for all requests. Oftentimes, once fully trained, the accuracy of the focused bot can be greater than almost all of the staff besides a handful of senior managers who have lived and breathed a hotel for years. In Crocombe's case, the system is split between general information and contractual information relating to a reservation or other exchange of monies, with the chatbot for general information and the structured booking engine for reservations.

While other related tactics to encourage direct bookings may include the strategic sequestration of inventory and information sent to the OTAs so that the richness of content is always greater on the hotel website, generally most customers will go wherever the experience is the most frictionless (speed of service) and the most personalized (quality of answers). Direct integrations into the restaurant or activity bookings are one such elaborate way to increase the level of convenience as is offering more loyalty perks or remembering details from past interactions with the website.

Still, getting an AI from the sandbox testing phase to the 80% confidence interval then to >95% calibration requires a lot of work by the entire team that cannot be understated. However, this can be achieved relatively quickly, as in weeks and months rather than years or decades, with focused testing prior to launch and in the early days of being online with real guests.

With the arms race already underway, Crocombe advised that, in the case of ChatGPT's applications, hoteliers need to 'move fast and break things' because getting to the 95% interval won't happen by itself, but it can be achieved relatively quickly.

These narrow AI use cases are called 'generative' because they take 'generations' to perfect; unlike humans where every generation is about 30 years, here each successive iteration can take days or even hours. Moreover, beyond competing against the OTAs, it's highly likely that one of your competitors is about to (or has already!) launch its own advanced chatbot, allowing it to jump to the top of the comp set over your own brand, particularly in converting lookers to bookers direct rather than through a third-party distributor.

Estimating the Impact on NOI

To demonstrate the longtail of what these Gen AI tools can do, let's consider a simple hypothetical situation for a leisure-dominant, independent resort with 200 keys, average yearly occupancy of 75%, ADR at $250, OTA commissions (including preferred and members additional commissions) at 28% and direct channel CAC at 2%.

Since reopening from the COVID, Crocombe has introduced a myriad of strategies and tactics such as website widgets promoting direct bookings, 24/7 live chat, room packages and new loyalty programs that have grown his direct business from 20% (pre-pandemic) to 45%. But he sees ChatGPT bots as offering the biggest potential to convert lookers to direct bookers, targeting 65% direct bookings with a full rollout of ChatGPT-enabled chatbots online. With these numbers, we can then look to see the overall size of the prize in terms of increasing direct bookings from 45% to 65% within a fiscal year.

Applying this 20% delta, we can deduce the net revenues increase as follows:
200 keys for 365 days/year at 75% occupancy = 54,750 room nights sold
55% (100% minus 45%) of 54,750 room nights at $250 ADR = $7,528,125 revenues at start
35% (100% minus 65%) of 54,750 room nights at $250 ADR = $4,790,625 revenues at end
OTA room bookings shifted to direct channel = $2,737,500 gross revenues
CAC difference (28% OTA commission minus 2% direct channel costs) = $711,750 savings

Yes, there are some assumptions baked in here, particularly as this supposes a one-to-one conversion of OTA to direct reservations with no attrition to total occupancy. Regardless, a half-million-plus boost to net revenues is something that should make any hotelier perk up. This is doubly true when you consider the unit economics of this channel shift where the vast majority of this savings in net revenues flows straight through to NOI.

Benefits Beyond Net Revenues

Using whatever market cap rate expansion or compression percentage you want, the long-term effect is safety for owners in terms of asset valuation growth. For the Cook Islands, the cap rate hovers around 10%, which means a multiple of 10 for this NOI flowthrough savings that can increase the value of the hotel by approximately $7 million.

Moreover, we must also consider TRevPAR growth, whereby it's reasonably assumed that the guests who book direct versus the OTAs will also have a greater ancillary spend per guest – particularly for resorts – and will be more likely to contribute to the brand via return visits to the same property or others in the portfolio. Less readily quantifiable, but still significant, benefits of encouraging this channel shift include better guest satisfaction that will translate into more word of mouth to help grow occupancies and fewer chargebacks for which evidence points to the majority of these emanating from third-party bookings.

To close, this gain to net revenues from the embrace of GenAI should by itself act as a mic drop for any hotelier looking to optimize NOI in a profound way over the next few business cycles. But as Crocombe bolded and underlined throughout our many conversations, this is only the start.

You can point to every single line item on a P&L or every single process within every department and there is undoubtedly a way that AI can deliver a quantifiable ROI for any hotel. It's just a matter of starting with one objective and seeing it through to completion then looking for the next application and the next until, before you know it, you have transformed the hotel into an AI-first self-learning and self-optimizing hotel.

Saving Labor with Conversational AI and a Mindset for Automation

Here's the hard truth: the labor shortages that hotels are confronting were not necessarily caused by the pandemic so much as accelerated, meaning the staffing problems for many properties are going to persist for many years to come. There are a lot of geopolitical and demographic forces supporting this thesis, but for hotels it translates into wages continuing to tick up, finding (and keeping!) good managers becoming increasingly hard, and automation becoming all the more mandatory in order to fulfill the service promise.

From the title, part of our job as strategic advisors is to not only help independent properties and small groups evaluate the new systems or platforms that best fit into their existing tech stacks in order to ramp up automation, but to think one level higher in terms of embedding an *automation mindset* into the culture at the managerial and executive levels.

Team Augmentation Through Automation

There is still a lot of stigma against the word 'automation' as hoteliers feel it means sacrificing service due to the removal of 'high touch' interactions between guest and staff. The opposite is in fact true; with further and further automation, hotels enable more of these high-touch encounters because their teams are liberated from the minutia of repetitive, interruptive tasks.

Nowhere demonstrates the need for a mindset shift better than the advent of 'Conversational Artificial Intelligence.' In a nutshell, this technology replaces the IVR (interactive voice recording) and supplements your reservation teams with a *near-perfect AI-driven voice* for guests to converse with.

It's important to note here, based on what was previously stated relates to having an automation mindset, the word 'supplement'. The conversational AI offloads the repetitive, basic guest inquiries like, "What time is the pool open?" so that the live agents deliver better quality service when they are patched through to the guests – shorter wait times and more time to develop rapport with the customer in order to increase call satisfaction or generate more revenue sold per call.

Solving for Call Abandonment

We saw this in action during our latest demo with John Smallwood, CEO of Travel Outlook, which has just debuted Annette™, a virtual assistant harnessing the power of conversational AI. Besides what this tech can do for labor savings and building revenues, what Smallwood also emphasized is the voice bot's ability to *protect brands against call abandonment* while always providing information to guests that is precise and 100% correct.

The reason call abandonment is such a critical issue right now is that we now live in an *increasingly attention-deprived world*. People have so many options vying for their eyes and ears that if you don't engage them right away they are gone. This pertains to the cacophony of travel search (shopper's paralysis) driving the resurgence of trusted travel advisors; it gives credence to the rise of chatbots; and for voice it means that guests have zero patience for holding on the line.

So, as guests are now exceedingly harried, from a service perspective, conversational AI solves this challenge on two fronts. First, prospective guests aren't hit by a convoluted IVR or kept waiting; they are immediately put through to an uncannily human-sounding voice that fully understands them. Second, for guests already in-house, voice bots can help facilitate any calls down to the front desk. Nowadays, it's all about *speed and simplification*, and that's what we saw in Annette and this principle should underline all other forms of automation that hotels pursue.

The Big Picture for the Voice Channel

The world has moved on to texting and everyone's on social media, so why does voice matter? Well, for one the baby boomer generation still prefers the voice channel when booking hotel rooms. And based on statistics from the United States, which shows that they control 50% of the nation's total wealth, it's a fair bet to assume that other advanced economies have similar behavioral patterns. Namely, the boomers prefer voice, so you have to *follow the money*. This for us makes any automation that can maintain service standards for this channel while solving the staffing problems a top priority.

The next thing of note from our demo with Annette was how it understood slang, colloquialisms, multiple dialogue threads, muffled voices, foreign languages and difficult-to-understand accents. All of this helps to make the call far more time-efficient with guests because the AI can understand them in cases when a live agent may ask the guest to repeat or clarify.

Working on the ground with hoteliers, one common objection we've often encountered when suggesting any form of outsourcing for the intake team or service call operations is that the external partner won't be able to answer the questions as well as the onsite agents. But put yourself in the guest's shoes; they value their own time above all else, so most times they don't care whether they are speaking to a real person or a virtual assistant so long as they get the information they need as quickly as possible.

In this sense, the big picture for voice bots harks back to the *centaur model* for AI-based workflows. Like the Greek mythological beast, the horse body (conversational AI) does all the grunt duties, freeing up the human head (live agents) to focus on meaningful work.

Embracing an automation mindset and having a vision of achieving a centaur model in the workplace is thus also one of staff retention. Teams can be easily demotivated by the repetitive, interruptive busywork that AI and robotic process automation (RPA) can now do. That's not why they decided to become hoteliers; they want to be front and center with guests, and they want to engage in challenging, creative work.

We hope that you can see from this example why the abovementioned objections towards further automation no longer apply. On the customer side, hospitality needs a myriad of automation tools in order to enable its teams to have high-touch encounters with guests and develop real relationships with them. Then on the internal customer side – that is, your staff as well as your managers – Smallwood concluded our discussion by noting, "Part of the rationale behind the Great Resignation movement has been a disengagement from the work due to the monotony of it. Our conversational AI tools are but one critical piece in the pie to help make employees more productive with their time and more connected to their roles so that ultimately they want to stay with the hotel."

Machine Learning from PMS Data Extraction Enables Personalization and Segmentation

We posed the question of how primary data extractions from the property management system (PMS) can be used for machine learning (ML) to the grow a hotel or heighten productivity. With a range of astute viewpoints from respondents, there are two main themes that the answers revealed.

The first major use case is personalization. This may seem obvious as it's been at the core of all AI thought leadership and company AI explorations for quite some time, but it nevertheless deserves some unpacking. What AI enables is the democratization of guest personalization, whereby having a solid backbone of smart automation technologies can allow hotels to deliver towards a specific guest or specific guest context.

Here are some examples of where ML can be applied to PMS data when combined with guest data from other key sources like the CRM or POS:

- Analysis of a guest's booking history, billing details and preferences to predict service requirements or what will 'surprise and delight' during the next reservation with the brand, in addition to helping with error recovery situations or with any service that would be aided by being able to respond in real time
- Beyond algorithmic rate optimization recommendations, which many RMS vendors already excel at, ML can help define upselling strategies and purchase propensity algorithms
- Bridging the gap between sentiment analysis and rate strategy to develop models for enhanced dynamic pricing and agile personalized marketing, by, for example, rapidly identifying high-value customers and using one-to-one offers to entice trial, knowing that the lifetime value of said customers will far outweigh any loss leader incentives
- Similar to customized marketing, with the right models loyalty programs can be specialized to offer more attractive and individualized perks, rather than adhering to the classic model of tiered loyalty member classifications

Related to all guest personalization applications, the next evolution of this is the development of enhanced or AI-guided segmentation and micro-segmentation. This isn't to say that the traditional mainstays of leisure, corporate and group no longer apply, but they are too broad to work as optimally as possible in today's hyper-fast, neuromarketing-driven world. Data connections and structuring allows ML to test assumptions and make recommendations about what actually motivates various guests to buy or spend on ancillaries.

Here are some ways that ML can help with customer segmentation:

- Create audiences or microsegments to verify or modify human biases about a hotel's ideal customers so that companies can more effectively find high-value guests or develop more productive marketing offers
- Comp set benchmarking to reveal which properties are direct competitors for each given segment as well as highlight areas for improvement
- Using topic or sentiment analysis, as derived from sources like social media listening tools or the CRM, to find relationships with PMS data in order to guide rates, packages and marketing

As you can see from just these three, AI-enhanced segmentation has many similarities to what can be done on the personalization front. No doubt there are plenty more use cases that will be made apparent as hotels deepen their exposure to ML, GenAI and other tools. Common throughout, and especially for PMS data extraction, is having strong integrations or interfaces, or using a customer data platform (CDP) or robotic processing automation (RPA) to connect all the siloed databases together.

To close, if there was a third area to touch upon for where primary data stores like the PMS can have applications for hotels in the present day, this would be team efficiencies. For instance, in accounting, AI can now help with error detection in financial audits or invoice processing. For housekeeping, predictive room status changes and more accurate occupancy expectations can help to define the cleaning priority list or more flexible start times, while merging data from major citywide events can help with long-term staff scheduling. Thirdly, a large language model (LLM) may soon be used to interpret SOP manuals or operations guides in order to facilitate faster customer support, micro training and the ability for team members to ask questions when focused on a specific task. Lots of applications, so best reach out to your tech vendors to learn more!

Segmentation Recommendation Engines as the Next Big AI Tool for Hotels

Customer segmentation has been critical from day one for the modern hotel industry. More recently, with numerous data sets being merged due to technological advances, brands are starting to get quite granular with their KYC (know your customer) in terms of understanding where guests are coming from (channels and geography), why they are selecting your property (leisure, corporate, conference and so on) and what their buying (packages, upselling offers, onsite ancillary spend or others).

Layering on artificial intelligence tools on top of all this data can now allow hotels to do far more than even five years ago within this burgeoning field of micro-segmentation, but this requires some understanding of how AI works (as well as a lot of techie acronyms).

To start, we must grasp how all this data is coming together. In contrast, with the dawn of application programming interfaces (APIs), disparate systems used by different operations could be strung together by structuring data field imports into a centralized storehouse. The PMS has always been a likely candidate for this nexus.

Still, increasingly it's the customer relationship management (CRM) because of this system's propensity to position all data around unified guest profiles and to incorporate above-property inputs.

Common friction points for working with APIs has been that an IT professional needs the spare time to set up each interface, and then maintain all those established connections with each subsequent software update. With each new system added to the tech stack, this quickly becomes resource-intensive. Here, a specific type of AI called robotic processing automation (RPA) has already proven itself by acting as a robot that can directly replace double entry work that has to be done manually because two systems haven't been integrated to talk directly to each other.

And it gets far better. Once you have all this data imported, cleaned (to remove duplicates) and structured into proper data fields, you now have an enormous treasure trove of numbers. While this database is far too vast for a pair of hotelier eyes to pick out patterns, the AI specialty of machine learning (ML) is designed precisely for that task. You give it the data; it finds the patterns, however, hidden they may be to the human overseer. The more data you give it, the more patterns it can potentially find and the more accurate its predictions will be.

Besides looking at vast amounts of data and then giving insights into that data, the key to ML is that it can produce a predictive model to optimize for desired future outcomes. Then, once that model is tested out in the field, the best AIs can then use the new data as feedback to improve their own modeling algorithm, further enhancing their predictive power to better optimize for a stated objective.

Where hotels have already seen the most lucrative applications for ML is in the revenue management system (RMS), with massive data sets comprising external and internal inputs are computed into an algorithm that can then recommend to the revenue director what pricing will optimize for rooms revenue, occupancy or now total revenue per guest stay.

It's this whole notion of recommendations that brings us to the concept of having ML interpret not only how to adjust nightly rates or what response to provide for a website chatbot, but also to look at the multitude of guest profile data and then come back with its own set of microsegments for your revenue, sales and marketing teams to interpret and pivot their planning accordingly.

As of now, all of us are operating under a given set of established business assumptions based on how we were trained and our experience working in hotels. We see the world in terms of leisure, corporate and groups, and many of us have become locked into these guest segments. Recommendation engines based on ML don't have those same limitations and thus can provide a fresh set of eyes on what your real segments are.

Perhaps this latest technology will help your hotel find an edge over the competition or allow you to deploy the advertising budget more effectively. Maybe it will give you suggestions on what packages will work better for attracting leisure guests or what types of groups are most winnable for your meetings and events business. Just as AI helps us to rethink business assumptions, neither of us would dare assume to know what such a tool would find buried within your hotel's data.

Our advice is to first chart a path for connecting all your systems, and only then investigate these more advanced ML tools. At the same time, you will also have to confront the cultural, more existential scenario of what happens when the AI finds microsegments that contradict those that your teams are working off. We live in exciting times!

Turning Up the Dial Knob on Hotel AI

With the dawn of ChatGPT and others of its ilk, the two of us have remarked upon how this chic AI's acronym (Generative Pre-trained Transformer) shares its letters with another more-seasoned GPT term – General Purpose Technology. Almost serendipitously, both inscribe applications across a variety of industries, jobs and tasks with creative destruction at every turn going back farther than electricity's conquest over steam power.

ChatGPT is but one of many new platforms currently available with this 'general purpose' – tools that can help hotels in numerous ways and across different departments. Hoteliers at all levels should be worried about this creative destruction, but not for the reason you think.

Natural, Inevitable Automation

Let's start by drilling into some specific roles, revealing where this fear may come from. Importantly, getting in the heads of individual actors and their incentives will help to reveal an organization's internal politics and its resistance to the changes that will ultimately prove to be beneficial in the long run.

Senior managers working behind the scenes may worry that their spreadsheet-analyzing, meeting-attending and email-answering days are numbered as system integrations become increasingly sophisticated and RPA (robotic process automation) takes hold. The reservations and front desk departments may fear both chatbots replacing their guest messaging duties and conversational AI supplanting the in-house call center. Next, revenue management AI analytics continues to gain both intelligent recommendations and judgment capabilities.

As for physical machines, the two of us foresee a day when runners and housemen are substituted by delivery bots while line cooks at fast-casual restaurants may soon be endangered by ceiling-mounted robotic arms. Yes, there was also an aborted, near-past attempt to automate laundry's clothing-folding task, but we chalk that up to 'too soon'. Think robot maintenance workers like they already have in Japan. You may even have programmatic, on-demand guestroom fitness based off the plethora of AI-driven wellness products hitting the market.

Look back in time, though, and you'll see that this has been the pattern for a long, long time. Automation to therein derive heightened per-employee output is, after all, at the pinnacle of business goals. And for this reason alone the future of hotels is wholly intertwined with technology. Hotels don't employ elevator operators anywhere, do they? What about switchboard operators? Capitalism being what it is, innovation is perpetually at your doorstep, and it favors the fast movers.

Knob Not Switch

Speaking of switchboards, implementing a new automation tool in a moment-by-moment recollection of events never looks like a light bulb going on and off at the flick of a finger. It only appears this way in hindsight long after the events have transpired. That is, we are never instantaneously 'turning off' jobs as an implemented technology replaces key tasks previously executed by humans. It's more like a volume knob on an amplifier turned slowly, but inevitably, to 11.

We'd like to claim this music analogy as our own, but credit where credit's due we gleaned it from our work with audiophile and CEO of Travel Outlook, John Smallwood, when helping implement the company's new conservational AI voice bot, Annette™, at a full-service resort on the East Coast.

Leveraging the latest in natural language processing, this is an AI that can understand human speech, multi-pronged questions and hard accents, and then respond accurately, eliminating the need for an IVR (interactive voice recording) and hours of live agent time devoted to answering basic guest inquiries.

But before any of that could happen, a key financial objection ruled the day: the live agents could already answer every question quite adeptly and upsell effectively, rendering said automation as a major risk to gross revenue performance. Looking at the numbers, it was prudent to stay risk-averse as a potential for high six-figure cost savings via automation could nevertheless compromise more than seven figures worth of revenue. If it ain't broke, as they say.

Enter the dial knob as an assurance of task replacement, not job replacement. In the case of Annette, we planned to automate only the vanguard of the guest interaction, getting executive team buy-in by reframing the discussion in terms of the voice channel customer experience. Replacing the IVR was an easy sell as most guests are mildly to strongly annoyed by these. More substantially, the lack of button pushing, being kept on hold or having to wait for a live agent to type information into a system is a real timesaver for guests. The conversation AI was thus trained to handle the top-of-the-top funnel – those initial, repetitive inquiries like "When is your restaurant open?" before passing calls over to the reservations team when warranted.

Besides winning on the call satisfaction side, intake teams were then freed from the monotony of answering these repetitive questions over and over again, which worked to boost morale and give them more time to patiently sell the product and drive TRevPAR via the cross-selling of other non-room amenities. No job was removed, only tasks that no employee really ever wanted to do in the first place.

Concurrently, we developed a roadmap to crank up the volume on Annette and give this bot more general purpose as the executive team became more comfortable, starting with in-house guest calls then deeper support for restaurant, spa and golf bookings along with helping on the hotel bookings side. Maybe group sales support one day, who knows!

Digital Centaurship

Several futurists have famously quipped, "Productivity is for robots." Unpacking this, we can see that we are on the verge of becoming something akin to centaurs, with the rote tasks at a hotel far better performed by workhorse-like automation tools (the horse torso) and liberating the hotel manager for creative thinking or being more face-to-face with guests (the human head).

Even today, general-purpose technologies like Annette and ChatGPT are only limited by the imagination and willingness of the humans behind them. That said, the risk with all this talk of mythical beasts and creative destruction is that hotels cannot simply automate for automation's sake. This will inevitably result in an average product that has no allure to guests and is simply a commoditized product at the mercy of market forces. The best hotels maintain their edge by being edgy, and this 'branding' starts and stops with your teams.

The purpose of technology must first and always be shrewdly focused on improving customer success. That much is obvious, but less so is that as we shift the relative returns of hotelier skillsets towards technology, we risk alienating the people who are drawn to hospitality over other industries.

Speaking from experience, we've seen associates and frontline teams become demoralized by all the tech rollouts that aren't accompanied by continuing professional development (CPD) programs that both explain the why behind the tech and make the job more dynamic.

For instance, with the dawn of kiosks and tablet-based check-ins, front desk agents can be retrained as 'guest success agents' or simply 'hosts'. Much like how the introduction of ATMs allowed bank tellers to focus more on personal customer support and the marketing of other bank services, by removing a lot of the 'transactional tasks' that front desk clerks must do, you now have a roving lobby team ready and willing to chat with guests and upsell them on ancillary amenities like your latest chef creations in the restaurant or a new spa package.

But this ability to upsell presupposes that you are educating your own teams on what else is happening around the property and that you are motivating them to care. Thus, AI-based automation also implies a rethink of your CPD, succession planning and employee wellness policies as well as the consolidation of data around a single source of truth and core platforms for easy interpretation and frictionless selling. Unless you do that, as the title implies, guests will gravitate towards those properties that have it all figured out, regardless of the chic AI toolkit you have deployed.

Ultimately, hotels will forever be people-oriented businesses because customers want to emotionally connect with other humans. That's where we need to go, and technology will only help us on the journey. You should only really be worried if your organization is complacent to act in this grand shift because when things shake out in five to ten years' time there will be winners and a lot of losers.

The Paradigm Shift in New Economic Value from AI-Powered Hotel Websites

Throughout the history of technology adoption, a new invention doesn't necessarily take off because of direct, apples-to-apples savings versus the old guard, but rather because of the new value that this innovation unlocks, at first on an incremental then later on an exponential basis.

The most studied example of this was the advent of electricity brushing up against the entrenched steam power-oriented factories during the turn of the 20th century. In pitching their wears to factory owners, electric motor companies saw little success by citing the one-to-one cost savings from shifting away from coal, wood and other means of localized steam generation. The nuisance of exchanging machinery was simply too great – both financially and emotionally – for the factory owners.

Instead, the electric motor salespeople realized success when they emphasized how electricity enabled a groundbreaking reconfiguration of manufacturing processes within the factory floor, moving away from cramped, multistory buildings in the heart of the city and into flexible, single-floor arrangements that could be cheaply built in the suburbs. One early adopter who saw the potential for this new design paradigm was Henry Ford with his electric-powered assembly line, and the rest is, well, history.

This same narrative played out during the late aughts with the battle of Blackberry's email-specific mobile phone versus the newer app-driven iPhone, or with the dawn of Netflix's streaming service that usurped Blockbuster's video rental stores. This value-driven innovation principle is relevant today as we transition from a static internet of one-size-fits-all websites into ones that use artificial intelligence (AI) to match the website content to each guest's needs as this guest moves through the customer journey.

To showcase how AI-enabled websites and integrated booking engines (IBEs) can unlock substantial new economic value for hotel properties, we sat down with Frank Reeves, Chief Evangelist at SHR Group, to discuss the company's next-generation website and IBE platform called allora.ai. Reeves is also the co-founder and CEO of Avvio (the developer of allora.ai) which was acquired by SHR.

Static Versus Contextual Websites

While framing the advent of next-gen hotel websites within the context of steam giving way to electric power may seem a bit grandiose on the surface, this comparison of historical events to inform predictions about present-day outcomes for hotel tech trends is in fact similar to what the machine learning (ML) propelling allora.ai have been doing for quite some time now.

The more contextual data and interactive feedback the system has – as derived from the entirety of guests accessing websites or going through a hotel's IBE built by allora.ai – the more the platform learns what a guest might want. The outcome here is that the ML can better predict the optimized orientation of a website's content in order to achieve a specific goal, such as boosting reservation conversion rate.

As Reeves puts it, our current websites are 'static digital brochures'. A customer enters, and while tracking mechanism like pixels may tell the analytics platform where this user came from (IP address, mobile versus desktop, organic versus paid ad and so on), the website doesn't react or A/B test how the information is presented in order to better fit the context of the customer.

Now, however, with an AI engine powering a website, a hotel can present information that's fully personalized to each guest, no matter which stage of the customer journey they are presently on.

Consider the following diagram of the customer journey:

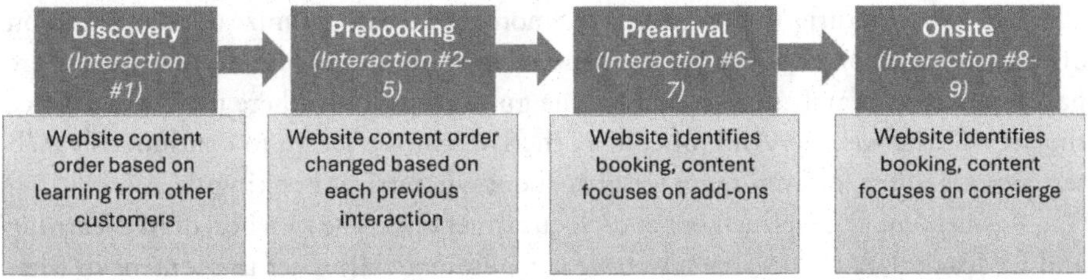

How might this look like in practice within only those initial stages of interaction for now?

- *Interaction #1 (discovery).* The AI can recognize the country where a customer is searching from and, if it's overseas, rewrite the content to state, "Enjoy our spa after a long-haul flight."
- *Interaction #2 (early prebooking.* With the initial clicks acting as a profiling baseline of interests, the AI can showcase a review of the hotel's dining outlet from someone in the user's country
- *Interaction #3 (early prebooking).* Now with an expression of intent around dining and spa based on user clicks and country of origin, the AI can bring to the top the "Food and Spa LOS" package
- *Interaction #4 (late prebooking).* Now with the intended travel dates plugged into the IBE, the AI can highlight guestroom and suite reviews from past guests in the user's source country
- *Interaction #5 (late prebooking).* Bringing together every interaction and learning about the prospect, the AI can reorient the rates and packages to create a hyper-personalized experience

When you consider the website up until the point at which a guest departs the hotel, a lot can happen that can influence hotel revenues. Importantly, it's the context of the guest that's changing. A person who lands on a website during the initial discovery or dream phase may not have the intent to book just yet; they are simply on a fact-finding mission. When they exit a static website after this first or second interaction, traditional metrics record this as a lost customer, even though this isn't necessarily true.

Suppose that during the first browse, this particular user seems especially interested in the spa as determined by what they click on and time spent on certain webpages. Armed with this information as well as previous learnings from past interactions with other similar customers, the allora.ai platform would then rearrange the website's information to better personalize it for what's deemed to be a spa seeker. For example, upon returning to the website, wellness-oriented imagery would be prioritized in the homepage slider, while rows of spa content would appear ahead of rows about, say, golf or F&B.

The Flywheel of Feedback Data

The more a user returns to the website, the more the AI can optimize the configuration of content based on how the prospect interacts. This also applies to the IBE, where past reservation searches are stored for the guest to pick up where they left off once they revisit the website. And, of course, the IBE can be set up to continuously A/B test various offers for even more insights about what drives bookings.

Refinement after refinement at each customer click, the flywheel of ML learning and feedback data means that a website can automatically cater the content to what each individual wants to help move them down the sales funnel and, ultimately, into a finished reservation. Managers can also set up rules to incentivize results, such as having the website display a direct booking discount or F&B credit when a user returns for, say, the fourth time onwards or after two weeks have passed since the first viewing.

Finally, it goes without saying that all these content optimizations help immensely with a channel shift away from the high-commission OTAs. No third party will ever be able to offer as personalized and as pleasurable a user experience, resulting in reduced costs per acquisition and greater net revenues.

As a digression here, it's important to consider why many customers prefer the OTAs in the first place. Yes, there's the convenience of aggregating all properties in a location, but it's also because of guest frustration with a brand.com. Website hyper-personalization via an AI backbone fixes this issue, really bringing the hotel's hospitality into the online realm.

Websites for Beyond the Sales Funnel

The value that AI-powered websites will add to the prebooking phase is by itself remarkable because of how it can help brands to micro-segment customers within the sales funnel, so much so that marketers can now accurately separate the upper funnel from the lower funnel or even the 'upper-upper funnel' with specific insights at each partial phase on what motivates guests to move in the right direction.

But, why stop at using websites solely to drive guestroom and package sales? What can an AI-powered website do to boost ancillary spend (TRevPAR) or keep the relationship going after departure?

"Take a London hotel that we work with, for example," commented Reeves. "We observed from both past guest behavior on this brand's website and from the totality of interactions across all hotels using the allora.ai platform that travelers who had already made a direct booking and who originated from the United States have vastly different needs leading up to arrival over those travelers coming in locally from within the United Kingdom. Monetarily speaking, past US travelers highly favored F&B content, so prioritizing the display of various dining options for incoming guests from the US resulted in more prearrival F&B revenue per guest and more on-premises utilization."

To expand on this example a bit further, the true power of ML comes not only from how past users interact with your own website, but also from how all users across all websites have behaved. It's this combination of macro (systemwide patterns) and micro (feedback on your own brand.com) that has allowed allora.ai to attain a minimum efficient scale for any new property to leverage past learnings.

Such a blend of macro and micro opens a wholly novel website functionality: reducing cancellations. Because the system knows who is more likely to cancel a reservation during the prearrival phase based on past cancellation data from all travelers at all properties on the platforms, managers can use this information to proactively send out cheerful reminders in the days leading up to arrival or even send out additional incentives to those 'risky' guests such as F&B vouchers.

Mapping Value for the Whole Guest Journey

The analog of a flywheel spinning across the entirety of the customer journey to unlock value at each stage really works here. Each website or booking engine interaction provides feedback to fuel improvements for future interactions.

This can be broken down as follows:

1. Discovery. Apply learnings from past website visitors and systemwide patterns to make a better first impression with a new user, encouraging them to revisit versus book through an OTA
2. Early Pre-booking. Rearranging content based on dream phase interaction and use ML to deduce what content best optimizes for continued engagement and conversions
3. Late Pre-booking. Further personalize the website and IBE content, possibly adding a booking incentive to further encourage direct sales versus one made through a third party
4. Early Pre-arrival. Optimize the display of add-ons based on what's known about a guest in order to maximize revenue on the books, which also helps with staff scheduling
5. Late Pre-arrival. Defend against possible cancellations through website personalization that accentuates how great the onsite experience will be combined with other one-to-one offers
6. Onsite. Act as a virtual concierge to relieve onsite teams by displaying the most relevant information as well as the most relevant add-ons to further amplify more property usage and TRevPAR

7. *Early Post-Departure.* Show a thank you note and other departure information to amplify how the onsite experience was perceived, meaning higher guest satisfaction and better reviews
8. *Extended Loyalty.* After some time has passed, entice return visits by highlighting what's new onsite in relation to the context of the guest's past stay

Optimization Increases Valuation

To close, consider how a hotel can get 'more juice from the squeeze' at each point in this chain by leveraging the latest in artificial intelligence and machine learning. Every optimization works to increase automation so that teams can be more productive per unit time while also providing those teams with more accurate insights to inform other operational improvements.

At discovery and prebooking, we're talking about increasing the conversion rate versus the competition and driving more traffic away from the OTAs, enhancing both gross revenues and net revenues that flow through to net operating income (NOI). At the prearrival stage, we're talking about TRevPAR and fewer cancellations, both of which also augment NOI. Then for onsite and beyond, we're talking about how the website can lead to better satisfaction scores which in turn enhance word of mouth and return visits to further lower future customer acquisition costs.

Taken together, all this acts to boost the overall economics of a property and its long-term asset valuation. If the static brochure websites of yesteryear are like steam power, then ML deployments truly are the electricity upgrade your hotel needs for the decade ahead.

Every Hotelier in Every Role Must Now Understand Technology

Traditionally, aspiring hoteliers enter the industry because they have a passion for service. And we have groomed them as such. But as the post-pandemic period has so resolutely proven, that time is resolutely over.

Gone are the days when a GM or rooms division manager could pawn tech problems or new integrations off to IT personnel. Yes, those technical wizards are still instrumental to the smooth functioning of all parts of the tech stack. Two areas where these managers will forever be vital are cybersecurity and building two-way software connections or using APIs to bring data from one system into a central hub.

Now, though, because our properties are exceedingly reliant on various software to optimize our operations, it behooves every hotelier in every department to not only understand the many intricacies of those platforms already deployed but also to investigate further technological upgrades so as to 'future proof' the hotel.

As has often been remarked about the pandemic, many of the resultant trends affecting hospitality are ones that would have transpired regardless, but that the evolution occurred over a matter of months and not years. Such trends as online training, mobile keys, contactless check-in and check-out, digital payments, guest messaging apps, online sentiment analysis, robust CRMs, smarter maintenance work order systems and housekeeping optimization software all existed prior to COVID, but there was no gun to our heads, so we didn't act.

The next decade for hotels and resorts will be defined by those organizations that are able to strip away the 20th century mentality of good service only being possible via high-touch interactivity with the guest. Many of the pandemic-born traveler behaviors are here to stay and customers will continue to prefer those properties that embrace the convenience (and safety) of no-touch service delivery.

While the pandemic is over and we think we can get back to business as usual, the sad truth is that there's no going back. Accepting this and embracing its implications necessitates a profound cultural shift within your organization so that you can continue to find technological solutions that will put your hotel(s) at the forefront year after year.

Here are some steps you can take to make that happen:

- At the most basic level, all managers should be invited to share their thoughts on any pain points they are experiencing so that tech solutions can be identified to solve those needs
- Embracing tech must start at the top for acceptance at the lower rungs to occur, and thus both owners and GMs should encourage new tech discussions within executive committee meetings
- Set up specific monthly or bimonthly meetings to review what can be done to enhance operations in every single department
- Share technology articles internally, either peer-to-peer via email or LinkedIn, or posted on the company bulletin
- Cross-departmental presentations that can be added into any town hall whereby one team members gives a quick overview of the tech they use and how it helps
- Siloed thinking must not only be discouraged but also reprimanded so that managers feel empowered to share what ideas they conjure up or what articles they read, all of which may benefit another department not specifically under their purview
- Going one step further, perhaps it should be a part of every hotelier's job description to read about the latest and greatest developments, either with a smaller time allotment set aside each week or something that is to be done outside of regular office hours
- Traditionally, only IT directors, GMs, asset managers and owners have had the privilege of attending tradeshows focusing on tech, but perhaps there's room here to motivate team members from other departments by letting them attend once in a while
- User conferences or virtual training seminars designed to widen the usage of the full feature set within a current platform should be heavily promoted

- While you likely have little power over what schools teach their students, all younger or new hires should be screened for their aptitude and attitude towards enterprise platforms
- Senior executives must know tech – no exceptions – with some form of testing, oral or written that assesses a broad understanding of core software and common physical devices, required prior to signing on any new director or team leader
- Climate change is not something hotels can ignore, with automation tools that affect numerous operations helping to curve energy usage and realize some cost savings in the process, and be conscious of this global movement must become a part of your culture in order to derive technological solutions that will help

Above all, what should be stressed is how technology can help reinforce the vision for the future of the organization and any properties owned or managed. Thinking ahead ten years, what does a popular urban hotel look like? What new amenities and features does it have that are only pipedreams today? How is technology incorporated into the guest experience in ways where it is presently lacking? And how would this be different for a resort?

This is not meant to be an ultimatum, but these are the questions you simply must ask in order to prime your hotel for the decade ahead – again, future proofing. It is as much a knowledge problem as it is a cultural one. Embrace tech on all levels because every department will ultimately benefit and because you never know where the next break though will come from.

NEXT-GENERATION TECHNOLOGY

As the flagship hotel for the Hudson Yards development, Equinox Hotel New York combines the best of this trendsetting fitness brand with its luxury and invisibly high-tech sleep chambers.

Tech Will Turn Limited-Service Hotels into Vending Machines

From humble beginnings in the early '60s, as of 2020s vending machines blossomed into a $35 billion industry for the United States alone. Pretty much anything that can fit into an automatic dispenser, and meets the branding criteria, is now sold that way.

Thinking about our current hospitality problems, vending machines are totally immune to labor market hiccups. One rep can service multiple units across a wide geography, while newer vending machines monitor utilization to thereby eliminate stockouts and further optimize labor. Importantly, once installed such automated machines enhance profit margins by reducing both fixed and variable costs. Can this mode be applied to limited- service properties to drive profitability? Let's investigate.

Learning from Vacation Rentals

Without drilling into any specific statistics, the broad trend from the past year shows that short-term rentals (Airbnb, Vrbo, Homestay, onefinestay, Sonder, Homes & Villas by Marriott and their ilk) grew in overall market share to comprise roughly a third of all stays for the United States. Key benefits include variety, flexible room configurations, and a direct appeal to the modern tempo of travel.

Variety is easy to understand; each room, apartment, villa, or rental house is typically distinct in some way, adding a new zest to the discovery phase as well as to the onsite experience (which also feeds into the flexibility value proposition). But what do we mean by 'modern tempo', especially in the face of how COVID has altered or catalyzed certain trends?

The modern tempo of travel is fast, automated, and frictionless (with in-person contact largely seen as a point of this friction), and this extends across all segments and star ratings. Guests will still enjoy meeting new people and chatting while abroad, but they no longer want to waste time on 'transactional' conversations. They don't want to line up at the front desk for check-in. They want to be able to reserve dining or spa appointments off a website or app without any human interactions. They want a frictionless journey so that their time is better allocated towards meaningful experiences.

Technology Can Moderate Prices

It's worthwhile at this point to digress a bit and look at the macroeconomic forces that support our thesis of how some hotels will inevitably come to resemble vending machines. We're all familiar with terms like 'disruption' and 'creative destruction', but another, more-foundational kindred spirit to ponder is straightforward 'deflation' – basically, when prices go down.

Essential for you to note, technology naturally works to deflate prices because of the new efficiencies that are derived from said innovation, namely increased labor productivity (automation that augments output per worker), improved supply chains (either through better methods of transportation or access to new markets) and faster information flows (to reduce price asymmetry).

Automation and cheaper supply costs mean that a hotel can reduce its overhead and charge less while maintaining its margins, thereby making it more competitive. And to the third reason, consider the price and guest sentiment transparencies brought about by the OTAs and review websites that have resulted in hotels no longer being able to get away with overcharging customers. Comparative information is now too widely available, meaning that a property's rates will gradually be forced down as members of the comp set continually undercut each other to gain market share.

Voluminous economics tomes have been written on this principle. In hospitality, to fight this race to the bottom, we brand, we rebrand, we advertise, we package, we renovate, we personalize, we unveil new amenities and so on. But for certain properties at the economy and midscale, commodification inevitably occurs, with the guest only looking for a bed in a quiet room where the lowest price is the law.

Eliminating Most Onsite Labor

In a deflationary world propelled forward by rapacious technology, the hotel with the fewest expenses wins because such businesses are able to charge less while sustaining profitability or, alternatively, only somewhat undersell the market while diverting lots of cash back into R&D and marketing. For this, the only way forward is replacing labor with cheaper SaaS costs.

For what can and should be done now, getting rid of transactional conversations means applying technologies to automate nearly everything, freeing up existing staff to perform other tasks (like having convivial chats with guests) or reducing their numbers wherever possible. Obviously, this applies more to the limited and select service side of things and not so much for upscale, resort, convention or luxury properties where 'high touch' service is a hallmark reinforcement of branding.

So, what happens when we try to turn a limited-service hotel into a vending machine? A tad extreme, but a time will come soon when properties can use technology to eliminate all onsite staff, save for security, maintenance and housekeeping (although the latter two can also be outsourced to on-demand services). Such a hotel would have an envious EBITDA!

Let's examine all the daisies in the tech chain that can make this happen, either today or very soon in the future.

- *Search.* Mapping platforms can now automatically update all OTA content while AI-driven revenue management products can analyze travel intent data in real-time then yield rooms up to the minute. With these tools in place, a revenue manager working at a corporate office can run more than a dozen hotels at once.
- *Reservations.* Besides using a seamless booking engine, intake can be fully outsourced to call centers or AI-based voice services along with integrated chatbots for SMS or social media. You won't need a reservations time save for a front office manager who can also work out of a regional office to handle complains or complex bookings for multiple properties.

- *Property management.* There's no need to host on-prem and devote IT resources to maintaining your own servers. Cloud-everything is the way forward, especially for your PMS for which there are a plethora of secure options already on the market.
- *Prearrival.* Advances in CRMs, CDPs and open APIs allow for rich data integrations so that hotels know their guests before they arrive and offer bespoke, one-to-one upsells, with all of it automated through a robust PMS or communications platform of choice.
- *Check-in and check-out.* This can be wholly contactless to eliminate the front desk. Mobile keys will reside in a digital wallet (accessible via a phone, smartwatch or smart ring) as prompted by a prearrival check-in portal. Or, in the rare case that a guest doesn't do this in advance, a kiosk will be available in the lobby.
- *In-Room.* AI-based voice command speakers can act to address guest questions instead of a live agent at the front desk or concierge. Everything in the room will be IoT-controlled while casting to the TV to access a guest's preferred streaming service will be made increasingly frictionless.
- *Food & Beverage.* While onsite restaurants are critical for four stars and above, for midscale and economy hotels, online food ordering like Uber Eats, Grubhub, and Doordash will suffice. Once you set up the drop-off rules for security, you can eliminate this entire department.
- *Parking.* It will all be self-park with automated ticketing and monitoring. Realistically, though, most guests will be using Uber or Lyft to get around.
- *Housekeeping.* This can be only upon guest departure for short stays. Or, via integrations to the PMS, you can let the guest choose between no stayover cleans and leaving fresh towels at the door or daily cleaning for an extra charge. Using existing systems, room attendant routing can be optimized with cleaning schedules updated in real-time and pushed to a staffer's phone.
- *Accounting.* No cash transactions will be allowed on site, and mobile payments will become the norm. Moreover, new centralized payment operations platforms are emerging to expedite audits, workflows, reporting, clearing and reconciliation so that, much like other departments, accounting can be moved to a regional office with one controller for multiple properties.
- *Recruitment.* Networked on-demand labor platforms are emerging that verify and onboard staff members, giving HR quick access to a large pool of potential hires with little extra work.

The End of Onsite Administration

What's fascinating here is that, in a vending machine model, there's no need for a front desk manager, rooms division manager, executive housekeeper, or even a general manager. Let that sink in. Hotels at the low end of the spectrum will only need a regional manager who oversees the guest value chain and runs the IT team that safeguards all the connections that make this end-to-end automation a reality.

This may seem revolutionary, but it's a matter of survival in the face of heightened competition from new brands, the rise of home-sharing, and impending commodification. Instead of reacting day by day, think of our current staffing shortage as a wake-up call to truly rethink your operations and drive the bottom line. Technology is the salvation for owners, and with the expectation of a modern tempo your guests will thank you for it or not even notice.

Planck's Principle and Hotelier Skepticism for Blockchain

We've already seen many of the various cryptocurrencies grace the front page of major news outlets. This trend will continue into the future and, by our predictions, for the rest of everyone's natural lifespans who happen to be reading this article. Pure hype or not, the technologies underpinning these altcoins are going to keep expanding and maturing as the applications for blockchains are too great to ignore.

Prior to any college-level lessons about the exact inner workings of blockchains, decentralized hyperledgers, algorithmic hashing, non-fungible tokens (NFT) and mining incentivization via proof of work, there's an even more basic mental step that must first take place. Ruminating on a very broad level about any trepidations within companies or resistance to investigating how best to deploy blockchain technologies (beyond viewing bitcoin as a diversified portfolio hedge against fiat currency's current hyperinflation trajectory), it's critical to recall a famous quote by the physicist Max Planck who discovered quantum electron valences and inspired Einstein.

The short paraphrasing of this quote is, "Science advances one funeral at a time." Now known as Planck's Principle, the argument is that new advancements in humanity's collective knowledge don't occur by winning over the opposition to any singular concept, but by letting the opposition die out in order to allow for younger, more receptive minds to flourish and build upon the new discovery. Just think about all the initial (and perhaps ongoing) cynicism to such concepts as Darwinian evolution, the heliocentric solar model, vaccines, the Internet, cell phones, plant-based diets or even the seatbelt; blockchain and cryptocurrencies are following a similar path.

If you are skeptical about bitcoin, ethereum, dogecoin, decentralized finance (DeFi) and the power of blockchains in general, ask yourself, with Planck's Principle in mind, whether your apprehensiveness is born out of an intrinsic rigidity to new processes or a bona fide rational argument for why this new technology is total bunkum. It takes a lot of introspection, and frankly courage, to confront the former of these two dispositions in order to then accept where the future is actually headed.

As most of us were raised and trained on the idea of centralized finance and placing our trust in fiat currencies as backed by the economic power of sovereign nations, it makes sense that a quantum mental leap is necessary in order to grasp the true potential for blockchain. With this in mind, though, if you are open right now to investigating what blockchain can do for your organization, then that already puts you ahead of many of your competitors who are stuck in Planck's opposition.

Think of the applications. Would DeFi help to reduce accounting costs, minimize chargebacks and eliminate the need for a PMS hosted onsite? How might a hotel's own brand-coin help increase loyalty? How about revamping the gift shop so that all inventory was ethically sourced and in small batches as verified by a blockchain? What if you set out to create an 'NFT hotel' (after the current NFT bubble has burst) whereby all the artwork in every space is unique while also growing a secondary asset class that might also appreciate alongside the physical property itself?

These are but a few examples. By pondering how blockchain will help streamline operations and grow revenues today, you are already positioning your brand to have a first mover advantage tomorrow.

Notice that we haven't even explained what a blockchain is? We're not suggesting that you absolutely need to start implementing blockchain right away – especially if you can't already picture how it works. Rather, take the time to learn about how it works (independently from this article) so that you will be ready once the technology has gained more maturity. An internet article here and there, or perhaps even a book on that subject, may suffice – slow and steady learning while keeping a curious mind.

The bottom line is, regarding your feelings about it, our hope is you will accept that blockchain technologies are here to stay. Deal with it. And if you deal with it fast enough, you may gain a solid edge for your competitors who happen to stay in the opposing camp according to Planck's Principle.

How ChatGPT Can Evolve Hotel Search

A shocker that's still making waves to this day was the unveiling of ChatGPT, a groundbreaking artificial intelligence chatbot that is the most adept to date at intimating human conversational versatility when delivering answers to any number of questions or creative requests. Compounding this is the news that Microsoft – an investor in OpenAI, the company behind ChatGPT – may be looking to incorporate this chatbot into its search engine, Bing, as a means of gaining market share versus the Google juggernaut.

Whether it is specifically ChatGPT or another service, it's inevitable that advanced AI will soon be deployed into customer-facing entities like travel and hotel search. Hence, what should your hotel brand be aware of, and how can you prepare?

To see how a chatbot like this can evolve hospitality web searches, you first have to know a bit – and only just a bit – about how the underlying software works. While admittedly, we are not experts in the field of AI research, we emphasize to hoteliers that knowing how to use a piece of technology is far more important for our purposes than specializing in how it works.

For example, the majority of us know how to drive a car, and yet how many of us can fix one? That's the mechanic's job. It's our job to source the mechanic we trust the most and pay them for their services. Apply this relationship to each hotel company and its respective vendors, tech or otherwise.

Nevertheless, there are some AI fundamentals that everyone should know. In this case, the acronym GPT stands for 'Generative Pre-trained Transformer' which means that the chatbot (in this case, GPT-3 or the third iteration) comes already trained using the full breadth of language-associated data on the internet as put through the cogs of 175 billion parameters in order to generate text-based information for its users.

The results are answers that are both highly realistic in terms of how an actual human would respond and highly accurate in terms of addressing what the user initially wanted. This GPT function is also reinforced with additional learning processes so that it gets more realistic and more accurate the more times it is used.

The Leisure Guest Right Now

To understand how this can specifically increase the utility and customer convenience of travel searches, let's first examine the current behavior for how customers find then select a given hotel.

Currently, the holy grail of any brand is to be so top of mind that a guest directly accesses your website (or another owned channel) to complete a booking – no commissions and only first-party data. Think room blocks for a big event, corporate subscriptions, prearranged tours or browsing properties within a brand's portfolio. However, this is often not the case when it comes to FITs.

Picture the average leisure guest looking for their next vacation. They spend time deciding their dates; they spend time in the 'dream phase' of choosing their destination; they spend time lining up flights or other means of travel that meet their needs. Frequently, they go back and forth on these values in order to optimize costs and any other form of agony. Hotel selections are probably downwind of all this, resulting in a host of customers who are relatively brand-agnostic yet have specific criteria already in mind – availability, location, budget, exclusive offers, room features, onsite amenities, and so on.

The cross-comparisons herein to find the best fit can lead to dozens of browser tabs open at once, featuring a milieu of Google search, Google Maps, OTAs, Airbnb, TripAdvisor, brand.com, travel blogs, and other resources. While this 'sense of discovery' is part of the fun, it can also induce 'shopper's paralysis' – too much choice that sharply stresses the brain. If only there was a better way...

The Leisure Travel Opportunity

Given how versatile ChatGPT is as well as its capacity for further learning and refinement, such a vacationer can replace much of this helter-skelter travel search behavior with a simple chatbot conversation, akin to how numerous people today might call up their trusted travel advisor to outsource this decision-making mental fatigue.

You type in your search specifications and give some guidelines as to how deal-breaking each criterion is; then the AI returns with a narrow scope of recommended properties for you to further prod at with additional questions. (As a caveat, ChatGPT is still in beta but based on its preliminary outputs in the domain of creative writing, it isn't a stretch to suppose that, in time, it will get good that interpreting your travel needs to deliver quite personalized hotel suggestions.)

Now let's add some layers. Mix ChatGPT with 'conversational AI' language recognition and you have a very convenient and wholly automated form of voice-first hotel search – that is, no typing required. Next, throw in a virtual reality (VR) or mixed reality (MR) headset and you have a fantastic way to use emerging metaverse platforms to sift through immersive 3D representations of hotels or travel destinations, as guided by your voice-primary interactions with the chatbot software.

Content as Always King

Whether it's Google, Microsoft, OpenAI or another leading tech company, most of this development is beyond any of our control. The best we can do is stay abreast with the latest news, comprehend the overall direction and then prepare accordingly.

In this case, the best way forward is to know that what's always in your direct control is the 'content' about your brand that you then upload to allow these algorithms to crawl. We put the word content in parentheses for a reason here; particularly with the dawn of the metaverse, content itself is evolving.

For the past two decades, the meaning of web content has come to involve text descriptions, images, metadata, search engine optimization, paid search, user generated content, third-party reviews (and your responses to those reviews!), rate mapping to affiliates, social media, blogs, videos and so on.

Now, we all have to consider how our written words or imagery will be interpreted by AI – whether a text bot or a voice bot – so that our hotels are favorably presented, both in accordance with customers' expectations about our properties as well as in adherence to given brand directives.

Lastly, hotels have to start thinking in 3D – recruiting vendors who can translate the physical site or individual objects into 'digital twins' so that these assets are ready to be deployed into a virtual world once the metaverse has (sooner than you think!) achieved a critical mass of consumers using their VR headsets to secure their next hotel reservation. The future is happening fast, so start planning now.

Generative AI Will Reorient Guest Behavior Around Chatbots

There's a sea change for the travel world happening on the heels of the AI craze, but like previous innovations, we may be overestimating its impact in the short term and underestimating its impact in the long term. To see just how much generative AI will change how travelers find their accommodations and the level of service that guests will come to expect, we must first look back to inventions in the near past to build a trendline for what's coming.

First, if you're old enough, think about how you discovered your chosen hotel before and after OTAs like Booking, Expedia, Priceline and Agoda became household names with extensive, worldwide distribution. Travel guides, travel magazines and travel agents likely all had a much stronger influence on where you decided to go to back in the day. As the OTAs gained network effects, brands with a smaller footprint suddenly gained a new channel through this to frictionlessly sell inventory, while travelers benefited from a portal through which to conveniently discover new products in new destinations.

If you think of the OTAs as a simple line market, by bringing buyers and sellers closer together, they worked to expand the total volume of hotel inventory sales. Concurrently, TripAdvisor and other review websites came to provide a baseline of trust for consumers in a positive feedback loop – that is, more reviews have meant more trust in the platform and more trust in hotels with lots of good reviews, thereby incentivizing more travel to new hotels and more reviews on the platform.

Next, consider the sharing economy. Airbnb and its ilk have further propelled global travel numbers to astonishing new heights starting in the 2010s by incentivizing growth within the vacation rental market. The response from traditional hotels has largely been more hotel brands to serve different customer niches, more technology deployment, better amenities and a shrewder focus on quality service. Similarly, one could point to the growth of social media travel influencers and the opening up of previously unknown destinations as well as a new channel through which to reach lifestyle consumers.

The point throughout is that technological innovations that attain global scale inevitably reorient consumer behavior, with a few common threads from all development to keep in mind:

1. More hotel product diversification and segmentation
2. More destination access, distribution and travel volume
3. More expectations for enhanced service and flexibility

Further Democratizing Travel Products

With these broad strokes as a framework, it's far easier to predict how the hospitality-specific chatbots and robotic process automation (RPA) tools that are leveraging machine learning and generative AI will change the ways that travelers discover new destinations and book their accommodations as well as how hotel guests will want to purchase additional experiences from their host hotels.

Newer hotel systems developed within the past decade have been able to use advances in cloud-hosting services and APIs to outcompete legacy software by offering nimbler platforms at drastically cheaper prices. We often label this progression as 'democratization' because the lower costs enable ever-smaller businesses to reap the benefits from using the technology.

To start, ChatGPT-esque clones will become synonymous with other elements of a hotel website like the top navigation and booking engine, so much so that such a feature will move from value-add to customer expectation, where eventually more bookings may come through the chat thread than through a search initiated through the classical booking engine. Just as user-friendly website development tools like WordPress and Squarespace democratize website creation, these chatbots will only further enable small hotels or other tourism operators to maintain a great digital storefront without the high costs of human-based customer service.

From there, it isn't hard to imagine a curated AI built with OpenAI's GPT being used, not just for basic guest inquiries and facilitating bookings via interfaces but to natively power direct reservations and back-of-house workflows for properties of under, say, 10 rooms, supplanting the need for a PMS, booking engine and ops platform. You may be skeptical that such a leap will take place sooner rather than later, and yet a recent example of this is Jurny's announcement of an AI-enhanced PMS powered by GPT-4.

Further, diminishing tech costs without any major sacrifices to service, such systems might empower more small hotels and vacation rentals in little-known destinations where the economics currently don't work. Moreover, the tech cost savings might be redeployed to finance other more capital-intensive operations, enabling additional product nichification to serve emerging segments like digital nomad, glamping-adjacent or wellness-primary travelers.

Over-Tourism Breeds Travel Redistribution

With an increasingly vast network of travel products and various incentives for people to go abroad, we now have enough macroeconomic data on this self-perpetuating cycle to see how technology has accelerated the modern problem of over-tourism, with knock-on effects being unaffordable real estate, disruptions to local culture and contributions to global warming.

Despite the damage that has been brought by over-tourism, under-tourism is a far worse problem because of how it can impair a destination's economy, diminish trade, and increase crime. By democratizing access to technology for SMB operators in second-tier cities, rural areas, and developing countries, AI can enable tourism redistribution and thus act as a solution to this challenge.

These sorts of changes may seem to occur at a glacial pace and not necessarily affect your hotel. And yet, they still do. The easier it is for someone to shift a house into a viable vacation rental business, the more likely it is to happen. And while the growth of travel over the past two decades as supported by technology implies an ever-expanding total addressable market for worldwide travel, this says nothing about the products that get left behind because they didn't adapt fast enough and got caught in a death spiral of flatline revenues and no capital leftover for a brand refresh.

Amongst financial circles, we often say and have heard is, "The hotel industry isn't overbuilt; it's under-demolished."

To close, here's a broad, sequential list of what to investigate with regards to AI so that you don't end up on the latter end of this adage:

1. Start with a chatbot or enhanced AI assistant to facilitate basic inquiries on the website
2. Expand this chatbot to handle on-prem guest requests via SMS or within the branded app
3. Deploy a conversational AI to do the same for the voice channel and replace the IVR

4. Investigate how RPA can further reduce manual work to free up the team's time for other tasks
5. Recruit a semantic analysis engine to guide operations from prearrival and post-stay remarks
6. Connect the chatbot and conversational AI so that they can handle reservations on the website
7. Connect both so they can handle ancillary bookings for restaurants, spas and activities
8. Use an AI tool for dynamic pricing, channel management, upselling and attribute-based sales
9. Roll out an AI-powered platform for loyalty and one-to-one return stay offers
10. Look out for new systems that are using AI to do all this under a single, unified interface

Generative AI Agents Promise to be a Boon for Hotel Operations

As of now, the common sentiment around Generative AI (GenAI) and the use of large language models (LLMs) or generative pre-trained transformers (GPTs) for hospitality is centered around chatbots and their ability to answer guest inquiries and, in some cases, complete standard room reservations. While we all inherently grasp that there are applications far more advanced than these already-advanced functionalities, standing above the rest are the AI agents that can be trained to perform specific and rather complex tasks.

You might ponder why we don't already have these available to us, but as Oracle highlighted in a recent article on the subject, it is best to proceed cautiously, even as a series of powerful AI tools have already been deployed on the Oracle Cloud Infrastructure (OCI) for departments including HR, finance, sales, front desk, SCM and marketing. To answer why caution is advised regarding some potential risks in having bots run operations without human oversight, we can look at one example: a recent court case involving the Canadian travel industry where an AI hallucination caused a lot of headaches for Air Canada, the country's leading airline.

In this case, a passenger was told by the AI chatbot that they could apply for a reduced bereavement airfare retroactively within 90 days of the flight date. However, this contradicted the corporate policy as stated on the website, which did not allow refunds for travel that had already transpired. The AI had imagined or 'hallucinated' something that was inaccurate.

During the subsequent trial, Air Canada was found responsible for the policy as stated by its AI chatbot under the guise of 'negligent misrepresentation'. It had to honor the refund.

To add my own notes on the case, this is hardly the first or the last time we will see a hallucination cause problems for a company. And the chances for creating an inaccurate pattern or model only grow as we start to expand the uses of AI into the territory of 'agency'. For instance, GenAI has been cited as a tremendous tool for automating tasks such as scheduling housekeepers or juggling room reservation assignments. But what if there's a mistake and room attendants are told to start their shift at 3am or a group room block ends up scattered across an entire 500-key hotel? As a human, I'm already biased in what unfortunate scenarios I can imagine; it's difficult to predict what an AI will hallucinate because they don't think quite like we do.

This all said, the benefits of AI agents are far too great to ignore and hotel tech leaders are devoting plenty of resources to QA to minimize the risks, which brings us to an important term for hoteliers to keep in mind regarding the deployment of AI agents: retrieval-augmented generation (RAG).

While out-of-the-box LLMs and GPTs are trained on vast quantities of data, RAG aims to limit the range of responses from an LLM to only those available from your own enterprise data sources or 'internal knowledge base'. Per its namesake, RAG works to 'augment' a human prompt or query into a foundation model by 'retrieving' then adding into that prompt the contextually relevant data in order to 'generate' a specific AI response or task to be performed.

Whether this augmentation is ruled-based, semantic-based or dependent on AIs interacting with APIs, RAG holds the most promise in the near future to extend the capabilities of GenAI immensely for hotels while limiting the risk of hallucinations or the improper handling of transactional data. By giving accurate context to prompts, AI agents can then be tasked and trusted with the use cases that have long been promised but seldom delivered.

Some ideas for where AI agents can take us:

- Personalized room amenities based on guest preferences
- Conversationally driven custom reservations
- Predictive maintenance with prescriptive repair schedules
- And yes, organizing team shifts to more efficiently run a property without making anyone wake up in the middle of the night

There's obviously a ton more happening under the hood to make these technologies a reality; ask your vendors what their RAG roadmap is and how they are supporting this next-level automation.

Segmentation Recommendation Engines as the Next Big AI Tool for Hotels

Customer segmentation has been critical from day one for the modern hotel industry. More recently, with numerous data sets being merged due to technological advances, brands are starting to get quite granular with their KYC (know your customer) in terms of understanding where guests are coming from (channels and geography), why they are selecting your property (leisure, corporate, conference and so on) and what their buying (packages, upselling offers, onsite ancillary spend or others).

Layering on artificial intelligence tools on top of all this data can now allow hotels to do far more than even five years ago within this burgeoning field of micro-segmentation, but this requires some understanding of how AI works (as well as a lot of techie acronyms).

To start, we must grasp how all this data is coming together. In contrast, with the dawn of application programming interfaces (APIs), disparate systems used by different operations could be strung together by structuring data field imports into a centralized storehouse. The PMS has always been a likely candidate for this nexus. Still, increasingly, it's the customer relationship management (CRM) because of this system's propensity to position all data around unified guest profiles and to incorporate above-property inputs.

Common friction points for working with APIs has been that an IT professional needs the spare time to set up each interface, and then maintain all those established connections with each subsequent software update. With each new system added to the tech stack, this quickly becomes resource-intensive. Here, a specific type of AI called robotic processing automation (RPA) has already proven itself by acting as a robot that can directly replace double entry work that has to be done manually because two systems haven't been integrated to talk directly to each other.

And it gets far better. Once you have all this data imported, cleaned (to remove duplicates) and structured into proper data fields, you now have an enormous treasure trove of numbers. While this database is far too vast for a pair of hotelier eyes to pick out patterns, the AI specialty of machine learning (ML) is designed precisely for that task. You give it the data; it finds the patterns, however, hidden they may be to the human overseer. The more data you give it, the more patterns it can potentially find and the more accurate its predictions will be.

Besides looking at vast amounts of data and then giving insights into that data, the key to ML is that it can produce a predictive model to optimize for desired future outcomes. Then, once that model is tested out in the field, the best AIs can then use the new data as feedback to improve their own modeling algorithm, further enhancing their predictive power to better optimize for a stated objective.

Where hotels have already seen the most lucrative applications for ML is in the revenue management system (RMS), with massive data sets comprising external and internal inputs are computed into an algorithm that can then recommend to the revenue director what pricing will optimize for rooms revenue, occupancy or now total revenue per guest stay.

It's this whole notion of recommendations that brings us to the concept of having ML interpret not only how to adjust nightly rates or what response to provide for a website chatbot, but also to look at the multitude of guest profile data and then come back with its own set of microsegments for your revenue, sales and marketing teams to interpret and pivot their planning accordingly.

As of now, all of us are operating under a given set of established business assumptions based on how we were trained and our experience working in hotels. We see the world in terms of leisure, corporate and groups, and many of us have become locked into these guest segments. Recommendation engines based on ML don't have those same limitations and thus can provide a fresh set of eyes on what your real segments are.

Perhaps this latest technology will help your hotel find an edge over the competition or allow you to deploy the advertising budget more effectively. Maybe it will give you suggestions on what packages will work better for attracting leisure guests or what types of groups are most winnable for your meetings and events business. Just as AI helps us to rethink business assumptions, neither of us would dare assume to know what such a tool would find buried within your hotel's data.

Our advice is to first chart a path for connecting all your systems, and only then investigate these more advanced ML tools. At the same time, you will also have to confront the cultural, more existential scenario of what happens when the AI finds microsegments that contradict those that your teams are working off. We live in exciting times!

Will That Be Cash, Card or Crypto for Your Booking?

Recently, we've seen cryptocurrencies go from theoretical speculation among circles of computer geeks to a popular dinner conversation topic with a much more diversified pool of investors. Whether you deem this asset class viable over the long term or the purest form of bubble just waiting to burst, the sheer growth alone dictates that this is not a monetary system you can ignore any longer.

No doubt you've read on your own time about bitcoin, ethereum, dogecoin, cardano, litecoin, filecoin, chainlink and a plethora of other digital coins. Now is the time to consider how to operationalize these emergent aspects of what's being called 'Web 3.0'. That is, how do these coins affect your hotel? More specifically, would you accept payment for a hotel reservation in the form of a cryptocurrency?

The first aspect for consideration has nothing to do with quotidian transactions per se, but with balance sheet decisions at the ownership level. At its core, bitcoin, the most popular and oldest crypto is not designed to be money but digital gold – a store of value that's left in a vault and you simply 'point' to it as a means of, for example, securing a line of credit in some other liquid form. In this sense, hotel owners can make a reasonable case – in line with numerous other large cap companies – to treat established cryptos like gold and allocate a portion of their cash reserves or quarterly net profits to these assets both as an investment and as a hedge against pandemic-related hyperinflation.

Second is for all senior managers to understand the technologies that power digital coins (which also helps to explain why certain cryptos like bitcoin are akin to digital gold and not digital cash) because they have applicability beyond just payments and wealth accrual. Think loyalty program incentivization. A word of caution here is that grasping how these hyperledgers work – algorithmic hashing calculations, mining, proof of work, proof of stake, gas fees and so forth – is not something one can learn in a day, so best to start now, at least intermittently, in order to have some working knowledge prior to when it becomes necessary.

As it relates to the third and final consideration, let's unpack this cash versus gold utility regarding whether or not to accept payments in cryptocurrency. Paper money works because it's fast (you hand it over on the spot) and portable (lightweight and fits in your pocket), and because you inherently trust the government behind it. Similarly, a centralized credit card processor such as Visa or Mastercard has built up the infrastructure over several decades to be able to handle thousands of transactions per second and diligently mediate disputes, thereby making these systems great for regular payments.

On the other hand, Bitcoin and Ethereum (capitalized here to denote the platforms and not the coins themselves) are setup to have per-second processing rates that are several orders of magnitude smaller. This is because the algorithmic calculations required to verify transactions and add them to the block require huge amounts of computational energy; it's simply untenable to move at the same pace as a major credit card company. The difference is that blockchains are 'trustless' whereby, in lieu of putting your faith in a centralized authority like American Express or the US Government, every node powering the chain must approve of the transaction in order to adjoin the new block.

As of right now, the infrastructure doesn't really exist for digital coins to be utilized for day-to-day payments by the average person. Can you imagine waiting ten minutes for the next block to be added to the Bitcoin chain in order to authenticate a customer's hotel room payment and settle their folio? This is only appropriate when the purchases are large and infrequent like a car or house.

Instead, there are a handful of cryptos, stablecoins (that is, cryptos fixed or tethered to a given fiat currency), rollup solutions (for off-ledger or second-layer transactions) and central bank digital currencies (CBDCs) that are emerging as blockchain-verified methods for everyday transactions. Once these are widely available, you can then expect a full range of wares both hard and soft that will support rapid bill settlements while also automatically converting from whichever digital coin the consumer has into your desired unit of account. Concurrently, however, you can also expect some younger guests to demand that your hotel to enable digital coin transaction.

So, to circle back to the question posed in the title, should your hotel accept cryptocurrency payments? The short answer is not yet.

The real answer is that we are at a crossroads and there could be a strong first-mover advantage for whichever hotel brand decides to be the forerunner into this space. True, there may be some backlash from people citing the energy consumption of cryptocurrencies and their contribution to global warming, along with some acrimonious remarks from the taxmen. But such a hospitality organization would endear itself to a host of globetrotters who also happen to be crypto investors looking for hotels that are amenable to these alternate forms of cash.

Ultimately, what we stress is to spend some time learning about blockchains and cryptocurrencies. Yes, there's a lot of hype, but that doesn't mean they are going away. And that presents an opportunity to grow another revenue vertical ahead of the competition.

How Hotels Can Dip Their Toes in the NFT Waters

With all the hype concerning blockchains, cryptocurrencies, nonfungible tokens (NFTs) and the dawn of the metaverse, now is the time for hotels to reflect on how these rapidly growing trends will come to impact our industry. How can they enhance the guest experience? When's the right time to act? And above all, will these help grow revenues or asset values?

What are Nonfungible Tokens?

As per the title, this brief post is about NFTs which are unique (nonfungible) digital identifiers (tokens) that bestow their owners with specific access to pieces of property, rights (including commercial usage) or services. This uniqueness is verified and upheld using blockchains with transactions for NFTs completed in cryptocurrencies; both of these terms are out of scope here, although we highly suggest you spend some time getting caught up on how they work.

Right now, NFTs are in an early adopter honeymoon phase, with the crypto community trading digital artwork for exorbitant prices while the outside world looks on in astonishment at what are merely innocuous, iterative jpegs of bored-looking apes. Our gut says that there is indeed a bubble, but it isn't tulip mania on repeat because the technology underpinning NFTs have profound, versicolor applications. The key word from the definition above is 'access' which can be practically anything.

Why Do NFTs Have Value?

Further examining the Bored Ape Yacht Club (BAYC) offers a prime example for where the technology is headed and where the potential value is for hotels. In case you haven't heard, the total traded value of all BAYC collectibles just crossed $1 billion USD. Per its website, BAYC is a 'limited NFT collection where the token itself doubles as your membership to a swamp club for apes'.

So, you pay for one of 10,000 limited edition NFTs with the distinct profile picture of a funny-looking primate as your visual proof of ownership. But that's the surface scratch – the Trojan Horse if you will.

This token also gives you dedicated access to a members-only community which for BAYC includes entry to a private Discord server (a fast-growing social media currently with over 350 million users) where you can communicate directly with a myriad of (fellow BAYC NFT owner) celebrities. As of now this list includes the likes of Jimmy Fallon, Mark Cuban, and Eminem; if you win a BAYC NFT auction tomorrow, you also gain an inside track to talk with these bigwigs.

Moreover, because the core identifier is unique, the jpeg is wholly and only yours to use across other digital mediums, most significant of which will be in future virtual reality metaverses, on augmented reality platforms or in mixed reality experiences. As Gary Vaynerchuk, another NFT evangelist, puts it, this is akin to buying a custom character skin or other aesthetic modification for a freemium game, only because of blockchains it tracks across all games and all platforms for as long as the internet exists.

Three Hotel NFT Use Cases

There's a ton that we've brushed over in how this works, but based on the above, our hope is that your gears are churning. Hotels are well-positioned to take advantage of the NFT explosion because we are already in the business of creating unique experiences for our guests. Not every stay would qualify, but simply thinking in terms of digitized, unique access should spawn some use cases.

1. *Augmenting unique experiences.* Say you run a 200-room property across several categories, without any singular keys that have boundless amenities and stratospheric price tags. Technically, that's 73,000 (200 times 365) unique stays per annum – not exactly 'limited edition'. Instead, suppose you do indeed have an unquestionably exclusive product – such as a presidential suite or villa – whereby you can stipulate that any guest who stays there for minimum one week (duration can vary) receives an NFT to earmark the occasion that, importantly, also bestows said guest with special access to a variety of other perks. What exactly those perks are depends on the brand, but some basic ideas include entry to a members-only online community as per BAYC, entry to private lounges in the real world, free room upgrades, complimentary airport shuttles on all future stays at any location or early access to future product launches. And because each NFT is unique, so too can the perks be delineated by year, edition and so on.
2. *Loyalty program marketplaces.* From the previous use case and the basic ideas listed off, the smart question is to ponder why you need the blockchain or NFTs to unlock all those perks when your current guest profile and loyalty program tracking software will suffice. The answer is markets. NFTs give their owners the ability to sell their privileged access underwritten by the token to the highest bidder. That in turn creates residual value for the hotel stay long after the onsite experience has been rendered complete. In a world where brand relationships are eroding, NFTs can bolster a loyalty program because an owner can then sell their access to future perks, reinforcing the incentive for purchasing in the present. And those loyalty-based NFTs need not be earned only through the purchase of one-off experiences but can also be achievable much like our current tiered, points-based programs. Again, it depends on the brand.
3. *Digital twinning.* As of now, VR tourism already exists and doesn't necessarily require unique tokens because its main purpose is to whet the traveler's appetite for something else. The act of producing a 'digital twin' is to create an identical, online replica, which has already found solid applications in modeling predictive maintenance for complex machines like mining equipment or passenger airplanes. While the metaverse will inevitably spin off into every form of wild and weird virtual reality or augmented layering of our corporeal earth, one of the first steps for hotels will likely be the photoreal mirroring of physical places within a blockchain-based online world. Within these nascent ecosystems, cryptocurrencies will be the mediums of exchanges, while digital property rights

and, for our industry's sake, unique hotel stays, meeting spaces or access to other exclusive virtual activity can be governed by NFTs, if the experience warrants it. And you never know, having a digital twin may give you insights on how to improve operations at the physical property much like other industries are currently using digital twinning.

4. *Capital raises.* Think back to the AAirpass program launched by American Airlines in the 1980s where for $250,000 passholders received unlimited first-class tickets on any of the airline's flights worldwide. If you identify as a frequent flyer and can foresee yourself to be that way for the next few decades, this price is actually quite economical. Using NFTs, you can build such lavish programs aimed at high-net-worth individuals – think a million dollars for a lifetime of stays in any room or suite at any branded property with all F&B included – but also stipulate within the underlying smart contract that each pass resale comes with a new incremental price floor as well as a percent of sale owed to the hotel. The end result is you get a big cash inflow that you can use for present needs like renovations or debt service balloon payments with the promise of future stays and meals as well as strong incentives for a secondhand marketplace and some form of residuals back to you at each resale.

Circling back to the opening questions, it may be a bit early to act because the virtual economy of cryptocurrencies, NFTs and the metaverse is very much the Wild West that has yet to coalesce around a select few universal protocols. Still, this shouldn't prevent you from putting the inklings of a plan together that trains your team on what these new technologies are and the opening strategy for taking advantage of them. This will be a very lucrative space in the near future, so prepare accordingly.

Hotel Previsualization as a Metaverse Use Case for Right Now

The hype over the metaverse has been put through the wringer recently as epitomized by Facebook/Meta's tumbling stock price and the reveal that Decentraland (one of the much-touted virtual worlds spearheading the metaverse movement) only had a daily active user in the hundreds. Yikes!

But even with these sobering reminders of the tech hype curve, hotels should not disregard the metaverse just yet as the travel industry is one of the prime beneficiaries of this technology with applications that your brand can realize for gains in the next few years.

Defining the Metaverse for Right Now

Before unpacking those use cases, it's important to first unpack what is encompassed by the term 'the metaverse'. Right now, the use of the term is less so pertaining to an object, singular technology or technological milestone that we will one day have in our lives, so much as it's a process of realizing those dream one step at a time.

For instance, when we talk about 'hotels in the metaverse', we aren't necessarily describing the establishment of a wholly digital hotel constructed in an interconnected virtual world that can feasibly take advantage of business-to-avatar (B2A) revenue opportunities with sound economic projections. Instead, we are taking more about a siloed, privately hosted 'digital twin' (as the name implies, a 3D replica existing somewhere online) of a property existing in the real world with a variety of functions for each of the key stakeholder groups (owners or executives, frontline staff and guests).

This digital twin may be connected to or ported over into a virtual world at a future date, but right now the focus is on how activities in the metaverse can grow revenues or save costs, with quantifiable results on a quarterly income statement, once there's enough data to verify either way.

With this as an objective, what a digital twin lets anyone do is previsualize the hotel – that is, view it on a 2D monitor (so no expensive VR equipment is necessarily required) as a virtual walkthrough prior to setting foot onsite. Following this line of thought opens up two profound guest-facing use cases with big upside potential.

Hotel Previsualization for Event Planning

Start by imagining your current sales cycle for a prospective event, from tradeshows, website activities and RFPs through to CRM workflows, site visits and contract negotiations. Throughout, what any event planner wants is the confidence that the space will serve the event's needs and those of all attendees. If there's trust, then the hotel is more likely to sell a bigger package, whether that's in the form of a larger room block, a more elaborate venue setup or additional catering.

Having a digital twin of your hotel available for event planners to peruse helps build this trust. And such twins can be freely accessible via a portal off the website or your sales team can walk the prospect through the virtual hotel during a live demo. The next step here would be to overlay specific table configurations so that a planner can see, for instance, the difference between rounds and long tables or evaluate the attendee flow between a cocktail reception area and the main banqueting hall.

Moreover, such 2D environments let an event planner envision what adding another 10% to 20% more guests would look like – both in the venue spaces and in the room blocks – helping justify the higher total spend. Just like test driving a car or trying on clothes before purchasing them, the metaverse builds trust in the hotel product to close the sale.

Hotel Previsualization for Leisure Travel

This idea of garnering trust extends to the transient segment, both for the booking phase and for prearrival upselling. The first domain – the dream phase of travel research as it's often called – has long been extolled as a use case for VR, both by multinational hotel chains (such as the Best Western Virtual Reality Experience) and destination travel organizations. But why do you necessarily need the headset?

With any new technology, you have to adapt it to what customers are already using. Right now, prospective hotel guests have a desktop, a mobile phone and a myriad of email, SMS and social media through such to send a link that opens to a 3D rendering of a hotel within a 2D monitor. This can work to add some more interactivity to the reservation process and be used to encourage direct bookings.

When it comes to the prearrival phase – roughly from 14 days out to the intended date of arrival – resending this link that opens to the digital twin can lead to several other opportunities right when your incoming guests are best primed to take advantage of upselling offers. Specifically, you can prompt them with an attribute-based selling (ABS) offer by highlighting specific guestrooms within the 3D replica environment along with their price tags. Or, if you want to sell spa services, you might include a link that directs guests to tour those facilities.

Beyond Incremental Sales

On the cost savings side of things, the metaverse has already been noted for its potential to ramp up the efficiency of staff training in order to decrease CPOR. Concurrently, such alternative training methods may also increase morale by reducing the pressure one faces once staffers are on the job. The problem here is a lack of access to the tech while offsite (whether that's a desktop or inexpensive AR/VR headsets). And while they're onsite, there's no substitute for the real thing.

This is not to say it can't be done, but we should be realistic with our approach and previsualization appears to be far more lucrative. To that end, you can use your digital twin to plan for an upcoming renovation by swapping furnishings in and out to get a sense of their impact, all while conducting some bot-driven heatmapping for spatial optimization. This use case can ensure that the remodeling proceeds smoothly while satisfying all parties, although the frequency of any renovation dictates that this may not be of recurrent utility for any individual property.

We already mentioned the B2A buzz term which inscribes the sales of wholly digital items directly to a person's avatar. Similarly, hotels can setup a physical to digital (P2D) offer whereby real-world purchases also grant the guest perks in the metaverse. As the inverse of this, digital to physical (D2P) is what may describe the commerce strategy behind what citizenM and Millennium Hotels & Resorts did with their NFT launches in Spring 2022 – sell NFTs touting access to their metaverse properties but also with perks that can be unlocked in the real world such as discounts or free drinks. Either way, there are companies testing the waters and it's time that you have a plan for where you think the potential is with this technology trend.

Ways That Hotels Can Make Money from the Metaverse (Part 1)

The metaverse seems to be all the rage right now, but is it just hype or will it actually take off and have a viable economic purpose within the next few years? Of note, we are looking at the next few 'years' and not the next few 'decades'.

Right now, the skepticism is palpable. Many see the entire ecosystem of cryptocurrencies, NFTs and the metaverse as one giant Ponzi scheme built upon the promise of a libertarian future as led by hyperintelligent futurists with innumerous other young, get-rich-quick wannabes drinking the YouTube Kool-Aid. The doubters raise some good points, but ultimately our sentiment is that the bulls will win because blockchain applications for businesses are too lucrative to disregard.

Never ones to recommend artificially derived beverages like the aforementioned Kraft Heinz-owned pop culture icon, our purpose here is instead to look at these new technologies through the clarity of a refreshing freshly blended fruit smoothie, preferably consumed on a tropical beach somewhere. The hospitality applications specific to the metaverse are indeed manifold in terms of building the plumbing for revenue streams based on strong guest demands within the 'next few years'. Therefore, it's important that you know what can be in order to see what you should do in the here and now.

As a caveat emptor, the most apt word is 'plumbing'; with any investment in this space, you are banking on a future that is still gestating with the focus on laying the pipe that has the versatility to enable your organization to seize upon that future with a first-mover advantage.

While we're always available for a consultation to see what's applicable for your property and your brand's specific needs or budget, the first step is to list off some of the ways that the metaverse can be used to initiate new revenue streams, serve as add-ons to current sales models or as cross-selling tools.

1. *An Extension of the Experience Economy.* We're both keen acolytes of Joe Pine and Jim Gilmore's 'The Experience Economy' which goes at lengths to describe how businesses will benefit most from looking at the customer's time as the most-limited resource. When you think in terms of 'time well spent', it reframes all your operations from the guest's exceedingly shrewd and hasty point of view. Guests value their time above all else and will therefore gravitate to those brands that in turn treat it with adoration. In this sense, the metaverse can be seen as merely the shiny new toy in the experience economy, whereby creating a virtual reality (VR) space for your hotel to exist in is but one more way to augment your service offerings and increase perceived value to drive bookings.
2. *Digital Twinning for Maintenance Efficiency.* There are a lot of great tools out there right now to help with preventative maintenance and the streamlining of work orders. The metaverse can help by imbuing a stronger sense of predictability into your engineering department via a 'digital twin' which is a clone of your physical property and all its mechanical components in the virtual world so that you can better monitor FF&E wear and tear. And with better monitoring, you can then develop better models for anticipating when certain devices will need repairs, all to limit negative reviews, optimize labor and reduce purchasing costs.
3. *Digital Twinning for Spatial Orientation.* Distinct from the previous use case, with a digital twin you can map out the flow of guests and staff through your property to improve route planning for various operations

or optimize the furniture orientation of other revenue verticals like your lobby bar and pool area. Which tables or chaises get the most traffic? Do those seating arrangements correspond with the highest spends per guest? Having a digital twin can give you an extra overlay to evaluate how customer positioning and traffic flow relate to F&B sales. While the maintenance use case is more about cost savings, this latter case can also help to increase the in-room experience by identifying the dead spaces or A/B testing alternate orientations to drive ADR and guest satisfaction.

4. *New ways to sell and enhance meetings and events.* It starts with enhanced virtual site visits whereby a metaverse clone of a hotel can be passed along to prospects so that they can 'window shop' a venue for a corporate retreat or wedding reception in lieu of or as an adjunct to a guided virtual tour and physical site visit. Then for the event itself, there are those who can't make it and are currently reliant on videoconferencing options. For these remote attendees, the metaverse gives you the option to replace a laptop camera feed with a wholly immersive environment.
5. *The Layering of Augmented Reality Experiences.* There's that word again – experiences. While not strictly an application for the metaverse per se, this would involve the coding of certain additive features into a hotel space that are only visible using augmented reality (AR) glasses. An extension of this would be to create a mixed reality (MR) experience that incorporates aspects of a virtual world with the actual world via AR. For those experiences, a hotel can charge a guest via a rental fee for a pair of Apple Glasses (still a rumor but hopefully to be unveiled later) or a hotel can act as the chef to a BYO(AR)D experience where any AR device owner can hop on and get the benefit via a gated – that is, paid-for – access code.

Stay tuned for five more applications in the second part...

Ways That Hotels Can Make Money from the Metaverse (Part 2)

Lengthy and chunky explanations of each specific use case compelled us to make this a two-parter consisting of a total of ten potential ways that hotels can get in on this latest tech craze.

To recap our thoughts, the metaverse is indeed controversial, and it is easy to shrug off traditionalists as just another online craze. Instead, we see it as a way to augment experiences in the real world and enhance brand advocacy. Moreover, the examples we present are ones that have applicability in the near future and not some distant decade where you've already retired.

As a final word, before getting into these latter five, some alphabet soup is in the order. If you're confused about the difference between augmented reality (AR), virtual reality (VR) and mixed reality (MR), know first that you are far from alone and plenty of other articles have been written to help distinguish each. Secondly, you should read up on non-fungible tokens (NFTs) insofar as how blockchains can support unique ownership of digital and physical assets.

1. *Lead User Innovation.* This is a term that deserves its own article specific to the hospitality space. Basically, it describes how your most loyal guests or 'evangelists' as some tech companies codify them will come to find new and extraordinary uses for your product that you never thought of or intended for. The metaverse can help you embrace the ingenuity of these individuals by giving them the space to interact with your brand in many more fun, fascinating and possibly perverse ways, all of which are tracked digitally and hence can be used to create actionable inferences for the physical product.
2. *A Bonus for Tokengating.* The future is all about the 'gating' or closing off of digital content for nonsubscribers. In this sense, 'tokengating' is simply the use of NFTs to govern who has access to a physical location, ownership of an asset or visibility of a digital construct. While you can create, say, a private lounge that only owners of a specific NFT will be allowed to enter, the prospects of MR and the metaverse introduce the possibility of even more added perks, specifically the access to certain areas or items that other non-NFT owners cannot interact with.
3. *Boosting the Concept of Transformative Experiences.* As the next generation of the Experience Economy, there is the notion of the 'Transformation Economy' where customers evaluate brands based upon how well products improve their overall livelihoods. So, can you use technology to ensure that a guest leaves a hotel better off than when they arrived? Without digressing too far into the wellness side of things, one metaverse-oriented application would be virtual exercise or yoga classes. Each room comes equipped with a VR headset and tracking suit, and guests can log in to an immersive digital environment for an on-demand training session with a highly skilled instructor, all without having to go through the logistics and inconvenience of meeting in person. In this sense, it's a bit like what Peloton has done but much more personalized. Moreover, depending on the sensors in the equipment used, such sessions can be much more responsive to incorrect movements, presenting the opportunity for an upsell related to physiotherapy corrective measures.
4. *Cataloguing Experiences as a Post-Departure Gift.* By deploying a digital twinning model to record aspects of the hotel stay, you can gain more data on a person's onsite experience while the blockchain technologies underpinning the metaverse clone can ensure that that data is kept private to only the guest. For this use case, the data can drill down to the minutia of point-to-point decisions made on property, nutrition or wellness information and memorable highlights of the trip. All of these can be catalogued in the metaverse for future access, with the ultimate loyalty goal of having guests leave a property in person but never really checking out. As a somewhat extreme example, a bride and groom want to revisit the place of their nuptials

on their anniversary at the exact moment when they said, "I do," but must rely on the metaverse to offer that meticulously timed experience because the rigors of life prevent them from doing so in real life.

5. *Further Incentives for a Loyalty Program.* While you mull over all the previous ideas, you can see that not only are there applications for the metaverse to improve your physical product, but also to encourage guests to revisit your property, especially when you also incorporate gamification techniques. For instance, what if you only allowed access to various parts of your metaverse hotel clone to certain tiers of your loyalty program? Each tier could be determined from points accumulated not just from purchases on-prem in the physical world – rooms, suite upgrades, spa treatments, F&B, gift shop, golf and so on – but also, through the integration of all your various digital channels, incorporate online actions such as responding to a survey, social media mentions or getting friends to click on a bespoke referral link. This is but one use case that could have some lucrative applications. Next, you can throw in the idea of token-gating certain AR-based experiences to particular loyalty tiers, and then you have the makings of a compelling, modern rewards program.

Luddites and the Modern Hotel Industry

While many hotel brands may still yearn for those pre-pandemic days of 'high touch' hospitality where passionate, attentive and well-trained associates delivered service with a smile, those times are over.

Technology will be a cornerstone of operations going forward – and an increasingly dominant one at that – with what was considered the time-honored standards of service firmly in the past. This may be hard to grasp in terms of what it means for the future of your organization, so we present the Luddites as one historical example with profound lessons for how to stay ahead of the curve when it comes to hospitality trends and guest expectations.

History hasn't been kind to the Luddites, nor has it been accurate. Our modern interpretation of these people is, in fact, wrong, and knowing the real story will help you to understand both their motivations and their actions in the moment – and not through the omniscience of hindsight – as well as why they are important at this pivotal moment for the hospitality industry.

A Bit of Historical Misinterpretation

Today, the word 'Luddite' has taken on a pejorative meaning for any individual who is tech-phobic or who refuses to 'get with the program' of any new digitized or digitalized way of life. At the time when they were most active in Great Britain around the first two decades of the 1800s amidst the nation's rapid industrialization, they were branded as terrorists, albeit with good intentions.

Throughout civilized history, creative destruction sucks for those on the losing end of the technological evolution, and the coal-fired factories popping up throughout England were putting a lot of craftspeople out of work – not to mention introducing abysmally horrid working conditions for the burgeoning class of poor, urban laborers. The Luddites started out as a virtuous protest movement to protect the economic interests of the recently unemployed, hoping to strike a balance between the newly wealthy industrialists in the cities and the usurped, largely rural artisans.

But radical factions soon emerged within the Luddites, engaging in guerrilla sabotage throughout the countryside, which angered the aristocracy (who were now making a fleet-load of money off the growth in domestic production and exports), inevitably getting the whole group outlawed. As history is written by the victors – in this case, the capitalists – we are left with the homogenized interpretation of the word. Luddite now connotes being tenaciously opposed to most forms of technological progress, and yet we glaze over the events leading up to this boiled-down definition. The Luddites weren't necessarily abhorred by technology; they started off as pacifists with the goal of protecting displaced businesses, seeking compromise in the face of rapid, unchecked change.

Lessons for Dealing with Home-Sharing

Consider how the Luddite movement organically grew from noble intentions into something more combative and what might apply from this example to our industry's current model. Oftentimes, we are so set upon preserving a way of operating that, instead of innovating internally for long-term survival, we are leaving ourselves vulnerable to systemic creative destruction from outside forces.

Nothing demonstrates this better than the rise of home-sharing platforms, as lead by Airbnb. Is your chosen action in the face of this global creative destruction to complain and seek out more protectionist laws from various governing bodies (that is, oppose new technology)? Or do you consider Airbnb as simply another iteration of supply and demand, where an influx of guestroom supply (home-sharing units) inevitably forces all current supply (hotels) to become better in order to justify their prices?

If the past two decades have taught us anything about technology companies, it's that they move significantly faster than the law. As such, the best action is not to be a Luddite and pin your hopes on punitive fines and injunctions – as those might take years to come and travelers will have shifted behaviors by then – but to adapt.

Important to consider in how you respond, here are three of the characteristics that make these new home-sharing entrants more adaptable to the current economy:

- Home-sharing inventory is introduced and managed on a one-to-one basis, thus requiring far less capital for onboarding, brand differentiation, and refurbishment, not to mention a more laissez-faire organizational structure that greatly reduces managerial requirements.
- The tech stacks underpinning these home-sharing platforms are more nimble, less complex and better integrated, together making it faster for

inventory to be brought online, cheaper to manage (less labor and SaaS costs) and easier to use by the end consumer.

- In a positive feedback loop, home-sharing platforms are training the next generation of guests not to expressly value a traditional hotel's 'high touch' service, instead preferring a hands-off experience with fewer amenities but truly unique living spaces.

The message here isn't to abandon ship. By listing these three advantages, our hope is that you can help discern what necessary changes you can make to appease the shifting interests of younger guests and what attributes will serve as bona fide defensible moats for your property well into the future.

Embracing Tech for High Touch

In speeches given to crowds around the world – both before and after the pandemic – we have steadfastly remarked that a hotel's team is its greatest strength. Despite any hints from the above that high touch is dying, the optimal solution is one of embracing technology so that your teams can be even more high touch than ever better (or hands-off if that's what the guest wants).

Reminiscing on the good old days of hospitality, the GM used to be front and center, knowing all guests by name and directing an orchestra of service to personalize the experience. Now, most managers are bogged down by emails, meetings, maintenance issues and all other matters that might stymie the development of real rapport along with the nurturing of a vibrant social atmosphere.

By building better tech stacks, you help to shift the guest-staff dynamic from transactional back to interpersonal. Whereas most home sharing units are going the way of keypad entries and only virtual contact with the host, you want your guests leaving your property thinking, "Wow, they treated us like genuine friends and really made our stay special." Ironically, this lofty goal echoes an early Airbnb intracompany slogan: a friend not a front desk.

Of course, there are innumerous other ways beyond service that can help a hotel resist creative destruction. Think physical aspects like location, golf courses, spas, restaurants, marinas, inspirational décor, themed rooms or lobby art. Perhaps you also have (or can develop) strong supply-side relationships, good branding or exclusive access to other entities.

Any tool in your shed can work but still keep in mind the true lesson of the Luddites. It's honorable to want to protect what has worked in the past, be it an operation, a SOP or a corporate structure with specific managerial roles. Nevertheless, change is inevitable and innovation is essential. If you don't strive to meet customers where they are headed, then someone else will.

WELLNESS & LONGEVITY

Embarking on a low-nine-figure expansion that will include multiple hotel properties and a full medi-spa, an integral feature will be Appenzeller Huus Gonten's staff accommodations that feature their own wellness facilities to induce long-term team retention.

How Real Wellness Programming Builds Perpetual Revenues with TheLifeCo

Our hypothesis is that wellness will play a leading role in many hotel brands' growth over the coming decades. Populations in advanced economies are getting older, meaning more demand for medical tourism or health span extension programming. Concurrently, there is an ever-growing interest in wellbeing-boosting and antiaging activities, scientific research and products following the work-life reset that was the pandemic.

While there are numerous other factors at work here, we consider wellness to be the *hotel trend of all trends* because, simply put, if you don't have your health then nothing else matters.

Rather than drone on in abstract about what properties can do in the domains of nutritional programming, sleep programs, in-room fitness, onsite physiotherapy, yoga, mindfulness, saunas, thalassotherapy, cold therapy, forest bathing or a host of others, what better way to learn than from a proven example of success?

For any hotel financier or developer out there, such a case study that shows positive results is all but necessary to consider a huge capex that may not reveal any significant payout within two or quarters. Engaging in the wellness space has this challenge: the benefits may not be immediate, but they can potentially be so lucrative that they match or exceed rooms revenue stream itself.

To help elucidate how to make wellness financially successful, we interviewed Ersin Pamuksuzer, Co-Founder of TheLifeCo, a branded wellness resort with two properties in Turkey (Akra Antalya and Bodrum) and one in Thailand (Phuket), with more in the pipeline. TheLifeCo specializes in multi-night guided chronic disease management, nutrition, detox and weight loss itineraries, where guests follow a strict weeklong (or longer) regimen tailored to the individual that encompasses all meals, all activities, onsite therapies and diagnostic testing.

While your first thought may be that this level of wellness is out of scope for your brand or is only a niche amenity, consider the following: *over 90% of guests to a TheLifeCo property end up returning* or visiting another property in the brand, with both the Bodrum and Phuket resorts selling out at least three months in advance during high season.

Defining Low Wellness and Alternative Medicine

To understand the potential for wellness as an enduring profit center, it's important to get to the root of what distinguishes TheLifeCo from other hotel's programming. At present, what most of us imagine as wellness is, as Pamuksuzer points out, in fact a more narrowcast spa concept often labeled by evangelists as 'low wellness' or 'pampering' – mani-pedis, facials, massages, and so on. Real wellness is so much more.

This 'low' labeling is not to besmirch these traditional spa amenities – they are veritable revenue generators in their own right – but they are not *transformative experiences for the guest* and thus they do not breed true loyalty. Understanding what we mean by transformative in this sense is absolutely crucial, whereby an activity, amenity or multi-day regimen is not only about making the customer feel good in the moment but enhancing their life satisfaction for years to come.

In the case for TheLifeCo, this transformation is accomplished through 'alternative medicine' programming – that is, holistic treatments or integrated health techniques that aim to heal the entire body and mind, not just a specific ailment or injury. The goal with any of these multi-day regimens to give guests 'healthcare' so that they can avoid having to go to the hospital for 'sickcare'.

For instance, an extended water fast may not have the precision of a modern clinical trial for a pharmaceutical drug in order to authenticate its efficacy, and yet its cleansing, restorative power has been documented in historical texts and codified into religions for thousands of years. Or, as the two of us like to pithy say for all manner of intermittent fasting, "You can't fix a car with the engine on."

The problem is that going without solid meals for 72 to 96 hours is very, very, very, very hard, and almost impossible to do at home with the diversions of family, friends, a pantry full of snacks, work stressors and that Uber Eats order only two clicks away. TheLifeCo offers a calm, curated, safe and distraction-free environment where guests can undergo the bodily transformation enabled by a water or green juice-only cleanse.

What You Can Do

Your property may not be in an exotic locale, and luring guests in for a full week LOS may be too big of an ask for your target audience, but there are nevertheless wellness applications for every brand in every hotel category.

Some tips from our conversation include:

- If there's a wellness center nearby that's continually reaching full occupancy, engage them to become the partnering overflow property
- Specifically for a water-only or green juice detox, any room with a minibar can be reoriented to only include allowable items so that any guest can purchase a 'mini-cleanse' as an add-on
- People plan for wellness-first trips much farther in advance than regular vacations or corporate travel, meaning that your marketing must likewise pivot to this L2B timeframe
- Everyone wants to abscond to Southern Turkey or Thailand while the weather is scorching hot, but if a hotel sells out quickly during peak season, the parent brand should have a process (automated or manual) for recommending these waitlisted customers to book another date range or another property in the brand for the requested dates, all so that these prospects stay engaged and don't start researching competitors
- Rethink your core audience and lookalike guest profiles as new wellness-driven customers are coming from all over the world (with Pamuksuzer remarking that TheLifeCo has seen a recent uptick in guests originating from Africa as wellness gains popularity there)

To this last point, consider the Global Wealth Report by Credit Suisse, which notes that there are over 62 million millionaires worldwide as of the end of 2021, with much of that growth happening outside of Europe and North America. Not only should you be taking a global view with your brand strategy, but also start to think in terms of *the only thing more valuable than money – time.*

As people accrue wealth beyond a certain point, day-to-day monetary needs become less important and we aim to increase the *quality* of how we spend our time (great experiences) as well as the *quantity* of quality time that we have (healthspan).

Above all for how hotels can get started, Pamuksuzer emphasizes, "People have souls; they're fragile, especially during a fast or detox program. To make any wellness offering successful, a hotel brand must start by fundamentally grasping this emotional vulnerability. If a company is only in it for the ancillary spend, that's all they'll end up getting – 'ancillary' that never comes close to rooms revenue. But if a hotel brand embraces a wellness-first mindset, then this will echo through every amenity and every team member. Guests will feel it and reward you with not just repeat business but lasting loyalty."

Corporate Wellness as a Next Big Profit Center with TheLifeCo

Wellness has tremendous potential for hotels, as is being made abundantly clear from the litany of articles on the matter in recent months. Part of that potential stems from the all-embracing, or rather ambiguous, definition of the word. It's healthy eating; it's spa; it's fitness; it's mindfulness; it's sleep; it's nature; it's medical diagnostics; it's all of the above. However, one theme throughout for hotels is that the focus skews to the individual or one-on-one (mostly leisure transients), less so to group activations.

Here's what's common knowledge. On the leisure guest side, wellness amenities can protect rate through brand differentiation as well as boost ancillary spend (TRevPAR). With good marketing, value-added packaging, and frictionless payment rails, these amenities can also be harnessed for business or leisure guests or to appease emerging segments like extended-stay digital nomads. Then, for the back of the house, employee wellbeing programming is becoming instrumental as a nonwage incentive to attract talent, minimize turnover, and maximize productivity (for example, by reducing paid sick days and presenteeism).

On the backburner in this expansive conversation is how to make wellness work for corporate events and retreats, both to improve the effectiveness of those meetings for attendees as well as to activate a new revenue stream for the hotel. To find out from an expert on how this is done, we interviewed Ersin Pamuksuzer, founder of TheLifeCo, a leading detox wellness center and hotel resort brand based out of Turkey that has also built a successful, evergreen corporate events vertical over the past two decades.

The Potential Benefits for Hotels

Before looking at how TheLifeCo approached this market and how to get underway with your own hospitality brand, let's unpack the 'why' behind corporate wellness in terms of how your organization can benefit, which will then influence your go-to-market approach.

1. *Product differentiation.* Lots of hotels offer meeting and events packages; it's a competitive industry. While price and the negotiation skills of your sales team will always be top considerations, offering wellness add-ons helps a hotel stand out, both for buyer-side event planners who must whittle down the selection as well as for top-of-funnel product awareness.
2. *Increased per-event spend.* All those wellness substitutions or add-ons work to justify a bigger contract. Some amenities like the spa, restaurant and gift boutique also have the potential to increase per-guest spend from those same corporate group visitors as each looks to enhance their individual stay during their downtime.
3. *Off-peak occupancies.* Business travelers are the saving grace of midweek revenues throughout the world, and setting up wellness amenities can thus breed new life into seasonal properties by giving groups a reason to visit outside of peak.
4. *Upgraded room categories.* Current room types can be remodeled with specific wellness amenities like air ionizers, herbal teas, circadian lighting, biohacking devices and health-focused minibars to generate higher nightly rates or as an incentive via packaging, prearrival upselling, error recovery events or complimentary upgrades to loyalty members.
5. *Auxiliary activations.* With a successful onsite corporate wellness program comes the possibility of offering extensions to clients, either at their offices or as a cosponsored event at a place that's more convenient for their workforce. Successful programming can also be productized and sold to other partnered hotels – for example, upgrading then cobranding a floor of guestrooms at a property in another city.
6. *Word of mouth throughout.* In today's world of perpetual noise and dwindling attention spans, you breakthrough not just with shrewd programmatic advertising or brute force media spends, but with memorable messaging. What we know, in a general sense, is that the more a guest uses a property, the more satisfied they are and the more likely they are to recommend to friends. As wellness increases this utilization, it follows that corporate wellness experiences will give your hotel yet one more avenue to maximize word of mouth, haloing back onto leisure performance.

Why Corporate Wellness Right Now

Numerous other sources have already shown over the past year that there's been a broad shift in the nature of work since the pandemic ended. Most poignantly for knowledge workers is the sharp rise in awareness for mental health issues and the need for better work-life balance. As Pamuksuzer identified, companies still aren't largely acknowledging the 'context of the individual' where any person, employee or executive, brings their personal issues into the job and this is inevitably reflected in their work.

And so we're clear, here are the workforce costs associated with mental health issues:

- Low job site productivity and poor team communications
- More sick days and more absenteeism
- Employee burnout and increased turnover
- Managers leaving suddenly for no obvious reason, creating leadership gaps
- Decreased intrapreneurship and team empowerment

In medical circles, mental health is now often associated with psychoneuroimmunology – or as others like Deepak Chopra have termed the 'bodymind' – whereby emotional stress causes physical damage such as a depressed immune system or generalized lethargy. And the reverse is also true: bad diet or a lack of exercise can advance underlying mental health issues or lead to undesirable workplace moods.

Combining the scientific recognition for this profound body-brain connection along with the mounting problems of mental health and 'talent-side pressure' within the labor market, companies all over the world have a present-day need for employee wellness in order to keep their teams at maximum productivity. But luckily, they can now source professionals who can deploy medically proven techniques to ameliorate the issue.

Know and Narrow the Target Buyers

Getting off the ground with any wellness venture is the hardest part, so it's best to narrow the focus, both in terms of aligning the amenities or offerings with what your brand stands for as well as the specific type of customers you pursue. While mental health is currently at the forefront, the obstacle for sales is that many corporate leaders lag behind in doing something about it.

Instead, Pamuksuzer's strategy has been to focus on those that already understand the benefits insofar as limiting the abovementioned drawbacks. Based on past performance, the business has largely come from high-margin companies with a mostly knowledge-based workforce. These prospects can be tech or finance, for instance, but they would probably come from the manufacturing sector. Still, as seeing is believing, it's inevitable that other companies will follow once they see the results.

In the early 2000s, TheLifeCo started by offering full-day sessions at corporate offices (mostly in Istanbul) using its internal team of facilitators, with each centered around meditation classes to get people in a more placid state of mind followed by a strategy workshop. Often this involved carving out a dedicated space within the office or renting a nearby conference center as well as training a 'wellness champion' within each client organization who would help corral the troops to maximize each event's success.

After executives saw the results of these onsite wellness seminars, they were far more receptive to the prospects of buying an offsite retreat package at one of the TheLifeCo's properties – in Turkey, these being situated in Bodrum and Antalya. Pamuksuzer also invited HR directors down to a branded resort to personally experience the leisure amenities firsthand as a form of targeted familiarization trip.

The promise has always been that a multi-day offsite filled with wellbeing and business seminars elicits exponential gains for a company's overall workforce productivity.

Corporate Retreat Programming

As for what actually happens at these offsites, each retreat is tailored to the individual client, but there is a turnkey curriculum underlying them all for cost efficiencies and proper staffing coordination. TheLifeCo deploys a variety of its leisure guest-focused services such as healthy F&B, supervised fasting, IV supplement administration and flexibility classes, which are then mixed in with professional development sessions on efficient communications, attaining a better work-life balance, finding one's job purpose and passion negotiations.

It all starts by assessing each company's needs and budget to then map out what each itinerary would look like. From there, TheLifeCo has developed a Rolodex of trained facilitators and external partners who can deliver on any specific client request or scheduling requirement.

Significantly, once this wellness package is put together, the price tag is often double what the quote would be for a non-wellness corporate retreat. In other words, the revenues are there for the taking, but it is a matter of developing that groundswell of specific services, facilitators who can render those services and highly focused marketing for these offerings.

Sleep Science at the Forefront at The Benjamin Royal Sonesta

"We believe in the importance of sleep. If a guest doesn't get a good night's rest they are less inclined to return." That profound statement came courtesy of Simon Chapman, Complex General Manager for The Benjamin Royal Sonesta, who oversees the hotel's Rest & Renew Sleep Program in collaboration with Dr. Rebecca Robbins, a medicine professor specializing in sleep science and author of "Sleep for Success" (2011).

We sought out Chapman for an interview because we deem sleep amenities to be a great tool to attract new guests and to support higher rates. While this is nevertheless true, the importance of sleep harks at something far more profound. In competitive urban markets like New York (especially the neighborhood of Midtown East), there are dozens of properties within a few blocks of The Benjamin, so ensuring that guests start their day as refreshed as possible is first and foremost an opportunity for building loyalty, return visits and positive word of mouth.

Advanced sleep programs have become quite trendy in the post-pandemic years because there is now a mainstream awareness of the importance of sleep in bodily restoration, immune system support, and overall longevity. Significantly, these programs needn't be overly expensive to execute.

To give you a sense of what to expect for FF&E and SOPs at your own hotel as you investigate the setup of a sleep program, here is what has been deployed at The Benjamin Royal Sonesta:

- Curated pillow menu including anti-snore, buckwheat, cooling cloud, five-foot body cushion, lullaby, satin beauty, Swedish memory, sleep for success side pillow, sleep for success back sleeper and water-filled
- On-demand meditation offering a variety of ten-minute mindfulness or mantra sessions via guestroom phones
- Sleep masks, ear plugs, blackout curtains and noise machines
- Work-down and wake-up calls

The most important takeaway from this list is that the execution of a successful sleep program involves comprehensive additions, blending together room amenities that all guests benefit from such as the blackout curtains as well as the on-demand meditation.

During our interview, we asked about ROI because generally the contributions to gross revenues from wellness additions are difficult to measure. In other words, barring the feedback related to the onsite sleep amenities within Medallia (the CX platform that The Benjamin uses), how do you know that guests find these features to be actually meaningful? How can you directly quantify whether or not someone is booking at the hotel specifically for its sleep amenities?

These are indeed hard questions to answer! The data shows that the Rest & Renew program has meaningful added value for the brand. According to Chapman, the initial sample of feedback has all been positive when asking guests specific questions about the sleep amenities or within sentiment analysis. Based on the success of the program, Sonesta International has partnered with Dr. Rebecca Robbins on other sleep initiatives throughout the brand portfolio.

As an interesting observation, Chapman noted that the periods of highest demand for the curated pillow menu are during holiday weekends when leisure travelers have remarked that they relish the chance to try a pillow they might not get a chance to experience back at home. This anecdote reveals another fundamental hospitality lesson: hotels should strive to be better than home, with sleep programs helping inspire guests to transform their daily habits when they aren't traveling.

But for scrupulous ROI calculations, Chapman said that to get a sleep program off the ground it will always need determined internal champions. Luckily, there are many within Sonesta who prioritize sleep and have applied the Rest & Renew Sleep Program across the entire portfolio as a way to differentiate the brand from competitors and provide guests with a great night's sleep.

And for this reason, it's our hope that you look to hospitality leaders like Simon

Chapman and Sonesta to see where the industry is headed and what else you can do to improve the onsite experience without breaking the bank. Ultimately, if your guests win by getting better sleep, then you will get rewarded with loyal repeat guests and stronger rates.

Sleep-Friendly Hotel Design Always Starts with the Bed

It's said that the average person spends a third of their life in bed, so wouldn't it make sense to optimize this time by getting the best sleep experience possible?

When framed this way, the answer may seem obvious. But most of us don't yet view bedding in the same luxury limelight as cars, clothing or jewelry – goods that we spend far less actual time inhabiting than our beds. But as sleep science gains in popularity, this behavioral gap presents a hugely lucrative opportunity for hotel brands to provide guests with a far better sleeping experience than they would ever dream of getting at home, and then charging appropriately for it.

While the design of a sleep-friendly guestroom can integrate many different features and amenities, we're focusing specifically on the bed because of how fundamental the physical mattress is for everyone's life and thus for the overall hotel experience. No doubt many of you, like the two of us, have suffered from poor sleep at times, so beyond examining the latest advancements in bedding appliances our hope is that this article also inspires you to think more deeply about how you sleep in order to feel refreshed while traveling and at home.

To show you what's possible and to explain the revenue opportunities for enhanced sleep systems at hotels, we interviewed Barry Van Doornewaard, Founder and CEO of FreshBed, the manufacturer of a proprietary *sleep system* with allergy-friendly functionality, active HEPA ventilation, thermoregulation and humidity controls built directly into the bed to profoundly improve the guestroom experience.

Why Sleep Right Now

Looking back at the history of hospitality, the provision of a good night's sleep is nothing new. It is a core facet of hotel operations because, on a deeply emotional level, if a guest does not sleep well at your hotel they are unlikely to return, while your TripAdvisor score may also suffer.

Nor is the notion of upgrading a hotel's guestroom beds a novel concept; just look back at the success of Westin's Heavenly Bed program first introduced in 1999. More recently, *sleep tourism* has become its own thing wherein travelers specifically seek out hotels for their restorative sleep programs. Rosewood Hotels & Resorts has its Alchemy of Sleep experiences; Park Hyatt has debuted a 'sleep suites' product tier; Six Senses offers multi-night sleep wellness packages, Sonesta is rolling out its Rest & Renew Sleep Program brand-wide; and in this particular instance, FreshBed is the supplier for the recently opened RH Guesthouse in the West Village neighborhood of New York.

So, what's the craze all about? Or, more explicitly, why should your hotel brand prioritize an investment in sleep-friendly design and technologically advanced mattresses and bedding appliances ahead of all the other possible ventures out there?

Here are some converging factors:

- *Sleep science* has gone mainstream, with plenty of recent research indicating just how critical good sleep is for bodily restoration, cognition, fat loss and the immune system
- Awareness for the benefits of *sleep efficiency* and high-quality sleep has also gone mainstream, with people of all walks of life now possessing a basic understanding of terms like deep sleep, REM, sleep hygiene, circadian rhythm and melatonin
- Fueling this mainstream awareness is the growth of the wellness and longevity industries, wherein the pursuit of good sleep is a foremost goal to aid in antiaging and overall wellbeing
- The pandemic threw a lot of people off their natural sleep cycles for various reasons, with many now prioritizing healthy *sleep hygiene* in this post-pandemic era of work-life balance while others are more conscious of air purification techniques used by hotel rooms
- Chasing the demand for quality sleep while traveling, many hotels beyond just the few mentioned above have already deployed upgraded *sleep programs*, turning this specific area into an arms race wherein only the cutting edge will now be effective at winning market share

To dwell on the last point about demand, the return on an investment in sleep programming can be broken down as follows:

1. At the base level, ensuring that guests get the best sleep possible protects a hotel brand from guest churn and boosts loyalty
2. A new sleep program can be used as part of a marketing campaign to increase product awareness and drive customer acquisition
3. Given how meaningful quality sleep is for travelers nowadays, room upgrades in this direction can strongly justify increases in nightly rate, either across the board for all guestrooms or by carving out new sleep-friendly room categories that can be packaged, upsold and used in error recovery situations
4. As a central pillar within the broader banner that is wellness, the introduction of an advanced sleep program can help a brand to pivot deeper into the wellness space in order to capitalize upon a series of alternate revenue streams in the future

How Beds Can Improve Sleep Quality

We all know that old mattresses that sag in the middle or have lumps can negatively affect sleep by contorting the body into an uncomfortable position, thereby increasing the time it takes to fall asleep, causing interruptive wakefulness during sleep as the body reorients itself and perpetuating lower back pain. But another aspect influencing sleep quality that isn't as widely understood is the ***bed microclimate*** created from the body's heat between the sheets, the comforter and the mattress.

To explain the issue of room ambient temperature versus the microclimate formed between the sheets and the mattress, Van Doorneward commented, "From a recent study, the European Bedding Industry Association found that the second biggest sleep disorder (52%) is having an improper bed climate, which is most likely to occur when body heat gets trapped by high-thread-count-linens, excess room humidity, plastic covers that prevent ventilation out the sides of mattresses or others. In these cases, as the temperature increases around the sleeper throughout the night, it can lead to restless leg syndrome, perspiration, conscious or unconscious wakeups, and poorer recovery."

"From scientific research, we now know that the ideal bedroom climate for recovery should be relatively cold (between 18C and 22C) and dry (around 50% relative humidity)," continued Van Doorneward. "Innovative sleep systems like FreshBed allow guests to personalize and optimize these two variables under the duvet so that temperature or moisture levels never become disruptive in the middle of the night, while the delivery of HEPA-purified air further enhances sleep quality. Altogether, this can improve sleep quality by up to 50%."

One other critical property of moisture is that water residues allow microbes and dust mites (or even bedbugs!) to flourish on pillows, comforters, duvets and mattresses. This then impacts air quality – and potentially introduces allergens into the environment – around the bed to further weaken sleep. Over the long-term, moisture also hastens the deterioration of the mattress.

Given the positive correlation between enhanced climate control and sleep quality, installing a *smart thermostat* in the room would be a worthwhile first step to bring the guestroom to a cooler, optimal temperature for sleep (and also helping reduce energy costs when the room is unoccupied). But ambient temperature doesn't necessarily help modulate the bed microclimate under all those linens and a thick duvet. More site-specific controls within the bed are needed to market a guarantee of improved sleep to guests successfully.

This precision is what elevates manufacturers like FreshBed from mere beds into sleep systems that can elevate the hotel experience and allow hotels to charge more for that guarantee significantly. Whether linked to the smart thermostat or through another *connected hotel app*, guests can set their own bed temperatures while the silent air purification filters capture microbes and curtail humidity, all to dramatically improve sleep quality and provide more peace of mind to travelers who may not sleep well while abroad. Then, as an added bonus for the hotel, the reduced moisture levels increases the lifespan of the mattress to lower the long-term replacement costs.

Luxury Travelers Prioritize Sleep

There's a reason why luxury hotel brands like some of the ones previously mentioned are starting with the mattress. Yes, contemporary sleep systems come with a higher unit cost, but the argument in favor of implementation always comes back to how central the bed is for guest satisfaction.

You can throw all the bells and whistles at a guest – fancy furnishings, great views, gargantuan room sizes, exquisite F&B, a world-class spa and so on – but everyone sleeps in roughly the same space, and if this experience isn't perceived as restorative then the guest isn't likely to come back.

In this sense, the rise of sleep tourism speaks to a broader change in the mindset of the luxury traveler; it's less about wealth and demography, and more about lifestyle and identity regardless of age or cultural background. For instance, van Doornewaard pointed out that the promotion of FreshBed installations at the RH Guesthouse became an instrumental support for the launch campaign into the crowded market that is New York City as well as for justifying the hotel's $2,200-plus nightly rates.

While the benefits of good sleep are becoming more commonplace, this information is still unevenly distributed, with the luxury traveler more sensitive to its importance. For instance, just think of the risks of getting a bad night's rest for a high earner like a stockbroker or a neurosurgeon. For the financier who relies on as little as a 1% edge over the market, any temporary cognitive drain can cost them immensely, while for the doctor it's potentially a matter of life or death.

For these reasons and many others, the guarantee of getting a proper sleep while traveling is something that people are willing to pay for, and it is an aspect of the guestroom experience that customers are now specifically looking for when selecting their hotels. The pursuit of the best sleep and the bed possible is an arms race that will inevitably seep through all hotels in all market segments, so best to get ahead of the curve while you still can.

Hotel Guestroom Redesign to Help Insomnia Sufferers

Do you currently suffer from insomnia or have previously gone through a period of restless nights? Our hope in writing this is firstly to educate on what causes insomnia so that you can avoid the strain this ailment may cause and secondly to show a possible direction that hotel owners or executives can take to help insomnia sufferers as part of an advanced sleep program.

On the heels of scientific breakthroughs over the past decade to deduce how sleep works and why it's so important for one's health – with a seminal book on the matter in "Why We Sleep" (2017) by Dr. Matthew Walker that is definitely worth the read – hotels around the world have commendably unveiled or upgraded their sleep programs as a key brand differentiator. Especially in urban markets catering to weary-eyed business guests, 'sleep friendly hotels' may soon become its own lifestyle niche.

Following a renovation, guestrooms now include a blend of the various sleep hygiene SOPs such as blackout drapes, circadian lighting, air purifiers, quieter HVACs, sleep-promoting teas, specific minibar products that aid in promoting sleep, sleep-oriented bathroom amenities, eye masks, noise-dampening building materials, pillow selections, smart temperature controls, moisture-controlled mattresses, breathable linens, vitamin-infused showers, on-demand meditation, nighttime stretching instructions, mindfulness apps, use of organic cleaning solvents, all-in-one tablet room controls that integrate all the various sleep tech enhancements or access to onsite sleep specialists.

These sleep programs are both a defensive move to maximize the chances of a good night's rest – which in turn boosts guest satisfaction and loyalty – as well as a proactive one to deepen a brand's association with wellness as a means to distinguish the product from competitors or to justify a higher nightly rate by 'guaranteeing' better sleep.

Insomnia Isn't Bad Sleep Hygiene

A heavy disclaimer at this point: we are not trained medical professionals nor do we have any accreditations related to sleep science. Rather, we are both utterly fascinated with how the mind works, while disparate bouts of insomnia in the past have led our curiosity to intensively research this emerging field. Moreover, understanding some of the mechanisms of insomnia will help you redesign the hotel experience to better help your guests.

While upgrades like the abovementioned ones that promote good sleep hygiene are important for elongating the deep sleep a guest experiences – that is, the part of total time asleep when the body is most active in self-repair and immune system restoration – and boosting sleep efficiency by helping reduce the frequency of brief bouts of nocturnal wakefulness, bad sleep hygiene is not necessarily a core driver of insomnia, whether the effect is difficulty getting to sleep or difficulty staying sleep.

Instead, and irritatingly for those looking for a quick solution to their woes, insomnia is multifaceted condition with numerous instigating causes and perpetuating factors that only the one-on-one work with a psychologist specializing in sleep disorders and chronotype mapping could properly diagnose. In fact, the only regimen that is clinically shown to actually work in correcting insomnia conditions is CBT-I (cognitive behavioral therapy for insomnia). All other practices or products can help but seldom tackle the core drivers.

What we know is that insomnia is a mental disconnect from the natural rhythm of the day that involves feelings of worry, anxiety, rumination, or depression that the brain comes to associate with the act of sleeping, then combined with other considerations that may deprive a person of a proper night's rest.

The ambiguity of direct cause and effect here may be better understood through examples.

1. The initial grief of losing a close relative or a major illness in the family may initiate a series of sleepless nights, while bad sleep hygiene practices and early evening caffeine intake would then prolong this temporary period of stress so much so that the brain's circuitry shifts to no longer favor falling fast asleep upon hitting the mattress, instead identifying the nighttime hours as ones for mental acuity and processing anguish.

2. The near-perpetual stress over one's job security can act as the insomnia spark, while any amount of evening consumption of alcohol to calm the nerves in that moment can both reduce the quality of sleep (alcohol is a sedative, after all) and induce a minor form of obstructive sleep apnea by weakening the muscles of the tongue, altogether prolonging interruptive sleep to the point where the brain rewires itself to believe this disruptive pattern as the norm.
3. Many of us during the work-from-house glut of the pandemic used our beds for sleep, watching television, reading, answering emails, scrolling through the void of social media, attending videoconferencing calls and perhaps even working out. Over time, our brains then came to associate the bed with more than just its two primary purposes (sleep as well as the other 'S'), especially if someone is engaging in high-stress or cognitively straining aspects of their job responsibilities from bed. It's no wonder we presently have so many people in the post-pandemic era complaining about difficulties getting to sleep and, indeed, it's hardly a coincidence that we're witnessing a surge in demand for enhanced guestroom sleep programs.

While the two of us are perpetual fans of all the various upgrades hotels are enacting to proper the most sleep-hygienic guestroom stay imaginable, it's critical to understand that this alone will not reverse insomnia. It will, though, provide 'peace of mind' which will help, and indeed many people sleep better away from their home beds specifically because the mental connection between the stressful home life and trying to drift to sleep is severed by geographic transplantation.

To that end, any and every sleep hygiene upgrade should be on the table, and they should be advertised front and center so that guests can anticipate a calm, quiet night:

- Smart mattresses and bed systems that can control the microclimate
- Breathable, soft, hypoallergenic linens and blankets
- Dedicated pillow concierge for guests to try different firmness levels
- Blackout curtains, often with IoT room controls
- Sound dampening and light-absorbent furnishings and wall materials
- Thermostats that can minimize HVAC noise while lowering the temperature to the ideal range
- Circadian lighting that is intuitively accessible from the nightstand
- Bespoke sleep amenities like herbal teas, facial creams, pillow sprays and sleep masks
- Upgrades to the minibar to include sleep-friendly snacks and calmative beverages

Don't Worry Be Sleepy

While a select few hotel brands have actually hired dedicated specialists to act as onsite sleep coaches who can properly assess sleep disorders, then proscribe CBT-I or other mindfulness methods, this is impractical for most properties given the labor requirements. Instead, brands should focus on providing 'peace of mind' by implementing various sleep hygiene practices into their brand standards, and then marketing them appropriately by telling guests not to worry or be anxious about getting a good night's sleep because the hotel has their back.

As we know that insomnia is largely associated with brain overexcitement or an inability to process lingering thoughts during one's normal waking hours, then we can use this theory to redesign or upgrade a hotel's sleep program with specific features and messaging for insomnia sufferers. Here are a few ideas where it's hardly a one-size-fits-all approach but more about what fits your brand, your target customers, and your budget.

1. *Great lounge chairs.* Without one's home office setup, the temptation to answer emails from bed is far more pronounced, but this can be a death knell for poor sleep while traveling due to the mental association of the bed with work. To decouple this pathway, hotels should promote their comfortable divans or lounge chairs that perfectly serve the transitionary state between wakefulness and sleep. Another aspect of this improved lounge chair would also be a small side table for resting a laptop or notebook as well as an amber-hued portable nightlight (where too often these are now built as bed attachments to thereby prompt working from bed).
2. *No visible alarm clocks.* Waking up in the middle of the night is more common than you are conscious of. But the sight of a clock can cause you to worry about getting enough to be refreshed for that morning's events to the point where you have a cortisol release that inhibits you from falling back asleep – a bit of a self-fulfilling fallacy. The solution here is to install alarm clocks or tablets that have a night mode where the screen is dark and the time is only revealed when the guest touches the screen or a button.
3. *Ergonomic working areas.* Many hotels claim to have office desks in the room, but these are often so dated and uncomfortable that they all drive guests to work from the bed. Correcting this may require a guestroom PIP, or better access to a revitalized business center, living room or club area where guests can focus on working efficiently with access to other amenities like snacks, beverages, printers and auxiliary computer monitors.
4. *Angling the television.* If the TV is bolted to the wall facing the bed then where do you think you are nudging guests to watch TV from? While watching TV from bed is a more passively engaging activity versus writing work emails or texting on the phone, it's nevertheless a trigger for people with sleep issues. Fixing this one is hard in that it may require articulating mounts or repositioning the sofa, but something to consider.
5. *Stimulating environments.* While blue light from screens has been rightfully demonized of late for their ability to disrupt the circadian rhythm, what's even more important to attenuating this cycle with the 24-hour day is

direct access to morning sunlight. While modifying a property's exterior is probably not in the cards, educating on the importance of daytime sunlight exposure and directing guests to quiet places where they can get their daily fix without leaving the environs would be greatly appreciated by future travelers.

6. *Alleviating afternoon tiredness.* While I'm sure the barista at your favorite café may disagree, due to caffeine's average half-life within the body of 12 hours, late afternoon or evening coffee consumption should be strongly avoided in order to maximize sleep quality. Instead, hotels should elsewhere for ways they can help address that midafternoon bout of tiredness we all experience, with options ranging from access to an outdoors setting or a quick walking route to healthy snacks, a greater selection of decaf coffee options and nootropic herbal teas.
7. *Electrolytes.* Of course, poor sleep is associated with bad nutrition. In vogue right now are the various magnesium supplements as well as the classic milk of magnesium, whereby a deficiency in this specific mineral has been widely researched with regard to sleep quality. While sleep is far more than just this particular substance, what's implied here is that hotels looking for a cheap addition to augment their sleep programs might investigate some of those electrolyte pack providers or other sleep-friendly beverage vendors.
8. *Exercise.* Through pure 'sleep inertia', if you exhaust your body during the day by using more calories, it's going to be significantly harder not to feel sleepy come nightfall. Yet, when we're traveling we often do not prioritize exercise or feel as though we have access to the right facilities to keep up with our at-home levels of exertion. Hence, hotels looking to boost their sleep programs would be wise to simultaneously look at their in-home exercise programming as well as the ease of access to the fitness center.
9. *There's an app for that.* Whether it's an app that offers guided mindfulness, meditation or light stretching programs for some evening relaxation, or one focused explicitly on CBT-I or NSDR (non-sleep deep rest) for helping someone process racing thoughts and relieve any anxieties over getting proper sleep, there are software solutions that can be applied to insomnia. While we haven't yet encountered one specifically for obstructive sleep apnea or other interruptive sleep conditions, a hotel could create some on-demand oropharyngeal (that is, tongue muscle) exercises or sketch them onto a piece of cardstock as part of the downturn service.
10. *One-click sleep mode.* While on the topic of integrated tech, modern guest-facing tablet providers can now help hotels set up preset room modes, acting as universal remotes for all the various technologies in place. As it concerns insomnia sufferers, the most critical here would be the goodnight button that simultaneously lowers the curtains, turns the temperature down, silences any noises and dims the lights. Another would be an intermediate evening

mode that sets the lights to a low-intensity amber hue that prepares the mind for sleep.

There's obviously a lot more that hotels can do to help guests naturally drift off to sleep to then wake up feeling both refreshed and fully satisfied with their choice of hotels. But alas, insomnia can take months to propagate and months to course correct, so the best hotels can do is act as centers of inspiration so that guests want to keep coming back.

The key here is crafting your messaging around peace of mind. Insomnia or not, guests are willing to pay extra for some form of guarantee that they will get a good night's sleep. This is a huge opportunity for hotels to boost rate and carve out new product categories. So, do what you can and your customers will inevitably reward you as well as spread the good word about how great a rest they got.

Sleep Architecture as the Central Concept for Sleep Tourism Revenues

With sleep science reaching the mainstream over the past few years, numerous hotel brands have unveiled fancy new sleep programs in an arms race to win over travelers looking for accommodations that will help them get a full night's rest while aboard.

But the rise of sleep tourism needn't be limited to only luxury hotels that have the capital to devote a gargantuan sum per key to noise-dampening materials, new air purification systems or state-of-the-art bedding systems that have built-in temperature and moisture controls. Rather, any brand can build a strategic plan for deploying affordable sleep enhancements to their rooms and their onsite services.

But to be strategic in the true sense of the word, and not just remixing amenities arbitrarily based on what the competition is doing, the most important term to have a base understanding of is 'sleep architecture'.

Lest we forget that it has only been a decade or so that society has started to approach sleep not just as an unconscious and unnecessary aspect of life but as perhaps the most vital period of the 24-hour cycle. This is when the body goes to work on building muscles or restoring other organs, when the immune system is most active to prevent disease propagation, when hyperemotional states are reset to baseline and when memories are transferred from short-term to long-term storage. The latter of these two processes mostly occur during rapid eye movement (REM) sleep while the first two repair pathways largely occur during deep or slow wave sleep (also called non-REM sleep).

Sleep architecture describes the controlling operator in the brain that determines the daily rhythm of when you feel tired when you should wake up, when you should extend the duration of sleep and how to allocate the time you are asleep to REM and non-REM.

As an example, let's say your regular sleep-wake cycle is 10:30 pm to 5:30 am and you had a heavy barbell squats day at the gym. As you're drifting off that night, the brain says to itself, "Okay, we have seven hours here and we did a lot of damage to our musculoskeletal system today, so let's devote more time to slow wave repair at the sacrifice of REM-based memory codification." Bundling a big gym day with lots of important meetings may result in some important information conveyed during those meetings being forgotten because the brain prioritizes non-REM repair tasks.

Once you understand that the architecture of sleep is all about maintaining a rhythm and the allocation of limited resources, you can begin to design some sleep programming for your hotel that is highly personalized, customizable, and more effective – and thus more meaningful and valuable – based on a guest's needs on any particular evening. Here are some ideas to inspire you with what you can do for programming as lensed through the principles of sleep architecture:

1. *Melatonin supplementation.* Ostensibly the most renowned sleep aid and one that's being studied as a longevity supplement, several hotels are now including melatonin-based beverages, low-dose pills or powder additives as part of the minibar or in the sundry. The issue with this supplement is timing; take it too late and in too high a dose (which is very easy to do) then you will likely wake up quite groggy, especially if your sleep rhythm hasn't adjusted to a new time zone. As such, melatonin wouldn't be recommended for someone arriving in the wee hours of the morning and looking for something to settle the nerve before drifting off. Instead, a signature herbal tea with chamomile, passionflower, lemon balm or other natural ingredients will work far better to gently lull you to sleep. Then on the techie side, there are quite a few devices, especially those in the IR (infrared) and PEMF (pulsed electromagnetic field) areas that claim to extend REM and promote deep wave, so that you can maximize whatever your body and mind need after an intense travel day.
2. *Circadian lighting equipment.* It's becoming common knowledge that we should all limit blue light and stick with amber-red wavelengths at night to get a good night's sleep. Sleep architecture tells us the answer in that you have a bodily clock that is sensitive to blue light. A few hotels are keen to meet this need, upgrading their lighting systems with non-overhead, dimmed evening lights as well as ones that can adjust into the red spectrum to set the mood for sleep. A far cheaper amenity is to offer blue light-blocking glasses. Sleep architecture also tells us that these solutions may not do the trick. Suppose your daily rhythm is to wake up at 6 am EDT in Toronto then you head out to Vancouver on a business trip for the week. You eat right, you settle into your room, and you wake up at 3 am PDT. Counterintuitively, to bring your clock back three hours to the West Coast tempo, you may want some softer, balanced yellow light in your room alongside a non-caffeinated energizing tea to extend your bodily clock.
3. *Bedding customization.* When you start regularly tracking your sleep, one of the first things you may discover is that you wake up and move around quite frequently during the night. These can be 'unconscious wakeups' while the latter is often ascribed as a form of 'restless leg syndrome'. The cause of

these can be poor nutrition, stress, acute bodily pain, room temperature, moisture, bad air quality, uncomfortable linens, uncomfortable mattresses, uncomfortable pillows, or any combination of these. What we do know is that these sleep interruptions can negatively affect bodily repair and REM cycling. Enter a host of new-age suppliers ready to help solve these issues. You have uber-expensive mattresses with built-in temperature controls being deployed at luxury hotels. You have pillow concierge services where guests can sample different firmness levels. You have smart thermostats that can better help to keep the ambient temperature at the scientifically preferred 19C. You have more breathable linens. You have materials that don't emit volatile organic compounds (VOCs) and more effective HVACs. Combine these features with sleep tracking wearables and your guests can see the overnight benefit to their health in terms of improved sleep quality scores.

4. *Food menus.* The current heuristic for getting the best possible sleep is the 3-2-1: no food three hours from sleep, no water two hours out and no screens one hour out. By doing this, it means that your blood is never being redirected to your digestive tract to absorb food and can squarely focus on repairing the body during slow-wave sleep. This alone means that in general snacking before bed is bad for the health, but alas, sleep architecture suggests that the answer needs to be individualized. To start, if you regularly snack before bed then this has become a part of your daily blueprint; interrupting this by not snacking when combined with the stressor that is a foreign bedroom can be enough to cause a cortisol or adrenaline release at times when they aren't conducive to falling fast asleep. Given these rhythmic challenges, hotels can best serve varying guest needs by designing sleep-friendly food menus comprised of light, nutrient-dense and easily digestible snacks.

To close, we hope this wasn't too far into the weeds of the science of sleep. This is still an emerging field but as you can see there are numerous applications for our industry. Above all, what we are witnessing is a great societal push for more awareness of the importance of quality sleep, and this will ultimately compel hotels to start designing services and amenities that cater directly to this guest demand. Hence, you best start building a sleep strategy for your hotel and understanding sleep architecture will help to ensure that you develop a highly fruitful plan.

Wellness Floors as a Steppingstone for Enhanced Mixed Use Revenues

The core revenue stream for every hotel brand will always be heads in beds. But increasingly for luxury, premium and upscale properties, a strong reason to visit is required to convince customers to select you versus the competitor. With the OTAs, metasearch, short-term rentals and a litany of other travel resources, guests have near-endless optionality for accommodations. Your hotel must forge a striking identity, with the wellness industry now assuming a central role in a brand's strategy for attracting guests and commanding above-market rates.

Not just as a reason to visit to feed the rooms revenue ledger, the sheer broadness and flexibility of the term 'wellness' allows nearly any brand to play in the space. Within the word's comprehensive definition as products or services that enhance an individual's health or well-being, there are applications for traditional spas, the guestroom, F&B, M&E and activities. As such, having a long-term wellness strategy is critical for TRevPAR growth (revenue per guest including all ancillary spend) as well as that of a hotel's overall profitability mix and asset valuation.

What we're seeing as a trend within this trend is the proliferation of the concept of 'wellness floors'. Another term with some ambiguity, two main categories can comprise said floors, and it's up to you to decide which has the most feasibility for your brand, your property and your capital budget.

The first definition of a wellness floor is a straightforward rebranding of the spa. The traditional 'spa' connotes massages, facials, manicures, pedicures, treatments, sequences of different treatments (now commonly called rituals) and a calming atmosphere with high-end finishings. While guests still want those services, a wellness floor can incorporate whatever the owner or designer fancies and any number of the latest health crazes. Moreover, such upgrades can help to sell day passes to locals to further bolster the revenue mix.

Mineral bathing, contrast therapy and sauna circuits are in vogue right now, so a renovation can look to build out some cold plunges, ice baths, steam rooms, halotherapy (salt) rooms, infrared saunas or even cryo chambers. And speaking of advanced treatments like spending three minutes in a -150C tube, there's also hyperbaric oxygen treatment (HBOT), cyclic variations in adaptive conditioning (CVAC) systems, deprivation tanks, soundscapes, neuro-acoustics and lots more ways to awe guests with the latest sci-fi devices.

Wellness can also mean fitness, with hotels spending a pretty penny for state-of-the-art exercise equipment as well as looking for yoga, breathwork or dynamic movement practitioners who can lead group classes or provide guidance on in-room workout programming for guests who may not have time to hit the gym. Finally, wellness most certainly means food, with many of these redesigned floors also including a bespoke food outlet with a health-conscious menu likely centered around more informal dining and plant-based items that don't require a full kitchen to prepare.

To cover off the next key pillar of well-being – sleep – brings us to the guestroom and the second category of defining a wellness floor. Like the club floor concept, this is when a hotel upgrades one or two guestroom floors specifically as wellness-oriented inventory as a means of introducing another product tier for enhanced packaging, upselling and rewards.

We highlight sleep because that's where most hotels are realizing the most traction with these single-floor or single-section renovations. Think temperature-controlled beds, circadian lighting, a pillow concierge, your choice of breathable linens, blackout curtains, noise-dampening materials, branded eye masks, enhanced bathroom amenities, vitamin-infused showers, air purifiers, access to sleep tracking tech, sleep-inducing stretching routines on the TV, sleep-promoting turndown services, and custom herbal tea blends with ingredients like chamomile or passionflower.

Wellness floors need not be themed solely around sleep, though. Hilton's Five Feet from Fitness and IHG's EVEN Hotels, amongst others, have both tapped into a lucrative niche by designing exercise-centric rooms alongside a myriad of other onsite services for the traveler who wants to maintain their at-home fitness routines but may not necessarily have the time for a full gym session. Even more niche, you can outfit certain room stock ahead of arrival with heightened F&B such as wellness-oriented minibars, elaborate coffee service, on-demand supplements or all the requirements for a multiday juicing detox.

So, whether it's a spa wellness floor renovation, a guestroom wellness floor renovation or a full-scale PIP that factors in both, the point herein is that there's lots of territory for any brand – even those more firmly in the midscale or economy segments – to deploy some wellness-oriented amenities to support rooms revenues or help diversify incomes away from strictly heads in beds.

Which path do we recommend? That depends entirely on your brand vision. But because each brand is different and because wellness can be many different things to different people, when done right your hotel can realize tremendous success from this burgeoning industry.

The New Frontier of Integrated Welltech for Hotels

Every industry has its jargon and its acronyms. For hotel technologists, this is the PMS, CRS, POS, IBE, CRM, BI, AI, ML, PCI, as well as financial KPIs to monitor like GOPPAR, GSS or CPOR. While useful as heuristics for discussing business challenges, over time such technical details can unknowingly narrow one's focus to the point where it limits one's appreciation for concurrent trends in other industries. Specifically for our purposes today, when hoteliers hear the word 'technology', they may conjure images of the abovementioned alphabet soup, and yet there's a whole other parallel world of spa ('spatech'), fitness ('fittech') and wellness technologies ('welltech') that are just waiting for hotels to take notice.

Why notice? Cite whatever stat and the story is the same: the wellness industry is booming. As one tool in the trade to capitalize on this growth, welltech nevertheless has capex considerations but also the promise of sizable ROI.

Framing this from the macro before getting to the micro, what you should know for this megatrend is that the rate of medical research discoveries is compounding (especially now with the help of artificial intelligence) and these findings about how to spot bodily irregularities or improve one's health are slowly but surely disseminating into the public sphere. This process is occurring both with people of all ages or dispositions who are opting for healthier lifestyles as well as through entrepreneurs who are introducing new wellness products in order to serve this ever-increasing wellness market.

With many of these new products and companies opting for a direct-to-consumer business model, our homes are destined to become 'high-tech health hubs'. The challenge therein that hotels face is straightforward: as one does at home, one will expect at their chosen accommodation.

While it may be easy to shrug this off as a topic of concern for those brands and executives solely focused on the spa or spatech spaces, lest we forget the technology adoption life cycle which compels new trends, styles and habits to naturally but inevitably shift from niche (dedicated spa goers or wellness junkies) and luxury (early adopters with lots of disposable cash) to all other categories as economies of scale and induced demand work their magic.

Even as we must contend with the burgeoning marketplace for welltech, the hospitality industry is already derided for being a tech laggard – unfairly so, in our opinion, given the complexities of managing a live property's tech stack. Yet now, with the proliferation of all these fancy smart furnishings and devices available at home, hotels that don't have a wellness strategy will be lag even further behind as consumers start voting with their wallets for health-oriented lodging brands.

Another essential element for figuring out how to incorporate welltech in hotels pertains to how many of these tools can be scaled in a labor-light manner. There's spatech that can be assembled in a treatment room for a 'set it and forget it' guest experience; of course, there are wellness apps with minimal unit economics; and there are handheld or wearable equipment that can be made as an in-room brand standard or upsold rentable.

So, what kinds of welltech are consumers looking for? As technology now pervades all things, this term 'welltech' is quite the umbrella for anything and everything like:

- *D2C apps.* Offering various health tracking, nutrition, mindfulness and wellbeing functionalities
- *Club management.* On the B2B software side, it goes without saying that advances are being made in the systems that ensure operations proceed smoothly, with AI now being embedded to drive staff and equipment efficiencies
- *Cosmetics.* Leveraging the latest research and technology in health-promoting ingredient purity, stability and bioactivation to produce high quality serums, creams and also fragrances to tap into the aromatherapy wellness niche
- *Supplements.* Still the Wild West in terms of regulation and precision, new brands are emerging that emphasize good manufacturing processes for the latest in vogue longevity pills
- *Light therapy devices.* Whether handheld, wearable or mounted, running the range of infrared and red light therapy through to sad lamps and IoT circadian room lighting
- *Hydrotherapy machinery.* Applicable more so as spatech but nevertheless a consideration as part of a total sensory activation for a new wellness program

- *Soundscapes.* Yet more sensorial experiences that can run the gamut of curated environmental music through to binaural beats and neuroacoustics
- *Biophilic design.* Hinging on the conceit that being in nature promotes good moods, hotels now have more live plants, living walls and artificial or digital greenscapes, yet all this still relies on BOH maintenance and energy management systems
- *All things fitness.* This banner can include new types of machinery to enhance exercise in various ways, handheld fitness devices, muscle recovery products and mobility tracking apps
- *Massage devices.* With some fittech overlap, this can be chairs, handheld massage guns, compression suits that amplify lymphatic drainage or even vibration plates
- *Sleep tech.* Whether that's cooling mattresses, bedside air purifiers, sound plates underneath the mattress or wearables that monitor your sleep
- *Body scans.* Whether looking at muscular imbalances, fat disposition, bone density (DEXA) or movement mechanics, a lot of personalized health advice can be driven by scanning the body
- *Diagnostics.* Whether from drawing blood to look at one's epigenetics and multicancer early detection (MCED) or evaluating one's gut microbiome from a stool sample, hotels can play a key role in introducing guests to the incredible world of preventative health screening

From that quick list alone, you should at least get a sense of how big the world of welltech is. But no matter what device, app or six-figure spatech equipment you purchase, all of it still relies on the core hotel tech stack for effective commercialization.

Some technology questions to consider as you refine your wellness strategy:

1. How are you marketing and packaging these new amenities?
2. Can you merchandise these wellness activations as prearrival upselling offers, on-prem purchases via the hotel app, or other stages of the guest journey?
3. How will you use your wellness offers to encourage brand loyalty and return visits?
4. Operationally speaking, for handheld device rentals, how do you manage inventory, delivery, cleaning and attachments to the guest folio?
5. For consumables like supplements or cosmetics, do they work with your procurement systems?
6. To help make your branded app a one-stop shop, can partnered wellness apps integrate for frictionless guest access?
7. How can you use your existing market intelligence data feeds to spot upticks in wellness travel consumption as well as segment your wellness-primary and wellness-secondary guests?
8. Are you able to map the ROI of your wellness investments through a long-term total revenue metric such as customer lifetime value?

As you can see from these eight questions, for this new frontier of welltech at hotels, it all still relies on your core stack to make any programming a financial success. Knowing that the opportunities out there are quite lucrative for early adopters in this area, what we advise is that you start by learning the jargon.

There's a ton in the welltech lexicon and also in the theory behind how all these devices and diagnostics work, so it won't happen in a day. Once familiar, you'll then have a better grasp of what's required from your traditional hotel technologies to guide your technology investments so that whichever wellness applications you deploy are a resounding success.

A Framework for the Wild World of Welltech

When it comes to hotel wellness, we often start with the total addressable market (TAM) to get people's attention. As of 2022, the Global Wellness Institute estimated the global wellness economy at $5.6 trillion, with an 8.6% CAGR to reach $8.5 trillion in 2027. That's a tremendous opportunity and huge growth, all stemming from many personal factors that can be summarized in the phrase, "If you don't make time for your wellness, you will be forced to content with your illness." That is, consumers are voting with their wallets for healthier lifestyles, and as they do at home they will expect from hotels.

Wellness Relies on IT

Where this intersects with hotel technology is that, first and foremost, any and all wellness programming must now be operationalized in a labor-efficient manner, and then merchandized effectively across the entire guest journey in order to generate throughput and profitability. Connected systems and centralized data are thus the engine that powers the wellness experiences that hotels can offer onset.

Before getting into the wellness technology (welltech) applications, here are some more specific ways where IT professionals become essential for commercializing hotel wellness going forward:

- Using marketing systems that can seamlessly merchandize wellness offers or experiences within the prebooking, prearrival, onsite and post-departure stages
- Configuring APIs, a CDP or RPA to increase the data connections so that you can better segment or target your loyalty guest pool with news or offers related to wellness
- Smart staff scheduling to enable flexible shifts and personalized service delivery as well as learning management systems for faster onboarding
- Task automation so that the spa therapists or other wellness practitioners can focus on the guest
- Investigating machine learning or related tools that provide features like multivariate testing, dynamic availability, sentiment analysis itinerary builders or one-to-one marketing offers

What we would also stress with any strategic discussions about wellness is that this area can provide a strong 'reason to visit' for a property that will induce more demand for overnight stays. Tracking this reason to visit nowadays means having strong analysis and reporting tools so that you can examine metrics like TRevPAR, ADR, direct booking share, LOS and lead time pace to see how this ancillary programming is actually performing and supporting the bottom line.

Welltech as Innovative Labor-Light Experiences

Let us first say that the most important element of wellness is (and will remain as such for quite some time) touch. That is, the emotional rapport that's built between the guest and the staff, which for wellness is most likely to occur within the spa.

The problem, however, is that great spa professionals are in short supply. Hence, the advent of welltech, in all its various forms, presents hotels with a way to augment their wellness footprints in a scalable way that's largely untethered by the traditional requirement to staff up. Welltech can therefore present itself as 'set it and forget it' spa technologies (spatech), items in the guestroom that promote better sleep (sleeptech), electronically-enhanced gym equipment (fittech) and advanced diagnostic machinery that can tell guests more about their genetic or epigenetic makeups. (foodtech can also be included here, but that's a whole other can of worms!)

Spatech in Focus

Focusing specifically on spatech, this obviously pertains mostly to those hotels that already have a spa or wellness center. While it may be possible for resorts with some available land to build out a new facility (with the right capex and municipal approvals in place), this is orders of magnitude harder for an urban property to do. Nevertheless, spatech may work to round out other traditional spa treatments or thermal bathing experiences, as well as also present an opportunity for converting a no-longer-viable space like a retail outlet or a tucked-away business center.

To start, know that there are dozens of great spatech suppliers, but the machinery that lets a spa practitioner set a guest up then be largely hands-off for the next 20-30 minutes can come with a hefty price tag. In that sense, what we advise is to focus first on the senses to create themed experiences for guests. The most well-practiced application here would be to look for ways to augment a contrast therapy-focused spa (thermal bathing, sauna, salt room, experiential showers, ice baths, snow rooms) with an infrared (IR) sauna or pod and IR-heated loungers or relaxation chairs. Related to this, while cold exposure is increasingly being cited as beneficial for the body, cryotanks and cryofacials require training and direct staff interactions (for safety reasons at least).

If we dwell on the use of light wavelengths for a moment, IR is but one range that can be used to help guests feel better as part of an add-on experience. Red light therapy (RLT) has been used for pods or blankets, or for handhelds and wearables that can also be put in the guestroom. And if you're looking for something even more sci-fi, non-thermal laser (NTL) has promising results for more medical treatments.

Circling back to the senses, beyond light and cold, there's sound in the form of meditation pods, binaural beats that can be added into other experiences and gravity wave equipment, while cycling air pressure or oxygen concentrations in the air (CVAC and HBOT) present emerging applications to offer guests welltech treatments that are both cutting edge and effective.

Sleeptech as the Foundation

Within the longevity community, the evidence is increasingly pointing to sleep as the foundation of bodily health. Without high-quality sleep, our moods deteriorate, our cognition suffers, our immune systems are weakened and weight loss becomes increasingly harder. We all know this to some extent, and yet traveling often leads to disrupted sleep rhythms (especially when jumping continents).

This has led to the rise of sleep tourism, and indeed for every property the incorporation of sleeptech presents a relatively efficient way to help guests get a better night's rest. After all, only some people will use the spa, but every hotel guest wants good sleep. For this reason, while sleep is at the core of one's wellbeing, for hotel brands it's also an opportunity that's evergreen ("Everdream?" We joke…).

What hotels can do to formulate their sleep programming is to start by looking at each of the elements that influence quality sleep hygiene. For climate, you want noiseless HVACs with advanced filtration for cleaner air, in addition to smarter controls so that the ambient temperature can be attuned to optimal levels for slow wave then REM sleep cycles. Next, we return once more to lighting wherein the overhead LEDs are often laden with blue light that tells the body that it's daytime. Cove or low-positioned, softer lighting helps from a design standpoint, while the gold standard is to switch to circadian-adjusted bulbs that can transition to red-amber to imitate sunset and the onset of sleep. While discussing design, other factors may include motion-activated lighting around the bedframe so that no overnight lights need be turned on during nocturia events. Even something as simple as having blue light-blocking glasses available shows that you care.

Getting more advanced, beds are no longer just mattresses but full-on bedding systems. Many of the leading manufacturers can now include temperature and moisture controls as well as built-in air filters to remove carbon or dust particles. Wearables in the form of wristbands and smart rings are also now in vogue as they can provide great data for guests on factors involved with sleep architecture such as blood oxygenation levels, wakefulness after sleep onset (WASO) and heart rate variability (HRV). Finally, for activating other senses in a positive, sleep-enhancing way, think gravity wave installations under the mattress, calming soundscapes or vitamin-infused showers.

Then All the FitTech

As you might already be able to tell, welltech is indeed a wild world insofar as all the various options and vendors for those options that you have at your disposal, from gargantuan machines in your spa through to the apps and smaller devices that guests can rent or are packaged into offers. There's a bit of shopper's paralysis, and that's why we built the framework around hotel system connections, then sleeptech and spatech. Those are the best places to start for building out a plan for using technology to enhance your revenues from wellness over the next five years. Nevertheless, it's a wild world, and to round out the conversation of areas you can investigate, let's touch on the aforementioned diagnostics, fittech, foodtech.

For fittech, the primary step before evaluating your options is to think of your fitness center as a reason to visit rather than checking the box. How can you uplevel this amenity so that it is a brand differentiator? You can look at state-of-the-art machinery to complement the classic gym setup of dumbbells, strength trainers, and cardio machines with your choice of isometrics, isotonic, or off-balance trainers. But as any fitness brat well knows, recovery is just as important as the workout itself, with a whole new breed of massage guns, vibration plates, compression pants, RLT wraps or cold packs to help you reduce the chance of joint injury or muscle strain – all of these can be packaged or made rentable.

And for when it comes to mobility-related issues, one emerging area to look at might be augmented reality (AR) movement tracking, gait analysis and sports analysis to offer personalized corrections either alongside a trainer or independent of one. Finally, mobility issues via muscle imbalances along with body fat composition and bone density can be diagnosed using scanners like the dual energy x-ray absorptiometry (DEXA) for more precise suggestions.

And Ending with Revenues from Diagnostics

This last point about DEXA brings us to diagnostics, which is a domain where hotels can realize huge gains by cluing guests into their genetic and epigenetic (which genes are turned on and off) makeups in order to help them adjust habits back at home as well as to augment the rest of the guest stay. If there's a biomarker, there's a test you can take to know more about yourself. Significantly, people are willing to travel to specific destinations and pay for elaborate multi-night packages that incorporate these sorts of screenings along with consultations or personalized recommendations.

For instance, the field of nutrigenomics looks into factors like the people who specific lack a gene that facilitates the efficient absorption of vitamin B12 into the body, implying that said individuals would benefit from B12 IV therapy or sublingual tablets. One may glean this from a test at a regular clinic or one purchased off the internet, but hotels can also help customers discover these sorts of bioindividual characteristics that can impact their long-term health.

Yet other longevity-clinic-in-a-hotel setups are offering gut microbiome assessments that can have implications as profound as those uncovered by genomic sequencing. An example here would be that only roughly half of all people have the right bacteria to convert the beneficial ellagic acid in pomegranate seeds into the postbiotic urolithin A that's being studied as a strong mitochondrial booster, indicating that those people without this specific strain would benefit from urolithin A supplementation.

Hormone blood panels can also inform hormone replacement therapy (HRT) alongside peptide treatments – both of which are becoming popular offerings at high-end resorts building out clinics. Next, epigenetic clock tests can give a good baseline for how lifestyle factors are impacting a person's longevity over time. Key here is that one biological clock test is fine, but taking one repetitively year over year will help to keep people on track with their health goals.

After all, you can only manage what you measure, and what better way to manage it than to go on an annual retreat as a check-up in an idyllic location? For the last time, it's a wild world, but there's a method to the madness. Luxury hotels around the world are already building programs that help guests discover their own bodies to improve their wellbeing…and they're charging thousands of dollars per night for these experiences. What we're suggesting is that every hotel can play at this game; it's just a matter of theming your approach and have a strategic vision.

The Five Freebies of Wellness and Where Hotel Tech Fits In

One core thesis we have for the future of hotels is that wellness as a profit center will come to equal or exceed room revenue. So, what can your hotel do to start up a wellness vertical that continuously improves upon itself with a healthy rate of return?

We've closely examined the mountains of nutritional, pharmaceutical, psychological, exercise, sleep, meditation, and longevity science to see what programs will work for any property or brand based on its category, location, available capital, and business objectives, then compiled these principles into a list of the "five freebies of wellness." By studying these techniques, hoteliers can see which ones will add value to their brand and best motivate guests to buy. As you'll see, all of this rests on technology – to increase KYC ('know your customer') and guide brand initiatives; to automate basic tasks so that your team actually has time to figure all this out; and to decide what wellness apps or devices to deploy.

The Five Freebies of Wellness

There's lots of information out there about what to eat, supplements to take, exercises to do and so on. From our own exploration, we've identified five major groupings of activities that are zero-cost and are based on the interconnected parts of the body that these aim to bolster.

1. *Muscles, Bones, Ligaments & Tendons.* Planks, pushups, sit-ups, pullups in the park, HIIT, sprint drills, stairs drills, plyometrics, isometrics, yoga, stretching and any other bodyweight exercises
2. *Circulation, Heart, Lungs and Other Blood-Healing Organs.* Intensive heat exposure, cold showers, low-intensity cardio, long walks while maintaining proper posture, gardening, nasal breathwork, breath hold exercises and even laughter therapy

3. *Digestive Tract.* Herbal tonics or juices and intermittent fasting whether it's an 8:16, a 5:2, one meal a day, protein cycling or a proper multiday abstinence
4. *Skin (considered the largest organ in your body by weight).* Suntanning (but not sunburning…there's a difference), sweating, face yoga or stretching
5. *Brain, Spirit & Other Endocrine Organs.* Meditation, CBT, mindfulness, breathwork, socializing in person, grounding (also known as earthing), forest bathing, being near water, periodic caffeine withdrawal and digital detoxing (especially from social media or the news)

But with numerous freebies at everyone's disposal, why aren't all of us doing them consistently?

Why Wellness Rests on Tech

The main reason why we aren't engaging in these freebies on a daily basis is because we're busy. The limiting factors in our lives are always time and attention, and thus we compromise.

But something changes when we travel. Our routines are interrupted; we're more open to trying something new. Hence, the two of us propose that hotel guests will increasingly be looking for their chosen hotels to provide wellness amenities baked into the nightly rate and as add-on experiences.

With so many different forms of wellness and health-promoting projects to choose from, technology is what will tell you where to apply capital and what can be deployed at scale without a proportional increase in demands on labor. Here are some ideas where tech will become instrumental in this process:

- *Unified guest profiles.* The consolidation of siloed guest data is the lynchpin of all future services, amenities and programming that you create. These can be built within the PMS or CRS, or fed into a CRM or BI platform using a CDP and direct interfaces. Only once you have this connected can you start asking questions and getting prescriptive answers. As a basic example, by building a good bridge between the restaurant POS and PMS, you will not only know what percentage of hotel guests dined at your restaurant but also who opted for the healthier menu options. If you notice an update in the latter, it can help guide menu expansions and packaging creation.
- *Upselling platforms.* While the core driver for bookings will likely remain for most hotels as the location, nightly rate, room availability, distribution and value-added promotions, many guests will nevertheless be primed to purchase additional services from their chosen hotels in the weeks and days before arrival. How will your incoming guests know what's available at the exact time when they are ready to buy? Cross-selling tools like well-configured prearrival emails and guest communication platforms that can push notices to SMS or texting apps can ensure that customers receive your

upselling messaging through the medium they prefer. Moreover, testing within these systems will allow you to refine your approach by giving you more data on the conversion funnel. What lead time from the arrival date generates the most clicks on our prearrival cross-selling email? What channel, whether email or WhatsApp, generates the most conversions for additional service purchases?

- *Staffing and dynamic availability.* Whether it's yoga, guided meditation or one-on-one consultations, a critical step is the automation of any practitioner's hours with the portal that guests book through. Most hotels simply don't have the bandwidth to manually herd all these third parties then, through double entry, offer this time-based inventory to guests through an online booking engine (that hopefully can also seamlessly charge to the reservation folio) so that they can complete a purchase without having to get a spa receptionist on the phone. Next comes 'dynamic availability' which is also critical whereby you use intelligent tools to recommend what days of the week and times of day you should offer specific treatments or classes. The idea here is profit maximization for spa services (you don't want a loss leader manicure eating up a primetime Saturday afternoon timeslot when you could sell that for a couples massage) as well as making informed decisions about when your guests would be most receptive to buying said service (scheduling a yoga class for 10am on Saturday is very different than 10am on Wednesday).
- *Profiting from the five freebies.* Guests want inspiration and this alone means you can set services and amenities that can either be sold or baked into the nightly price in order to drive ADR growth. For muscles, think bespoke in-room exercise programming that connects to custom classes through an interactive TV. For circulation, you could build a new wellness center with an infrared sauna and ice plunge tank, but something simpler would be a breathwork module built into your hotel app that can interact with an in-room IoT device to keep guests on track. For the mind, guided meditation apps abound while sensory deprivation tanks and sound therapy chambers are both reaching the mainstream. There's so much you can do in each area!

It's All About Data Plumbing

While there are many possibilities for paid-for wellness programming based solely on the five freebies—in the restaurant, in the guestroom, in the spa, advanced medical machinery, or on demand throughout the property—it all comes back to the 'data plumbing'.

For instance, it's a lot of work to set up something as simple as a yoga class. You need to find an instructor, secure their timeslots on an ongoing basis, block off a classroom space, itemize the required equipment, and complete any necessary renovations. But all that will be meaningless if the classes aren't visible to incoming guests, aren't easily bookable or don't align with your primary guest profiles. The systems and the plumbing between them are what will make your wellness programs sing.

Hence, the first step is to build these data connections. Once you know your guests (KYC), you can personalize the marketing delivery then test and tweak your way to profitability.

Wellness Revenues for Any Hotel Brand Starts with Tech

60-word summary: Wellness is an incredibly lucrative profit vehicle for hotels in any category with many different types of amenities and packageable offerings available to fit your brand. The issue is labor, wherein many of these wellness activations require lots of staffing to oversee. However, get a grip on your tech stack and automations will lay the foundation for success.

Wellness is now at the forefront both as a back-of-house means to retain talent and for the front of house as a way to support higher rates or grow ancillary spend. For this article, the focus is on the latter of these two as our thesis is that wellness as a profit center will come to rival the rooms ledger for many brands. But in order to activate new programming and support it with continuous improvement, a solid tech foundation has to be there first.

Why Wellness Now?

While 'wellness' itself is quite an ambiguous and omnibus term, that also means there are elements within wellness that can work for any category.

Just consider a few of your options:

- Health-conscious cuisine, herbal teas and antiaging supplements
- Traditional spa treatments like massage, facials or acupuncture
- On-demand, in-room fitness or stretching programming
- Guestroom sleep programs with circadian lighting and smart beds or pillows
- Yoga, meditation or breathwork classes and other forms of group mindfulness
- Guided intermittent fasting regimens and water or juice detoxing
- Contrast therapy with saunas, hot tubs, ice baths, cryotubes or hyperbaric chambers
- Forest bathing, self-guided hikes and all manner of exploring the great outdoors
- Light and sound therapy involving near-infrared exposure or sensory deprivation tanks
- Cacao ceremonies and using borderline-legal psychedelics like psilocybin or ayahuasca
- Physiotherapy and other one-on-one functional restoration sessions
- Educational experiences like culinary or aromatherapy classes
- Genome analysis with one-on-one nutritional and chronotype advice
- Onsite counseling for blood work, epigenetic testing or microbiome analysis

Indeed, there's lots of space to play within, but why now specifically? For this there are a variety of factors all converging over the next few years.

While the two of us would write a whole other longform essay on these that brings in OECD statistics, for your concentration's sake, here's another list:

1. Awareness for at-home wellness boomed during the pandemic lockdowns and people are looking to persist with these lifestyle adjustments
2. The rise and persistence of remote work means that people have gotten off the proverbial hamster wheel, with a newfound pursuit for a healthier work-life balance leading to more demand for products that help this balance
3. The medical research around longevity and what causes aging is accelerating in both its findings and its acceptance amongst mainstream practitioners, thereby increasing the supply side of clinicians, dietitians and all manner of personnel who can fulfill wellness roles at hotels
4. Baby boomers are both entering retirement in droves and starting to experience chronic illnesses, making them a demographic primed for wellness products and medical tourism
5. With their more malleable brains, the younger generations (Y and Z) are increasingly foregoing 20th century mainstays like excessive drinking, cigarettes, lots of refined sugar and deep-fried foods that are proven to be key aging factors
6. Corporations are pushing for more employee wellness and mental health programming in order to retain talent, thereby helping feed the market for corporate retreats or wellness-oriented ancillary spend budgets for business travelers
7. As all these abovementioned factors work concomitantly to raise both the supply and demand sides, it democratizes the pricing for numerous wellness products, acting as a positive feedback loop on awareness and demand

But What About Staffing?

Okay, we've identified the diverse range of programming a hotel brand can potentially undertake, as well as some broad, global factors that justify their setup. But because many of these are high touch by their nature, who is going to administer and render all these services?

Concurrent to the seven identified macroeconomic forces, we can also confidently say that the labor challenges the hospitality industry is facing right now aren't going away any time soon. Hence, why would a hotel executive even consider ramping up wellness product offerings when they are having trouble cleaning rooms to put more heads in beds?

This is the core question because it not only affects frontline teams earning hourly wages but also salaried managers. On the administration side, many hotels don't have the 'bandwidth' in terms of executives will time to spare to formulate what the wellness program would look like, let alone operationalize it within SOPs and training.

And yet, if hotels don't innovate within the wellness space, they are not only missing out on this astoundingly lucrative vertical, but it may also compromise future brand positioning. That is, given the rising demand for travel wellness offerings and amenities, not evolving the brand in this aspect means that nightly rates may be commoditized because there's no meaningful 'reason to visit' one property versus another.

The Solution to Wellness Is Technology

Much like the great strides that hotels made to modernize their tech stacks during the early phases of the pandemic, more is still needed to both automate the monotonous, coordination tasks that associates are currently performing as well as free up managers' time to focus on the planning, implementation and continuous improvements of any wellness programming. In this sense, it's all about time management so that you can more adroitly redeploy existing resources to new tasks.

Within this, however, is another fundamental goal that we call 'data plumping' or the establishment of rich system integrations to help clean and structure all guest data across multiple profit centers into one centralized storehouse. Once you do this, you will then have profound insights on your existing customers so that you can more accurately predict what new product offerings will be measurably productive insofar as generating more loyalty, more ancillary spend or more awareness.

On this note, we leave you with four general ideas for how and where tech will become instrumental for the development of a profitable wellness arm to your hotel brand:

1. *Unified Guest Profiles.* The consolidation of siloed guest data is the lynchpin of all future services, amenities and programming that you create. These can be built within the PMS or CRS, or fed into a CRM or BI platform using a CDP and direct interfaces. Only once you have all these siloed systems connected can you start asking questions and getting prescriptive answers according to KYC (know your customer). The game here is to more accurately assess what guest segments spend the most onsite and what they are already spending the most on. As a basic example, by building a good bridge between the restaurant POS and PMS, you will not only know what percentage of hotel guests dined at your restaurant but also who opted for the healthier menu options. If you notice an update in the latter, it can help guide menu expansions and packaging creation.
2. *Upselling Platforms.* While the core driver for your brand's bookings will likely remain for most hotels as the location, nightly rate, room availability, distribution and value-added promotions, many guests will nevertheless be primed to purchase additional services from their chosen hotels in the weeks and days before arrival. Thinking contextually, how will your incoming guests know what's available at the exact time when they are ready to

buy? Cross-selling tools like well-configured prearrival emails and guest communication platforms that can push notices to SMS or texting apps can ensure that customers receive your upselling messaging through the medium they prefer. Moreover, testing within these systems will allow you to refine your approach by giving you more data on the conversion funnel. What lead time from the arrival date generates the most clicks on our prearrival cross-selling email? What channel, whether email or WhatsApp, generates the most conversions for additional service purchases?

3. *Dynamic Availability.* Whether it's yoga, guided meditation or one-on-one consultations, as stated above a critical step is the automation of any practitioner's hours with the portal that guests book through. Most hotels simply don't have the bandwidth to manually herd all these third parties then, through double entry, offer this time-based inventory to guests through an online booking engine (that hopefully can also seamlessly charge to the reservation folio) so that they can complete a purchase without having to get a spa receptionist on the phone. Then comes 'dynamic availability' wherein you use intelligent tools to recommend what days of the week and times of day you should offer specific treatments or classes. The idea here is profit maximization for spa services – for example, you don't want a loss leader manicure eating up a primetime Saturday afternoon timeslot when you could sell that for a couples massage – as well as making informed decisions about when your guests would be most receptive to buying said service – for example, scheduling a yoga class for 10am on Saturday is very different than 10am on Wednesday).
4. *Inspirational Transformation.* Guests want inspiration from their chosen hotels so that they can 'transform' their own habits back at home, and this alone means you can set services and amenities that can either be sold or baked into the nightly price in order to drive ADR growth. For a tech-centric exercise example, think bespoke in-room exercise programming that connects to custom classes through an interactive TV. Already mentioned, you could build a new wellness center with an infrared sauna and ice plunge tank (big capex and staffing requirements for safety), but something simpler would be a breathwork module built into your hotel app that can interact with an in-room IoT device to keep guests on track. Finally, to grow within the now-popular mindfulness space, guided meditation apps abound while sensory deprivation tanks and sound therapy chambers (two more expensive yet techy options) are both reaching the mainstream.

Medical Tourism as the Next Evolution for Wellness

Let's look ahead at the large-scale demographic shifts as generations get older and are supplanted by younger cohorts. What emerging trends will define travel for the decade ahead?

Hoteliers are well-aware that we are now living in the 'experience economy' whereby, unlike the more materialistic age of decades past, consumers define their identities and their journeys on this planet by the places they visit, the activities they partake in and the events they attend. The experience economy will be reflected by an undercurrent of 'traveling with purpose'. Instead of whimsically going for the sake of going, guests of all types and segments will preplan and build an itinerary with specific goals in mind and not leaving anything to chance.

The question then is: for what express purpose will guests stay at your hotel? Every hotel can, and should, have a different answer.

And while there are innumerous answers to this question – all of which can present lucrative revenue opportunities if the execution is great – it's too much for one article to cover. So, let's focus the conversation on 'wellness' – that is, properties aiming to distinguish themselves by offering a place for visitors improve their physical, mental or spiritual health.

If we look at how wellness has evolved over the past century, it started with the spa, which could either be utilized as a way to build adjunctive revenues for the hotel (customers book rooms then opt for a spa appointment to fill their day) or a reason in its own right to visit the property then haloing back onto room reservations (people want to visit the spa and book a guestroom in order to experience it).

As the concept of the spa gained steam (both metaphorically and literally), individual hotels had to further upgrade their programs in the face of heightened worldwide competition. This was done through such initiatives as more elaborate treatments, healthy food and beverage offerings or partnerships with local, organic product purveyors.

Success breeds more competition, and the cycle begins anew. In pursuit of unique approaches to the market, hotels and resorts have sought out all manner of treatments, products and devices that will allow people to feel rejuvenated, uplifted or even healed from an ailment. With the coming evolution of health technologies, it's again time for hotels and resorts reinvent their wellness programs in order to stay ahead of the curve and keep the guests coming.

The Decade Ahead

What's different now is that there are several remarkable medical advancements that are reaching a point of maturation and economies of scale to thus make them accessible for hotels to utilize as a unique reason to visit – that is, using the spa or wellness program to drive room occupancies.

Particularly in the areas of genomics and AI-based treatments, hotel brands can become wellness pioneers to attract a new demographic of high-paying guests and grow TRevPAR. As a broad example, consider the aging boomer generation which will increasingly be on the lookout for a 'healing journey' or ways to prolong their livelihoods no matter the costs.

Some thoughts and trends for the future of wellness include:

1. *Digital detox.* This is not exactly anything cutting edge, but it can still be given a contemporary makeover. We are satiated with screens and media, and many of us are looking for a retreat to calm our nerves. Beyond merely policing the use of cellular phones in public areas, the notion of a detox can extend to bespoke eating regiments, heartrate and activity level monitoring, room features that enhance one's quality of sleep (for instance, red-hued nightlights or vitamin-infused showers), meditation classes or, if the property is rural, nature hikes (where the futuristic spin would be to incorporate augmented reality into said treks).
2. *Technology-aided physiotherapy or sports clinics.* Why simply go to the local chiropractor once a week when you can take two weeks off to combine a vacation with daily corrective treatments for a more lasting impact on the body? These types of resorts already exist, but now machinery such as gait analysis or ultrasound muscle activation scanners can be put through an artificial intelligence program to both accurately deduce the cause behind any musculoskeletal pains and develop more effective therapies. In the realm of sports, imagine an AI-based golf swing assessment program that uses state-of-the-art wearables or an infrared camera to generate a step-by-step improvement plan within seconds, all to complement in-person coaching.
3. *Surgery recovery centers.* Whether cosmetic or otherwise, why spend days or weeks recuperating in a spartan, urban hospital that's devoid of character (and likely doesn't supply gourmet meals) when you can instead devote this time to being in a more inviting setting? Indeed, hotels all over the world are already merging with surgical operation centers to offer a tranquil place for patients to recover while also accessing the full range of onsite amenities. Particularly for reconstructive surgeries of the head or face and body augmentation procedures, guests may not want to immediately return home and would prefer to heal in the relative anonymity of a suite or private resort that's away from the public eye.
4. *Drug or psychiatric rehabilitation.* Many resorts already specialize in this area, and new approaches to physical and mental restoration are on the forefront. We now understand much more about how the combination of a peaceful environment, proper diet, regular exercise, mindful reflection and cognitive behavioral therapy can lead to greater self-esteem, more self-control and a better life outcome. Further, novel classes of medicines are emerging to help the brain form new synapses and reverse any degradative pathways. For one, cannabis is all the rage right now and has been shown to offer a myriad of health benefits. The rapid pace of global legalization will offer hotels a range of ways to capitalize on this relatively cheap, recreational drug. Next, considered as 'the next marijuana', the active component of psychedelic mushrooms (psilocybin) and, to a lesser extent, LSD are both in clinic

human trials for curing addictions, trauma and various other ailments via 'micro-dosing'.

5. <u>*Stem cell treatments.*</u> Despite any theological consternation over the sourcing of said cells, this is already a multibillion-dollar business. In very simple terms, when you inject these undifferentiated components into a part of the body alongside the correct growth factors, stem cells will help 'fill in the gaps' and revitalize the entire area – think near-immediate relief of chronic and debilitative joint pain, smoothing of facial wrinkles, the regrowth of hair follicles for baldness or even correcting damage to the nerves that control locomotion. Such injections still have a recovery period as the body incorporates these cells, thereby necessitating the demand for comfortable accommodations, great cuisine, entertainment and additional rehabilitative treatments while on the mend.
6. <u>*Biohacking.*</u> With PCR sequencing becoming widely available and the advance of CRISPR-based gene therapies as well as a deeper understanding of epigenetic-influenced health factors, we are on the verge of bringing together a great hotel stay with DNA-specific treatments and dietary regiments. This is often labeled as 'biohacking' because we are using medicines that target specific sequences in an individual's genome or the protein structures within the nucleus that switch genes on or off. Biohacking can also involve numerous other biochemicals that enhance one's body or mental capacity as well as cybernetic augmentations. Expect these highly targeted treatments, with a few of the more outlandish cyberpunk implants, to have a mounting presence in the news over the next decade as these technologies are perfected.

Two Caveats

Whether or not you elect to pursue wellness within one or more of these pillars to differentiate your brand, two closing remarks must be emphasized.

First, whatever you do, you should commit wholeheartedly. Many hotels attempt to pass themselves off as wellness centers while only offering lip service to the term. While this can work in an adjunctive capacity to help round out another key reason to visit – be it location, F&B, golf and so on – oftentimes a half-hearted activation of wellness results in resources and energy diverted away from more lucrative revenue opportunities.

Second, none of the above comes cheap. Each requires huge upfront capex and ongoing opex in the form of facilities, equipment, medicines, doctor salaries, nurse salaries, management, administration and liability insurance. Nightly rates will have to be marked up appropriately to cover this cost, which means that marketing budgets will also need to swell in order to reach the niche, wealthier target audiences for these kinds of services.

Broadly speaking, the overall thrust for all these trends, wellness or otherwise, is the continual need for innovation no matter the property, as well as the use of technology to personalize the guest experience. If you choose to embrace wellness, then you will inevitably need to start incorporating one of the above in order to stay relevant. Or, if wellness isn't your forte, then you will still need to hone your brand's specific appeal over the next few years in order to find that x-factor for your property to not strictly compete on a purely monetary basis via a straight rate comparison.

To conclude, we ask again, why will guests choose your property above all others? What is compelling them to pay more than the competition for the chance to stay with you? Answer that and your job will become that much easier.

How GenAI Can Enhance Hotel Wellness Programs

Generative AI (GenAI) as led by the lustrous ChatGPT is rightfully front and center in the news because there are seemingly endless possibilities for how these pretrained models built on large data sets can help speed up various processes at a hotel or enhance the guest experience. But while it's fun to bloviate in generalities about how the world will be transformed inside of five years as these algorithms pierce the veil of general intelligence, right now on the ground we need narrow use cases for these technologies.

And for that, one specific area where we are passionate is in wellness. Particularly with today's labor conditions, hotels should be on the lookout for solutions that can build revenue per guest (TRevPAR) while also being as labor-light as possible.

The Longevity Revolution

Concurrent to the advent of GenAI, another revolution is happening that's receiving notably less media attention, largely because it's mired in complex medical science with an alphabet soup of acronyms and terminology that require lots of time to comprehend. The 'longevity revolution' is the banner term to describe the medical practitioners, researchers and biohackers who are working to deduce the root causes of the hallmarks of cellular aging and how aging has a near-omnipresent influence on pathologies ranging from cancer and dementia to arthritis, osteoporosis and balding.

The hope isn't necessarily to reverse aging or make humans immortal (for now at least) but to deliver antiaging treatments and regimens that will help people live longer, healthier and free from early-life causes of mortality like sudden-onset heart attacks or severe viral infections on immunocompromised individuals. For hotels, the word of choice here is not only 'treatment' which implies applications for traditional spa offerings but also 'regimen' denoting a reorientation of one's lifestyle around wellness-oriented habits. That is, as wellness gains popularity, people will come to adopt healthier habits, thereby increasing demand for wellness products.

And this trend is already underway. Spas all over the world are evolving into wellness centers that marry a variety of alternative medical approaches and all the latest welltech. Indeed, from our experience working with luxury properties as part of the Mille Club program (with 'mille' coming from the Italian for a thousand to connote hotels with ADRs at over $1,000), advanced wellness programming is quickly becoming a make-or-break element to give guests a strong reason to visit the hotel in the first place.

Wellness is indeed a tool to drive product awareness, while it can also be used as part of a broader strategy to support room rate and TRevPAR growth. In this sense, GenAI is also a tool. Combining the two gives hotels a highly lucrative path to drastically increase a brand's wellness footprint.

When looking at near-term applications for GenAI in hotel wellness, we see this happening first through intelligent insights that a manager can interpret, then through AI-driven recommendations for people to implement or reevaluate, and finally through prescriptions where the AI is given full autonomy over selected workflows.

GenAI in the Back of House

While the front-facing welltech may steal the limelight, the workhorse for GenAI will predominantly lie in the BOH where it can be deployed to help a hotel's already incredible wellness team be even more incredible by optimizing their time and efforts according to what motivates them to come into work each and every day – helping guests with their wellbeing goals.

Here are three concepts to consider.

1. *Automated marketing and bookings.* What good is a wellness center if no guest knows about it? What good is a receptionist at the spa entrance if they're always on the phone with guests trying to reserve treatments? What good is a spa package if guests can't get the appointment time that they want because they didn't book far enough in advance of their arrival? GenAI can help by letting spa practitioners focus on their guests and not have to worry about promotions. GenAI can do this by offloading a lot of the automated marketing and ecommerce rails, delivering these prompts in a manner that considers the 'context' of the individual customer. That is, some guests will want to immediately reserve their treatment times after booking their rooms, while others will want to be upsold in the days preceding arrival, and yet others will wait until they reach the front desk to sort this out.
2. *Dynamic availability and dynamic pricing.* The former term denotes the use of past booking data to optimize a wellness center's time-based inventory so that the highest profit margin treatments are assigned the most popular timeslots throughout the week, where nowadays all of this scheduling can be attenuated by natural language processing (NLP) sentiment analysis to drive customer satisfaction. Similarly, while every hotelier is familiar with dynamic pricing for rooms, this too can be adroitly deployed for other profit centers with the granular yielding controlled by an AI, should the hotelier desire to go this route.
3. *Staff and guest scheduling.* Unlike hotel rooms, wellness centers must be very careful to throttle visitor occupancy so that guests aren't discouraged by treatments being unavailable due to specialized practitioners being off duty.

> Meanwhile, practitioners may become demoralized if they have no one to help. Looking beyond dynamic availability, GenAI will come to the rescue in the form of flexible and predictive team scheduling that optimizes for both guests' needs as well as each practitioner's requested hours.

"Generative AI emerged not just as a supporting tool but as a transformative ally. Through meticulous Hotel AI audits, we can unveil bespoke solutions poised to elevate the guest wellness experience," commented Vincent Somsen, a GAIN Advisor who leads the company's AI innovation division. "Think of personalized meditation and relaxation sessions curated based on a guest's stress levels, preferences and mood, ensuring a rejuvenating mental retreat. Or consider rooms that adjust in real-time to a guest's physiological state, from lighting and temperature to aroma. Or how about the benefits of tailored in-room exercise routines that cater to a guest's unique fitness goals and physical requirements, complemented by holistic dietary plans devised from an amalgamation of health metrics, dietary preferences and wellness goals. At the helm of this welltech transformation would be the 24/7 AI Wellness Concierge, always ready to assist, whether to book a spa session or recommend a therapeutic local nature trail. Any way a hotel brand decides to proceed, it will always come down to providing a comprehensive, AI-enhanced journey for holistic health and wellbeing."

The Future for the Front of House

Expounding on Somsen's remarks, where AI is already helping medicine and wellness is in making sense of vast reams of data to help discern patterns about a person's 'biochemical individuality' which encompasses their genome, their epigenome (which genes are turned on and off) and all accompanying biomarkers. While GenAI will play an important role in near-future lifesaving medical treatments, wellness centers at hotels will also benefit from all this research as more people come to seek out preventative techniques to stave off any last-minute interventions.

Here are three possibilities:

1. *Personalized guest wellness itineraries.* As a natural extrapolation from optimized guest and staff scheduling as well as dynamic availability, the future of this entire process may start with a conversation about what the guest's wellness goals are for their visit, which a GenAI will compute alongside any provided health data to come back with a limited selection of suggested multi-activity itineraries for the guest to then authorize. Right now, this is largely done manually through the setup of spa packages, but GenAI can take this to a hyper-personalized level that takes into account how certain treatments may affect the guest's bio-individual composition.
2. *Functional nutrition.* Right now, nutrition is still a bit like the Wild West, with some proponents of veganism as the best way to eat and others now extolling a nose-to-tail, ancestral diet as the way to go. The optimal way is likely somewhere in the middle and comprised of nuanced differences for

each guest based on their genetics, epigenetics and contextual goals while traveling. GenAI is quickly becoming capable at computing the multitude of bio-individual data to arrive at specific recommendations for modifying any dish to optimize nutritional benefits while still remaining within the framework established by the guest's stated goals.

3. *Computational therapies.* Bringing it all together, when you combine AI-driven functional nutrition with a bespoke guest itinerary, a step further is to customize each treatment to optimize a guest's biomarkers based on all personal data submitted to the hotel. Perhaps this is as simple as adjusting the time in the infrared sauna to be five minutes longer with a customized remineralization beverage served to the guest immediately afterwards. Or for the more futuristically inclined, it may involve the on-the-spot creation of a bespoke blend of raw ingredients to produce a skin cream that's perfectly attuned to that guest's moisture levels. For either case and numerous others, GenAI will inevitably act as the computational backbone to deliver this degree of personalization at scale.

Ultimately, with any technology of tool, we must always revert back to the 'why' behind the 'how'. For all things wellness, our foundational goal is to help our guests improve their wellbeing, and hopefully this inspires you to look at how you can use the astounding advances by the recent batch of generative AIs to further serve that core purpose.

How Web3 and the Metaverse Support Hotel Wellness

With the grand unveiling of the Apple Vision Pro, as well as the previous PSVR2 and Meta Quest 3 news, it's time once again to look at what's possible (and what's practical) for the next-generation internet. While an article could solely focus on the metaverse applications – that is, the use of AR, VR, and MR interoperable digital spaces – to enhance wellness, we rope in web3 and blockchain technologies here because there are many interesting overlaps.

Undoubtedly, there is some skepticism about the applicability of these two emerging fields for hotels, especially in the near-term where so many tech tasks take precedence. This is why we have focused this discussion specifically on wellness, a space where hotels are already excelling at adding more value to the guest experience and where there's still tremendous potential.

What we also emphasize with the intersection of web3, metaverse systems and wellness, is to consider what economists call *induced (or latent) demand*. It isn't just about developing a hotel in the metaverse or upgrading the spa to capture more of the current total addressable market (TAM) relative to the comp set; it's about understanding that as these fields mature, access to more robust out-of-the-box solutions will emerge and prices will drop, consequently leading to an increase in customer demand. The pie will get larger, as they say.

With respect to induced demand, first consider Apple Vision Pro's visionOS. This spatial operating system will likely serve a similar role as the original app store, enabling developers to make progressively more useful tools purpose-built for Apple's mixed reality headset, in turn opening more doors to further development and newer applications for all metaverse devices – a virtuous circle. Analogously, as wellness techniques become more mainstream and scientifically proven to be beneficial for one's health, more practitioners and researchers will enter the field, leading to more access and newer discoveries that will further propel more interest.

Alas, these are mere predictions and, to be our own devil's advocate, no one really knows which way the wind will blow. Nevertheless, by ideating all the possibilities, it will help hotels to narrow the field down to the probabilities.

Next-Generation Loyalty & Rewards

Blockchain-based tokens are often proposed as a way to take hotel loyalty or rewards programs to new heights, with the key advantages of reduced administration costs and *points interoperability* that will boost perceived value through the creation of secondary, market-making exchanges for these points. Regardless of the data piping that allows guests to earn or redeem, though, the program is only as good as the hotels and offers behind it.

Wellness offerings can enter the picture here because they encourage significant ancillary spend and work to fulfill the desire for experiential travel, all of which can be made more conveniently accessible to customers on the loyalty platform through tokenization that can seamlessly convert between local currencies and different property management systems. Moreover, think about third-party, non-hotel wellness businesses that may have their own loyalty programs where web3-governed interchangeability can synergize cross-selling for your hotel from their customer base. Finally, wellness offers might also bundle perks in the metaverse, all of which can be *token gated* via NFTs for lower cost administration.

Mixed Reality Wellness Onboarding

As demand for hotel wellness products grows, what becomes the rate-limiting step is not price or facility costs per se, but access to skilled labor. Just as many other roles can hire for passion then train for skill, this rule can also apply to wellness-oriented recruitment processes, but some of the procedures are so specific that onboarding time then becomes a challenge.

Where all the fancy metaverse-related tech comes into play is by offloading much of the training from live sessions or shadowing, allowing rookies to train virtually and on their own time. As the sensing hardware gets more advanced and cheaper, this opens the doors for AI or remote-human-assisted tactile guidance and testing for all SOPs. Furthermore, because we live in the age of information access and not necessarily information retention, having a library of AR or VR tutorials can help with rapid onboarding just prior to the service delivery. Call it *bite-sized learning*, as enabled and gamified by cutting edge tech. This becomes especially important when hotels attempt to cross-train across departments as an incentive to retain good team members through continuing education.

Exercise & Physiotherapy

On the guest-facing side of mixed reality, movement tracking and working out in a digital environment are the obvious applications, especially with the growth of *wellness-secondary travel* broadly defined as people wanting to stay active while traveling for other purposes. Again, labor challenges dictate that the best way to do this at scale is through on-demand exercise programming where guests can work out from their rooms or the gym while being personally guided by AI or remotely by a trainer.

While there will be many direct-to-consumer services that specialize in the above for in-home fitness, differentiating a hotel brand will come through access to top-tier practitioners educated in various schools of physiotherapy or bodily alignment. A foremost scenario where MR tech can help is by reconnecting a guest with the same instructor across multiple properties within a brand.

For instance, a guest develops a rapport with a physiotherapist at a branded resort on one Caribbean island, then is able to get a virtual reassessment by that same physiotherapist when visiting another resort in the same brand, with in-person assistance from another practitioner for a hybrid, value-added experience. And on the note of hybrid, on-prem trainers might use an AR-guided AI for more precise body tracking and exercise recommendations, where this aspect is already showing lots of promise in sports training.

Web3 Fractional Ownership

All these futuristic opportunities to use next-gen tech to enhance your wellness programming are nothing without the capital to get them started. While fractional ownership as a means of fundraising can be completed without putting everything on the blockchain, the key advantages of Web3 include reducing administration costs via smart contracts, increased asset trace ability as an incentive for purchase, and the establishment of a *decentralized autonomous organization* (DAO) for voting rights on future project direction.

Applying tokenization to fractional ownership can be quite complex, both algorithmically and legally. There's no avoiding those challenges, but one source of trepidation that can be overcome is the misperception of cryptocurrencies as having extremely volatile values. To escape this, an ownership token need not be diluted down to an amount designed for everyday transactions but kept in the five-to-six figure range, which will limit total subscriptions and ensure the DAO remains 'thoughtful' with its balloted decisions (or multipronged decisions which can involve *quadratic voting*).

Virtual World Previsualization

Here's where the term 'try before you buy' enters the picture. That is, the more a customer interacts with a product beforehand, the more likely they are to make the purchase. Imagine setting up a lifelike *digital twin* of your wellness facilities that guests can access via a portal as part of the prearrival upselling process, allowing them to tour the spaces but also preview select treatments. Such twins might also integrate with a tokenized loyalty or rewards program from the previous use case.

Then on the management side, virtual renderings of wellness spaces can aid in modeling a new build or renovation. Drafting software to generate floorplans will still be needed, but digital twins help to reduce costs by allowing decision makers to better envision how the space will work so that consensus is achieved faster and there are fewer corrections needed later on in the development process.

Mixed Reality Experiences

To close out, the key obstacle that hotels will face when trying to grow new sources of revenue beyond increasing ADRs will come down to labor supply in order to render services complete. Applying a hybrid approach that aids existing teams through immediate access to tutorials or remote AR guidance can then help with other wellness-oriented experiences like cooking classes, aromatherapy, sound therapy or guided mindfulness sessions.

While many of these examples may seem impractical for today, overall the point here is to show the wide range of possibilities that together will drive more consumer acceptance of next-generation technologies like blockchain and the metaverse, which will then inevitably increase access to vendors that can turn these hypotheticals into fully realized profit centers. It's often hard for humans to evaluate exponential trends where the principle of induced demand throws current TAM estimates under the bus, so for now just follow the news and develop a strategic approach for when the time is right.

Know Your 'Omes' for the Coming Merger of Hotel Tech and Welltech

When most of us are primed with the term 'hotel technology', we conjure thoughts of the PMS, guest profile data, inventory distribution, cabling infrastructure, energy management, credit card processing, cybersecurity and the like. But as more and more brands start to integrate advanced wellness practices into their spas or rooms to drive guest satisfaction, longer LOS and total revenue, hoteliers and IT professionals would be wise to have a cursory understanding of the vast world of technologies that are helping evolve and expand the footprint of wellness at hotels.

We caution this not as a recommendation to go out and study medicine for four years, but in order to better see this secular trend as it's unfolding and so that you know how to best align your own property or brand's hotel technology in order to make any advanced wellness programming an unbridled success. The biological sciences come with their own jargon and alphabet soup much like hotel tech, after all, and if you are struggling to grasp the terminology or interpret the results from some new landmark research paper, then it becomes all the harder to seize the opportunity for your own brand's growth.

This megatrend we speak of is, of course, wellness, where within this broad, ambiguous word is the implication that people all over the world are discovering (and rediscovering) healthy lifestyle practices so that they can live their days with more vitality, heightened cognition, less sickness and better moods. Over the past two decades, the advent of 'welltech' has entered this zeitgeist, introducing a plethora of health-promoting machinery and diagnostic tools that all the leading hotel spas have already deployed or have investigated deploying.

But the real catalyst over the next decade for the continued growth of wellness practices and welltech acceptance stems from the discovery of the epigenome which to this day is rewriting everything we know about how our bodies work and is influencing the way people think about their lifestyle choices.

Some Background on the Omes

This word 'epigenome' may be unfamiliar to you, but it's unlikely that 'genome' is. This latter term was introduced just over a century ago as a portmanteau of 'gene' from the Greek root for 'creation' or 'trait' and 'ome' which for our purposes comes from the Greek for 'body' or 'collection'. With 'epi' meaning 'above', epigenome thus translates to 'the collection of elements that are on top of a person's body of traits'. In other words, the epigenome comprises those substances in every cell of our body that attach to our DNA and influence which genes are expressed or not expressed.

What's groundbreaking with the recent research into the epigenome – and by 'recent' we mean roughly over the past 15 years – is that while a person's genome is determined at birth and set for life, the epigenome is malleable to changes that reflect environmental and lifestyle factors. The analogy we like to use here is that if your genetics is a switchboard then your epigenetics is the switchboard operator.

The next earthshattering development was in discovering that epigenome changes within specific organs can influence disease progression and the directionality of tissue aging while certain population-level epigenetic patterns correlate with one's chronological age (read: Horvath Clock). Combining these breakthroughs with the latest million-dollar equipment that can detect individual atoms – as well as the internet that allows researchers to coordinate across continents and a ton of machine learning – and today we can measure 'epigenetic biomarker proxies' in order to estimate someone's 'biological age' or how old their bodies actually are compared to their physical time on this planet.

All this has led to an explosion of medical research as scientists tease out the nuances of how life works and how to help people with better treatments or early detection of various ailments. Starting with genomics and epigenomics – or the study of the genome and epigenome, respectively – we now have a variety of 'omes' and 'omics' as these subjects are becoming increasingly specialized:

- Chromosomics. Modeling the elements that constitute the architecture of a chromosomes
- Transcriptomics. Studying the entirety of RNA transcripts produced by activated genes
- Proteomics. Studying the entirety of proteins in one's body and how their functions change
- Metabolomics. Examining all the metabolites or byproduct molecules and how they interact
- Secretomics. Examining all the body's secreted molecules or hormones and how they interact
- Connectomics. Mapping the trillions of connections amongst the brain's neurons and other cells
- Interactomics. Looking at how RNA, proteins, metabolites, hormones, drugs and others interact
- Spatial-omics. Looking at how all the various molecules interact in 3D space over time

If that isn't enough 'whoa' for you, consider a series of recent connectome studies where they now estimate the human brain has 80 billion neurons and over 80 billion support cells, identifying over 3000 different types of specialized cells and with geometric complexity of branched connectivity. That's where we are now in the research, and the best is yet to come.

But What Does This Have to Do with Hotels?

We aren't expecting you to memorize the above terms, although any one of these can easily lead you down a multi-hour Wikipedia rabbit hole. Rather, know that all this has only happened in the past two decades. We listed these terms off to show you just how far this rabbit hole now goes. And the rabbits are only digging faster and faster.

That is to say, all over the globe, doctors and scientists – our proverbial rabbits – continue to work ceaselessly to decipher the hidden mechanisms of biological systems and evolution in order to find new treatments, formulate better diagnostics, and deduce those habits that will improve the lives of every human being. With each study or scientific invention being cumulative – that is, building off what's come before – we now have access to technologies that let us test hypotheses at lightning speed relative to only a few years ago. Hence, it isn't unreasonable to expect the pace of medical discovery to hasten in the decade ahead.

Where hotels can play in all this is in embracing and encouraging lifestyle changes for the better. Researchers continue to test how factors like nutrition, intermittent fasting, exercise, sleep, mental health and specific stimuli like red light therapy (RLT) can influence a person's epigenome, with the pursuit of attenuating certain hallmarks of aging and disease progression. With each new study that's published, it is adding to the vast body of evidence pointing to some habits as being health-promoting and others as being health-disrupting. And then, with each new study or meta-analysis (a study of other studies), that information trickles into the newspapers, literature, and onto the airwaves for us to consume and adjust our lifestyles accordingly.

As the recent explosion of the wellness industry has indicated, people of all walks are starting to understand that lifestyle equals life outcome and that welltech can help to ensure one is as healthy as possible. This 'welltech' can mean the aforementioned RLT devices that have now been shown to stimulate the dermis layers of the skin and release subcutaneous melatonin (the molecule of sleep and a powerful antioxidant). Welltech can also mean other sensorial activations like massage guns, compression boots that promote lymphatic drainage to improve the immune system, soundscapes, meditation apps or binaural beats to promote certain types of thought patterns.

Then for diagnostics, welltech can imply sending your guests an epigenome test kit so that a clinician or wellness practitioner can interpret the results to offer personalized meal plans and supplements once the guests are on premises. Or you may give guests DEXA scans to indicate muscle imbalances for a precise exercise program. Together, this is an immense field with a bevy of technologies worth exploring.

The Intersection of Hotel Tech and Welltech

Yes, some hotels will always be heads in beds, with wellness not even in consideration. But the metrics behind this megatrend are blatantly signaling that travelers are now prioritizing their health while abroad. We see this in the growth of sleep tourism and the wellness retreats industry. We see this in chefs reinventing their menus with ever-healthier options. We see this at the luxury end with traditional spas morphing into antiaging clinics that offer all of the aforementioned welltech and plenty more.

Ultimately, whatever welltech and advanced wellness programming your teams recommend, purchase or install must have a seamless integration with the systems that serve and connect the hotel. For instance, what good is that fancy new cryochamber if your guests can't book it online, your digital signage isn't talking about it, your staffing software can't effectively schedule in the practitioners trained to operate the machine and your marketing team can't incorporate spa vouchers into their packages?

Next, consider the CRM and how merging various databases such as the PMS, spa and F&B POS can inform which guest types would be most likely to reserve a wellness-oriented offer. This not only gives you a clearer path for targeted marketing but also when we talk about lifestyle habits this explicitly suggests multiple occasions over a longer stretch of time. That is, in order to experience the full benefits of joining a yoga class while at a resort, using a welltech device or going through a multi-day sleep restoration program, it's best if the guests return every so often for a tune up.

Whether it's through automations, distribution support, building lookalike audiences and other factors, hotel technology is critical to enable all these welltech activations and maximize wellness revenues. And as the TAM for hotel wellness continues to grow, it behooves all IT teams to understand a bit more about how welltech works in order to envision then predict what the requirements are for the systems that will act as the engine for this vertical.

In this sense, thinking about all the new omes and omics that have emerged is one way to humble the mind and to think long-term about where medicine and, soon after, guest demands are headed. A decade ago, the word epigenome was only mentioned in niche medical laboratories; now, the word is casually tossed around in gossip magazines alongside others like biohacking, adaptogens and nootropics. Over the grand scheme of things, this is a 50-year merger of hospital and hospitality that is still in its infancy, and the hotel brands that will reap the rewards will be led by those IT professionals who have a working knowledge of both sides of this union.

Placing Wellness and Sustainability as Core Hotel Values with the Fairmont Mayakoba

Article originally published in October 2023 and the indicated activities by the Fairmont Mayakoba at the time of this writing may not reflect current company practices.

Spread across a sprawling 45-acre ocean-facing campus with 401 rooms and suites, the five-diamond, AAA Fairmont Mayakoba has long been on our bucket list of resorts worth visiting. Just outside of Playa del Carmen in the heart of the remarkably popular sun destination that is the Mayan Riviera (especially for Canadian snowbirds like the two of us), the Fairmont Mayakoba property intrigued us because of its diverse array of amenities, its sustainable luxury approach within the broader Mexican hospitality industry and its core focus on authentic wellness experiences.

But it wasn't until we caught wind of the special program set up ahead of International Yoga Day that we expedited the conversation and an official familiarization with the resort. In particular, to celebrate this day, the Fairmont Mayakoba rolled out a yoga program specifically for kids. Not only is it adorable, but it's incredibly valuable because such early life exposure to yoga will help to inspire people at a younger age to learn about the vast importance of bodily alignment, flexibility, balance, mid-body awareness and emotional self-reflection.

Upon sitting down with Silvia Ferrer, the resort's Director of Marketing and Public Relations, who plays a key role in the ideation and implementation of the Fairmont Mayakoba's wellness programming design, the two of us remarked that we wished these sorts of kid and teenager-oriented classes existed back when we were young. But as we quickly learned, this was just the latest facet within a far, far greater ecosystem that the property has cultivated, touching on every single operation and employee.

The more time we spent with Ferrer, the more we learned about just how embedded wellness and sustainability are within the Fairmont Mayakoba and Fairmont's brand DNA. As was pointed out, that's really the only way to be successful with these pursuits; make them a core value then the whole team will always give them the attention they deserve with every single task or plan. Therein, this property's work offers a powerful lesson for the global hotel industry in terms of how to create an aspirational place of work and how good core values create a virtuous circle for ongoing success.

A Subtle Example of Wellness in the Brand DNA

Let's start small, as often the little details are what distinguish the greatest properties around the world. When first crafting the on-premises guest experience, having wellness as a core value meant that it wasn't compartmentalized as a spa-only affair. The approach to F&B, the guestroom design and the arrival experience had to be top considerations, of course, but the team also gave a lot of thought to imbuing the entire customer journey with wellness elements to make it an immersive theme.

This being a tropical resort, having wellness at heart meant that the team had to ponder how a guest's five senses would be positively influenced at every turn as they moved about the grounds. Specifically, certain plants that are both calmingly fragrant and reflective of the local environment (thus also reinforcing the pursuit for sustainability in all matters) were strategically positioned so that passersby would benefit from their scents as they walked from place to place. In essence, this engineered the resort for total relaxation.

Almost imperceptibly, such scents nudge guests into better moods and help to alleviate stress. But the word 'passersby' implies not only paying visitors but also the onsite teams that grace the same corridors as they go about cleaning rooms, delivering service orders or, for managers, walking to the next meeting.

With so much emphasis nowadays on employee wellbeing, we often forget that wellness programming is not just a way to increase ancillary spend per guest (TRevPAR); it's a cardinal way to improve the livelihoods of teams so that they are more motivated to excel in their roles. With any new plan put forth, it's the attention to all the little details that will make the program a success, and this will only truly happen if the team embraces

Making Every Stay Different Through Sustainability

Upon asking about what's next for the Fairmont Mayakoba on the wellness front, Ferrer was quick to rifle off a near endless list of new experiences and updates to current ones, avidly recapping in mere seconds the thousands of hours of work from her team to set these all up. Importantly, she remarked that given all the hospitality investments into the Yucatan spurred on by the soon-to-be-open intercity Tren Maya, the Fairmont Mayakoba must adopt an attitude of continual reinvention to stay competitive, with a key driver of that being not only wellness, great F&B and a series of onsite concerts featuring some world-class names (including Ricky Martin), but sustainability itself.

The fundamental rubric for this is Accor Planet 21 wherein Fairmont has pledged to become one of the top environmental leaders in the world. But sustainability need not be siloed into only a BOH energy management assessment or an ecosystem impact study. Embracing it as a core value at the Fairmont Mayakoba has resulted in a layered approach, asking "Am I helping the planet as well as the local culture?" which has helped inspire new ideas for eco-conscious guest activities, making sustainability fully visible to customers while also offering unique excursions to encourage repeat visits.

For instance, one layer of this program has been arranging for daytrips into the local Mayan communities, teaching guests about their traditional way of life with an emphasis on how these cultures exist in harmony with nature and how nothing goes to waste. And yes, there's great food, too. Oftentimes, visitors to the Mayan Riviera go from the airport to the resort then back to the airport, and don't develop a real connection to the land or its people. Such excursions change that and offer something unforgettable.

Connected to this is another initiative to help preserve the local communities. Pack for a Purpose is an original program at the Fairmont Mayakoba where guests are invited to use the extra space in their luggage for supplies that are needed for projects supporting disadvantaged local children and nonviolence towards animals, with the incentive of 10% off the regular room rate. Ferrer noted that this is a big win-win as travelers are initially motivated by the discount but then come to realize the positive impact they are having while the locals get to see the true depth of the hotel's advocacy.

Third of note is the property's partnership with Oceanus, an organization dedicated to reef restoration. The excursion here is a scuba diving trip but with the extra element of planting corals that will grow to full size over the course of a decade or longer. To track this progression as a memento for the experience, post-departure guests can log in to a web portal to see exactly how their specific coral is taking shape.

Finally, as with all the wellness pursuits, these sustainability touchpoints also endear the hotel to its teams, creating an aspirational place to work. Locals want to see their communities thrive in real time, and there's an opportunity through these eco-conscious programs to draw young minds back into the hospitality industry.

Transformative Experiences Require Property Evolution

The nature of wellness is evolving, as are sustainability requirements, and together this means a competitive game of one-upmanship amongst hotels, both to keep attracting guests and to continue to promote hospitality as an aspirational career path. Through the examples that Ferrer showed from our time together, when you have these two principles as part of the brand DNA, it ensures that no practice or excursion ever becomes 'stagnant' – that you remain a step ahead

An indispensable aspect to making this happen is the concept of 'transformational experiences' where it's not just about the onsite excitement but leaving a lasting impression that improves the guest's livelihood back at home long after they've departed. The Oceanus program fulfills this premise as guests not only have the once-in-a-lifetime chance to help replenish a coral reef, but they can revisit that moment years afterward, serving as a constant reminder that we humans are caretakers of the earth.

And with the notion of transformation in mind, we closed our meetings with Ferrer on the topic of food because, while spa-based wellness experiences or yoga are indeed very cool, not everyone is so inclined to partake. But everyone eats. And at a luxury resort, the food and beverage programming has to be a star of the show.

Unlike other properties, the transformational angle where the Fairmont Mayakoba team starts is by asking, "How can we teach people to eat better?" From this outlook, every menu is constantly reevaluated in collaboration with Spa Director,

Jessica Lonngi, who offers her healthy recommendations based on each individual guest's dietary needs. Yes, the burger and fries continues to make an appearance, but the option to follow a more nutritionally dense path is always present for the guest to try then take their learnings home with them.

The end result of this convergent focus on wellness, sustainability and guest transformation are reflected in experiences like the unforgettable, customized cenote excursion that Fairmont has created via a local partnership that's wholly sustainable and changes every quarter. Thus, a trip to the Fairmont Mayakoba in, say, October 2023 is different than one in March 2024 and together they are both different than one taken in December 2024. The same guest, couple or family can visit the same property time and again without ever being short on new things to do or different ways to experience the amenities. But this is only possible when there's a process in place for continual renewal and passionate teams like the ones Ferrer leads underpinning each step of the implementation.

A Case Study in Upleveling Rooms and Expanding Wellness at the Fairmont Tremblant

Article originally published in January 2024 and the indicated activities by the Fairmont Tremblant at the time of this writing may not reflect current company practices.

As background for those not from Canada, Tremblant is a picture-perfect ski village under two hours northwest of Montreal in the Laurentian Mountains. With numerous small hotels, chalets, lodges and short-term rentals to choose from, Tremblant is perhaps the closest thing that North America has to a charming French of Swiss alpine town, wherein the 312-key Fairmont Tremblant has always stood at the luxury resort pillar of the destination since its opening in 1996.

Yet even with this lofty status, renovations are an inevitable and compulsory part of keeping pace with global hospitality trends and providing guests with a perennially exceptional onsite experience. How does a flagged resort do this right? At the luxury end, it's never just a matter of checking the brand standard boxes, but of making the property even more of a destination unto itself no matter the season.

In this case, the Fairmont Tremblant executed on two fronts simultaneously: carving out a portion of the rooms to become part of the elevated Fairmont Gold category as well as building an outdoor, terraced thermal circuit and foodservice. Just launched this past November 2023 following a seven-month renovation, we interviewed General Manager Anne Marie Johns to guide the details of this case study so that any reader – owner, hotelier or otherwise – can understand the nuances that go into making a PIP like this a true success.

The Hotel Within The Hotel

Fairmont Gold represents an exclusive lifestyle hotel floor consisting of elevated rooms and suites, a specially reserved reception desk (and sometimes even a separate hotel entrance), as well as access to club lounge amenities such as deluxe daily breakfast, afternoon tea snacks, evening canapés, a curated honor bar, boardroom access (in select locations) and cozy reading rooms (again, in select locations). These private floors within a larger property are part of a global trend that many brands have adopted in recent years, with Fairmont Gold as the innovator.

What Fairmont Hotels and other brands have realized is that in today's experience-driven luxury travel market, memories and time are more valuable than money or elasticity to nightly rates. Hence, it's no longer just about the in-room experience and the property amenities, but also about creating a more intimate space that's tucked away from the crowds. Such a haven with VIP F&B privileges adds a strong element of flexibility wherein Fairmont Gold guests can enjoy the destination on their own terms by giving them the convenience of delectable culinary delights.

For the Fairmont Tremblant, while the renovation itself was only seven months' long, the property's Gold floor was temporarily closed wherein a PIP was already in the works before the pandemic hit. Given the touch-and-go nature of travel restrictions in the province of Quebec throughout 2021 and 2022, the renovation was hard to time in accordance to what the brand standards for luxury travelers required. Ultimately, the renovation saw an upgrade of the existing Fairmont Gold Lounge and private reception on the seventh floor overlooking the ski slopes. All 34 Fairmont Gold rooms and suites were also renovated, including the addition of four new guestrooms and two signature suites, into what's dubbed a contemporary chalet-chic style that mirrors the natural beauty of the surroundings.

Contrast Therapy as a Pillar of Hotel Wellness

As the two of us quip, when it comes to contrast therapy, mineral springs and thermal bathing, North America is two decades behind Europe and APAC in terms of cultural appreciation and overall footprint.

From a study conducted by the Global Wellness Institute in 2018 on the global presence of thermal and hot springs spas, in the previous year Europe had 5,967 of these establishments totaling $21.7 billion in revenues while Asia-Pacific had 25,916 facilities amounting to $31.6 billion in revenues. For comparison, North America had only 302 establishments for $0.7 billion.

While one could argue that this relative absence in Canada and the United States is due to cultural differences from the Old World, the success of more recent thermal spa facility launches within major North American markets or at destination resorts since that study was published suggests that this is still rife ground for hotels to seize the opportunity and expand their wellness businesses in this direction.

For a ski village like Tremblant, adding a thermal circuit makes complete sense, as it fits perfectly with the average traveler purpose to that destination. In the case of Fairmont Tremblant, the renovation here involved a revitalized outdoor pool terrace exclusive to hotel guests that's designed as a slope-side haven with a hot whirlpool overlooking the mountain-scape, a seasonal waterfall and a cool plunge pool. The hotel also installed a custom light therapy component within the pools that can be circadian-adjusted to optimize the mood according to time of day. Thirdly, given the bodily shock that can occur for a novice to ice baths, Johns emphasized that special team training was required to ensure guest safety.

While we could write a whole other article on the cardiovascular benefits of hot-cold contrast bathing, remember that the emotional goal of all this is bodily relaxation, translating to guests feeling better, sleeping better and more satisfied with their overall onsite experiences. Notably, such a warming-up facility allows the property to more fully embrace its ski-in, ski-out access through its vibrant après-ski menu, thereby increasing F&B revenues per guest in the process.

Thinking bigger, though, there is the matter of having a strong 'reason to visit' for a given destination or hotel. While the town of Tremblant has stark seasonality due to its winter orientation, the year-round operation of the thermal facility at the Fairmont Tremblant helps it to drive occupancies regardless of whether or not there's snow on the mountain.

Overcoming Situational Challenges

In speaking with Johns, this renovation wasn't all smooth sailing from ideation to opening, and her team had to overcome many obstacles to usher this in on a timeline. As aforementioned, the ever-capricious COVID variants caused several delays, and then the post-pandemic inflationary costs of construction and material costs added even more anguish. Ultimately, the renovation for both the Fairmont Gold hotel within a hotel and the addition of the outdoor pool terrace cost just under $9 million.

While Johns has now conquered the challenges of post-pandemic construction and launch, the market of Tremblant still comes with its peculiarities. For one, it only has a total hotel room inventory of about 1,600, wherein this small size can lead to heightened variability in rate yielding. Then there are other external forces such as Porter Airlines (a mid-sized, regional flyer operating mostly out of Ontario and Quebec) cancelling its in-season direct flight from Toronto to Tremblant.

Despite this challenge, Toronto continues to be a key origin market for the Fairmont Tremblant, with most guests either flying into Montreal first or driving the whole way. Overall, heading into the reopening, Ontario represented roughly 30% of customers for the property, with another 30% from Quebec, 30% from the United States and 10% international – a healthy mix overall. Porter's removal of that flight route decreases the ability for Torontonians, a primary feeder city, to plan a quick getaway. It isn't a totally lost market, but Johns continues to focus on a mix of Toronto, USA and international segmentation with a longer look-to-book window as well as luxury distribution networks into key markets that can sustain the elevated price points of the Fairmont Gold rooms and suites.

As we're still very much in the post-pandemic period where travel is rapidly evolving, Johns noted another important trend that may apply to other destinations based on her team's observations over the past year. The rise of remote work and flexible hours in the office has meant that more and more guests have decided to stay longer, punctuating their Tremblant-based workweek with a few days of good skiing or on-premises relaxation, all while avoiding the weekend crowds and ski hill lineups. Significantly, though, the Fairmont Gold amenities and the presence of a thermal bathing area further incentivize this increase to LOS, particularly for the slower, midweek nights.

In the grand scheme of things, the combined capital improvements of a higher-tier hotel experience via the Fairmont Gold product and the outdoor pool terrace help to give the Fairmont Tremblant reliance against any market forces by making the property the destination unto itself. The town of Tremblant will always be ski, but adding unique touchpoints as we've described mean that this hotel will always have a reason to visit beyond just the mountain. And that's a takeaway that any hotel can learn from, in addition to a reason for anyone to visit no matter the time of year.

Thoughtful Sleep Program Setup at the Deer Path Inn as an Example for All Independent Hotels

Sleep tourism may be a relatively new buzz term, but for hospitality it isn't really anything novel; it's an extension and more deliberate expansion of what hotels aim to achieve each and every night. After all, one of the hallmarks of guest satisfaction, and a core part of any hotelier's duty of care, is whether or not the guest slept well. Knowing this principle, leading brands are engaged in an arms race of sorts to meet the increasing cultural appreciation and prioritization for sleep amenities. Often lost in this conversation, though, are independent hotels.

The Deer Path Inn, a 57-key, four-star property in Lake Forest, Illinois, on Chicago's North Store, is one such example where the introduction of a thoughtful and appropriately themed sleep program serves to show that any hotel can, and should examine how they can upgrade their amenities to appease modern traveler demands. Sitting down with James Barnett, General Manager of the property since September 2023, we talked through the full extent of the new sleep program as well as its context within the broader evolution of this now 95-year-old historic inn.

Property in Focus

On the approach to its centennial anniversary coming up in 2029, the Deer Path Inn recently completed a full-scale property improvement plan (PIP) in 2015, where ownership and the management group, Charlestowne Hotels, worked hand-in-hand to ensure that the building's heritage and its significance for the North Shore's growth over the past century were both preserved, even as they went down to the studs in order to properly update many of the rooms and facilities. As an Australian who has also spent many years in London's hospitality scene, Barnett was well-versed with how the expressiveness of a hotel's heritage can directly and indirectly heighten brand awareness and revenues.

Like so many historic hotels around the world, the team behind the Deer Path Inn has a great sense of responsibility in being a steward for the city around it. Embracing its British countryside theme meant carefully sourcing furnishings and finishings for the latest renovation in order to maintain that antique charm and match previously used materials, while also adding archival photography or other refurbished pieces to the guestrooms and public spaces like the signature restaurant, The English Room. With the adjacent Garden Room and conservation area along with the secluded Courtyard patio, together these F&B outlets contribute nearly half of total revenue.

This contribution highlights an interesting aspect about the property's unique segmentation mix; for hotel guests this is at approximately 60% leisure, 25% corporate and 15% group as Barnett recalled. Besides in-house guests, the Deer Path Inn certainly draws in a sizable local crowd for dining and its event series, while most travelers are booking because they adore the upscale, storybook décor and exceptional service. For instance, even to this day a member of the team calls every guest ahead of their arrival. These touches offer a clear value-add above the local comp set and even for properties closer to Chicago's downtown core.

Transients can include, for example, local getaways from within an hour's drive, midweek corpora or those visiting the area for graduations, while the inn has strong relationships with nearby businesses looking for an intimate yet stately venue for C-level retreats. Then for wedding parties, for which the inn hosts many, the whimsical backdrops of the various venue spaces can host up to 175 attendees. Taken together, for the setup of the sleep program, staying true to its heritage and to current guest expectations has meant focusing on embellishing their culinary expertise and English-inspired theme.

Sleep Program in Focus

"The last memory a guest has of a property when checking out in the morning is how well they slept the night before," commented Barnett. "If they don't get good sleep, that will emotionally transfer back on to the host property. The senior team has understood this since well before the last major PIP, and from the beginning of that refurbishment set aside budget for a selection of higher-end mattresses, linens and bedding supplies known to elicit better sleep."

This simple yet wholly relatable concept acted as the impetus for the new sleep program that Barnett oversaw. Indeed, it's supported by psychology through what's called the 'peak-end rule' where people are most likely to remember the peak of a given experience as well as its ending. It follows that if you fumble the departure – the ending of a hotel experience – then that mishap may outweigh other positives during the course of the stay.

With respect to helping guests get better sleep in order to improve the end experience, the Deer Path Inn's specific offering here is called 'A Good Book & A Spot of Tea'. True to its name, it includes a bedtime tea service, snacks and a curated 'Sleepy Sips' playlist, along with a book selected for guests by the Lake Forest Book Store. The property's Chief Spirits Officer has also crafted a complimentary lavender mocktail and will offer a trio of cocktails inspired by English authors (Charles Dickens, Jane Austen, William Shakespeare). Lastly, the inn has partnered with luxury loungewear clothing line Sleepy Jones to debut its own branded Deer Path Inn PJs, available in the gift boutique as well as on their ecommerce channel.

While it may seem relatively straightforward to focus on the bedding, herbals and inspired cocktails, this belies the multitude of work that happened behind the scenes in order to verify the program and keep it in harmony with all the other elements that together constitute the guest experience. For example, the inn consults with sleep experts, while they also involved members of the housekeeping team throughout the process to ensure operational feasibility. Above all, Barnett noted that they relied on firsthand feedback and personal interactions with guests to guide both the PIP and the sleep program's rollout. Such is an advantage that only independents can really have: a deep relationship with key guests and the flexibility to adapt to their individual requests.

Part of a Larger Mission

While the sleep program was only recently debuted, unofficially it has been in works on an evolving scale since the early planning for the PIP in 2015. It is part of a broader strategy that's focused on maintaining a unique, time-honored sensibility that uplifts the community. Sleep is but one spoke on this wheel.

"As an independent, we still have to play to our strengths," added Barnett. "At only 57 rooms, we may not have the widest range of amenities like some of the larger chain hotels or resorts, especially when it comes to outdoor space or wellness programming. But we punch far above our weight when it comes to unique charm, dining, service, events and, especially with the official launch of our new sleep program, in-room relaxation."

The broader strategy that includes the PIP and the sleep program is culminating in the centennial, where Barnett is now focusing on overseeing a new summer event series in the central courtyard as a way of highlighting the hotel's history and giving back to Lake Forest. This includes the 'Summer Soirée' that plays homage to traditional British innkeeping and 'Dine Like It's 1927' with menus inspired by what the hotel would've served during the Roaring Twenties – and also with some help from the local preservation society to ensure they're getting it right. This will then lead into a large New Year's Eve party which the hotel in all its time has never hosted before.

Overall, the point is that a sleep program doesn't necessarily have to be any major pivot for any property. With the continued growth of sleep tourism, these programs can bring together the best of what a property already does in the areas of service, F&B, wellness or technology. And per the peak-end rule, sleep programs should thus be on every hotel's radar, but they can also be a part of a greater multi-year strategy, especially when a PIP is being mapped out. Independents like the Deer Path Inn are showing that with the right strategy and thoughtful planning this can be executed in a way that enhances the onsite storytelling and overall experience.

Sleep Architecture as the Central Concept for Sleep Tourism Revenues

With sleep science reaching the mainstream over the past few years, numerous hotel brands have unveiled fancy new sleep programs in an arms race to win over travelers looking for accommodations that will help them get a full night's rest while aboard.

But the rise of sleep tourism needn't be limited to only luxury hotels that have the capital to devote a gargantuan sum per key to noise-dampening materials, new air purification systems or state-of-the-art bedding systems that have built-in temperature and moisture controls. Rather, any brand can build a strategic plan for deploying affordable sleep enhancements to their rooms and their onsite services.

But to be strategic in the true sense of the word, and not just remixing amenities arbitrarily based on what the competition is doing, the most important term to have a base understanding of is 'sleep architecture'.

Lest we forget that it has only been a decade or so that society has started to approach sleep not just as an unconscious and unnecessary aspect of life but as perhaps the most vital period of the 24-hour cycle. This is when the body goes to work on building muscles or restoring other organs, when the immune system is most active to prevent disease propagation, when hyperemotional states are reset to baseline and when memories are transferred from short-term to long-term storage. The latter of these two processes mostly occur during rapid eye movement (REM) sleep while the first two repair pathways largely occur during deep or slow wave sleep (also called non-REM sleep).

Sleep architecture describes the controlling operator in the brain that determines the daily rhythm of when you feel tired when you should wake up, when you should extend the duration of sleep and how to allocate the time you are asleep to REM and non-REM.

As an example, let's say your regular sleep-wake cycle is 10:30 pm to 5:30 am and you had a heavy barbell squats day at the gym. As you're drifting off that night, the brain says to itself, "Okay, we have seven hours here and we did a lot of damage to our musculoskeletal system today, so let's devote more time to slow wave repair at the sacrifice of REM-based memory codification." Bundling a big gym day with lots of important meetings may result in some important information conveyed during those meetings being forgotten because the brain prioritizes non-REM repair tasks.

Once you understand that the architecture of sleep is all about maintaining a rhythm and the allocation of limited resources, you can begin to design some sleep programming for your hotel that is highly personalized, customizable, and more effective – and thus more meaningful and valuable – based on a guest's needs on any particular evening. Here are some ideas to inspire you with what you can do for programming as lensed through the principles of sleep architecture:

1. *Melatonin supplementation.* Ostensibly the most renowned sleep aid and one that's being studied as a longevity supplement, several hotels are now including melatonin-based beverages, low-dose pills or powder additives as part of the minibar or in the sundry. The issue with this supplement is timing; take it too late and in too high a dose (which is very easy to do) then you will

likely wake up quite groggy, especially if your sleep rhythm hasn't adjusted to a new time zone. As such, melatonin wouldn't be recommended for someone arriving in the wee hours of the morning and looking for something to settle the nerve before drifting off. Instead, a signature herbal tea with chamomile, passionflower, lemon balm or other natural ingredients will work far better to gently lull you to sleep. Then on the techie side, there are quite a few devices, especially those in the IR (infrared) and PEMF (pulsed electromagnetic field) areas that claim to extend REM and promote deep wave, so that you can maximize whatever your body and mind need after an intense travel day.

2. *Circadian lighting equipment.* It's becoming common knowledge that we should all limit blue light and stick with amber-red wavelengths at night to get a good night's sleep. Sleep architecture tells us the answer in that you have a bodily clock that is sensitive to blue light. A few hotels are keen to meet this need, upgrading their lighting systems with non-overhead, dimmed evening lights as well as ones that can adjust into the red spectrum to set the mood for sleep. A far cheaper amenity is to offer blue light-blocking glasses. Sleep architecture also tells us that these solutions may not do the trick. Suppose your daily rhythm is to wake up at 6 am EDT in Toronto then you head out to Vancouver on a business trip for the week. You eat right, you settle into your room, and you wake up at 3 am PDT. Counterintuitively, to bring your clock back three hours to the West Coast tempo, you may want some softer, balanced yellow light in your room alongside a noncaffeinated energizing tea to extend your bodily clock.
3. *Bedding customization.* When you start regularly tracking your sleep, one of the first things you may discover is that you wake up and move around quite frequently during the night. These can be 'unconscious wakeups' while the latter is often ascribed as a form of 'restless leg syndrome'. The cause of these can be poor nutrition, stress, acute bodily pain, room temperature, moisture, bad air quality, uncomfortable linens, uncomfortable mattresses, uncomfortable pillows, or any combination of these. What we do know is that these sleep interruptions can negatively affect bodily repair and REM cycling. Enter a host of new-age suppliers ready to help solve these issues. You have uber-expensive mattresses with built-in temperature controls being deployed at luxury hotels. You have pillow concierge services where guests can sample different firmness levels. You have smart thermostats that can better help to keep the ambient temperature at the scientifically preferred 19C. You have more breathable linens. You have materials that don't emit volatile organic compounds (VOCs) and more effective HVACs. Combine these features with sleep tracking wearables and your guests can see the overnight benefit to their health in terms of improved sleep quality scores.
4. *Food menus.* The current heuristic for getting the best possible sleep is the 3-2-1: no food three hours from sleep, no water two hours out and no screens one hour out. By doing this, it means that your blood is never being redirected

to your digestive tract to absorb food and can squarely focus on repairing the body during slow-wave sleep. This alone means that in general snacking before bed is bad for the health, but alas, sleep architecture suggests that the answer needs to be individualized. To start, if you regularly snack before bed then this has become a part of your daily blueprint; interrupting this by not snacking when combined with the stressor that is a foreign bedroom can be enough to cause a cortisol or adrenaline release at times when they aren't conducive to falling fast asleep. Given these rhythmic challenges, hotels can best serve varying guest needs by designing sleep-friendly food menus comprised of light, nutrient-dense and easily digestible snacks.

To close, we hope this wasn't too far into the weeds of the science of sleep. This is still an emerging field but as you can see there are numerous applications for our industry. Above all, what we are witnessing is a great societal push for more awareness of the importance of quality sleep, and this will ultimately compel hotels to start designing services and amenities that cater directly to this guest demand. Hence, you best start building a sleep strategy for your hotel and understanding sleep architecture will help to ensure that you develop a highly fruitful plan.

Hotel Longevity: Wellness Versus Illness

Accredited to Joyce Sunada's, "If you don't make time for your wellness, you will be forced to make time for your illness."

The crux of this segment is to help you, the hotelier, profit from the ongoing convergence of scientific research, medical technologies, supply chains and societal awareness that are leading to a revolution in life-extending possibilities. With that mouthful said, the focus should nevertheless be the here and now because, to put it squarely, why worry about popular aspects of the 2040s when you're triaging daily staffing shortages, inflation, and a possible swath of cancellations from the latest COVID variant?

And so, for the year ahead, the in-vogue trends of human longevity or antiaging have the most pertinence for a hotel within the confines of what we presently codify as a wellness program. Therein, with this coronavirus still top of mind for everyone, it's important to look at the difference between the words 'wellness' and 'illness' because they are being redefined as mirror images of the same intracellular functionality, with the direct application being upsell programs for your guestrooms and spa that work in both capacities.

Without a biology degree, the most straightforward way to explain this is that it's all connected. Problems with your heart not only affect performance in the gym but can also decrease your cognition, depress your immune system, trigger hair graying or cause digestive issues, often in a self-perpetuating, positive feedback loop. The reverse pathways are also true, where a long-haul influenza-like disease can preoccupy the body to the point where it lacks the bandwidth to perform regular maintenance on a myriad of other processes.

A good analogy here is to think of your body as an office desk or email inbox. When you're overloaded with quick tasks that require your immediate attention and nonstop meetings, you seldom have the time or energy to focus on the intensive, purposeful projects that will actually benefit the brand in the near or distant future instead of simply keeping the lights on for one more day at a time.

For your own googling pleasure, look up the 'informational theory of aging' or the 'mitochondrial theory of aging' (the energy creation units existing in every cell of every animal on the planet), along with a few similar other postulates that are attempting to explain on a molecular level how systemic aging, chronic diseases and general bodily breakdown occur. By helping reframe every part of the body as one unified machine, the hope is to develop techniques – that is, wellness programs – that act to fix everything all at once, leading to fewer visual signs of aging, more brainpower and longer lifespans.

In this sense, illness is the inverse of wellness. All those kale smoothies, frantic Peloton workouts, CoQ10 supplements, guided meditation sessions and lavender bubble baths work to amplify a human's baseline functionality. By doing so, individual units of the body, much like your email inbox, aren't bogged down by minutia and can more adeptly pivot to whatever problem the randomness of the world throws its way, be it a carcinogen in that cheeseburger you just ate, a free-floating virus particle that lodges in your nostril or one of the quintillion rays of UV light bombarding our planet that happens to cause a mutagenic break in the DNA of one of your skin cells.

Wellness is your best defense against the chaos of the universe. It's also often the cheapest where, as the proverb goes, an ounce of prevention is worth a pound of cure. Eating right, exercising and giving up smoking will save you from heart surgery a decade or two later. And as luck would have it, millions of people, or dare we say billions, are waking up to this principle and incorporating it into their livelihoods.

Knowing that this antiaging enlightenment is ramping up means that guests will soon come to not only want but expect wellness programs from their chosen hotels. And if you don't have these value-adds set up and properly marketed in one capacity or another, your property will be immediately disqualified.

To those who think we're speaking in tongues, yes the 'heads in beds' mentality will persist for limited and select service properties. There will always be the customer who's just looking for a comfy bed in a quiet room – no frills whatsoever. But this hospitality segment will increasingly suffer from commoditization, squeezing the ADRs you can charge and forcing you to cut corners until your hotel is essentially a vending machine for travelers.

The future of luxury or upscale travel will be defined by experiences, of which wellness programs will play a huge contributing role in how much enjoyment, satisfaction or meaning each guest derives from their hotel stays. Moreover, we see this trend seeping into the four-star and corporate mindsets where guests progressively want such amenities as in-room workout equipment, wholly organic meal options, or sleep-promoting room enhancements.

To close, we propose that, because antiaging is increasingly on people's minds, wellness should therefore be on every hotelier's radar, no matter the star classification, as a way to safeguard brand equity as well as increase per-guest revenue capture by offering various upsell opportunities that play into this disposition. As for specific tactics and programs, for that, we could write a 300-page dissertation that would be out of date the moment it hit the press, so do your own internet-based research and brainstorm amongst your peers what can work for your specific organization.

Hotel Longevity: Sleeping on a Pile of Profits

What hotels don't promote a good night's sleep nowadays? While the offerings have gone from the erstwhile novel introduction of Westin's Heavenly Beds to today's perfunctory pillow concierge, hotels have yet to tap this well fully. Those brands that do wholeheartedly continue down this path will come to realize tremendous revenues for their efforts.

Even though we've known for millennia that sleep plays an important part in our moods, energy levels and even appearances, 'sleep science' is only now reaching the mainstream, so much so that 'sleep tourism' – defined as traveling for the express purpose of enhancing one's sleep quality – is a fully marketable segment with travelers willing to pay thousands of dollars for multi-night packages.

With the modern world bombarding with blue-light-heavy screens every moment of our waking lives, people of all demographics are increasingly recognizing this (hopefully) daily activity as critical for determining the following day's productivity and its role in supporting the immune system and bodily longevity.

As more people begin to adopt effective sleep hygiene techniques at home, they will come to expect such programs to exist at their hotels of choice. Particularly if you aim to attract the largely affluent antiaging or wellness-seeking crowd, building a robust sleep program that permeates a variety of operations is mandatory.

We argue that as this trend becomes commonplace in households, hotels must stay one giant step ahead to wow guests and elevate the brand, either to substantiate higher ADRs or to cross-sell sleep-oriented products. It's an arms race; the more sleep science awareness there is, the more travelers will come to demand great amenities from all properties (and not just wellness resorts already renowned for these programs).

Here's a laundry list of sleep-enhancing ideas you can consider, some cheap and others not:

- Linen, bed and pillow types known for their quality in this regard
- Soporific herbal teas like chamomile or passionflower available in-room or on-demand
- Clinically safe, over-the-counter sleep aids like melatonin or valerian root also available as a guestroom amenity or as an on-demand service
- Specific F&B options designed and promoted for their sleep-improving qualities

- Nutritionists, herbalists, hypnotherapists, RMTs, physiotherapists or any other manner of 'sleep experts' available for onsite consultations
- Purposefully designed spa treatments with products available for purchase in the gift shop
- Convection saunas, infrared saunas, steam rooms, and relaxation lodges
- Onsite yoga, meditation, mindfulness, breath-work, or group healing classes
- In-room guided programs per the above or others like progressive muscle relaxation (PMR)
- Bathroom amenities with ingredients known to enhance sleep or even nasal oil applications
- Mineral or vitamin-infused showers proven to relax the body
- Circadian lighting that naturally shifts from blue (morning) to amber (night)
- Smart thermostats that lower the temperature in the middle of the night to prolong sleep
- In-room noise minimalization, which may require better windows, new HVAC or thicker doors at a high capex to do right, or easier-to-implement noise canceling equipment that provides for adaptive sound masking
- In-room aromatherapy, including dispersal machines, soaps, incense, candles (be careful), oils, and fabrics, for calming scents like lavender or jasmine
- New-age bedside electronics that offer everything from the melodic sounds of crashing ocean waves help you doze off to intuitive alarm clocks that connect to the room controls via IoT
- Dedicated relaxation spaces like a cozy fireplace library or green-walled naturalistic lounge
- Soothing activities like Zen Garden or mandala art classes
- Wearable bedtime devices such as a smartwatch or smart ring that monitor a guest's vitals during sleep as well as connect back to an AI that can then offer algorithmic recommendations for the following night or modify room controls in media res via IoT
- Even more sci-fi, advanced health diagnostic tools like a metabolome bloodwork assessment (noninvasive via skin-contact sensors) that gives a picture of all metabolites in the body then returns specific dietary, medicinal and exercise regiments

Although many of the above may require a bit of PIP, the mix and match you choose ultimately depends on your brand and who you want to attract. Be advised: the wealthier the prospect, the more sleep amenities you must have in place to win them over. This is because such guests are likely already accustomed to the more prevalent ones and will continue to seek out innovators.

In all recent asset management assignments, building a wellness program or augmenting the existing one has been a topic of discussion, with a sleep as a central topic therein. We conduct this exercise because we know that a good night's sleep is a leading factor in guest satisfaction, but also because of the aforementioned upsell opportunities and long-term brand equity support.

Rome wasn't built in a day, though, and neither will your sleep program. Determine what can be done given your budget and what fits with your locale, then map it out in phases so that your team can properly execute on all new SOPs and add-ons. You can even start by carving out a new room category specifically marketed for its sleep benefits.

Whichever direction you determine, know that there's a way to increase or at the very least protect your revenues. Don't believe us? Sleep on it then decide.

Hotel Longevity: Getting More Wellness Revenues from Men

The longevity revolution holds a lot of promise. Still, with labor challenges, supply chain nuisances, and a never-ending looming recession that may handicap the current travel recovery, hotel brands need practical solutions for the here and now. Per the title, let's consider taking what you have and tweaking your services or messaging to ramp up select demographics.

In the interim, between the current post-pandemic revenge travel and the launch of radical new antiaging treatments, traditional wellness and spa services like massages, facials, and mani-pedis continue to be a profound growth vertical for hotels. Still, the totality of 'wellness' goes far beyond the four walls of your spa treatment rooms, incorporating F&B, in-room amenities, public space elements and curated activities, meaning both more work for you to appease this demand as well as huge profits when done right.

The pandemic has only accelerated this trend as people have been compelled to explore the broad concept of mindfulness, reorient their workout routines, cook healthy homemade meals or learn about the benefits of good sleep habits. For the decade ahead, these at-home adjustments will seep into guest expectations, with many travelers looking for transformative wellness programs as a value-add and eventually as mandatory in their hotel selections.

There are many opex and capex decisions to be made in order to take advantage of this burgeoning trend, but for now we ask what you are doing to activate the other half of the population that is likely to be underserved by your current wellness amenities. Before embarking on an elaborate upgrade to your spa or implementing a new plant-based food menu, there are many tweaks you can make to increase revenues from men. As we will see, these will also serve the dual purpose of differentiating your brand in the face of inbound competition as everyone else looks to get in on the wellness craze.

Men as the New Wellness Profit Center

To give you a sense of the potential here, let's outline some stats:

- According to ISPA data (2019), men are more likely than women to choose body services (30% compared to 24% of women), fitness or sports services

(29% compared to 10% of women) and hydrotherapy (20% compared to 11% of women)

- A British market survey found that men in their thirties lead the spending on male grooming products, ahead of men in their forties, who part with an average of £70 ($115 USD) a month
- Recent 2022 reports have shown that 49% of spa-goers in the US are men, with these figures up from the 29% of men using spas in 2005
- Forecasted by a study from the American Med Spa Association (2018), men are going to go from 10% of the marketplace to 30% in the next decade due to the rising spending power of male millennials, with the data suggesting men are outspending women by 13% in med spas
- According to the Wellness, Spas, Health and Travel 2030 survey, solo men have made it to top three in terms of key target segments for wellness in the Middle East and in Asia

As you can see, not only is there an opportunity from motivating more men to use your spa services or select your property due to its wellness program, but there's also an even bigger fish in the worldwide growth of this industry.

Hinted at from the previous mention of the pandemic-born lifestyle changes, one of the largest contributors to the ever-blooming TAM (total addressable market) for wellness will be its convergence with longevity and preventative science – treatments, foods, supplements, exercises and activities proven to counteract advanced-stage diseases like cancer, diabetes, blood flow disorders, arthritis, dementia and visual signs of aging.

Hotel brands are primed to get in on this longevity revolution as we have the resources to develop synergistic programs that bring together multiple beneficial programs under one roof. To learn more about how hotels can get this off the ground, we collaborated with Laszlo Puczko, founder of HTWWLife, an international intelligence and advisory group focused on wellness travel.

"Gone are the days of 'pampering' and similar verbiage that seldom appeals to the more masculine orientations," started Puczko. "To start, reframe your existing spa nomenclature to focus on the health and wellbeing benefits in terms of destressing, bodily rejuvenation, vitality, mental clarity, muscle recovery or improved sleep. This also extends to your visual messaging and advertisements by ensuring that all genders and a greater diversity of demographics are represented, not just women aged 25 to 45. Note that men prefer to choose offers that have clear outcomes and results. In this sense the term 'spa' may represent only some space in the hotel and not what it can functionally do for men."

As an extension of this, think couples and mixed groups. With evidence overwhelmingly supporting the notion of communal experiences enhancing personal wellbeing, leisure guests will be looking for those amenities will social aspects included. Conversely, the solo corporate traveler and remote worker are yet two more untapped segments for wellness where specific services aimed towards a 'quick recharge' or 'midday mindset reset' can generate incremental demand.

Protecting Then Growing Your Brand

Beyond this core repositioning, expansion and evolution will inevitably involve building out a plan, recruiting more specialized labor and devoting budget for a serious renovation. While these upgrades can heighten demand, facilitate more cross-selling and boost ADR, understand that they are foremost a defensive measure. Due to both the lucrative size of this space as well as shifting guest expectations in the wellness direction, your competitors will also be forced to chase this cash cow.

It is hardly a zero-sum game. Part of the reason why the TAM for wellness will continue to grow is because of a customer-accessibility positive feedback loop where more entrants in the industry will, in turn, elicit more awareness and demand, then more overall consumption will draw in more entrants and lower costs through economies of scale. Still, it's up to you to be first past the post and to differentiate your brand through new well-being-oriented services that aren't offered by the hotel down the street.

Luckily, there are manifold prospects available nowadays to serve this need under five wide categories:

1. *Treatments.* The spa will persist as the cornerstone of any holistic wellness program, but that doesn't mean you shouldn't explore new treatments, cutting-edge equipment, trending ingredients and gift shop sales opportunities. Local partnerships are expected, but now global supply chains can let you source niche longevity-promoting products previously unavailable.
2. *Therapies.* You can go the route of advanced stem cell injections or related clinical therapies like platelet rich plasma treatments, but these have both a substantial setup cost and serious labor restrictions. More attainable might be those programs addressing the modern conveniences of consistent temperature controls and junk light from computer monitors. Consider ice baths, infrared saunas, hyperbaric chambers, red, yellow or blue light immersions or sound-dampened meditation pods, all of which are gaining popularity.
3. *Nutrition.* The awareness for feeding high-octane fuel into our engines has peaked, meaning that F&B is a mandatory element of this conversation. People want to eat cleaner, know where their foods are sourced and are going plant-based both for health and to protect the environment. Beyond servicing the vegans, vegetarians and flexitarians, you can value-add existing menus by offering supplements, freshly blended juices or spice-integrated shots designed to boost the immune system.
4. *Sleep.* As the restorative effects of a good night's sleep are beginning to be understood on an anatomical level, so too are the in-room features progressing. Think circadian-attenuated smart lighting, vitamin-infused showers, napercise classes or even something as simple as ensuring that calming herbal teas are available.
5. *Activities.* Group of private classes for yoga, meditation, mindfulness and physiotherapies are seeing swells in demand. But also think about the

experiential side, where travelers are increasingly valuing the calm of serene beach setup or guided nature hikes to let them get those forest-bathing benefits.

Male-Oriented Wellness in Practice

As you can tell, wellness has a litany of possible revenue verticals for your brand to capitalize upon; it's more a matter of developing a congruent slate of features across a variety of operations for a cohesive brand identity. Key towards getting revenues from men, though, is to state all these amenities in terms of their health benefits.

To close, Puczko offered one such example from South Korea. The Dr. O & Ananti private clinic at the Ananti Cove in Busan, Korea, offers personalized treatments for well-aging and both internal and external well-being. This nation has long valued skincare, grooming and healthy lifestyle choices as we see in the products that reach our Western shores, but it's important to note that these values exist equally for both women as well as men. Hence, the guest journeys at Ananti Cove are tailor-made for each guest, with the wellness programming itself being gender-neutral.

Looking at the current slate being introduced to attract men to the wellness world, there are indeed some great innovations. You may find it to be unexpected that men actually opt in for such experiences, but a slight twist or tweak – like beer and stretching, eco spas or kilted yoga led by a couple of Scotsmen – may be just the ticket for big revenues in the near-term.

Hotel Longevity: Loyalty Escape Velocity

With the rise of wellness, anti-aging, and longevity, one of the top outcomes for any individual traveler is to extend one's active years on this planet (healthspan) to have time to enjoy the many places, cultures, cities, foods, arts, and hotels that are on offer. Otherwise, what's the point? And if everyone is living healthily into their geriatric years (or later), then this has profound and highly lucrative prospects for your loyalty program.

Longevity Puts More Value into Loyalty

The term 'escape velocity' was popularized in physics and astronautical parlance to denote the force required to drive a rocket beyond the punitive pull of Earth's gravity, which would 'free' the object from crashing back down into the ocean somewhere. More recently, the renowned futurist Ray Kurzweil used the term 'longevity escape velocity' to denote the point at which medical technology allows humans to be freed from the inevitability of aging and death.

While immortality is still very much in the realm of sci-fi and not sci-fact, we are making abundant strides to say without any doubt that average lifespans are getting longer (COVID statistical skewing notwithstanding), particularly in highly developed nations and amongst affluent communities. Knowing with certainty that you have many more years of adventure ahead of you before your joints become rickety, your immune dips to a point of abject vulnerability and travel insurance becomes an expensive obstacle alters the very core of how you select your destination as well as your lodgings.

Where this 'longevity escape velocity' affects hotels is in the brand advocacy efforts that we undertake to make 'customers for life'. It's a costly gambit to deliver exceptional service for a 75-year-old guest when the average mortality is around 82. That actuarial equation tips when average mortality rises by a decade or two.

In such a scenario, the work you put in towards winning that septuagenarian and have them sing your praises via word of mouth, word of mouse, or return visits can deliver exponentially more ROI because said customers' lives are lasting that much longer and they thus have more time to support your brand. Moreover, we're talking healthspan here and not just lifespan, which means that those newfound years of advocacy aren't necessarily mired by dementia; your guests remember your hotel with clarity and can cognitively regale their respective social circles on the merits of staying at one of your properties.

In Silicon Valley, the apt term for this would be 'customer lifetime value' (CLV), with the formula attempting to calculate how much revenue is based on average sales value, number of transactions, and retention timeframe. As longevity takes hold, it would be as if that third input doubles or triples, which in turn delivers a multiple on CLV.

Customer sentiment is a double-edged sword, though, and the negative end also grows a fat tail as longevity gains traction. That is, when lifespans increase, so too is the time that a slighted guest has to besmirch your name. Hence, in a world where antiaging becomes the norm, even more extensive efforts must be taken to protect your brand from the consequences of bad reviews and word of mouth.

Planning for Today

This brings us to the present. What can you do now?

First, know that the relentless march of scientific progress will most likely lead to numerous antiaging breakthroughs in the coming years and decades, and this will more significantly benefit the members of the current millennial and centennial generations as the recipients of this cumulative knowledge. We already see this taking effect insofar as the increasing number of young people who are vegan, vegetarian, don't smoke cigarettes, drink less, regularly exercise, take longevity supplements, or engage in other life-extension activities. Efforts to win over these cohorts now could pay dividends for far longer than what the current mortality figures would suggest.

This isn't to exclude the boomers and Gen Xers from the discussion. They also have access to the same medical treatments, supplements, and instruction as their more youthful counterparts, in addition to a treasure chest of disposable income to throw at a well-marketed wellness resort, spa or any other longevity products you attempt to cross-sell.

Your Action Plan

So, what you can do in the here and now is to outline the entirety of the guest value chain then look for ways to enhance personalization, loyalty growth and vehicles for promoting your wellness vertical. Technology is a necessity for your teams to automate repetitive tasks to free up their time for better service delivery as well as to start imbuing predictive analytics to the total customer experience.

With the guest value chain mapped out, you can start looking at all the touchpoints to see where real-time software platforms can either enhance the relationship or at least give you more data to know your guests better for future interactions. Fill in or upgrade the gaps one by one or look for ways to consolidate your tech stack and data, both of which make it easier for future enhancements.

Above all, we stress with the concept of loyalty escape velocity that with the prospects of slower aging comes more travel options. It's not exactly a direct relationship between augmenting average mortality and increases in CLV. Guests will be harder to impress because of their prolonged youthful attitudes, and you're going to need to step up the level of service and relationship-building to stand apart as a memorable brand. And the time to start is now because, well, we aren't getting any younger.

Hotel Longevity: The Transformation Economy for Post-Retirement

Now firmly into this series, it should be apparent that an underlying effect of the nascent longevity revolution is that people are going to live longer. But not only that, their healthspans are going to increase – the years where they are active and able to travel, in opposition to their 'diseasespans'. This has profound implications for every part of our society, foremost of which is the concept of retirement.

If you were to travel back to the 1800s and ask an elderly gentlemen – back then, an 'elder' might be someone in their fifties – what he planned to do once he retired, he would give you a puzzled look.

Retirement as an institution for the masses didn't exist before the labor movements established it during the turn of the century. Prior to this and the advent of pensions or government support programs, you worked until the day you died or were too feeble to leave bed. And due to lifespans and healthcare systems at the time, there was no need for retirement as people tended to die off before they could even contemplate a life after their working years!

Knowing that retirement is a relatively modern luxury, how can we purport to have gotten it right the first time around without continuous adjustments? The very notion of a hard stop at age 65 is based on outdated mortality tables, where that specific number was determined based on a fiscally manageable number of post-retirement years where the ex-worker wasn't to have much of a third act. Now that retirees are living into their nineties and the number of centenarians is ticking up, the age at which someone ends their full-time professional career is likewise due for a review.

The Transformation Economy and the Baby Boomers

This brings us to the concept of 'The Transformation Economy'. Coined by Joe Pine and Jim Gilmore, who also defined 'The Experience Economy' in the early 1990s, transformation goes a step further than the notion of people pursuing 'time well spent' through experiences in what can be thought of as 'time well invested.' Transformation denotes experiences that pay dividends with compound interest, where one's own future incorporates the achievement of some significant aspiration.

In other words, people want activities that are not just entertaining, interactive and memorable. People want experience that will ultimately improve their livelihoods and bestow meaning, purpose or ikigai as the Japanese would call it. In Maslow's hierarchy of needs, transformative experiences are ones that self-actualize – the tip of the pyramid.

What we're seeing as longevity creeps into our social fabric is that people retire – settling into the whole lackadaisical lifestyle of daily crosswords, long walks, dining out all the time, tai chi in the park, aquafit classes and lots of television – but then, right as the grim reaper would come knocking as per 20th century actuarial tables, the retiree is still within their healthspan yet bored with the slow pace of it all.

So, the long-lived retiree now enters a post-retirement phase. They want to reengage their minds with hobbies, community volunteering, mentorship and emeritus positions in companies – activities that transform. Therein lies a huge opportunity for hotels to develop programs appealing to this mindset.

A big trend that will continue over the next two decades is the mass retirement of baby boomers, so much so that it's estimated that one in six people on the planet will be over the age of 65 by 2050. Notably for boomers, they are perhaps the wealthiest generation relative to other cohorts, and their retirement brings with it a lot of disposable income cocked and loaded for purposeful travel. Members of this group will likely start with the fully catered cruises and grand tours through Europe or Asia, but eventually their demands will look for ways to incorporate some form of giving back while traveling to new or known destinations.

Societal Transformation Activities

Think volunteerism programs, vocational excursions where you can try out new jobs or, if you operate a resort, ecotourism activities either prepackaged or as a marketable add-on. In addition to the business or organizational transformations that are happening in workplaces around the globe, this harks at the notion of 'societal transformation' whereby people derive meaning by helping others and making a difference, whether that involves the local community or improving the environment.

You might scoff at the idea of people wanting to scour a beach picking up trash while on vacation but take a step back and consider it through the lens of the post-retirement transformation economy. Another ecotourism possibility is 'sharing the catch' where travelers pay an admission fee to assist the crew on a sustainable fishing charter. As two more possibilities, rural properties can also incorporate a 'working farm' or add a beekeeping experience once an apiary is built.

For urban hotels, consider how you can partner with local colleges or high/ middle schools. As professional boomers exit the workforce, they are taking with them so much specific industry knowledge that will be 'sitting on the sidelines' without a proper mentorship vehicle for it to be disseminated. Imagine you are visiting a city and in between high dining, museums and shopping trips, you also have the opportunity give a guest lecture at a nearby high school, with all logistics arranged through your accommodations provider so that it's a relatively frictionless value-add to your hotel stay.

This may be the 1% inspiration and leaves out the 99% perspiration to get such a program set up. And yet, the early adopters will not only develop an attractive reason to visit for boomers but also get lots of local street cred and word of mouth – a true win-win. While undoubtedly you have other more pressing matters, the burgeoning trend of post-retirement aspirations is nevertheless one that intrepid hotel brands will find a way to leverage in interesting and highly lucrative ways.

Hotel Longevity: The Silver Tsunami and Dependency Ratio Revenues

Some have estimated that by 2050, one in three people will be over the age of 65 in many advanced economies, namely most of Western Europe, Japan, South Korea, New Zealand and a few others. Just think about how this grand shift will permeate through your daily life. For instance, you go for your daily walk and there's an outside chance you don't see a single 'young' person.

Yes, that's 2050 – a long way's off. So, why care? Well, demographic shifts of this nature aren't like flipping on a light switch (or punctuated events like pandemics, world wars and supervolcano eruptions). They happen gradually, often at a glacial pace that only economists can accurately describe in hindsight. While this one-in-three stat is for 2050, expect to see this become an ever-present issue within a decade's time. Knowing is half the battle, and now it's time to pivot your business accordingly.

This burgeoning and global change to demography is what's been catchily labeled as 'The Silver Tsunami', although we specifically put the word 'young' in quotations in the opening paragraph because when everyone is old then youth becomes the outlier. (As a digression, the word 'silver' is also presumptuous because it assumes that by 2050 we won't have the longevity science, practices and technology to effortlessly reverse hair graying.)

Our purpose with this column is to first calm your mind at what can seem on the surface to be a paralyzing long-term development. In fact, it's the opposite; it will usher in a prodigious new profit center for hotel brands that rivals or even exceeds rooms revenues, if these companies play their cards right. While your organization can go the route of medical tourism (people traveling specifically for a healthcare treatment with the hotel experience as secondary) or antiaging wellness (hotel experience primary with longevity programming as the auxiliary incentive), let's discuss a third vertical that relies upon the 'dependency ratio'.

A term ripped straight from economics textbooks, the dependency ratio describes a national or multinational percentage of the total citizenry that falls outside of the highly productive Working Age Population (WAP) – today defined roughly as ages 18 to 65 – and is thus 'dependent' on those in the WAP for all matter of sustenance, be it food production, shipping, manufacturing, software development or caregiving services. The higher the dependency ratio, the more strain there is on those left in the WAP to provide a great tax base to support public goods (like infrastructure projects, pension funds or hospitals) and the lower the overall supply of labor (which can in turn lead to sector-specific labor crises, salary inflation, commodity disruptions and numerous other macro-effects).

Within this broad definition are plenty of nuances as we pan the looking glass onto a specific country or issue related to aging:

- For various socioeconomic reasons, advanced economies are notorious for diminishing birth rates, meaning fewer 'replacements' into the WAP as aged workers exit via retirement
- While Japan has long been cited as the canary in the coalmine for what will happen to all other advanced economies, the Silver Tsunami is actually a global progression where emerging market economies are steadily taking advantage of modern medical advances in the form of better public healthcare systems to catch up to the West in terms of average lifespans, and this in turn is contributing to their citizens adopting 'Western lifestyles' which include lower birth rates
- A big issue with increasing lifespans is the rising incidence of 'end stage diseases' such as dementia, Alzheimer's, Parkinson's and other ailments that impair self-subsistence, thereby incentivizing WAP labor to shift to caregiving roles and straining supply for other industries
- Also important to any population graying and dependency ratio discussions is how the travel insurance industry will adjust their premiums to offer a non-prohibitive means for the majority of the elderly population to continue exploring the world (and not just the wealthy), particularly when framed according to the 'economic gravity' of not having as many WAP travelers available as prospective customers to sustain their revenues
- A declining WAP and the need for more 'high touch, low skill' caregivers will put increasing pressure on robotics and AI development in order to maintain domestic output and growth, not to mention the probability of sweeping changes to immigration policies in advanced economies

Always the optimists, the Silver Tsunami, combined with the strides being made in longevity practices, present vast and highly lucrative opportunities around the world to target local, regional, and international guests for wellness experiences, with applicability for all hotel categories. This truly is an evergreen territory that any hotel company can investigate as a new source of long-term revenues.

Knowing that our planet is destined for a much higher dependency ratio above the present day, the question then is how do you prepare your hotel brand to profit from all this?

Focusing only on catering to dependents, there are plenty of opportunities in the near-term:

1. Accessibility will become a primary determinant for hotel bookings, meaning that you need to adjust your messaging on the website, in marketing materials, in prearrival communications and through the retraining of chatbots to dispel concerns and raise booking confidence
2. With the make-or-break nature of accessibility for many travelers' purchasing decisions, some hotel companies may benefit by pivoting to become the brand of choice for this graying demographic, centering their offerings around 'all accessible rooms' where every guestroom or suite is configured with new amenities, safety features and IoT integrations that give peace of mind to the elderly, along with a myriad of value-added, on-demand caregiving services
3. Also given the rising demand for caregivers, there's an opening for new hotel brands that blend traditional guestroom and extended stay products with offerings more indicative of long-term care facilities so that specialized eldercare labor can be shared amongst the two verticals
4. Building on the notion of chatbot and machine learning tools combined with the long-term dwindling of the WAP, hotels should start to investigate their options for robot workers to help offload the more rudimentary houseman and runner operations
5. Rising dependency ratios can lead to increasing numbers of multigenerational travelers where working age guests bring along a senior family member (or other dependent) and will be influenced by onsite caregiving services, wellness programming targeted at the elderly, the ability to book adjoining rooms directly off the website and any packaging that mixes these together to offer more perceived value or convenience to the booker

With those five mentioned, hopefully it's clear that every brand needs to map out their plan to capitalize on this global trend. To close, take a moment to consider the decades-long effects from the recently introduced 'Time Bank' concept in Switzerland where young people can volunteer by helping the elderly and thereby accrue 'time credits' for when they too are older. The dawn of the Silver Tsunami, and any resultant labor issues, is not a battle that hotels need fight alone; it is a challenge that all industries and businesses will face to varying degrees. Yet, as always, there are lucrative first-mover advantages to those hotel brands that start evolving their services and features for these dependent travelers.

Hotel Longevity: Nature Knows Best

With all matters related to the longevity revolution – in particular how the graying of the population will result in the growth of verticals like hotel wellness and medical tourism – often it's best to go back to our roots.

A significant part of the antiaging, wellbeing and healthy living narrative stems from comparisons of modern, urban, helter-skelter life to that of our ancestral past before the agricultural revolution when we were all hunter-gatherers spending our days in communal tribes of no more than 150 people. By applying this comparison to a hotel's design, programming or branding, you can make a property far more welcoming and profitable in its wellness pursuits, and in fact many of these organic or nature-leaning suggestions can be done on a limited budget.

As evidence, we see this ancestral narrative reflected in the prominence of paleo or ketogenic dieting where the theory is that humans are ill-suited to digest most grains, cereals and pulses that were only domesticated within the past several millennia. We see it in cold plunges and ice baths, where the easy explanation – one that excludes biochemical discussions of heat shock proteins and mitochondrial activation – is centered around the fact that warm water is uncommon in nature. This philosophy is also a component of mindfulness and meditation, where neurologists have shown the health benefits of quieting the mind that is so often induced into an anxious state by our overstimulated environments.

The point herein is that as awareness for returning in part to the ways of our ancestors increases and people start to adjust their lifestyles to be more attuned to a more primal state, travelers will come to demand then expect their accommodations to likewise evolve in stride.

This particular aspect within the larger trend of hotel wellness should thus be on every brand's agenda as they look to evolve their product offerings over the decade ahead. In fact, there's a whole field of study (albeit some would deem it pseudoscience for the moment) emerging related to 'nature therapy' that looks at how specifically being amongst nature can rejuvenate the body, mind and spirit.

Nor is this a trend that only well-capitalized resorts can seize upon to guide their next big renovation. The notion that nature knows best has a multitude of wellness applications that any hotel in any category can incorporate without overwhelming capex.

Yes, some directions and programs are more expensive than others, and of course many will lean heavily into the luxury destination end of the spectrum. Still, this should not preclude economy, select-service or midscale properties appeasing primarily corporate and group guests from devising a plan with nature in mind. In fact, the opposite is true where incorporating more of these biomimetic elements can be just the ticket to revive a staid product.

Below is hardly an exhaustive list of what's possible. Instead, it's inspiration as to the breadth and flexibility of what can work for your brand, your target audience and your budget.

1. As a rather direct interpretation of *nature therapy*, develop programming for your guests to get out in a natural setting, like a horticultural tutorial, a la carte picnics or outdoor exercise class
2. Similarly, the idea of *forest bathing* is becoming popular where a guided hike or group meditation amongst the terpene-laden aero biome of a forest offers substantial health benefits
3. For urban properties, and especially after COVID brought attention to this matter, high quality *ventilation* (like HEPA filters) that fill guestrooms with clean, purified air are becoming marketing points unto themselves and key booking drivers for urban hotels
4. Urban hotels can also aim to *bring nature inside* with live plants, living walls in the lobby, biomimicry in selected artwork or art installations, themed wallpapers, green-spectrum décor (the color our brains most associate with nature), or types of biophilic design or tailored scents of pine, citrus and aromatic flowers that can be disbursed on demand through in-room devices
5. Nature has long been incorporated into cultural design styles like *Feng Shui* (Chinese), *Godai* (Japanese) or *Hygge* (Scandinavian) that often emphasize exposed woods, stone, the presence of water, proper flow in furniture orientation, ample natural light and optimized bed spaces
6. New science is also emerging around the concept of *negative ionization therapy* where the friction from recurrently running water (like that of waterfalls, heavy rainstorms or ocean waves) generates negatively charged ions in the air that calm our bodies, and this effect can be artificially recreated with small devices that can be hidden away in guestrooms
7. On this notion of resetting a body's natural charge, *earthing* or *grounding* – the simple act of touching your body to solid earth unencumbered by rubber-soled shoes or socks– is becoming a popular practice and ripe messaging fodder for any rural property
8. All this talk of being amongst nature or next to running water, other more esoteric forms of wellness like *halotherapy* – the breathing of tiny, restorative salt particles – can also serve to differentiate your wellness program or as an in-room, on-demand offering
9. With the awareness around the detrimental effects of artificial blue light from computer screens on sleep habits, *smart lighting* or *night lighting* is becoming a highly sought-after room feature so that travelers can program LEDs to shift into the amber-red hues to help set wind down or, alternatively, get a jolt of blue light in order to power through jetlag
10. Building on this idea of smart room tech is the progression towards a *connected room* that incorporates IoT devices that can restore a guest's sleep patterns to a natural state and offer a host of other wellness product integrations, namely

the aforementioned smart lighting, aromatherapy devices, smart mattresses and temporally modulated thermostats

11. Ancestral living also extends into your fitness programming through what some call *primal workouts* or *high intensity interval training* (HIIT) where the principle is that short bursts of varied, full-body heavy lifting help to maximize the metabolic benefits of exercise
12. Finally, getting back to nature obviously includes a rethink of your F&B strategy, incorporating not only more organic ingredients and paleo-friendly dishes but also *nose-to-tail cooking* whereby organ meats (however unpalatable they may seem at first) have been shown to be jampacked with key minerals or vitamins far above many fruits and vegetables

Perhaps you may deem these dozen territories as mere bells and whistles; perhaps there's a morsel here that can work for your brand. Regardless of your opinion on the growth of hotel wellness, it should be abundantly clear that there are many ways to get involved and creatively incorporate various schools of thought into your next big remodeling or product unveiling. Above all, when in doubt just look back at what our ancestors were accustomed to then proceed from there.

Hotel Longevity: Add Some Biohacking Foods

Prioritizing health, nutrition and wellness are a long-term trend, but how can any hotelier distill this multi-decade progression into one or two action items that can elicit measurable results over the next few quarters? You may not have a spa or capex for wholly new programming, so start small and start with F&B – an operation that nearly all hotel guests experience during their stays.

When it comes to food, the term 'biohacking' encompasses any and all additions to the plate that can literally hack the eater's (or drinker's) internal biology to elicit a positive health benefit – 'superfoods' as a synonym in this regard. Typically, these are smaller additions seldom comprising the bulk of the caloric intake but help to catalyze the macronutrient processing of the primary meal components.

To give you an idea of this, let's list some off, along with more scientific terms to substantiate their advantages, then run through how to market and measure these superfoods to evaluate whether or not there's a larger appetite for more wellness programming within your brand.

1. *Garlic* (contains sulfurous thiols that are antimicrobial, although not the best for the breath)
2. *Turmeric* (plenty of documentation on its anticancer effects)
3. *Apple cider vinegar* (blunts insulin response following carbohydrate intake)
4. *Caperberries* (highest in quercetin, a longevity antioxidant also found in onions and fruits)

5. *Parsley* (contains PQQ and apigenin which promote energy restoration in the cells)
6. *Cilantro* (a powerful chelator that removing heavy metals; tastes like soap for some people)
7. *Brazil nuts* (very high in selenium which is important for mercury chelation)
8. *Spirulina* (contains the anticancer molecule phycocyanin and helps chelate aluminum)
9. *Marine collagen* (vegan form of bovine collagen; over 30% of bodily protein is collagen)
10. *Edible flowers* (providing a whole color wheel of antioxidants and other beneficial compounds)

Besides your career goals as a hotel operator, we hope you start incorporating these foods into your diet. And the ten biohacking foods here are hardly an exhaustive list, so part of the experience is exploring all the other superfoods at your disposal (check out gac fruit from Vietnam which contains extremely high levels of lycopene, the predominant polyphenol in tomatoes).

Perhaps, though, you can already envision how these may play out as menu additions. Some ideas:

- Most breakfasts contain a yogurt bowl with some combination of fruit, nuts and seeds, where a dollop of Brazil nuts or spirulina can be a two-dollar extra
- At the smoothie bar, spirulina and marine collagen are already proven add-ons often priced at three or four dollars more per scoop
- Collagen, vegan or animal-derived, is now often sold under the buzzy 'bone broth soup' which can be great for winter menus
- As practically the only two salty fruits, caperberries and olives would make for a nice appetizer
- With people looking for alcohol alternatives, turmeric has been a mainstay when sold as 'golden milk' (nut milk, turmeric, cinnamon, ginger, black pepper and honey all boiled together)
- Likewise for dieters and as a digestif, apple cider vinegar, lemon juice, honey and sparkling water combine well into a restorative tonic
- For parsley, cilantro and edible flowers, these can all be sold as individual add-ons to a salad or main or combined as a 'fresh herbs and flowers' addition

From these ideas, you can see that nothing here is breaking the bank and nothing here is going to add seven figures to the bottom line either. Instead, it's about testing the waters.

Is there potential, both for future expansion of the healthy food options for your restaurant or as room service offerings? How would you know whether it's time to carve out a second restaurant devoted to nutritional eating? How receptive would these health-conscious diners be for other wellness products beyond F&B like spa, sleep programs or in-room fitness? These are the strategic questions we answer as part of any consulting assignment, then develop a plan for rolling out

Let's focus on the singular example of offering a handful of Brazil nuts as a $2.50 extra to the yogurt bowl (with the assumption that this is well-typeset in both the physical and digital menus so that it's visible). Restaurant guest purchases of this add-on will be recorded within the POS; from there you can do a basic before-and-after comparison to determine whether the availability of Brazil nuts was purchased in a significant amount and also if this addition increased total sales of the yogurt bowl.

Connecting your POS to the guest profile data in your PMS (whether it's a two-way integration or piping the data into a third entity like a CRM) allows for even more end-to-end feedback and analysis. If you know an overnight hotel guest purchased the Brazil nuts addition, you could set up an automated workflow within your post-stay survey platform to specifically ask about whether they would pay for other health-minded products during their trip as well as what their preferred products would be.

In this sense, the minutia can inform a greater whole. The two of us are very bullish on wellness for hotels, but this takes on numerous different forms depending on the brand. To discover what's best for your organization, you have to test and you have to measure, and the additional of a few biohacking foods can help you do just that.

Hotel Longevity: Boomers to Soon Boom

In this ongoing column on the growth of wellness as a profit center for hotels, one concurrent trends to be cognizant of is the aging of the baby boomer generation – ostensibly the wealthiest to date that is, at present, entering the prime travel years of early retirement. This generational shift intersects with the longevity revolution in many interesting ways that hotels can capitalize upon.

First of note is that because boomers are relatively richer than other generations, it behooves hotel brands to follow the money by developing branded programs and marketing campaigns that target this cohort, especially when there are 77 million of them in the United States alone. But this strategy is often at odds with growing wellness revenues because the burgeoning awareness for wellness and healthier lifestyles is largely happening amongst the younger generations who are not 'set in their ways'.

Not to stereotype too hard, but it is much harder to convince an older traveler with firmly cemented habits to be swayed by a wellness program so that they select your brand over the competition or are willing to pad their hotel stay with wellness-oriented activities. Speaking from personal experience amongst the two of us authors, we have Adam (millennial) who spent five year convincing Larry (boomer) to stop putting milk in his coffee (for your information, commercial pasteurized milk can be inflammatory and not really all that good for your bones) and to get off of the dogma of 'three square meals' in favor of an 8:16 intermittent fasting regimen.

But while you can't teach an old dog new tricks, necessity is the mother of invention. To put more bluntly, nothing will make a person adopt healthier habits faster than a severe, acute medical scare.

In this case, we have two concurrent trends:

1. Boomers are getting older, which means a higher chance of both becoming chronically sick and looking for a manageable solution to said sickness, whether preemptive or post-hoc.
2. Awareness for the efficacy of wellness and alternate medicine practices in illness prevention is likewise rising, as is accessibility to practitioners.

Right now, the numbers may suggest that guests are only coming to your hotel for leisure or business or as part of a group, and not much else. Have faith; the combination of these two major trends alone will mean more demand for wellness programming, with the wealthy boomer generation leading the way in making longevity practices a booming business for hotels.

Within this grand progression, it's important to also codify the difference between 'wellness primary' and 'wellness secondary' guests. The former are those that travel specifically to a destination for some form of medical tourism or transformative experience. The latter are traveling for other purposes but nevertheless want to stay healthy as they go.

This distinction is important on a strategic level in determining your overarching brand direction, particularly in how it intersects with another prominent trend – the rise of bleisure or workcations. As mentioned in a further column, retirement at age 65 itself is a relatively new concept, and even wealthy boomers who have the means to fully retire may opt for part-time emeritus roles or simply want to actively manage their equity portfolios while abroad (especially if they are relying on dividends as a part of their retirement income). And so, with the rise of bleisure, you now have a growing cohort of middle-aged or older professionals who keenly want to stay healthy while traveling in order to uphold their business or familial responsibilities.

Great; we've covered the demographic trends. What can your hotel do about it over the next two years?

In our view, it all comes back to the data. If your systems aren't connected to deliver rich guest profiles (whether within the PMS or pushed into a CRM), you won't know what your customers really want. You won't be able to identify any of the wellness primary or wellness secondary guests who have already traversed your premises. Moreover, you need data integrations to test whether small, incremental changes to your operations are having a meaningful effect on revenues. Third, if your teams are too busy handling the minutia of your existing operations, they won't have time to learn new SOPs so that you can develop a full-fledged wellness program.

While we don't want to get too far into the weeds of technology for this short article, the direction is nevertheless clear. You need your existing teams to be as productive as possible and fully empowered through automation technologies. Simultaneously, you can develop a roadmap for implementing a wellness program that is already fitted to what you know about what your customers want and what your budgets can allow. To this end, always keep in mind some of these long and slow, but also permanent, trends and where your brand fits into the bigger demographic picture.

Hotel Longevity: An Example to Get You Started

Top three takeaways:

- Building wellness revenues for a hotel requires a commitment to the long term.
- Know your customer and what will work within their preexisting travel motivations.
- Initial results show revenue potential, better guest satisfaction, and likelihood to return.

Look at any global statistic and you'll see that wellness for hotels is becoming popular as well as profitable ($4.9 trillion in 2019 according to the Global Wellness Institute). Our mission with this series is help hotel companies existing within any category or segment realize the best path forward for capitalizing on this booming trend.

Notably, by incorporating wellness into various operations, brands can both grow revenues per guest by introducing wellness-oriented add-ons to a hotel stay and, more defensively, prevent brand attrition as the increasing number of wellness-minded travelers 'vote with their wallets' for properties that fit with their newfound lifestyles. That said, there are two fundamental, magnetic-core-level obstacles that companies without any prior exposure to wellness face.

While these are hardly insurmountable, it's important to first consider:

1. *Shopper's Paralysis:* Beyond just spa, wellness is a bit of a catch-all term, bringing together healthy eating, sleep hygiene, mindfulness, yoga, breathwork, nature therapy, physiotherapy, the latest hype around extreme temperature exposure and a slew of others. Where should any given brand start? How do they know their current guests will appreciate these new amenities? How do executives justify big capex upfront that may only have a long-term payout 'if' things go according to plan? This 'paradox of choice' can prevent the development of a solid plan even before it gets soft approval.
2. *There's No Silver Bullet:* Will wellness be the saving grace for your hotel? Will it immediately become a vertical with topline revenues on par with the rooms' ledger? Just as the results from a healthy diet aren't immediately perceptible and compound over time, the financial benefits from wellness programming are likewise attained over the long run. Thus, any entrance into this space requires patience, planning and a full-fledged commitment so that there's time to refine the offerings and build awareness.

Accept That There's No Overnight Successes

If it's so hard, why bother starting? The potential is there, but also it's an arms race. For instance, if the competition debuts a new sleep program that allows them to charge more and win over your customers, you risk commoditization. Hence, to answer both of these abovementioned existential obstacles and generate consistent profits in the process, wellness necessitates a mentality shift at the owner, investor and finance level with a full pivot within the brand DNA in order for it to work.

Instead, the strategy taken and plans implemented to profit from wellness will look different for each and every hotel depending on the brand, target customers, hotel category, property location, property size, available capex and a myriad of other factors. And then you have the biggest variable of all, which is time. Say you develop a long-term vision for what wellness looks like for your brand five years from now. How do you get started? What are the early steps that will generate buzz and some form of measurable returns so that everyone at the top can foresee a worthwhile payout in the future?

Sorting through these inputs to design a roadmap for continuous operational improvements and a deepening into the wellness space is something we've helped independent hotel owners with during recent consulting assignments. Without knowing your own situation, the best we can do is to illustrate how this works with a specific example so that you can extrapolate what might work for you.

Consider a West Coast Rural Resort

The property was a British Columbian remote, forested resort with just over 50 rooms that made its bread off of middle-aged couples and nuclear families driving up for two-night or three-night stays, along with a smattering of groups and small weddings during summer. The signature restaurant was the same attraction, achieving well-above-breakeven results even though it wasn't a big draw for nearby residents (as a fine dining locale, it was priced out for regulars and seen as a special occasion place).

While the pandemic restrictions on international travel and subsequent rate yielding helped the resort realize its best topline performance ever for 2021, the sagacious owner knew the party would soon be over. With a desire to buffer the occupancy drop as borders reopened, the two of us proposed the idea of using wellness and outdoor activities as a way to both give guests a clear, marketable 'reason to visit' (or 'revisit' as much of the efforts were low-cost digital retargeting of existing customers via newsletters, social media and paid search) and drive ancillary spend.

At its current size, the financials didn't support the buildout of a full-service spa facilities (nor did we want to go through the arduous process of getting municipal approval). Luckily, from a previous remodeling, there was a lower-level fitness room populated with a few machines and dumbbells that was carved out of three former guestrooms – ones that were usually the least desirable and predominant cause of guest chagrin. Besides that, skepticism reigned as current metrics showed that most visitors just wanted to lounge out.

Indoors Wellness First

With limited budget and a dearth of preexisting cultural buy-in, the roadmap we developed was all about 'less is more'. So, we chose to set up only one program for: indoors, outdoors and personnel.

While we initially looked into offering strong incentives to have guests visit a nearby yoga studio (packages, shuttles, discount vouchers, promo codes), besides costs the main obstacle was that this wouldn't be frictionless with respect to the established reason that brought the majority of visitors to the resort – cozying up in a room, great cuisine and maybe a saunter about the grounds decided in the moment. Classes had to be onsite and available on-demand.

Thus, the solution involved the following:

- Low cost transformation of fitness room into an onsite studio by removing equipment
- Scheduling software for both third-party practitioners and for guest to book their spots (nothing fancy insofar as direct bookings, only holding a spot with folio settlement at check-out)
- To start, the hybrid yoga and meditation classes were only made available during peak leisure periods of Friday afternoon through Sunday late morning
- Updates to entire digital marketing presence so that guest awareness was high
- Instead of only purchasing yoga mats and making them available in the studio, these were conspicuously placed in a corner of each room as a strong on-premises nudge
- Team retraining primarily involved personally introducing the marketing team to the practitioners coming onsite (so selling would be done from experience), and instructing the front desk agents to inform guests about class availability, costs and booking

Outdoors Wellness Second

As a British Columbian resort, the property was blessed with verdant land and already had a few trails carved out on-premises, in addition to several fantastic provincial parks within a short drive. The problem was that they were just trails and guests often didn't know they existed. Similar to the yoga program setup, fixing this required multi-pronged awareness updates and making it all frictionless.

Starting as simple as possible by focusing on hiking and biking, we oversaw the following actions:

- Decorative signage for the on-premises trails
- Illustrated hiking map created then expressed both in print at the front desk and on the website

- Purchase of a handful of mountain bikes available as a zero-cost rental item, requiring an update to the inventory management system as well as the drafting of some legalese
- More digital marketing updates and team retraining

The Cultural Shift

Both of these programs were designed to be low cost because we knew that the direct return would likewise be small and also hard to measure. Besides the yoga class bookings and volume of bike rentals, we also looked at softer metrics like the number of inquiries, both those made digitally during the prearrival stages as well as those made verbally while guests were onsite and any comments made during online guest reviews.

While we would like to say that it was an immediate success, the results were best described as consistently moderate. That is, only about a third (30%) of all leisure guests expressed any form of interest (significantly lower for other segments) in the classes or the trails, with a 5% conversion rate for class bookings from the total customer pool.

However, most remarkable was that satisfaction scores amongst the guests who self-declared that they used the studio or the trails were significantly higher. Moreover, while it's still too early to evaluate this for certain (under two years of data), we have already noted a greater likelihood of these wellness-activated guests returning in greater frequency to the property – this done by retargeting based on class purchases connected to the guest profiles within the PMS.

With this data at our disposal, the owners became believers. Extensions were drawn up including more classes, guided outdoor experiences, a rethink of the minibar to include healthy F&B and the setup of a small locally sourced, wellness-oriented gift boutique at the front desk (requiring more training and procurement systems updates). But we also used this wellness programming to bolster the team by setting up monthly team-only classes and promoting a passionate guest service agent into the resort's activities coordinator to help design future programming.

For you, the conclusion should be that you can indeed achieve reasonable returns in the near-term. It doesn't have to be a loss – often called 'wellness for the sake of wellness' – if you start small by working within the physical boundaries of your hotel as well as the mental boundaries through which your current customers are approaching your brand.

Hotel Longevity: Demographics Alone Will Make Wellness Worth Trillions

The problem with slow burn trends like the current aging out of the baby boomers is not so much that we fail to predict them but that we often cannot account for them in a readily quantifiable and obviously actionable manner on a quarterly or annual financial statement to thereby jumpstart the necessary adjustments to adapt a business.

This failure to pivot is what caused Blockbuster and Kodak to file for protection – two examples of Adam Smith's silent hand of pervasive, irreversible, indirect and often unpredictable market evolutions. In hindsight, we ask ourselves, "How could they not have seen it?" But this thinking is a bit naïve as it doesn't account for entrenched culture and the need to protect the cash cow.

Wellness has blossomed to the forefront of cultural and hotel industry awareness, and yet the two of us believe that we are all still greatly underestimating just how big the total addressable market for this space is. Per the title, we put in the trillions, far above its current global footprint.

However lofty we estimate this TAM, though, properties and brands the world over remain entrenched in a straight 'heads in beds' mentality that could one-day mark spell doom to their business viability. Our hope is that you start planning now while we're still at the 'elbow of the curve' with this growing trend so that you aren't pushed out like some bygone company.

Wellness Population Dynamics

Silent-hand economic changes are just that – hidden from plain view. So, let's spell this baby boomer situation out in a sequence of events for you to understand how to make money from it all. As a note, we are speaking in general about the globe's advanced economies, although each country offers its own nuances within a broader trend.

1. Boomers are currently retiring and exiting the working-age population (WAP), and they will continue to do so over the next decade.
2. Because boomers started having fewer children on average than previous generations, there are fewer replacement workers and consumers amongst Gen X+Y+Z to maintain the WAP's ratio within the total population.
3. A shrinking WAP means overall labor supply shortages, thereby increasing the price that labor can command (albeit this says nothing about the influences of technological unemployment, global supply chains, immigration or industry-specific demand changes).
4. As boomers get older, they will incur more age-related diseases, increasing the demand for healthcare services and workers in this sector.
5. With a shrinking WAP and more elderly demanding healthcare services, this leads to inflation of those services as supply can never keep up with demand, with this reflected in greater direct-to-consumer costs, more expensive insurance, an inability to find labor in this sector, high costs of labor, increased wait times at the hospital or a greater levy on taxpayers to maintain standards.
6. As they are also currently the wealthiest generation, many boomers can tolerate this 'healthcare crunch' scenario by being able to afford the ever-higher prices, and yet paying these premiums often only adds more fuel to the fire of inflation.
7. While some may be able to stomach this medical system inflation, others, whether boomers or part of another cohort will be incentivized to seek out

alternative methods, practices and products to support their healthcare and well-being needs.

From these seven steps, we paint a picture of why the economics of baby boomers getting older will in its own right compel people to start incorporating wellness into their lives as a means of precluding themselves from needing ever-more-expensive healthcare services.

Then there are concurrent trends converging to further propel consumers to buy wellness products:

- Far greater awareness and access to healthier eating, exercise and supplementation options
- Mainstream acceptance of wellness practices like yoga, meditation and contrast therapy
- Scientific research that is proving various wellness, fitness and nutrition practices as beneficial to one's lifespan and healthspan (that is, the good years you get on this green earth)
- Economies of scale of functional genomics to advance our medical understanding of human longevity and then apply this knowledge in the real world

How Wellness Protects Your Business

Great, we've driven the point that the future belongs to wellness. But within there, it's worth describing the ways that wellness programming can protect your hotel's room rates versus competitors, add new revenue streams and help to reduce overall labor costs.

What we stress, though, is that as the demand and cultural appreciation for wellness inevitably grow over the next two decades, this programming only becomes all the more crucial.

1. Wellness amenities are a means to differentiate hotel brands on a feature-comparison basis, first preventing rate commoditization and then helping to command higher rates relative to the market
2. New wellness programming can work to refresh the marketing presentation and inventory distribution in order to diversify the target audience and customer segmentation
3. Wellness amenities and services can be packaged or cross-sold to boost TRevPAR (total revenue per guest) as well as to increase LOS
4. Devoting more resources to employee wellbeing will help to buffer inflationary wages, increase team retention and stave off productivity losses from sick days, absenteeism or presenteeism

To close, all this is coming at it from a thousand yards away. We all know wellness is coming and it's going to be big, but to meet it head-on will require a lot of work right now to set your hotel organization up for more success in the coming years. It takes a shock to the system to change an entrenched culture, but that's exactly what's required.

Hotel Longevity: Transformative Culinary Experiences

You are what you eat. Every day, more people are coming to appreciate food as more than just fuel but as medicine that can restore the body, slim the waist, steady the mood, elevate cognition, and even reverse chronic diseases. This burgeoning wellness way of life is also reflected in various dietary trends like plant-based or keto as well as buzzy meal additives like probiotics, superfoods, nootropics or adaptogens.

We argue that hotels must not only shift their F&B programming in stride with these cultural changes but also that there are specific ways within this food-as-medicine trend to activate new revenue streams and greatly enhance loyalty.

Longevity Lifetime Value

One of the beauties of pursuing the giant wellness pot of gold is that this segment of customers has, in the aggregate, a substantially longer lifetime over other groups of people. While it's easy to say that eating healthy, exercising, meditating and the like will all help you to live longer and have more healthy years within that lifespan to devote to travel (what's called 'health span'), many hotels still aren't properly incorporating this in their loyalty strategies.

On an individual basis, one person with a predilection for wellness may give you five to ten more years of potential room reservations over another person who doesn't value wellness. What's more, there is a positive correlation between wellness and wealth, which makes sense when you consider that heightened intellect, reduced sickness and augmented quotidian energy levels that stem from healthy habits can all enable greater workplace productivity as well as more income-earning years.

In other words, wellness-oriented guests will probably have more disposable cash over other customer segments to allocate towards elevating their hotel stays. So, wellness not only means more customer lifetime value (CLV), but also a higher average guest spending across multiple profit centers – seems like a win-win.

The Nutritional Challenge

With the awareness for food as medicine ever-increasing – that is, the number of potential guests who have realized the value of healthy eating and, likely, other related activities that promote longevity – one of the largest obstacles that said consumers face is they don't know where to start. The pandemic also catalyzed this growth as we were all forced to expand our home kitchen repertoire.

Changing habits is hard. Compounding this is that there's a lot of conflicting nutritional advice out there. Then adding jet fuel to it all are the food and beverage providers who have hijacked the term 'healthy' with marketing labels such as 'all natural', 'low calorie' and 'low fat'. Who has time to read the full ingredient list? Who has time to understand what each ingredient does to the body? Who has time to research the specific sourcing and quality of each ingredient?

It's all very intimidating. The biggest barrier to adopting healthier eating habits is thus not knowing how to incorporate healthier ingredients and food preparation methods into one's daily routine. Wouldn't it be great if there was a place that assumed the role of being an inspiration by offering people a fun, dynamic and convenient way to learn about healthier eating habits so that said consumers could bring those lessons home?

Transformative Experiences

The question alludes to what we call a 'transformation' – an activity or experience that is not only enjoyable now but that leaves a person better off from where they were at the outset. Hence, teaching hotel guests about great food through live demonstrations, an immersive tasting and an interactive cooking class is what we would denote as transformative culinary experiences.

Many properties already offer foodie-related activities that likely bring together local partners to weave in an authentic cultural narrative about the area. Keep going with this, obviously, but then take it a step further by thinking about ways to leave a lasting impression on guests through the lens of improving how they eat at home.

The world is your oyster, and oysters just so happen to be a superfood! A wine tour can incorporate wellness elements, as can a farm tour, cheesemaking class, healthy baking class, guided tea ceremony or chocolate confectionary tutorial. Urban or rural, there's always a way to fuse what's local or what's on the theme with interactive education into something that's inspirational. Such experiences can then be reinforced through packaging with onsite vouchers, arrival amenities, departure gifts, other merchandising opportunities in the gift boutique and other wellness activities like mindfulness classes or spa facility access.

One of the best examples of a post-pandemic transformative culinary experience is Silversea's S.A.L.T. program. The acronym stands for Sea and Land Taste, where the onboard dining menus and interactive cooking laboratories adjust with each new destination and are then combined with an onshore excursion accompanied by one of their food experts. Yes, this is a cruise line, so the economics are different, but there's no reason a hotel can't emulate this on a smaller scale.

Access Is Everything

The key to any experience of this nature is to make them accessible or visible with easy payment rails. Most hotels struggle to capture ancillary spending beyond meals at the restaurant, so going to the next level of designing experiences that are also well-attended is out of scope.

Get the technology ironclad first. Are these packages visible on the front-end website and then easily purchased on the booking engine? Are you talking about them in your marketing channels? What's your communication process with public relations to get the word out? Given that many guests are only prime for upselling in the days preceding arrival, do you have these experiences available as add-ons and how are you telling guests about them in this context? Similarly, how are you telling them about last-minute experience availability once on site, whether through the hotel app, in-room tablets or digital signage?

Then consider other components in the tech stack. How are all the various elements of a purchased package parsed out to other software? Given that classes are time-based inventory, how do guests reserve spots? How are you prompting them to reserve a spot in advance of their stay? How are you managing to staff? For any physical good, how are you managing this within the inventory system?

Lots of questions, but no one said this was easy. What you will find, though, is that answering these to help make experiential offerings more 'turnkey' will also help solve a lot of other upselling and labor productivity issues along the way. So, while targeting wellness guests may be a win-win, addressing your tech stack to better enable the required service enhancements makes it a triple crown.

Hotel Longevity: The Growing Demand for Mobility Training

Is fitness a primary booking driver for hotels? Unless it's a lifestyle brand known explicitly for its exercise programming like Equinox or EVEN, the answer is a resolute 'no'. We can confidently say that a traveler's purpose will most likely always center around location first, with price as a close-second attribute, for all those outside the luxury segment. However, there are a few significant trends that hoteliers should consider with respect to fitness that will influence how guests choose their properties and the rates they can command.

Fitness-Tertiary Travelers

The greatest overall force is that there is now a vast body of evidence for the relationship between consistent exercise and the maintenance of one's good health. Just as it's common knowledge that smoking is bad for nearly all life outcomes, the word is out amongst members of every demographic group that exercise is beneficial, regardless of whether one chooses to do it.

The key word here is 'consistent' in that it's also recognized that a pittance every day is often better than a pound every week or month. This is the basis for the maxim, 'Sitting is the new smoking', whereby a lack of low-intensity activity throughout the day – for instance, going for a brief walk once an hour to move the blood around – is now deemed a recipe for congestive heart disease amongst other ailments. The need to uphold one's at-home regimen is already spurring more guest desire to stay active while travelling, especially in an on-the-go manner via quick in-room guided workouts or yoga stretching routines versus blocking off hours at time to head down to the fitness center.

Despite the rollout of these new fitness-oriented guestroom features, for most guests, they aren't a 'must have' but a 'nice to have'. Similar to how wellness-oriented travelers are segmented, while we may define 'fitness secondary' guests as those who choose a location first for various reasons and then narrow the query down to those hotels that have excellent exercise programming, most customers will still fall into the 'fitness tertiary' camp, with location, price and other considerations coming ahead of one's curiosity for features that enable working out while abroad.

Within the broader wellness umbrella, this alone makes a far stronger argument for focusing on operations like healthy F&B (because everyone eats) or high-margin ancillary add-ons like selling more spa treatments and experiential activities with a wellness component. Therefore, the business case for fitness-oriented branding requires different factors to make it worthwhile.

Boomer Sarcopenia

The most salient concurrent driver is the aging of the baby boomers – the wealthiest generation on the planet for the rest of the 2020s – wherein a hallmark of bodily aging is a natural decline in muscle mass as well as muscle responsiveness, with 'sarcopenia' as one of a handful of medical terms to codify this steady, decades-long progression.

Sarcopenia explains why one's grip strength is used as a marker for lifespan. For one, a firm squeeze is a heuristic for upper body muscle mass which is correlated with the level of activity a person maintains as they age and the health of the circulatory system.

But equally as significant is the 'healthy user bias' within scientific research on grip strength in that upper body muscle helps to prevent a fall from being fatal and therefore prolongs the lifespan of those that regularly lift weights versus that don't. While the occasional trip or accident is a matter of chance, when you are able to do a pushup or forcefully brace onto a nearby tree branch, you are thus able to use your upper body strength as a 'preventative' force to lessen the momentum of a fall, reducing the damage of the impact. Lest we forget that it was only a century ago – before the days of acute healthcare – when 'falling on the stairs' or 'tripping on the sidewalk' was a common cause of death.

The medical community recognizes this relationship and doctors all over the world now recommend weightlifting to their patients. However, age-driven sarcopenia is usually accompanied by the loss of integrity in the joints, ligaments and tendons, leading to chronic pain that can prevent someone from working out at a high intensity. The big opportunity for hotels and resorts therefore resides in wellness programming that caters to the management and amelioration of this pain by way of various forms of physiotherapy, massage therapy, mobility training, isometrics, yoga, Pilates, stretching classes, aquafit classes and tai chi.

Strength Versus Stability

In any discussion of physical exercise, it's important to differentiate between strength training and stability, mobility or balance work, with the latter arguably far more important for longevity and overall quality of life.

When we speak of weightlifting, many still have a stereotypical image of brooding hunks doing bicep curls or chest presses. Far less often do we mentally conjure that of balancing on one foot, squatting on a BOSU ball or using a TRX suspension system. And for reference, when we speak of 'mobility' we are referring to someone's strength combined with their flexibility, as reflected in their ability to comfortably move their body across a wide range of motion at each discrete joint.

While classical barbell weightlifting is better able to drive up the heart rate and induce muscular hypertrophy for a metabolic, fat-burning boost, mobility and stability exercises work to improve mind-body connectivity, joint elasticity and the responsiveness of individual muscle striations (the units within a muscle) to thereby promote better bodily alignment and smoother joint tracking across the entirety of one's range of motion. To put it bluntly, without joint stability, you would be in near-constant pain, preventing you from vigorously exercising and inevitably shortening your lifespan.

A simple way to think about this would be like comparing the human knee to a train chugging a track with two rails. That screeching sound a train makes as it rounds a curve results from an imbalance of weight or momentum on one side versus the other, which can be seen as analogous to the perceived pain from an uneven loading on the medial or lateral meniscus within the knee joint. Many in this situation would opt for a knee brace, but that's only palliative and doesn't correct the underlying issue. The real solution is to realign the loading of weight back onto the middle of the train tracks – in this case, the center of the knee – by looking at how certain muscles of the thigh are firing in tandem as well as the holistic functionality of the hip and ankle muscles.

Hotels Inspiring Change

If only everyone understood the fundamental importance of mobility, every single physiotherapist would have a full schedule and we'd have sweeping tax incentives in place for seeking out these professionals. Alas, we're still coming out of the 20th-century educational system where gym teachers were basically goons not smart enough to teach any other subject. As it relates to travel, there's a profound shift in one's frame of mind as they are removed from the hamster wheel of familiar surroundings.

Hoteliers naturally know this; guests are more receptive to new experiences they might not otherwise consider when at home. With the proper messaging and contextual targeting, a case can be made for both on-demand mobility training regimens as well as the incorporation of onsite guided experiences and group classes that are either packaged or served up as an extra expense.

The luxury resort segment excels in this area by weaving physiotherapy practices with their broader wellness-primary and wellness-secondary programming. But with the overall aging of the population combined with the increasing number of younger travelers who recognize the value of exercise, the demand is there for hotels to deepen their fitness branding.

While improving joint stability, balance and bodily mobility to thereby reduce joint pain and help to prevent fatal falls require vigilant consistency throughout one's daily habits, hotels can be centers of inspiration to elicit that change for the better. This is what we would codify as 'transformative experiences' – those activities offered by hotels that encourage guests to improve their overall livelihoods, therein having a second-order effect of augmenting loyalty and customer lifetime value as said guests return for the next 'booster' of inspiration.

So, to return to the opening question, is fitness a primary booking driver? Currently, no, but it can be, and importantly it should be, because all it takes is one bad fall, assisted by sarcopenia and a loss of balance, for your life to change forever. An ounce of prevention is worth a pound of cure, as they say. The most successful hotel brands in the near future will be those that identify a growing niche and work to serve it with approachable and appropriate experiences, and hopefully from reading this article, you can see why demand for onsite fitness and mobility training will increase as time goes on.

Hotel Longevity: There's No Silver Bullet and That's Great for Business

While longevity researchers continue to unravel the intrinsic mechanisms of how to permanently stave off chronic disease, prolong human life, and even reverse aging, it's becoming increasingly apparent that there is no single cure to every ailment – not yet, at least.

That is to say, there is no silver bullet treatment that anyone can pay a medical practitioner to quickly take a decade off their biological clock (that is, healthspan) or extend the maximum upper age limit beyond roughly 125 (that is, lifespan). While this lack of a present-day panacea is frustrating for doctors, it's a brisk business for wellness hotels as we will soon see.

To put this in scientific terms, while advanced practices like induced pluripotent stem cell treatments, therapeutic peptides, proscriptive exercise, caloric restriction and specific supplements like resveratrol have all been shown to help attenuate signs of aging (often only in studies on rats, not humans), in isolation their long-term effects with regard to elongating either healthspan or lifespan are questionable. A great quote to sensibly rationalize this predicament goes as follows, "If there was one single application that could human life by 50 years, evolution would have figured it out 50 million years ago."

Instead, the evidence continues to reinforce that the best way to be as healthy as possible is through holistic lifestyle change. For example, the Mediterranean diet has long been a gold standard for promoting vitality – lots of greens, fresh herbs, fruit, nuts and fish – but what's often missed in this conversation is what complements this nutritional regimen including consistent, moderate exercise, a cultural emphasis on socialization, slow eating, time spent outdoors and a cumulative lack of stress.

Adopting these daily habits requires a mindset shift that conflicts with modern pill culture. Luckily, the 20th-century mentality of waiting until a problem causes serious illness is giving way to a 21st-century ideal of treating the body like a garden – consistent care with just the right balance of water, sun, fertilizer, probiotics and pruning. And as more guests start to seek out this consistency while traveling as part of this new-age lifestyle, it will mean a steady rise in demand for wellness products at hotels.

Put another way, because longevity and staving off chronic disease requires continuous attention and real effort, hotel brands can thus position themselves to develop recurring revenues from this vertical with the proper attention given to service, personalization, packaging and loyalty or rewards offers.

Let's put this in real terms so that you can visualize how to operationalize human longevity and wellness for hotels. Consider a relatively benign hot mineral bath at a spa. Any balneologist could cite multiple studies showing that these are good for relaxation, improving skin elasticity and relieving joint pain. But the positive effects from a single spa day – whether actual or simply placebo – fade quickly, and thus to realize a long-term effect then long-term exposure is required.

This is simple principle behind exercise, diet, saunas, supplements, meditation, red light therapy and practically everything else short of stem cells or peptides. Deriving healthy revenues from this is far easier said than done, though, as hotel teams must simultaneously deliver an experience that feels good in the moment and also has a convincing lure to elicit return visits for the real health benefits.

From our work in wellness-oriented rebranding and property redesigns, here are some common topics of importance to help generate those return visits:

1. *Technology.* With today's ongoing labor battles, every piece of automation is important. But more so than that, it's about data interfaces and customer segmentation to more narrowly define retargeting and loyalty offers so that hotels can more conveniently fit into a person's wellness habits and the frequency of visitation they desire.
2. *Theme.* Wellness is an umbrella term for so many different practices. To be memorable, brands must tell a simple, cohesive story about their product offerings – one that's also congruent with their existing customer base. Nowadays, integrations are essential for building a rich, structured database for KYC (Know Your Customer). A core focus is what will allow for word of mouth and ensure that you are delivering great experiences for those core focuses before branching out.
3. *Context.* Oftentimes it's not just about the promotion or the messaging but when and how that offer is presented to the guest. A wellness-primary guest will be more likely to purchase a package and book an appointment far in advance of arrival while a wellness-secondary guest may only be receptive to cross-selling upon arrival. Again, various tech tools can enable contextual delivery and A/B testing.
4. *Commitment.* Just as changing one's lifestyle to promote health requires a person to actively alter their habits until they become ingrained, the pursuit of profits from wellness won't happen overnight. It requires a

long-term pledge and a cultural change so that any established program is not quietly abandoned but continually improved. When starting with any new programming, as Voltaire said, "Perfect is the enemy of the good." Sometimes it's better to launch then tweak and tweak and tweak rather than hold off on getting market feedback.

While involved with a hotel wellness brand redesign project or speaking about wellness at a conference, it's all but inevitable that someone will ask one of us, "What's the one thing I should do to be healthier?" Our answer often baffles those still stuck in the 20th-century mold of silver bullets: just think.

More people every day are waking up to a new way of thinking about their own health – one of proactive vigilance and not of reactive reliance on a pill or surgery to solve every problem. As this continues to happen – as people adjust their mindset to one of the regular habits oriented around wellness – there will be profound benefits for the hospitality industry as these individuals seek out hotels for inspiration as well as restoration. It's a big trend that will play out over a decade, but it's happening regardless, so find a way to make it work for your topline.

Hotel Longevity: Measuring the Customer Lifetime Value of Wellness Guests

The holy grail of any hotel brand's tech stack is likely to be the creation of a 'unified guest profile' with the various data points on an individual piped and structured within a CRM so that teams can more meaningfully improve the guest experience in order to, candidly, drive more revenue, more profit and better asset valuations.

For some, that improvement is onsite personalization – something as simple as knowing a certain guest likes extra pillows and ensuring this is fulfilled prior to said person's next arrival. For others, it's looking at what services and amenities are best able to grow the business, especially when lensed through the goal of increasing ancillary spending on a per-customer basis (TRevPAR). Ultimately, what any hotelier wants is higher nightly rates, more on-property utilization and guests that boast about the property to friends or are much more likely to return.

The singular metric that brings this all together is the customer lifetime value (CLV) which in hospitality's case computes the total amount of present-day revenues that a hotel is projecting to derive from a single guest. Our hypothesis is that wellness-oriented customers have a significantly higher average CLV than non-wellness guests, which will help to quell any doubts about achieving a positive ROI on wellness investments. For this reason, every hotel should be investigating their options with regard to attracting travelers with a wellness mindset as well as actively cajoling guests to drink the wellness Kool-Aid.

Equation Breakdown

To statistically verify this hypothesis is more a task for a PhD candidate with a whole semester on their hands, but we can nevertheless do some convincing back-of-the-envelope estimation by evaluating each component with the formula used to calculate CLV. For simplicity, we'll use an equation that's specific to a single hotel consumer while not incorporating other elements like churn rate, profit margins and the discount rate of money.

CLV = (avg. spend per stay) x (projected stay frequency per year) x (remaining healthspan in years)

To grasp this, let's plug in some basic numbers for a twentysomething, corporate, heads-in-beds guest:

- Average spend per stay = $500 (representing an average length of stay of two nights with no F&B or other ancillary spend)
- Annual stay frequency = 1 (meaning this guest is projected to come once a year, with this measurement being brand-wide and not just for a singular property within a group)
- Remaining healthspan = 45 ('healthspan' being the healthy years that one has left in their life where they are able to travel without assistance and not remaining lifespan)
- CLV = $22,500

Obviously, there are a lot of assumptions here in terms of what's used to equilibrate the average spend per stay, how we are evaluating this guest's future travel frequency (especially given scenarios like changing jobs and no longer visiting that city regularly) and the actuarial science behind how many more good years of travel this guest has in front of them.

Nevertheless, the objective is to grow CLV, using the micro-analysis of a single person's contribution to the hotel's ledger to inform macro considerations to guide operational development. If we can boost the CLV for the individual by playing around with these three variables, then it stands to reason that we can chart a course for boosting CLV across the board.

Wellness Boosts All Three Variables

Once our simple version of the CLV formula has been broken down into these three variables, it's easier to see where wellness adds value and also calculate some conservative estimates for just how much. Of course, this will vary by guest, by guest context (midweek business trip versus a family vacation), by the property, by the package purchased, by brand, and by location, but we can still make some general conclusions.

For average per-stay spend, take the aforementioned example with its $250 per night rate but change the guest context to a wellness-oriented getaway at double occupancy. Let's also suppose that this property doesn't have a spa facility as not every hotel does, nor is it logical to assume one can be retrofitted within this current structure. For ancillaries, we're going to add an upsold 'sleep well' turndown service at $15 per night and two couples' dinners off the new health-minded prix fixe menu totaling $150 including alcohol per night. Together, that's already an increase of 66% to $830 per stay.

Next, for frequency, it is hard to beat the reservations volume of a road warrior executive who travels every week or every other one and has their loyalty program of choice. In the post-pandemic world, these are a dwindling breed. For most other guest contexts, though, wellness programming offers a veritable 'reason to visit' independent of a pure-location rationale like a work trip. Unwinding, rejuvenating, recharging, digital detoxing and staying fit while abroad all contribute to the emotional thrust of why guests choose wellness-oriented brands over others. Let's take frequency up by 25% to 1.25.

The third variable is where things get interesting. While the science is still out on extending human life beyond its current limits as defined by mortality tables, we do know that staying healthy is the best way to reduce causes of early death like congestive heart failure, thereby extending healthspan. Put another way, if the maximum lifespan is held at 100, wellness habits would work to allow a consumer to sustain their vigor for 90 of those years rather than having chronic ailments hinder regular travel beyond age 80. With this 10-year bump, it brings the remaining healthspan to 55 years.

Now to bring it all together:

- Average spend per stay = $830
- Annual stay frequency = 1.25
- Remaining healthspan = 55
- CLV = $57,062.50 (a 254% increase)

To restate, there are lots of assumptions built in here to get to a 2.5 times boost, not to mention net profit analyses that are necessary because many of these wellness services are expensive to execute. But even if we pare down some of the boosts, the positive revenue effect should be patently clear.

Most significantly, what we emphasize from this examination of CLV is to look at the 'lifetime' and not necessarily with a quarter-over-quarter mindset. As well, a caveat is that these rough calculations speak nothing to the amount of work you will need to do to figure out which direction to take your wellness programming, define all the SOPs, train your team and market it all so that guests are actually aware of your brand's newfound reason to visit.

CONCLUSION

Tucked away in the Cook Islands, The Rarotongan Beach Resort & Lagoonarium is also highly innovative, using its technology to offer guests one-of-a-kind experiences that maximize their enjoyment of this tropical paradise.

What You Can Learn from More Than a Thousand Articles Written

Our first published article on hospitality debuted in early March 2011. In October 2020, we published our sixth book entitled, 'More Hotel Mogel.' In each article, we offer a morsel of education and inspiration for hoteliers based on what we've gleaned from our ongoing consulting work for hotels, resorts, and technology firms. (Note: we also published a seventh book, 'In Vino Veritas. A Guide for Hoteliers and Restauranteurs to Sell More Wine' in October 2022. This book was a departure for us, reflecting our love of wine.)

While it was exciting to see our name in print back then, now with a thousand articles under our belts it has become just a matter of routine, albeit a fantastic one at that and something we will always take great pride in. And if you are avid reader of ours, we apologize for all the hours we've taken away from you when you could be focusing on more pressing matters!

Reflecting upon what we've reported on and what trends we've noted, it's fascinating to see how those stories developed over the years with many still evolving as we speak. Flipping through the pages of the six books we've composed on hospitality management, we felt that it was time to look back on what we've experienced over the past decade and what we can expect over the next few years (all in no particular order).

1. *Hotels sell experiences, not just accommodations.* Exquisite food and beverage, spa, wellness, golf and other ways to involve the guest in your property have all become critical factors in business success. Moreover, the need for local activity partners is all the more critical to marketing and brand loyalty.
2. *The local community is your breadwinner.* Thinking of your lobby nowadays as a living room and how you welcome your neighbors will pay big dividends. Now more than ever, your 'hyperlocal' constituency is a vital important source of business as well as word of mouth generation for incoming travelers.
3. *Does a brand name mean anything anymore?* More than a dozen new brands were launched over the past nine years. Can you name them all? If you can't then do you think your guests will be able to? All this reeks of customers having too much choice in what we refer to as the 'paradox of choice' as well as a lack of deepening brand relationships or 'brand dilution'.
4. *Marketing gets repositioned to the digital realm.* Right or wrong, traditional advertising has run its course. For most hotels, channels like newspapers and magazines have become too expensive. Broad-based advertising is narrowcast while measurement and analytics have sadly taken the place of bold positioning and strategy.
5. *The OTAs have moved from enemy to invaluable channel partner.* We're not sure if the average reduction in OTA commissions was a result or a precursor to this attitudinal change. At the same time, metasearch is also a strong factor in any rate decisions.
6. *The mobile world has taken over.* These days, who would even consider a website that is not mobile friendly? Now we build for mobile first, other

screens second. Instrumental now is to have a speedy, intuitive mobile experience to best assist during the travel research and booking phases of the customer purchase pathway.

7. *The sharing economy has grown at a monumental rate.* When we started this journey of the pen, Airbnb was basically a couch-surfing platform for millennials. Now totally mainstream, this distribution network, and others like it, has over 10% of the worldwide marketplace and more rooms available each night than the sum of all the major chains combined. With such inventory, when Airbnb sneezes, the world quivers.
8. *There's a tech for just about everything.* Highlighted from the recent wave of IoT-based innovations, shiny new toys abound like room keys or in-room safes that respond to smart phones, thermostats that recognize your guests' movements to help save on the energy bill and a host of other applications that synchronize operations with your PMS. The beauty of technology, and why we continue to be a big proponent of it, is that all these vendors have the potential to save hotels on costs as well as improve the guest experience to offer a key point of product differentiation.

Top Lessons from the Series 'The White Lotus'

A popular satirical miniseries from HBO is par for the course from the network that is par excellence for dramatic television. While it's mostly focused on the intricate relationships and intersections of its well-drawn cast of characters as well as its thematic focus on rich versus poor, as it revolves around a heavenly Hawaiian resort, it is worth the watch for any hotelier.

For those who haven't yet caught up on all the episodes, let's just say that an entirely separate article could be written about the smarmy, jaded, hilarious and increasingly unhinged hotel manager, Armond, but there are far more important lessons to glean from *The White Lotus*. Namely, the series touches upon more than fifty shades of the phrase, "The customer is always right."

When election season rolls around, we love to talk about 'the silent majority', but this show highlights 'the very vocal minority' in that when a hotel guest repeatedly requests something from a staff member through a progression of similar questions, it should be immediately clear that the underlying message is that this matter is of the utmost – and emotional – importance to said guest.

Often, staffers aren't empowered to grant such requests, instead offering an apology and hiding behind hours of operation, availability or another company policy. Other times, they aren't trained on how to improvise a suitable 'yes and...' to counteroffer a guest with appropriate compensation. And yet other times, it's the manager or supervisor on the receiving end who is too harried to give the necessary amount of mental energy to such incessant requests from a disquieted customer.

Whether it's a roadside motel or a tropical beachside paradise, guests want experiences, and they ask questions in order to maximize their own experiences. In the opening episodes, there are several key instances when the characters persistently ask for a way to augment their vacations, and it's when those requests aren't satisfied in a meaningful way that said guests act out into unpredictable ways, ultimately damaging the hotel's reputation or leading to additional corrective measures – that is, more labor needed to address the situation.

The show demonstrates that the reverse is also true. When characters are indeed presented with a compromise in the form of a duly profound experience, said guests become overtly enamored with the host property. Building upon the aforementioned adage, if the customer is right, then proving them correct will make them truly yours – brand advocacy at its finest. This is what we often call a 'wow' moment and hoteliers should look for ways to create them both grand and minute.

What we stress through this is that, even in the operationally erratic times that are the post-coronavirus era of hospitality, you have to develop the right services, training and technologies to build experiences that optimize a guest's satisfaction.

To draw upon examples from the series without any spoilers, develop a flexible protocol to always have a fitting alternative ready for when a guest's specific request cannot be met. If you cannot guarantee a specific room request, then offer another that's a true apples-to-apples equivalent. Or better, ensure that your technology is fully functional so that requests of this nature are tracked and rendered, with proper team accountability throughout to reinforce training where need be. The same can be said for spa appointment availability.

For those resort properties offering a bevy of spa, dining, golf, activities and other onsite experiences or area attractions, you must do your best to not leave these as laissez-faire additions that guests attempt to purchase at check-in or whimsically on the morning of when they want said experience. In a labor-efficient market, activities and appointments need to be booked as far in advance as possible to make sure a guest's experience does not suffer any setbacks after they have arrived. For this, there's now a myriad of integrated pre-stay software to help automate these upsells. Or you can go the lo-fi method by making members of your front office team personally email or call guests in advance to develop a thorough itinerary for their stays.

The White Lotus features plenty of other lessons besides a discussion of how to effectively service guests. And if anyone has their own Armond-esque stories, we'd love to hear them.

Fun Tech: Brainstorming the Hotel of the Year 2030

Right now, there are so many advances taking place in the realm of technology that it's hard to keep up. Specific to owners and senior executives, asking 'what if' is always fun for how these developments can help evolve the hotel in the pursuit of greater occupancy and growing ADR.

Importantly, though, hotels must consider how they are inevitably going to set aside capex for this progress, both as a defensive play to stay apace with guest expectations and as a means of enhancing brand awareness through buzzworthy early adoption. The hospitality industry has traditionally been a laggard when it comes to technology, but with all the shifts compelled by COVID perhaps it's finally time that we become a vanguard for progress.

The list below is not one of things that will definitely happen. Rather, it's hypothetical, and only designed to get you thinking about what trends a decade from now will be hot topics in for hotels:

- *Electric vehicles* galore with ample *charging stations* in every parking lot and even such offshoots like electric golf carts, along with a general stigma of those 'oil luddite' hotels that lack the necessary EV accessories
- *Autonomous vehicles* as the next step after EVs, whereby brands can more cheaply facilitate shuttle services for guests such as transportation from the airport to the hotel and sightseeing tours based upon a preprogrammed route with designated stopping points
- Superefficient *internal recycling systems* using a series of integrated, IoT technologies to monitor water usage, temperature controls and lighting as well as other potential enhancements like *solar panels* feeding into the grid or onsite processing of plastics, food waste and sewage through a combination of fungal and insect-based bioconversion
- *Voice automation* in guestrooms and dining establishments that not only makes smart recommendations but also integrate into BOH inventory systems to manage orders and kitchen processes more effectively
- Newer, smarter *metasearch travel channels* requiring a rethink of your distribution strategy like, for instance, Amazon which may decide to leverage its multitude of data to make bespoke booking recommendations or Netflix suggesting whole preplanned trips based off one's past streaming activity
- Payment support for *cryptocurrencies*, perhaps also encompassing your brand's own *inventory management blockchain* to verify the source of all goods onsite or unique digital art pieces as authenticated by *non-fungible tokens*
- *AI-based exercise or sports training programs* which take the SaaS model of companies like Peloton one step further by offering personal performance feedback based on sensory motion analysis for everything from a basic plank position to a golf swing
- *Augmented reality* or, in some cases, *virtual reality* training and entertainment rooms that can add as a versatile repurposing of windowless spaces
- *DNA-based wellness* including personalized nutrition, exercise or therapy regimens as enabled by CRISPR gene editing technologies
- *Drone delivery* of drinks and snacks to the pool, to a beachside cabana, up to your suite's terrace on the ninth floor or practically anywhere on property where the aviation authority will permit these flying robots
- *Robot room service* and housekeepers, with the former already a possibility for basic, contactless delivery or pickup of items while the latter is likely still very far off in the future

- *Autonomous agriculture* to cost-effectively maintain an onsite herb garden, vertical heirloom vegetable farm or fruit orchard using a combination of AI-driven management systems and drone or robot workers
- *Modular turnkey construction* of freestanding cabins, villas or whole hotels, as aided or manufactured wholly by industrial 3D printers and potentially using upcycled plastic waste products as the core building materials
- *Lab-made meats* as an ethical, and increasingly (potentially) cheaper, alternative to the real thing, again facilitated by the use of 3D printers in the kitchen
- In fact, some brands may decide to turn their gift shops into interactive design studios where *mini 3D printers* are utilized to give guests personalized mementos for their time onsite
- An all-in-one, consolidated *hotel management system* that amalgamates the PMS, CRM, CRS, RMS, booking engine, payment gateway and other software used by individual departments under one platform while cutting SaaS costs in the process
- *Space hotels* as promised by the likes of SpaceX, Virgin Galactic, Blue Origins and Orbital Assembly or, at the very least, easier access to short trips around the Earth

The hope is that this list inspires you to think long-term about the future of the hotel industry and ways that you can use technology to differentiate your brand and augment the guest experience. While not all of this will become reality by 2030, it would nevertheless make for an invigorating team discussion.

Hotels Must Embrace Creative Destruction with an Emphasis on *Destruction*

The new economy presents numerous challenges for hotels with the three biggest elephants in the guestroom being post-pandemic fluctuating occupancies, supply chain issues and labor shortages. None will be resolved overnight and there are effects on travel that are here to stay. What's key is to keep adapting which often requires short-term pain for long-term gain.

Often, it's hard to properly visualize the near or far-off future where you want to take your brand or your property because to get there you have to disrupt normal operations, creating more work or increasing costs in the process. To help you think more objectively about this time preference – sacrificing the ease of steady-state management in lieu of unsettling this balance to better prepare your organization for coming shifts in traveler behavior – we turn to the now-classic economic theory of creative destruction.

First expressly coined by the Austrian economist Joseph Schumpeter around the time of World War II, the concept has been central to evolutionary capitalism where even Charles Darwin remarked earlier that the "extinction of old forms is the almost inevitable consequence of the production of new forms." The creative part comes in primarily through technological ingenuity where new, more efficient inventions displace old methods of productivity or a workforce in a now-defunct field.

In other words, real innovation is never complete without destroying something else. We are in still the throes of a rapid evolutionary event because of the pandemic and its aftermath – that has accelerated dramatic changes in travel demands and behaviors. Survival requires destruction in one or more creative ways.

By now you should accept that there is no going back to the way things were in 2019 (i.e. prepandemic), and this will require some emotional strain to see you through to the future. We could drone on about all the forces at play that you're likely tired of hearing about at this point. Instead, let's look at the painful destruction your hotel may have to face in order to thrive in the new economy.

1. *Lean teams mean furloughs can become permanent.* Yes, we're using the F-word, in that the rapid pace of technological upgrades stemming from the first lockdowns onwards naturally mean that numerical roles within hotel companies are no longer needed. With a smorgasbord of connective automation and machine learning tools, a hotel can now imbue enough baseline output into its tech stack to no longer have to pay for a full bench of mid-tier 'paper pushers'. This allows a property to replace monthly administrative overhead with a SaaS expense, often resulting in a ten-to-one savings going straight to the net operating income. With this added buffer, hotels can put more money in the capex budget or operate out of the red at a lower occupancy. Such a change is emotional painful because it means letting go of friends and perhaps long-time colleagues, not to mention the cultural disruption. In the face of technology now being able to do so much for so cheap, hotels must rejig their entire organizational structure, each manager's job requirements and the overall succession plan. Or, as an alternative to terminating employments, hotels must redefine what each role encompasses so that the software does the grunt work while managers are asked to take on new responsibilities.
2. *Guestrooms need serious renovations to meet new demands.* After the destruction of the organizational chart comes the physical tearing down of walls. Some related and pervasive trends that can justify a gargantuan property improvement plan are the rise of remote work and the need for extended stay accommodations as well as the continued influences on travelers from short-term rentals. The age-old concept of 'heads in beds' will still exist, but it will comprise a smaller slice of the pie with some properties feeling the squeeze by becoming uncompetitive or commoditized to the point of insolvency. Guests increasingly want livable, hybrid travel options – quiet rooms with big desks where they can plunk down with a laptop and take a video call, access to services that become critical for any stay longer than a week or perhaps a small kitchen so that they aren't beholden to eat out for every single meal. Most hotels weren't built for these conversions, thus requiring

big bucks to carry out. And yet without this conversion, the property will slowly but assuredly die.

3. *Then re-imagine your public spaces.* With so much automation in the form of mobile check-in, mobile keys, kiosks, and guest messaging apps, do you even need a front desk anymore? How could you transform that space so that it becomes a meaningful touchpoint for the modern guest? How can you remodel your business center to meet the demand for remote work? What are guests looking for when it comes to experiential shopping and how can you adapt your gift shop to address this shift? Instead of maintaining a costly restaurant, would you ever consider shuttering it and partnering with a food delivery app? What about a gated club lounge only for members or premium package holders? We're just scratching the surface here but as you can see the answer to each question unavoidably necessitates a heavy coin purse.
4. *Wellness becomes universal.* We all understand the effects that the pandemic had on us – hospitalizations, long-haulers or deaths – but it's much harder to measure the second-order effects like loneliness, job burnout, depression, mental health issues, alcoholism, drug abuse and, in rare cases, suicide. In search of remedies beyond telehealth and a prescription, people all over the world have turned to wellness and its multifarious combinations of clean eating, exercise, stretching restorative activities, meditation, breathwork, sleep hygiene and a bunch of other de rigueur interests. Hotels that don't engage guests in this capacity will be missing out on a huge source of ancillary revenues as well as strong method to protect the brand against the heads-in-beds commodification problem. And yet, to do wellness properly will require a total overhaul of normal operations and a cash injection to make it happen.

These are just four macro-trends that may or may not need to be addressed depending on your locale and how you fared during these topsy-turvy times. Underlying each is that in order to innovate in a way that will reposition your brand for long-term viability, you have to dismantle some aspect of your current operations. In this way, creative destruction is the same as what any gym-goer will tell you, "No pain; no gain."

GLOSSARY OF TERMS

Although not all terms and acronyms below have necessarily been used in this specific book, all are nonetheless important to grasp for the hospitality industry, especially as this industry comes to intersect with various other sectors.

Given how vital technology is becoming for hotel operations, many of the terms are related to this field, for which you should aim to have a base understanding.

2FA: Two Factor Authorization; becoming standard in identity and credit card verification processes, this involves the requirement of two different forms of personal substantiation in order to allow a given action to take place.

3DS: Three Domain Secure; a protocol for ecommerce payment security that involves three forms of authentication based on who the customer is (for example, a thumbprint or facial scan), what the customer has in their possession (for example, a physical credit card or unlocked phone with a digital wallet) and what the customer knows (for example, a four-digit pin code).

ABS: Attribute-Based Shopping; a newer form of querying specialized or individual products within a broader product category that's becoming increasingly lucrative for the hotel industry to sell unique rooms as well as stay-independent services.

ADA: Americans with Disabilities Act; a civil rights law in the United States that came into effect in 1990 that has profound implications for necessary hotel physical design features and website functionality, with other countries passing similar laws in other years.

ADR: Average Daily Rate; a calculation of the total room revenue for a day divided by the number of rooms sold, generally excluding ancillary revenue such as F&B, spa, parking and so on.

AI: Artificial Intelligence.

Aparthotel: The portmanteau of the worlds 'apartment' and 'hotel' to describe hybrid accommodation units that combine elements of both residential modalities, often used interchangeably with 'condotel'.

API: Application Programming Interface; denoting the ability of two disparate pieces of software to communicate and share data with each other.

AR: Augmented Reality; utilizing one's smartphone or specific eyewear to layer over a physical space with digital constructs.

B2B: Business to Business.

B2L: Business to Leisure. Programs targeted directly at the end-use, or guest.

BAR: Best Available Rate; the lowest available nightly rate on any given date.

BEO: Banquet Event Order; the full, itemized list of every F&B and non-F&B component for a social group event or meeting.

BI: Business Intelligence; a modern reporting system that relies on numerous data interfaces and forms of AI to analyze a complex entity such as a hotel property or make comparisons amongst multiple hotels.

Bleisure: The portmanteau of the words 'business' and 'leisure' to describe hybrid guests who combine both of these core travel purposes, now often used interchangeably with 'blended travel'.

BLE: Bluetooth Low Energy.

BNPL: Buy Now, Pay Later; a recently introduced form of installment payments, typically in four or six payments, that is now being added as an option to ecommerce purchases.

BOGO: Buy One Get One.

BOH: Back of House.

BTG: By The Glass; typically reserved for selling wine for which different pricing from a merchant may be available.

BYOD: Bring Your Own Device.

CAC: Customer Acquisition Costs; the expenses that are directly associated with attaining a given customer, new or existing, as measured by a conversion or booking, where for hotels these costs are typically advertising or third-party commissions.

CAGR: Compound Annual Growth Rate.

Capex: Capital Expenses.

CBDC: Central Bank Digital Currencies.

CDP: Customer Data Platform; a type of system that is specifically designed to manage and centralize the interfaces amongst all the various entities within a hotel's technology ecosystem.

CMS: Content Management System; the 'back-end' of a modern website, allowing for revisions without directly involving a programmer.

CNP: Card Not Present.

Comp: Room or other product given on a complementary basis, used as a noun or as a verb such as, "This guest's room was a comp."

Comp Set: Competitive Set; all the other accommodation providers that are within the same geographic territory and targeting the same demographic as a specific hotel.

COVID (also pandemic): Coronavirus Disease 2019; the infectious disease caused by the SARS-CoV2 virus that became a pandemic with worldwide economic repercussions.

CPACE: Commercial Property Assessed Clean Energy.

CPD: Continuing Professional Development; a broad term encompassing the ongoing education that employees or business owners undertake to help advance their careers.

CPOR: Cost Per Occupied Room.

CRISPR: Clustered Regularly Interspaced Short Palindromic Repeats; a revolutionary form of editing DNA that holds vast promises for gene therapy and other future forms of medicine.

CRM: Customer Relationship Management; now used to denote the guest profile systems where amalgamated data can be leveraged for key insights and specific marketing techniques.

CRS: Central Reservation System; a database housing all guest data as well as facilitating hotel bookings that is accessible across multiple screens and updated in real-time.

CVAC: Cyclic Variations in Adaptive Conditioning; a wellness treatment using fluctuating air pressure to train the body within a pod similar to a hyperbaric oxygen chamber.

D2C: Direct To Consumer.

DAO: Decentralized Autonomous Organization.

DND: Do Not Disturb.

DofM (also DOM): Director of Marketing; can also be referred to as the Director of Sales and Marketing (DofSM).

EBITDA: Earning Before Interest, Taxes, Depreciation and Amortization.

ECOM: Executive Committee; for other industries this might denote 'ecommerce' but for hotels this typically refers to a weekly or regularly scheduled meeting for all the various department heads to regroup.

EOY: End of Year.

ESD: Electronic Safety Device; a small, wearable accessory that can be used as a panic button and to pinpoint someone's location in case of emergencies.

ESG: Environmental, Social and Governance.

EX: Employee Experience; examining the employee's wellbeing within a given workplace situation, understanding that this has profound implications for their overall productivity as well as the quality of the customer experience (CX).

FAM: Familiarization; a tour organized for travel agents or media representatives to introduce a destination or property so that these individuals are knowledge in relaying its selling attributes to their customers or readers.

F&B: Food and Beverage; referring not only to the outlets, but also catering and room service.

FF&E: Furniture, Fixtures and Equipment.

FIT: Free Independent Traveler; as in leisure guests who are not part of a specific group, wholesaler or tour operator package.

FOH: Front of House. That part of the hotel experience that is guest-facing, as compared to BOH or back of house being those activities that do not directly interface with the guest.

GDS: Global Distribution System; a computerized system generally utilized by airlines, car rental companies and hotels, and managed by traditional travel agents.

GEMS: Guest Experience Management System.

GM: General Manager; in some properties there are variations, with a multi-tiered senior management team including a Managing Director and a Hotel Manager (other variations exist).

GOP: Gross Operating Profit.

GOPPAR: Gross Operating Profit Per Available Room.

GUI: Graphical User Interface.

Home Sharing: Used somewhat interchangeably with the sharing economy for the accommodations industry to define alternate lodging providers who operate expressly through online marketplace platforms.

HNWI (also HNW): High-Net-Worth Individual; wherein there are also Ultra-High-Net-Worth Individuals (UHNWI) denoting people with investable assets in excess of $30 million USD.

HPOR: Hours Per Occupied Room.

HVAC: Heating, Ventilation and Air Conditioning.

IBE: Internet Booking Engine.

IoT: Internet Of Things; describes the process by which regular electronic devices can now be equipped with an internet connection in order to give holistic data on a situation as well as coordinate further actions back through the device.

ISBF: Internet-Based Service Firm.

IT: Information Technology.

IVR: Interactive Voice Recording.

KPI: Key Performance Indicator.

KYC: Know Your Customer.

L2B: Look To Book; hotel jargon describing roughly the average number of days from when a customer first looks at a property or makes an initial inquiry to when they confirm a reservation.

LCD: Liquid Crystal Display; a form of flat-panel display technology that has since been largely outmoded by LED and OLED technologies.

LED: Light-Emitting Diode; used to describe today's common form of flat-panel television.

LEED: Leadership in Energy and Environmental Design; a prestigious green building certification

program that is used worldwide.

LIFO: Last In, First Out.

LLM: Large Language Model.

LOS: Length Of Stay; defining how many nights the average guest stays at a given hotel.

LPAR: Labor Per Available Room; a cost metric used in conjunction with RevPAR to calculate the gross profit of each individual room.

MDR: Merchant Discount Rate.

MICE: Meetings, Incentives, Conventions and Exhibitions; an all-encompassing term to denote the meetings and events industry, and acting as a critical segment for many hotels.

MinPOR: Minutes Per Occupied Room; specific to housekeeping to define the average guestroom cleaning time so as to evaluate costs and scheduling.

ML: Machine Learning.

MOD: Manager On Duty; when the general manager is not in-house, his or her replacement becomes the MOD.

NFC: Near Field Communications.

NFT: Non-Fungible Token.

NLP: National Language Processing.

NOI: Net Operating Income.

OCC: Percentage Occupancy; the ratio of rooms in use to total rooms in house. Often, complementary (house use) rooms and out-of-service rooms are not considered in this calculation.

OLED: Organic Light Emitting Diode; for our purposes this technology concerns low energy flat-panel televisions with bright color output and high contrast.

OMS: Operations Management System; often used interchangeably with 'ops platform' to signify the hotel platform that interacts primarily with the PMS to expedite departments that directly affect the guest experience such as housekeeping and front desk and maintenance dispatch.

Opex: Operating Expenses.

OTA: Online Travel Agency; agencies operating primarily through the Internet. Typical examples are booking.com, hotels.com or expedia.com.

P&L: Profit And Loss.

PCI DSS: Payment Card Industry Data Security Standards.

PIP: Property Improvement Plan; a catch-all term to signify major renovations or a hotel refresh, often scheduled into multiple phases to prevent the need for a property closure and to ensure smooth operations throughout the process.

PMS: Property Management System; the software used to internally manage and integrate rooms, revenues and ancillary services.

POS: Point of Sale; being the data accumulated through cash registers and computers located throughout the property.

PPE: Personal Protection Equipment; including items like gloves, face masks and face shields, all designed to protect against the spread of infectious diseases.

PR: Public Relations; the department within a hotel organization responsible for communicating with media representatives and influencers to generate awareness for a given product.

QR: Quick Response; as in 'quick-response code' to denote the two-dimensional matrix barcode that's compatible with phone cameras.

RAG: Retrieval-Augmented Generation.

REC: Renewable Energy Certificate.

Re-marketing: A type of digital advertising whereby customers are targeted with ads specifically designed based on what they previously searched or what websites they browsed.

RFID: Radio-Frequency Identification.

ROAS: Return On Advertising Spend.

ROI: Return On Investment.

RevPAG: Revenue Per Available Guest; calculated by totaling guestroom revenue and all other profitmaking streams then dividing by the maximum capacity of guests; used mostly for resorts or all-inclusive providers.

RevPAR: Revenue Per Available Room; calculated by taking the total guestroom revenue and dividing it by the number of rooms times 365, or the number of days in the revenue period.

RevPOR: Revenue Per Occupied Room; calculated by taking the total guestroom revenue and dividing it by the number of rooms occupied; generally more useful in analysis of properties with a high proportion of ancillary revenue such as a spa, food & beverage or golf.

RFID: Radio-Frequency Identification.

RM: Revenue Manager; responsible for analyzing competitive rates and advising the general manager on setting room rates to maximize yield on occupancy.

ROB: Revenue On Books.

RPA: Robotic Processing Automation.

RSI: Repetitive Strain Injury or Repetitive Muscle Injury (RMI); chronic injuries incurred through a high frequency use of a specific body movement causing pain in the joints or muscles.

RWD: Responsive Web Design; a website that detects what device (computer, tablet or mobile) is accessing it and automatically configures the information for an optimal viewing experience.

SaaS: Software as a Service; the payment for licensed use of a given system or platform on a monthly or annual subscription basis.

SDK: Software Development Kit.

SEM: Search Engine Marketing; this is activity undertaken to promote a property's website through paid-for marketing activities such as Google Adwords, Bing Ads, banner or display advertisements and other activities such as remarketing.

SEO: Search Engine Optimization; the process of enhancing how a property is found when using search terms within Internet search engines. Typically, this refers to the 'organic' or unpaid portion of this process, which involves elements of the website that are recognized by Google (or Bing) in rankings.

Sharing Economy: Also known as the gig economy, this umbrella term is most often used to describes businesses that facilitate peer-to-peer exchanges of goods or services for payment, most often conducted via an online portal that acts as a marketplace.

SOP: Standard Operating Procedure.

SSO: Single Sign-On.

STR: Smith Travel Research; a foremost travel and hospitality marketplace intelligence organization, whereupon the company's STAR Reports are often used as performance benchmarks.

TA: Travel Advisor or Travel Agent.

TAM: Total Addressable Market.

TLDR: Too Long, Didn't Read; a contemporary shorthand to denote a summary of a longer passage.

TRevPAR: Total Revenue Per Available Room; also known as 'total revenue' which includes revenue from room reservations as well as all ancillary amenities such as F&B and wellness sold on premises, in addition to stay-independent revenues such as that from spa day guests or online gift cards.

UAV: Unmanned Aerial Vehicle; also known as a drone.

UGC: User Generated Content; most often used to describe the comments, photos and videos posted by individual users to a social media network where a product acts as the subject matter.

USP: Unique Sales Proposition; mainly utilized for sales and marketing to define what special brand qualities can be promoted to help differentiate a company from its competition.

UX: User Experience; shorthand for how a person navigates through a website.

VIP: Very Important Person; a person who is 'VIP'd' typically receives a special welcome amenity, upgrades and personalized reception from a key member of staff. The individual is typically tagged in the property management system.

VR: Virtual Reality.

WBE: Website Booking Engine; now used interchangeably with 'integrated booking engine' (IBE) and 'booking engine' (BE).

Welltech: Combination of 'wellness' and 'technology'.

WFA: Work From Anywhere; a contemporary acronym that has emerged since the pandemic given the rise in remote work where knowledge-based jobs can be performed from practically anywhere including hotels, although this is most often 'work from home' (WFH).

ACKNOWLEDGEMENTS

For the writing of this third book in the Hotel Mogel Series – as well as our eighth book overall – we first want to thank Ronna Mogelon, Larry's sister, who oversaw the editing of the manuscript for this book as well as Samantha Mogelonsky, Larry's daughter and Adam's sister, who contributed the cover graphics. As with many hotels around the world, Hotel Mogel is also a family affair. None of this could be complete without a mention of Maureen Wright, Larry's spouse and Adam's mom, who put up with all of these shenanigans!

As hospitality is a business wholly reliant on collaboration and teams, this book would not have been possible with the heartfelt contributions from hoteliers from around the world who we interviewed over the past few years. In alphabetical order by last name, this includes Davide Barnes, James Barnett, Giacomo Battafarano, Marc Bauer, Jeremy Buffam, Analia Capurro, Philippe Champagne, Simon Chapman, Janis Clapoff, Tata Crocombe, Shearvon Devenish, Sharmin Dharas, Gaurav Dutta, Silvia Ferrer, Carlo Fontana, Amanda Frasier, Phillip Haller, Mark Hope, Chris Hunsberger, Anne Marie Johns, Stephen Johnston, Shannon McCallum, Antonio Mejia, Nicholas Messian, Brandon Morrison, Teresa Muk, Ronn Nicolli, Chris Norton, Ersin Pamuksuzer, Jim Peters, Laszlo Puczko, Gregor Resch, Julius Robinson, Francesco Roccata, Toby Smith, Marc Speichert, Vikram Sood, Anil Taneja, Wayne West III, Dean Winters and Hans-Peter Veit.

Next, as technology, design and other areas of expertise for the industry were also such a large part of this book, we would like to extend our gratitude to the industry suppliers and all the other intelligent individuals who directly contributed to the writing of this book. In alphabetical order by last name, this includes Conner Erwin, Saar Fabrikant, Adam Glickman, Michael Kessler, Steven Moore, Alessandro Munge, Frank Pitsikalis, Andreas Posmeck, Laszlo Puczko, Frank Reeves, Jeff Robbins, Michelle Russo, Bruno Saragat, John Smallwood, Vincent Somsen, Robert Stevenson and Barry Van Doornewaard.

To close and reemphasize, the hotel business is one of people. We are honored to have so many friends in this business who provide an endless stream of ideas for us to write about. To all those colleagues and clients who we've had the pleasure of knowing over the years, we sincerely thank you for making us the humble (and hopefully knowledgeable!) hoteliers that we are today.

ABOUT THE AUTHORS

Larry and Adam Mogelonsky are a father-son consulting team constantly in search of ways to perfect the hotel experience for existing luxury and independent properties as well as for new luxury and upmarket developments. Sometimes that means incorporating new technology or new amenities as part of a PIP – in particular these days, wellness, as this book has demonstrated – but more often than not this means optimizing the assets a property already has to exude a true sense of the word 'hospitality'.

After a formal education in engineering and business plus a stint as a brand manager at Procter & Gamble, Larry's first brush with the hotel industry was during his half-dozen years at a top ten advertising agency where he was the team leader for the Four Seasons Hotels & Resorts account. Smitten with the hospitality bug, Larry then founded LMA Communications Inc. in 1991 as a boutique firm specializing in hotels and tourism with clients across the globe.

Since its inception through to its sale in 2015, LMA was recognized with over 75 Adrian Awards from HSMAI (Hospitality Sales and Marketing Association International) for its creativity and strategic business acumen, as well as being awarded TravelClick's Worldwide e-Marketer of the Year. He was also named a Top 30 hospitality educator by International Hospitality Institute.

Before joining his father in the family business, Adam attained an undergraduate degree in pre-medicine and was working as a therapist/personal trainer for several years. Starting as a copywriter and digital strategist right at the time when social media was becoming a major marketing platform for brands, Adam rose over the years to become an account director for LMA's various hotel clients, working on projects beyond only marketing and into operational support.

Upon the sale of LMA, Larry and Adam formed Hotel Mogel Consulting Ltd. as a way of helping solve critical issues and working closer with property owners, developers, operators and industry suppliers. Together, they strive to offer the best strategies for their clients, all while never losing sight of the core drivers of a great hotel experience and what will lead to long-term success. Working primarily in the luxury hotel space, their core philosophy is to look at a hotel's 'reason to visit' as an emotional driver for continuous business growth and as a central objective that informs all other improvements or actions.

Concurrent to their consultancy practice, both Larry and Adam are active hospitality writers and public speakers, with articles written by Larry then edited by Adam and multiple speaking engagements given by Larry around the world each year. To-date, they have published over 1,500 unique articles in a variety of trade journals and magazines while also producing seven prior books addressing operational and marketing issues for hoteliers. Both Adam and Larry are active speakers, with Adam focusing on wellness and human longevity's applications for hotels and technology, while Larry delivers keynotes on guest experience, operational luxury, and market trends.

Both Adam and Larry reside in Toronto. Larry lives with Maureen and their 160-pound Bouvier des Flandres named Hondo, while Adam lives downtown mere blocks from all the greatest hotel developments in this booming city. Contact them at adam@hotelmogel.com and larry@hotelmogel.com.

Printed in the United States
by Baker & Taylor Publisher Services